Industrial
Democracy
in America

Ideological Origins of National Labor Relations Policy

"The discussions of every age are filled with the issues on which its leading schools of thought differ. But the general intellectual atmosphere of the time is always determined by the views on which the opposing schools agree. They become the unspoken presuppositions of all thought, the common and unquestioningly accepted foundations on which all discussion proceeds.

"When we no longer share these implicit assumptions of ages long past, it is comparatively easy to recognize them. But it is different with regard to the ideas underlying the thought of more recent times. Here we are frequently not yet aware of the common features which the opposing systems of thought shared, ideas which for that very reason often have crept in almost unnoticed and have achieved their dominance without serious examination. . . .

"When this is the case, the history of ideas becomes a subject of eminently practical importance. It can help us to become aware of much that governs our own thought without our explicitly knowing it. It may serve the purposes of a psychoanalytical operation by bringing to the surface unconscious elements which determine our reasoning, and perhaps assist us to purge our minds from influences which seriously mislead us on questions of our own day."

F.A. Hayek, The Counter-Revolution of Science: Studies on the Abuse of Reason *(1955)*

Industrial

 Open Court
La Salle, Illinois

Democracy in America

Ideological Origins of National Labor Relations Policy

HD
4508
.D54
1987

Howard Dickman

OPEN COURT and the above logo are registered in the U.S. Patent & Trademark Office.

© 1987 Howard Dickman. All rights reserved. No part of this publication may be reproduced, stored in a retrieval system, or transmitted, in any form or by any means, electronic, mechanical, photocopying, recording, or otherwise, without the prior written permission of the publisher, Open Court Publishing Company, La Salle, Illinois 61301.

Printed and bound in the United States of America.

Cloth: OC876 10 9 8 7 6 5 4 3 2 1
ISBN: 0-8126-9002-8
Paper: OC881 10 9 8 7 6 5 4 3 2 1
ISBN: 0-8126-9008-7

Library of Congress Cataloging-in-Publication Data
Dickman, Howard. Industrial democracy in America. Bibliography: p. Includes index. 1. Trade-unions—United States—History. 2. Collective bargaining—United States—History. 3. United States—Social conditions. I. Title.
HD6508.D54 1986   331.8'0973   85-21460
ISBN 0-8126-9002-8   ISBN 0-8126-9008-7 (pbk.)

Acknowledgment is made for permission to quote from *The Counter-Revolution of Science* by F.A. Hayek, © 1952 by The Free Press, a division of Macmillan, Inc. Copyright renewed 1980. Reprinted by permission of the publisher.

To my mother and the memory of my father

Contents

Acknowledgments

Several years ago, Sylvester Petro suggested to me that a review of the ideas responsible for the labor relations policies of the 1930s was long overdue. I am profoundly grateful for the time he has since taken to read and comment on the various drafts of this study, for his suggestions, criticisms, and unstinting encouragement—and above all, for his patience. But I absolve him from any errors of fact or interpretation that have found their way into the book.

I thank the Liberty Fund, especially A. Neil McLeod, for generous financial support throughout the life of this project; and I appreciate the assistance of the Earhart Foundation, especially Antony Sullivan, for making it possible for me to finish this book at the Social Philosophy and Policy Center, at Bowling Green State University. Also, a very special thanks to Fred Miller, Jeffrey and Ellen Paul, and John Ahrens, for creating at their Center such a hospitable and stimulating climate for serious scholarly endeavor.

I would like to acknowledge the following individuals, who responded to all or parts of this book with much useful advice: Thomas Haggard, Robert Hessen, Burton Folsom, Harold Livesay, Leo Troy, and Elizabeth Welborn. Thanks, too, to Joan Kennedy Taylor, for her enthusiastic support and sage counsel; to William M. H. Hammett, for an encouraging word; and to David Ramsay Steele, for editorial effort above and beyond the call of duty.

Norwalk, Connecticut
July 1986

Industrial
Democracy
in America

Introduction

Americans generally have ambivalent feelings about unions and collective bargaining. Many people credit labor unions with raising the living standards of millions of workers since the New Deal—even with making a middle class out of what had been an impoverished and immobile class of wage earners. But unions are also held responsible for pricing American products out of domestic and international markets and their members out of jobs. Union political power is credited with much of the extension of the welfare state since the 1960s; but unions are also blamed for the inflation and high taxes that have financed federal social programs. Unions are praised for introducing democracy into industry, securing for their members some voice in the conduct of their working lives, thus checking and balancing what many believe is the otherwise arbitrary and despotic power of employers. But many unions are themselves accused of corrupt and undemocratic practices, and of not really representing the interests of their members, or of the "working class" as a whole. The general feeling is that unions were and still are "necessary," but that "Big Labor" has become *too powerful.* But there is a profound reluctance to inquire very deeply into the *source* of union power. There is even less interest in reassessing the arguments that have been, and still are, advanced for granting to unions the power they do have.

This book will explain and re-examine the reasons that have been put forward in favor of unions, in order to understand why American society came to favor collective over individual bargaining, and to account for the peculiar legal structure our system of collective bargaining—our system of industrial democracy—assumed as a result of the Wagner Act (also called the National Labor Relations Act, (49 Stat. 445), or NLRA) in 1935.[1] I emphasize the word "peculiar," because majority-rule unionism, the structural core of our collective bargaining system, existed nowhere else in the world. Even now, few industrialized nations vest in a single union the exclusive legal right to override individual contractual preferences and establish employment relations for all workers under its jurisdiction, whether these workers are members or not.

As an historical essay, my interpretation of the origins of national labor relations policy is neither a comprehensive intellectual history of 19th and 20th century social reform, nor a narrative, blow-by-blow history of the organized labor movement in America. It is a little of both. To understand why collective bargaining came to be favored over individual bargaining, I will re-examine, in an historical context, the arguments for and against competitive labor markets: are individual laborers in a disadvantageous bargaining position with regard to employers in modern industrial society? And if they are, can unions help them to do better? Or is some other restructuring of the economy the answer? To account for the Wagner Act itself, I will explore several alternative models of industrial democracy which existed at the time of, or before, the Great Depression, insofar as these alternatives informed or affected the choices Americans made in the 1930s.[2]

In this introduction I will: explain why the Wagner Act was a watershed in American life; present an overview of the economic and political arguments which underlie it; and summarize the contents and logic of this book.

The Wagner Act drastically altered the legal framework of the market economy in America; in so doing, it transformed the very meaning of unionism and collective bargaining as they had hitherto been known. We are still accustomed to regarding a union as a private, voluntary association —the 'agent' of its members who deal with employers through it. Negotiations between these organizations and employers are still referred to as 'free collective bargaining'. The rules governing employment that emerge from these negotiations are called 'contracts'. But this language, while it more or less did describe the situation before 1935, is misplaced when applied to collective labor relations conducted under applicable Federal (or similar state) law today. For the essence of American national labor relations policy is a commitment to compulsion—to compulsory unionism.

This claim will no doubt seem strange, even perverse. Most people today understand compulsory unionism simply as the 'closed shop'—the arrangement whereby an individual must be a member of a union *before* he can be hired by any given employer. This was, to be sure, the primary meaning of compulsory unionism as it existed before 1935, and the Wagner Act did nothing to hinder, and much to assist, the spread of closed shops throughout the economy.[3] Yet in 1947 the Taft-Hartley Act prohibited the closed shop, although it permitted other kinds of 'union security agreements'[4] which accomplished nearly the same monopolistic ends.

But it is a mistake to define compulsory unionism solely as the closed shop or other forms of union security agreements. Philosophically, the equation of compulsory unionism with the closed shop begs a vital question: is any particular closed shop really the result of compulsion, or is it the result of a voluntary agreement between an employer and a union? If this was or is the case, it makes little sense to regard such an agreement as unfairly coercing any individual employee by interfering with his right to work. No one has a right to employment with any given employer except on the terms an employer and employee mutually agree to. If an employer has voluntarily agreed to hire only workers who have previously joined a union, that becomes a term of the employment offer along with any other. On their face, the federal or state laws (or common law doctrines) that prohibit closed shops or other union security agreements in the name of free competition are themselves the opposite: they interfere with freedom of association and are instances of compulsion.

But the prohibition of the closed shop is only one example where the fiat of the state has supplanted the contractual freedom of individuals. Our labor relations policies are deeply committed to compulsion in virtually all their dimensions, especially in light of the several far-reaching, monopolistic privileges granted to unions by the labor laws.

The broad commitment of national labor relations policy to compulsion, where freedom once ruled, is best understood by considering four of its major principles: the "right to organize," or anti-discrimination principle; the "duty to bargain," or compulsory collective bargaining principle; the enforceability of collective agreements (particularly union security agreements) as "contracts"; and the all-important principle of exclusive representation by majority rule.[5]

The 'right to organize' that labor relations law secures today is a very different breed of right than that which the common law recognized in 19th century America or England, the two countries whose legal and economic traditions are most germane to this study. But to understand the difference, a little background is necessary.

Throughout most of human history, men have existed under one form or another of personal or governmental tyranny. Individual workers were rarely free even to make their own employment contracts (as individual employers were rarely free to charge whatever prices they wanted for the goods they produced), no less to make employment bargains in groups. By the end of the 18th century the right of the individual to make his own bargains was secured, particularly in England. Nevertheless, the common and the statute law, reflecting organized society's traditional fear of concentrated economic power (and the wishes, no doubt, of politically powerful employers), prohibited individual workers from organizing or joining unions to negotiate collectively the wages, hours, and working conditions under which they would individually accept employment. Combinations of workers were indictable, wherever they existed, for unlawfully conspiring to interfere with 'the free course in trade', with non-union employees' right to work, with employers' right to manage their businesses as they saw fit, and with the general 'public policy' or 'public interest' in competition. These ancient prohibitions were relaxed in the first quarter of the 19th century in England, as liberal, individualistic ideas and ideals became ascendant in law and public opinion. The right of individual workers to organize into groups, or combinations, was secured.

Individual liberty of contract and the general principle of free association were also among the founding ideals of the American Republic. But their applicability to labor combinations, given the common law in England (which was the basis of American common law and which was hostile to combination in the last quarter of the 18th century) was unsettled. There was no national, that is, federal, policy. In some states, statutes modeled on the English Combination Acts of 1799 and 1800 summarily outlawed unions as criminal conspiracies. In other states, judges achieved virtually the same result by interpreting 18th century common law precedents against the crime of conspiracy in restraint of trade. In still other states, unions came under the ban less for the mere fact of combining or for the abstract ends they sought, than for the lawless, and frequently violent means they used.[6]

A crucial case in Massachusetts, *Commonwealth* v. *Hunt* (1842), recognized the individual worker's right to organize into unions, and did so in the context of a journeyman bootmakers union's threat to strike to maintain a closed shop. Chief Justice Lemuel B. Shaw, reasoning as economists in England did a generation earlier, concluded that since

> every free man, whether skilled laborer, mechanic, farmer or
> domestic servant, may work or not work, or work or refuse to
> work with any company or individual, at his own option, except
> as he is bound to contract

it was *not* "criminal for men to agree together to exercise their own acknowledged rights" in a labor union "in such a manner as best to subserve their own interests." Shaw's affirmation of union legitimacy was eventually accepted by all other state and federal courts as *the* common law in America. His justification of the closed shop was not.[7]

Nevertheless, the 'right to organize' recognized in *Commonwealth* v. *Hunt,* in common with other constitutionally protected freedoms, was primarily a legal claim that "ran" *against the government*—a claim that the government refrain from doing something *to* an individual (or group of individuals), but not a claim that the government do something *for* an individual (or group) at someone else's expense (i.e., at the expense of someone else's freedom of action or of his material resources). As such, the right to organize implied no positive (or what we would call today, affirmative) obligations on employers or non-union workers (outside the criminal law). Workers were free to organize or join labor unions. Employers and nonunion workers were free to ignore them. Employers could refuse to employ union laborers, discriminate against them in their employment policies, and generally decline to 'recognize' or negotiate with their organizations. The 'negative' right to organize, in short, implied nothing about the positive power or ability to organize in the face of employer hostility or reprisal, or the indifference of nonunion workers.

Recognition of the 'right to organize', even in the negative sense, left unresolved the lawful limits within which unions could exert their organized power in pursuit of their ends. It left unresolved which of their ends—higher wages? shorter hours? employment of union members only?—were lawful. It left unsettled the question of means. Indeed, candid discussions about the strike itself were (and still are) rare. What is a strike? Is it a concerted *withdrawal* of employees' services from an employer, a refusal to work—in other words, a primary boycott (A refuses to deal with C)? Or is it a concerted series of actions (such as picketing) designed to keep an employer from operating his business by inducing *others* to keep from dealing with (or working for) him—in other words, a secondary boycott (A attempts to persuade B not to deal with C)? If a strike is merely a withdrawal from the workplace, isn't this simply equivalent to quitting? And if it is something more, doesn't the right to strike imply some kind of property right in a job superior to an employer's right to hire and fire whomever he wants?[8]

At any rate, the negative 'right to organize' reflected less a belief that unions were necessary in order for individual workers to get fair wages and working conditions than it did a commitment to the principle and value of freedom of association and of competition generally. Since combination by investors or employers was tolerated and permitted, there was no compelling reason to prohibit it by employees.

As belief or confidence in competition waned during the 19th century, the idea grew that unions were not merely tolerable, or desirable, but were *indispensable* if workers were to obtain fair wages and working conditions. Union proponents insisted that the 'right to organize' under the common law was not enough. The state, they urged, must also positively restrict employers' freedom *not* to associate with unions or their members—because such discrimination interfered with the workers' 'right to organize', and decreased their ability to negotiate better wages and working conditions. It is this *positive* right which the Wagner Act secures.

The positive right to organize contradicts the traditional meaning of rights and of legal equality. It compels employers to associate with (that is, to retain) workers whom they otherwise would not. Indeed, the National Labor Relations Board (NLRB) may order an employer to hire or reinstate a dismissed worker (or pay damages to him) if it finds the employer dismissed him out of anti-union prejudice. The 'right to organize' principle in modern labor relations law is a form of forced association—of compulsory unionism. On the other hand, there is no such thing as the NLRB ordering an employee *to work* for an employer.[9]

The 'right to organize' establishes compulsory unionism in two other senses as well. First, Section 8 of the NLRA made it an "unfair labor practice" for an employer "to refuse to bargain collectively" with a union chosen by a majority of his employees. This is the 'duty to bargain', that is, compulsory collective bargaining, the second major principle of the Wagner Act. Negotiations *mandated by the government* are not "free collective bargaining."[10]

The other sense in which the 'right to organize' commits national labor policy to the principle of compulsory unionism concerns the status of the closed shop. Here again, some background is necessary.

Before the 1930s, employers could, with rare exceptions and in the absence of a fixed contract of employment, fire workers for any reason, or for no reason, just as employees could, with rare exceptions, quit at any time, for any reason, or for no reason.[11] Employers could insist that workers agree to refrain from joining a union as the price of getting or keeping their job (the so-called "yellow dog contract"), or they could insist that workers join a company union to get and keep their jobs. The closed *nonunion* shop was everywhere lawful; and employers could, in certain circumstances, get injunctions from federal or state courts to prevent unions from inducing workers to breach these yellow dog contracts (that is, to prevent them from attempting to organize the employees of their firm).[12]

The lawfulness of union attempts to seek or to maintain closed *union* shops—through strikes or strike threats, or through other forms of primary or secondary boycotting (violent or nonviolent), to keep employers from hiring anyone but members of a particular union, or to get employers to discharge workers who were not members of a particular union, or not members of any union—was *not* so well established. Some states permitted unions' nonviolent attempts to get or maintain a closed shop, reasoning that these were within the right of workers to advance their own interests. The economic 'harm' that this monopoly might or did inflict on other workers, employers, or the public at large was incidental. But other states regarded this behavior as an unlawful conspiracy in restraint of trade under the common law, or (on the federal level) under the Sherman Act.

Unions insisted that the closed union shop was properly within their contractual rights; and that the 'harm' these agreements had on nonunion employees was either irrelevant (since no nonunion employee had a right to any given job) or was outweighed by the benefits enjoyed by organized workers as a result of the closed-shop agreement (or indeed, by the benefits to the public at large from having collective employment relations). Unionists also claimed that the closed shop was not merely permissible or desirable, but, given the employer's otherwise untrammeled right to hire and fire workers at will, and given the ever-present fear of free riders,[13] that closed shops were indispensable to the survival of unions.

The Wagner Act reflected the desires of organized labor to monopolize work through closed shops in a variety of ways. For our purposes here, it should be noted that the NLRA specifically permitted unions to require workers (through pressure on unwilling employers) to join unions as the price of getting their jobs, but it specifically prohibited employers from requiring workers to agree *not* to join a union as the price of getting their jobs. In other words, there was, under the Wagner Act, no right not to join unions legally analogous to the right to join a union; and employers had no legal right to refuse to bargain with a union over its demand for a closed shop.[14]

The Taft-Hartley Act (61 Stat. 136 (1947)) did not sweep away closed union shops to the same extent that the Wagner Act had earlier abolished closed non-union shops. The law formally recognized a worker's 'right not to organize', and it banned those union security agreements whereby a worker had to join a union before he was hired. However, other union security agreements (such as the agency shop, which requires a worker, after he is hired, to pay union dues) remained lawful. On the other hand, Section 14 (b) of the Taft-Hartley law permitted states, if they chose, to outlaw virtually all kinds of union security agreements. Eleven states had these so-called "right to work" statutes before Taft-Hartley; nine others have since passed similar laws.[15]

The Wagner Act's third radical departure from the common law of the free market concerned the legal status of the collective bargain. Prior to the New Deal, collective agreements were only rarely enforceable in law courts as contracts. Most unions refused to incorporate and were therefore legally incapable of entering into *any* contractual relations with employers. Even where a union was incorporated, judges rarely, if ever, discovered any legally enforceable promises that the union could or did make to employers in return for the employer's recognition of or assent to the union's terms. Lacking "mutuality," or "consideration," these collective bargains were only "gentleman's agreements"—they were legally unenforceable.[16]

After the Wagner Act, employers were legally compelled to live up to the collective bargain. But as far as the union was concerned, Section 13 made it clear that nothing in the law was to "be construed so as either to interfere with or impede or diminish in any way the right to strike."

The fourth major principle of the Wagner Act is exclusive representation by majority rule. This was arguably the most revolutionary departure from the common law of free markets. Section 9 (a) of the Wagner Act states that

> Representatives designated or selected for the purposes of collective bargaining by the majority of the employees in a unit appropriate for such purposes, shall be the exclusive representatives of all the employees in such unit for the purposes of collective bargaining in respect to rates of pay, wages, hours of employment, or other conditions of employment: *Provided,* That any individual employee or a group of employees shall have the right at any time to present grievances to their employer.

(The National Labor Relations Board decides in each case the "unit appropriate for the purposes of collective bargaining" (Section 9 (b)). *Majority rule prohibits individual workers or minority groups from making their own employment contracts except as the exclusive bargaining representative allows, and only on such terms as it finds acceptable.* This applies to workers who would have preferred another union and to workers who would prefer *no* union. The collective agreement negotiated by a majority representative *must* govern *all* employees in the appropriate bargaining unit, whether or not they are members.

The champions of exclusive representation claimed in its favor that majority rule "is in accord with American traditions of political democracy, which empower representatives elected by the majority of voters to speak for all the people."[17] But the wholesale restructuring of private contractual relations through a political device like majority rule is a drastic and radical repudiation of another American tradition at least as old as democracy, namely freedom of contract. Legislatures have, to be sure, interfered with contractual freedom in America since colonial times. But the majority rule principle in labor law was unprecedented, in that it vested in some men the power to establish employment relations for other men, without their consent.[18]

By virtue of unions' exclusive (that is, their legally-created monopoly) bargaining rights, the rules of collective bargains bear less affinity to voluntary contracts than they do to the public laws of the state. "Like the legislative branch of the government, effecting changes in the law," as one advocate of the Wagner Act explained, the terms of the collective agreement

> bind the employee to each change effected irrespective of the employee's intent in the matter. Nor can the employee [or the employer] by any individual contract alter the rules governing his employment fixed by the collective agreement entered into by the union elected by a majority of the employees in the unit any more than a citizen by private contract can alter the laws enacted by the legislature.[19]

"Unions," as another sympathetic scholar contended, *"are not private organizations but are governmental agencies garbed with the cloak of legal authority":*

> A union, in bargaining, acts as the representative of all workers within an industrial area. . . . It negotiates a contract which becomes the basic law of that industrial community. In making those laws, the union acts as the worker's economic legislature. After the laws have been made, the union is charged with their enforcement. . . . It is the worker's policeman and judge. The union is, in short, the employee's economic government. *The union's power is the power to govern.*[20]

The affinity of exclusive representation to *political* rule is neither casual nor accidental. On the contrary, it is the climax of a long-standing and deeply-rooted impulse to democratize, that is to *politicize,* the workplace. Workers, many felt, ought to and must have "a voice in determining the laws within industry and commerce which affect them, equivalent to the voice which they have as citizens in determining the legislative enactments which shall govern them"—a voice which, the proponents of unionism argued, they did not have in a regime of individual bargaining.[21]

This book is, in large part, an extended investigation, and critique, of that claim. But I should like to sketch here, as briefly as possible, the essential logic of three far-reaching theories which historically constituted the rationale for industrial democracy, both here and abroad: a theory of laborers' bargaining disadvantages under competition; a theory of income redistribution through collective bargaining; and a theory of unions' proper legal relations with employers, other workers, and the state in a modified capitalism.

The demand that employment relationships be structured on a political, not a contractual, model is based first of all on the belief that the interests of employers and employees are naturally antagonistic and not symbiotic, and that in this conflict of interest employers possess all the advantages, all the 'bargaining power'. In some age long past, proponents of this theory typically claimed, the need of workers and employers for each other was more or less equal. This was no longer true in modern industry "where one establishment employs a large number of workmen," since "the employer can discharge a single workman with comparatively slight inconvenience, while the workman loses his whole means of subsistence."[22]

But when the parties to a contract do not stand equal in power and position, as two leading champions of industrial democracy argued, *"legal freedom of contract merely enables the superior in strategic strength"* to arbitrarily *"dictate the terms"* and force the inferior in bargaining strength to "accept the lowest possible terms." Employers are *able* to force wages down to "the barest subsistence" level, because of their greater bargaining power. But they don't have any real freedom in the matter either, because competition between them and other employers in the market to sell goods *forces* them to cut wages down to subsistence.[23] From whatever direction, the result is supposed to be the same: wage competition under individual bargaining condemns the mass of propertyless, powerless men to lives of poverty, dependence, and subordination.

Unequal economic power, if this theory is pushed just a bit further, *is* political power. Social theorists who championed market transactions over legal controls were mistaken, because the distinction between voluntary exchange for mutual benefit and unilateral political coercion is nebulous, if not wholly illegitimate. The reasoning behind this arresting conclusion is simple. The crux of *governmental* power is a legal monopoly of the use of physical force, and its essential exercise is to compel an individual to act in a manner he otherwise would not freely choose. But the crux of an employer's economic power is *his* legal monopoly—that is, his ownership—of the means of production and subsistence; of life itself. When you control a man's subsistence, you control his will. Hence, the argument goes, the 'bargain' employers offer workers is not 'you perform this service for me and I will pay you so much', but 'you do this for me, or you will not work, and you will starve and die.' This choice, according to the critics of competition, is no different than the 'bargain' offered by a despot or a highwayman, namely, 'give me what I demand of you, or suffer confiscation, captivity, or death.' The bottom line is the same. The employment relationship is a political one; "industry," the dean of American reform economists wrote late in the 19th century, is a "despotism."[24]

But despotism breeds rebellion in economic affairs just as surely as it breeds rebellion in political affairs. Thus, the arbitrary, 'minority rule' of employers, particularly their refusal to allow workers to unionize, is the root cause of "industrial strife or unrest" [NLRA, Section One], or more plainly, of union violence. Social peace, on the other hand, is possible only when social relationships are ordered justly; and the basic principle of social justice is democracy. The democratic principle, as the popular social reformer Henry Demarest Lloyd declaimed in a widely read encomium to organized labor,

> must and will rule wherever men co-exist, in industry not less surely than in politics. *It is by the people who do the work that the hours of labour, the conditions of employment, the division of the produce is to be determined. It is by them the captains of industry are to be chosen,* and chosen to be servants, not masters. It is for the welfare of all that the co-ordinated labor must be directed. Industry, like government, exists only by the co-operation of all, and like government, it must guarantee equal protection to all. This is democracy, and democracy is not true only where men carry letters or build forts, but wherever they meet in common efforts.[25]

Laborers must be organized, this theory of democracy implied, because only through unions can laborers redress employers' greater bargaining power and resist arbitrary treatment. "Singly the employer can stand out longer in the bargain" than the unorganized worker, a mid 19th century trade union theorist explained, "and as he who can stand out longest in the bargain will be sure to command his own terms," unions put workers "on something like an equality in the bargain for the sale of their labour with their employers."[26] Organization is "essential," Chief Justice William Howard Taft agreed many years later, "to give laborers opportunity to deal equally with their employer."[27]

Unionization is an irreducible *first* step if employees are to exercise *any* voice in making the economic rules under which they live. Accordingly, collective bargaining nominally concerns wages, hours, and other working conditions like grievance procedures and promotion policies. But logically speaking, there is no aspect of employers' decision-making power, no 'management prerogative', which is not ultimately up for grabs. How can there be, since there is scarcely any significant decision involving the disposition of a firm's assets—the price of its products, where and how they are marketed, how the firm is organized, how and under what conditions its capital is raised, or where the plant is or will be located—that does *not* directly or indirectly affect that firm's employees? Employers today, it should be added, are already under a legal duty to bargain about most of these matters; the rest are probably only a matter of time (and the shifting political complexion of the National Labor Relations Board and the Supreme Court). Union control of the workplace is the final, logical goal of industrial democratic theory.

The second theoretical pillar of modern industrial democratic doctrine is an 'underconsumptionist', or 'purchasing power' theory of unemployment under capitalism. Historically, industrial democrats of virtually every stripe in this country (as well as abroad) have insisted that the fundamental cause of business crises and their accompanying unemployment is an allegedly progressive 'maldistribution of income' bottomed on employers' greater bargaining power in the labor market. Workers, this theory holds, do not receive as wages the income or purchasing power necessary to 'buy back' as consumers the ever-growing output of industry. Wages lag behind profits and consumption lags behind production. If the market is left to itself, the system as a whole will break down. One bankruptcy will cause another, and another, in domino fashion, as purchasing power contracts and an ever-widening wave of unemployment engulfs the economy.[28]

According to the "theory of collective bargaining," as it was aptly named in 1930 by W. H. Hutt, unions can and do remedy this allegedly inherent tendency toward instability and unemployment through collective bargaining. The idea here is that unions can and do redistribute national income (the proceeds of production), obtaining higher permanent real wages than would otherwise prevail under individual bargaining, and *for all workers.* The higher wages won by organized workers are paid out of employers' profits (or investors' interest, or landowners' rent), *not* by other organized or unorganized workers, whose real wages or purchasing power are reduced by higher prices, or by increased unemployment and an accompanying downward pressure on wages (wage rates and earnings) elsewhere. This theory flies in the face of the reasoning of virtually the entire classical and neo-classical schools of economic thought, according to which the analysis of union economic power is essentially no different than the analysis of any business cartel or monopoly: any redistribution of income which accrues to the monopolists or cartel members is at the expense of the rest of society.[29]

If the "theory of collective bargaining" is right, it follows that unionism and collective bargaining perform a vital public service above and beyond the benefits organized workers win as individuals. Collective bargaining as an institution balances or stabilizes production and consumption in the economy as a whole. The implication here is that unionism and collective bargaining, which arose as a protest against capitalism, are essential to the preservation of capitalism![30]

Given this basic analysis of what is wrong with competition in labor markets, and how what is wrong can be righted, it is readily apparent why national labor relations policy is *not* based on individual contractual freedom, on purely voluntary unionism, or on strict legal equality of treatment between employer, union, and worker. These are precisely the values and institutions industrial democrats reject as untenable in light of modern economic conditions.[31] In the theory behind our labor relations, individual freedom and equality before the law are subordinate to the principle of special privileges for the group; and in practice, industrial democracy in America is a system designed to increase *union bargaining power.* Union power is the principle that integrates the four major provisions of our law of collective bargaining, and union power is the value which our national labor relations policy was (and still largely is) designed to secure.

Thus, the 'positive' right to organize was never intended to protect an *individual* worker's free choice of a bargaining representative. It was, and is, an instrument to encourage "the practice and procedure of collective bargaining" [NLRA, Section One], by making it more difficult for employers to resist. Similarly, Congress rejected truly voluntary collective bargaining for the same reason that it rejected the 'right not to organize'. "Without" the employer's "duty to bargain," its supporters insisted, the employees' "right to bargain would be sterile."[32]

The same 'instrumentalism' explains why industrial democrats in America ultimately chose majority rule over individual bargaining rights or other collective bargaining systems (like proportional representation, members-only collective bargaining, or the dual and rival union arrangements) which existed and still exist elsewhere in the world. In the eyes of their champions, unions in America were too weak to survive without some form of monopoly guarantee like exclusive representation. Workers in this country were too individualistic or insufficiently 'class conscious'; and unions themselves were wracked by factions and rivalries they were either unable or unwilling to overcome in order to meet the common enemy, capital, with a united front. Individual bargaining or minority representation would weaken union power fatally, since employers would be encouraged to resist, evade their "duty to bargain," and count on existing division within the ranks of the workers to make strikes or strike threats fizzle. Looked at from this angle, the principle of exclusive representation is simply another *kind* of union security.

Nevertheless, insofar as the theory of industrial democracy is concerned, the majority rule device practically commits the labor relations policy in this country to a species of "one party" government. Not only are minority groups (or individuals) excluded from any direct voice in making their own contracts, but they are excluded from any role in the "legislative process" of collective bargaining itself. Moreover, while the workers in a given bargaining unit can (and more than occasionally do) "decertify" a majority representative, there is no mechanism for periodic "recertification" of the bargaining representative analogous to the periodic election provisions of every democratic polity. As originally enacted in 1935, the NLRA provided no legal guarantee that these majority

representatives—these 'private governments'—would themselves operate democratically, or even represent the interests of the majority of
workers in the unit.[33]

The Wagner Act drastically changed the rules of the capitalistic game,
but the kind of compulsory unionism established during the New Deal did
not go quite so far as the logic of industrial democracy might imply. To
understand why is to understand something important about the ultimate
character of the American system of industrial democracy.

The right to organize, for instance, was said to be sterile without the
employer's duty to bargain. But even though employers are compelled to
bargain with majority representatives, they are not under a duty to agree to
union proposals, or even under the duty (at least formally speaking) to
make concessions on a single union proposal. Employers may bargain "in
good faith," but nevertheless negotiations may reach an impasse, break
down, and a strike break out. Why doesn't this fact render the right to
organize any less sterile? Why not compel agreements?

Similarly, the law compels all employees (in an "appropriate bargaining
unit") to accept collective *representation* not of their own choosing and
to yield up their individual contractual rights when a majority chooses a
union. But if unionization is indispensable, why doesn't the law compel *all*
employees to accept union representation? Why doesn't it compel all
employees to *join* unions as well?

Finally, while the law prohibits employers from interfering with the
"right to strike," it does not guarantee that any given strike will be
effective. So why doesn't the law, in order to make the "right to strike"
really effective, prohibit employers from operating a struck plant with
supervisors, nonstriking workers, or permanent replacements, in any or in
all instances? This is, after all, what the logic of the strike—and the reality
of the picket line—is really all about. When organized workers strike and
picket, their message to employers is *not,* in the overwhelming number of
cases, 'accept our conditions, or do without *our* labor services', but
'accept our conditions, or do without *any* labor services'.

The Wagner Act did not directly compel universal compulsory unionization or compel collective agreements throughout the economy. It is not
likely that legislation to achieve this goal would have succeeded, even in
the radical 1930s. But very rarely, if ever, did anyone even propose such
legislation (and if they did, not very loudly). The champions of industrial
democracy wanted to *achieve* universal compulsory organization. For the
most part, however, they wanted a system of law and public policy that
would enable unions to obtain this goal *by themselves,* through strikes or
other actions, aided where necessary by special legal privileges when,
where, and to the extent necessary, but otherwise with the direct
intervention of the state kept to the minimum.[34]

The reasons are easy enough to grasp, but important enough that they bear stating. Political power in a democratic society is virtually never granted to any individual or group, public or private, without accountability following sooner or later in its wake. If the government gives you some form or another of subsidy or specially privileged status, it will sooner or later demand the right to regulate or control you. This is a political version of the economic maxim, "There is no such thing as a free lunch." The experience of regulated industries such as the railroads is an outstanding example of this principle. The government big enough to give you anything you want, as one recent president put it, is big enough to take away everything you have.

Historically, the leadership of the organized labor movement was well aware of the danger. Samuel Gompers consistently refused to countenance *any* compulsory arbitration scheme, on the reasonable ground that if the government could compel employers to accept an arbitration award, it could compel unions to accept it too—by outlawing strikes. For that matter, as discussed later in this book, unions won an enormous legislative victory, even before the New Deal began, with the passage of the Norris-La Guardia Anti-Injunction Act in 1932. The Norris-La Guardia Act virtually suspended the federal antitrust statutes insofar as these laws had previously reined in union power. The organized labor movement was much too perspicacious to risk its gains by fighting for some state-engineered, universal compulsory unionism.

I have discussed the case for industrial democracy as if it were a unitary theory implying a single solution to the problem of labor relations in a competitive, industrialized society. But it was and is not. The outer legislative limits of the American system of industrial democracy help put the character of the system into sharper focus and provide the structure for this study.

When Henry Demarest Lloyd contended that it "is by the people who do the work that the hours of labour, the conditions of employment," and "the division of the produce is to be determined," he neglected to specify *which* people. By all workers for all workers, as in socialism? Or by the workers in each industry for that industry, as in syndicalism? What is to be the role of the union in industry, if the former? And what is to be the role of the state, if the latter? And if neither syndicalism nor socialism, then what?

Lloyd's own version of industrial democracy combined socialistic rhetoric with a somewhat fuzzy mixture of socialistic, syndicalistic, and corporativist legal reforms. But Lloyd's mixing of elements was not unique. Each of the three theories that rationalized industrial democracy theory in this country (the theory of bargaining disadvantage, the theory of income redistribution through collective bargaining, and the theory of private government) arose out of diverse 19th century and early 20th century European (and English) radical and reformist ideas. And our *system* of industrial democracy is modeled, to a lesser but still quite significant degree, on elements of the labor relations policies first put into practice in Europe and England. Virtually every criticism of individual contractual freedom in the labor market, and every means for overcoming the alleged deficiencies of competition, was first proposed abroad before it came to influence Americans. The evolution of these ideas, their institutionalization abroad, and the various avenues through which these ideas and practices were absorbed or assimilated here, occupy the remainder of the book, as outlined in the next few paragraphs.

Since the case *for* industrial democracy, in any version, was and still is cast largely as a case *against* individualistic competition, chapters one and two survey the theory and legal policies of the market economy with regard to individual and collective bargaining in the labor market, as the market economy arose in England and America, within the context of English common law.

Classical economists of the late 18th and early 19th centuries helped liberate individual workers from traditional legal shackles on their freedom and mobility. These thinkers regarded competition as the best and even the only way to justly reward individual effort, promote rising living standards, and protect the interests of workers and consumers alike. The "market," as a 20th century market economist wrote, *was* "a democracy where every penny gives a right to vote."[35] They insisted that the people rule the system and choose the "captains of industry" to serve them. But economists of the capitalist persuasion insisted that the people exercise their rule through consumer choice, through the competition of employers for labor, and through the competition of employers to sell goods cheaply. This was the social process that insured fair wages consistent with full employment and an ever-rising purchasing power for the mass of men, achieved through more and better goods sold at lower prices. Imbalances of supply and demand in the system (which result in idle resources and unemployed men) were temporary and self-correcting through the price system, at least so long as the price system is permitted to exist and function freely.

The original concept of economic liberty, and the original defense of freedom of contract, did not assume that men had to be equal in position or wealth in order for the bargains between them to be fair. It assumed only that they were equally free. In fact, the defense of freedom of contract is impossible if one assumes social or economic equality is a necessary precondition, as Justice Peckham of the United States Supreme Court observed years ago:

> No doubt, wherever the right of private property exists, there must and will be inequalities of fortune; and thus it naturally happens that parties negotiating about a contract are not equally

unhampered by circumstances. This applies to all contracts, and not merely to that between employer and employee. Indeed, a little reflection will show that wherever the right of private property and the right of free contract coexist, each party when contracting is inevitably more or less influenced by the question whether he has much property, or little, or none; for the contract is made to the very end that each may gain something that he needs or desires more urgently than that which he proposes to give in exchange. And, since it is self-evident that, unless all things are held in common, some persons must have more property than others, it is from the nature of things impossible to uphold freedom of contract and the right of private property without at the same time recognizing as legitimate those inequalities of fortune that are the necessary result of the exercise of those rights.[36]

Nevertheless, economic liberalism, as it was espoused by Adam Smith and his followers, contained some equivocal, even contradictory elements that critics of the market—who denied that individual competition led to a fair and democratically controlled economy—took up and developed at great length and variety during the rest of the 19th century and on into our own.

Adam Smith defended the free market as an institution that produced and maintained a *harmony* of interests in society. But he also pioneered a theory of labor's bargaining disadvantages to which virtually every critic of competition pointed as demonstration that *conflict* of interest is the rule of capitalistic society. Secondly, Smith's own 'labor theory of value', though eventually discarded by liberal economists, dominated 19th century socialist and syndicalist conceptions of the wages system, and was the point of departure for the various underconsumptionist theories of unemployment under competition. Thirdly, the "wages fund" doctrine which Smith pioneered, and which his followers developed, was the single greatest obstacle to union-oriented theories of collective bargaining in the first half of the 19th century.

The wages fund doctrine, analyzed at length below, could be taken to mean any number of things. As a bare arithmetic formula, it meant merely that at any given time the average wage in the economy *as a whole* was that part of the nation's capital stock used to pay wages, divided by the working population. The implications of this seeming truism for labor unions caused a great deal of controversy.

Classical economists insisted that "strikes cannot raise wages" and that "wages cannot rise except as profits decline." Now these two statements can refer to the relative shares of national income accruing to wage earners and profit (or interest) recipients, in which case the second claim is necessarily true, and the first claim almost certainly but not necessarily and certainly not self-evidently true. Or they can refer to real (or money) wages in the sense of an absolute amount, in which case the second statement is false, and the first statement is false as well—at least insofar as the wages of *some* wage earners are concerned. But the various meanings attached to the wages fund were not always clearly distinguished, and this led to confusion.

Finally, Smith's ambiguous attitude about the ultimate justification of the "system of economic freedom"—whether it was an individual's natural right to liberty, or whether it was the utility of competition for society *in general*—opened the moral and philosophical door for the opponents of economic liberalism in the 19th century.

Chapters three and four explain the two leading alternative "exploitation" theories of wage bargaining under capitalism as these evolved in Europe and America during the early and middle decades of the 19th century, and as these theories resulted in two leading, but different versions of industrial democracy: syndicalism and socialism.

Syndicalists and socialists both insisted that the conflict between 'labor' and 'capital' under competition was irreconcilable and irremediable; both sought abolition of the wages system and of private ownership of the means of production; and both explained the unemployment problem in terms of laborers' radically unequal bargaining power and consequent inability to 'buy back' the product of industry.

In most other respects the two theories are in opposition. Syndicalism is a 'collectivism of the group', implying worker (actually union) control of industry. Socialism is a 'collectivism of society', implying control of industry by and on behalf of society as a whole. Syndicalists view socialism as just another form of industrial despotism; socialists regard syndicalism as fundamentally anarchic and unworkable—a 'monopoly capitalism' of the unions.

Chapter five discusses the decline of the wages fund doctrine, the 'bargaining power' and 'indeterminacy' theories of wages which took its place, and the relation of these to versions of industrial democracy that saw in collective bargaining a 'middle-of-the-road' alternative to unfettered capitalism or socialism. Trade union theorists and their sympathizers insisted that the conflict of interest between 'labor' and 'capital', while inherent in a competitive society, was not irreconcilable or irremediable. Through organization, workers could supposedly be made 'equal' to their employers; and once equalized, "their position is not one of opposition, but of mutual interest."[37]

Chapter six explores the rise of reformist, pro-union industrial democratic theories in late 19th century America through a discussion of two different, but extremely influential 'economy of high wages' doctrines that came to challenge both classical and neo-classical economic theory. The corporativist-oriented theory of 'regulating the plane of competition' through special privileges granted to producer groups on the basis of majority rule was developed by leading progressive economists in the 1870s and 1880s and was an important historical source for both the National Industrial Recovery Act and the Wagner Act some fifty years later. The 'eight hour' theory of wages developed by trade union theorists was a source for and justification of the idea that labor market restrictionism can *increase* employment, production and consumption and stabilize capitalism; and it, too, influenced New Deal labor policy.

Chapter seven explores union-oriented labor relations reforms as they emerged in England and Europe late in the 19th century and on through the first decades of the 20th century. Many of these systems arose in the context of a powerful 'anti-statist' intellectual and cultural movement best dubbed 'pluralism.' The theory of legal pluralism and the kinds of labor law reforms it engendered were well known to American progressive intellectuals and trade union leaders; chapter eight assesses the impact pluralist legal reforms abroad had on Americans in the first three decades of the 20th century, and it discusses the legal and constitutional collision which occurred in the so-called era of 'government by injunction' when the champions of industrial democracy sought to undermine and overturn the inherited legal protections of individual contractual rights in America.

A climate of opinion favorable to compulsory unionism existed in America by World War I, but the structure of national labor relations policy as we know it today did not coalesce until the political and economic crisis of the 1930s. Chapter nine surveys the most important legislative and administrative precedents for the Wagner Act; discusses the debate over some of the important provisions of the law; and assesses the Supreme Court's treatment of exclusive representation by majority rule in the 1930s and 1940s.

1. Putting Wages into Competition: The Rise of Individualistic Economic Policy

 Do the interests of employers and employees conflict, or are they complementary? Do employers possess all the advantages in employment relationships, or is their bargaining power checked and balanced by competition? Is the 'public interest'—the interest of all men collectively and the interests of each man individually—better served by letting each man make his own employment bargains according to his individual judgment, or by a policy of social control? If economic exchange is to be controlled in the interests of 'society at large', how and by whom will the control be implemented? And if economic exchange is to be free, what legal institutions best preserve individual autonomy in the competitive marketplace? May individuals pursue their own interests by any means except force or fraud? If so, may groups of individuals do the same?

Implicitly or explicitly, every human society, at whatever stage of economic development, must and does answer these questions. The answers have more often than not reflected ideas or attitudes suspicious of, even hostile to, principles of individualism and freedom of contract. Only in the 19th century, and even then imperfectly, did the policy of generalized political and economic freedom take root, most notably in England and America. The purpose of this chapter and the next is to explore some aspects of the rise of competitive individualism, particularly in England and America, including the dominant rationale for competition and the treatment of combination in the labor market by liberal political and economic thinkers. The pro-competitive theories and practices discussed in these chapters will then serve as the background for describing the evolution of industrial democracy theories, which are the antitheses of industrial individualism.

Organic Collectivism and the Traditionalist Society

Economic liberalism arose partly in reaction to the implications of what I will call, in this book, the social and economic theory of (and the policies usually derived from) 'organic collectivism'. Organicism denotes a vision of human society that has deep philosophic roots in the West. It is a vision whose assumptions are common to a remarkably wide variety of otherwise disparate forms of social organization, such as feudalism, absolutism, mercantilism, or modern socialism. Society is compared metaphorically to a unified organism, much like the human body: individuals are the cells, arranged into social classes, which are the organs. Thus the social group, not the individual person, is the basic unit, the building block of social reality in the organic society. The structure of society, like the relationship of cells to organs and of organs to the body, is hierarchical. There are the rulers and the ruled, each bound to the other by mutual obligations "in which the lower serves the higher and the higher directs and guides the lower."[1] The needs of the community or of its constituent groups, as these needs are defined by secular and religious authorities, take precedence over any contrary individual interests, needs, desires, or rights.

In societies animated by organic collectivist ideals, the individual essentially *belongs* to society. He may act only as society allows and then only in a manner consistent with the interests of the group. As one philosopher has characterized this notion, the individual exists "to be sacrificed by and for the collective whenever it—or its representatives—deems this desirable."[2] With this general outlook, the pursuit of individual gain and advantage is typically regarded with deep suspicion if not outright hostility; all the more so when economic exchange is regarded as a zero-sum game (an activity where one profits only at the expense of another) and the total wealth of society is regarded as fixed.

Individuals in traditionalist, organic societies in the West were all theoretically equal 'in the eyes of God', but they were *not* equal in their rights. On the contrary, as one historian has put it, society was

> composed of distinct classes, each with its appointed office to perform, each established in a practically fixed and unchanging position by religious sanction and tradition, and all co-operating like the members of a corporeal body to sustain the life and discharge the destinies of the nation.[3]

Each individual was bound to serve society in some ascribed capacity or position; he was, in turn, served by others assigned to other niches in the social order. The system promised social and economic security, at a price—liberty and abundance. Except for a tiny minority at the top, the philosophy and practice of organic collectivism had no room for individual geographic, occupational, or social mobility.

The apposite social concept of this economic and political system, "the key word of this structure was 'status'."[4] Status in law denotes either the legal capacity to act or a recognized legal position acquired by that capacity, such as trustee or employee. In liberal societies, all men are presumed free and equal in their rights, and thus have *full* legal capacity. They acquire their positions in society through the free exercise of their faculties. In the organic society, status defines a sphere of social space into which an individual was placed, usually by birth, wherein he was conceded certain rights but compelled to accept certain unchosen obligations. Status, in other words, implied some diminished (or enhanced) capacity. A person did not so much possess status as he was possessed by it.[5]

Traditionalist society coordinated the relationship of class to class and the relations among individuals within each class to prevent or regulate what the rulers regarded as self-interested, 'antisocial' behavior that interfered with what the rulers thought to be the health and good order of society as a whole. The instruments of control varied greatly from class to class; in severity, incidence, and duration over the centuries; and from country to country. The full social and political implications of status in traditional, organic societies, as well as their change over time, is beyond our present concern. Here we are concerned only with the economic implications. In the following pages, some aspects of the social control of economic activity in England before the late 18th century are discussed, particularly those controls directly affecting the labor market: statutory wage and price controls, and the guild system. The legacy of these institutions is vital for understanding the rise of competitive individualism, unions, and industrial democracy.

Incomes Policy in the Traditionalist Society

The statutory regulation of wages of common agricultural labor in England began in the middle of the 14th century as a response to the emergency shortage of labor caused by the Black Death. And like more familiar, contemporary price-fixing measures adopted in response to economic emergencies (such as rent control), it outlived the emergency—in this case, for some 400 years.[6]

The Plague presented an unprecedented opportunity for common agricultural laborers and tenants to escape their customary position of economic subordination to the landlords. Many workers deserted their place of birth or work in search of higher wages offered elsewhere by desperate, labor-starved, and opportunistic landowners. The Crown, on behalf of those politically powerful landowners who were presumably less able, or unwilling, to compete, attempted to re-establish the old, customary wages and guarantee an adequate supply of cheap, servile agricultural labor. Statutory wage maxima were periodically renewed until the great Elizabethan Statute of Artificers (5 Elizabeth, c. 4 (1563)), which discarded national maxima and ordered justices of the peace to regulate and adjust (assess) local wages according to local conditions, particularly the price of food, and completely rewrote the labor code.*

Economic analysis demonstrates that price ceilings transform scarcities into shortages, since they whet demand while they discourage supply. Labor markets exhibited this principle perfectly. Maximum wage rates caused more labor services to be 'demanded' at the lower price than there were workers willing to accept employment at them. But below a certain wage rate laborers, like the suppliers of any other good, will not and do not offer their labor for sale (actually, in the case of labor, for rent). Economists call this phenomenon a 'reservation price', the price below which workers will 'reserve' or withdraw their labor from the market. Thus, soon after the initial controls took effect, what one might call the 'Robin Hood' effect emerged. Men tried, with greater or lesser success, to evade the law, and as the government explained,

> [I]f their masters reprove them for bad service, or offer to pay them for the said service according to the form of the said statutes, they fly and run suddenly away out of their services and out of their own country, from County to County and town to town, in strange places unknown to their said masters. And many of them became staff-strikers and live also wicked lives, and rob the poor in simple villages, in bodies of two or three together.[7]

The solution to this problem—which was perceived right from the

---

*See the Appendices below for texts of several important statutes.

start—was *compulsory labor*. All able-bodied men and women under the age of sixty, not otherwise employed or with a livelihood, had to serve as agricultural laborers to whoever required their services. Any vagrants who refused a job could be carted off to jail by the sheriff until someone agreed to put them to work. It was a crime to leave one's job without a reasonable cause (such as nonpayment of wages) before one's term was up, and it was a crime for anyone to employ someone who broke his labor 'contract'. Indeed, it was even a crime to give alms to beggars, lest they escape the necessity of working for a living. The penalties for beggars breaking the labor code were at times particularly severe, including variously whippings, mutilation, slavery for life, even death.[8]

The labor laws were not well-differentiated from poor relief. When the state came to assume the burden of relieving the poor (previously a religious function, until Henry VIII began expropriating the wealth of the monasteries in the 1530s), the two became intertwined. The function of the poor laws was as much to put people to work as it was to alleviate distress. Since relief was administered on the local level, laws were adopted to restrict to their place of birth individuals likely to become public charges. These 'laws of settlement' backfired, since they obstructed the efforts of laborers to escape poverty by seeking work elsewhere.[9]

Duration of Employment

The statutes that fixed wages also regulated the terms of employment in English agriculture (and later, in many trades as well). By custom, as well as by law, hiring was normally for a year, and employers could not normally dismiss their workers at any time, without cause. Neither could workers quit their jobs at any time, without cause. Even by the end of the 18th Century, Blackstone explained in his *Commentaries* that

> If the hiring be general, without any particular time limited, the [common] law construes it to be a hiring for a year; upon a principle of natural equity, that the servant shall serve, and the master maintain him, throughout all the revolutions of the respective seasons, as well when there is work to be done as when there is not.[10]

While concern for employee welfare may have been one reason for this rule, the labor system as a whole established by these statutes—compulsory labor at fixed prices—makes it clear that keeping laborers in a straitjacket was the dominant motive.

Food Supply and Trade

Local authorities regulated the price of foodstuffs and supervised the distribution system. 'Engrossing' was singled out for special discriminatory treatment. The engrosser was a speculator. He purchased crops before they were harvested, or before they reached the town market. The engrosser sold to forestallers—wholesalers who conducted exchanges outside of the town market to avoid the "stallage" fee owed to the (monopoly chartered) owners of the marketplace—and to regrators—black-market retailers who bought from forestallers or engrossers. The practical effect, and perhaps the purpose, of the laws against engrossing, forestalling, and regrating, was to confine the marketing of foodstuffs into narrow geographic markets.[11]

Wages and the price of food were deliberately set to keep laborers poor, according to the precepts of a widespread notion later dubbed the 'theory of low wages', or the 'utility of poverty'. The belief on the part of the ruling classes was that workers who enjoyed an increase in their living standards would 'selfishly' choose leisure over additional work, thereby decreasing the supply of those goods which added to national wealth. "Every one but an idiot," in the classic words of an agricultural progressive Arthur Young (1741-1820), "knows, that the lower classes must be kept poor, or they will never be industrious . . . they must (like all mankind) be in poverty or they will not work."[12]

The Guild System

Wage controls and compulsory labor for the lowest classes of agricultural workers were among the harshest characteristics of a socioeconomic order that did not recognize the principle of occupational freedom for anyone. On the contrary, the right to pursue trades or crafts within the incorporated cities was typically vested in semi-autonomous, economically self-governing, occupational and geographical cartels—the merchant or craft guilds. These cartels controlled and regulated entry into their respective professions, policed production and quality standards, set retail prices and regulated apprentices' and journeymen's wages, and arbitrated disputes among the guild members.[13]

In contrast to later times, secular and religious authority looked on the elimination of competitive rivalry in the various trades and crafts as a positive social good. The guild monopoly was rationalized as necessary to 'protect the unsuspecting public from shoddy goods and unscrupulous artisans', on the theory that unrestricted competition would force producers and traders to cut corners to seize one another's business and exploit the hapless consumer.

Guilds also existed to protect the social and economic status of merchants and craftsmen—probably their true *raison d'être*. In a society which valued security over liberty, the guildsmen were entitled to a customary, secure position in the social order, *a property in their job or way of life.*

The guilds controlled entry into a trade through apprenticeships, and after 1563, the Elizabethan Statute of Artificers 'nationalized' the system (as it denationalized wage controls), generally making seven-year apprenticeships the legal minimum. Apprenticeships were supposed to protect consumers by insuring that only competent artisans could practice a craft. But by raising a legal barrier to entry, they undoubtedly protected the guildsmen's rights to enjoy an income partially due to monopoly. Guilds, moreover, charged premiums which kept even qualified journeymen (who had completed apprenticeships) from becoming masters. And the guilds attempted to keep the apprenticeship system from becoming a source of cheap labor (and thus a means to undercut the cartel) by limiting, or getting the government to limit, the number of apprentices a master might employ together with hired journeymen.[14]

Competition between guilds for work had to be suppressed. According to a prevailing idea, there was only so much work to go around and it ought to be shared. Thus "artificers" and "handicraft people," a 14th century statute (37 Edward III, (1363)) declared, must "hold them every one to one mystery," [craft] on pain of fine and imprisonment. It was only fair, a town ordinance of 1534 explained, that each ought to "keep and occupy his own proper craft or occupation wherein he hath been brought up, so that by their doing *every one of them may live by the other.*"[15]

Competition within the guild also had to be severely limited. Just as modern unions exist to secure for their members a 'property right in their job', so too did the kernel of the guild ethic, that "none should seek an unfair advantage over his fellows" embody "the principle that every burgess should have a share in trade 'sufficient for the maintenance of himself and his family'." Each guildsman was presumed to have a right to the custom of his patrons, and it "was strictly forbidden to entice a servant away from the service of his master or a customer from a dealer" by price competition, or by deviating from guild work rules or production standards. The result, in one historian's view, was an all-pervading system of coercion that "enveloped the life of the mediaeval craftsman in a network of restrictions, which bound him on every side hand and foot," and "did not suffer the minutest detail to escape its rigid scrutiny and observation." Guild communalism embodied "in its regulations a whole social system, into which the individual was completely absorbed by the force of public opinion and the pressure of moral and social conventions." The guilds' private rules carried the force of public law; and in extreme cases, recalcitrant guildsmen who cheated in one way or another to gain an advantage could be expelled from the trade.[16]

Guild work rules and the jurisdictional demarcations separating crafts and trades brought about and tended to perpetuate an artificial and uneconomic division of labor. This problem, plus the slow realization that the guilds themselves, and not competition, exploited consumers, led to the decay of the system as a whole.

The work rules of the guild system are strikingly reminiscent of modern union featherbedding practices and jurisdictional disputes. Carpenters, for instance, were prohibited from doing "masonry, plumbing, daubing or tiling"; shoemakers (or as they used to be called, cordwainers) were not supposed to *repair* shoes, which was reserved for cobblers. Drapers cut cloth for one use, shearmen and tailors cut and sewed garments; at one point, the bakers of white bread were not allowed to bake black bread![17]

Guildsmen protected what they believed to be their property rights by recourse to law courts, when that was possible. If it was not, they took the law into their own hands. In the 14th century, for instance, a merchant complained that

> because he sold his merchandise at a less price than other merchants of the town . . . [his competitors] assaulted him, beat him and ill-treated him and left him there for dead, so that he despaired for life.

Similarly, the "Dyers g[u]ild undertook to work only at certain rates; and when a number of dyers refused to be bound by these rates, the g[u]ild hired Welshmen and Irishmen to waylay and kill them."[18]

Journeymen who organized against their guildsmen employers also employed violence. Thus a clergyman described a 16th century picket line:

> twenty-one journeymen shoemakers . . . assembled on a hill without the town, and sent three of their number to summon all the master shoemakers to meet them, in order to insist upon an advance in their wages threatening that 'there shall none come into the town to serve for that wages within a twelve month and a day, but we woll have an harme or a legge of hym, except they woll take an othe as we have doon.'[19]

The situation on the European continent may well have been worse; as one historian of the guilds explained, violence reached formidable proportions as "bloody battles for the monopoly of work in a particular town often took place."[20]

Technological change occasioned new instances of social strife, as consumer choice collided with the principle of property in a job. A famous case involved the threat "fulling" machinery posed to woolen "cappers." The cappers petitioned the English Parliament, claiming that material felted by machinery was inferior to their own handiwork. Twice Parliament attempted, each time unsuccessfully, to protect consumers from the allegedly shoddy product of machinery—testimony to the real fact of the matter, which was that fulled caps were not really shoddy, only cheaper.[21]

Regulating Monopoly: Common Law and Competition

One of the public rationales for guild control of manufacturing was to protect the consuming public against the exploitative potential of an unrestrained competitive system. Nevertheless, even in the 14th century the Crown recognized the abusive potential of legally established monopoly, and began to regulate the ordinances of guilds, their agreements to fix prices, and their attempts to restrict output (which guilds attempted to achieve typically by limiting the number of hours of work per day).[22]

In the 16th century, Parliament passed the Bill of Conspiracies of Victuallers and Craftsmen (2 & 3 Edward VI, c. 15, (1548)), a turning point in the history of the guild system, and perhaps in the history of the economy.* It prohibited agreements (conspiracies) of victuallers (food sellers) and "artificers, handicraftsmen and labourers" to fix prices for their output, labor, or hours of work (as the case may be). There were fines, and for second or third offenses, jail, the pillory, and even loss of one's ears, for conspiring to sell victuals "at unreasonable prices" or limit output or work "contrary to the laws and statutes of this realm, and to the great hurt and impoverishment of the King's majesty's subjects." The law also prescribed the *dissolution* of any "corporation" (that is, "any society, brotherhood or company of any craft, mystery or occupation of the victuallers above mentioned") which engaged in an unlawful conspiracy.

This statute sought to prevent combinations or conspiracies from interfering with prices, hours of labor and output, etc., which were *themselves* fixed or regulated by positive law. What about agreements between merchants, traders, or laborers to fix the prices and output of services or goods which *were not* regulated by law? This issue must be deferred to the next chapter, when the common-law principles governing combinations or conspiracies 'in restraint of trade' in England and America

---

*The complete text is reproduced as Appendix 2 below.

are taken up. In the meantime, some important developments in the common law regarding competition and monopoly are worth noting.

A few generations after the Bill of Conspiracies of Victuallers and Craftsmen, some landmark decisions *under the common law*, which were largely due to the influence of Sir Edward Coke (1552-1634), established a 'public policy' in favor of competition. The famous antimonopoly cases decided at the turn of the 17th century did not revolutionize the English economy. But they are an important milestone in the legal history of competition in product and labor markets.[23]

The Merchant Tailor's Case (*Davenant* v. *Hurdis,* Moore 576, K.B., 1599) grew out of a jurisdictional dispute between two guilds. Merchant tailors and clothworkers both claimed rights to "finish" cloth, but the latter were more efficient and gradually won a greater and greater share of the trade. The clothworkers were helped along by wealthier merchant tailors who preferred to subcontract the process out to them rather than do it themselves or throw the business to the poorer merchant tailors. These poorer merchant tailors accused the clothworkers of 'stealing' their jobs and battled the 'scabs' through "litigation, and requests that Parliament settle the matter by legislation," and street violence.[24] In the meantime the Merchant Tailor's guild sought to end the conflict by adopting a 'share the work' bylaw, under which all merchants who subcontracted the finishing process had to give half their work to indigent fellow-guildsmen.

Davenant was a merchant tailor who defied the bylaw and sued the guild when the guild's agent attempted to seize his property to pay the fine. He chose Sir Edward Coke, the Attorney General of England, to argue his case.

Coke challenged the lawfulness of the guild's share-the-work plan because it tended to create a monopoly of the trade. The guild might, after all, confine *all* cloth dressing to themselves and throw the *clothworkers* out of work. This, according to Coke, would be illegal, on the grounds that bylaws establishing monopolies or tending to monopolize markets were contrary to the common law.

The Attorney General's argument was the *point d'appui.* How, the guild's attorney argued, could guild *bylaws* be against common law and void, unless the guilds themselves—which had existed for centuries, under the aegis of King and Parliament, precisely to monopolize trade—were against common law and void?

The guild probably had the better legal argument. Nevertheless, none of the judges was disposed to agree with the defense attorney, and the court decided that a "rule of such nature as to bring all trade and traffic into the hands of one company, or one person, and to exclude all others, is illegal." (p. 591).

The Merchant Tailor's Case established that there were common law principles against monopolistic practices, good even to police the behavior of those monopolies established by positive law. In the famous Case of Monopolies (*Darcy* v. *Allen*, 11 Co. Rep. 84b, Moore 671, K.B., 1599, decided 1603) Coke directly challenged the authority of the Crown to establish monopolies in the first place.

In this case, Queen Elizabeth granted to one of her favorites an exclusive monopoly to manufacture and sell playing cards. Unlike monopolies being granted to various merchants for foreign trade, however, this monopoly applied to an established industry, and threw many businessmen and their employees out of work. They sued, and Coke trumped the new card-makers, getting the Court to decide that the monopoly *grant* was "against the common law" and "utterly void." "All trades," the Court held,

> which prevent idleness (the bane of the commonwealth) and exercise men and youth in labour for the maintenance of themselves and for their families . . . are profitable for the commonwealth, and therefore the grant to the plaintiff to have the sole making of them is against the common law, and the benefit and liberty of the subject . . . and the common law, in this point, agrees with the equity of the law of God, . . . by which it appears, that every man's trade maintains his life, and therefore he ought not to be deprived or dispossessed of it, no more than of his life. (pp. 86a-87a)

Monopolies, said the Court (adopting Coke's language), were "not only a damage and prejudice to those who exercise the same trade, but also to all other subjects," that is, the consuming public; for "the price of the commodity will be raised . . . [and] the commodity is not so good and merchantable as before." (p. 86b) No classical or neo-classical economist could put it better.

Seven years later Coke, then Chief Justice of the court of common pleas, drew out the implicit logic of the two previous cases. He claimed that the Courts had the authority under the common law *to overrule an Act of Parliament*—he asserted, in other words, the right of judicial review. In *Dr. Bonham's Case* (77 Eng. Rep. 646, K.B. 1610) Coke invalidated the London College of Physicians' attempt to penalize Bonham for practicing medicine without a license. Despite that guild's clear Parliamentary authority to do so, Coke claimed that

> it appears in our books, that in many cases, the common law will controul . . . Acts of Parliament, and sometimes adjudge them to be utterly void: for when an Act of Parliament is against common right and reason, or repugnant, or impossible to be performed, the common law will controul it, and adjudge such Act to be void . . . (p. 652)

Finally, in the *Ipswich Tailor's Case* (11 Co. Rep. 53a, K.B. 1614) a guild's apprenticeship rule that excluded a tailor from working was voided. The Court announced that at

> common law, no man could be prohibited from working in any lawful trade, for the law abhors idleness . . . and . . . all monopolies, which prohibit any from working in any lawful trade . . . (p. 53b)

were unlawful.

Most historians agree that Coke was actually *making* new common law in these cases. The historical precedents Coke used to bolster his arguments were not impressive, when they weren't plainly wrong. Nevertheless, Coke's principles, once *they* became precedents, moved the common law in a direction favorable to freedom of enterprise.

Even so, the decisions in these anti-monopoly cases did not create laissez faire. In the first place, the guild system survived the 17th century legally unscathed. Apprenticeships, the legal regulation of prices, wages, and output, the restrictions on geographical mobility, all continued intact; and Coke's attempt to establish the right of judicial review of Acts of Parliament did not become part of the English legal tradition, as it would of the American. The great anti-monopoly crusades of that century ended when *Parliament* assumed, and in succeeding years exercised, the monopoly-granting power hitherto the preserve of the Crown.

Even more importantly, the common law protections for freedom of trade existed *within,* and were applications of, a fundamentally *regulatory* tradition—they were *not* a recognition of any absolute natural rights existing anterior to civil society, which the common law saw as its duty to protect. The economic "freedom which the common lawyers favored," as a legal historian explained, "was freedom from arbitrary restraints *not sanctioned by the law,* whether those restraints were imposed by the *voluntary acts of contracting parties,* or were imposed by persons acting without legal authority."[25] But this freedom of an individual, another jurist noted, was "compatible with countless restraints imposed by law for the benefit of his fellow subjects individually, or of the public generally, or of himself."[26]

Hence, the common law "right to work" turned, in no trivial sense, on a *public policy abhorring idleness* (which, in another context, was not inconsistent with compulsory work), rather than on a policy favoring unlimited occupational freedom. Put another way, the juridical recognition of the harmful effects of monopoly turned as much on a public policy favoring *low prices* (an effect) as on a public policy favoring *competition* (a cause).[27] The difference is significant. A policy in favor of low prices is legally compatible (as a policy of free competition is not) with statutes fixing maximum wages. The full significance of the difference—the difference, that is, between what economic freedom the common law was willing to protect in the name of "public policy" and that which a consistent, laissez-faire, individual *rights* policy would recognize—will become clearer in the next chapter, when the laws against combinations and conspiracies (of labor and capital) in restraint of trade are explored.

The Rise of Economic Liberalism . . .

The early 17th century anti-monopoly cases, decided on common law principles, established a 'right to work' against the *arbitrary* exercise of government power, and against the *arbitrary* exercise of private monopoly power secured by government privilege. The more radical notion that *any* interference with a person's liberty to dispose of his person or property as he alone saw fit *was itself arbitrary* evolved much more slowly, and on the level of political philosophy, not in the common law.[28]

The most important of the 'libertarian' philosophers was John Locke (1632-1704). He argued that each man had an equal, natural right—derived from his right to life—to acquire and dispose of property, including his own labor, which the laws of the commonwealth should recognize and protect. The end or purpose of "law is not to abolish or to restrain but to preserve and enlarge freedom." "[L]iberty," according to Locke,

> is to be free from restraint and violence from others . . . to dispose and order as he lists his person, actions, possessions, and his whole property, within the allowance of those laws under which he is, and therein not to be subject to the arbitrary will of another, but freely to follow his own.

Government, Locke maintained, ought to secure equally to all men a "perfect freedom to order their actions and dispose of their possessions as they see fit, within the bounds of the law of nature, without asking leave or depending upon the will of any other man." Government power was strictly limited; it

> is not, nor can possibly be, absolutely arbitrary over the lives and fortunes of the people . . . for nobody can transfer to another more power than he has himself, and nobody has an arbitrary power . . . to . . . take away the life or property of another.[29]

Natural right and natural law ideas were common currency in England and America by the end of the 18th century, but Lockean ideas had also migrated to France via Voltaire and Montesquieu and spread through the "laissez-faire" doctrines of the Physiocrats. "God," wrote A.R.J. Turgot (1727-1781), a leading physiocrat, colleague of Adam Smith, and Comptroller General of France, "by giving to man wants, and making his recourse to work necessary to supply them, has made the right to work the property of every man, and this property is the first, the most sacred, the most imprescriptable of all."[30] The philosophy of royal absolutism, according to which the right to work at a trade was a royal privilege which the King might sell and that his subjects were bound to purchase from him, was (in the memorable words of the physiocrat Abbé Beaudeau) "the most odious maxim which the spirit of domination and rapacity ever invented."[31]

The Scottish social philosopher and political economist Adam Smith agreed. The "property which every man has in his own labour," he wrote,

> as it is the original foundation of all other property, so it is the most sacred and inviolable. The patrimony of a poor man lies in the strength and dexterity of his hands; and to hinder him from employing this strength and dexterity in that manner he thinks proper without injury to his neighbour, is a plain violation of this most sacred property. It is a manifest encroachment upon the just liberty both of the workman, and of those who might be disposed to employ him. As it hinders the one from working at what he thinks proper, so it hinders the others from employing whom they think proper.[32]

Libertarian, natural rights arguments grew increasingly common in 18th century England, and so too there were a growing number of philosophers (such as Bernard Mandeville) who were willing to concede that the pursuit of individual self-interest was ethically legitimate, at least to the extent that it had socially beneficial consequences. Adam Smith's unique contribution was to systematically investigate the advantages to society— the public interest—of permitting relatively unfettered self-interest full sway in the marketplace. Breaking decisively with the assumptions which have typically governed the traditionalistic economic order, Smith and his followers stressed that individual happiness *and* social well-being were best served when men were left free to pursue their own self-interest. The value of self-interest and competition in the social order was, above, all the premiss uniting the natural rights and utilitarian defenders of economic liberalism and distinguishing them from their anticapitalist predecessors—and successors.[33]

. . . Which Lifts All Boats

According to Smith, the pursuit of self-interest did not lead to social disorder, but was actually a means for social integration. Even though buyers and sellers were naturally rivals in the market, there was an important philosophical sense in which their interests did *not* conflict. When men exchange goods and services freely and are unable to force one another to act against their judgment of what is in their own self-interest, exploitation disappears and they discover that their interests are *complementary*. The nexus between individual self-interest and social advantage was Smith's observation that it will readily occur to each man to 'interest' himself in, and find some means of satisfying, the desires of other men, should he wish them to serve his interests. "Whoever offers to another a bargain of any kind," he wrote, "proposes to do this. Give me that which I want, and you shall have this which you want . . . "[34] In a free marketplace, men cooperate on the basis of mutual advantage and incentive instead of acting in response to mutual (or unilateral) coercion and fear.

Competition preserves the "harmony of interests" in the individualistic economic order. Should a buyer offer less than a seller is willing to accept, the seller must be free to seek out a competing buyer; and the original buyer must be free to seek out a competing seller. Should a seller ask more than a buyer is willing to pay, the seller must be free to seek out a competing buyer; and the buyer must be free to seek out a competing seller. Each must be free to seek out someone with whom to cooperate for their mutual advantage.

The higgling between buyers and sellers causes the actual price at which commodities are bought and sold to gravitate toward a "natural," or (what is now more commonly called an) equilibrium price. This price equates the quantity supplied with the quantity demanded; every willing seller finds a willing buyer. It is the price where 'the markets clear'; the price at which there will be no unsold goods and no unsatisfied buyers. If the actual price is higher, buyers will not take all that is offered, and sellers will have to lower their price to vent unsold goods. If the actual price is lower, more goods will be demanded than are being willingly supplied, and the price will be bid up by unsatisfied buyers.

Though Smith did not use the terminology, he and his followers regarded the natural, or market-clearing price arrived at in the market as the 'socially just' price as well, insofar as it is the 'social product' of the system of free exchange. The equilibrium price does not satisfy sellers *unilaterally,* for they would be happier to get more. It does not satisfy buyers *unilaterally,* for they would be happier to pay less. But since neither can compel the other, the natural price is the uniquely satisfactory, socially harmonious rate of exchange. The analysis is the same for buyers or sellers *unwilling* or *unable* to buy or sell at the market-clearing price; and the market for labor services is no different. Freely contracted wages at mutually satisfactory rates tend toward an equilibrium, market-clearing level where there are neither unsatisifed buyers (employers) nor unsatisfied sellers (employees). This equilibrium wage rate defines the condition of voluntary full employment within an industry; and equilibrium wage rates, as later economists have argued, define the condition of voluntary full employment across the economy as well.[35]

Economic liberals such as Smith insisted that the profit motive was 'socially virtuous'; it would lead men to so dispose of their property and labor in a manner consistent with the greatest good of the greatest number—of consumers. Greater profits will be earned in producing those goods and services consumers demand *most* urgently; capital *and* labor will be attracted *to* employments that *best* serve the public (as the individual members of the public determine), and *away* from employments which serve less urgent consumer demands.

Freedom in the labor market, Smith claimed, leads laborers to allocate themselves geographically and occupationally on the basis of the 'net advantageousness' of the various employment opportunities open and known to them. This movement, or mobility, of laborers toward some pursuits and away from others, is much like the movement of capital in the economy, save that greater or lesser money profitability is typically less important in the former than in the latter case. A worker, for instance, might choose to accept a lower wage in his home country, with its familiar surroundings, language, and culture, rather than migrate to a strange land where wages are higher.[36]

The "net advantageousness" or profit-and-loss mechanism by which labor and capital shuffle and reshuffle themselves in response to changing consumer preferences, technological developments, or discovery of new resources depends crucially on inequality of reward. If wage and profit differentials are not permitted to exist, there will be little or no incentive to move or to change. Economic freedom, in other words, implies inequality—of reward, of position, of values. The equality of opportunity in a competitive economy means nothing except the equal liberty to compete in product or labor markets. And as far as society is concerned, either individuals allocate themselves geographically and occupationally in accordance with their own wage and non-wage preferences (guided by consumer demand), or they must be allocated by others.

In common with other 18th century liberals, Smith denounced the theory of low wages. Men did not respond to rewards differently just because they were laborers or capitalists; and as the profit motive led entrepreneurs to greater endeavors, so too did workingmen put forth greater effort if lured by the prospect of greater reward. Indeed, Smith noted that "when they are liberally paid by the piece," they "are very apt to over-work themselves." The just and proper policy of the great society was an *economy of high wages*—that is, an economy of rising living standards for all.

> Servants, labourers and workmen of different kinds, make up the
> far greater part of every political society. But what improves the

circumstances of the greater part can never be regarded as an inconvenience to the whole. No society can surely be flourishing and happy, of which the greater part of the members are poor and miserable.[37]

Smith contended that capital and labor must *both* be free, if the market is to work properly. The "pretence" that apprenticeships and guilds were necessary to protect consumers "is without any foundation. The real and effectual discipline which is exercised over a workman" is "that of his customers. It is the fear of losing their employment which restrains his frauds and corrects his negligence." Exclusive guild corporations only weaken "the force of this discipline." It was an open secret that "in many large incorporated towns no tolerable workmen are to be found, even in some of the most necessary trades. If you would have your work tolerably executed, it must be done in the suburbs, where the workmen, having no exclusive privilege, have nothing but their character to depend on . . . "[38]

The innumerable controls and regulations on food, Smith pointed out in his famous "Digression on the Corn Trade," were neither in the interest of producers or consumers—indeed, even the much-despised speculators and middlemen served the very important public interest of smoothing out wide swings in supply and demand (over time and space).[39]

Capital and Labor: The Wages Fund

Free economic exchange, according to Smith and his classical economic followers, was mutually beneficial; and even though buyers and sellers were natural rivals, nevertheless, on the 'system' level, their interests did not fundamentally conflict. The examples Smith used to demonstrate the symbiotic nature of economic exchange were typically drawn from exchange between producers and consumers. But what about the relationship between laborers and employers? Were the interests of laborers, or 'labor' as a class, and capitalists, or 'capital' as a class, in conflict, or were their interests complementary and symbiotic as well? What about bargains between capitalists and laborers? Did inequality in economic position vitiate or destroy the case for competitive contracting in these markets? And what about the role of combinations—of unions?

Smith defended competitive contracting between individual laborers and capitalists on grounds of natural justice and social utility. And he offered this defense in the context of a society where disparities of income, wealth, and political power between laborers and employers were quite pronounced. Nevertheless, in his famous chapter, "The Wages of Labour," as elsewhere in *The Wealth of Nations,* Smith's treatment of the relations between capitalists and laborers included several ambiguous discussions which were of great significance for the later development of industrial democratic theory—indeed, some of the more important radical criticisms of competition, which we will be exploring in later chapters, arose straight out of *The Wealth of Nations*.

On what we might call the 'macro' level, Smith's analysis of the forces determining real wages (living standards) in the economy—an analysis that in the hands of his followers came to be known as the 'wages fund' doctrine (the term is not in *The Wealth of Nations*)—clearly supported the 'harmony of interest' doctrine, and implicitly denied any fundamental significance to bargaining power or strikes by unions as vehicles for working class advancement. But on another, 'micro', level, dealing with the actual process of wage setting, Smith seemed to contend that employers, after all, *did* possess overwhelming advantages.

The gist of what came to be known as the wages fund doctrine is the proposition that the average real wage (not the relative distribution of national income between wage earners and capitalists, but the absolute amount) was strictly and impersonally determined by the market, particularly by the proportion of capital to population. The demand for all labor was the entire amount of 'circulating' capital all employers spent to employ laborers. This fund of working capital was, at any point in time, a sum fixed and predetermined by prior savings. All circulating capital which *could* be paid out in wages (without decreasing anticipated or realized profits, thus checking the accumulation of capital and hence diminishing real wages in the future) *would* be paid out. Competition between employers insured that result. The aggregate supply of labor was simply the laboring population, a number also fixed at any time. Competition between them for jobs implied exhaustion of the wages fund as well. So, the average real wage for the economy as a whole was strictly determined by the law of supply and demand—the division of the wages fund by the labor supply. The concept of the wages fund is thus analogous, although in an imperfect way, to the modern notion of national income per capita.[40]

The only way to increase real wages was to increase the rate of capital accumulation faster than the rate of population increase. "The demand for those who live by wages," Smith wrote, "necessarily increases with the revenue and stock of every country, and cannot possibly increase without it."[41] The rate of capital accumulation (or its deaccumulation) is the fundamental determinant of employment and wages in the economy, a determinant exercised through the demand for labor (employment). In "years of scarcity" wages will sink as self-employed or independent workmen seek employment while employers are at the same time letting workers go. "More people want employment than can easily get it; many are willing to take it upon lower terms than [in] ordinary [times]." But "in years of plenty" the demand for those who live by wages "is continually increasing," and the "scarcity of hands occasions a competition among masters, who bid against one another, in order to get workmen, and thus voluntarily break through the natural combination of masters not to raise wages."[42]

Capital accumulation, in other words, makes the payment of higher wages *and* the receipt of greater profits possible; competition between employers for (now more) relatively scarce labor, and between employers to sell their products, makes higher wages and lower prices necessary. On this level, then, there is a fundamental harmony of interest between 'labor' and 'capital' (normally looked on as rivals in any particular bargain, or as rival claimants to the relative distribution of the proceeds of industry). The prosperity of both depends on the accumulation of capital—the goose that lays the golden eggs—and the circumstances which permit and encourage this accumulation, such as the security of private property and contracts, and the potential to reap profit.

The increase in the demand for labor which results from an increase in the accumulation of capital will, as Smith was aware, raise the price of labor. Thus, *ceteris paribus,* the "increase in the wages of labour necessarily increases the price of many commodities, by increasing that part of it which resolves itself into wages, and so far tends to diminish their consumption both at home and abroad." Higher wages that result from this case were not, however, a social evil. The "same cause . . . which raises the wages of labour, the increase of stock, tends to increase its productive powers, and to make a smaller quantity of labour produce a greater quantity of work." By economizing on labor, employers rearrange the division of labor so that the "increase of" labor's price is more than compensated for by the diminution of its quantity per unit of output. The enhanced productivity results in a great increase in total output, which, as Smith and his followers developed in greater detail, reduces prices, and in so doing increases real purchasing power. This increased purchasing power increases the demand for output, and, *pari passu,* the demand for laborers to produce it. There was no 'lump of labor', no fixed amount of total social wealth which had to be shared, lest some go without work.[43]

Economists after Smith identified the "funds destined for the payment of wages," or for the "maintenance of labour," as a 'wages fund'. And since the wages fund was part of employers' *capital,* economists from Adam Smith to John Stuart Mill explained that *wages were paid from capital*—or, to put this another way, that employers' capital was the source of workers' wages. What the economists meant by the word 'source' was the following. Wages, in the final analysis, are not money, but the things money can buy (output). Since capital is the source and (at least one) limit of output, it necessarily follows that *all* wages are paid from *all* capital. (It would miss the point entirely to object that the *source* of wages, in this aggregate sense, is the revenue employers get from selling output.)

Now the meaning of the idea that wages were paid from capital, explained in the previous paragraph, is little more than a restatement of the truism that *all* production in an economy is necessarily limited by the amount (and quality) of capital (and technological know-how) in existence. This version of the wages fund idea, at least on the surface, concerns only the amount of real wages in the economy as a whole, and not the relative distribution of wages and profits in the economy, or within an industry or firm.

Nevertheless, there was another interpretation of the wages fund that led in an entirely different and more controversial direction. Adam Smith, as well as many of his followers, illustrated the meaning of the idea that the wages fund maintains the laborer with the example of agriculture.[44] Farm laborers must be paid (that is, they must subsist) during the growing season, even though their employers do not realize any income until after the harvest. Hence laborers' wages must be advanced out of employers' previously accumulated cash savings. What a farmer can pay to laborers is therefore limited—or so it was argued—by what he had saved from previous years.

Now this 'period of production' analysis seems to imply that on a 'microeconomic' level the capital in the hands of any *given* employer is *both the source and the limit of his own* employees' wages. Nevertheless, the theorem that 'the *real* wages of any *particular* set of laborers' is fixed or 'predetermined' by *their own* employer's capital is "an entirely different proposition" from the aggregate interpretation given previously. It was a proposition that caused much confusion about the significance of labor combinations and strikes in relation to the wages fund (taken up in the next chapter).[45]

Capital and Labor: Bargaining Power and Strikes

When he looked at the impersonal social mechanism operating in all wage transactions, Smith made little reference to the idea that workers would get the short end of any wage bargains. But when he looked at the mechanism for setting individual wage transactions, Smith depicted competition very much in terms of unequal bargaining power; in this context he did seem to believe that employers held all the aces.

"What are the common wages of labour," Smith wrote, "depends every where upon the contract usually made between those two parties, whose interests are by no means the same. The workmen desire to get as much, the masters as little as possible." But

> [i]t is not, however, difficult to foresee which of the two parties must, *upon all ordinary occasions, have the advantage in the dispute,* and force the other into a compliance with their terms. The masters, being fewer in number, *can combine much more easily;* and the law, besides, authorises, or at least does not prohibit their combinations, while it prohibits those of the workmen. We have no acts of parliament against combining to lower the price of work; but many against combining to raise it.[46]

Smith furthermore contended that while "[i]n the long-run the workman may be as necessary to his master as his master is to him, . . . the necessity is not so immediate." The employer's built-in advantage is the worker's poverty. The worker, Smith wrote, cannot wait. His resources are scanty, and in

> all such disputes the masters can hold out much longer. A landlord, a farmer, a master manufacturer, or merchant, though they did not employ a single workman, could generally live a year or two upon the stocks which they have already acquired. Many workmen could not subsist a week, few could subsist a month, and scarce any a year without employment.[47]

The bargaining advantage that employers' greater wealth allegedly gave them could be used to beat wages down to very low levels, although Smith believed that in "disputes with their workmen" it was "impossible to reduce, for any considerable time, the ordinary wages even of the lowest species of labour" below subsistence. The subsistence wage must also be sufficient to marry and bring up a family, or "the race of such workmen could not last beyond the first generation."[48]

It is not easy to square Smith's 'micro-economic' discussion of wages and combinations with his 'macro' discussion of the forces which determine wages.

First, Smith explained those "circumstances"—a continually increasing accumulation of capital—"which sometimes give the labourers an advantage, and enable them to raise their wages considerably above" subsistence. In the growing economy, where the increase of revenue and stock "furnishes employment for a greater number than had been employed the year before, the workmen have no occasion to combine in order to raise their wages," since the "scarcity of hands occasions a competition among masters, who bid against one another, in order to get workmen, and thus voluntarily break through the natural combination of masters not to raise wages." Similarly, in a later discussion, Smith observed that an investor in new trade or manufacture

> must at first entice his workmen from other employments by higher wages than they can either earn in their own trades, or than the nature of his work would otherwise require, and a considerable time must pass away before he can venture to reduce them to the common level.[49]

So in a progressing economy, competition worked to the advantage of employer and employee alike. In a stationary economy, however, Smith concluded that the increase of the labor supply would lead to a "competition of the labourers," which, along with "the interest of the masters," "would soon reduce" wages to the "lowest rate which is consistent with common humanity." With a dearth of capital, employers could not be "obliged to bid against one another" for workers. But in slack times, "where the funds destined for the maintenance of labour were sensibly decaying," wages would fall naturally. One can easily imagine the occasional employer combination in any of these circumstances operating to delay an increase in wages or make a decrease more rapid. Nevertheless, it would certainly seem that the power of combinations of masters to fix prices was subordinate to the larger, impersonal economic forces determining competition throughout the economy.[50]

Did Smith actually believe that employers *ordinarily* combined to lower wages—that employer "monopsony" [a monopoly of buyers] was the common state of affairs? (If so, then the inter-employer competition implied virtually everywhere else in his treatise might be likened to a "grin without a cat.") Or did Smith refer to *extraordinary* occasions—that is, to labor *disputes* brought on by a combination of laborers?

His discussion was extremely elusive. At first, he seemed to say that employer combination was the norm. "We rarely hear," he wrote,

> of the combinations of masters, though frequently of those of workmen. But whoever imagines, upon this account, that masters rarely combine, is as ignorant of the world as of the subject. *Masters are always and every where in a sort of tacit, but constant and uniform combination, not to raise the wages of labour above their actual rate.* To violate this combination is every where a most unpopular action, and a sort of reproach to a master among his neighbours and equals. We seldom, indeed, hear of this combination, because it is the usual, and one may say, the natural state of things which nobody ever hears of.

This frightening observation, however, turns out to be little more than the obvious *interest* or *desire* of employers not to pay more than the going rate. For Smith adds immediately the following proviso:

> Masters too *sometimes* enter into *particular* combinations to sink the wages of labour even below this rate. These are always

conducted with the utmost silence and secrecy, till the moment of execution, and when the workmen yield, as they sometimes do, without resistance, though severely felt by them, they are never heard of by other people.[51]

Smith finishes this discussion with some observations about combinations of workmen. He believes that sometimes they are "defensive," that is, organized in response to employer combination. But they "sometimes too, without any provocation of this kind, combine of their own accord to raise the price of their labour," in response to "the high price of provisions" (brought about, one supposes, by inflation or poor harvests) or in response to "the great profit which their masters make by their work." Smith notes that

they have always recourse to the loudest clamour, and sometimes to the most shocking violence and outrage. They are desperate, and act with the folly and extravagance of desperate men, who must either starve, or frighten their masters into an immediate compliance with their demands.

The upshot, according to Smith, is that employers call in the authorities to put down the violence. In any event, strikes rarely succeed, "partly from the interposition of the civil magistrate, partly from the superior steadiness of the masters, partly from the necessity which the greater part of the workmen are under of submitting for the sake of present subsistence."[52]

Finally, while Smith did not speak directly on the justice or expediency of the various statutes prohibiting combinations by laborers, there is reasonably strong evidence that he was *not* in favor of prohibiting them. First, in the passage quoted earlier, Smith noted that while labor combination was prohibited, employer combinations were not (or so he believed: see chapter two *infra.*). Second, Smith believed that the law should treat individuals impartially, regardless of their station. Third, on the question of combination *in general,* he came out for a policy of laissez faire:

People of the same trade seldom meet together, even for merriment and diversion, but the conversation ends in a conspiracy against the public, or in some contrivance to raise prices. It is impossible indeed to prevent such meetings, *by any law which either could be executed, or would be consistent with liberty and justice.* But though the law cannot hinder people of the same trade from sometimes assembling together, it ought to do nothing to facilitate such assemblies; much less to render them necessary.[53]

The classical economists' analysis of strikes will be deferred to the next chapter, where the law governing combinations in England and America is taken up. The followers of Smith agreed, in the main, with him that strikes generally fail of their purpose—but not necessarily for the reasons (government suppression) that Smith adduced. Nevertheless, what Smith said about workers' bargaining power, employer combinations (monopsony), and employers' alleged ability to reduce wages to subsistence, constituted an important legacy to the radical socialist and syndicalist critics of capitalism—who purported to demonstrate that employers kept wages at subsistence at all times, whether they combined or not.

Labor Theories of Value and Exchange

There was another profound, and profoundly ambiguous, legacy Adam Smith bequeathed to 19th century defenders of industrial individualism and to their critics, the industrial democrats: the 'labor theory of value'.

Somewhat as Locke wrote about the origins of private property, Smith contended that labor was the *cause* of value, in the sense that labor must be expended to make something into an economic good. This 'labor cost' theory of value, we might call it, amounted to the claim that

> The real price of every thing, what every thing really costs to the man who wants to acquire it, is the toil and trouble of acquiring it. . . . What is bought with money or with goods is purchased by labour, as much as what we acquire by the toil of our own body . . . Labour was the first price, the original purchase-money that was paid for all things.[54]

Smith also wrote that labor *measured* value, in two separate senses. *Before* private property in land or the accumulation of capital, all goods produced by labor would, according to Smith, exchange on the basis of equal *quantities* of labor expended to produce them—though he was careful to add, *only when the labor was of the same type.* The reason for this important proviso was that not all labor *was* of the same type. Characteristics such as severity, "dexterity," or "ingenuity," which must be acquired—we might add that the ability to acquire them is not equally distributed in the population—put a premium on the produce of specialized labor. Therefore, "the produce of one hour's labour" of one kind "may frequently exchange for that of two hours labour in the other."[55]

Nevertheless, if one is concerned with the distribution of income in the primitive economy, Smith contended that prior to "the appropriation of land and the accumulation of stock, the *whole produce of labour belongs to the labourer.* He has neither landlord nor master to share with him."[56]

But even after the division of labor, according to Smith, labor still measured value, at least insofar as the value of commodities exchanged is related to the labor of other men which the commodity can (indirectly) purchase. This might be called Smith's 'labor purchase' theory of value:

> The value of any commodity, therefore, to the person who possesses it, and who means not to use or consume it himself, but to exchange it for other commodities, *is equal to the quantity of labour which it enables him to purchase or command*. . . . Labour, therefore, is the real measure of the exchangeable value of all commodities.[57]

Whether one looks at it from the standpoint of cost, measure, or purchase, labor seems to be some *thing* that is *itself* exchanged. And in succeeding years, as will be explored in chapters three and four, the critics of competitive capitalism developed this idea in a radical direction. Many insisted that labor was the *only* source of value and the *sole* claim to remuneration—and that the sharing of the produce of labor with landlord and master was a form of theft of the "surplus value" created by the laborer but stolen by the landlord and capitalist because of their monopoly control of access to the means of production and subsistence.

Moreover, some influential critics of capitalism denied that there was any just difference between types of labor. Seizing on the Physiocrats' notion that "exchange is a contract of equality, equal value being given in exchange for equal value,"[58] some asserted that there is injustice in free exchange, even if both parties are *mutually* better off after having freely bargained over a wage or a price, unless the two parties are 'equally' better off. This concept is at odds with the basis of self-interested economic exchange. Transactions occur precisely because A values something that B has *more* than he values something of his own, and vice versa.

Rights or Utility?

The late 18th and early 19th century case for an individualistic social policy was neither fully worked out, nor entirely free from ambiguity. The tension between the 'natural rights' and 'social utilitarian' justifications for freedom in the marketplace is one of the best known and most important of these ambiguities.

Smith believed that freedom of contract was *both* just *and* socially expedient, a theme taken up in case after case where he denounced various restrictions on competition. "There was," to Smith, as one scholar recently put it,

> no trade-off between "efficiency" and "equity" in the more

familiar modern sense. As a general principle of social order, the freedom of individual choice would produce efficiency; but it would also be a central attribute of any social order that was just.[59]

Nevertheless, Smith was far from being an unqualified advocate of egoism or self-interest. For that matter, neither was he an unqualified advocate of natural rights or laissez faire. He favored government provision of some basic services (such as public education or poor relief, as long as such relief did not interfere overmuch with labor mobility) and government building of roads and canals; and he was willing to countenance some (though not many) government restrictions on individual freedom where, as he put it in one instance, these "might endanger the security of the whole society." Yet the grounds for providing public education or relief of the poor are far from apparent on the principles of natural liberty. It may be in the interest of A that B, C, D, etc., be educated or fed; that is not the same as saying that B, C, or D have the *right* to A's property without A's consent. What crime has A committed to justify depriving him of his property? Does he have title to his property by right, or only by the sufferance of the arbitrary wills of a majority of other men?[60]

There was a strain of natural rights political theory in the 19th century, kept alive by men such as Frédéric Bastiat in France or Herbert Spencer in England. But the 'main line' of liberal political economists and social philosophers, beginning with Jeremy Bentham, abandoned the moral language of natural rights as the basis of (and justification for) individual freedom. They opted, instead, for "social utilitarianism," for the idea that the greatest good of the greatest number is the basis for permitting or disallowing individual freedom.[61]

The significance of this—what one scholar has called the moral revolution in 19th century economic science—is plain. Rights in utilitarian theory are not recognized by society as inalienable, but created by society and protected only insofar as the individual good or happiness secured therefrom adds to, or at least does not subtract from, social good or happiness. In any contest between the individual and society, however, utilitarianism lends itself easily, if not necessarily, to a kind of legislative democratic majoritarianism that tramples utterly individual liberty and legal equality[62] in the name of social welfare.

Just how far this philosophy differs from the ideas underlying the American Revolution was made fairly plain by the American novelist and Benthamite John Neal. In his notes to Jeremy Bentham's *Principles of Legislation,* Neal averred that he would "recognize no duties, no rights, in opposition to . . . [t]*he greatest happiness principle,*" including those which the American Revolution were fought:

No! for I acknowledge no rights that can interfere with the *greatest* happiness of the *greatest number*—none whatever, not even that of 'life, liberty and the pursuit of happiness'—to borrow the awkward, and either very unmeaning or untrue phraseology of most of our constitutions. If it be better off for the greatest happiness of the greatest number that a man should die, whoever he may be, and whatever he may be, *cut him off without mercy.* And so with his liberty, and so with his property.[63]

Utilitarian economists and social theorists replaced the natural rights of man with the happiness of the mass of men as the basis of their defense of free markets and of the free society. In so doing, they subtly but unmistakably undermined the defense of private property and contracts as these institutions were defended by natural rights theorists such as John Locke. Utilitarians reinvigorated the dichotomy between private right (individual self-interest) and public good (collective interest) that previous generations of liberals had struggled to surmount and opened the way for those who, with a very different perception of man, society, and the economy, turned liberalism on its head.

The 18th century legal commentator, Sir William Blackstone, argued in the first book of his famous *Commentaries on the Laws of England* (1765-1769), that "the public good is in nothing more essentially interested than in the protection of every individual's private rights."[64] In succeeding generations, various democratic collectivist philosophies argued, in essence, that "abolition" should replace "protection." In succeeding chapters, their reasons will be explored. In the meantime, the next chapter will take up the treatment in law and economic theory of workingmen's combinations in England and America. For unions first obtained legitimacy when capitalist ideas and ideals were ascendant, even though these organizations, and their intellectual champions, ultimately refused to accept the limits capitalism imposed on collective action.

2. Competition and Combination: From Criminal Conspiracy to Free Association

 This chapter will explain how and to what extent labor combinations achieved legitimacy in England and America during the first quarter of the 19th century, while the liberal, pro-competitive ideas discussed in the previous chapter were ascendant. In succeeding chapters, the anti-competitive, pro-industrial-democracy theories that arose in reaction to economic individualism will be explored, together with the demands that wages be once again taken out of competition. The significance of the policies governing and limiting combinations in the free market will become apparent in later chapters, as pro-union forces pressed them to the limit, and beyond.

Combinations 'In Restraint of Trade'

The Anglo-American legal tradition was, from a very early period, suspicious of and hostile to private *combinations* of employers or laborers to advance their economic interests at the expense of what were deemed the interests, or rights, of the public at large. The "common law favored 'low' prices rather than free prices, and accepted as a matter of course that all important prices would be set by political or corporate authorities."[1] More generally, the economic "freedom which the common lawyers," or the common law, "favored was freedom from arbitrary restraints *not sanctioned by the law*, whether those restraints were imposed by the *voluntary acts of contracting parties*, or were imposed by persons acting without legal authority."[2] A 'pure' laissez-faire standard—with individuals free, as long as they do not employ force or fraud, to make contracts to obtain or dispose of property, *alone or in groups*, on *whatever* terms are mutually agreeable—never existed in the common law. Common-law rules evolved over the centuries to favor a great deal of contractual freedom, but such rules were always subject to the legislature's overriding, if ill-defined, 'police power'. This statement is true for America as well, even after the adoption of the federal constitution, the implications of which will become clear only in chapter eight.

The history of restraint of trade, as the history of anti-combination law, is complicated. But the legal history of unionism cannot be understood without some grasp of the broad issues involved. The fairly substantial body of law regulating or prohibiting combinations, contracts, and conspiracies in restraint of trade developed in the context of, and was meant to preserve the structure of, a *noncompetitive* economy: an economy in which individual capitalists and laborers were *not* generally free to make such price or wage bargains as they chose, and where entry into trades, occupations, or crafts was *not* generally open to anyone on equal terms. But the evolution of a competitive economy did not result in the abrogation of conspiracy law, and labor unions (in England and America) tangled with it throughout the 19th century.

Workmen who sought to raise their wages, or otherwise collectively determine the conditions under which they would individually accept employment, fell afoul of more than one body of law prior to the 19th century. There were statutes fixing wages and prices and regulating the activity (including the hours of work) of legally authorized guilds. There was a body of judicial decisions concerning combinations, or agreements in restraint of trade. There was a slowly evolving, and slowly expanding, law of criminal conspiracy in general; and, finally, there was the eventual application of the common law doctrine of conspiracy to 'economic crimes'; that is, to activities deemed unlawfully 'in restraint of trade'.[3]

The wage- and price-fixing statutes discussed in the previous chapter implicitly outlawed combinations to defeat the purpose of the laws, and at least in one case (34 Edward III, c. 9 (1360)) did so explicitly. But in 1548, a comprehensive Bill of Conspiracies of Victuallers and Craftsmen (2 & 3 Edward V, c. 15) clearly banned agreements among food sellers, handicraftsmen, laborers, and artisans to fix prices or (among the latter four groups) to limit the hours of work. Beginning in 1720 with a statute applicable to journeymen tailors (7 George I, stat. 1, c. 13), a series of statutes outlawed combinations to raise wages or lower the hours of work in *specific* trades or industries—often in response to arson, violence, vandalism, and riot by unruly groups of workers.[4]

These several statutes outlawing labor unions were codified in 1799 (39 George III, c. 81) and in 1800 (40 George III, c. 106, which repealed the previous statute).[5] The Combination Act of 1800 declared all contracts or agreements between workers to get higher wages, lessen the hours of work, restrict output, prevent or hinder an employer from hiring anyone, or generally to control or affect an employer's "conduct or management" of his business in any way to be "illegal, null, and void." The Act subjected the individuals engaging in such behavior to three months in a common jail or two months at hard labor in a house of correction. Any attempt by workers through combination to raise their own wages or to prevent any other worker from seeking employment, or to induce, persuade, or threaten someone presently employed to quit his job—and thereby, to breach *his* employment contract (employment at that time in England was customarily for a definite term, or, if of indefinite duration, required notice by either side to terminate)—was a *crime*. Insofar as what we would today call the closed shop was concerned, it was a crime for a workman or journeyman "who, being hired or employed, shall, without any just or reasonable cause, refuse to work with any other journeyman or workman employed or hired to work therein."

The Combination Act of 1800 (and the other statutes that preceded it) was only one source of law affecting trade combinations. Guild bylaws had been regulated by government since the early 16th century. These were *lawful* combinations; nevertheless, their behavior (and by implication, that of anyone or any group who would pressure a guild to change its behavior) was subject to restraint as well.

There was yet another body of common law, involving so-called 'contracts in restraint of trade', which eventually affected trade unions, although it originally had nothing to do with them.

Suppose A wants to sell his business to B, perhaps because he wants to retire or move. B may want A to agree *not* to turn around and set up another business in competition with his old one, and A will typically be quite willing to agree not to compete. If A did start a new business after selling his old one, the new business would reduce the prospective earning power and profits of the old business, particularly if A had previously built up 'good will', earning the loyalty of old customers. The possibility of A starting up a new business would reduce the price he would get from B for his old business. But whatever A or B agree to, C or D are still free to enter the market.

At a very early period in the history of common law, virtually all of these kinds of agreements not to compete were unlawful, on the following grounds: they deprived the individual A of his livelihood and the means for supporting his family, they deprived the public of the benefit of another (unwilling) competitor, and they tended to establish a monopoly. The feebleness of the rationale for this government 'restraint of trade' (for after all, it is the law, and not A and B, that is restraining a trade) is plain. If B cannot get an enforceable promise from A not to compete, he will likely neither buy A's business nor set up his own. The net result is that A retires or moves, unable to reap the rewards of his enterprise and thus deprived of a property right just as surely as if he was prevented from selling a piece of land. And needless to say, if *all* agreements not to compete are unlawful, then it is impossible for trade unions to exist.

This onerous doctrine evaporated after the famous case of *Mitchel* v. *Reynolds* (1 P. Wms. 181) in 1711. Common law judges thereafter evolved a kind of 'rule of reason' that permitted and enforced these kinds of agreements not to compete in a fairly wide variety of circumstances, though not in every case.[6]

The trickier set of circumstances—which also has direct implications for trade unions—involves agreements, combinations, or contracts between A and B not to compete, when *both* were already in business (such as in the case of a cartel, or even a merger); and trickier still are the cases where the agreement, combination, or contract between A and B is the means for thereafter capturing the business of C. This involves another, related, branch of the law, "conspiracy," but before this is explored, it is worth taking a detour to consider a puzzling question historians as well as lawyers have brooded over. The 18th century statutes (as well as the codifications in 1799 and 1800) prohibiting trade combinations in specific industries were mentioned several paragraphs back. Were combinations of laborers to raise their wages or lessen their hours of work *also* illegal *at common law*, even in unregulated trades or industries? Although not everyone who has studied this problem would agree, I think the answer is yes.

Conspiracy

The general crime of conspiracy dates from the late 13th century. In 1305, an important statute (33 Edward I, stat. 2) was passed whose sole aim was to prevent *combinations to obstruct justice*; that is, to "falsely and maliciously" promote indictments or acquittals. Moreover, in the early days at least, the crime of conspiracy was not said to exist until its object had been accomplished.

In the 17th and 18th centuries, the general crime of conspiracy expanded. In the first place, *the agreement or combination itself* to perform a criminal act became the offense; it was no longer necessary to actually *commit* the crime. The conspiracy itself was a separate, substantive offense at common law, not punished in the same way as would be the actual commission of the crime. The penalty for conspiracy might possibly be harsher than the penalty for committing the activity which was its object, since conspiracy was a felony, but some crimes might be only misdemeanors. Once a conspiracy was set in motion, every act in pursuance thereof, however otherwise innocent or unlawful, was considered part of the plot. Each co-conspirator was criminally liable for the acts of all the others; liability, to borrow a phrase from the civil law, was joint and several.

Much more important was the evolution of what I will henceforth call, for lack of a better name, the "conversion" principle or principles. Under the law of conspiracy, some acts that, if done by an individual alone, would be merely tortious—civil wrongs for which the tortfeasor could be sued—might be criminal, that is indictable, if done by a combination. Second, and much more controversially still, there were certain activities an individual could lawfully do alone (such as fix a price on his own goods), which, if done (or even contemplated) by a group of individuals, would *not* be lawful.

The different legal treatment of individual and group behavior raises a most difficult and controversial issue in the theory and policies of a liberal society, only some of the complexities of which can be hinted at here. The conversion principle poses the age-old dilemma of the legitimacy of government power—but in reverse. Philosophers have long pondered whether men justly *acquire* by association into a government a right to coerce other men that they would not otherwise legitimately possess individually. The law of conspiracy turns, in a sense, on the question of whether men can *lose* by association the legally protected rights, privileges, or powers to act that they otherwise have as individuals. Judges in conspiracy cases have to consider whether there are certain acts that are 'absolutely lawful', or 'lawful in themselves'—regardless of whether they are done by an individual or a group, and regardless of the motive or intent of the actor or actors—or whether acts, performed by an individual or a group become lawful or unlawful according to circumstance, including the circumstance of combination.

By and large, legal and social thinkers have *denied* that group acts are (necessarily) juridically identical to the same act performed by individuals in isolation, and they have affirmed that the differences were sufficiently important to justify different treatment. For businessmen, the primary significance of the conversion principle was, and continues to be, its restraint on their concerted efforts to raise prices, mutually restrict their trade, or compete aggressively against rivals. For laborers, the primary significance of the conversion principle has been its impact on their right to organize into unions, and even more important in modern times, on the use of their organized power through primary or secondary boycotts.[7]

The significance of the conversion principle in conspiracy law for the economic activities of combinations *at common law*—to return now to the issue of combinations by traders not to compete, or to compete aggressively against those not in the combination—became apparent in the 18th century. In 1716, a legal authority claimed that "[t]here can be no doubt, but that all Confederacies whatsoever, *wrongfully* to prejudice a third Person, are highly criminal at Common Law"—a singularly unhelpful definition which left out the most important desideratum, the exact meaning of the term "wrongfully."[8] A few years later, in the leading case of *The King* v. *The Journeymen-Taylors of Cambridge* (8 Mod. 10 (1721)), the Court of the King's Bench declared illegal *at common law* a combination of journeymen tailors to raise their wages, not so much on the grounds that it unlawfully prejudiced other journeymen or the employer, but because it injured society through higher prices. Even though a *statute* passed one year previously outlawed such behavior, the court held that it was not for refusing to "work under such rates, which were more than enjoined by the statute," but "for *a conspiracy* to raise their wages . . . which is an offence at common law." (p. 12, emphasis in original)

What was happening generally in the later 17th and 18th centuries was that judges exercised the 'police power', presumably the province of the legislature, to censure behavior merely on the grounds of its being "contrary to public policy."[9] As Lord Mansfield explained this vision of judicial activism in 1774, "[w]hatever is contrary, *bonos mores est decorum* [to good manners], the principles of our law prohibit, and the King's Court, as the general censor and guardian of the public manners, is bound to restrain and punish." (*Jones* v. *Randall,* Lufft 384, 385 (1774, K.B.)) Price and wage fixing were not good manners; and a few years later this same Mansfield solidified the precedent established earlier in the century by the Journeymen-Taylor's case, holding that

> persons in possession of any articles of trade may sell them at such prices as they individually may please, but if they confederate and agree not to sell them under certain prices, it is conspiracy; so every man may work at whatever price he pleases, but a combination not to work under certain prices is an indictable offence. (*King* v. *Eccles,* Leach C.C. 274, 1783)

By the latter half of the 18th century in England, in short, labor unions, and employer cartels,[10] were probably common-law criminal conspiracies, regardless of the specific anti-combination statutes.

Unions, the Wages Fund, and Strikes

The public policy assumptions governing both the common law decisions of the 18th century and the statutes outlawing unions were not universally held. In the first place, as Lord Francis Jeffrey (a champion in the movement to reform the Combination Act of 1800) noted, even though the law prohibited combinations of both employers and employees, the practical effect of the law was uneven:

> A single master was at liberty at any time to turn off *the whole* of his workmen at once,—100 or 1000 in number—if they would not accept the wages he chose to offer. But it was made an offense for the whole of the workmen to leave that master at once, if he refused to give the wages they chose to require.

"It is evident," according to Jeffrey, "that in this there was no equality or fairness."[11]

Moreover, economic liberals who followed Adam Smith were generally opposed to the assumptions governing a decision such as *King* v. *Eccles.* A labor union, the popular and influential economist John Ramsay McCulloch (1789-1864) reasoned, was analogous to a partnership or joint-stock company. There should be no legal presumption against either:

> Capacity to labour is to the poor man what stock is to the capitalist. But you would not prevent a hundred or a thousand capitalists from forming themselves into a company, or *combination* who should take all their measures in common, and dispose of their property as they might, in their collective capacity, judge most advantageous for their interests:—why then should not a hundred or a thousand labourers be allowed to do the same by *their stock?*

"There is no good reason," he concluded, "why workmen should not, like the possessors of every valuable and desirable article, be allowed to set whatever price they please upon the labour they have to dispose of."[12]

McCulloch, whose views are fairly representative of the classical school as a whole in this period (in America as well as England), explained how the operation of competition would *limit* the effects of union activity to the achievement of ends which *were* consistent with the market.[13]

The wages fund analysis demonstrated, according to McCulloch, that the interests of wage earners and of their employers were not fundamentally in conflict. Both benefited from unimpeded capital accumulation and competition:

> At first sight it does indeed appear as if their [the capitalists'] interests were opposed to those of the labourers; but such is not really the case. The interests of both are at bottom identical; and it has been already seen that all the wealth of the country applicable to the payment of wages is uniformly, in all ordinary cases, divided among the labourers.

McCulloch pointed out that "when wages are increased, profits are at the same time most commonly reduced," a statement that is necessarily true insofar as the division of national income is concerned. But this did not mean for him, or for any other classical economist, including Ricardo, that the absolute amount of wages and profits could not increase together.[14]

The "average amount of subsistence falling to each labourer, or the rate of wages," McCulloch explained, "wholly depends on the proportion between capital and population." Indeed, the average wage was simply a matter of long division between, on "the one hand," the "quantity of necessaries and conveniences, and, on the other, the work-people, among whom they are to be divided." Within this framework, therefore, "no means" exist

> by which wages can be raised, other than by accelerating the increase of capital as compared with population, or by retarding the increase of population as compared with capital. And every scheme for raising wages, which . . . has not an increase of the ratio of capital to population for its object, must be completely nugatory and ineffectual.[15]

The implications of the wages fund analysis for *strikes* seemed to be simple. Since strikes do not increase the rate of capital accumulation or decrease the rate of population growth, it follows that they cannot *raise* wages—bearing in mind here that we are talking about wages in the form of the aggregate wealth (wage goods) of society available to all wage earners. Nevertheless, it was perfectly obvious to economists that the (money) wages of *some* striking workers might, at least temporarily, be increased, though only by setting in motion forces which would come back to haunt them.

First, despite a mythical notion that has grown up about classical economic reasoning, neither McCulloch nor any other significant classical economist assumed that competition in the labor markets worked 'perfectly', in the sense that the automatic adjustments of price to changing conditions of supply and demand occurred *instantaneously.* On the contrary, markets, including labor markets, were active processes through which the actors searched for 'natural' or equilibrium prices. McCulloch wrote that "voluntary combination, unaccompanied by violence," was "a fair exercise of the right of judging for themselves on the part of the workmen" if the actual rate of wages paid them was "unduly depressed," or temporarily "below the natural and proper rate of wages in the branch of industry to which they belong." In this case, according to McCulloch, "the claim of the workmen for an advance is fair and reasonable," and it could be achieved by a simple, peaceable combination:

> Few masters willingly consent to raise wages; and the claim of one or a few individuals for an advance of wages is likely to be disregarded as long as their fellows continue to work at the old rates. It is only when the whole, or the greater part, of the workmen belonging to a particular master or department of industry combine together, or when they act in that simultaneous manner which is equivalent to a combination, and refuse to continue to work without receiving an increase of wages, that it becomes the immediate interest of the masters to comply with their demand. And hence it is obvious, that without the existence either of an open or avowed, or of a tacit and real combination, workmen *would not be able to obtain a rise of wages by their own exertions, but would be left to depend on the competition of their masters.*[16] (emphasis added)

The case outlined by McCulloch illustrated the desirability of combination, and of a public policy of not interdicting workmen "from adopting the only means in their power of doing themselves justice."[17] It did not, to his mind, demonstrate that combination was *necessary*—since the competition among employers would eventually raise wages anyway to their "natural and proper rate." The basic reason was the mobility of capital.

The rate of profit, like the rate of wages (or prices), tends toward uniformity; and it follows that an above-normal profit *due to a below-normal wage rate* creates a competitive imbalance which employers will exploit by bidding wages up. In McCulloch's words,

> When the wages paid to the labourers in a particular employment are improperly reduced, the capitalists who carry it on obviously gain the whole amount of this reduction, over and above the common and ordinary rate of profit obtained by the capitalists who carry on other employments. But a discrepancy of this kind could not be of long continuance. Additional capital would immediately begin to be attracted to the department where wages were low and profits high; and its owners would be obliged, in order to obtain labourers, to offer them higher wages. It is clear, therefore, that if wages be unduly reduced in any

branch of industry, they will be raised to their proper level, without any effort on the part of the workmen, by the competition of the capitalists.

Nevertheless, unions might make competition work more expeditiously:

> When they are allowed freely to combine, their combination may occasion an immediate rise of wages; but when their combination is prevented, more or less time must always elapse before the high profits caused by the undue reduction of wages become generally known, and consequently before capital can be attracted from their businesses. And hence it is clear, that every attempt to prevent combination in such cases as this, is neither more nor less than an attempt to hinder workmen from making use of the only means by which their wages can be speedily and effectually raised to their *just level.* It is committing injustice in behalf of the strong, at the expense of the weaker party.[18]

What *was* the natural and proper rate of wages in any particular department? For McCulloch, it was the same as what we would call today a market-clearing price. It was the rate *at which no laborers would voluntarily leave their jobs elsewhere to enter the new one;* or, to look at it from the employer's point of view, it is the lowest rate at which employers can satisfy their demand for (that is, get and keep) a workforce. In other words, if workers attempted to strike for a higher-than-natural rate—a purpose which McCulloch deemed "improper and unreasonable"—the competitive process insured that they would ultimately fail. Laborers elsewhere would be only too glad to replace them (with or without the employer's urging). Moreover, "owing to the influx of other labourers into their business during the *strike,* they [the workers] will probably be compelled to accept of a lower rate of wages than they previously enjoyed." McCulloch added that employers would probably require the strikebreaking workers to agree to (what we would call) a yellow-dog contract to protect themselves against strikes in the future.[19]

Of course, even supposing employers could *not* get new workmen to break a strike, the added cost of the combination's rates might also induce them to use machines as strikebreakers. According to McCulloch, the "substitution of machinery for manual labour, and its improvement has done more perhaps than anything else to put down combinations in manufacturing employments." In a free trade nation, imports could also break strikes; or else capital might flee to another country.[20]

At any rate, McCulloch, along with the other economists in England, France, and America who followed his analysis of strikes and their consequences,[21] did not see very much that combinations could do to ameliorate their members' working conditions or increase their wages.[22]

Yet classical liberals did insist that workers had the right to freely associate, and the right to engage in peaceable demonstrations.

The Combination Acts of 1824, 1825

The Combination Act of 1824 (5 George IV, c. 95)* completely repudiated the Combination Act of 1800 and decriminalized trade unions. This legislation resulted from agitation and support by liberal, individualistic opinion.[23]

The statute of 1824 expressly repealed all the earlier anti-combination acts. It declared that combination to fix or increase the rate of wages, lessen or alter the hours of work, decrease output, "induce another to depart from his Service before the End of the Time or Term for which he is hired, or to quit or return his work before the same shall be finished, or not being hired, to refuse to enter into Work or Employment," or otherwise interfere with an employer's management of his enterprise would henceforth *not* be liable to indictment or prosecution for conspiracy, "or to any other Criminal Information or Punishment whatever," whether the indictment be made "under the Common or the Statute Law." Furthermore, it exempted combinations of *employers* who sought to reduce wages, or increase the hours of work, or interfere with another employer's management of his enterprise from indictment or prosecution as a criminal conspiracy, under the common or the statute law as well. The statute did outlaw violence, threats, or intimidation by a person or by a group to "wil[l]fully or maliciously force another" to leave his work, conform to the rules of a combination, or interfere with an employer's management of his enterprise.

The Combination Act of 1824 rendered unions immune from prosecution (under the common or statute law of *criminal* conspiracy) for engaging in a very wide variety of non-violent strike and strike-related activity, including, presumably, strikes or strike threats to induce an employer to discharge, or not to hire, nonunion men (a closed shop). The statute did not spell out, and thus presumably left up to the judiciary, what exactly constituted "threats" or "intimidation"; nor is it exactly clear why the terms "wil[l]fully or maliciously" qualified the force, violence, threats or intimidation which the statute banned.

Many proponents of this law, including its foremost champion Francis Place, had long expressed the idea that the disorderly, violent strikes

---

*See Appendix 5 below.

occurring in the late 18th and early 19th centuries were the *result* of the unfair and unequal laws which prohibited employees from combining to resist employer combinations. The legitimation of labor unions, in this view, would demonstrate the futility of collective action and lead to their demise. But granting individual workers the freedom to organize into unions did not lead to industrial peace. It precipitated a wave of violent strikes. Alarmed at what it had helped bring about, Parliament in 1825 passed another Combination Act (6 George IV, c. 129) that governed English collective labor relations for almost the next half century. (This statute and the decisions of the common law judges under it also influenced the evolution of American common law governing combinations.)

The Combination Act of 1825* continued the repeal of the various *statutes* (up to 1800) that had made the existence of labor combinations a criminal conspiracy. It also exempted from prosecution or penalty under "any Law or Statute" (significantly, it did not mention the common law) any persons "who shall meet together for the sole Purpose of consulting upon and determining the Rate of Wages or Prices," or the hours of work "which *the Persons present at such Meeting or any of them,* shall require or demand" for their own work of any employer. (emphasis added)

Nevertheless, the Combination Act of 1825 broadly prohibited any person (and hence any group of persons) who "shall by Violence to . . . Person or Property, or by Threats or Intimidation, or by molesting *or in any way obstructing another,* force or endeavour to force" anyone, whether a member or not "to depart from his Hiring, Employment or Work, or to return his Work before the same shall be finished," or to "prevent or endeavour to prevent" any worker from taking any job, or to conform to the laws of any labor union (for example, work at union rates or pay a fine). It banned any one (or any group) from the use of violence, threats, intimidation, "or by molesting or in any way obstructing . . . force or endeavour to force" any employer from running his business as he saw fit. (emphasis added)

Commentary

Whatever else it did, the Combination Act of 1825 did not put the genie of union violence back in the lamp. Throughout the rest of the century, the

*See Appendix 6 below.

English government constantly had to grapple with labor violence. The economist Nassau Senior, for instance, investigated labor relations in the 1830s, and concluded that these organizations utilized "intimidation and a system of annoyance or injury to the property or persons of those who oppose, and in most instances of those who do not assist in the combination" *as a matter of course.* Arson and sabotage were the usual punishments meted out to employers and employees who did not capitulate to strikers' demands and attempted to operate their factories during a strike. Occasionally, "masters opposed to particular combinations" were "wounded, maimed, or assassinated" by union members or hired thugs. But violence, threats, and intimidation were the usual methods reserved for nonstriking workers; the "obnoxious workmen, having little property, suffer in their persons the punishments rising from simple assaults to blinding with vitriol and beating to death." Senior wrote these words in the 1830s; he might just as well have written them of the 1840s, 1850s, or 1860s.[24]

There is one oddity about the Combination Acts of 1824 and 1825 (or for that matter, about the earlier statutes) that deserves comment. Terms such as 'strike' or 'picketing', are nowhere present. Especially in the case of the term 'strike', this presents a curious problem in interpretation which has rarely received the attention it deserves.

Throughout the years in which the various theories of industrial individualism and industrial democracy were debated, the analysis of the legality, whatever the limits, of the strike always started with an observation similar to that of Lord Jeffrey previously quoted, who complained about the inequity of a law permitting an employer to dismiss all his workers at any time, for any reason, while making it unlawful "for the whole of the workmen to leave that master at once, if he refused to give the wages they chose to require." This was, and is, always considered inequitable, *because it denies 'labor's sacred right to strike'.*

Yet it is questionable to equate an employer's mass dismissal of his workforce with the strike—that is, with the concerted 'withdrawal' of workers from their jobs. When an employer dismisses his workforce, there is no longer *any* employment relationship between him and them. When an individual or a group of workers 'withdraws' from the workplace (again, except insofar as an employer, in his own discretion, may care to treat it otherwise), why shouldn't he (or they) be regarded as having quit, and thereafter as having *no legal relationship whatsoever* with the firm?

When workers strike, even under the mildest, most peaceful circumstances imaginable (such as no picket lines) they do not regard themselves as having terminated the employment relationship. The essence of the strike, in the minds of the strikers as well as in the minds of most employers (or the public at large), is the *unilateral* assertion of a claim that the employment relationship is not terminated. But how can this be squared with the notion of contract, which is always a *mutual* undertaking?*

Combination and Conspiracy in 19th Century England

The Combination Act of 1825 limited the use of a union's organized power far more severely than did its predecessor of 1824. In fact, it generally *revived* the common law of conspiracy in trade disputes, making an exception only for the right of workers to agree *among themselves* not to work below a certain rate (or above a certain number of hours a day), but otherwise pretty generally rendering unlawful any attempt to get *anyone else* to adhere to their demands, particularly other workers. Juristically, the rationale for the distinction was expressed by William Erle, a leading judge, in a case in 1851. Under the Combination Act of 1825,

> the law is clear that workmen have a right to combine for their own protection, and to obtain such wages as they choose to agree to demand. . . . [But] a combination for the purpose of injuring another is at once a combination of an entirely [different] nature, and the law . . . gives no sanction to combinations which have for their immediate purpose the injury or hurt of another. (*Reg.* v. *Rowlands,* 5 Cox, C.C. 436, 460, 461)

The bare act of combining after 1825 was not a crime. But virtually anything beyond that was of doubtful legality—a simple, peaceable strike to get a closed shop, for instance—since it might be interpreted as a conspiracy to injure nonstriking workers, employers, or the public, by denying to them the benefits of an unobstructed labor market.

Even a spontaneous walkout was not necessarily legal. The Master and Servant Act of 1823 (4 George IV, c. 34)† made it a crime for an individual

*Consider the following as a kind of (provocative) thought exercise. Why is a strike *called* a 'labor dispute'? Suppose a union, none of whose members are (or were ever) employed in a firm, sets up a picket line and attempts to oust the current employees (let us suppose they are members of another union) and install themselves, such as in a jurisdictional dispute. If their placards say, "Firm X Unfair to Labor," would not most of us recognize (and discount) the phony nature of the message? But if we do *not* agree that the situation is essentially the same in *any* strike, is it not because of some hidden notion about property rights in a job? Why do we equate the term 'lockout' with the term 'strike'? Do employers who lock workers out ever picket their homes to get them to come back to the factory, or prohibit them from taking work elsewhere?

†The complete text is given as Appendix 4 below.

to breach his employment contract by leaving his work before his term was up (although an employer who broke his side of the bargain was guilty only of a civil wrong). This law, plus the injunction in the Combination Act of 1825 against forcing—or perhaps even inducing—anyone to leave his work before his term was up, or to return his materials (as in the 'putting-out' system) before he was finished working on them, heavily qualified the right to combine or the 'right to strike'. According to some contemporaries this situation helped usher in employment contracts *terminable at will*.[25]

Because it became very important in later years in both England and America, the post-1825 law of conspiracy, as it impinged on the act of inducing someone to quit, and on the legality of contracts in restraint of trade in the labor field, is worth discussing at this point.

In the leading case of *Reg.* v. *Rowlands*, Judge Erle affirmed the principle that a combination of workingmen would be in restraint of trade and liable for indictment as a criminal conspiracy if they "conspired together for the purpose of inducing workmen to leave" their jobs "contrary to their contracts" of employment, when such contracts ran for a definite term. (p. 462)

The 1850s inaugurated another, related series of English cases and precedents about 'inducing a breach of contract' that ultimately affected the law of collective labor relations in America, particularly 'yellow-dog contracts' in the so-called era of 'government by injunction'. (These will be discussed in chapter eight *infra*.) The leading case here was *Lumley* v. *Gye* (2 Ellis & Blackburn, Q.B. 1853), involving an opera singer who broke her exclusive contract to perform for a certain impresario. While the English court would not compel her to perform, it held that the employer could *sue* the individual *who had induced her to breach her contract*. The legal principle involved here was that if an individual who broke his (or her) employment contract (and eventually, the doctrine was extended to *other* contracts, such as the ordinary commercial contract) was liable for damages, the individual who knowingly, "maliciously" induced or procured this breach of contract could *also*, in certain circumstances, be sued for damages in tort. Judges reasoned that anyone who was an accomplice to a legal wrong was

> a joint wrongdoer, and may be sued, either alone or jointly with the agent . . . He who maliciously procures a damage to another by violation of his right ought to be made to indemnify; and that, whether he procures an actionable wrong or a breach of contract. (pp. 232, 233)

The reasoning in back of this controversial doctrine (for it is controversial) was something like the following. It would be a strange legal system indeed—to make an extreme (but telling) analogy from the criminal law—if the law could punish a hired assassin but not the individual who let out the contract. An individual who precipitated such a violation of individual rights cannot claim 'freedom of contract' or 'freedom of speech' as a defense. He cannot plausibly claim that all he did was communicate a desire, unaccompanied by a threat (indeed, in the instant case it is accompanied by an incentive), and that, as he did not pull the trigger, what he did was a perfectly peaceable and entirely lawful act which the government had no right to prevent.

Essentially, the rule of law that evolved after *Lumley* v. *Gye* amounted to the following: if there was an already formed, legally binding contract between A and B, B is liable to pay A for damages if he breaks his promise, and C is liable to pay A for damages in tort, if C knew about the contract and, without a just cause or excuse, induced or caused B to break the contract. The just cause or excuse might be a legal or moral duty such as the case of a doctor who advises a miner (employed by the term) to cease working in the pits because it is endangering his health or, perhaps, the instance of someone who induces a battered wife to get a divorce. But one's own financial gain (or, in the case of a labor dispute, the gain of a group) would not and logically could not, standing alone, serve to privilege such otherwise tortious action.

On the other hand, the principle whereby C is liable for B's behavior because C induced or procured it is not one that can be applied in all social or economic circumstances, regardless of context, lest equally vital values and freedoms disappear. The primary value or freedom here is the obvious one, freedom of speech. When does the mere communication of ideas about the desirability or necessity of reform become an incitement to riot? And in the case of contract law, is every case where C induces B to break off contractual relations with A a tort? What if B is only a customer of A, who can buy or not buy from A as he pleases? What if B is an employee of A (and C, a union official or striking worker), but an employee at will who can quit whenever he wants? If B can leave his employment without breaking an agreement, is it unlawful for C to persuade or induce him to do so?

To return to the 1850s. *Hilton* v. *Eckersley* (6 Ellis & Blackburn, Q.B. 1855), involved the legality of a combination of *employers* set up to defend themselves against labor unions. The unions were apparently practicing 'whipsaw' tactics, striking one employer while continuing to work for, and pay strike benefits from the dues of the workers of, other employers. In response, the employers formed a cartel to present a united front to the union, presumably by declaring a general lockout in the case of a strike against any single employer. Each employer posted a bond to insure that he would abide by the decision of the majority. The case turned on the legality and enforceability of this 'pooling' agreement. The decision had ramifications not only for labor law, but also for the law of contracts in restraint of trade generally.

In the absence of the Combination Act of 1825, the Court declared that it would have found the employers' combination "illegal and indictable at common law." (p. 53) The statute clearly exempted the combination itself from indictment as a conspiracy in restraint of trade. But the Court held that "the bond is void, as being against public policy"; the combination, while legal in the sense that it was not *punishable,* was not of such a nature that "the breach" of the contract "can be enforced at law." (p. 54) Crompton, the judge who spoke for the court, clearly meant this principle to be a general one that would also make unenforceable agreements between workers as well "not to retire from the strike, or to pay a weekly subscription to it, or to pay a penalty if [any one of them] went to work without the leave of the majority of a meeting, or disobeyed the dictation of the delegates." (p. 56)

In dissent, Judge Erle claimed that since the "agreement is legal, it follows that it may be enforced by law," and that "[c]onsiderations of [public] policy confirm[ed]" his view. (pp. 60, 61) By *not* enforcing agreements, particularly those of workmen, Erle hypothesized that the parties making them would only "resort to social persecutions, fear and force" to make them stick. It would be far better, he wrote, to bring them within the purview of the courts:

> If the agreements could be enforced by law, they would be made with a knowledge of rights and liabilities: and the enforcement of them would be within the limits of the law, and for the most part free from purposeful evil. If the law protected them, it would be for the law to decide whether they were in restraint of trade beyond what was required for the protection of any lawful interest; and, if so, to declare them void for the excess. (p. 61)

Nevertheless, after *Hilton* v. *Eckersley* the general understanding in England and America came to be that, even if they were not otherwise illegal, agreements between employers, or between laborers, or between employers and unions, to fix prices or wages were *not enforceable,* as being contrary to the public policy favoring competition.[26]

The Combination Act of 1825 recognized the right of workingmen to organize and allowed unions to "meet together for the sole Purpose of consulting upon and determining the Rate of Wages or Prices" or the hours of work which *they* "require or demand" of any employer, but otherwise severely limited any attempt on their part to prevent *any one else* from making whatever contracts they individually wanted. And thus in the next forty-odd years English unions continued to be prosecuted under the criminal conspiracy laws.

From Criminal Conspiracy to Civil Conspiracy

A turning point came in the period 1868 to 1875 (perhaps not coincidentally, exactly the period during which the classical economists' wages fund doctrine went into eclipse; see chapter five *infra*). The English union federation, the Trades Union Congress, together with valuable allies such as Frederic Harrison, attempted through a Royal Commission to convince both the public and the Parliament that the unions deserved a much freer hand.[27]

The Trade Union Act of 1871 (34 and 35 Victoria, c. 31) declared that the "purposes of any trade union shall not, by reason merely that they are in restraint of trade, be deemed to be unlawful, so as to render *any member of such trade union liable to criminal prosecution for conspiracy or otherwise."* (Section 2, emphasis added) This law also redefined the legal status of the trade union. A majority of the Royal Commission suggested giving unions full corporate status, and legally separating their benefit and strike funds (in order to protect union members' pensions from suit by employers or by union officials' commingling). But the minority, led by Frederic Harrison (and clearly reflecting the desires of trade union officials themselves) prevailed. The law allowed unions to register under the terms of the Act and acquire a limited form of corporate status. They could sue or be sued in their common name, and could enter into binding contracts. But no legal separation of benefit and strike funds occurred, and courts were specifically *prohibited* from enforcing a collective labor agreement as a contract. Nor could the courts entertain suits by workmen to force union officials to abide by union rules, or suits by unions to collect dues or extract penalties from workers for violating union rules.[28]

The Trade Union Act of 1871 sought to eliminate criminal conspiracy from trade unions and trade disputes, and presumably, to permit organized laborers a much wider area for collective action. But the ink was hardly dry on this law when an English court (in 1872) held, in a case involving a strike of gas stokers (a publicly regulated utility), that the threat by employees to simultaneously break their employment contracts (in the instant case, for the purpose of reinstating a worker previously discharged for union activity) was so highly unlawful as to be *indictable,* even though the individual workers, if they had done so singly, would only be liable to a civil suit.

This decision caused an outcry, and Parliament replied with the Conspiracy and Protection of Property Act (CPPA) in 1875 (38 and 39 Victoria, c. 86).* The new statute abolished the common law of *criminal conspiracy* in restraint of trade from labor disputes, except in certain

*See Appendix 7 below.

cases where a breach of an employment contract would "endanger human life, or cause serious bodily injury, or . . . expose valuable property whether real or personal to destruction or serious injury," or where it would disrupt certain public utility services. It was no longer a *crime* for an *individual or a union* to threaten to break an employment contract, or to induce another to break his employment contract. The CPPA sharply pruned back the always-controversial "conversion principle" in conspiracy law. No "agreement or combination by two or more persons to do or procure to be done any act" *in a trade dispute between employers and employees* would any longer "be indictable as a conspiracy *if such act committed by one person would not be punishable as a crime.*" (emphasis added)

After 1875, restraint of trade in the context of labor disputes was no longer a crime. Nevertheless, if the intent of the authors of the CPPA was to recreate the world of trade disputes as it existed after the Combination Act of 1824 but before the Combination Act of 1825, it failed. For English law courts in the next twenty-five-odd years essentially recreated the position of unions circa 1825 to 1875 by reproscribing virtually all of their *decriminalized* activities under the laws of *tort* and *civil conspiracy*!

Inducing another to break his employment (or other) contract was no longer a crime, but, recalling the case of *Lumley* v. *Gye* already discussed, it might still be a tort. Depending on the circumstances, even if it was not a tort when committed by an individual, it might be tortious if committed by a combination, depending on the 'purpose' or 'motive', as divined by the judiciary. Moreover, English law courts from at least as early as 1868 were willing to use their equity powers, that is, their power to issue injunctions, to restrain these torts.[29]

Several cases after 1875 (not all of them, to be sure, involving trade union disputes) established the general principle that, as one judge put it, while "[m]erely to persuade a person to break a contract, may not be wrongful in law or fact," nevertheless

> if the persuasion be used for the indirect purpose of injuring the plaintiff, or of benefitting the defendant at the expense of the plaintiff, it is a malicious act which is in law and in fact a wrong act, and therefore a wrongful act, and therefore an actionable act if injury ensues from it.[30]

Attempts to induce the breach of ordinary commercial contracts were held to be tortious. But in the labor field the tort of inducing a breach of contract was applied to employment contracts *at will* as well as employment contracts by the term. And in one instance, a Court declared that to protect the right to a free course in trade it might be a tort to induce "persons not to enter into contracts" in the future![31]

This last extension was soon repudiated. As one law lord explained, it "seems to have been regarded as only a small step" to extend the tort of interference with contracts to apply prospectively; but "there is a chasm between them." After all,

> in the one case the act procured was a violation of a legal right, for which the person doing the act which injured the plaintiff could be sued as well as the person who procured it; whilst in the other case no legal right was violated by the person who did the act from which the plaintiff suffered: he would not be liable to be sued in respect of the act done, whilst the person who induced him to do the act would be liable to an action.[32]

The tort of interfering with *prospective* contractual relations is one that a legal system must define with great care, else it will swallow advertising, indeed all competition, along with unionism.[33]

From Traditionalism to Freedom of Contract in America

In America, the evolution of free market ideals and policies, and the treatment of labor combinations, recapitulated the pattern in England.

Although a learned American historian has claimed that "capitalism came" to this country "in the first ships,"[34] colonial America was more nearly one of the "last outposts of medieval economic thought."[35] The Protestant fathers of the New England colonies subscribed fully to the organic world view, and to the ideals of a status society, as described in the previous chapter. Individualism and the pursuit of self-interest were, to their way of thinking, an execration; when an early attempt to organize Massachusetts Bay on socialist principles failed, that colony's eminent historian gloomily concluded not that communism was evil, but that men were too corrupt to live in accordance with the dictates of self-sacrifice.[36]

Seventeenth century colonies, especially in New England, experimented with a variety of wage and price controls to maintain a status-bound, hierarchical social order. But the authorities in chronically labor-short North American colonies usually lacked the Mother Country's ability to enforce them. Whenever Massachusetts Bay leaders tried to fix wages, its first governor complained, laborers "would either remove to other places where they might have more, or else being able to live by planting, and other employments of their own, they would not be hired at all."[37]

Wage and price controls gradually faded by the end of the century in both North and South, although the authority to impose them did not. Compulsory labor also existed at times in the early history of the colonies, particularly for agriculture (and not only for black slaves), as it did in England. Furthermore, a fairly substantial portion of the white labor supply in the colonial era came over as voluntarily indentured servants. During the course of their indentures, white laborers could be compelled by judicial process to perform their personal service contracts—that is, ordered to work. For those not bound by indenture, the duration of employment in agriculture and domestic service was often "by the term," that is, yearly. But apparently many common laborers in America were, from the earliest days, hired "at will"; and even where the hiring was yearly, employment (as in England) could be ended earlier, either by worker or employer, as long as notice was given.[38]

The guild system failed to take hold in America, although the colonies were themselves the creatures of foreign trading companies, which were legally created corporate monopolies. First, the colonies were settled at a time when the guilds were under attack for their abuses. Second, urban society in 17th century America was far too primitive and underpopulated to support a guild system's elaborate division of labor. Merchant and craft guilds, with apprenticeship systems, developed in the larger cities of America in the 18th century (particularly in specialized trades such as printing, shoemaking, tailoring, hat making, and among the teamsters), and the journeymen of these guilds formed the nucleus of the early 19th century trade unions. But American guildsmen (or would-be industrial monopolists) were incapable of obtaining from London a domestic monopoly against goods imported from their politically more influential competitors in England. Occupational freedom also existed as the general rule in America on the eve of the Revolution. There were few legal restrictions on entry, even into professions like law and medicine.[39]

Natural right and pro-competitive ideas were profoundly important assumptions among the Founding Fathers (as well as among thinking Americans generally), many of whom were well-read in the political philosophy of John Locke, the 18th century libertarian tract writers, or the liberal economic doctrines of Adam Smith and the Physiocrats.

At the time of the Revolution, there was widespread opposition to government-granted monopolies. Several states outlawed them in their constitutions, although no one sought to abolish the police power of the state legislatures, a major vehicle, then as well as now, for "interventionist," anti-competitive regulations in the name of protecting the safety, health, morals, and general welfare of the public. The police power, no less taxation or eminent domain—the three sources of government power in the economy—were considered inherent and necessary attributes of sovereignty, and they remained undisturbed in state governments.

Nevertheless, the framers of the U.S. Constitution sought to limit government interference in private affairs by carefully enumerating (and thus excluding, by implication, what was not enumerated) specific powers in the federal government on the one hand, and by prohibiting or qualifying the economic powers of the states on the other. Provisions in the Bill of Rights further sought to protect economic liberties, by curtailing Congressional power, lest any future Congress assume it had such power.[40] Since these constitutional protections of economic liberties constituted some of the fundamental legal lineaments of American capitalism, a few of them are worth review.

The Fifth Amendment prohibited Congress from seizing private property (eminent domain), *unless* it was "taken for public use," and only if "just compensation" were paid. This provision was intended to restrain the federal legislature from seizing individual A's property and then turning it over to individual B merely for B's private use and enjoyment. The federal "takings" clause echoed common law decisions and government practices in England and in the American colonies.

Article I, Sections 9 and 10, prohibited Congress and the states (respectively) from passing any *ex post facto* laws (that is, retroactive laws); and Article I, Section 10 prohibited the states from passing any "law impairing the obligation of contracts." Although the exact scope of these two clauses protecting individual rights was not altogether clear, and has led to an immensely complicated case law and historical controversy, there is powerful evidence that the *ex post facto* provision was intended to operate in the *civil* as well as in the criminal law. This interpretation (which the Supreme Court rejected, in a controversial case in 1798) would have restricted the power of both federal and state governments to interfere with the disposition of private property.* Similarly, the contracts clause presupposed a general, 'natural' right to enter into contracts (that is, to acquire private property), although the clause itself protects only the enforcement of contracts already formed; and that, too, only of 'lawful' contracts.[41]

Article IV, Section 2, states that "citizens of each state shall be entitled to all privileges and immunities of citizens in the several states." The privileges and immunities clause deserves mention because, as Circuit Court Judge Bushrod Washington (nephew of George Washington) made clear in the 1820s, the 'right to work' free of state interference was among

---

*If the *ex post facto* clause applied generally, for instance, it might be constitutionally impermissible for the states and the national government to shut down previously lawful businesses, such as the production and distribution of alcohol, oleomargarine, or gambling; or it might convert such police power regulations into instances of eminent domain—which, by making taxpayers compensate investors and other property owners for legislative expropriation, would radically restrict this activity.

the fundamental civil liberties of the American citizen. These privileges and immunities, "which belong, of right, to citizens of all free governments; and which have, at all times, been enjoyed by the citizens of the several states which compose this Union" were primarily economic:

> . . . Protection by the government; the enjoyment of life and liberty, with the right to acquire and possess property of every kind, and to pursue and obtain happiness and safety; subject nevertheless to such restraints as the government may justly prescribe for the general good of the whole. The right of the citizen of one state to pass through, or to reside in any other state, for purposes of trade, agriculture, professional pursuits, or otherwise; to claim the benefit of writ of habeas corpus; to institute and maintain actions of any kind in the courts of the state; to take, hold and dispose of property, either real or personal. (*Corfield* v. *Coryell,* 4 Washington's Circuit Court 1823, 6 Federal Cases (No. 3230) 546, 551-552)

In the 19th century, legislators and judges time after time affirmed the individual's 'right to labor' as a natural, inalienable right that the law of the land was duty-bound to protect. Even so, a rigorously consistent laissez-faire policy existed neither in judicial practice nor in juridical theory. The legislative branch of government was always conceded the "police power" (in the American context, to be sure, within the bounds of constitutional safeguards). Thus, in a much cited opinion (*Allgeyer* v. *Louisiana,* 165 U.S. 578, 589 (1897)), Justice Peckham explained that

> liberty . . . means, not only the right of the citizen to be free from the mere physical restraint of his person, as by incarceration, but the term is deemed to embrace the right of the citizen to be free in the enjoyment of all his faculties; to be free to use them in all lawful ways; to live and work where he will; to earn his livelihood by any lawful calling; to pursue any livelihood or avocation, and for that purpose to enter into all contracts which may be proper, necessary, and essential to his carrying out to a successful conclusion the purposes above mentioned.

Nevertheless, this same judge admitted earlier that "[i]ndividual liberty of action must give way to the greater right of the collective people in the assertion of well-defined policy, designed and intended for the general welfare." (p. 585) Where to draw the line? Peckham didn't say. And as we shall see in chapter eight *infra.*, the inability or unwillingness of judges to limit the otherwise limitless capacity of legislators exercising the police power to regulate the labor market made American industrial democracy constitutionally possible.

On the eve of the American Revolution, the individual laborer's right to contract for the sale of his own labor (his right to make his own bargains) was firmly entrenched in law and custom, as was the individual businessman's right to fix prices for his own products. But how far American law (common or constitutional) protected the rights of *combinations* was very much up in the air since, in the absence of federal or state legislation to the contrary, the English *common law* (at least the common law as it stood up to 1776!) "ruled" in America also. The applicability of the English common law of conspiracy to labor combinations had yet to be tested.

Evolution of American Common Law on Labor Combinations, 1806-1842

The tests came in a series of state cases between 1806 and 1842, in which journeymen trade unions in various crafts were indicted as criminal conspiracies. Virtually every combination in these years hoped to obtain, or retain, a monopoly of the labor supply through a closed shop (the unions themselves, it should be noted, were typically not open to all outsiders). And as in England, violence and intimidation were very much a part of these unions' strike-related activities.[42]

Violence or its threat colored the views of judges about unions in conspiracy cases, and helps account for many of the decisions. But the important legal question was whether workers had a right to organize at all, or whether a combination of workers to raise their wages or otherwise better their own interests was *automatically* a criminal conspiracy. The first reported case, *Commonwealth* v. *Pullis* (the Philadelphia Cordwainer's Case, 1806), reflected the authority of the English Journeymen-Taylors Case of 1721. The prosecution argued that a combination to raise wages was unlawful *per se,* and the Recorder's Court Judge Levy agreed. "A combination of workmen to raise their wages," Levy instructed the jury, "may be considered in a two-fold point of view: one is to benefit themselves . . . [and] the other is to injure those who do not join their society. The rule of law condemns both."[43]

The decisions in cases after 1806 did not generally follow Recorder Levy's stringent construction. Except insofar as state law prohibited them, virtually all the courts granted workmen the common law right to organize for mutual protection and betterment. But virtually none of them granted unions the right to seek or maintain the closed shop through strikes or strike threats.[44]

The climax of the early conspiracy cases came in 1842 with the celebrated decision in *Commonwealth* v. *Hunt* (45 Mass. [4 Met.] 111

(1842)).[45] This case involved a union of journeymen bootmakers that secured the discharge of a workman by threatening a strike, but did not otherwise use or threaten violence to enforce their demands. After carefully considering the English precedents, Chief Justice Lemuel Shaw held that the union was not an indictable conspiracy at common law, *nor was their threatened strike to maintain a closed shop an unlawful exercise of power.*

Reasoning as the liberal economists in England did a generation earlier, Shaw wrote that "every free man, whether skilled laborer, mechanic, farmer or domestic servant, may work or not work, or work or refuse to work with any company or individual, at his own option, except so far as he is bound by contract." (p. 133) "In this state of things," he concluded, "we cannot perceive, that it is criminal for men to agree together to exercise their own acknowledged rights, in such a manner as best to subserve their own interests." (p. 130)

What about the law of conspiracy? Shaw described a criminal conspiracy as "a combination of two or more persons, by some concerted action, to accomplish some criminal or unlawful purpose, or to accomplish some purpose, not in itself criminal or unlawful, by criminal or unlawful means." (p. 123) And by unlawful, Shaw clearly meant conduct or behavior that might only be actionable by a private suit, such as for fraud, breach of contract, or tort.

Shaw claimed that what the union was after, "to induce all those engaged in the same occupation to become members of it," was "not unlawful" since "the power" this state of affairs would give the organization "might be exerted for useful and honorable purposes." It

> might be used to afford each other assistance in times of poverty, sickness and distress; or to raise their intellectual, moral and social condition; or to make improvement in their art; or for other proper purposes. (p. 129)

The combination "agreed not to work for any person, who," after due notice, "should employ any journeyman or other person not a member of" (or who broke the rules of) their "society, after notice given him to discharge such workmen." These were not unlawful means, even though these "measures . . . may have a tendency to impoverish another, that is, to diminish [his] gains and profits." (pp. 128, 134) Like the rivalry of competitive merchants, the harm in this case to nonunion workers (or presumably to the profits of the employer) was *damnum absque injuria*—a harm but not a legal injury (a harm for which the law provides no cause of action).

Commonwealth v. *Hunt* applied the principle of freedom of association and contractual liberty about as far as any 19th century American judge was willing to apply it to labor unions. Yet Shaw did not eliminate, nor did he intend to eliminate, the law of conspiracy in restraint of trade as it applied to unions (or to any other group in the economy). Violence, of course, remained an unquestionably unlawful means to obtain any purpose, however lawful. And Shaw did not mean to foreclose judicial inquiry into the purpose or purposes of a combination, observing that a labor

> association might be designed for purposes of oppression and injustice . . . injurious to the peace of society or the rights of its members. Such would undoubtedly be a criminal conspiracy, on proof of the fact, however meritorious and praiseworthy the declared objects might be. (p. 129)

Moreover, Shaw was careful to distinguish between the facts of the case he was deciding and one where a group of workers "engaged for a certain time" (p. 131) combined to break their employment contract or to induce an employer to break another employee's contract, where the contract was for a term. In the latter case, the combination would be unlawful and indictable.

Taking Wages Out of Competition: The Anti-individualistic Impulse

Not all state courts followed Shaw's defense of the closed shop. In the following years, strikes or strike threats to obtain or maintain a closed shop were held in some states (as in England during this period) to be an unlawful attempt to injure other employees, employers, or the public interest in competition.[46]

These developments will be discussed in chapter eight, in the context of the attempts by unions and other proponents of industrial democracy to abolish 'government by injunction'. Now it is time to turn to that large and influential group of thinkers who insisted that individualism, contractual liberty, and competition were *not* in the best interests of individual wage earners, nor in the larger interest of society as a whole; and who sought to reimpose the pattern of collective control that characterized the economies of England and Europe prior to the rise of economic liberalism.

The crucial error the economic liberals and other individualists had made, according to these 'neo-collectivists', was their unwillingness to see that property ownership conferred overwhelming bargaining power upon employers. Competition between radically unequal bargainers, the opponents of the market argued, practically made a mockery of liberty of contract and destroyed the alleged harmony of interests the classical economists spoke of. Inequality transformed the natural rivalry between buyers and sellers of labor into an irreconcilable conflict between social classes—a conflict which, if left unresolved, would uproot civilization in a bloody chaos.

Solutions to the alleged contradictions between the theory and the reality of capitalist individualism were many, but in the early decades of the 19th century there emerged two major axes or trends around which all later writings in one way or another revolved. Syndicalists (and to some degree so-called 'utopian socialists') perceived the democratic solution to class conflict and oligarchical rule under capitalism in *worker* control of industry. Socialists advocated social (usually that meant *state*) control of industry. But both agreed that private ownership of the means of production must go, and both contended that unionism and collective bargaining were an unacceptable compromise with the wages system, however valuable as a first step toward its overthrow. Nevertheless, syndicalists and socialists pioneered the crucially important theories of labor's unequal bargaining power and class conflict upon which union-oriented models of industrial democracy in Europe and America ultimately came to rest.

3. Labor's Powerlessness Under Competition: Industrial Democracy as Syndicalism

 "[I]f there be one ... doctrine more contrary to truth than any other," the influential businessman-turned-radical-intellectual Robert Owen claimed in 1820, "it is the notion that individual interest ... is a [more] advantageous principle on which to found the social system, for the benefit of all, or of any, than the principle of union and mutual cooperation."[1]

Owen's assertion was the moral leitmotif of all 19th and 20th century collectivist critics of capitalism.[2] Whereas economic liberals saw voluntary exchange as mutually beneficial, these 'neo-collectivists' saw it only as exploitation and coercion: as a kind of zero-sum transaction where what one side gained the other side lost. Conflict, not harmony, ruled the marketplace. Competition was, to their way of thinking, the *antonym* of cooperation, since it made enemies of us all. The following rhetorical passage captures the flavor of this 'dog-eat-dog' perspective. "You are going into business?" asked Louis Blanc, a popular French journalist and politician in his inflammatory pamphlet, *L'Organisation du Travail* (*Organization of Work*). "Good: but where will you get your customers?—I will take those of my neighbour.—Then your neighbor will die.—What can I do about it? If it had not been he, it would have been I."[3]

As Blanc's comment well attests, anti-capitalistic radicals did not limit their protest to the operation of competition in labor markets, but generally denounced the immorality of free exchange in all markets, whatever the position or status of the traders. Nevertheless, it is the individual laborer's alleged lack of bargaining power—and the implications of this idea for poverty, for unemployment, and for the irreconcilably adversarial relationship between wage earners and employers—which is crucial for the history of theories of industrial democracy.

There was very little agreement among capitalism's 19th century radical critics about what should replace the 'system of natural liberty'. Some wanted to nationalize and redistribute the land; others constructed smaller or larger agrarian, communal utopias where the lines between anarchism, syndicalism, and socialism were indistinct. Some were 'individualistic' anarchists, others communitarian anarchists; still others insisted that the abolition of poverty and exploitation required a highly centralized socialist state. Some hoped to achieve their new world by the voluntary withdrawal of small numbers of men and women to serve as a model for the rest; others believed that the state could transform society by financing workingman cooperatives through cheap credit; still others, that citizens could vote themselves into an economic democracy. A few looked forward to violent revolution.[4]

The visions of industrial democracy described in this chapter and the next are similar, however, in that they necessitated the abolition, not the reform, of the wages system. The class conflicts which the radical critics of capitalism believed to exist they also believed to be irreconcilable. Theirs was a vision not so much of the laborer's unequal bargaining power as one of the laborer's utter powerlessness. The trade union, in their view, ought to exist as a vehicle for social and economic revolution; anything less was futile, even dangerous. Nevertheless, it is the *radicals'* critique of the wages system (if not their programmes) that supplied the theoretical foundation for union-based versions of industrial democratic *reform*.

Private Property in Land: A Contradiction

The late 19th century intellectual historian Anton Menger suggested that there were two kinds of critics of competitive capitalism. One emphasized the laborer's "right to the whole produce of [his] labour" as a basic principle or goal on which to reconstruct the social order. The other emphasized the superior right of every individual to "subsistence."[5] The former view inclines one toward syndicalism, a politico-economic system where organized workers own and operate the means of production. The latter view inclines one toward socialism, a politico-economic system in which society *as a whole* controls the means of production.

Menger's distinction is not necessarily the best (and certainly is not the only) way to classify radical critics of the wages system, and it is not an unfailing predictor of a given individual's political commitment. But there are enough differences between the two types' respective approaches to the problems of the wages system, the conception of equality that informs their version of an ideal socio-economic order, and the legacies they bequeathed to modern, unionist-oriented versions of industrial democracy, to justify separate treatment. Using Menger's distinction, we discuss the syndicalists in this chapter, leaving the socialists for the next.

In the late 18th century and the early decades of the 19th, the dominant 'exploitation' or 'surplus value' theory (the idea that under the wages system employers rob workers of some or most of the value of the product that they, the laborers, create) grew out of an anti-Lockean assault on the legitimacy of private property in land. This agrarian critique was spearheaded by three English pamphlet writers: Thomas Spence, William Ogilvie, and Dr. Charles Hall.[6]

The attack spread, via Robert Owen, the single most important Anglo-American radical theorist, and his numerous followers, the Owenite or Ricardian socialists, to an all-out rejection of private ownership of any means of production.[7] Agrarian and Owenite ideas spread to American radical intellectuals generally, including many leaders of the politically-oriented labor movement of the 1820s, 1830s, and 1840s. At the same time, French social theorists, particularly Charles Fourier and Pierre Proudhon, espoused a fundamentally similar critique of private property in land and capital. The ideas of these two individuals also attracted followers and disciples in America.[8]

In the 17th century, John Locke wrote that the earth was mankind's common heritage. But this heritage, he insisted, was not commonly owned. Ownership began when an individual "mixed his labor" with the land; and the individual did not need society's permission to possess unowned land on which he mixed his labor. While Locke spoke of limits to the amount of land an individual might justly own or engross for his own use to the exclusion of others, there was nothing in his theory that implied equal land ownership by all the earth's inhabitants.[9]

The 18th century agrarians did not agree. They argued that the earth was society's *common property,* and that an individual must first obtain permission from society before he could use or possess it. But in no case could an individual actually *own* the land, *since his labor did not create it.*[10]

Private property in land was, according to the agrarians, incompatible with the right to life—or, to put it more exactly, it was incompatible with a *guaranteed* subsistence, such a guarantee allegedly inhering to all individuals in a state of nature. After all, "if the first occupants have occupied every thing," as Proudhon put it, "what are the newcomers to do? What will become of them, having an instrument with which to work," their labor power, "but no material to work on? Must they devour each other?" This was monstrous; therefore private property was "impossible" to square with justice. It was *theft*.[11]

Many American radicals agreed. Denouncing both John Locke and Thomas Jefferson, Thomas Skidmore announced that man had a right *to property*, not merely a right to acquire it—for without property, "the rights of life and liberty are but an empty name."[12] As George Henry Evans observed, if man is deprived of his "right to land enough for his subsistence," he is placed "at the mercy of those" who do own land.[13]

Private property in land, according to these writers, destroyed social harmony by dividing society into two irreconcilably conflicting social classes. Landowners were literally land *lords* who, controlling access to the means of subsistence, kept the landless at the very margin of subsistence and consumed the fruits of their labor. Income from land—all rent—was a monopolistic exaction, a surplus of value created by laborers but denied them by the landowner.[14]

But private property in land was only the first 'contradiction' of capitalism.

The Bargaining Power Paradigm Generalized: The Capitalist as Landlord

One might suppose that, since capital, unlike land, can be augmented indefinitely, it would constitute an *escape valve* from the social pressure-cooker of landless masses rubbing elbows with a tiny group of landowners. Capitalists would compete with landowners for laborers, to the latter's advantage. Not so. "*Capitalists,*" Thomas Hodgskin claimed, "have long since reduced the ancient tyrant of the soil to comparative insignificance, while they have inherited his power over all the labouring classes."[15] *Ownership of capital, in other words, was equated with ownership of land; and in both cases ownership of the means of production was equated with a monopoly of the means of production.*

This identification of ownership and monopoly is the key to the indictment of the wages system. Employers, the radicals argued, did not compete among themselves *as employers*—even though they did compete among themselves to sell output. Paraphrasing Adam Smith, William Thompson assured his readers that indeed

[a] universal and always vigilant conspiracy of capitalists, of

necessity the most intelligent, exists everywhere, because founded on a universally existing interest, to cause the laborers to toil for the lowest possible, and to wrest as much as possible of the products of their labor to swell the accumulation and expenditure of the capitalists.[16]

The wages system, according to this way of thinking, can be envisioned through a kind of paradigm: a single employer (or a small cartel of noncompeting employers) confronts a group of desperate, propertyless laborers who have no alternative but to accept the particular wage 'bargain' offered by that employer. Bargaining power in this context meant the existence of alternatives, of choices, and wage-earners had none.

These writers depicted individual wage-contracting less as bargaining than as extortion; less a matter of friendly (or even unfriendly) *rivalry* between *traders* than as the presentation of non-negotiable demands in a matter of life and death. "If you will labor for me in such and such a way," Charles Hall characterized *any* employer's offer to *any* potential employee, "I will give you out of those things such as you stand in need of" *to live;* "but unless you will do these things which I require of you, you shall have none of them" and will *die*. There was in all this no "voluntary compact equally advantageous on both sides, but an absolute compulsion on the part of masters, and an absolute necessity on the part of the workman to accept of it." The employer's profit "might be considered just as the taking so much from the workman by the master."[17] Or, as the Jacksonian labor leader William Heighton exhorted a group of trade unionists, the employer was simply a thug:

> Necessity compels us to work for such prices as are offered, and pay such prices as are demanded for everything we need; we must either do this—resort to fraud or theft, or perish by hunger and nakedness. Where then is the difference between our relative situation and the accumulating class, and the traveller and the highwayman?[18]

Some Americans went even further, comparing 'wage slavery' unfavorably to chattel slavery. The master, after all, was inclined by his own self-interest to guarantee the slave's personal subsistence; but not so the industrial employer or farmer. This refrain was most often voiced by the Southern apologists for their peculiar institution, but some Northern radicals agreed to it as well (though none of them explained why no unemployed northern millhands or farm laborers ever retraced Liza's steps across the Ohio River ice flows *into* Kentucky to escape their plight).[19]

Combination (monopsony) on one side, competition on the other; can there be any doubt, cried Louis Blanc in 1840, that the system was "for the people a system of extermination"? In a passage of his famous and widely-

read *Organization of Work,* Blanc vividly and sarcastically depicted the
wage system as a hideous race to the bottom, a virtual slave auction:

> [An entrepreneur] needs a laborer: three apply. 'How much do
> you ask for your work?' 'Three francs, I have a wife and children.'
> 'Good, and you?' 'Two and a half francs, I have no children, but a
> wife.' 'So much the better, and you?' 'Two francs will do for me; I
> am single.' 'You shall have the work.' With this the affair is settled,
> the bargain is closed. What will become now of the other two
> proletarians? They will starve, it is to be hoped. But what if they
> become thieves? Never mind, why have we our police? Or
> murderers? Well, for them we have the gallows. And the fortunate
> one of the three; even his victory is only temporary. Let a fourth
> laborer appear, strong enough to fast one out of every two days;
> the desire to cut down the wages will be exerted to its fullest
> extent. A new pariah, perhaps a new recruit for the galleys.
>
> Can anyone assert that these conclusions are exaggerated . . .
> Who would be blind enough not to see that under the reign of
> free competition the continuous decline of wages necessarily
> becomes a general law with no exception whatsoever? . . . A
> systematic lowering of wages resulting in the elimination of a
> certain number of laborers is the inevitable effect of free
> competition.[20]

The Economy of Low Wages: Underconsumptionism and Unemployment

Robert Owen and his followers insisted that individual bargaining in the
labor market guaranteed an economy of low wages, not an economy of
high wages, and located in this alleged contradiction between the theory
of economic liberalism and its practice the cause of poverty and persistent
unemployment.

"Every master manufacturer," Owen contended in a memorable passage
of his address "To the British Master Manufactuers: On the Employment of
Children in Manufactories" (1818),

> considers low wages to be essential to his success. By one master
> or another, every means are used to reduce wages to the lowest
> possible point, and if but one succeeds the others must follow in
> their own defense. Yet, when the subject is properly considered,
> no evil ought to be more dreaded by master manufacturers than
> low wages of labour, or a want of the means to procure
> reasonable comfort among the working classes. These, in conse-

quence of their numbers, are the greatest consumers of all articles; . . . when wages . . . are low, all classes suffer . . . particularly the manufacturing interest; . . . It is therefore essentially the interest of the master manufacturer that the wages of the labourer should be high . . . which is not possible under the existence of our present practices.[21]

Low wages were thus 'bad for business', since they retarded sales. Owen also implied that low wages, long hours, and poor working and living conditions were not conducive to workers' efficiency in factories. In his own mills at Lanark—among the most efficient and productive in England—he had reduced the hours of work from thirteen to twelve, and eventually to ten, hours a day. Owen insisted that employers' failure to care for workers' welfare—their payment of very low wages and their insistence on very long hours of work—was costing them money. "I have expended much time and capital upon improvements of the living machinery," he wrote in the prefix to his "Third Essay on the Formation of Character," and he asserted that better wages and working conditions more than paid for themselves through higher output.[22]

But what about the social benefits of capital accumulation and technological innovation? Did they not, as Smith and his followers claimed, augment the fund destined for the payment of wages, thus increasing the demand for labor and raising wages? The critics of competition did not think so. Under the competitive system, they argued, machinery only made things worse. As Owen put it in 1820, during the famous slump after the close of the Napoleonic wars, the "steam engine and spinning machines, with the endless mechanical inventions to which they have given rise, have . . . inflicted evils on society, which now greatly overbalance the benefits which are derived from them."[23]

Some went so far as to claim that machines would take away everybody's jobs. "*Invention,*" the trade union leader William Heighton asserted in 1827,

which is capable of being made the fertile source of an immense profusion of wealth, is . . . a source of the most abject poverty, wretchedness, and starvation . . . [because] under the influence of *competition* and invention . . . the U[nited] States [will saturate the market] with a superabundance of all kinds of wealth, until the demand for labour shall have ceased and they can obtain wealth no longer . . .[24]

Thomas Skidmore seconded him; mechanical "improvements supersede, sooner or later, in a great measure, all demand for the labor of the poor; it dries up their resources faster than it multiplies them . . ."[25]

While this was an extreme position, it was nevertheless a common belief among the critics of capitalism that persistent unemployment was inevitable under competition, because workers, as wage earners, were systematically deprived of the income necessary to purchase, as consumers, the output of industry.

In making this claim, the neo-collectivists challenged a basic 'macroeconomic' principle of classical economists, most of whom denied that a *general* imbalance between production and consumption—a 'general glut' or overproduction—could arise on the market. Although the production of particular goods could always be too large in relation to demand, most classical economists denied that the supply of goods in general could ever outstrip the demand for goods in general. The reason was that the supply of goods in the aggregate created the demand for them. This principle is known as Say's Law. What the principle means for our purposes is this: the supply of a particular good offered on the market is the source of the incomes (paid out to owners of each 'factor of production', laborer, capitalist, or landlord) that constitute the purchasing power, or the demand, for *other* goods. The supply of all goods, therefore, is the source of the demand for all goods; in shorthand (actually, a rather dangerous shorthand), "supply creates demand."[26]

Critics (here, and as amplified further in chapter four, *infra.*) of competitive markets have always (for many reasons, only some of which are relevant for this study of the origins of industrial democracy) denied that the principle that J. B. Say, James Mill, and others identified *operated* in such a manner as to prevent general imbalances between production and consumption.

"[T]hat the producer may live," Proudhon asserted, *"his wages must repurchase his product."* He explained that

> [a] contractor pays one hundred thousand francs for raw material, fifty thousand francs in wages, and then expects to receive a product of two hundred thousand francs,—that is, expects to make a profit on the material and on the labor of his employees; but if the laborers and the purveyor of the material cannot, with their combined wages, repurchase that which they have produced for the contractor, how can they live?[27]

The resulting imbalance between profits and wages—or looked at from a different angle, between production and consumption—meant that employers blindly built up inventories of goods which they would eventually be unable to vent at a price which would even pay their cost of production, no less yield a profit. The result would be panic, bankruptcies, further unemployment, lower purchasing power, and ultimate collapse.

"[C]ompetition," John Gray explained in a highly significant passage of his *Lecture on Human Happiness,* *"limits the quantity of wealth obtained by individuals,"* that is, individual laborers. The *"quantity of*

wealth obtained by individuals collectively, composes the aggregate quantity obtained by the whole community"; and *"[t]his aggregate quantity forms the"* market *"demand"* for all goods. But *"demand limits production"* under the wages system to a quantity of social wealth far below that necessary to keep all laborers employed, and to satisfy all social needs. Capitalists produce only so much as *"they can dispose of at a profit,"* not *"how much . . . would be required to supply the wants of mankind."* Competition leads, in short, to the great paradox of poverty in the midst of potential plenty.[28]

Are Unions the Answer?

While Owenites, Proudhon, and other proponents of 'cooperation' had high hopes for trade unions, it was only for their revolutionary potential— only for their *future* role as cells of the new society. They were bitterly critical of labor combinations as they then existed and functioned within the framework of a competitive society, recognizing in these unions the same narrow, monopolistic, 'selfish' spirit they decried everywhere else.

William Thompson was the follower and colleague of Robert Owen most responsible for forging "the alliance of Trade Unionism and Owenite Cooperation that came to dominate working-class activity in the years immediately after the Reform Act of 1832."[29] But he *accepted* the limitations of the wages fund doctrine. Thompson asserted that the "highest price which Free Competition will enable Unions of the industrious to obtain for their labor, is not any thing like the products of their labor, but" only

> that rate of remuneration which will permit the capitalists in their line of industry to reap the same profits that other capitalists in the same line, or in other equally hazardous lines, reap from their capital.

These combinations, he reasoned, "merely ward off a portion of the avoidable evil of the Competitive System." "Every one of the Industrious Classes . . . who wishes to ward off from himself and his fellow-creatures this portion of evil," he added, "ought to be a member of such voluntary and peaceable associations."[30]

Unfortunately, the combinations then extant were anything but peaceable, voluntary, or otherwise imbued with a consciousness of what we would call class solidarity. Thompson denounced as "vain and unjust" unions' attempts to protect the privileged position of their members by excluding "the young just entering life," the "poor foreigners," and the "under-paid agriculturists and common or day laborers and their children." These unions were organized as much against other workers as they were against the employer; their victories were "unjust" gains secured by a "conspiracy" "of the well-paid . . . against the ill paid,—of the few against the many of their brethren."[31]

Thompson asked rhetorically if the unions were right to "resort to *force*—law-supported as to apprenticeships, or illegal as to intimidation." He answered that "in all cases" these methods were "equally hateful." Unions must not, as they were attempting to do, "put down the competition of the great majority of the Industrious, and thus erect a bloody—for force will lead to blood, and without blood no aristocracy can be supported—*aristocracy* of Industry." This would make *them* oppressors, with the result that

> unskilled laborers would every where form a league with the capitalists; and being the majority in point of physical strength, and having, moreover, justice and the legally armed bands of the country on their side, they would by the under–bidding of their labor defeat everywhere all the efforts of Trades-Unions, local, general, and central, to keep up the remuneration of the skilled, *i.e.,* of easy, labor, to what the average rate of profits would afford.[32]

Thomas Hodgskin also abjured monopoly. He denounced the guilds in Germany, for instance, and hoped they would "be abolished by the rest of society refusing to submit to them."[33] John Bray admitted that "much tyranny and injustice was inflicted by both sides on individual workingmen and individual capitalists" during labor disputes.[34] According to Proudhon, compulsory association "places fetters on the liberty of the laborer," and hides "a secret intention of robbery and despotism."[35]

Securing the Right to the Whole Product of Labor: Industrial Democracy as Syndicalism

For those agrarians who thought they might roll back the tide of history and escape the factory system altogether, the solution to the social problem was the nationalization of land.[36] Others recognized the impracticability of this notion, if for no other reason than that there were too many people. Nevertheless, if society could not guarantee to each individual what was allegedly his natural, rightful due—namely *land* enough for subsistence—it might still guarantee him a *job* at a living wage.

Thus the followers of Charles Fourier were willing to leave property in private hands, so long as society secured every laborer a job.[37]

Owen and Proudhon emphasized the importance of agriculture to their new societies, but they were not pastoralists. Their ideas about democracy and cooperation in an industrial setting evolved toward syndicalism.

After the collapse of his microcosmic "New Harmony" settlement in America in the 1820s, Owen, as one of his biographers explained, "began to dream of a society in which the unions" might spearhead a social revolution, "dominating the industries they covered, and ultimately replacing the State by a network of interrelated producer's co-operatives."[38] The more Owen contemplated the unions' revolutionary potential, the larger his vision:

> He had six departments at New Harmony, and now he proposed more. Each Trade Union was to be transformed into a national one to carry on the employment with which it was associated. The Agricultural Union was to take possession of the land, the Miner's Union of the mines, the Textile Unions of the mills.[39]

J. E. Smith, one of Owen's eager followers, explained that the so-called Grand National Consolidated Trades Union the Owenites established in the early 1830s was intended ultimately to transform the very notion of political society. In place of the House of Commons there would be a "House of Trades":

> We shall have a new set of boroughs when the unions are organised: every trade shall be a borough and every trade shall have a council of representatives to conduct its affairs. . . .[40]

In France, Louis Blanc imagined a nationwide system of "ateliers sociaux" (social workshops), sponsored by the government and run by the workers. These would eventually evolve into autonomous, self-governing syndicates, while the state simultaneously evolved into an industrial cartel. As one historian explained it:

> The workshops of all the trade associations (ateliers sociaux) are to be united into one organisation, all those of the same trade depending on one central agency. This would allow prices to be fixed for the different factories, thus preventing competition between them. At the head of all the industrial and agricultural, there would be a supreme council . . .[41]

Proudhon's theory of "mutualism" involved reorganizing society along syndicalist lines through private cooperatives that would be financed by a private "Bank of the People." Democratic self-government, Proudhon insisted, requires the end of the employer-employee relationship. A man, if he is a wage earner in a large industry, is "subordinated, exploited: his permanent condition is one of obedience and poverty." But if he becomes a citizen in an industrial democracy, with a "voice in the council" of the industry

> he resumes his dignity as a man and citizen, he may aspire to comfort, he forms a part of the producing organization, of which he was before a slave; as in the town, he forms a part of the sovereign power, of which he was before but the subject.

The workers must form a general association; and "[e]very industry, operation or enterprise, which by its nature requires the employment of a large number of workmen of different specialities, is destined to become a society or company of workers." In the new society a "railroad, a mine, a factory, a ship are to the workers who use them what a hive is to the bees, at once their tool and their home, their country, their territory, *their property.*" The syndicates, or communes, would police themselves and contract with each other through a kind of collective bargaining. But the system as a whole would be virtually anarchic, as there would be no superintending, sovereign state.[42]

Virtually all of the agrarians, utopians, and syndicalists of the early 19th century believed passionately in one form of labor value theory or another. But they developed the labor theory of value differently than had John Locke (in his labor theory of property) or Adam Smith, in order to foster social and economic equality.

Smith, it will be recalled, wrote that in a society prior to the appropriation of land and the accumulation of capital "the proportion between the quantities of labour necessary for acquiring different objects" would regulate the exchange ratios between them (their prices). "In that original state of things the whole produce of labour belongs to the labourer," since the laborer "has neither landlord nor master to share with him."[43] Since the neo-collectivists rejected the institution of property in land and capital, they claimed that labor, in William Thompson's words, was "the *sole* parent of wealth" and the only just claim to remuneration.[44] The *"laborer,"* Proudhon concluded emphatically, had the right to the whole product of his labor; he *"retains even after he has received his wages, a natural right of property in the thing he has produced."* The "error and surprise, not to say deceit and fraud" of private property and the wage contract changed nothing.[45]

Smith also wrote that, even in the primitive state, not all labor was *alike,* nor would it be compensated equally; and of course in a developed economy the "quantity of labour commonly employed in acquiring or producing any commodity" would *not* measure its price.[46] Here, too, Owenites and others disagreed, insisting that *all labor was of identical worth.* "Labour," Bray wrote, "is neither more nor less than labour." There were no differences in types or kinds of labor that justified differential or unequal rewards. "Men have only two things which they can exchange with each other, namely, labour and the produce of labour." "[S]trict justice not only requires that all exchangers be *mutually,* but that they should be *equally* benefit[t]ed."[47] John Gray put it in a nutshell: "All just contracts have for their foundation *equal quantities of labour . . .* "[48]

Robert Owen was apparently the first to contend that human labor *time,* the "natural standard of value," could be directly applied to modern society *in place of money* as a medium of exchange.[49] But the American anarchist Josiah Warren first put the principle into practice. Warren established a "Labor Time Store" in Cincinnati, Ohio, in the late 1820s. Each individual received a "labor note" in exchange for his goods signifying the number of hours and minutes spent producing the item in question; the labor note served as money to obtain goods similarly priced.[50] Robert Owen's "National Equitable Labour Exchange," instituted in London a few years later, was a larger and better known version of the time store.[51]

Exchange on the basis of labor time neatly solved (or at least neatly appeared to solve) a variety of social problems in one fell swoop. First, of course, it was just; each worker obtained the whole produce of his labor. Second, labor exchanges preserved basic social equality because they precluded the existence of antagonistic classes. Finally, labor exchange would cause the presumed gap between production and consumption to disappear, along with unemployment. Adequate purchasing power to consume all goods would be simultaneously created and distributed.

Commentary: The Bargaining Power Doctrine

The critique of the wages system described in this chapter rested crucially on the assumption that competition between employers to sell product exists while competition between them to purchase the services of laborers does not. This is contrary to the everyday experience of individuals who leave one job for another elsewhere, and it conflicts with such a mundane phenomenon as the recruitment of highly or specially skilled workers in short supply at wages much in excess of the average. Whether they are shopkeepers, mine operators, computer manufacturers or fast-food managers, employers (past and present) must adjust the wages, hours, and working conditions they offer in order to get, and keep, a workforce adequate to their needs. As John Stuart Mill complained (in an essay otherwise very sympathetic to the opponents of capitalism), "even the most enlightened" of the socialists "have a very imperfect and one-sided notion of the operation of competition." After all, "if it is competition which keeps the prices of labour and commodities as low as they are, it is competition" of employers for workers "which keeps them from falling still lower."[52] Wage earners do have choices, and the expansion of industry and trade multiplies them. They are not powerless. The single-employer paradigm used to describe the fundamental reality of the wages system is a Chimera.

Moreover, holding both assumptions simultaneously (that employers compete to sell output but do not compete to buy inputs) commits one to all sorts of queer conclusions, some of which can best be explained by reconsidering Louis Blanc's famous depiction of the wages system as a kind of auction for work. Suppose, as he said, an entrepreneur needs one worker, but three apply. What *will* happen to the other two? Will they starve or become thieves? Or will they find employment elsewhere?* The race to the bottom, as Louis Blanc, or for that matter as Adam Smith himself, envisioned it is flawed in principle. "Let a fourth laborer appear," Blanc wrote, "strong enough to fast one out of every two days; the desire to cut down the wages will be exerted to its fullest extent." But why do employers stop at two francs? And why must they wait for the fourth laborer?

If employers are *not* responsible for paying a 'living wage'—as they are not—one must suppose that they literally meet secretly in some giant wage-fixing conspiracy. If not, then as Edwin Cannan pointed out, the entire subsistence model based on monopsony does

> not inquire how the fact that the labourers would die out if they did not get sufficient to support a family prevents the masters from pursuing their advantage in the bargain so far as to bring the wages below that level. It cannot be the interest of the individual master prevents him from using his individual advantage to the utmost, since *he does not rely on his own workmen's children,*

---

*The choice, in short, is not, "Work for me, on my terms, or starve," but rather, "Work for me on the terms I offer, or work for one of the thousands of other employers on the terms they offer." If the response be made (as it would be by the socialists, as discussed in chapter four *infra*) that the former proposition can simply be amended to say, "Work for *the employing class as a whole* . . . ," the reply is that *any* society always gives the individual the choice of doing what society requires of him, or starving. The employment decisions of capitalists are generally not arbitrary, but reflect the competing wants of consumers (which we may take here as a metaphor for society as a whole) in a world of scarce resources and limitless wants. I should like to thank David Ramsay Steele for making this point.

but can draw on supplies from elsewhere. Does the combination of masters take the *future* supply into account, and decide, 'We must not press for too much, or where will our sons get their labour from?'[53]

Not even William Thompson believed that *all* employers *actually* met *in camera* to establish wages adequate to evoke a supply of laborers across the generations. But unless one supposes they did, the race-to-the-bottom model fails to explain how society under the wages system can survive at all from one generation to the next!

Furthermore, contrary to what Robert Owen claimed, or to the necessary implication of Blanc's auction, it is very hard to imagine that *all employers* are so blind to the productivity implications of extremely low wages and extremely long hours that they ignore it entirely. If some (or even if many) employers ignore the decline in output or the increase in shoddy work produced by a demoralized gang of starving drudges incapable of putting in a decent day's work, it does *not* follow that all employers have to match them in order to survive competitively. The incentive would be to cream off the best of the workforce by offering a higher wage, and then to outproduce the competition.[54]

Finally, the race-to-the-bottom model simply ignores a fundamental economic theorem: the lower the price, the greater the quantity demanded. If the bid is lowered, all three unemployed workers in Blanc's little parable might be employed—if not by the first entrepreneur, than by another, whose opportunity to expand output (by taking advantage of lower input (labor) prices) might now become practicable.

Nevertheless, the critics of competition would insist (much as in later years the champions of unions did insist) that wage-cutting was necessarily a generally deflationary force, reducing purchasing power in the economy generally so much that expansion elsewhere in the system could not occur. Here we will discuss the hypothesis that "machinery reduces employment"; in a later chapter the doctrine that laborers' wages (the major component of aggregate demand) must fail to keep pace with the social product (the aggregate supply) will be discussed. In both instances, the shortcomings of the neo-collectivist analysis are essential for understanding the deficiencies of their theories, particularly their inability to explain the rising living standards of wage earners in England, Europe, and America throughout the 19th century (during a period when trade unions were insignificant in numbers and influence). More recently other examples of this process have occurred in Japan, and subsequently in other Asian countries, where real wages increased dramatically, despite a toothless union movement.

Commentary: Technology, Employment, and Real Earnings

Classical economists generally denied that technological improvements, and particularly machinery, had a harmful effect on total employment, aggregate purchasing power, or the living standards of wage earners. Most (though not all) of them concluded that while machinery might temporarily displace certain workers, and lead to a reallocation and a recomposition of the industrial workforce, it would not cause permanent unemployment.[55]

In the first place, machines can often increase net employment in the industry where they are introduced. Machinery is introduced because it lowers production costs. These savings are passed on to consumers (that is, to other workers, who make up the bulk of consumers) via competition, as lower prices. Lower prices elicit greater demand, occasioning an increase in production and the need for more workers. This process, McCulloch explained, had taken place in key industries such as cotton textiles.[56]

Nevertheless, output might not expand sufficiently to increase employment in *that* industry; in fact, machines might reduce net employment in that industry. Nevertheless, the declining prices of output implies greater real wealth for consumers. Consumers' now-enhanced real 'purchasing power' is released to demand *other* goods (or new ones). The increased demand and consequent growth of production and employment in *other* industries, that have, in a sense, been indirectly aided by improvements elsewhere (not those, of course, in competition with the first!) is the crucial reason why economists then and now reject the theory of permanent technological unemployment. (For that matter, the competitive mechanism whereby real wealth is created and augmented by lower costs is the very heart and soul of any theory of noninflationary growth.) As McCulloch put it, "though we may have enough of one commodity" whose prices have declined because of technological improvement,

> we can never have what we reckon enough of *all* sorts of commodities ... The revenue set free by the fall in cottons would not be permitted to lie idle in our pockets. It would be applied to purchase, either directly by the parties themselves, or indirectly by those to whom they might lend it, an additional quantity for something else. The total effective demand for labour, or the produce of labour, would not, therefore, be in the least degree impaired.[57]

Unquestionably, in England as in America (and elsewhere), competitive pressure, whether due to machinery or anything else, can, will, does, and did reduce both the nominal wage rates and often the nominal and real earnings of some segments of the workforce. In the early days of the factory system, the highly skilled artisans often lost ground. But this did not imply that nominal wage rates *for all workers* declined, still less that the real wages (living standards) of the working class as a whole suffered as industrialization proceeded.

On the contrary, capital accumulation and technological change permitted the employment of hitherto unemployed or underemployed—or in the case of agricultural labor, very low-paid—workers at wages *higher* than they could previously obtain. There was, as the economist W. H. Hutt has put it, a kind of "leveling-up" process. Population increases may have led to a statistical "dilution" of rising per capita output and incomes; but this did not imply declining absolute living standards.[58]

In America, for instance, immigrants from abroad swelled the bottom layers of the population. This was both an effect and a cause of rapid economic growth; it was a sign of general economic health and rising opportunities. Yet if one looked at the 'distribution of income' or the 'distribution of wealth' in a static context and saw an increase in 'inequality' and greater numbers of poor people (i.e., an increased proportion of income earners or wealth holders below such-and-such a cutoff point), one might think that things were getting worse and worse.[59]

Looking at the broad changes in the early decades of the 19th century from this perspective also helps illuminate the situation of the artisans in America who organized into unions to fight the 'monopolists' prior to the Civil War.

As the population and the settled area of the country increased, transportation improvements knitted expanding markets closer together, necessitating a recomposition of the increased manufacturing labor force. The opportunity was seized by a rising class of 'merchant capitalists' (i.e., merchant wholesalers and retailers with spare capital to invest—often to manufacture a line of goods they previously sold) in league with men of technical know-how. Gradually, production for an impersonal market replaced the small master craftsmen making goods on a custom-order basis—the so-called "bespoke trades," where goods were not produced until customers specifically ordered (spoke for) them.

On one plane, competition between producers forced the prices of luxury goods down; and as manufacturers economized on their costs, so too did the wage rates decline for the journeymen who worked for and with the masters to provision these markets. Far more significantly, a change occurred in the very composition of the goods produced for sale; factory methods began to supplant household manufacture and small shops for the general consumer market (in towns and also in farming areas).

A likely explanation for what happened is that the total employment in any given industry increased as demand for labor bid in unskilled workers (including women and children). In these industries, the total wages paid out (that is, the number of employed times the wage rate times the number of hours times the number of days worked per annum) also probably increased. But the position of the skilled journeyman in the workforce undoubtedly suffered. Not only were his wage rates lowered to match the greater productivity of less-skilled machine tenders; but, to judge from some of the complaints voiced, the number of hours he worked may have increased as well, as the pace of industry speeded up (although the number of hours would probably not have exceeded the available alternatives for unskilled laborers elsewhere—such as common farm labor). The skilled workers' total wage envelope may have declined as well, if rates fell relatively faster than the number of hours worked increased.

Most importantly, the journeyman's prospects for becoming "his own boss" faded (at least in the field in which he served his apprenticeship). Thus, a combination of falling income and insecure social status (albeit in a more fluid and generally improving social order) could, and probably did, engender feelings of deep social injustice. As one philosopher-historian imaginatively described it,

> The workers would be notified that a reduction in wages would take place, and the immediate response would be an indignation meeting, usually culminating in a disorderly quitting of work and a refusal to come back save at the old wages. *There was no reasoned theory as to why the men should receive what they had always been receiving; there was merely a feeling of outrage that time-honored customs were being violated by the new masters,* and with perhaps a connecting of the phenomenon with the 'monopolists' and the holders of the United States Bank bonds . . .[60]

Along with the yeoman farmers, journeymen artisans considered themselves not only as potential masters, but as the very backbone of the republican order. They, and their spokesmen, identified and interpreted any unfavorable change in *their* economic or social prospects as an unfavorable change in the status of the "producing" or "laboring" class *as a whole.*

Organized to protect their status, the leaders of and spokesmen for trade unions in the ante-bellum period complained long and loudly about monopoly—particularly about monopolies created or sustained by special government privileges, which, they reasoned, "facilitated the mistreatment of labor." But there is something peculiar about their crusade. The monopolies they complained about exploited workers *as consumers,* but they were largely irrelevant to workers *as workers.*[61]

The industries experiencing labor organization and militancy (such as boots and shoes, textiles, ironmaking, and printing,) were not monopolistic, but rather open and competitive. Moreover, with the exception of the tariff (and tariffs, it must be kept in mind, are a boon to all domestic producers and their employees), the growth of the factory system owed far more to technology and expanding markets than it did to bank monopolies or special corporate charters.

When trade unions in that era objected to *monopoly* in their industry, what they in all probability were objecting to was *competition,* which was pushing aside inefficient producers—and which was making it less likely that their members would become "their own bosses." This was a protest at what was perceived to be their permanent status as wage earners. The only real alternative was itself some form or another of special privilege which would protect the monopoly of the skilled—their particular jobs, or their opportunity to go into business themselves. And the commitment of many leaders of organized laborers to democratic, cooperative production as an alternative to the wages system lasted for a very long time. It changed only gradually as the American Federation of Labor superseded the syndicalist-oriented Knights of Labor as the "spokesman" for organized workers in the 1880s. The AFL settled on collective bargaining rather than on worker ownership as the most viable means to control the market in its favor.[62]

Commentary: The Right to the Whole Product of Labor, Equality, and the Conundrums of Syndicalism

The problems with the version of the labor theory of value[63] put forth by the various radical critics of capitalism discussed in this chapter are also worth exploring, since its shortcomings are clues to the inadequacies of the practical or proposed attempts to realize any version of industrial democracy based on it.

In the first place, the champions of the strict labor time theory did not seem to worry about honesty. The individual worker, guild, syndicate, or industrial union in the cooperative commonwealth might simply lie about the actual time necessary to produce the commodity in question—a circumstance which apparently occurred, even among the presumably idealistic participants in Josiah Warren's experiment.[64] But it is the *kind* of lie labor timers have the incentive to tell that is so deadly. When labor time replaces money as the medium of exchange, a premium is put on goldbricking.

Similarly, as Smith insisted, even in the pristine state of nature not all labor is of identical worth. Little reflection is necessary to realize that ten hours whittling stick figures from wood is not quite the same as ten hours spent moiling in a factory, cultivating fields under a hot sun, hunched over a hand loom, digging coal underground—or writing books. The attempt to divorce differential rewards from labor whose products are valued by consumers differently makes the rational allocation of productive resources impossible. In practice, the cupboards of labor exchanges would soon be stripped bare of those commodities for which demand is strong but for which the time spent in production is onerous (or for which the skills are scarce), but piled high with fingerpainting and modern poetry. Jobs requiring the least application will be glutted while those with more exacting standards, unable to offer higher compensation, will go begging. There will be bureaucrats and sociologists aplenty, but few engineers and plumbers. Within each field, equal remuneration again presents a great incentive for shirking or coasting. The result would be production gluts and dearths—exactly that type of "imbalance" of production and consumption denounced by the opponents of inequality (but without a price system to order and balance supplies and demands).

A strict labor time theory, in short, raises all the problems of incentives that have always been a staple, and decisive, objection to schemes for social reconstruction based on equality. Moreover, if the various syndicates were allowed to freely bargain among each other without a sovereign state to regulate the process, the likely result would be anything but equality.

Many proponents of cooperation recognized this last problem. In a conflict between the putative goals of an industrial democracy organized along syndicalist lines—equality—and the means by which it is organized—voluntarism—which has priority?

The Owenites faced this issue, but treaded gingerly. John Bray admitted that "the testimony of experience goes to prove the general truth of" the incentive "objections" to equalitarianism. Nevertheless, Bray opted for the doctrine his mentor was so famous for espousing, a doctrine which eventually became *the* standard rejoinder: environmental determinism. *A structural transformation of the material basis of society would produce a transformation in men's character—abolish profits, you abolish selfishness.* In the new society, handclapping would replace cash:

> If it be contended that men will not do their duty to their fellows without being spurred on by a stimulus more or less connected with their animal wants—that if the men of all trades and professions receive the uniform rate of wages, a carelessness will be engendered as to whether much or little is produced—that if all be insured a future provision, they will become indifferent to

present exertion . . . there will be a Public Opinion to give its award to particular actions.[65]

Anyway, according to Bray, payment by time (salary) was replacing piece work in many fields of endeavor, without (so he claimed) any ill effects:

> In almost all trades, the workmen now receive a stated weekly sum, although the powers of production of various individuals differ considerably; and yet such uniformity in the rate of payment does not encourage idleness.[66]

Oddly enough, this argument of the Owenites and others seemed persuasive to even so eminent an economist as John Stuart Mill. Yet it is a discouragingly naive fallacy. Bray, and the others who subscribed to this defense of the labor time theory, neglected to mention that not all time under capitalism is paid at the same rate; and those who do shirk under time payment systems risk dismissal.[67]

William Thompson wrote in one place, somewhat obscurely, about a tendency "to increase human happiness, if all species of cheerful exertion for the common good were *equally* remunerated" by prior agreement.[68] But he came down ultimately on the side of utility, for elsewhere Thompson wrote that only *"[w]herever equality does not lessen production"* should it "be the sole object pursued. Wherever it decreases really useful production . . . it saps its own existence and should cease."[69] We might say that he was willing to countenance only so much inequality as was necessary to insure maximum production. But how can this be determined except by a competitive market?

A third position was outright voluntarism, equality be hanged. Hodgskin best exemplified this approach. Though he doubted "whether one species of labour is more valuable than another," or "more necessary," he did not believe there was any "principle or rule," such as equality, "for dividing the produce of joint labor among the different individuals who concur in production, *but the judgement of individuals themselves.*"[70] In other words, one is worth what one can fetch.

Proudhon was also more of a "voluntarist" than an egalitarian. Although he claimed, or seemed to claim, that labor *time* was the proper unit for measuring just exchanges, for the most part he more or less endorsed free bargaining à la Hodgskin.[71]

A similar spectrum of belief existed in America among the radical intellectuals and others influential in the labor movement. For every outspoken egalitarian such as Thomas Skidmore, there were probably a dozen Stephen Simpsons, who claimed that

> [i]t is a perversion of the aims of the enlightened advocates of

labour, to represent that they are contending for an *equality of wealth,* or a community of property. Our object is as remote from that, as the existing system of extortion is from justice . . . we could not advocate an equality of possessions, without committing an infraction of the rights of others—and being guilty of that very injustice, of which we now accuse *capital.* Equality of rights to what we produce, is not equality of possession—for some will produce more than others.[72]

At any rate, trade unionism as it really was and is (as opposed to unionism as some intellectuals wistfully want to make it), was and is voluntarist, not egalitarian. Unions bargain for their members or for those whom they purport to represent: they do not bargain for the whole class of workers. And they do not hesitate to ask for more than the average wages of their fellow workers elsewhere.

Nevertheless, whenever the (collective) voluntarist principle takes precedence over equality as a principle of exchange and income distribution in an industrial democracy that is organized along syndicalist lines, serious problems arise. How can one syndicate of producers prevent the formation of another competing syndicate, whenever the first fails to satisfy the aspirations of the former's members (say, if it becomes undemocratic), or the preferences of the members of other syndicates who consume its products? If free formation of new voluntary co-operatives is allowed, one is on the slippery slope to capitalism. But if competition is prohibited, how can society as a whole protect itself from the mutual exploitation of predatory syndicates? The "bargaining power" of the railroad syndicate, after all, will be more formidable than that of the union of toymakers.[73]

The conundrum of syndicalism amounts to this: How can the inefficient, stagnationist potential of a modernized guild system be prevented? The advocates of industrial democracy by voluntary cooperation had no answer. The state socialists believed they did.

4. Labor's Powerlessness Under Competition: Industrial Democracy as Socialism

Socialism demands that "[a]ll the means of production" be "in the *exclusive* control of the organized community."[1] The substantial difference between socialism and syndicalism, and the much closer relationship of unionism to syndicalism than to socialism, should be immediately apparent.

Nevertheless, the doctrinal contributions of modern socialists (most of whom recognized the modern nation state to be the most likely representative of the organized community) to the ideology of 'adversarial', compulsory unionism were important. In Europe, socialistically-inclined intellectuals had and still have a major influence on the direction of the organized labor movement's political programme. In America, socialist criticism of competitive capitalism had a significant impact on the ideology of many union leaders, even if the socialist proposal to abolish private ownership of the means of production did not. Socialists had a much better developed theory of unemployment than did the utopians or the syndicalists, and the socialists' vision of class conflict rationalized violence against employers, the capitalist state, and insufficiently class-conscious workers, which the Owenites *et al.* were unwilling to condone.

This chapter will explain some distinctive socialist contributions to union radicalism; describe socialists' reasons for rejecting syndicalism and their various views about collective bargaining; and assess several criticisms of socialism as a principle of economic organization.

Socialisms and Socialists

The understandable tendency today to interpret socialism almost exclusively through the lens of Marx and the Marxians must be put aside in any historical investigation of the sources of industrial democratic thought. There were several influential versions of socialism that predated Marxism and competed with it in the 19th century, or for that matter, in the 20th. Many socialists were radical egalitarians and democrats; but many were meritocrats who believed in rule by elites. There were champions of violent revolution, but there were many who sought to revolutionize the social order gradually, through education and democratic political change. Many socialists were avowed atheists, seeing in religion and the churches the main prop of the private property order and thus the greatest obstacle to the achievement of their aims. But there was a sizeable, and very influential, group of Christian Socialists who located the fundamental source of all socialist ideas in the Judeo-Christian ethical heritage.[2]

There were Marxists, of course: but among these there were revisionists and nonrevisionists, and later, Leninists, Stalinists, Trotskyists, and others. There were socialists such as Daniel De Leon, who donned a syndicalist frock for tactical reasons. And finally, insofar as the institution of unionism and collective bargaining is concerned, many socialists believed that socialism could arrive only if the *entire* working class organized into one big union for the final showdown with the capitalist order. But others saw great merit in partial, industry-by-industry, compulsory unionism as a vehicle for transporting society toward socialism.

In France, despite radical egalitarians such as Rousseau, there was an influential group of socially conservative, inegalitarian socialist theoreticians: Claude Henri de Saint-Simon, an atheist who nevertheless sought to restate "the essence of Christianity, in accordance with the needs of the new industrial age";[3] Auguste Comte, founder of "sociology," the "science of society," which he conceived as a direct challenge to what he thought of as the incorrect, "metaphysical" methodological individualism of classical economics, and the man who coined the term, "altruism";[4] and a group or cult known collectively as the Saint-Simonians, who were convinced that competitive capitalism was "anarchic" and in need of replacement by a planned, "rational" social order run by a scientific-technocratic elite.[5]

In Germany, major 19th century socialist (and extreme statist) thinkers such as Johann Gottlieb Fichte, G. W. F. Hegel, Johann Karl Rodbertus,

Ferdinand Lassalle, Karl Marx and Friedrich Engels all opposed the capitalist social and economic order because of its alleged ethical deficiencies—namely, its legitimation of egoism. And on this last point, many of them were simply drawing out a logical political implication of the moral thought of Immanuel Kant, the single most influential philosopher in 19th century Germany.[6]

Nineteenth century English socialism was chiefly inspired by Owen and the Owenites, though among intellectuals, such aesthetes as John Ruskin, Thomas Carlyle, and Matthew Arnold exercised a hold. But late in the century a group of so-called Fabian socialists grew up around the civil servant Sidney Webb and his social-worker wife Beatrice Potter. The Webbs' distinctive and very important contributions to the theories and practices of Anglo-American industrial democracy warrant separate treatment and will be discussed in later chapters, but the underconsumptionist theory of John A. Hobson, a Fabian fellow-traveler, will be discussed here.[7]

There were few state socialist thinkers of importance in America prior to the Civil War, but in the 1870s and 1880s French and German socialism (and Christian Socialism) gradually permeated the culture.[8] The intellectual pioneers were Laurence Gronlund, a revisionist Marxist whose *The Cooperative Commonwealth* (1884) "was the first attempt by an American Socialist to write in English a comprehensive yet simplified analysis of Marxism for the man in the street";[9] and Edward Bellamy, a Comtean whose utopian novel, *Looking Backward, 2000-1887* (1889), as well as its sequel, *Equality* (1897), was to the shaping of pro-socialist "popular opinion" what "*Uncle Tom's Cabin* was to the anti-slavery movement."[10] Daniel De Leon, a university-professor-turned-revolutionary-agitator and a founder of the revolutionary industrial union, the Industrial Workers of the World (IWW) is also worth mention.[11]

Bargaining Power Revisited

Socialist opponents of competition who proclaimed the necessity for a planned social order analyzed laborers' position under capitalism in terms not dissimilar to those utopians and syndicalists discussed in the previous chapter. But there were differences in emphasis that led to substantive differences in the programme for reform.

Many socialists sidestepped the problem interemployer competition posed for the credibility of the claim that workers had no choices and employers could arbitrarily set wages. They indicted the alleged domination of labor by capital in *class* rather than in *personal* terms. "Today," the Saint Simonians contended in the late 1820s, "the entire mass of workers is exploited by the men whose property they utilize," because the worker

> can exist only under the conditions imposed upon him by a class
> small in numbers, namely the class of men who have been
> invested through legislation, the daughter of conquest, with a
> monopoly of riches, which is to say, with the capacity to dispose
> at their will, even in idleness, of the instruments of work.[12]

Sixty-odd years later, according to the Webbs, the situation hadn't
fundamentally changed, since

> the monopoly of which [workers are] here impatient is not that
> of any *single* individual, but that of the *class itself.* What the
> workers are objecting to is . . . a . . . feudal system of industry . . . of
> . . . domination of the mass of ordinary workers by a hierarchy of
> property owners, who compete, it is true, among themselves,
> but who are nevertheless able, as a class, to preserve a very real
> control over the lives of those who depend on their own daily
> labor . . . [the worker is] free only to choose to which master he
> would sell his labor—free only to decide from which proprietor
> he would beg that access to the new instruments of production
> without which he could not exist.[13]

The interemployer competition which *did* exist was, according to the
socialists, fast becoming obsolete. The process of competition was itself
liquidating inefficient capitalists and concentrating control in an ever-
smaller number of noncompeting hands. *"[B]ig industry kills small
industry,"* the Saint Simonians concluded by the end of the 1820s (as
would Marx a generation later, and as would each succeeding generation
of socialists right up to the 1980s):

> What has been happening in England justified this assertion and
> proves that the concentration of workshops and instruments of
> work increases steadily *as the direct consequence of competi-
> tion.*

This allegedly irresistible tendency toward the emergence of one big
monopoly "prepare[s] the elements of the universal association of the
future." *Socialism, in other words, is inevitable.*[14]

Underconsumption, Unbalanced Production, and the Need for Planning

The Owenites, and syndicalists like Proudhon (it will be recalled from
the previous chapter), explained unemployment as the result of a

deficiency of markets; explained deficiency in markets as a result of inadequate aggregate demand; explained inadequate demand as the result of inadequate wages; and explained inadequate wages as the result of unequal bargaining power between 'labor' and 'capital'. Their solution was that workers in the future must receive the 'whole product of their labor', undiminished by profit, interest, or rent.

The concept of 'unbalanced' production and consumption was a central theorem of socialism as well. But socialist theoreticians asserted that it was not sufficient that the workers in a *given* industry be able to 'buy back' the product of *that* industry, nor even that the working class *as a whole* be able to repurchase the output of industry *as a whole*. Production itself *must be planned* or coordinated by social authority in order to *guarantee* that there are no unmet social needs nor any superfluous, unwanted goods.

The German Johann Karl Rodbertus offered at mid-century a powerfully influential underconsumptionist theory of unemployment and the trade cycle, bottomed on laborers' lack of bargaining power, that established the case for socialism most lucidly.[15]

Rodbertus admitted that the standard of living of the working class had increased over the years. Nevertheless, he insisted that poverty, or 'pauperism', was a "social, that is a relative matter," consisting

> in the inability of anyone to supply himself with the requisites needed in his own station of life; and as the wants of the working class increase with its rise in general social standing, *poverty may be said to increase, even though the actual amount of income stays the same.*[16]

Employers' greater bargaining power kept wages hovering at the subsistence level—even though the level was a *moving, culturally determined one*. This, as Rodbertus's student Ferdinand Lassalle put it, was the essence of the "Iron Law of Wages," under which

> the average wages always remain reduced to that rate which in a people is barely necessary for existence and propagation; a matter governed by the customary manner of living of each people.[17]

Marx similarly explained that, while *"the price of labour will be determined by the cost of production,"* the tendency "does not hold good for the *single individual* but only for the race."[18] Transient increases in real wages above the minimum caused by fluctuations in supply and demand result, à la Malthus, in larger working class families (an increase in the supply of labor), that, because of competition, cause wages to decline again toward the social subsistence level. If wages should drop below the minimum, the labor supply would shrink and average wages would increase. The shrinkage would occur not only from absolute destitution and starvation. If wages declined below a certain level, young workers would postpone marriage and family, since they would not be able to support them in a (culturally-defined) decent way.

Nevertheless, to return to Rodbertus, while wage earners may well receive higher *absolute* real wages in periods of prosperity (when the demand for labor is increasing), *inequality* between the economic classes continues to increase. The employing class still gets *relatively* richer. This was Rodbertus's famous "Law of Diminishing Wage Share," the foundation of his trade cycle theory.

This law he defined in the following manner. "[W]hen the distribution of the national product is left to itself"—in a laissez-faire economy—the laws of supply and demand "produce this effect: that with increasing productiveness of the labour of society," due to a greater division of labor, accumulation of capital, better technology, and so forth, "the wages of the labouring class become an ever smaller portion of the national product."[19]

Rodbertus demonstrated the meaning of the law with an eminently plausible example from agriculture. Suppose, he said, "100,000 labourers produced 10 million bushels of grain 50 years ago, but to-day produce 20 million bushels"; but suppose each laborer received the nominal wage equivalent of "50 bushels as wages . . . as he did 50 years ago." In other words, 50 years ago the laborers received, in the aggregate, wages which could purchase 5 million bushels of output [100,000 × 50], or 50 percent of the output. Fifty years later they still receive in the aggregate wages which could purchase 5 million bushels of output—but the laborers' "relative share of the product" has sunk "to half of what [it was] before." (Five million bushels is only 25 percent of 20 million bushels). Rodbertus correctly observed that their relative share would still "sink even though the quantity" of their wages "should rise to from 60 to 80 bushels." Their "share of the product" would "be maintained" only if their wages [that is, what their wages could buy] "were increased in direct proportion with the increase in productiveness—if they increased from 50 to 100 bushels." Only then would their share or output remain stable, at 50 percent [100,000 × 100 = 10 million, half of 20 million] of "the gross product."[20]

Marx appeared to agree with this analysis. There are periods, he wrote, when both profits and wages increase. But Marx added that profit as a share of real social income *always* "rises in the same degree in which wages fall" and *always* "falls in the same degree in which wages rise." This was, to be sure, merely a truism, but he added that "[r]eal wages may remain the same, they may even rise, nevertheless relative wages may fall." Marx illustrated this concept with a different example. Suppose that as the result of competition in product and labor markets "all means of subsistence" have fallen by "two-thirds in price, while the day's wages have fallen but one-third." The real wages of the working class—their purchasing power—have increased. Nevertheless, "wages have decreased in proportion to the gain [profit] of the capitalist," whose surplus value has increased; "for a smaller amount of exchange values, which he pays to the worker, the latter must produce a greater amount of exchange values than before." The share, or value, of capital has increased relative to the share, or value, of labor; and the "distribution of social wealth between capital and labour has become still more unequal.... the social position of the worker has become worse."[21]

The law of diminishing wage share, according to Rodbertus, unlocks the mystery of the trade cycle. Private entrepreneurs base their (uncoordinated) investment plans for future production on past and present experience, broadly on the assumption that the various groups of commodities demanded by different social classes "will," as one student of his work explained, "be wanted in their old proportions," that is, "the things wanted by the working class will require the same portion of the productive power of the country, and likewise with the things wanted by the other classes."[22]

But the gradual *change* in the proportional mix of income shares which occurs as production gets underway throughout society means that these production plans, *ex post*, are misguided. The purchasing power available to the wage earning classes will *not* ultimately be sufficient to buy up the new, and much larger, supply. The tendency will be toward a "[c]ontinuous overproduction of one group of commodities" (commodities produced for the market whose consumers were predominantly workers) which leads inevitably to commercial crises. "Failure and bankruptcy stare in the face the makers of commodities which are not covered by purchasing power." The crisis in one sector causes unemployment, and hence a contraction in the purchasing power, in that sector; competition between newly unemployed workers in the other sectors beats down purchasing power in others, which eventually engulfs the entire economy.[23]

So what emerges is a flood of unsalable goods *and* a mass of starving men, a paradox of 'poverty in the midst of plenty'. As Rodbertus put it, "simultaneously with superfluity, four-fifths or five-sixths suffer want." The fundamental social problem is that owners of capital produce only insofar as it is privately profitable to do so; but a faulty distribution system means that production for profit stops well short of the satisfaction of social needs. People produce under capitalism "not with a view to satisfying the needs of labor, but the needs of possession; in other words, they produce for those who possess."[24]

John A. Hobson expounded his underconsumptionist theory of the trade cycle later in the century, in scores of books and articles published after 1889 that were avidly read in America. (Some were published in American journals of opinion). Hobson's general views on social reform were enormously influential among the men who charted the course of the New Deal, including its labor legislation. Many knew him firsthand; still others received their education in his thought through Hobson's major American disciple, the Catholic progressive reformer Monsignor John A. Ryan.

Hobson's theory of the trade cycle was similar to Rodbertus's (although Hobson rarely referred to underconsumptionists that preceded him, and it is not clear if he read Rodbertus), except that he dropped the latter's assumption that capitalists and workers consumed different *kinds* of commodities. Hobson contended that disproportionate rates of increase between savings and consumption (which Hobson called spending) *in general* were sufficient to generate the deadly imbalance between aggregate supply and demand that ineluctably led to depression and unemployment.

In the version of his theory relevant for our purposes,[25] wages (which constitute the bulk of consumption demand) lag behind profits (which constitute the bulk of investible savings) during a boom. As the income from production becomes more generally maldistributed in favor of the "rich" (those who are profit, interest, or rent recipients), a greater and greater proportion is invested in production facilities, the output of which cannot all be marketed (at prices which repay the cost of production and yield a profit). Eventually, therefore, consumption of final goods falls off relative to their production; and this slackening of consumption demand touches off a crisis in capital goods industries. Employment in these businesses contracts, reducing purchasing power; competition of the unemployed for work elsewhere beats down wages and purchasing power still further.

It is difficult to exaggerate the degree to which American as well as European socialists and nonsocialist reformers—such as Robert F. Wagner or Franklin D. Roosevelt—leaned on one version or another of the underconsumption doctrine as the basis for their belief in the social and economic necessity of income redistribution through government power, via taxation, or via the promotion of collective bargaining.[26]

Edward Bellamy, for instance, made underconsumption the showcase of his critique of capitalism. He explained the theory brilliantly in an often-reprinted extract from *Equality* (1897), the "Parable of the Water Tank," itself a noteworthy metaphorical anticipation of the claim that capitalism constitutes a kind of "trickle-down" economics.[27]

Daniel De Leon's famous speech of 1905, the "Socialist Reconstruction of Society" (on the preamble to the IWW), was even more well-known in America, and even throughout the world.[28] From census figures (supplied by the National Executive Committee of the Republican Party, no less!), De Leon purportedly proved that labor's share of the national income had declined since the Civil War, despite the increase in national wealth and income. (De Leon also asserted that the working class was getting absolutely poorer.)

What De Leon did was to compare the value of the total product from the manufacturing sector of the economy for each decade (after 1860) with the total wages paid in that sector. The results, he announced, exposed "a good portion of the naked and hideous reality" of capitalism. Labor's share of national wealth, he claimed, was never more than one-fifth, and had displayed a marked tendency to decline even below this paltry figure. His conclusion was clear and forceful: there was no harmony of interest between labor and capital:

> The working class and the employing class have nothing in common . . . the condition of the Working Class is one of hunger, want and privation, that from bad it is getting worse and ever worse; that the plunder levied upon them mounts ever higher; [and] that not only does their relative share of the wealth they produce decline, but [that] the absolute amount of the wealth that they enjoy shrinks to [an] ever smaller quantity in their hands.

Apologists for the established order, who pointed to the increasing aggregate wealth of the country, were "guilty of that worst form of deception that consists in stating a half truth and suppressing the other half;" they were "swindler[s]." De Leon added parenthetically that the "positions" of those who believed that the real wages of workers individually or on the average had deteriorated and those who believed that they had improved were "irreconcilable." And he laid down the challenge; if "the latter" thesis, that wage earners' living standards had improved, "be true, or even approximately true . . . then the . . . Preamble" of the IWW (as well, presumably, as the organization's critique of capitalism itself) "fall like the baseless fabric of a nightmare."[29]

Socialism vs. Syndicalism: The Right to the Whole Product of Labor

Socialist theoreticians depai.ed from syndicalists much more profoundly than might appear if one were to focus only on differences in emphasis about whether it was a capitalist, or 'capital', that exploited labor, or only on the mechanics of the trade cycle. The leading socialist theoreticians denied utterly that there was *any such thing* as an individual worker's 'right to the whole product of his labor', or that organized workers could or should control industry directly.

In the first place, *qua* socialists, virtually all of these writers shared one fundamental assumption with their precapitalist collectivist predecessors, namely the idea that society was an organism of which individual human beings were only subordinate cells.[30]

On the 'social view of man', as it has been called, an individual had no 'right to the whole product of his labor'. Production was a social process, and as such, *there was no such thing as individual labor.* Indeed, all *income was essentially unearned,* and the "total product of the labour of society belongs to society as a whole."[31]

The individual's earned share was a laughable pittance. The reason? Bellamy explained that

> [t]he element in the total industrial product which is due to the social organism is represented by the difference between the value of what one man produces as a worker in connection with the social organization and what he could produce in a condition of isolation.

What this *means* is that

> [i]f the modern man, by aid of the social machinery, can produce fifty dollars' worth of product where he could produce not over a quarter of a dollar's worth without society, then forty-nine dollars and three quarters out of every fifty dollars must be credited to the social fund to be equally distributed.

But even of *that quarter dollar,* the individual had no *real claim to a cent!* After all, "society" fed, clothed, and educated him before he could act on his own. Therefore, he owed "society" *everything.*[32]

The bottom line of this social calculus was clearly set forth, particularly in the philosophy of Auguste Comte. Morally, "we must eliminate *Rights,* as in philosophy we eliminate causes." The

> social point of view . . . cannot tolerate the notion of *rights,* for such notion rests on individualism. *We are born under a load of obligations of every kind, to our predecessors, to our successors, to our contemporaries. After our birth these obligations increase or accumulate, for it is some time before we can return any service.* . . . Positivism [the name Comte chose for his philosophy] urges us to *live for others.* This, the definitive formula of human morality, gives a direct sanction exclusively to our instincts of benevolence, the common source of happiness and duty. [Man must serve] Humanity, whose we are entirely.[33]

Gronlund was quite explicit in explaining that socialism was a complete repudiation of everything the American Revolution stood for:

> [I]t is . . . important that thoughtful people should know that

philosophic Socialists repudiate that theory of 'natural rights', and insist that the lesson . . . in our own Declaration of Independence must be unlearned . . . *It is Society, organized Society, the State that gives us all the rights we have.* To the State we owe our freedom. To it we owe our living and property . . . the State may do anything whatsoever which is shown to be expedient.

He added that "as against the State, the organized Society, even Labor does not give us a particle of title to what our hands and brains produce."[34]

Socialism vs. Syndicalism: Planning vs. Anarchy

Based on this 'social view' of man, socialists contended that the solution to the problems they believed were endemic to a capitalistic society required central economic planning.

One of the most lucid expositions of this alleged need appeared in the "Doctrine" of the Saint-Simonians, in the 1820s. "[P]roduction", they declared,

> must be so organized that short supply or glut need not be feared in any of its branches. [But] [i]n the present state of affairs, where the distribution [investment?] is made by capitalists and owners, none of the conditions is either being or can be realized except after a large number of trial and error attempts, frequent blunders, and sad experiences. And even then the result that is obtained is always imperfect and momentary. Each individual is left to his own limited knowledge and no common view presides . . .

If the means of production are socialized, however, the problem will be solved. The planning body

> is then entrusted with these functions that are performed so poorly today. The institution is the trustee of all the instruments of production. It presides over all material exploitation, and therefore is in a position to have a total view which permits it to see all parts of the industrial workshop at once. Through its branches it is in contact with every locality, with every kind of industry, and with all the workers. It can therefore take into account general and individual needs, and direct manpower and industry where [it is] most needed. To be brief, it can regulate production, bring it into harmony with consumption . . .[35]

Rodbertus added, years later, that planning was necessary to insure that "the share of each" social class remain "a fixed, unalterable quota of the product . . . be the increase in productiveness what it may." It was only just that the needs of the poorer, more numerous members of society be met before the desires of the rich for luxuries be satisfied.[36]

Other socialists wanted to *do away with social classes altogether.* But whether they wanted a classless society or not, the common thread among the socialist theoreticians of industrial democracy was the necessity to centralize ownership and investment of all economic resources in order to guarantee full employment by balancing production and consumption, and to guarantee that goods were produced to satisfy social needs, and not merely to satisfy the desires for entrepreneurial profit.

A planned economy is as incompatible with syndicalism as it is incompatible with free trade unions, and for the same reason. What socialist theory guarantees to each individual is not the product of his labor, but subsistence—it guarantees him *a* job (actually, it would compel him to work), but would not guarantee him any *particular* job.[37] There could be no such thing as a worker's (or workers') *property in their jobs,* and there is no room in socialist theory for the control of an industry *by the workers of that industry.* The interests of 'society as a whole' take precedence over any lesser, constituent social group.

All European socialists commented, even if obliquely, about the incompatibility of syndicalism or trade union autonomy with the demands of a planned economy; and so did American socialists such as Bellamy and Gronlund. But the American socialist John Spargo, in the 20th century, denounced the syndicalist 'heresy' as (allegedly) championed by the IWW, or its European cousins, in the most outspoken terms:

> As socialists we are as utterly opposed to the exclusive control of the means of transportation by the workers who happen to be engaged in transportation as we are to the present system. The transportation system concerns not alone the workers engaged in that branch of service, but all the people of the nation. Moreover, the Syndicalist utopia must inevitably resolve itself into an industrial caste system in which the workers engaged in industries of most vital and primary importance to the life of the nation will rule [through the strike threat] all the rest of the people through the strategic positions they occupy in the industrial scheme.[38]

Syndicalism or independent trade unionism would also pose an insuperable obstacle to the principles governing the distribution of income and the allocation of work under socialism.

Broadly speaking, socialists tended to line up along two axes. Some were reasonably comfortable with at least some degree of 'meritocracy', rule by elites, and differential rewards (inequality of income). Others were much stricter in their egalitarianism.

The Saint-Simonians, Rodbertus, or Gronlund, to pick some representative examples of the first type, appeared quite willing to reward individuals differently on the basis of performance, at least *in each job*. 'From each according to his ability, to each according to his work' amounted to their operational principle of income distribution. They were willing to tolerate differences in reward for work performed, although they hoped to keep the income ranges between *different occupations* much closer than under capitalism.[39]

The egalitarians sought to distribute income according to a maxim first espoused by the 18th century Frenchman, Morelly: "From each according to his ability, to each according to his needs."[40] The moral "title of every man, woman, and child to the means of existence," Bellamy explained to his American readers in *Looking Backward,* "rests on no basis less plain, broad, and simple than the fact that they are members of one race— members of one human family, . . . joint inheritors, co-heirs" of the socially-produced fund of wealth. All must have the "same share" because all "make the same effort." The *same* effort, according to Bellamy, is "the *best* service it is in the power" of each "to give":

> All men who do their best, do the same. A man's endowments, however godlike, merely fix the measure of his duty. The man of great endowments who does not do all he might, though he may do more than a man of small endowments who does his best, is deemed a less deserving worker than the latter . . . [41]

This 'need' principle of distribution serves the cause of equality in only one, rather hyperrefined (and thoroughly arbitrary) sense. Only a moment's thought is necessary to recognize that distribution of the product of effort according to (socially defined) need must amount *in fact* to radically *unequal* distribution of income. The needs of the weak and the sick are much greater than those of the strong and healthy in mind and body. The latter's input will be anything but equal to those of the former— in any event, for as long as the abilities of the strong and healthy continue to be manifest (which, given the incentives of this system, will not be for very long).

How the pie is cut affects how big a pie will be baked under any social system; and socialists of all stripes faced the same problem of incentives that 'labor time' advocates puzzled over. How does one keep men from shirking *in each* occupation? How does one insure that the labor requirements are filled *in different occupations* according to 'society's' plan?

Many socialists proposed to deal with the latter problem by rendering subjectively unequal tasks relatively more equal, by reducing the "socially required" time spent doing them. In other words, they sought to lower the hours of labor constituting a "normal working day" in the disagreeable occupations. The utopian Charles Fourier apparently had something like this in mind, with his notions of making labor more "attractive," and individuals such as Rodbertus and Gronlund agreed, as did, to some extent, Edward Bellamy.[42]

Nevertheless, manipulating the hours of work might not do the trick. The next expedient proposed was the 'handclapping' method, espoused by some of the Owenites (see chapter three *supra*.) According to Bellamy, "the administration" of the socialist state "would only need to" declare some occupation "'extra hazardous', and those who pursued it especially worthy of the national gratitude, to be overrun by volunteers." But, when push came to shove, Bellamy admitted that *compulsory labor* would serve well enough as the final solution to the selfishness problem:

> the administration, while depending on the voluntary system . . . holds always in reserve the power to call for special volunteers, or draft any force needed from any quarter. . . . As for actual neglect of work, positively bad work, or other overt remissness on the part of men incapable of generous motives, the discipline of the industrial army is far too strict to allow anything whatever of the sort. A man able to do duty, and persistently refusing, is sentenced to solitary imprisonment on bread and water till he consents.[43]

The justification for compulsory labor followed ineluctably from the basic principles undergirding the socialists' ethical philosophy. One of the characters in Bellamy's novel explained the political implications of the morality of altruism with unusual candor. Under socialism, "a man who can produce twice as much as another with the same effort, instead of being rewarded for doing so, ought to be punished if he does not do so." Capitalist ethics would hold that "when a horse pulled a heavier load than a goat," the horse should get more hay; instead "we should have whipped him soundly if he had not, on the ground that, being much stronger, he ought to . . . " "It is singular," Bellamy had this character say with a "twinkle in his eye," "how ethical standards change."[44]

Bellamy's views were by no means idiosyncratic. Virtually every major state socialist thinker concluded that occupational freedom was dispensable if it conflicted with the state's economic plans.[45]

Socialism vs. Unionism: Violence and the Class Struggle

If individual men were to be subordinated to society under socialism, so too would their private associations and combinations. Hence, there was no place in the socialist society for the free, independent labor union, or for the 'right to strike' (however conceived). Many socialist writers saw the labor organizations that existed under capitalism as only a temporary, if useful, *destructive* force.

"Whether we think of ownership and control of all industry by one vast union of workers with centralized authority," the American socialist John Spargo wrote, or "a series of local industrial unions owning and controlling local industries" à la Proudhon, "the assumption that the labor union is by its very nature the proper unit of social government and administration is itself open to the most serious question." "To be absolutely candid about it," Spargo revealed,

> the *very nature* of the labor union, the work it *must perform* in present society, tends to unfit it for the part the Syndicalists would impose upon it. *Its work is critical and destructive.* It does not concern itself with the constructive work of industrial organization and management.[46]

This unflattering verdict on unionism should not be taken to represent complete disapproval of unions. On the contrary, Gronlund explained that the unions did serve one *very* constructive purpose, as far as socialism is concerned—namely that of inculcating its "central spirit . . . to wit, *that the interests of all workers are the same, that each must postpone his own advantage to the common good and each yield his individual prejudice and crotchet to the collective judgment.*"[47]

This spirit of subordination of individual right to group advantage was a fundamental characteristic of socialism, as it was and is the essence of the argument made on behalf of compulsory unionism. The new ethic was best inculcated through education. But if that didn't work, it might just as well be accomplished through intimidation or social terrorism.

On the issue of violence in labor disputes *as such,* spokesmen for *avowedly* revolutionary organizations—such as the Industrial Workers of the World—minced few words. The blunt testimony of Mr. Vincent St. John, its General Secretary and Treasurer (before the U.S. Commission on Industrial Relations in 1915), is a case in point:

Q: If, in carrying [your purposes] out, it is necessary to destroy property, would your organization countenance that?

A: If the destruction of property would gain the point for the workers involved, that is the only consideration we would give to it . . .

. . .

Q: Would that same reasoning apply to questions of violence against persons?

A: Certainly.

. . .

A: . . . and as far as the destruction of property is concerned, the property is not ours. We haven't any interest at all in it; it is used simply . . . to

make the lot of the workers, as a class, harder; and the only property that we have, experience in the past has shown that the
employers, as a class, are not at all particular whether they injure
our property or not. They take us into the mills before we have . . .
even the semblance of an education, and they grind up our vitality,
brain and muscular energy into profits, and whenever we can not
keep pace with the machine speeded to its highest notch, they turn
us out onto the road to eke out an existence as best we can . . . the
employing class . . . has not shown any respect at all for our
property, . . . it is not incumbent upon us to show any respect for his
property; and we do not propose to do it; and we do not propose to
make any bones about having that attitude clearly understood; . . .
And the same holds true with regard to life and violence. . . . if life
happens to be lost in strikes that we are implicated in, the blame
generally, and has been up to date, on the other side. But we are not
going to tell our membership to allow themselves to be shot down
and beat up like cattle. . . . Violence . . . as a general rule, is forced on
them as a simple act of self-defense.

. . .

Q: Take the case of workers filling the place of strikers . . . If your people
believe that by committing acts of violence against the people who
take the places, they would cause a determination of the struggle in
favor of the strikers, then you would countenance such violence?
A: Certainly.[48]

An overt, unashamed and unabashed defense of strike violence for the
'larger aims' of the class struggle was not uncommon among state
socialists, both in Europe and in America, and no doubt had, over time, an
important effect in softening up and inuring (as well as intimidating)
public opinion to what would otherwise be an intolerable state of social
affairs.[49] The famous journalist Henry Demarest Lloyd, for instance,
declared that "[t]he workingmen are often wrong, but theirs is always the
right side." If "ruffianism stains both sides, . . . the blackest half of the guilt is
theirs—the great, the rich, the wise, who use it to make the poor poorer
and to still further wrong the wronged."[50]

Lloyd appeared before the Congressional investigation of the famous
Anthracite Coal Strike of 1902 to testify on behalf of the United Mine
Workers (UMW). He did not bother to deny that bloodshed had occurred.
Nor did he even make the claim (otherwise repeated *ad infinitum* and *ad
nauseam* in those days, as today, by the proponents of unionism) that it
was *employers* who started the slugging. But he *did* claim that

What violence there was . . . we charge in the gross and in the
main upon those who held in their hands the control of the
livelihood of a whole population and refused to negotiate or
reason with them. The denial of arbitration . . . was itself a
monstrous act of violence. The far less immoral physical vio-

lence that followed . . . was precisely what would have been foretold by any student of human nature . . . Draw the picture of what you call the anarchy of the five months of last summer as black as you choose; the blacker is the condemnation of those who, for two generations, have ruled these regions as masters.

What of innocent bystanders? There were none, least of all workers who did not go out on strike, or scabs. Strikes were incidents of war, class war, to Lloyd's way of thinking. Non-striking workers were class traitors.[51] "Trade-unions," Lloyd insisted in a major speech that so captured the fancy of the nonsocialist American Federation of Labor that they reprinted it for popular distribution,

> exist to maintain the only sacred right to work. The only right to work which is sacred is the right to work for the good of all, and not to make others idle and unhappy. The unorganized workman cannot make a free contract. The workingman who is too ignorant and crabby to join the union . . . has no sacred right to take away the work of other men. He has a sacred right to his own work, but not to theirs. If he refuses to become a citizen in the Commonwealth of Labour, he makes himself an alien.[52]

Socialist unionists like the popular, even revered Eugene Debs—a veteran of many a violent confrontation—constantly defended labor violence in terms of the class struggle. (Debs's reputation as a pacifist is based on his resistance to the struggle between *mutually* armed nations, as in World War I; a picketer's baseball bat cracking the skull of an unarmed nonstriker or scab evoked no protest from him.[53]) And socialist lawyers who represented violent unions in their all-too-frequent scrapes with the courts occasionally sought to claim a privilege for their clients' behavior on the ground of military necessity![54]

According to some socialists, all criminal activity on the part of striking workers was always *caused* in the last analysis by the social system. Capitalist society, Bellamy claimed, has no

> moral right to forbid stealing or to punish robbers, for the whole economic system was based on the appropriation, by force or fraud on the part of a few, of the earth and its resources and the fruit of the toil of the poor. Still less [has] it [the state] any right to forbid beggary or to punish violence, seeing that the economic system which is maintained and defended necessarily operated to make beggars and to provoke violence.

"The logic of the strike," he added, is "the overthrow of the irresponsible conduct of industry, whether the strikers [know] it or not." The forces of law and order, whose "principal function" was, according to Bellamy, the "suppression of strikes with bullet or bayonet," were engaged in political repression. Or, as we might say, those who are captured for stealing, violence, or other invasive acts are political prisoners.[55]

Socialism vs. Unionism: The Question of Collective Bargaining

The attitude of socialist thinkers toward collective bargaining usually depended on their views about how the overthrow of capitalism might best be achieved. The revolutionary position on collective bargaining, particularly collective bargaining as practiced by the American Federation of Labor, was best laid out by individuals like Daniel De Leon, who loathed it and the federation together. The very concept of coming to terms with "Capital" was, to his way of thinking, an inherently counter-revolutionary one, a form of class collaboration. If a union should actually live up to the terms they managed to bargain for, employers, De Leon reasoned, would use collective agreements to "tie up" their workforce. Strikes by one craft, for instance, would be ineffectual, since other segments of the workforce would be bound to continue working, or "scabbing," as he put it.[56]

De Leon's critique of collective bargaining cut much deeper than a mere protest against craft organization. Even industrial unions would be co-opted from the revolutionary struggle if they abided by their agreements. Many industries stand in supplier relationships to one another: if the workers were bound to continue deliveries to a customer whose workforce was on strike, they too would be engaged in strike-breaking. Indeed, this ingenious analysis can be expanded indefinitely, to encompass scab-consumers who break a farmworkers' strike by continuing to eat, scab-patients and their Pinkerton ambulance drivers who crash picket lines on their way to the emergency room during a hospitalworkers' strike, perhaps even scab-bookwriters who criticize compulsory unionism.*

Those who preferred to see socialism arrive through ballots rather than bullets were more hospitable to collective bargaining, particularly if it was forced on employers via the state. Two important socialist thinkers were particularly prescient on this score, and they were among the earliest to propose compulsory bargaining between employers and unions possessing what amounted to exclusive representation rights.

Henry Demarest Lloyd was the foremost champion of a system of compulsory arbitration developed in the 1890s in New Zealand, whereby

---

*For an example of this kind of conflation, see Jack London's essay, "The Scab," *Atlantic Monthly* XCIII (January 1904): 54-63, reprinted in *Novels and Social Writings,* (New York: Viking, 1982), Volume II.

unions could haul employers into court for binding arbitration over wages, hours, and other working conditions. In this system, the awards handed down by specially appointed labor courts could be made legally enforceable on—that is, were judicially *extended* to cover—*all* workers and *all* employers *throughout* an administratively determined occupational or geographical jurisdiction, whether or not these unions commanded majorities or even pluralities among the workers in that jurisdiction. The "extension" device was incorporated, with modifications based on later experience in Europe, into the National Recovery Administration (NRA) in America in 1933 (for more discussion, see chapter seven *infra*).

The socialist theoretician Laurence Gronlund also looked favorably on the idea of converting trade unions into an "'estate of the realm' by giving them a privileged *status* in law, 'thus incorporating the working–classes into the constitution of the country'." He also believed in compulsory collective bargaining, since "strong trades-unions" were essential to the "success" of "obligatory industrial arbitration." For that reason, there should be laws "to 'persuade' every workman to join his trades-union, or other labor organization," by so arranging "conditions that it will be made as disadvantageous for him as possible to remain outside." The foremost condition was exclusive representation on the basis of nationwide, industrial unions. "Let the law," he wrote in 1898,

> grant to the unions and assemblies, when they are organized in a perfectly democratic fashion, as many high privileges as possible, in [the] last resort that of finally determining all labor-questions for all the workmen in the trade, whether they be inside or outside of the organizations. In that way the law will make the union or assembly the legal representative of the men, on an equal footing with the most powerful employer.

Eventually, he hoped this reform would make "the ideal of every true union man" come true; "an organization, controlling the entire labor force of the country; in other words, one National Syndicate of Labor."[57]

Commentary: The Distribution of Income Under Competitive Conditions and the Irreconcilable Conflict of the Classes

The socialists' indictment of the allegedly irreconcilable differences between the wage-earning and capital-owning classes did not go unchallenged by market-oriented economists. John Stuart Mill, for instance (though sympathetic to the aspirations of the poor and sensitive to the complaints of their would-be intellectual champions) nevertheless denied that poverty was increasing, either absolutely *or even relatively.* The socialists, he wrote, completely misapprehended the "proportions in which the produce of the country is really shared and the amount of what is actually diverted from those who produce it, to enrich other persons." Mill explained that the distribution of income is not so radically unequal as they claim; and the

> present system is not . . . hurrying us into a state of general indigence and slavery from which only Socialism can save us. The evils and injustices suffered under the present system are great, but they are not increasing; on the contrary, the general tendency is towards their slow diminution.[58]

One error Mill detected in their reasoning was a confusion between the personal wealth of the capitalist and the functional distribution of income in that capitalist's firm, or in the economy in general. If a capitalist invests 20,000 and earns 2,000, for instance, what he pays out in wages and salaries has to be compared, not to 22,000, but to 2,000; and

> [i]f we subtract from the gains of some the losses of others, and deduct from the balance a fair compensation for the industry, skill, and labour of both, grounded on the market price of skilled superintendence, what remains will be, no doubt, considerable, but yet, when compared to the entire capital of the economy, annually reproduced and dispensed in wages, it is very much smaller than it appears to the popular imagination.[59]

Mill caught sight of a general fallacy at the basis of the various 'laws' that socialists, syndicalists, and others claim to prove that income is progressively maldistributed under competitive conditions.

Consider first, in isolation, the hypothetical case of a single industry. We will assume that this industry is growing, that it is adding capital in the form of machinery which increases its productivity, and that it is becoming more 'concentrated'—i.e., that the more efficient capitalists are 'killing off' the less efficient.

At the beginning, the industry consists of 10 firms, each of which has one 'boss'. The boss is the owner as well as the manager. Each firm employs 10 workers. The output of the industry as a whole is 1 million units, each of which is sold for $1, so that the market value (revenue from sales) of all the output is $1 million. Eight hundred thousand dollars of this $1 million we assign to raw materials and other related (nonlabor) costs of production, so there is a $200,000 pie to be cut. We stipulate that each boss/capitalist earns as salary/profit $10,000, so that, in the industry as a whole, the 'profit' is $100,000 [$10 \times \$10,000$]. Each worker earns $1,000, so that, in the industry as a whole, 'wages' are also $100,000 [$10 \times 10 \times \$1,000$]. If we consider only that portion of the aggregate revenue paid out as wages or profit in that *single* industry, the 'share' of capital is equal to the 'share' of labor. (The personal distribution of income is, of course, 'radically' unequal.)

Assume that this industry expands its output and its sales for any number of reasons—say the introduction of new machinery, better transportation giving it access to broader markets, what-have-you. *Now* it produces and sells 10 million units, each of which is sold at 50 cents. The market value of the output sold is therefore $5 million. Competition, however, has "killed off" seven of the firms. The rich have become richer; each of the three remaining firms now has a boss/capitalist whose salary/ profit has leaped from $10,000 to $100,000. Employment in each (vastly enlarged) firm has increased from 10 to 150 workers. There are now 450 laborers in the industry (350 more than before), but each one of these workers earns $750, not $1,000. In other words, the profits of the owners are much fatter while the wallets of the new workers are 25 percent leaner, even while the 'productivity' of each worker has increased (productivity is defined simply as the ratio of physical output to "units" of labor input; in the good old days it was 10,000 units of output per worker [1 million units/100 workers], while now it is 22,222.22 units of output per worker [10 million units/450 workers]).

We now have, in this *one* industry, a much more "radically unequal" distribution of personal income. The three fat cats at the top haul down $100,000 a piece, while the larger group of drudges at the bottom eke by on only $750. But what has happened to the *functional* distribution of income (in the industry at hand)? The industry profit is $300,000 [3 × $100,000]; the aggregate payroll is $337,500 (450 × $750]. In other words, 'capital's relative share' of the industry's income has declined from 50 percent to 47 percent [$300,000/$637,500] while "labor's relative share" has increased from 50 percent to 53 percent. So much for any *law* of diminishing wage share.

It may be objected that the numbers in the example above were completely arbitrary. They were, as were those chosen by Rodbertus. His 'industry' was wheat farming, and he showed how the relative share *of the output* claimed by the farm laborers could fall. What he neglected to say was what share *of the output* constituted the landlord's *profit* (in his terminology, what was the nominal profit equivalent in bushels of wheat) in the early or in the later period, and how *it* behaved *relative* to that of wages. It could have decreased; it could have remained the same; or indeed it could have increased. Rodbertus never did say anything about the equivalent of the 5 million bushels of wheat not distributed in wages to the agricultural laborers 50 years ago, or the 15 million bushels of wheat not distributed to the agricultural laborers 50 years later. Was *all* of it profit?

Or was most of it paid out in production expenses? He asserted the existence of a *law,* followed it up with an incomplete illustration of its *meaning* for a single industry, and assumed that that was enough to make the case for the economy as a whole.

Marx's comments on this issue were even murkier. "Real wages," he wrote first of all, "may remain the same, they may even rise, nevertheless relative wages may fall." True; but then again, relative wages may stay the same; and they may increase. Yet after stating one possibility among several, Marx, simply glides into asserting the iron necessity of an arithmetic truism, namely that as a *share,* profit can rise only to the extent that wages fall.

De Leon purportedly demonstrated *empirically* that labor's share of the national income was only one-fifth, and that it had declined slightly over time. What he compared, however, was the wages paid workers (that is, the direct labor costs) in all manufacturing industries versus the value of all manufactured output. But manufacturers have other expenses to meet before they calculate profit: raw materials, semi-manufactured or manufactured parts, energy, administrative overhead, rent, interest on money borrowed to finance production, and so forth. There is a labor cost component of each of these factors of production as well.[60]

When economists *have* looked at the data correctly, they have found that payments to labor in the aggregate (not only in manufacturing, and also at each stage in the production process), rather than constituting one-fifth of the national income, is closer to four-fifths. Moreover, statistical studies conducted by a great number of investigators on the behavior of the relative income shares have shown *no* tendency for 'profits' to increase over time relative to 'wages' (regardless of the amount of unionization). Actually, the shares have remained relatively stable, while the real wages of laborers have increased enormously. (There has been some slight tendency over the decades for labor's share to increase, the result not of unionism, but of the decline of self-employment, particularly as the agricultural population has shrunk.) Even this isn't the same as saying that the share of income between 'labor' and 'capital' has remained relatively the same: after all, wage earners save, invest, and reap the rewards therefrom (or, in other words, not all income reported as "profit" accrues to nonwage earners).[61]

Hobson's ideas have also been subject to numerous criticisms. The progressive maldistribution of income that would make his theory tick is not empirically demonstrable. Moreover, as an explanation for the Great Depression, his theory was "inconsistent with the observed fact that the consumption industries continue[d] to prosper for some time *after* the depression [had] appeared in the capital producing industries." The crisis, whatever its cause, was "not precipitated by the sudden appearance of a glut of consumable goods."[62]

The idea that there is some law proving that labor's share of income declines, even in progressive conditions where the accumulation of capital and the demand for labor are both increasing, is, like the bargaining power doctrine, a Chimera.

Commentary: The Inevitability of Socialism and the Anarchy of Planning

The theory that competition (low prices) leads inevitably to monopoly (and to higher prices) and thus paves the way for the inevitable arrival of socialism has similarly enjoyed a reputation all out of proportion to its significance. John Stuart Mill recognized that (leaving to one side the possibility of government restriction of entry) there is definitely a tendency for concentration to occur in several industries where machinery, better organization, and other features, permit lower unit production costs, and that by and large these lower production costs are passed on to consumers (that is, to workers) in the form of lower prices.[63] But again, the emergence of an actual *monopoly* able to persistently enjoy supernormal profits *not due* to lower costs has rarely, if ever, been observed outside of those sectors where entry has been restricted in one form or another by the government. The tendency toward concentration is not universal in all sectors, and is counterbalanced, as it were, by the continuous expansion of the economy, particularly in less mature, more atomistic sectors.[64]

More to the point, perhaps, is not whether state ownership of the means of production is 'inevitable', but whether it measures up to its promise as a form of industrial democracy. Does it solve the problems it believes are inevitable under capitalism? Is it a viable solution to the dilemmas of syndicalism?

The Owenite socialist John Gray, it will be recalled from chapter three, was one of the earliest to float the idea that the problem of production had essentially been solved, but that the problem of distribution had not. In his formulation, competition unnaturally limited production. Entrepreneurs, he complained, never "ask themselves how much cloth would be required to supply the wants of mankind," or "how much cloth they have the power of making . . . All they ask, all they require to know, is *how much cloth they can dispose of at a profit* . . ." If competition were abolished, however, Gray insisted that *"everything that deserves the name of wealth shall instantly become accessible to all:* for we should then have as much wealth as we have the *power of creating."*[65] Similarly, Rodbertus intimated that planning an economy would be a piece of cake; the "wants of men in general form an even series, and . . . the kind and number of objects required can easily be calculated." "Provided we know the time that a person could afford to devote to the work of production," he wrote, "we could easily satisfy the needs of everybody."[66]

This is implausible, since it ignores the omnipresence of economic scarcity—the fact that *means* (material resources, labor, and *time*) are always scarce in relation to desirable ends. The "uniform series" of wants, easily ascertainable by the planning authority, exists

> only in the imagination. What we really find is a small number of collective needs combined with a great variety of individual needs. Social need is merely a vague term used to designate both kinds of wants at once. The slightest reflection shows that every individual possesses quite a unique series of needs and tastes.[67]

Mankind does not want only for coats; it wants coats of different styles and kinds, that are ever-changing. It also wants shirts with sleeves both long and short, with an infinite variety of button and collar styles, etc. The satisfaction of *all possible cloth requirements* (for coats and shirts) necessarily encroaches on the finite, scarce human and non-human resources that could be employed for the satisfaction of *all possible* non-cloth requirements (shoes, housing, what-have-you). The exhaustion of our productive powers would arrive far earlier than the satisfaction of all our wants.

The decisions that economic planners would have to make are of staggering complexity, as the economist F. A. Hayek pointed out years ago:

> The planning authority would not only have to decide between, say, electric light for the farmer or bathrooms for the industrial worker in town, but it would also have to decide whether, if the installation of electric light in a hundred farms is regarded as more important than the provision of bathrooms for fifty working-class families, they ought still to give the preference to the claims of the farmers if instead they might have provided sixty working-class families with baths. The planner will not only have to know whether an additional doctor or an additional school teacher is more urgently needed, but he will have to know how to choose if, at the cost of training three doctors, he can train five teachers, and how if at the same cost he can train six teachers and so on. A decision whether a housing scheme in one town or another ought to be started first, or whether the greater costs of building in the one place are more than offset by the greater urgency of the needs there, a decision whether the cost of dispersing population to a certain extent is greater or smaller than the aesthetic and cultural advantages thereby obtained, can only be arbitrary—that is, there are within wide limits no grounds on which one person could convince another that the one decision is more reasonable than the other.[68]

The real questions are these: who is to decide the trade-offs, and how are these trade-offs to be satisfied at the least possible cost in resources? Either consumers freely choose the ends to be satisfied (including their freedom to *change their minds* about what they have been accustomed to wanting if offered new or different goods or services on which to spend their money) or the *planners* choose, in accordance with some set of priorities that, whatever else these priorities are, they are not those of the individuals who will be forced to live with (and consume) the choices someone else makes. If consumer free choice is permitted, however, one cannot guarantee that all markets will always clear and that there will never be *any* misinvested funds or misallocated laborers (from the retrospective point of view). If balance, or full employment of all labor at all times, is the desideratum, then freedom of choice has to be done away with. Whatever kind of "democracy" one may purport to have in a planned economy, it is not the democracy exercised by consumers casting their 'dollar votes'.[69]

Theoretical economists after the turn of the century—the most important of whom was Ludwig von Mises—demonstrated that without private property and a functioning price system (including interest rates) *for capital goods,* it would be impossible for economic planners to rationally calculate the least-cost production methods for those stages of the production process far removed in time and space from consumer goods (cost here conceived in material and time, in terms of alternatives foregone). The planning authority could not tell if their own allocation of resources, to fulfill whatever production quotas they set, *better served* social needs *as they defined them* than any other plan. Central economic planning without property, prices and wages would be essentially irrational.[70]

In practice, those centrally planned economies that have evolved in this century could not and did not dispense entirely with prices. They have incorporated a price system, but of a defective sort, wherein prices are not allowed to allocate goods and services and labor in defiance of the 'plan'; these economies are characterized by what amounts to a universal system of price and wage controls. This has resulted in the shortages and gluts which economic theory would predict.[71]

Of course, it is difficult to take seriously any claim that socialism could even in theory be democratic or 'fair', particularly those brands whose authors subscribed to the 'need' theory of distribution. (They could hardly be efficient, for the problems of incentives under an equal labor time standard would be nothing compared to the problems of a regime which placed a progressive tax on ability.) The anti-capitalist Proudhon understood better than did John Stuart Mill the radically *immoral* nature of a regime dedicated to the altruistic proposition, "from each according to his ability, to each according to his needs." Proudhon correctly denounced this as the "exploitation of the strong by the weak." It would amount to a society, as one modern philosopher has explained, that operates on the maxim that "those who do not work, shall eat those that do." [72]

Neither Helpless nor Hopeless: Toward a Collective Bargaining Theory and the Birth of Modern Industrial Democratic Theory

John Stuart Mill, as discussed above, defended the role of competition in the economy against the gloom-and-doom prophecies of the socialists. Nevertheless, the commitment of this doyen of classical economics to the system of natural liberty was a hesitant and uncertain one. Particularly in the labor market, Mill came to gravely doubt the implications of the wages fund for the distribution of income under competition. Eventually, his doubts came to the surface, precipitating a crisis in economic and social thought whose ramifications we still live with today. Mill's recantation of the wages fund theory in 1869 made plausible the vision of an industrial democracy based on unions and collective bargaining—of unions that could "raise wages" and redistribute the national income more favorably to wage earners through the strike threat.

5. The Eclipse of the Wages Fund and the Birth of Modern Collective Bargaining Theory

 The common theme of the socialist and syndicalist critics of capitalism in the early decades of the 19th century was the utter powerlessness of the individual laborer and the necessity for abolishing the wages system. According to the wages fund doctrine developed by the classical economists, strikes could not 'raise wages'. The idea that unionization could permit workers to obtain a greater share of the national income was not generally acceptable.[1]

In 1869, John Stuart Mill announced in the pages of the prestigious *Fortnightly Review* that the wages fund was dead and "must be thrown aside." The remuneration of labor was not *strictly determined* by some pre-existing fund destined for the payment of wages; what could, and would, be paid was subject to bargaining and was therefore indeterminate. The "power of Trades' Unions may therefore be so exercised as to obtain for the labouring classes collectively, both a *larger share* and a *larger positive amount* of the produce of labour." Contrary to what generations of economists had taught, unions could after all redistribute the national income in favor of wage earners.[2]

Mill was the most famous social scientist in the English-speaking world, indeed in the entire world. His doubts about the wages fund were extremely significant for the history of industrial democratic theory, since they legitimized one of its major pillars, the 'theory of collective bargaining'. By calling into question one of the cornerstones of classical economics, Mill called into question the entire notion that there were determinate economic laws by which the likely effects of interference with competition could be predicted (and usually, on that basis, the policies rejected). In its stead, an 'interventionist' or 'regulatory' ethic became much more popular and plausible, pointing toward the idea of a 'middle way' or 'third solution' to the social problems of a capitalist society—that is, toward social reform short of social revolution. After Mill, social reformers urged that the state *should* use its power to intervene in economic relations on behalf of the poorer and weaker elements in society, and that it *could* do so without making things worse.[3]

Interventionist reform was, and typically still is, a matter of *direct* state control or regulation of the marketplace—a matter of setting maximum prices or hours of work, minimum wages, or redistribution via taxation of income already earned. Although its proponents did not typically use this terminology, we might say that these kinds of state actions sought to 'democratize' *the economy*—to achieve an 'economic democracy'. At the same time, reformers have also sought to rewrite the basic legal groundrules of the market to *empower groups* within society to 'get a better deal' for themselves; and unions have by far been the most important (though not the only) beneficiaries of this kind of intervention. Here we might say (again bearing in mind that this terminology came into common use only in the early 20th century) that reformers sought to democratize *industry*—to achieve an industrial democracy.

This chapter explores the criticisms of the wages fund that led to its downfall, and introduces some of the individuals and groups whose ideas influenced Americans favorably toward unionism.

The Wages Fund, Unions, and Strikes: A Recapitulation

The wages fund doctrine was explained in the first and second chapters of this study, and here only a brief recapitulation of its main tenets is necessary before the several criticisms levelled against it in the early and middle decades of the 19th century are discussed.

The gist of the wages fund doctrine is the proposition that the average real wage was determined by the proportion of capital to population. The demand for labor, in the aggregate, was the entire amount of circulating, or working, capital (savings) that all employers spent to employ laborers. This fund was, at any point in time, a sum fixed and predetermined by prior savings. All circulating capital that *could* be paid out in wages without decreasing profits, checking the accumulation of wealth, and hence diminishing future real wages *would* be paid out. Competition among and between all employers insured that result.

The *supply* of labor, in the aggregate, was also fixed at any point in time. It was simply the entire laboring population. Competition between workers for jobs also meant that no part of the wages fund would go begging.

The average real wage for the economy as a whole was, therefore, strictly determined by the law of supply and demand—in this case, by what amounted to the division of the wages fund by the labor supply. It followed that the only way to increase real wages was to increase the rate of capital accumulation faster than the rate of population increase.

Since the wages fund was part of employers' *capital,* classical economists from Adam Smith to John Stuart Mill explained that *wages were paid from capital*—or to put this in another way, that *employers' capital was the source of workers' wages.*

The concept that 'capital is the source of wages' is susceptible to two different interpretations. The 'aggregative', or as we might say, macroeconomic, interpretation is simply a recognition that all output in an economy is limited by the amount of its capital. (It is also limited by the quality of the capital, the level of technology, and the skill of its workforce.) The output of an economy *is* its wages, however, in two related senses. (1) Wages are ultimately not money, but the things money can buy; and (2) all income is ultimately derived from the sale of the 'social product'. As a kind of shorthand, therefore, it follows that wages are paid from capital, or that capital is the source of wages.

There is another possible interpretation of the concept that 'capital is the source of wages'. Classical economists from Smith onward illustrated the idea that the wages fund 'maintains labor' with the example of farm workers who are paid a subsistence during the growing season by advances from the farmer's cash savings. What these farm workers could be paid was limited by what the farmer had previously saved. The farmer could not pay any more, since he does not realize any income until after the harvest. Now *this* way of looking at the idea of a wages fund—a 'period of production' analysis—can be taken to imply that the capital in the hands of *each* employer is *both the source and the limit of his own employees' wages.* This 'microeconomic' interpretation is not at all the same as the 'macroeconomic' interpretation.

There was another important conclusion of wages fund doctrine, to wit, that 'strikes cannot raise wages'.

As explained in a previous chapter, a careful reading of McCulloch, Torrens, *et al.,* makes it clear that they *never* said that all strikes *always fail.* The ability of combinations to temporarily force the *rate* of wages above the "natural and proper," or market-clearing, rate was never denied. But if the wage rate were pushed above the equilibrium, it would have a "boomerang" effect of one sort or another.[4] New workers would be attracted into the industry; employers would mechanize; higher labor costs would be passed on to consumers (other workers); international competition would intensify; investment might be driven away. The old rate might be reasserted through the competition of other workers; or the higher wage rate might check the number of workers hired and thus *decrease* total payrolls; or higher wage costs might even strangle the industry. Since the amount of the wages fund was fixed in the short run, any augmentation of one set of workers' wages implied a diminution of the rest. Strikes could not redistribute income to the wage-earning *class*. In relation to labor combinations, in other words, the wages fund doctrine was less a part of price theory than it was a proposition about the distribution of income. Nevertheless, the opportunity for misinterpreting the dictum that 'strikes cannot raise wages' is obvious: a sophisticated conclusion about the ultimate incidence of a strike is a very different statement than a bare assertion that strikes always fail.

Early Objections to the Wages Fund

The wages fund doctrine did not lack for critics, even in the heyday of classical economics.[5] The basic objections to it revolved around the following, often interrelated, propositions. Many insisted that competition in labor and product markets did not work perfectly, and so the whole of what employers *might* pay with *no* boomerang effect was not usually paid out under individual bargaining. There was available for wage payments some amount of profit that was *unattainable* by workers except insofar as they organized and bargained for it. Other wage fund critics emphasized that wages were not paid from or limited by capital, but were paid from and limited by consumer income—by demand for output. Some critics asserted that higher money wages *cause* greater output, because of an alleged direct functional relationship between wages and productive efficiency. Finally, the American economist Francis A. Walker observed that an increased supply of labor, given fixed capital stock, *does not* imply lower output and real wages. It might be a source of higher real wages, since there is no reason to assume that the economy is in a region of diminishing returns.[6]

The German economist W. B. von Hermann's wage theory had a very long-lasting influence on the evolution of economic thought in his country. In his 1832 treatise, *Staatwirtschaftliche Untersuchungen* (Investigations in Political Economy), Hermann claimed that the source of workers' wages was the income of consumers, not the capital of employers, since the turnover of capital in many trades was quite rapid, unlike in agriculture. Thus, his idea was that "[w]hat the employer can pay the laborer, and what he will pay if competition is free, depends on what the consumers pay him."[7]

Hermann's theory expresses one truth of undoubted importance, namely that the demand for a product limits the wages that can be paid *in a given industry*. And in the hands of the marginal utility theorists of the 1870s and thereafter, demand became the powerful engine for neo-classical price theory in general, including the marginal productivity theory of wages. Nevertheless, Hermann's criticism of the wages fund missed the point. As the American neoclassical economist Frank Taussig explained very late in the century, consumer income *in general* is not and cannot be the *source* of workers' wages *in general*. This really amounts to reasoning in a circle. Consumers (or at least the largest portion of them) are themselves workers whose income is largely or exclusively wages. But this means that Hermann is claiming that wages are the source of wages! Taussig explained that Hermann confused nominal wages (money income) with real wages (commodities, or wage goods, or the things-money-can-buy).[8]

Moreover there was precious little in Hermann's ideas of comfort to unions. In the first edition of his treatise, he said that the wages fund doctrine disturbed relations between the social classes because it encouraged arrogance on the part of employers. Employers should not feel that they actually paid their workers' wages. They were only middlemen between workers and consumers. But Hermann did not say that employers' allegedly mistaken pretensions actually influenced the rate of wages they paid. In a later, second edition of his treatise, Hermann went even further. If laborers thought employers, and not consumers, paid their wages, laborers would be encouraged to participate in needless and harmful strikes.[9]

Although Hermann rejected the wages fund, he did not attack the classical economists' conclusion that strikes cannot 'raise wages.' Others did.

Strikes Can Raise Wages: Frederic Harrison and the Trade Unions

In 1860, one T. J. Dunning, an official of the Bookbinder's Union, published a noteworthy treatise that not only rejected the conclusion of wages fund theorists with regard to strikes, but put forth, in strikingly modern terms, the case for unionism and collective bargaining.[10]

Dunning did not claim that employers could arbitrarily set wages at whatever rate they pleased, and he did not demand the abolition of the wages system. He only claimed that unorganized laborers bargained at a disadvantage. "[B]esides the rate of wages, which results from the demand for it in proportion to its supply," he claimed, "there is a lower rate which may be the result of the necessities of the workman." In individual bargaining, this lower rate will be the one usually paid; but through organization, the higher rate can be struck. When workers organize, Dunning claimed, their bargaining power will be equal to that of their employers; and hence unions will achieve exactly that kind of 'harmony of interests' Adam Smith saw as the great virtue of a free society. When "all things" are "equal," Dunning claimed, the "position" of labor and capital would not be "one of opposition, but of mutual interest."[11]

Professor Frederic Harrison helped bring these 'conservative' trade union views to the attention of informed popular and academic opinion, and he spearheaded the attack on the wages fund in the early 1860s. Auguste Comte's leading disciple in late Victorian England, Harrison (along with several other 'positivists') was an influential advocate of labor unions and of social reform. A close confidant of the English trade union leadership, Harrison was appointed with their blessing to the important Royal Commission to Investigate Trade Unions (1867-1870)—out of which came legislation that fundamentally recast the law of labor relations for the remainder of the century.[12]

Harrison asserted that the wages fund was false because its conclusions with regard to strikes were demonstrably wrong. "It is an axiom of science," Harrison informed his readers, "that a strike can never avert a fall of wages," nor can it ever permanently increase wages, since the "rate of wages depends by eternal necessity on the state of the 'Wages-fund'." Rubbish! Strikes can raise wages, and the proof is that they do:

> Any one who will search the files of a working-class organ will find accurate reports of countless successful strikes over every part of England. [I have] a list of the successful strikes for one single trade in one year. This list contains more than eighty instances in which one union in that period had by actual or threatened strikes obtained increased wages, or, what is the same thing, shorter hours.

"How this is economically possible," he sneered, "had better be answered by those economists who first invent industrial laws, and then invent facts to fit them."[13]

Harrison did not claim that laborers had no bargaining power, and he did not claim that there was no competition between employers. "No doubt the influence of this competition is very great," he wrote, for "without it the workmen would be (what they occasionally are) at the mercy of the capitalists." Nevertheless, "the question is, whether" interemployer competition "is so great as to counterbalance all else on the other side, and establish an equality."[14]

He asserted that it wasn't. Laborers were far less mobile than their employers. Poverty and ignorance kept workers from taking advantage even of what opportunities were potentially available to them; their employers knew this, and were able to factor this knowledge into their wage offers.[15]

When Harrison said that the competition between laborers and capitalists was unequal, what he meant was that the competition between workmen for jobs (driving wages down) was of greater significance than the competition between employers for workmen (driving wages up). Labor, he said, was far more "plentiful" than capital; and

> with our redundant population and vast reserve of labour-power just struggling for life—that incubus of destitute and unemployed labour which lies so heavily on all efforts of our [unionized] artisans, hungering for their places, . . . [n]othing can prevent the dregs or Helotism of labour from continually underselling it.[16]

If, however, the need of employers for workers could be made more pressing and immediate, Harrison reasoned that bargaining could be made more equal. The "moment" workers "agree to act together, and to help each other in turn, the bargain is equalised; the need which each side has of the other is on a par, and the power each has to hold its ground is nearly equivalent." This, according to Harrison, was why strikes could and did raise wages. "Wages' questions are simply questions of time," and as "capital means insurance against time," so too was the union's strike fund.[17]

Commentary on Harrison

Something is missing from Harrison's criticism of the wages fund. He does not clearly distinguish between the *rate* at which wages are paid, the volume of laborers hired at any given rate of wages, and the total payrolls before and after a strike. Strikes over wages typically concern rates of pay (directly, or, as when the hours of work are the issue, indirectly.) They do not normally cover the volume of employment, the annual earnings of employees, or the amount of money employers expend on direct labor costs. They certainly don't consider who bears the ultimate incidence of higher direct labor costs. All of these 'distribution' questions are central to economic analysis. Harrison ignored them utterly.

But there is something else missing in Harrison's, and T. J. Dunning's, analysis. The trade union theory of equal bargaining power, Dunning explained, depends on making sure that "the buyer can get *no labour elsewhere.*" This is the assumption which, together with the assumption that the workers have sufficient reserves to stand out longer than the employer, assures that "the workman is sure to win."[18] Which workmen? Surely not the "dregs" of the workforce refused admittance to the combination in the first place, or anyone else prevented from taking the strikers' places. Both Harrison and Dunning (and presumably those on behalf of whom they spoke) apparently assumed that the essence of the strike was not the collective withdrawal of the strikers' *own* labor power to bargain for better terms, but their ability to prevent any others from taking their place.

The Wages Fund under Assault: Longe, Leslie, and Jenkin

Harrison was not the only individual in the 1860s to challenge the wages fund. Francis D. Longe, a government lawyer and student of European and English labor relations law, objected to it in a pamphlet of 1866, *A Refutation of the Wage-Fund Theory of Modern Political Economy, as Enunciated by Mr. Mill, M.P., and Mr. Fawcett, M.P.*[19]

Longe denied that there was any wages fund *"distinct from the general wealth of the country."* Payment in kind, profit-sharing arrangements, etc., all made hash of the idea that wages were 'advanced' entirely from employers' prior savings. Moreover, even if there was a fund, competition among employers would not distribute the whole of it. The "number of labourers whom any class of employers engaged in a trade . . . can employ . . . is determined by the *quantity of work they require to be done,"* but the quantity of work was rigidly inelastic, and an exception to the rule that demand increased as price decreased.[20]

Longe pointed to a group of farmers needing hands. Why should price competition affect the demand for labor?

> If ten thousand labourers did all the work they wanted to have done, e.g. all the ploughing, and harrowing, and reaping, & c., there might be any number of surplus labourers in the country, and their competition might reduce wages to sixpence a day, but the farmers would not employ more labour then they wanted, however cheap it was.[21]

Longe also apparently assumed that capital was immobile. Interemployer competition would not distribute "the aggregate capital at the disposal of the employers engaged in the different trades of a country as the supposed wage-fund" says it would.

How could the shoemakers compete with the tailors, or the blacksmiths with the glass-blowers? or how should the capital, which a master-shoemaker saved by reducing the wages of his journeymen, get into the hands of the master-tailor? or why should the money, which a reduction in the price of clothes enables the private consumer to spend in other things, go to pay or refund the wages of any other class of labourers belonging to his own country? It would clearly be just as likely to be spent in the purchase of foreign wine or in a trip to Switzerland.[22]

The combination of capital immobility and an infinitely inelastic demand for labor, according to Longe, undoubtedly rendered interemployer competition ineffectual for raising wages in a trade where these wages were, as McCulloch would have put it, temporarily and unduly depressed. Nothing compelled an employer to "give one farthing more than the smallest quantity of wealth or money for which they could get the labourers to do the work they wanted," except an "association" of laborers. Indeed, just the opposite was true; competition worked *only* to depress the price of labor:

[t]he employment of a portion of the labourers at a low wage, instead of tending to raise the value of the rest, would operate most powerfully to prevent the other employers, whose demand for labour was not satisfied, from giving a higher wage than the labourers already hired were receiving; for whatever additional wage they gave would be dead loss to them, as compared with the lower cost at which their rival traders were getting or had got their goods made, supposing at least that they were all supplying the same goods market.[23]

The Irish economist Thomas E. Cliffe Leslie also voiced this objection. "It is sometimes said that if the profits of a particular business are abnormally high, a consequent accumulation of capital resulting must raise wages in proportion." This was false, according to Leslie; "there is nothing to compel the recipients of high profits to make that particular use of them." They might spend the money on personal consumption, or invest it abroad.[24]

Although he rejected the wages fund, Longe was anything but a proponent of trade unions. "A true science of Political Economy would teach the labourer that the more work and the better work he gave his employer, the more would be the wages which his employer could afford to pay him." Since "the real value of the wages" the labourer obtains

depends upon the quantity of the necessaries and conveniences of life which they can purchase, labourers are themselves benefit[t]ed, as well as the rich or non-labouring class, by the cheapness of the labour employed on the production of the things which they require.

He was even more orthodox on strikes. Longe insisted that insofar as organized workers succeeded in getting a "wage for their work disproportionately high, as compared with that which other labourers are receiving," the effect would be harmful, since it would give "them a power of consumption to which they are not entitled"; increase "the price of things which other labourers buy or acquire"; or even drive "capital from their trade and send the consumer to another market."[25]

Commentary on Longe

Longe's theory of capital immobility rests on the assumption that capital cannot be *withdrawn* from one trade and re-invested in another in response to differential profits—caused, for instance, by below-market wage rates. Yet in his remarks about strikes he recognized that long and costly disputes drive capital away! Surely it is "abnormally high" profits that is the mechanism through which "shoemakers compete with tailors, or blacksmiths with the glass blowers"—the means by which "the capital" a shoemaker saved by lowering wages gets "into the hands of the master-tailor."

Longe's observations about the alleged price inelasticity of the demand for labor are best taken up later, when William Thornton's similar notions are addressed, but his criticism of interemployer competition deserves immediate comment. There is, to be sure, no incentive for one employer to pay "higher wages" *just because another pays lower wages* (at least if one assumes that both groups of workers are equally productive). But high wages and low wages are not the terms of the wages fund analysis of classical economics. Wages as costs of production *in relation to normal or competitive rates of profit* are what makes the doctrine tick. And within the context of classical theory, the existence of higher-than-normal returns *due* to lower-than-market wages *does* provide an incentive to bid up wages, or bid away the most productive workers, until normal prices, or rates of return, re-emerge.

Two years after Longe's pamphlet appeared, Fleeming Jenkin, a Professor of Engineering at the University of Edinburgh, criticized the wages fund in an article, "Trade Unions: How Far Legitimate." He amplified his views a few years later, in "The Graphic Representation of the Laws of Supply and Demand, and Their Application to Labour."[26]

Jenkin's basic point was that strikes may force an employer to raise wages and still keep the same number of employees, if his only alternative was losing his entire profits; and if an employer can "obtain an increase of price from the consumer" in partial compensation as a result, this hold-up process could continue. Even so, if an employer's "profits fall below a certain point, he will endeavour in all ways to direct the use of his fixed capital to other objects"; and "if wages rise and profits fall beyond a certain point, his contribution to the wages fund will diminish, and possibly disappear, owing to his ruin." And, of course, "no one will deny that in [the] face of falling profits and rising wages new investments in a particular trade will be checked."[27]

Despite these caveats, Jenkin suggested that the division of income between profits and wages, being "purely a question of bargain," could "legitimately vary, within very wide limits," particularly if the workers were organized.[28]

Yet Jenkin did not assume that the volume of employment was unresponsive to price. "It is the seller of labour who determines the price," he wrote, "but it is the buyer who determines the number of transactions. Capital settles how many men are wanted at given wages, but labour settles what wages the man shall have." Unions, in other words, may bargain some of their members out of a job; indeed, Jenkin added, collective bargaining "often does so."[29]

He saw no cause for alarm. Though "the quantity of labour . . . bought under" the circumstances of concerted action "will be less than when no reserved price is fixed," Jenkin wrote that

> it may be more advantageous to the salesman to sell a moderate quantity at a good price than a large quantity at a bad price. It may be more advantageous to labourers that a moderate number should be employed at good wages, than a larger number at bad wages.

In the long run, he contended, this admittedly artificially high wage rate will justify itself over a generation. The "cost of production of labour will have risen," and workers who fail to secure employment "will not marry, or will emigrate." Eventually a "new state of equilibrium between capital and labour will have been reached, and although production of wealth may have been checked for a while, it will afterwards progress as before."[30]

At any rate, strikes can undoubtedly increase employers' gross payroll costs, since "the reduced number, with augmented wages, may receive more than the larger number at lower wages." This was enough, according to Jenkin, to demonstrate the fallacy of the idea that there was a fixed, predetermined wages fund, and enough to legitimate trade union practice. Jenkin claimed that "it may be the interest of the workman to support his fellows out of work by a contribution from his gains, rather than by a reduction in his own requirements, to allow them to find employment." But was it in the interest of those who were bargained out of a job? Didn't they have any say in the matter? Jenkin didn't say; but the next, and most important, critic of the wages fund did.[31]

On Labour and the Wages Fund: Thornton's Critique

The climactic critique of the wages fund appeared in a long book published in 1869, *On Labour: Its Wrongful Claims and Rightful Dues, Its Actual Present and Possible Future.* William Thornton, its author, was a secretary of public works in the India Office.[32]

Thornton criticized the idea of a fixed, determinate wages fund, and he developed an elaborate rationale for the idea that the price of labor was *indeterminate*—that is, there was a range of prices (wage rates) that could be established by bargaining, within which *the quantity of labor employed would not vary.* He thereupon argued that only combination on the part of the laborers insured that actual wage rates would remain at the highest point on this range.

Thornton's essential argument against the idea of a fixed wages fund was a familiar one, namely its alleged inconsistency with the vulnerability of some employers—farmers at harvest time, building contractors facing deadlines, etc.—to extortion by a strike threat. The amount employers planned to spend on wages, raw material, or even on personal expenditure from profit varied with circumstance. Since "fixity or definiteness is the very essence of the supposed wages fund," the entire doctrine was invalid. "If" the wages *fund* is

> indeterminate, it cannot of course be divided, and might as well not exist for any power it possesses of performing the sole function of a wages fund, that, viz., of yielding a quotient that would indicate the average rate of wages.[33]

Thornton did not rest his case for the proposition that prices may vary without affecting the amount demanded *only* on the strategically timed strike threat. He argued, on the basis of an analogy, that certain technical characteristics of the labor market demonstrated that the price of labor could vary *generally* with no effect on the volume of labor demanded (employed).

Thornton asked his reader to consider a "Dutch auction." Suppose a group of fishermen want to sell the previous night's catch. The supply of fish is fixed *and it is perishable.* There are a small number of sellers who confront a larger number of buyers.

> The fish are divided into lots, each of which is set up at the *highest* price which the salesman thinks himself at all likely to get for it, and which, if necessary, he gradually *lowers* until he comes to a price which some by-stander is willing to pay *rather than not have the lot,* and to which he accordingly agrees.[34]

Thornton argued that if a cartel of sellers initiates and controls the bidding on this fixed supply, the price at which each lot is sold will likely be higher than if competitive buyers initiated the bidding at the lowest price they deemed likely to elicit acceptance by the sellers. Thornton's reasoning was thus. Assume there is *one* buyer who would be willing to pay as much as 8 shillings for a lot, but *no other buyers* willing to pay more than 5 shillings. If the sellers controlled the bidding, from the top down, so to speak, Thornton claimed it most likely that 8 shillings would close the sale (clear the market), since the buyer would snap up the lot at that price rather than risk losing it. But if the auction were 'English', with the bidding starting low, from the buyers' side, the sale price for the lot would "very possibly" not exceed 6 shillings. The sellers would never reap all they potentially could.[35]

Thornton drew two conclusions from this example. His first was that supply and demand do not *determine* price at all.[36] His second and less idiosyncratic inference was that *individual, unorganized laborers were normally in the position of the fishpeddlers, but that buyers—employers—controlled the bidding.*

Labor power was "perishable," Thornton wrote, and because of this fact, he insisted that it had no reservation price. It was perishable because it

> will not *keep*; . . . it cannot be left unused for one moment without partially wasting away. Unless it be sold immediately, some portion of it can never be sold at all. To-day's labour cannot be sold after to-day, for tomorrow it will have ceased to exist. A labourer cannot, for however short a time, postpone the sale of his labour, without losing the whole price of the labour which he might have exercised during the period of the postponement.

And it had no reservation price because the laborer could not afford to search for a better deal;

> very poor labourers are almost compelled to deal with the first customers [employers] who present themselves. They cannot wait for the chance of better customers, for they are in urgent need of immediate subsistence.[37]

But what about interemployer competition for laborers? Won't buyers seek out the sellers? Basically, Thornton said, they won't because they are in a tacit combination not to do so. At bottom, therefore, he fell back on the idea that "[i]n the absence of combination among the labourers, the rate of wages is settled arbitrarily by combination of employers." Thornton did not claim that this supposed cartel beats down wages to subsistence, however:

> [i]t does not follow that the rate of wages so settled should be lower than that which might have resulted from competition. The lowest rate which any set of masters ever arranged among themselves to offer was probably not quite so low as the very lowest rate which they might have offered without any danger of being outbidden by each other.[38]

The labor market, according to Thornton, is a mixture of competitive, noncompetitive, and anticompetitive elements in which the individual laborer is a very weak bargainer. For, except in the rare case when labor is scarce, employers

> are in the habit of combining instead of competing, and it is their combination which, in the absence of counter-combination among the labourers, then determines the price of labour, and determines it arbitrarily—*not indeed absolutely without regard to the relations between supply and demand, but without any uniformity of correspondence with those relations.*[39]

Apart from the validity of his analysis (which will be taken up later), Thornton engaged in a bit of sleight-of-hand here with regard to a fundamental assumption. He started his critique of the determinateness or fixity of the wages fund by reasoning as if the concept of indeterminancy referred to *market clearing*, or *full employment* prices. Recall: what a given employer spends on his *entire* labor force is supposedly not fixed; and so a bit of elbow-twisting can get more out of him, *for all*. But when Thornton comes to consider a positive theory of collective bargaining, it turns out that his concept of the indeterminancy of wages under competition is actually a theory of monopoly prices (in the vernacular of modern economists, it becomes a discussion of the indeterminateness of price determination between bilateral monopolists). He relaxes, without warning, his assumption about the effect of price on the volume of labor ultimately employed.

The shift was subtle, but unmistakable. With organization, he wrote that striking workers might, with reserves (a strike fund), "hold out as long or longer than the masters would choose to hold out," since the employer must also continue to pay interest on his indebtedness, or at least lose profits he might otherwise have made.[40] But do the employers hold out because no other laborers are willing to work at the old wages; or is it because our fishpeddlers on the beach prevented other boats from docking or kept the buyers from moving to another beach? And if it is the latter, wouldn't this be something else again that the full "'freedom of exchange with regard to labour by putting the workman on something like an equal position in bargaining with his employer'," the words of T. J. Dunning that Thornton approvingly quoted?[41]

Thornton resolves any doubt soon thereafter. Regardless of what union leaders or their champions say, Thornton admits that unions do seek considerably more than competitive equality. They demand nothing more or less than domination of the labor market:

> they have no notion of contenting themselves with an equal voice in the settlement of labour questions. They tell us plainly

that what they aspire to is 'control over the destinies of labour'—
that they want not merely to be freed from dictation but to
dictate, to be able to arrange the conditions of employment at
their own discretion; and facts are not wanting to indicate how
they would use such discretionary power if they had it . . .

How would they use it?

To enable themselves to get the highest obtainable wages, and to
do in return the least possible work, doing that little, too, with
the least possible inconvenience to themselves . . . such, stripped
of its various glosses, and represented in its natural colours, is
their simple scheme. This is the whole head and front of their
intending.[42]

"The single aim of trades' unions," Thornton concluded, "is to enable
themselves to dictate arbitrarily the conditions of employment"; and those
conditions amount to a very simple formula: more pay for less work. No
'reactionary', union-baiting employer could ever, or has ever, put it more
bluntly. But Thornton intended it almost as a compliment. Their aim, he
said, was entirely legitimate. Why? Because *employers,* given half the
chance, would dominate labor! Labor's claim is

the exact correlative of a right of Capital which has generally
been used directly against them, and which has almost always
been exercised with remorseless disregard of their welfare. What
need of further words to show that this correlative, must
necessarily be also a genuine, right?[43]

Clearly, some further words *are* needed here, because something has
been lost in the shuffle: the rights and the interests of nonunion laborers,
and those of consumers (not to speak of employers).

Toward the end of his treatise, Thornton distinguished and analyzed at
length six possible cases where, he believed, a union could through a
strike or a strike threat permanently increase the wage rate and the gross
wage payrolls an employer paid:

1st, in any trade of which, owing to some peculiarity in its nature
or character, the employers in the same neighbourhood have
virtually a monopoly: 2nd, in any trade for the prosecution of
which one country possesses a marked advantage over others:
3rd, in any trade the demand for whose produce happens, owing
to the growing wealth or growing number of customers, to be at
the time increasing: 4th, in any trade in which, without any
increase, and perhaps notwithstanding a considerable reduction
in prices, the increased productiveness of industry places an
augmented quantity of produce at the disposal of the masters,
and increases, consequently, their total sale proceeds: 5th, in all

trades whatever, provided the rise take place simultaneously and equally in all trades: and 6th, in any trade in which the scale of business is such, that a greater aggregate profit can be made in it at a low rate than in others at a high rate.[44]

But in no case did Thornton conclude that the bounty obtained through collective action would necessarily be enjoyed by all the striking workers, nor that it would be paid out of the profits of employers of labor alone. He ends up in the odd position of admitting and reaffirming what was actually the single most important insight of the wages fund doctrine.

> Whether a country be stationary or progressive, an exceptionally high rate of wages cannot be maintained in any particular trade, unless the workmen of all other trades are prevented from entering that particular trade, and endeavouring to get the same rate. *Unionism cannot keep up the rate in one trade, without keeping it down in others.* It cannot benefit one portion of the labouring population without, during a period of stagnation, injuring the remainder, nor even in a season of prosperity, without at least shutting out the bulk of the labouring population from the advantages secured for a portion.[45]

"[P]artial unionism," Thornton admits after all, "cannot benefit any part of the labouring population, except more or less at the expense of the rest." Nevertheless, since partial unionism was, he supposed, the only way to build up universal unionism (that is, the organization of the entire working class), it must be a good thing, because "whatever benefit universal unionism conferred on any labourers, it would confer on all."[46]

But wouldn't a universal union annihilate the market economy through a general strike, killing the goose to get at the eggs? Maybe it would; nevertheless, Thornton opined that

> [f]or all parties concerned, . . . there may be consolation in reflecting that a good while must elapse before it can have so much power to abuse, and that in the interval it may learn moderation enough not to use a giant's strength barbarously, when it becomes a giant.[47]

Mill on Thornton *On Labour*

John Stuart Mill responded to Thornton's treatise with a long, two-part review essay in the *Fortnightly Review.* Mill dropped a bombshell, for in this essay he recanted the wages fund doctrine, announcing that it was "deprived of its scientific foundation, and must be thrown aside." "The power of Trades' Unions," Mill concluded, "may . . . be so exercised as to obtain for the labouring classes collectively, both a *larger share and a larger positive amount* of the produce of labour."[48]

Mill's recantation of the wages fund had a very far-reaching affect on his contemporaries (though oddly, Thornton's treatise did not; it was not often cited, and it is not often discussed, even by historians), and understandably so, given its momentous conclusions.

Mill first took up Thornton's theory of indeterminacy and of laborers' bargaining disadvantages. Mill did not accept the idea that supply and demand *never* determined price, but he did agree that it did not operate in *all* cases to determine a *single* price. "The conclusion" to be drawn from Thornton's Dutch auction example, according to Mill, is

> not that the law [of supply and demand] is false . . . but only that . . . *there is some amount of indeterminateness in its operation*—a certain limited extent of variation is possible within the bounds of the law.[49]

Thornton's Dutch auction assumed a rather small number of buyers dealing with a rather small number of sellers as the basis for making his larger point, namely that "demand" does not increase "with cheapness." Mill asked "how many such cases really exist?" In general, he answered, very few indeed:

> [W]here buyers are counted by thousands, or hundreds, or even scores; in any considerable market—and, far more, in the general market of the world—it is the next thing to impossible that more of the commodity should not be asked at every reduction in price.

But is the *labor market* one of those "excepted cases" where "several prices all agree in satisfying" equilibrium? Can we agree "that the question between one of those prices and another will be determined by causes which operate strongly against the labourer, and in favour of the employer"?[50]

Mill's reasoning at this crucial juncture becomes difficult to follow. For what we might expect, namely an analysis of labor markets or of interemployer competition, is not what we get.

He begins by raising a possible argument favorable to Thornton (calling to mind Longe and Leslie). Perhaps the quantity of labor demanded is insensitive to price because the quantity of work is fixed. Suppose an employer

> buys as much labour and no more as suffices to produce the quantity of his goods which he thinks he can sell to advantage. A fall of wages does not necessarily make him expect a larger sale for his commodity, nor, therefore, does it necessarily increase his demand for labour.[51]

Mill seemingly *dismisses* this hypothesis. The increased profits in an industry that emerge from *lower labor costs* than might have been anticipated, even if they are not invested in *that* industry would be invested elsewhere, "where it will either be itself expended in employing labour, or will liberate some other person's capital to be so expended, and the whole of the wages-fund will be paying wages as before."[52]

Up to this point, Mill's observations are quite in the spirit of the wages fund. A sudden drop in wages paid would, after all, imply an *instantaneous* increase in the employer's theoretical "wages fund," but this does not invalidate the idea that the fund is "fixed" or "determinate." There is nothing whatever in the account, say of J. R. McCulloch, that assumes that adjustments do not occur with more or less rapidity (even if, for purposes of abstraction, these adjustments can be collapsed and considered as if they took no time). Nor, for that matter, did Mill accept Thornton's criticism of the validity of the law of supply and demand simply because it took some time for economic forces to work their will.[53]

But Mill unaccountably drops this approach when the issue of sudden, unanticipatedly *higher labor costs* arise. An employer in a vulnerable position hit with a strike or a threat of a strike might have no time to adjust the number hired and might have to increase the amount he paid in wages right up to the whole of his profit, indeed right up to the amount which might put him out of business; and this is *all* Mill feels is necessary to invalidate the wages fund. The secondary 'boomerang effects' are ignored. Mill's words were these:

> If we choose to call the whole of what he [an employer] possesses applicable to the payment of wages, the wages-fund, that fund is co-extensive with the whole proceeds of his business, after keeping up his machinery, buildings and materials, and feeding his family; and it is expended jointly upon himself and his labourers. The less he expends on the one, the more may be expended on the other, and *vice versa. The price of labour, instead of being determined by the division of the proceeds between the employer and the labourers, determines it. If he gets his labour cheaper, he can afford to spend more upon himself. If he has to pay more for labour, the additional payment comes out of his own income*; perhaps from the part he would have saved and added to capital . . . perhaps from what he would have expended on his private wants or pleasures.

"There is no law of nature," Mill concluded,

> making it inherently impossible for wages to rise to the point of absorbing not only the funds which he had intended to devote to carrying on his business, but the whole of what he allows for his private expenses, beyond the necessaries of life. . . .

Thornton, therefore, "has made it necessary for us to contemplate ... that employers, by taking advantage of the inability of labourers to hold out, may keep wages lower than there is any natural necessity for."[54]

It is not easy to understand how Mill could conclude that trade unions could "obtain for all the labouring classes collectively, both a larger share and a larger positive amount of the produce of labour" on the basis of such a slender reed as the vulnerability of some employers to strikes, ignoring all the secondary, 'boomerang' consequences his fellow economists pointed out. Did Mill believe that employers were unable to adjust the volume of their workforce in response to a change in factor prices? Did he think them incapable of finding alternative workers? Of substituting machinery and unskilled labor for skilled labor? And if so, what did this imply for a theory of indeterminateness?[55]

The strange thing is that Mill *was* aware of all this. For in the *second* part of his essay on Thornton, he proceeded to so qualify what he said about collective bargaining and the redistribution of income that one wonders what it was he recanted in the first part! The *very* wide limits within which wages may vary depending upon labor's collective bargaining power Mill now admits would apply *only* to a *universal union* of the entire working class. In the case of a partially organized workforce, "there is often a nearer limit—that which would destroy, or drive elsewhere, the particular branch of industry in which the rise would take place."[56]

Similarly, Mill denied that a possible mechanism through which higher wages could be paid—higher prices—could be generalized from a particular instance. A "real rise of general wages cannot be thrown on the consumer by a rise in prices." Without an inflation (an increase in the money supply), all prices cannot rise simultaneously; and even supposing this happened, *real* wages would not generally be higher than before. Any union wage gain made at consumers' expense through higher prices "is generally a gain made, wholly or in part, at the expense of the remainder of the labouring classes" in their capacity as *labourers in other industries.* Consumers, having to spend more on A, have less to spend on B, C; and as consumer demand falls off in B, C, so too will employment in them.[57]

At this point, Mill left off the economic analysis of collective bargaining to broach a broad question of public policy. How, he asked, can the restrictionist activity of a trade union—which admittedly hurt workers not members of it—be justified? How can the "distinct evil" union limitations on entry "be reconciled either with the obligations of general morality, or with the special regard professed by [unionized] labouring men for the interest of the labouring class?"[58]

Thornton had excused the harm unionized workers imposed on unorganized workers on the grounds that when all were organized in the bye and bye, the labor problem would allegedly be solved. In the meantime, all the law might rightfully forbid was overt violence.[59] Mill, employing his own brand of utilitarianism with a touch of Malthusianism, went even further.

Mill declared that the harm unions inflict on nonunion workers may be justified because the latter were a morally and economically inferior, but more numerous, class who, if allowed the freedom to do so, would only spoil things for their betters. Their willingness to live in degraded conditions, coupled with their unrestrained breeding habits, would drag everyone down to the level of abject misery, including the better sort of workman who had climbed to the top [Mill didn't add, on their backs]. Therefore, the unionist law of the jungle was a "not fallacious point of view, from which the apparent injustice of Unionism to the non-united classes of labourers may be morally vindicated to the conscience of an intelligent Unionist" and to other presumably enlightened individuals.[60]

Contemporary Reaction to Mill

"In matters of Political Economy," the Scottish economist James Stirling explained a year after Mill's essay appeared, "the present generation of Englishmen pins its faith to the sleeve of Mr. Mill. Any utterance of his, therefore, is an event, not only in the history of the science, but in the history of the nation."[61] And so it was.

Not all Englishmen pinned their faith on Mill, of course. His colleagues, Henry Fawcett and John Elliott Cairnes, continued to insist that the distributional consequences of the wages fund were essentially valid. Cairnes, in particular, conceded what Francis Longe had made such a point of, namely, that not all capitalists or wage earners competed *directly* with each other. But he failed to see why this changed the general implication of the wages fund with regard to strikes and the distribution of income.[62]

Stirling wondered where Mill's vaunted humanitarianism had gone. The scab, after all,

> is not an outlaw, to be cut off from personal freedom and protection of the law. He has his rights like his betters; and though too often treated like the leper of old, his chief offence is, after all, his poverty. But any stick will do to beat a dog; and the poor knobstick is the dog with a pan at his tail, which every passer-by must fling a stone at.[63]

For that matter, as T. S. Cree pointed out in a tightly reasoned paper several years later, Mill's own proposed euthanasia of the nonunion worker grossly libeled Malthus. "Mr. Malthus advocated self-restraint. He never proposed the destruction of the weak by the strong, in order that the latter should have more to divide." Nor, Cree added, was Mill's or Thornton's logic about the alleged benefits of universal unionist restrictionism at all compelling:

> [w]hat is aimed at is a limitation of the amount of labour in each trade. It is evident that, for such a limitation, a union of all labour is exactly the same as no union at all, while a union not of all labour, but of all trades, will create an enormous army of paupers. . . . The surplus men from one trade could not be absorbed by other trades, for these are also organised and occupied in getting rid of their own surplus.[64]

Cree questioned whether a defense of the basic workability or justice of individualistic bargaining at all required as a necessary condition that it be 'perfect', for example, that "labour should be perfectly mobile, that every labourer be perfectly informed, perfectly alive to his interests, and perfectly willing and able to go to the locality where he could sell his labour to the best advantage." This nowhere existed, and it did not have to exist; it was necessary only that marginal movements, including marginal movements over time, take place.

> I hold that something far short [of the assumption that all workers be able to move] is all that is necessary. If there are a few in each trade or each congested locality willing to change or to send out their sons to other places or trades, that is all that is needed to redress the balance

between the bargainers. And at any rate, he added, what is the point of arguing about perfect competition in the context of unions, when their whole aim is to subvert it?[65]

Commentary: Problems with the Theory of Collective Bargaining

Several years after Thornton's treatise and Mill's essay appeared, the English neoclassical economist Alfred Marshall re-evaluated and reworked Thornton's cases whereby unions might increase the wage *rate* and the *wage payroll* of any given employer or employee. In Marshall's formulation, these were

> *Firstly,* that there is no easy alternative method of obtaining the commodity which their trade helps to produce; and this generally requires (a) that they have control over the supply of labour in their trade and district; (b) that the commodity cannot easily be brought from some other district, in which the conditions of

labour are beyond their control; and (c) that there is no available mechanical or other contrivance by which the commodity can be produced independently of them: *Secondly,* that the commodity is one the price of which will be raised considerably by a stinting of supply, or in other words that the demand for it is not very elastic; *Thirdly,* that the share of the total expenses of production of the commodity which consists of their wages is small, so that a great proportionate rise in them will not greatly raise its price and diminish the demand for it. And *Fourthly,* that the other classes of workers, and the employers, in the trade are squeezable, or at least are not in a position to secure for themselves an increased share of the price of the joint product by limiting artificially the supply of their labour and capital.[66]

Marshall concluded that, in effect, there was an indeterminancy involved here in the redistribution of gains and losses, since the gains secured by organized workers in each and every case would come partly at their employer's expense, and partly at the expense of those consumers who were not wage earners. But they would come partly at the expense of working-class consumers, and partly also at the expense of workers dismissed in that trade, or as Mill understood, at the expense of workers dismissed in *complementary* trades.

Marshall agreed with T. S. Cree that a case for "universal unionism" couldn't serve as a defense for the defects of partial unionism. If *all* workers attempted to "gain by the general adoption of a mode of action which has been proved to enable one trade, under certain conditions, to gain at the expense of the others," the result would be *losses* (of output, wages, employment) spread progressively through the economy. The "influence which Unions exert on the average level of wages," Marshall observed, "is less than would be inferred by looking at the influence which they exert on wages in each particular trade." "When the measures which they take to raise wages in one trade have the effect of rendering business more difficult," he wrote, "they are likely to diminish employment in other trades, and thus to cause a greater aggregate loss of wages to other trades then they gain for themselves, and to lower and not raise the average level of wages." John Ramsay McCulloch would not have said it very differently.[67]

Theories of Industrial Democracy and Social Reform after Mill

The classical economists' wages fund doctrine fell into desuetude in the 1870s, although their neo-classical successors never accepted the 'theory of collective bargaining'; with the advent of marginal productivity theory (discussed in chapter six *infra*), the conclusions of the wages fund with regard to strikes and income redistribution remained essentially valid. Nevertheless, in Mill's wake one may observe an important transition in the general currents of social and economic thought. The proponents of individual bargaining were thereafter increasingly on the defensive. The clear vision of classical distribution theory about strikes and collective bargaining—indeed, about price controls and their effects generally— was befogged by a variety of reform movements and 'bargaining power' wage theories which emerged to supplant laissez faire on the one hand, and socialism (or syndicalism) on the other.

Three nonrevolutionary reform movements of late 19th-century England and Europe were particularly important for the growth of industrial democratic thought in America: German historicism and social liberalism; Christian Socialism; and Fabian socialism.

With few exceptions, German economic theorists after Hermann concentrated on the economic and social forces influencing the movement of wages for particular groups, but not informed by any general theory of price determination. By mid-century, proponents of this 'historical' or 'empirical' school were the dominant presence in the academy. And when classical economic theory reached its crisis in the 1860s—the impasse over the wages fund was one of its symptoms—their influence began to be felt outside Germany as well, most significantly, by a generation of American graduate students who studied with them after the Civil War at the great German universities.[68]

The 'historicists', many of whom were deeply inspired by the socialist theoretician Johann Karl Rodbertus, curtly dismissed what they called 'deductive', classical economic science on the grounds that it rested on what they believed to an empirically false proposition—that men were motivated exclusively or even primarily by 'greed' or 'self-interest'. But while they claimed that this was factually untrue, what they really objected to was the *morality* of self-interest.

Thus, the German historicists taught that men "are subject to moral law," which they defined as the morality of self-sacrificial duty; men "are stimulated by moral motives or should at least be guided by them." As Adolph Held, one of its leading theorists put it, the historical school "demands, above all, the abandonment [of the presumption] that man in his action is influenced only by egoism." The new economics

> demands that economic man shall be considered as [a] member of an organized society . . . and asserts that the existing system of law, as a whole and in its details, must be considered as a factor of the highest importance in the explanation of social phenomena.[69]

What this kind of emphasis on law and social institutions meant, however, is something very different from what economists who study these matters mean today. Historicists denied that economic laws based on self-interest are universally true for all times, for all people, and in all cases. They are true only relative to the particular historical period in which they were espoused; relative to some cultures; and relative to the particular class in whose interests, and by whose authors, they were formulated. What this usually meant was that if minimum wages, social security, national power, or protection of workers against exploitation, became the object of social policy, with a greater priority than maximum social wealth (within the framework of private property and free competition), the 'armchair', deductive economists of the classical school who claimed that price fixing, tariffs, and other interventions, would have harmful effects on total social wealth could be readily dismissed, partly on the grounds that they hadn't conducted an "empirical study" of the effects, and partly on the grounds that since the state was committed to other goals—say redistribution—their objections were irrelevant.[70]

Most of these historicists/institutionalists emphasized state controls of various sorts—tariffs, compulsory minimum wages and maximum hours, factory inspection laws, compulsory health and unemployment insurance—to overcome "the inadequacy of traditional theory and its failure in the presence of the turbulent demand of the times for social reform."[71] Nevertheless, there was an important minority faction among these *Kathedersozialisten* (Socialists of the Chair) who were strong proponents of unionism as a vehicle for working class amelioration. The leader of these 'social liberals', as they were called, was Lujo Brentano.[72]

Brentano—whose writings helped shape the views of the Webbs, and of Richard Ely and other American progressives —had an interesting theory of collective bargaining, echoes of which we still hear today. Organized workers, he claimed, could increase their real wages and the share of income accruing to the working class just so long as employers passed these wage increases through to consumers.

> [T]hat which a consumer offers for a commodity is by no means an inevitably settled amount. This amount is rather various according to the degree in which the consumer needs a certain commodity, and may possibly amount to this whole wealth. [The wages fund theory] . . . overlooks this possibility of rolling off upon consumers the higher wages demanded by the coalitions; it overlooks the fact that an employer will always be ready to expend more capital in the payment of wages as soon as the consumers replace for him the amount expended thereupon, and that in such a case it will always be possible for him, if he has no more than a certain capital, to procure capital by borrowing more abroad.[73]

Brentano denied that this procedure harmed other workers. There would be no *aggregate* decline in output, or employment, or purchasing power, because *the workers who received the increased wages would themselves demand goods and services as consumers.* At most there would be a wholesome and socially beneficial shift in the direction of production, away from luxury goods and towards the needs of the working class: a redistribution which would also be in the interest of manufacturers, since it would increase the market for their goods. "Accordingly," he concluded,

> instead of permanently inflicting upon the labourers of other industries an injury, an increase of wages in an isolated industry is permanently advantageous to the whole laboring class . . . an increase in wages of the laborers in coalition diminishes in no industry the wages of laborers; it diminishes solely the income of the consumers of the commodities produced by the laborers in coalition, causes a change in the persons of the demanders, and a change in the kind of production. The entire demand for commodities, however, remains unchanged in quantity . . .[74]

Brentano's theory rests on the fallacy, which critics were quick to pounce on, that the consumers who bore the incidence of higher prices were not themselves wage earners. But if they are, reshuffling an unchanged aggregate demand (assuming that it is unchanged) hardly constitutes a redistribution of real wages across socio-economic class lines.[75] Moreover, only in the case of dire necessities will "that which a consumer offer[s] . . . amount to his whole wealth."

Brentano at various points in his long and influential career strongly defended compulsory unionism, arbitration, an end to government 'repression' of strikers, and even a complete corporative reorganization of the economy. The leader of the social liberals regarded any effective government policy to protect the right of strikebreakers to work unmolested as a species of reactionary legislation which only furthered the interests of the capitalists. "What was needed," according to Brentano, "was not a tightening of government's restriction on unions but an abolition of those restrictions."[76] Those other doughty champions of industrial democracy, Sidney and Beatrice Webb, couldn't agree more. "[H]owever annoying such practices as picketing," including picketing en masse around a nonstriking worker's home, "may be to the employer whose objects are defeated thereby," they wrote, any attempt to curtail this kind of democracy in action was socially biased.[77]

The Webbs' seminal *History of Trade Unionism* (1894) was a landmark study of English labor organizations that set the standard for the teaching of labor history in England and America. *Industrial Democracy* (1897) was their magnum opus, a great synthesis of 19th century radical and social reform thought and an enormously powerful apologia for compulsory unionism.

Yet the Webbs, and their group of sympathizers, the 'Fabians', were first and foremost *socialists*. They never endorsed syndicalism; and whatever power they wanted granted to unions would always be, in theory at least, subject to the overriding authority of the nation-state.[78]

Christian Socialism was a third important strand of European and English social reform thought to influence Americans.[79] The Christian Socialists made a noteworthy contribution to the concept of industrial democracy: corporativism, essentially a revived, updated version of medieval social theory. Many Christian Socialists sought to steamroll individualism and re-integrate society by forcing all workers to join unions.

The "state," Bishop Ketteler taught 19th century clerics and laymen, "had the duty of furnishing by means of legislation the necessary assistance to the working class in organizing a corporative structure" in which "the new corporations would enjoy autonomy within their respective spheres."[80] "To be effective," his disciple Hitze believed, "guild organization must be compulsory for all industries, trades, and professions." Since it is "no longer possible to ignore the fact that a conflict exists between capital on one side and labor on the other," something had to be done lest violent revolution (and presumably those atheistical forms of socialism) arrive.

> There remains open to us no course but to acknowledge this conflict openly, to *organize* it, to give it *legitimate organs,* to assign it to a *recognized place where, under the eyes of the central state authority, the battle can be fought out.*[81]

The significance of this last, corporative approach for economic governance in America after the Civil War is the subject of the next chapter.

6. Approaching Industrial Democracy in America: The Economy of High Wages

 This chapter considers some important American intellectuals and trade union theorists in the late 19th century, whose ideas about labor unions and the role of the state in economic life contributed mightily to the rise of industrial democracy as a principal goal of economic reform. Post-Civil War era reformers accepted class conflict as the basic fact of economic life in a modern industrial society. But they did not seek to eliminate private ownership of the means of production, and they did not seek to abolish competition. Most wanted to reorganize and regulate competition *between organized groups* under the watchful eye of the state. Their outlook was more corporativist than socialist or syndicalist.[1]

The Passing of the Old Guard and the Sentinels of the New

"[W]hen men exchange services with each other," Arthur Latham Perry, Professor of Political Economy at Williams College, wrote in the 18th edition of his popular and widely read *Elements of Political Economy* (1883), "the just and comprehensive rule always will be" that each party is bound to look out for his own interest . . . and to make the best terms for himself which he can make. Capital does this for itself, and laborers ought to do this for themselves, and if they are persistently cheated in the exchange, they have nobody to blame but themselves.

"So long as capital and labor rest solely on their natural rights," he added, "neither can have the advantage of the other" and "the prosperity of each will build up the other." The public policy of a democratic society should be one of virtual laissez faire:

> The Legislature, whether State or National, cannot be too scrupulous in this whole matter, because the proper limits of legislative action on economical subjects are pretty narrow . . . in general, capital and labor should have the utmost liberty of action compatible with social security, and the *equal rights* of each will best be reached by leaving both to take care of themselves subject only to the general laws relating to person and property.[2]

Perry's individualistic sentiments were fairly common; one can find similar encomiums to economic freedom in college textbooks and essays written by his colleagues and contemporaries—men like Simon Newcomb, Francis Wayland, Amasa Walker, or William Graham Sumner. Except on tariffs, academic economists in America from the late 18th Century to the Civil War generally followed the procompetitive commitment of the classical school.[3]

But, even while men such as Perry and Sumner spoke, the intellectual ground was shifting beneath their feet. "The question of [individual] right," the influential sociologist Lester Frank Ward wrote in that same year (1883),

> can be disposed of with a word. . . . Not until we have succeeded in banishing the metaphysical conception of right . . . shall we be prepared to discuss intelligently the conditions of man's progress conceived as capable of accomplishment by his own efforts.

Social progress, as far as Ward was concerned, depended upon *collective* effort. 'Progressivism', as this attitude came to be known, rested on the belief that the economic growth achieved by individual effort within the framework of private property and competition—the 'system of natural liberty'—was *not* the avenue to social amelioration, but the road to inequality and tyranny. Progressivism *meant* a commitment to the exertion of collective force, typically through the state, on behalf of the majority. To the progressive mind, individual property rights were only a means for the unscrupulous minority to exploit the majority; the "so-called 'abstract rights' of mankind must be denied if society is ever to become the arbiter of its own destiny."[4]

Richard T. Ely, German-educated dean of the American progressive economists and one of the most influential teachers in America from the 1880s down to World War I, explained the new attitude. "The nation in its economic life," he claimed, "is an organism, of which individuals" and subordinate groups "in their economic life from parts." Individual rights and individual happiness were false idols that must yield to the general welfare. "Happiness is an end" that "must be subordinate to . . . service . . . for the sake of others," he wrote. This was "the aim of social ethics" and the first desideratum of government policy.[5]

Ely helped establish the American Economics Association (AEA) in 1885. This organization was modeled specifically on the *Verein für Sozialpolitik,* an association of German historicists and social liberals dedicated to economic interventionism and social reform, whose meetings he attended as a graduate student in Germany, and whose goals he wanted American economists to adopt. The "conflict of labor and capital," Ely wrote in the prospectus for the AEA, "has brought to the front a vast number of social problems whose solution is impossible without the united efforts of Church, state, and science." The "state," he insisted, was "an educational and ethical agency whose positive aid is an indispensable condition of human progress. While . . . the necessity of individual initiative in industrial life" was plain, "the doctrine of laissez-faire is unsafe in politics and unsound in morals; and [it] suggests an inadequate explanation of the relations between the state and its citizens."[6]

Ely's, and Ward's, sentiments were shared by a rising group of college professors who had taken their graduate training in Europe after the Civil War. Studying at first-hand the social reformist doctrines of the German historicists and social liberals described in the previous chapter, influenced by the Christian Socialists (and later by the Fabian socialists) and well-read in the literature of socialism and syndicalism, economists and social scientists such as John Bates Clark, Henry Carter Adams, and Simon Patten dedicated themselves to the task of establishing an economic democracy that would fulfill the promise of the political democracy they already knew.[7] They in turn taught the next generation of teachers and intellectuals—Ely's most famous student, for instance, was John R. Commons, the founder of "Institutional Economics" and an extremely important teacher and reformer in his own right.[8]

Their influence permeated not only economics, but sociology, law, and even philosophy, where their collectivist goals were aided by the growth of the American philosophy of Pragmatism. Though its ethic is relativistic and does not necessarily imply any political doctrine, Pragmatism, as John Dewey espoused it, amounted in practice to the 'social engineer' ethic—

the attempt to apply the scientific methods of experimentation and manipulation of matter to human beings and social institutions in the service of 'society as a whole'.[9]

In religion, Christian Socialism strongly influenced the growth of the 'social gospel'. This creed—the 19th-century version of today's 'liberation theology'—comprised clerics whose major figures, Washington Gladden, William Dwight Porter Bliss, Walter Rauschenbush, and above all, John A. Ryan, were dedicated to the reorganization of American society along collectivistic lines, in which unions would play a major role.[10]

Competition as a Form of Minority Rule: The Case Against Free Contracts

The argument against laissez faire and in favor of state intervention into the economy that most captured the progressives' fancy emphasized the dichotomy between 'negative' and 'positive' freedom. This dichotomy was best summarized by the English neo-Hegelian social philosopher and reformer Thomas Hill Green in his often-cited essay, "Lecture on Liberal Legislation and Freedom of Contract" (1881). Individual liberty, according to Green, should not mean "merely freedom from restraint or compulsion," but the "positive power or capacity of doing or enjoying something worth doing or enjoying, and that, too, something that we do or enjoy in common with others."[11]

True freedom was not 'negative', according to Green; it was not "merely freedom to do as we like irrespectively of what it is that we like."[12] Man is fundamentally a social being; and as such, Green insisted that the positive freedom "that can be enjoyed by one man or set of men at the cost of a loss of freedom to others" is antisocial and therefore false. Nor is "the mere removal of compulsion, the mere enabling a man to do as he likes, . . . in itself [a] contribution to true freedom." "True" freedom, "freedom in the positive sense" by which social progress is measured, is "the greater power on the part of the citizens *as a body* to make the most and the best of themselves"; it is "the liberation of the powers of all men equally *for contributions to a common good.* No one has a right to do what he will with his own in such a way as to contravene this end."[13]

The protections which government accords to the individual against force physical and fraud, otherwise leaving him a free hand to do what he will with his own, are merely abstract, formal freedoms. They not only form a small portion of liberty and democracy; in fact, they foster a regime whereby the great majority of men *cannot* effectively exercise free choice. *Economic coercion,* and not physical coercion, was the fundamental social problem of modern society.

Richard T. Ely asserted that "restrictions upon liberty are, for the most part, *outside of and beyond government."* The real problems are centered in the economy, because the real "restrictions upon our positive liberty of action are mainly due to the *coercion of economic forces,"* above all, "in and through the contract competitively formed." Indeed, "[w]herever modern slavery or a near approach to slavery exists, it assumes almost invariably the form of voluntary contract."[14]

Unfettered, individualistic competition, according to Ely and others, fostered *minority rule* in social and economic affairs—most notably, though not only, in the labor market. His analysis of this alleged problem set the stage for the kinds of reform the progressives thought were essential, if American society were to be rescued from class warfare and revolution and a new democracy—a new Republic, as it were—established.

The *"problem of the twentieth man"* was the key to the idea that minorities, and not majorities, ruled in the marketplace:

> Nineteen men wish to pursue a certain course of economic action, but are coerced competitively by the twentieth into a line of conduct which they dislike. Nineteen barbers in the city of Madison, Wisconsin, wished to close their shops on Sunday; the twentieth would not agree to close his, and consequently, all the twenty were, and still are, kept open. Nineteen men may desire to work ten hours a day, and may be coerced by the twentieth into working fourteen hours a day. Apparently they are all working fourteen hours a day because they choose to do so, but the choice is not a free one, in any true sense of the word. Even the twentieth man prefers to work ten hours a day, but yields to pressure for the sake of a temporary advantage, and so he is likewise coerced.

"The freedom which thus expresses itself in contract," Ely concluded, "is in certain cases like the freedom of a slave, who chooses to work rather than to suffer under the lash."[15]

The results were all too familiar. There had been a "long era of declining wages," John Bates Clark asserted.[16] Henry Carter Adams agreed: "Rodbertus was right." Laborers were receiving an ever smaller share of the wealth made possible by improved productivity.[17] Contrary to what the Arthur Latham Perrys of the world might say, Clark maintained "it is imbecile to reiterate that there is no possible ground for conflict between" capital and labor.[18] Unless they organized, Adams added, workers would "surely get the worst of any bargain," for "individualism" in labor markets was "social suicide."[19] "[I]ndustry," Ely stated simply, "is a despotism."[20]

Regulating the Plane of Competition

It did *not* follow that competition must be abolished, nor private property in the means of production socialized. "Competition," Henry Carter Adams wrote, echoing views shared by his colleagues, "is neither malevolent nor beneficient, but will work malevolence or beneficence according to the conditions under which it is permitted to act." Although competition has "not worked in the nineteenth century as Adam Smith, writing for the eighteenth century, said it would work," the socialists were mistaken in their belief that competition could or should be abolished. Given the right conditions, Adams agreed that competition guaranteed that "goods will be produced at the lowest possible cost," and that "the hope of personal gain leads to the best disposal of labor, to invention, and to the adoption of the best machinery." Both "unbridled industrial license" and "complete governmental control" were unacceptable, for "either of these methods leads to tyranny."[21]

What Adams, and those of his generation, sought was a "middle course" between laissez faire and socialism, which they felt would lead to "industrial liberty." The essence of this version of 'social reform without socialism' was that the state could and should *restrict* liberty—the liberty of powerful individuals—in order to *expand* liberty—that is, to empower other individuals as members of groups. Adams called the *kind* of course they charted "regulating the plane of competition," according to which the state should *regulate* and *restrict* the liberty of the anti-social minority in order to expand the power of a majority. When a "large body of competitors agree respecting some given method of procedure" but an unscrupulous minority is so positioned to frustrate their will, *"it becomes the province of the state to incorporate the wish of the majority in some practical law.* In this manner there is established a legal plane of competition higher than that which could be maintained in the absence of legal enactment." There, in a nutshell, was the road to democratize industry and the economy.[22]

The significance of this approach to social reform is vast. It is a theory of the *competition of groups* under the aegis of the state. It is a "middle course" between capitalism and socialism that borders on *corporativism;* and some progressives were perfectly willing to cross this border. John R.

Commons asserted that an authentic "constitutional" government "recognizes the existence of antagonistic classes and opens up its framework to the equal influence of the two or three [dominant] classes" in society. "A truly representative assembly," the founder of Institutional Economics asserted,

> would be one to which the different organized classes elected their own representatives as the older guilds elected their members of Parliament. Let the labor unions, irrespective of locality, come together and elect their members of Congress . . . These would be the true representatives of the wage earning class. Let the bankers elect their representatives by themselves. . . . Let the trusts elect theirs. . . . Such an assembly I should call representative in the original sense of the word.[23]

For Herbert Croly, editor of the influential magazine, *The New Republic*, compulsory unionism was a virtual necessity. Unions "cannot exercise the power necessary in their opinion to their interests without certain radical changes," namely "an economic and political order which will discriminate in favor of union labor and against non-union labor." Union claims were eminently just; if anything, the demands of the conservative, mainline American unions, such as those affiliated with the AFL, were too modest. Croly explained that a "man who repudiates with abhorrence the proposed revolutionary methods of syndicalism" as preached by the International Workers of the World "may still believe that it is infusing into unionism a necessary ferment and into modern economic civilization a necessary ideal." The "conscience and the intelligence of the American democracy" must not "fail to recognize the peculiar promise and nobleness of the syndicalist ideal," "an ideal," he added, "whose realization is necessary to democratic fulfillment."[24]

The search for the right mixture of legislation, group power, and individual freedom necessary to institute democracy in industry and throughout society has occupied economic and social progressives continuously from the 1880s to the 1980s. But before the kinds of industrial democratic reforms they espoused in the first half-century are taken up, some account must be given of what they hoped to accomplish in the labor market through state intervention and collective bargaining.

To fill the vacuum created by the demise of the wages fund, there were, broadly speaking, two general theories of wages around which American champions or sympathizers of social reform rallied. The one most popular with academics and intellectuals took as its point of departure a hypothetical nexus between higher wages and employee efficiency. The one most popular with trade unionists took as its point of departure a hypothetical nexus between higher wages and increased employment. Both theories justified wage regulation by legislation and by unions armed with the power of the state. Both grew in influence over the decades and dominated the thought of Americans on the eve of the New Deal.

The Economy of High Wages: An Efficiency Theory

For classical economists generally, the level of real wages—that is, material living standards—was *an effect* of previously accumulated capital, while the level of money wages in each industrial sector was the result of supply and demand. Capital, we might say, governs wages; wages govern, or more correctly, wages *are* the standard of living.

There is another possibility. Could the level of real wages—the standard of living—*be itself a cause of high or low wages?* Classical economists occasionally came close to answering this question affirmatively. Some of their statements became the background for an entirely new way of looking at how material prosperity can be obtained.

Ricardo, for instance, wished "that in all countries the labouring classes should have a taste for comforts and enjoyments" since in "those countries where the labouring classes have the fewest wants, and are contented with the cheapest food, the people are exposed to the greatest vicissitudes and miseries."[25]

McCulloch also observed that higher wages improved workers' "habits"; and "as they learn to form more exalted notions of what is required for their comfort and decent support," *their* "natural or necessary rate" of wages is augmented. What he meant in this context was that workers who did not receive a wage that would enable them to marry and raise a family *at a standard of living approximating their peers* would not do so. Thus, the supply of labor would eventually adjust itself to this new higher subsistence wage. Put in modern terms, as individuals grow wealthier, they will reduce the number of children they have, in order to maintain a certain lifestyle for themselves and their offspring. Low wages were dangerous since they habituated workers to a lower standard of living. According to McCulloch,

> [v]ery low wages, by rendering it impossible for increased exertions to obtain any considerable increase of advantages, effectually hinders them from being made, and is of all others the most powerful cause of that idleness and apathy that contents itself with what can barely continue animal existence.[26]

Adam Smith also commented on this phenomenon. "The wages of labour," he had written,

> are the encouragement of industry, which, like every other human quality, improves in proportion to the encouragement it receives. A plentiful subsistence increases the bodily strength of the labourer, and the comfortable hope of bettering his condition, and of ending his days perhaps in ease and plenty, animates him to exert that strength to the utmost.[27]

But if these observations were correct, perhaps the classical economists had neglected certain problems that competition could not solve and might even exacerbate. Suppose, the American economist Francis Walker asked in 1876, the wages of workers already on the margin of subsistence were reduced, for instance during a depression. Might this not result in a permanent decrease in their productivity? The worker might contract a wasting disease or suffer a permanent loss of general health and vigor; and even more importantly, his self-respect and ambition could be shattered. The return of economic prosperity, Walker claimed, *would not* restore all to the former state. Employers would "not find the same man" they previously discharged; "he [would] no longer [be] capable of rendering the same service" as before. They would not pay him higher wages because, in truth, he would not be worth them—and never would be.[28]

Walker thus asserted that the competition which reduced wages did not necessarily bottom out quickly and was not necessarily self-correcting. On the contrary, these "effects tend to remain and perpetuate themselves. When people are down, economical forces solely are more likely to keep them down, or push them lower down, than to raise them up." The degradation of living standards brought about by competition would cause workers to become less efficient, and the process would be cumulative and self-reinforcing.[29]

Walker concluded, as a general proposition, that wages and efficiency were linked; and that "every reduction of wages must, in some degree, diminish the efficiency of labor." Purely on grounds of economic efficiency, therefore, he argued that the state should never permit wages to drop below a subsistence level.[30]

If wages and efficiency were linked in one direction, why not in the other? If workers' wages were made higher perhaps workers would *become* more efficient? Perhaps wages themselves are an independent generator of increased productivity? As early as the 1840s, some claimed that the higher wages forced on manufacturers through a shorter workday had 'paid for themselves' through a more efficient workforce and had not resulted in any decline of output or increase in unemployment.[31]

Lujo Brentano, dean of the German 'social liberals', agreed. Citing several 'empirical' studies in the early 1870s, he claimed that "the curtailment of the workingday" (with the same wages paid as before) generally "leads to an increase in the national production." Brentano noted that increases and decreases in European coal production in the early 1870s correlated very closely with increases and decreases in average daily wages despite the lack of capital improvements in that industry. He concluded that increased 'labor productivity' could not have been possible "but for an increase in the average output of the workman *which was itself due to the increase of his wages.*"[32]

The policy implications were clear enough. Objections to legislatively established minimum wages or maximum hours—or to unions' resistance to wage reductions—were false economy.[33]

The Economy of High Wages: An Employment Theory

There was another 'economy of high wages' theory destined to persuade Americans of the justice and utility of industrial democracy. This one claimed that higher wages paid for themselves not by making workers more efficient, but through the expanded employment brought about when employers became more efficient.

This theory apparently originated in the Civil War era writings of the self-taught machinist Ira Steward. Steward's challenge to orthodox competitive theory influenced the American trade union movement, particularly as Steward's ideas were elaborated by George P. McNeill, a deputy of the Massachusetts Bureau of Statistics of Labor and an official of the Knights of Labor; the labor journalist Frank K. Foster, a leader of the AFL in Massachusetts; and George P. Gunton, the editor of Steward's unpublished manuscripts and a union journalist, educator, and magazine editor.[34]

Wages, Gunton wrote, are the "*price* of labor" and, like all other prices, are "determined by the cost of production." But while the price of labor "tends toward the minimum cost of production, it is the minimum cost not of the cheapest, but of the dearest, portion of the necessary supply." The dearest portion here, according to Gunton, was the subsistence wage of a family, which was the source of the labor supply. Gunton argued that the price of labor was the amount of wages necessary to maintain a family— according to a "socially accepted standard of living" that varied from country to country—and not that of the single laborer. This price regulated the supply of labor, at least over the long run. (The similarity of this reasoning to that of the classical economists described above should be apparent.)[35]

Trade union theorists concluded that the wages of labor was in the final analysis "determined by the habitual wants and customs or the social character of the people." "[I]t is not commonly the value of what is produced which chiefly determines the wage rate," Foster explained, "but the nature and degree of the wants of the workers, as embodied in their customary mode of living."[36] As Gunton put it, ultimately "social progress is neither more nor less than the change of human habits, or in other words, the increase in human wants."[37]

The implications were weighty. If the standard of living itself determined real wages, then the road to plenty lay, not so much through increasing the supply of capital by greater savings and the payment of the lowest wages possible, but through enlarging and stimulating consumption *demand* by the payment of the highest wages possible. "[I]nstead of the wages or consumption by the masses being governed by production, . . . the reverse is everywhere true, and *production is determined by consumption,* or wages." It was the 'demand-side' tail that wagged the 'supply-side' dog.[38]

Moreover, one could raise wages . . . simply by raising wages! The economy could be lifted by its own bootstraps. The crucial first step in this process was to reduce the hours of labor; for according to Ira Steward and his followers, "a reduction in hours [is] an increase in wages."[39] As one leader of what came to be known as the Eight Hour Movement put it, in "the eight-hour system employers must pay what they term ten hour rates to secure eight hours' work. On no other conditions can help be retained."[40] Eight hours work at ten hours pay should be sought through legislation, or if necessary, through strikes.

Shorter hours meant that workers had greater leisure. With this leisure, laborers would "cultivate tastes and create wants in addition to mere physical comforts."[41] The 'leisure' effect of a reduction in hours creates greater wants. But the 'employment' effect is what translates these wants into effective demand—and it is the heart of the doctrine.

Contrary to what the 'efficiency' intellectuals claimed, the union eight-hour theorists *did not* believe—nor did they want—that each individual worker would increase *his effort and output* to correspond, say, to a 20-percent increase in wages brought about by a 20-percent reduction in the number of hours he worked. Rather, he should produce the same as before. The sudden gap in output, however, will be bridged by employers hiring more workers. Samuel Gompers expressed this idea in a nutshell in 1887: "So long as there is one man who seeks employment and cannot find it, the hours of labor are too long."[42]

But if all these new employees that were supposed to be hired, plus all the old ones that were to be retained, *produced only so much as before,* wouldn't the cost of production shoot through the roof? Wouldn't that entail higher prices, lower output, lower profit, and greater unemployment? Not so. Eight-hour theorists reasoned that all new employees, along with the old ones, would now possess collectively a vastly larger reservoir of purchasing power. Employers would be eager to satisfy this huge market by increasing, not decreasing, the volume of production. And, since the "cost of making an article depends almost entirely on the number manufactured", costs and prices would decline.[43]

Mass consumption, in other words, causes mass production—but not the other way around (because, under competition, wages are kept down and markets remain too narrow or shallow to capture the economies of volume production). McNeill tied the whole doctrine up neatly in four simple propositions. "The demand determines the amount, the market determines the demand, the condition of the people determines the market, and the rate of wages determines the condition of the people."[44]

The larger volume of production in the economy cannot, it is true, be supported by the original capital stock. But urged on by the promise of markets, higher wages stimulate, cause, and permit manufacturers to profitably introduce more and better machinery. Not only 'will the opportunity lead them to do so, production costs will force them to do so, since

> the great pressure felt in the industrial world by the sudden arrest of the volume of production and its increased cost as a consequence of the reduction of time stimulates a thousand minds to overcome the difficulty by labor-saving inventions and devices.

Moreover, "greater managerial capacities are also brought into play, and the labor forces are organized and directed with greater efficiency and economy."[45]

The trade union theory does incorporate an efficiency effect of higher wages. It is not *workers* who become more efficient, but *employers* who are forced to become more efficient. "Labor-saving machinery," George McNeill explained in 1886,

> is never introduced until it pays; and it never pays until wages have advanced to that point that it is cheaper to have the work performed by machinery than by hand. High wages, then, invite more and more machinery, demand more and more goods, call for more rapid production, *lessen profits, and increase the purchasing power of labor.*[46]

Forty years (and a thousand articles, speeches, and strikes) later, the progressive economist Sumner Slichter revealed that this was indeed the "secret of higher wages":

the American people owe the unions a vote of thanks for striking or threatening to strike against wage cuts and thus forcing managements to make industry more effective.

Or as President Franklin Roosevelt explained the rationale behind his recovery program in 1933:

> [t]he idea is simply for employers to hire more men to do the existing work by reducing the work-hours of each man's week and at the same time paying a living wage for the shorter week....
> I am fully aware that wage increases will eventually raise costs, but I ask that managements give first consideration to the improvement of operating figures by greatly increased sales to be expected from the rising purchasing power of the public....[47]

The Two Theories Compared

Many American progressives in the early 20th century regarded the rationalization of industrial production through 'Scientific Management' techniques as a panacea for the social ills of industry. They had a hard time convincing trade union leaders that the sought-after efficiencies were anything more than a disguised 'speed up'. Just so: from the unionist point of view—always with at least one eye on its members' jobs—that is exactly what it was! The inconsistency between the two 'economy of high wages' theories is plainly that if laborers work harder, faster, or more efficiently as is predicted in the former, none of the employment effects hoped for in the latter will take place.

Nevertheless, the advocates of both schools agreed on one vital policy issue: the antisocial nature of wage reductions. Reformers who assumed there was a direct, functional relationship between wages and efficiency feared wage cutting because of its alleged effects on workers' productivity. Trade union theorists rejected wage cutting because of its alleged effects on the number of jobs. The "only possible result" of wage cutting, as one union spokesman put it in 1924, "is to further reduce the purchasing power of wage-earners" as a whole. But as "wage-earners compose a very large part of the whole public, consumption is thus further reduced and the market for goods" will be "made smaller," and this will be followed by still more unemployment.[48] All the progressive, unionist, and socialist underconsumptionists agreed. By the 1920s, many otherwise conservative economists were willing to concede the point. On the eve of the New

Deal, the lack-of-purchasing-power theory of unemployment had become the conventional wisdom.[49]

The Middle of the Road?

The economy of high wages, as interventionist intellectuals and as trade union theorists envisioned it, was a 'middle of the road' way of surmounting what they believed would otherwise be an intractable class struggle between labor and capital. Among trade union theorists, however, this led to a certain fuzziness in their rhetoric.

Ira Steward clearly hoped that the eight-hour system would be the first step in the *abolition* of "the capitalist, as we now understand him," although it would establish "in the good time coming" a utopia where "every man will be a capitalist" as a member of a cooperatively-owned industry, financed through the workers' greater savings. But would the increased wages resulting from a reduction in hours be paid for by the current *profits* of the employing class? It would not. Steward claimed that higher wages would come "practically, at the expense of no one," since "much of the increase is to fall upon the wastes of society," through elimination of inefficiency.[50] A milder social revolution would be hard to imagine, for it would take place without confiscation or redistribution.

McNeill, on the other hand, hoped that a reduction in hours and the accompanying increase in laborers' wages through the introduction of a true mass production/mass consumption economy *would* diminish "the profits upon his labor now obtained by the employer and middle-man."[51] He did not explain how or why. The 'economy of high wages' presumably entailed larger markets for employers' output; and even if the rate of profit per unit of output were reduced, this has no necessary implication for the total *amount* of profits earned by the employer (or by all employers in the aggregate), or for the *share* of national income as between profits and wages. On the face of it, the system sounds like the best thing that could happen—for businessmen. So while McNeill and others hoped that the higher wages would be a step toward the abolition of the wages system, the eight-hour system, assuming it worked the way they thought it would, might very well entrench capitalism even more deeply.

George Gunton welcomed this outcome. "The poverty of the laborer," Gunton wrote, "is not due to the inequitable distribution of the present wealth, but to the fact that the aggregate wealth produced is too small." True social reform involves not abolition of rent or profit, but an increase in "aggregate wealth per capita." The spread of mass production would concentrate capital in the hands of a smaller capitalist class, but it would at the same time increase the "consumable wealth" of the masses. *"[A]ll classes would become actually richer."* He claimed that

> [t]he laborer would get more wealth through his increased wages—the general consumer would obtain more through lower prices—and the manufacturer, while receiving a smaller per cent of the total product in profits, will actually obtain a greater quantity of wealth through the larger productions and extended business.

In other words, while a smaller percent of the national wealth "will go for profit," the number of those who live by profit will decrease even faster, so that "the capitalists" would become "both absolutely and relatively richer and relatively fewer in number."[52]

Was it not true, Gunton argued, that in "those industries where trade unions are best organized and exercise the greatest influence, strikes are fewest, wages are highest, hours of labor are shorter, and the relations between workers and employers most confidential and harmonious"? Didn't this fact alone prove that despite "all their defects," unions "have ever been real benefactors, *not only to their own members and the wage class, but to society*" as a whole? Gunton insisted that this was true. Unions were the saviors of capitalism; they had "really saved society from socialism." By "persistently forcing industrial reform they have prevented revolutions." The essence of Gunton's political economy was summarized in the following resonant statement of 1893:

> Organized capital is the means by which improved methods of production are developed and profits created, and labor organizations are the only economic power that laborers can employ to force capital to share this profit with the wage-workers.[53]

Approaching Industrial Democracy: Arbitration

Progressive economic reformers were similarly moved by a vision of unions as conservators of a new, regulated and 'humanized' capitalism. While the search for a proper mixture of legislative regulation and autonomous collective bargaining occupied the minds of industrial democrats for the better part of the next half-century, two possibilities sketched out as early as the 1880s are worth exploring here, insofar as they point to changes which eventually emerged in the 1930s. The first was 'arbitration'; the second was a corporativist scheme that the economist Henry Carter Adams called "industrial federation."[54]

Arbitration became popular after the great railroad strikes of the late

1870s, when urbanizing Americans were forced to confront for the first time the consequences of a disruption in the transportation system that now brought them the food they ate. In response to this menace, many states established arbitration boards, courts, and panels in the 1880s. Later in the 1890s, after the famous Pullman Boycott, Congress established an arbitration mechanism by the Erdman Act (1898) (discussed in chapter eight *infra*.)[55]

Nevertheless, arbitration systems always seemed to fall short of their proponents' hopes. In the first place, though American trade union leaders in the 1870s and 1880s typically endorsed 'voluntary' or 'legalized' arbitration, what they really had in mind was collective bargaining: direct, bilateral negotiations between employers and unions. They hardly ever endorsed a scheme whereby some allegedly neutral third party *decided* the rate of wages; and they almost *never* accepted the idea of giving a court of law the power to *enforce* a wage award, since that meant granting courts the right to limit strikes.[56]

If the leaders of organized labor were very wary of arbitration, employers were outspokenly (though not unanimously) against it. "There is nothing to arbitrate!" was their now-immortal cry.[57]

Of course, what they meant was that they would not *negotiate* or bargain collectively with unions. This policy, Richard Ely contended in an important essay published in the prestigious *North American Review* in 1886, was immoral, hypocritical, and incomprehensible. There "is no hope of a reign of peace in the United States," he claimed, until employers grant to unions *"full and free recognition,"* negotiate with them, and, if negotiations fail, submit to arbitration. Their current failure to do so, according to Ely, was due to employers' "[p]ride and arrogance," and their "failure to understand the true nature of labor organizations." The employers' pride and arrogance were demonstrated when "every attempt" on the union's part "to regulate the conditions of service" was denounced as "dictation."[58]

Businessmen, Ely wrote, insisted on their right to establish a price for the commodities they sold. They should not hypocritically deny the equal rights of workers to do so. How could they "overlook" the consideration that suppliers of labor had as perfect a right to say, "'under such and such conditions we will supply our commodity and under no others', as sellers of wheat have to name the terms of sale" to a miller? Why won't businessmen "receive any body of men who may represent labor just as courteously as [they] would any committee of men who desire to negotiate for the sale of other commodities, like iron or lumber"?[59]

Ely's assertion that businessmen's "pride and arrogance" explained their refusal to negotiate with unions is questionable, as is his claim that they didn't "understand the true nature of labor organizations." Perhaps these employers were dead set against "full and free recognition" and "arbitration" because they understood unions only too well. A businessman who recognizes the right of a supplier to name the terms of sale also reserves the right to refuse these terms and look elsewhere for alternative suppliers, and he expects the supplier to recognize his right to do so. But this is what unions did not generally concede. As far as the latter were concerned, recognition conferred perpetual bargaining rights to a particular organization.

A few years later, George Gunton, no enemy of the unions, explained this attitude with more candor than had Ely. "Experience," Gunton wrote, "has proved that to prevent others from taking strikers' places is an essential feature of the strike itself." The economic individualist might contend

> that when laborers go on strike they have given up their position and have no more claim to consideration than have total strangers. Therefore, their places are as absolutely at the disposal of their employers and open to new laborers as if each laborer had left individually and found work elsewhere.

Nevertheless, unionized workers who strike do not believe they have "severed all connections with the firm." They regard their action as "only a temporary cessation of work" that "creates no permanent vacancy." Gunton added that, from the union point of view, employers or non-striking workers who "absolutely refuse to recognize this view of their position" *are in essence denying that workers have the right to organize.* It is they, who deny the right of organized workers to exclude the unorganized from employment, who are guilty of "endangering the stability of society," and not the unions.[60]

Ely also ignored another problem. Unions would not accept, without a strike, any arbitration decision that *cut* their wages. Suppose, as the rising young labor leader Samuel Gompers testified before the Blair Committee of the United States Senate in 1885, arbitrators grant a wage reduction to a manufacturer who really needed it to compete with his fellow employers. "[E]ven though it" might appear to be fair, "if the workingmen in that case submit to the decision it will mean a general reduction of wages throughout the entire industry." This, Gompers insisted, was *unfair,* and could never be abided. Fair arbitration, "out of regard to the honest manufacturer and the laborer," would deny the claim. Indeed, any manufacturer who tried it "ought to be crushed out of existence."[61]

Approaching Industrial Democracy: 'Industrial Federation' as the Road to Industrial Peace

Arbitration, Henry Carter Adams contended in 1886, "is the machinery by means of which responsibilities may be *imposed* upon the legal proprietors of the world's capital." It was not, in his judgment, "the missing coupling between Labor and Capital, but is the . . . first step toward the overthrow of the wages system." For this reason alone, Adams concluded that "[w]orking-men are right in demanding it; employers also, if they judge wholly from the standpoint of their personal interests, are logical and clear-headed in opposing it." But achievement of industrial democracy and the end of the labor problem would require a new social form, which he called "industrial federation." This meant, to Adams, a corporative *integration* or partnership between organized labor and organized capital based on the recognition and protection of laborers' right to organize, and on what we would today call an explicit property right in their jobs. Adams's analysis of the labor problem, and his proposals to solve it, were seminal ones in the history of industrial democratic theory in America— anticipating some of the key assumptions of the Wagner Act by almost half a century.[62]

"The fundamental principle in the theory of Anglo-Saxon liberty," Adams wrote, "is, that the fruits of liberty can be reaped by him alone who has a voice in determining the conditions under which he lives." This was, in the last analysis, the "defense of popular government" and the basis for private property.[63]

When the great American and French political revolutions were fought in the late 18th century, democratic self-government was compatible with a policy of economic liberty because, in an age where "industries were numerous and small" and workmen themselves owned the tools of production, each could aspire to be his own boss. According to Adams, this was the "unexpressed premise" of Adam Smith's theory of "industrial individualism," the system of natural liberty. But the industrial revolution radically changed the situation. Democracy was no longer compatible with an unlimited "personal right to acquire property." Capital had been concentrated in a narrow class of men, while the majority had been relegated to a permanent, subordinate status as wage earners. History had brought forth a new kind of arbitrary, irresponsible power, since he "who controls capital controls men."[64]

But there is "no more reason for granting irresponsible control over this, the greatest social force of the day, than for permitting irresponsible control over the exercise of coercive powers of government." According to to Adams, capital, like all property, is a "social product." The "use of this social product should be granted to individuals only on conditions of strict responsibility to society." Democracy demands the social control of business; and society

> cannot hope for quiet and peace until the industrial organization is brought under the guidance of the same principle of control to which the religious and political interests of men have already been subjected.[65]

"Viewed historically," Adams concluded, "the labor movement of the present day must be considered as a step in the further development of individual rights," in essence a 'new individualism'. What is needed to resolve the conflict between capital and labor is the "further development of property rights" congruent with the needs of modern society—the right of workers to property in their jobs. What is implicit in the strike must be henceforth recognized as the foundation for public policy; what "workmen demand is such an organization of the industries to which they give their time that certain rights shall be granted to them, even though they are not proprietors," in the sense that those who invest money are.[66]

A worker's virtual property right in his job, according to Adams, is the mechanism whereby he could obtain job security. When men are granted "tenure of employment" and can no longer be dismissed by their employers for any reason, as they could be under the common law, "they may be said to be in the enjoyment of an *industrial home.*" Similarly, "if men are promoted from the ranks [that is, according to civil service rules] they may be said to have a vested interest in their industry."[67]

Even more importantly, Adams's reforms, which rest implicitly on a notion of job ownership, would entitle workers to claim a share in the decision making power at their place of employment analogous to that of an owner of stock. As Adams put it,

> if employees are consulted whether hours of work or the number of employed shall be reduced, . . . and if all these claims—as well as others naturally implied by them—should be so well established that an infringement on either side may be taken into the courts, the practical meaning of proprietorship in productive agencies will be radically changed . . .

The result will be "Industrial Federation," a kind of corporative reconstruction of the economy where private ownership of the means of production will still exist nominally, but where "proprietorship," that is *control*, will be shared by "employers and employe[e]s" who "are all to be found in the same organization."[68]

Adams apparently believed that the introduction of this democratic principle into American industry did not require "constitutional change, or a statutory enactment," but either could or should evolve through "common law development." The articulation or "clarification" of a worker's property right in his job "will take place through the evolution of collective bargaining and the formal labor contract." Each collective agreement will establish basic wages, "secure to each worker an industrial home," and "provide for a board of arbitration in each industry." This board, staffed with representatives of the union and of the employer, will be the source of industrial law. The individual worker's rights will arise from, and be construed and applied by, that collective body;

> it is likely that the by-laws of this court of arbitration and the decision which it renders upon such questions as are presented to it, will through a process of natural selection eventually come to be a common law of labor rights.

These rules, in turn, will be "so well established that infringement on either side may be taken into the courts" for enforcement.[69]

Industrial federation was the answer to the class conflict and industrial strife that were inevitable under the individualistic system. Presently, Adams claimed, the

> great body of workmen . . . have no property, privilege, or advantage that they can place in jeopardy as a pledge for the fulfillment of a labor contract, from which it follows that labor contracts, on one side at least, are bereft of responsibility, and consequently incapable of enforcement by the orderly proce- dure of English jurisprudence.

It was this fact which explained "the reckless manner in which workmen frequently urge their claims; and second, of the tendency on the part of employers to appeal to force." Workers have nothing to lose; employers have nothing else with which they can "appeal for the restraint of propertyless men."[70]

Collective bargaining and collective agreements would bring about industrial peace, by making the worker a "responsible person in the world of contracts," interested in the "orderly administration of industry." "Every contract, to be effective," Adams explained,

> must state or imply not alone the advantages to be secured by the consummation of the agreement, but also the nature and extent, of the loss to be sustained or reparation to be made, in case the agreement is not carried out . . . [the] exacting of the penalty recognized in the contract, (either expressly stated, or implied in the common law under which the contract is drawn) and voluntarily assumed by both parties to the agreement . . . is the means by which responsibility is brought to the support of voluntary association.

Provided that "the conditions are such that the compelling force of responsibility works in the same manner for both parties to the contract," that is, for laborers as well as for capitalists, Adams declared that socialism would not be necessary.[71]

In sum, Adams proposed to reconstruct the legal basis of capitalism along what would amount to corporativist lines. He would "require that employers . . . recognize unions and deal with the men in a body" and "be willing to submit all matters of internal organization to arbitration." The "men already employed in industry should have preference over men outside; and what is perhaps of most importance, all these should come to the workingmen as their right, and not by the grace of employers."[72]

Commentary: The Problems of Industrial Democracy

Ideas like arbitration or industrial federation appealed to intellectuals committed to the reconstruction of capitalism, and took their place alongside other *fin de siècle* visions of industrial democracy, like state socialism—as espoused by Edward Bellamy, Henry Demarest Lloyd, Laurence Gronlund, *et al.* In fact, there was a fairly widespread movement around the turn of the 20th century and thereafter quite favorable to corporativism, guild socialism, and other so-called "pluralist" schemes. These intellectual currents, discussed in the next two chapters, arose in Europe before they spread to America, and affected the labor relations systems of other industrialized nations before they did our own.

American reformers who sought to escape what they felt were the unfair shackles of the common law of employment (under which an employer could dismiss an employee at will for any reason, or for no reason) also proposed to grant workers a 'legal dismissal wage', regardless of union affiliation. This concept, which is embodied in the laws of many European countries (and has greatly increased in popularity in America in recent years) would extend to the individual worker, in the words of the sociologist Franklin Giddings, a right to "reasonable notice of impending dismissal . . . proportionate to the length of faithful service." If the notice was not given, "the employee should be entitled to a money damage"; if the worker failed to give notice, his "property right should be forfeited."[73]

Many criticized the notion that workers should be granted a property right in their jobs, whether directly by legislation, or indirectly, by forcing employers to 'recognize' unions. If employers are going to yield their common law right to fire employees summarily, will employees—can employees—yield their right to quit at any time? Do they automatically yield their 'right to strike'? And if the answer to these questions is negative, *why* would arbitration or collective contracts make the worker (or the union) a "responsible person in the world of contracts"?

"There is no power in the State to compel the performance of work under the terms of an [arbitration] award without recourse to practical confiscation and absolute slavery," Joseph Weeks, the foremost American authority on English and European arbitration systems, explained. In "the realm of labor to a degree unknown elsewhere, government exists only by the consent of the governed."[74] In most cases, as Professor R. H. Thurston of Cornell correctly observed in a rejoinder to Henry Carter Adams, "the proprietor has much to risk" by arbitration, "the employee little; the former must abide by the decision, usually; the latter, if not thoroughly honest, walks off if not suited."[75] Practically speaking, arbitration only bound employers. But even there it was defective, since employers could rearrange the size of their workforce and thus practically nullify the award, and the property in a job, that arbitration sought to preserve—at least for all the workers.

The legal dismissal wage concept suffered from a similar infirmity. Henry Farnham, a reformist professor of political economy at Yale, pointed out that it was a bootless method of making the laborers responsible; the laborers under Giddings's scheme didn't sacrifice anything real; they suffered no positive penalty. George Gunton added that, according to his experience with labor relations in America and his knowledge of England, the introduction of a time notice before a worker could quit—backed up, for instance, by the employer's right to withhold wages due—was usually resisted by workers, whether they were members of unions or not. The facts were that the "wage classes in general would rather take the risk of summary dismissal than forfeit the right of leaving their employment immediately when dissatisfied," or if organized, their right to strike.[76]

C. S. Walker, another reform-minded professor, proposed that employers be able to collect money damages from the "trades-union to which the laborer belongs," perhaps from a "trust fund," as a way of making Adams's concept of industrial federation work. The union, in that case, would become "a corporation furnishing labor . . . with the corporation requiring labor, pledging its fund in case of a breach of contract on its part or on the part of one of its members."[77] The concept was an intriguing one, and it would return again in later years. But it logically required unions to incorporate—a condition which, as will be discussed in chapter eight, both American and English unions mightily resisted.

There was another, related problem with Adams's version of industrial democracy, only dimly grasped during the years he espoused it. His idea of a property right in a job appears to rest on an individual worker's investment of time and skill. But the property right itself is defined and enforced by a union. This introduces a mare's-nest of tricky yet profoundly important questions. What is to be the legal relationship between the union member and his organization, or between union and employer? Should an individual worker be able to sue the union for failing to discharge its function of protecting his job property right? Adams didn't say. Should the employer, or indeed the union, be able to sue the employee for failing to live up to his end of the bargain, say by engaging in a wildcat strike? Adams didn't say. Should the employer or the arbitration court be able to sue the union for calling an unauthorized strike? What is one to make of a jurisdictional strike, where one labor organization forces an employer to dismiss other *organized* (or unorganized) laborers? What has become of the dismissed workers' job rights? What about a strike to establish a closed shop that entails dismissing nonunion employees? What about striking workers who prevent nonstriking workers—not 'scabs'—from exercising their right to work? Whose job property rights have precedence, and why? Adams didn't say.

Commentary: Regulating the Plane of Competition

The concept of majority versus minority rule, of freedom versus coercion in the marketplace, was the basic complaint social and economic reformers leveled against the competitive system. Quite apart from its implications for labor relations, one can see in this version of economic democracy the seeds not only of the National Recovery Administration (NRA) during the early New Deal, but the rationale for a great deal of contemporary regulation of industries and professions by state or federal agencies reflecting the 'wish of the majority in some practical law'—beginning, as some have argued, with the Interstate Commerce Commission, the nation's first federal regulatory agency (of which Henry Carter Adams was the first statistician). Unfortunately, the performance of these industrial-democracy-as-businessmen's-cartels has not lived up to its advance billing. Higher prices, lower output, reduced quality and indifferent service—all of the classic complaints of *unaccountability* raised against monopolies—have come to haunt the modern regulatory/administrative economy.

The reason may well lie in the appropriateness of the famous 'twentieth man' theory. Ely, Adams, and the rest of the progressive economists fundamentally misconceived the problem. Competition is not a matter of a coercive minority rule *by producers*. It is a system of democracy, of majority rule, of 'coercion', if you will, *by consumers*. As the economist John Maurice Clark pointed out in the 1920s, ironically before the advent of New Deal type regulation of the plane of competition,

> it would be truer to say that the consuming public can use one man out of twenty to coerce the other nineteen. The one man cannot coerce the others unless he has the consumers behind him. If competition did not exercise this kind of coercion, it would never reduce prices, weed out inefficient producers, and apply the spur of ruthless necessity to the others, all for the benefit of the public. In fact, if competition followed the will of the majority of the trade—phrase of speciously democratic sound—it would not be competition, but monopoly. Rule by the majority in a trade is precisely the thing the public is most anxious to prevent.[78]

The twentieth man willing to work a fourteen hour day does so not for a temporary advantage, but because he needs the pay; and, given his own needs and the other opportunities in the market, this is the best deal. On the other hand, the ability of the employer to get and keep a labor force willing to work those hours would reflect the conditions prevailing in the labor market generally, and not his using the twentieth man as a stick to beat the rest into line. Ely's melodramatic presentation notwithstanding, the fourteen hour day (which, incidentally, had mostly disappeared outside of some agricultural employment, without benefit of unions or factory legislation) would, in the instance he outlined, simply be the going rate.

Commentary: Do Higher Wages Make Employees More Efficient?

The various "economy of high wages" theories developed in the last decades of the 19th century by progressive intellectuals and trade union leaders were bulwarks for 20th century economic and social reform efforts, both in the area of collective labor relations, but also for the restructuring of labor markets by the state directly. For that matter, they are still widely held among the educated public. Nevertheless, there are many problems with these ideas.

There probably is some relationship between wages and the motivation of employees to work harder or more efficiently. The difficulty is that one cannot get a one-to-one correspondence. It would be nice if the relationship were functional; for, as the economist Nikolaas Pierson aptly remarked years ago, if "it were an established fact that the raising of wages was always and unconditionally a means of proportionally raising the quantity and quality of labour performed, then the social problem would, to a great extent, be solved." Alas, life isn't quite so easy; does anyone believe that, if wages were increased 50-fold tomorrow, productivity would increase to match?[79]

The neoclassical economist Alfred Marshall agreed with Francis Walker's claim that the tendency to lower wages was cumulative and self-reinforcing because of an efficiency effect, but he did not feel that a correlation between wages and industrial efficiency at the margin of subsistence could be extrapolated across the entire range of incomes. In his judgment, there were

> many trades in which a reduction of the hours of labour would certainly lessen the output in the immediate present, and would not certainly bring about at at all quickly any such increase of efficiency as would raise the average wage per head up to the old level.

And in these cases, "the resulting material loss would fall on the workers whose hours of labor were diminished."[80]

One of Marshall's younger colleagues guessed (and his guess has the ring of intuitive, if not demonstrable, truth) that the "higher the wages, and the higher the standard of comfort, the more uncertain does it become that the standard of efficiency will rise with every rise of wages, however slight, and rise correspondingly." At any rate, the 'empirical' studies which point to a correlation of high (or rising) wages and output even in the absence of a discernable improvement in capital stock, and conclude thereby that workers have become more efficient, prove nothing. Brentano, for instance, claimed that the increased wages in certain German mining districts had caused greater output. Looking over the same evidence, Davidson observed how the

> causal connection, in this instance, is almost surely from production to wages. Prices rose and the mine-owners and other employers, naturally desiring to take full advantage of the price rise, endeavored to increase their output. The employees were aware that prices were rising and demanded their share; and the employers, rather than face labor troubles at such a time, yielded their demand, being willing to sacrifice a part of the increased profit rather than lose the whole.[81]

Commentary: Do Higher Wages Make Employers More Efficient?

The key to the trade union version of the economy of high wages is what has come to be known as the 'shock theory': the pressure of higher production costs forces employers to become more efficient and introduce more and better machinery. Then they employ a greater number of workers at a higher rate of pay; this is what defines the mass production/mass consumption economy.

This notion became quite popular around World War I, particularly among those who, like Louis Brandeis, had long regarded "bigness" in business as a "curse" on the economy, a cause of generally inefficient and slothful management practices.[82] The economist Paul H. Douglas, for instance, hypothesized that higher wage rates imposed on them by an effective, industry-wide union (or the state) "might increase the efficiency of industry by transferring labor from poorly managed to better managed plants." (Although the implication here was probably even further concentration within the industry.)[83]

The kernel of truth in the shock theory is that the pressure of necessity from any quarter in the economy compels individuals to adjust to new conditions. But in general, the trade union theorists and their progressive followers who espoused the 'shock theory' committed a subtle yet grave error. They confused the *substitution,* that is, the *reallocation,* of capital from one sector to another as a result of higher factor prices in a given industry, with *net additions* to the stock of capital in the economy. Only the *latter* represents a pure social gain. If one industry, because of higher labor costs, now has to add to its capital stock by bidding capital away from another use elsewhere, that fact does not by itself imply any increase in the productivity of the economy *as a whole* (and probably implies a decline in overall productivity and output).[84]

On a related point, let us reconsider Gunton's claim (which has now become something of a cliché) to the effect that unions are the best thing that ever happened to capitalism. It may well have been true (as it still is generally true) that organized laborers are among the most highly paid, and among 'the most productive'. But there is considerably less here than meets the eye. Labor productivity is simply a measure that results from dividing output by input (in physical or value terms); it implies nothing about how hard workers work, or how skillfully. If higher wage rates result in the substitution of capital for labor, the 'productivity' of those who remain will, all other things being equal, increase. What about productivity elsewhere, in industries that now have access to less credit for capital improvement but more workers? Where industries employ organized workers whose skills are scarce, it is the scarcity of their skills that accounts for the height of their wages in relation to the average, and not *per se* the fact that they are organized, although being not-easily-replaceable certainly makes it easier for them to organize and stay organized. Similarly, unionized workers of no special skills in highly productive and profitable (including relatively less-competitive) industries may for *that* very reason enjoy relatively higher wages than elsewhere. (On the other hand, garment workers have been organized for decades, but their wages are fairly modest, even less than in many unorganized sectors of the economy, and certainly less than their brothers in steel or automobiles.) The ability of unions to capitalize, so to speak, on an already favorable supply and demand situation to extract even higher wages through cartel action may make them benefactors to their own members—at least some or most of them, for a longer or shorter time. It does not make them benefactors to wage earners as a whole.

The whole trade union approach ignores entirely the incentives for specific employers faced with higher unit labor costs, not to add to capital and maintain, or even increase employment, but to use capital to substitute for labor. Similarly, the 'purchasing power' argument *against* wage cutting assumes that the demand for labor in general is always inelastic—that reducing wage rates will never result in a proportional increase in employment. In other words, cutting wage rates will always reduce total wage payrolls and hence total purchasing power; or, in still other words, increasing wage rates, say by minimum wage legislation, will not result in net unemployment.

It is difficult, even impossible, to believe that these relations hold generally. One outstanding progressive economist, Paul H. Douglas, attempted to test the proposition about the inelasticity of the demand for labor empirically. In his landmark treatise, Douglas found that, should wages be "pushed up above the point of marginal productivity, the decrease in employment would normally be from three to four times as great as the increase in hourly rates," and that "it appears almost certain that . . . the total amount paid out in wages would . . . be less than before."[85] The irony here is that this work, hailed by economists throughout the Western world, appeared just as Western governments were implementing labor policies whose assumptions about wages and purchasing power conflicted radically with Douglas's conclusions.

Commentary: Are Competitive Wages Just?

The essential problem with all of the 'economy of high wages' theories was the same problem that plagued the critics of the wages fund who defended the 'theory of collective bargaining': an unwillingness to face the fact that employers, however vulnerable to higher costs in the short run, will eventually be able to adjust to new conditions. As Alfred Marshall explained, businessmen will always seek to arrange or rearrange the

factors of production (in the aggregate, and at the margin) in the direction
of the least costly methods in response to relative changes in factor prices.
Employers, he wrote,

> estimate the *net product* (that is the net increase of the money
> value of their total output after allowing for incidental expenses)
> that will be got by a little more outlay in this direction, or a little
> more outlay in that; and if they can gain by shifting a little of their
> outlay from one direction to another, they will do so.[86]

This process of substitution within a firm or industry, and across many
industries (over time), implies that the volume of employed labor is
indeed responsive to fluctuations in price. Like consumers, employers will
ultimately pay for something only what it is worth to them. In the case of a
worker's services, the price of a unit of a given type of labor tends to equal
its 'marginal product', defined as the value of its physical contribution to
output.

This 'marginal productivity theory of wages' evolved in the last decades
of the 19th century to supersede the wages fund concept, and it is the
theory of wages generally accepted by economists today.[87]

Economists explained the idea behind this theory by noting that with a
given supply of capital equipment, a point of diminishing returns eventually arrives where each additional laborer hired increases the total
product, but by a smaller amount than the last laborer did (added to the
previously smaller workforce). Even so, an employer will continue to hire
(demand) additional laborers just so long as the value of their output
exceeds the wage rate he must pay them. As Marshall put it, he
"endeavours to employ each agent up to that margin at which its net
product would no longer exceed the price he would have to pay for it."[88]
But the "product of the 'final'," or marginal, "'unit' of labor," as John Bates
Clark explained, "is the same as that of *every unit* separately considered."
In other words, each laborer of a given type is essentially interchangeable;
and thus the wage rate of the 'final', or 'marginal', laborer sets the standard
of pay for *all* of them.[89]

This process occurs across the economy as a whole, so that the "wages
of every class of labour tends to equal the net product due to the additional
labour of the marginal labourer of that class."[90] Should the wage rate drop
below the marginal product, the demand for labor will increase, since
employers will profit by bidding wages up and laborers away from other
pursuits (or from idleness); and should the wage rate rise above the
marginal product employers will discharge part of their workforce (and/or
adjust their capital), in order to bring the cost per unit of input in line with
its value. It thus follows, as John Bates Clark put it, that "if normal," that is,
competitive, "tendencies could work in perfection, it would be true not
only of each unit," that is, each laborer, "but of the working force as a
whole, that its product and its pay are identical."[91]

The author of these words attached a great deal of meaning to them. John Bates Clark began his scholarly career as an opponent of competitive capitalism, agreeing with his colleagues and contemporaries—men such as Richard Ely and Henry Carter Adams—that individual wage bargaining was unjust. But he re-evaluated a great deal of what he had earlier learned and taught, and underwent a major intellectual transformation in the later 1880s and 1890s. By the end of the 1890s, Clark emerged as an outspoken defender of the competitive system—more outspoken than his fellow neoclassical theorist Alfred Marshall.[92] As far as Clark was concerned, the marginal productivity theory of wages essentially demonstrated that laborers *did* receive the 'whole product' of their labor.

The common "indictment that hangs over society," Clark wrote in the opening pages of his internationally renowned treatise, *The Distribution of Wealth* (1899), "is that of 'exploiting labor'." "Workmen," claimed the radicals and reformers alike, "'are regularly robbed of what they produce. This is done within the forms of law, and by the natural working of competition'." But the marginal productivity principle demonstrates that workers *do* tend to get wages equal to the value of *their* contribution to the final output, regardless of their individual bargaining power or lack thereof. "However wages may be adjusted by bargains freely made between individual men," Clark wrote on the very first page of his treatise, "the rates of pay that result from such transactions tend . . . to equal that part of the product of industry which is traceable to the labor itself." Workers are *not* robbed, under competition, of the fruit of their labor: free bargains *are* fair bargains. The wages system does not exploit labor.[93]

Clark did not claim that competition was in fact anywhere 'perfect' or 'ideal'. But imperfect competition in the real world did not invalidate the general principle. "With an ideally complete and free competitive system," he claimed, "each unit of labor can get exactly what a final unit produces." But even with "an imperfect competition, it still *tends* to get that amount." That there were "opportunities for fraud in the distribution of wealth" Clark freely admitted; but they are "not the result of competition. The tendency of competitive forces is to repress" them.[94]

To realize just how fundamental a challenge he was posing to the theoreticians of industrial democracy, one might ask whether Clark was *seriously* claiming that the penniless, unskilled, immigrant laborer bargained equally with a mighty corporate behemoth such as United States Steel. Essentially, his answer would be *yes*—and for the same reason that an individual consumer "bargains equally" with Sears, Roebuck, & Co. In neither case did the laborer or the consumer actually 'haggle' or negotiate over price. But as long as there were competing employers or retailers, the individual, unorganized laborer or consumer had no *a priori* grounds for believing that he was being exploited. The fact that a corporation was large, even massive, did not imply that it possessed monopoly power. But even if the firm was a monopolist, it did not follow that it was a monopsonist (sole buyer) in the market for the type of labor it hired. As Clark explained, wages

> depend on the value that the final unit of labor can create *in the general system of affiliated industry*. If one industry were a complete monopoly it could not force wages below the rate fixed by the final productivity of labor in other industries. If one corporation owned every woolen mill in the world, while other industries were in the hands of separate and competing owners, the rate of pay in the monopolized industry would conform to the final productivity of labor in the others. This inter-groupal equalization of earnings is the thing that is of most importance to preserve.[95]

Business monopoly, of course, depresses wages. But it depresses the real wages of workers in their capacity as workers and consumers elsewhere in the economy through the misallocation of resources (*viz.,* less output, at a higher price). *The same is true of labor monopoly.* And its

> effect would differ from monopoly on the side of capital only in the fact that a favored class of laborers would get the benefit of the policy. This class would create a monopolistic gain and absorb it for itself, while all other laborers would pay tribute.

A monopoly of laborers was not a countervailing force to a monopolistic employer; it did not correct the problem, but exacerbated it.[96]

"Strikes now rely, in part," Clark observed, on a violent limitation of the labor supply. "They terrorize non-union men"; as far as Clark was concerned, this

> is so obviously intolerable that not a word should here be wasted in demonstrating what, in this connection, is the duty of the state. That would scarcely be a government at all that should refuse to exert its power in protecting men in their right to work.[97]

Contemporaneously, the English economist Philip Wicksteed explained that if striking workers had to prevent others from taking their place, that proved that the men who went out were *wrong* in believing that their wages were unfair:

> the justification of a strike must be that there are not a sufficient body of persons able and willing to do the work demanded at the wage offered. If the employers can find competent workers who will accept the wage they offer, that is an indication that, should the claims of the strikers be met, these others, able and willing to do the work on certain terms, would be driven to alternatives less eligible to themselves.

Although it was not popular to say so, Wicksteed affirmed that the hatred of the blackleg [scab], however natural, has no social justification, and if ever a Union has to invoke public odium to assist it in defeating the blackleg, it seems to shew that its position is economically unsound.

It was possible that the employer's use of scab labor might be only "a mere bluff," to break a strike, and that he would eventually dismiss them to take back the old workers, since the scabs might really be "inferior workmen," not "worth their wages." But then again, "if the blacklegs are really doing the work, they are demonstrating that the Unionist claim is for a position of privilege and is antisocial."[98]

The development of neoclassical economists' marginal productivity theories of wages, particularly with the heavy ethical content John Bates Clark attached to it, elicited a strong response on the part of progressive reformers. Marginalism challenged their critique of individual wage contracting and virtually reaffirmed the conclusions of the old, discredited 'wages fund' regarding strikes. The publication of Clark's articles in the 1890s, and particularly the publication of his treatise, touched off a lively debate within the economics profession in the first decade of this century—a debate which in one form or another still lingers today. The objections to the marginal productivity theory of wages would themselves require a book to explain. But a few of the longer-lived ones, particularly those raised by John A. Hobson and John A. Ryan, are worth discussing, particularly since they illuminate the fundamentally different world views of the industrial democrats and the industrial individualists.[99]

Hobson led the attack on marginalism from a socialist perspective. He asserted that the concept of specific productivity is philosophically misleading. Production was a 'social process', and all factors of production were 'equally' necessary. Take away labor, and capital is valueless; take away capital, and labor is valueless. Even on its own terms, Hobson added, marginal analysis failed to prove that capitalist exchange eliminated exploitation and surplus value. Since all laborers in the workforce are paid the rate of wages corresponding to the last, or final, or marginal, worker, didn't that show that all the earlier ones were fleeced? "The marginal" laborer "alone receives in payment virtually its whole product," he argued in the pages of the American *Journal of Political Economy;* "each of the others yields a surplus receiving the same payment as the last, but affording a larger product."[100]

Yet, as Thomas Nixon Carver pointed out, it won't do to say that, because both labor and capital contribute to production, "there is no way of finding out what each factor contributes." Hobsonians might say that that "is like trying to find out . . . how much of the cutting is done by the upper and how much by the lower blade of the scissors." But to

use this comparison is to show that one does not understand the problem. If one blade of the scissors were a little longer than the other, it would not require any so-called metaphysical or theoretical reasoning to see that the scissors might be improved by lengthening the shorter blade. If two workmen were to offer their services, one to lengthen the longer blade and one to lengthen the shorter blade, it would not take much of a theoretician to decide which workman it would be better to hire. The workman who would lengthen the shorter blade would add somewhat more to the cutting power of the scissors than the workman who would lengthen the longer blade.[101]

Marginalism does not explain "which of the factors produces the product when all work together, but rather what would happen if a unit of any one were taken away."[102]

Nor was the claim that intra-marginal workers were exploited very persuasive, either, since John Bates Clark had himself raised and answered the objection in his treatise. The product of any, and every, 'unit' of labor—that is, every laborer of a specific type—is the functional equivalent of every other, which is why, by definition, each is paid the same, and all are paid the same, as the marginal one. The 'earlier' laborers are not 'deprived' of any 'surplus' they created, for *no surplus exists*. The smaller marginal product of a larger workforce is due to the lesser amount of capital (or 'poorer quality' of capital) available per unit of labor *the entire larger workforce must use,* just as the greater marginal product of a smaller workforce is due to the greater amount of capital (or 'better quality' of capital) available per unit of labor which *the entire smaller workforce must use.*[103]

John A. Ryan did not attack the validity of specific productivity on technical grounds, but he denied that it carried the ethical or social connotations Clark said it did. "Even if the marginal productivity of any group of laborers under free competition exactly measured their actual productivity," social justice, that is, socialist justice, demanded that one take "needs" as the "primary title of award, as of ownership in general." Ryan denied that social policy should aim at securing each laborer the right to the whole product of his labor, and he argued that it should instead aim at securing a "decent living wage" through arbitration or legislation, "if necessary, and insofar as practicable," by lowering "profits and [raising] prices."[104]

Most economists who replied to this latter contention confined themselves to pointing out that price or wage fixing is simply an inexpedient method of bettering the lot of the poor. What does it avail the poorest laborers if, instead of a very low wage, they are, because of a statute or a collective bargain, *not hired at all?*[105] Yet few challenged Ryan's concept of social justice; few asked why, if an individual who baked a loaf of bread did not have the moral right to eat it, some other individual, whose only attribute was that he *didn't* bake it, had a superior claim.

Toward Industrial Democracy

The socialist journalist Henry Demarest Lloyd was generally well-disposed toward Henry Carter Adams's corporativist ideas about industrial democracy, but he was convinced that the professor was wrong to believe that the reorganization of American life would not require "constitutional change, or a statutory enactment," but could arise through "common law development." Lloyd was convinced that the kind of reforms they both wanted would not come "without invoking the help of the state";[106] and Lloyd was surely right. For even a voluntary arbitration scheme for the nation's railroads, such as the one the United States Congress adopted through the Erdman Act of 1898, necessitated a serious inroad into the constitutionally protected common law right of employers to discriminate against union labor. Full-scale corporativism would be something else again; and it would be close to half a century before the reform ideas of the 1880s were translated into reality. In the meantime, industrial democracy was already evolving in England and Europe.

7. Imperium in Imperio: Pluralist Models of Industrial Democratic Reform

 Industrial democracy arrived in European countries and elsewhere years before it did in America, and it gave American progressives and trade union leaders a bank of experience which they assimilated for their own purposes. The labor reforms mandating democracy in industry abroad arose from the belief in class conflict between capital and labor developed in the 19th century by socialists, syndicalists, and others discussed in previous chapters. But the direction of the changes instituted in the early decades of the 20th century were also influenced by a powerful spirit of 'pluralism'.

Political pluralism now connotes an attitude or spirit of 'tolerance' toward 'diversity' in a democratic society. Its original significance in late 19th and early 20th century political thought was different, however. Pluralism was then an attitude or spirit of profound intolerance toward state power generally, though it was not favorable to the rights of individuals, but to the rights of groups. The pluralist antipathy toward state sovereignty cut across the usual right-left political lines. On the religious and secular right, pluralism meant belief in one kind or another of corporativism, in which the economy (and even society itself) would be reorganized into compulsory economic groups that would conduct economic affairs under the supervision of the state—that is, some kind of tripartite entente of government, business, and labor unions. It was meant to ameliorate or reduce class conflict. On the left, pluralism sought to eliminate the capitalist class and parcel out control of the economy between guilds or syndicates of workers and the state. But unlike the state socialists, whose vision of the economy resembled a bureaucracy (such as the post office) or even an army taking orders from the top, left-wing pluralists sought a more decentralized, participatory democracy for industry and for society that would involve a much greater degree of control and operation by organized workers themselves.

Pluralism: Right and Left

The late 19th and early 20th century German legal historian and juristic theorist Otto Gierke helped set the stage for pluralist industrial democratic reform, both in its right-wing (corporativist) and left-wing (guild socialist and syndicalist) versions. An opponent of the authoritarian, state-worshipping Hegelianism saturating German social and political philosophy, Gierke championed the autonomy of spontaneously formed social groups: towns, guilds, religious associations, and corporations. Social groups, according to Gierke, were not mere creatures of the state, but were *real entities* anterior to the state that existed apart from the individual members. These groups, according to Gierke's famous *Genossenschaftstheorie,* possessed "natural rights" which "the state is in duty bound to respect, and which therefore constitute a real limitation upon the sovereignty of the state."[1]

Gierke's view of the sovereign state as a usurper of group rights appealed to a remarkably wide audience in Europe and even in America. In his own Germany and nearby Austria, for instance, the *Genossenschaftstheorie* influenced big businessmen/intellectuals such as Walter Rathenau, as well as radical, pro-union social democrats like the jurists Hugo Preuss and Hugo Sinzheimer. And it fit in well with the corporativist ideas of such important social liberals as Lujo Brentano.[2]

In England, the *Genossenschaftstheorie* struck chords of sympathy among individualistic liberals such as Frederic Maitland (who saw merit in Gierke's recognition that corporations were creatures of free association and contract anterior to the state) as well as among Christian Socialists such as John Neville Figgis. Figgis introduced Gierke's 'group right' theories to some of the rising young stars of the left-wing guild socialist movements as well—especially to influential scholars and teachers such as G. D. H. Cole and R. H. Tawney.[3]

In France, the *Genossenschaftstheorie* encountered an intellectual milieu already hospitable to pluralism. Corporativism—the compulsory organization of guilds for all industries, trades, and professions—was already the ideal of many Christian Socialists in France who argued that it was the best and only viable solution to the menace of 'atheistic' Marxism and 'selfish' capitalism.[4]

Even more important, however, a new, *secular* corporativism became increasingly popular and respectable. The world-renowned sociological theorist (and Comtean) Emile Durkheim (to take one well-known 'solidarist', as the secular corporativists were sometimes called) wrote about a "collective consciousness" or group mind, "existing outside of the individual," "possessing coercive power over him in the" spheres "of moral, legal [and] ethical rules." This collective consciousness, according to Durkheim, was necessary for the individual's mental health and well-being and for solidarity between the social classes.[5] The manifold evils of industrial society could and ought to be healed by creating autonomous, legally recognized and internally self-governing occupational groups—of capital and labor—who would jointly operate industry under state regulation. Eventually, the state itself should be transformed, from the present "aggregate of juxtaposed territorial districts," into an occupationally based body.[6]

Léon Duguit, Dean of the Law Faculty at the University of Bordeaux, was a major force in French legal thought before World War I and an internationally-known critic of the theory of state sovereignty. He was influenced deeply by Durkheim's sociological ideas, and Duguit became a major theoretician of corporativism whose ideas had a pronounced influence on the evolution of industrial democracy throughout Europe and even in America.[7] His most influential book in the English-speaking world was translated by the socialist Harold Laski—himself the single most widely read and admired political scientist in the Anglo-American world between the Wars.[8]

On the left, pure anarcho-syndicalist ideas in France remained powerful throughout the 19th century after Proudhon. Beginning in the 1890s, before the appearance of the IWW in America, syndicalism staged a strong revival in the French labor movement, after which it was picked up and popularized by such widely read writers as Georges Sorel, the would-be synthesizer of Marx and Proudhon.[9]

Pluralism vs. Sovereignty

The common ground of corporativism and syndicalism was their assumption that the occupational *group* (not the individual) was a, or even the, natural unit of human society. Thus, corporativists sought to replace investor control of industry under competition by a monopoly syndicate or corporation of employers and employees. The syndicalists or guild socialists (those who were not formally anarchists) sought joint control of industry through worker groups and the state. The necessary requirement of both was the abolition of the right of individual wage bargaining.

Another common ground between pluralists of the right and pluralists of the left was their antipathy toward the traditional notion of unified, 'monistic' state sovereignty as it had existed in Western political theory and practice since the rise of the European nation states, or more recently, since the 18th century democratic revolutions in America and France. In place of sovereignty, pluralists sought to interpose between the individual and the state groups that would protect him from the intrusive power of the centralized government, *but would exercise autonomous power over him as well*.

Pluralism, in short, was a vision of industrial democracy that amounted to what we might dub 'private government'—to a system in which the state would *delegate* to private social groups the traditionally sovereign legislative power to make rules for all individuals similarly situated in the economy—rules that overrode their contractual liberty.

With this end in mind, pluralists advanced two separate but interrelated arguments against state sovereignty. First, they argued that sovereignty (the unified, undivided power to command individual obedience to legal rules) was an unreal concept, and did not in fact correctly characterize the legal and political systems of modern, industrialized nation states. Second, they claimed that monistic sovereignty was incompatible with a healthy, free, self-governing society. Power in the state should be plural, not singular. It should be dispersed and decentralized, shared among many competing social groups.

Pluralists asserted that one could not locate the true sovereign power in modern nations such as Germany, England, or the United States. There were many bodies whose rules had the compulsive force of law—courts, legislatures, executive edicts, and administrative decisions of government agencies. Where, pluralists asked, was the *single* determinate human superior exercising indivisible, unified power?[10]

Sovereignty was incompatible with federalism, and pluralists claimed that it was also incompatible with constitutionalism. In a constitutional state, government power was defined and limited by written constitutions or unwritten legal conventions (such as due process of law). But all theoreticians of sovereignty, from Bodin to Hobbes to Austin, insisted that the sovereign will was *unlimited* and uncontrolled. So the concept of sovereignty therefore contradicted the theory of limited government; as Duguit put it, "it is absolutely impossible to understand how organic laws [constitutional laws] can be really laws since the state cannot address a command to itself."[11] Legislatures can and do overstep the bounds ·as defined by the constitution, and courts can and do sanction these transgressions. When this occurs, sovereign states reveal the ineradicable absolutism that is their true defining characteristic.

Left-wing pluralists went even further. According to many of them, the ruling class, which controls the state, was the true sovereign, and not some brainless abstraction existing in the ether. The ruling class in any society consisted of those who owned the means of production. As Harold Laski put it, "we always find that any system of government is dominated by those who at the time wield economic power."[12] Property owners are the true sovereigns under capitalism; their will is law. The capitalist nation states are societies *already* characterized by 'private government'— government of corporations, by corporations, and for corporations. That is what the laws protecting property rights and enforcing contracts are all about: *the government of laws is always and everywhere a government of men.*

States were not sovereign, and pluralists did not think they ought to be. Sovereignty, they argued, was incompatible with liberty and autonomy. According to Laski, for instance, laws were not necessarily just even under the best of circumstances; and on what grounds could the sovereign command submission by the citizen to an unjust law? Why ought a morally autonomous man bend *his* will (and knee) to the arbitrary will of another? "[P]ower," Laski asserted, "is held not for evil but for good, and deflection from the path of right purpose ought to involve the withdrawal of authority for its exercise." In his view, the state is "sovereign only where" individual "conscience is not stirred against its performance."[13]

Sovereignty was also incompatible with social justice. The capitalist state, according to Laski and many others, was devoted to freezing "the existing class-relations" by force. The "use of the injunction" by "American courts" on behalf of employers in labor disputes to break strikes and bust unions was, in his opinion, a prime example.[14] But in the struggle for democracy, G. D. H. Cole wrote, the oppressed had *no* moral obligation to obey the law:

> [a] public that acquiesces in exploitation has no rights against workers who are up in arms against it; the State has no right to intervene *as an impartial person.* The State should represent the moral sense of the community, and for the moral sense of the community to be 'impartial' in the great war between justice and injustice is for it to forfeit its right as a community.

Illegal strike violence, however "brutal," must be tolerated. Violence was no argument for "prohibiting strikes," in other words, but an argument for "altering the social system" to accommodate the wishes of those who engaged in it.[15]

The Question of Representation

In their assault on the morality of state power under capitalism, left wing pluralists were repeating what were, by that period in history, fairly common anti-capitalist clichés. Yet pluralists uncovered what they believed to be an even deeper flaw in sovereignty, and one which put them in conflict with mainstream socialists, whether of the Marxian or the Fabian variety. This flaw was the socialists' lack of provision for direct worker representation in the control of industry.

As the Spanish guild-socialist-cum-fascist Ramiro de Maeztu explained, workers in a bureaucratized, centralized state socialism would not be liberated from their present slavery. On the contrary,

> they will have done no more than change their masters and their form of government. The bureaucrats will replace the capitalists . . . [yet] the life of the masses, as at present, would be at the mercy of a few men.[16]

The socialists' error was their unthinking acceptance of the 18th century bourgeois model of political representation, as well as their notion that the state can act as the organized representative of 'society as a whole'. The "idea of democracy," G. D. H. Cole explained, "has become almost inextricably tangled up . . . with a particular theory of representative government based on a totally false theory of representation." The "false theory is that one man can represent another or a number of others, and that his will can be treated as the democratic expression of their wills." True representation in a democratized social order, one might say (though the pluralists would not have expressed it in this fashion), should be modeled on the relationship in contract law between a principal and an agent with a limited power of attorney. Political representation in a truly democratic society should be *functional*.

> It follows that there must be . . . as many separately elected groups of representatives as there are distinct essential groups of functions to be performed. . . . Brown, Jones and Robinson must therefore have, not one vote each, but as many votes as there are different questions calling for associative action in which they are interested.[17]

Industrial Democracy: A Corporativist Model

For socially conservative corporativists, of whom we may take Duguit as representative, social peace was to be achieved through private collective agreements to which the state would give the force of public law. For radical pluralists, of whom G. D. H. Cole (in his guild socialist phase) may be taken as representative, the collective bargain was a device to usurp capitalist power and ultimately to overthrow the system. In both versions, the obliteration of the individual worker's liberty to contract for the sale of his labor was central.[18]

According to Duguit, the state must have the power to guarantee "indispensable" public services, through force if necessary. But in all other spheres, it must relinquish its claim to sovereignty. It must no longer command, but rather *recognize,* the bylaws of organized workers and employers. The bylaws established by negotiations between employers and employees Duguit called "collective acts" or "statutory agreements."[19]

In a much-commented-on *Yale Law Review* article of 1918, Duguit explained that industry-wide "statutory agreements" ought to supersede individual bargaining rights and become "the *law* according to which individual labor contracts in a given trade shall be concluded." To be fully effective, he explained elsewhere, employers and workers should be "so strongly organised both in structure and numbers as to make the trades concerned almost a legally organised body."[20]

However—and this was crucial—society did not have to wait until all workers and employers voluntarily organized themselves. On the contrary, it should provide that the collective agreements of partially organized groups be given the compulsory force of public law, every act done in "violation of which will be declared illegal by the courts." The collective rules of the statutory agreement will bind even those who did not originally agree to them—much as in Henry Carter Adams's notion of "regulating the plane of competition."[21]

The statutory agreement, according to Duguit, would be the mechanism whereby the occupational group would ultimately gain representation in the state itself. In Duguit's version of corporativism, there would be a bicameral legislature. Representation in one House would be territorial; in the other, it would be occupational. But in both, eventually, the direct relationship of the citizen to the state would cease to exist. The individual would deal with the government, and would be dealt with by the government, only as a member of an organized class.[22]

Duguit explained that rules "which settle for an indeterminate length of time the situation of individuals and determine" their lawful "capacity under the aegis of a legal sanction" were "not a new phenomenon." He pointed to "times such as the feudal period when the idea of sovereignty as the *imperium* of the state was in some degree submerged" as a perfect example of what he was after. This corporativist model for industrial democracy, in short, was modeled on medieval feudalism, a social order he did not hesitate to defend. People have been grossly misled, Duguit claimed, by the *"clichés"* of "[f]eudal anarchy and feudal barbarism." Despite "the violence that disturbed it," he insisted "that the feudal régime was essentially both legal and contractual."[23]

Industrial Democracy: A Guild Socialist Model

Left-wing pluralists, such as the guild socialists in England and their like-minded intellectual contemporaries elsewhere, did not look on collective bargaining and the collective agreement as a device to *reintegrate* the social classes. On the contrary, they were the means for transcending capitalism by usurping the allegedly sovereign economic and political power of capitalist property owners.

According to Cole, for instance, collective bargaining should serve an agenda he called "encroaching control," "directed to wresting bit by bit from the hands of the possessing classes the economic power which they now exercise." In Cole's view, collective bargaining ought to substitute

> as far as possible for the present individual relationship of the employer to each worker, whom he, through his representatives, hires, fires, and remunerates individually, a collective relation to the employer of all the workers in the shop, so that the necessary labour is in future supplied by the Union, and the workers substitute their own collective regulations for 'hiring and firing' for those of the employer, and wherever possible, enter into a collective contract with him to cover the output of the shop, and themselves, according to their own Union regulations, apportion the work and share out the payment received.[24]

Eventually, unions would seize control of industry, at which point "National Guilds" (essentially industrial unions consisting of manual laborers, employed and unemployed, "brain workers" like technicians and administrators, etc.) would manage industry on behalf of the community as a whole. In the guild socialist society, unlike the corporativist society, joint control in the economy would not be shared between unions and employers, but between unions and the state. The latter might set production goals and prices, but the guilds would carry out the plans.[25]

"Worker control" became so popular a slogan on the left in the years before and during World War I that it even forced the Webbs—among the most bureaucratic of all the socialist thinkers—to make some concessions in this direction. After World War I they published an influential treatise, *A Constitution for the Socialist Commonwealth of Great Britain* (1920). The Webbs outlined a new, bicameral legislature in which both Houses would be elected on a geographic basis. The "Political Parliament" would administer justice, foreign relations, and defense; the "Social Parliament" would supervise the nationalized industries and possess the taxing power. Standing committees of the Social Parliament would supervise each sector of the economy; each committee would consist of two boards. One would be an information and planning body, the other would operate the industry. The board of directors of the operating committee would consist of representatives of workers, administrators, and consumers.[26]

The state, in both the corporativist and the guild socialist versions of industrial democracy, would not be sovereign. Individuals would obey the rules of their economic group or organization, which rules would have the force of law—and from which there would be no appeal to the State on the grounds that individual rights were being violated. What about disputes between groups? This would not be much of a problem. Pluralists believed that the structural transformation of society would render obsolete the causes of social conflict, and with it the need for coercion by a sovereign state.

Duguit, for instance, believed that men spontaneously grasped the objective need for rules of social cooperation, and that they would more or less automatically come to embrace the ideals of human solidarity.[27] Guild socialists tended to agree. Cole, to be sure, would grant to the ultimate political authority of the guild socialist society (which he called the "commune") the task "of co-ordinating the activities of the various functional bodies in Society," and he assumed it would possess some "coercive power," at least as great as the other "essential forms of association," to preclude anything like the "inconvenient . . . sort of cat-and-dog fight which went on between the Church and the State in the Middle Ages." Nevertheless, the commune would not be a sovereign; and all talk about coercion anyway was "nasty." Coercion, he contended, "is the consequence of social disorder, and the need for it largely comes, not of innate human wickedness," but of distorted social relationships, such as the class structure of capitalist society. "If we set our social house in order," Cole concluded, "the need for coercion will, I believe, speedily and progressively disappear."[28]

The Webbs also put great faith in participatory democracy as an alternative to the resolution of conflicts by force. Disagreements between the Parliaments, they wrote, would be resolved through committee meetings; and hence they spent few words on this issue. The Webbs were even less specific about the conflicts that might emerge between the state's planning directives and the wishes of the workers in the nationalized industries. It "will matter far less than at present exactly how the executive command" of society "is apportioned," they argued. As

> Democracy becomes more generally accepted . . . [decisions] will emerge . . . very largely, by common consent . . . reached by the cogency of accurately ascertained and authoritatively re- ported facts, driven home by the silent persuasiveness of the public opinion of those concerned.[29]

Left-wing pluralists, in other words, didn't dwell on the possibilities of strikes in nationalized industries. What if the arbitrators, to look at the Webb's scheme—those "disinterested professional experts" on whom so much faith was pinned—failed to convince the workers involved to accept the "accurately ascertained and authoritatively reported facts"? What if the workers concerned knew that, whatever the economic "facts"—for instance that their wages were much higher than sales could bear, or that there were too many of them—they could extort ever-greater subsidies from the Parliament by holding out? The Webbs didn't say. They naturally spoke about the right to strike remaining inviolable under socialism, but also about how each "vocational organization" would be "kept in order by all the other vocations, so far as concerns any claim to an unfair share of the national product," primarily through the threat of boycott. "Should the miners refuse to hew coal, the other crafts . . . will refuse to supply them with spirits, beer, picture-palaces and tobacco," which the Webbs seemed to believe would surely bring the miners quickly to their knees. Laski, in his lavishly praised 1925 treatise, *A Grammar of Politics,* danced around this issue also.[30]

Commentary: The Defense of Sovereignty

The pluralists' challenge to state sovereignty evoked sharp criticism by political scientists who insisted that the pluralists misrepresented the concept. Sovereignty, its proponents claimed, was essentially a *juridical,* not a *political,* concept, and only by confusing the two categories could it be equated with absolutism. Monistic sovereignty, properly understood, was not merely compatible with individual moral autonomy, but vitally necessary if the latter were to survive at all. Pluralism, its critics asserted, would introduce an element of anarchy into the social order that would pave the way, not for social peace and mutual cooperation, but for institutionalized class warfare, leading to dictatorship.[31]

Sovereign power, the American constitutional scholar and legal historian Charles MacIlwain explained, "as distinct from any other power is the highest legal power in the state, itself subject to no law." But the "term 'sovereign' has no proper application beyond the domain of law. It is purely a juristic term and it should convey a purely juristic idea. It has no proper meaning if carried beyond the sphere of law and into the sphere of mere fact."[32]

The distinction between *legal* absolutism and *political* absolutism was recognized by all the classic theoreticians of sovereignty, even those who were themselves *political* authoritarians also. But the defenders of legislative sovereignty *and* limited government—such as John Locke—pointed out that if a legislature, which under most circumstances had to be obeyed, overstepped its bounds, "there remains still in the people a supreme power to remove or alter the legislature."[33] The idea of 'popular sovereignty', in fact, summarizes the relationship between the juristic and the political meanings of the term, as Albert Venn Dicey explained in his *Law of the Constitution:*

> The word 'sovereignty' is sometimes employed in a political rather than in a strictly legal sense. That body is 'politically' sovereign in a state the will of which is ultimately obeyed by the citizens of the state. In this sense of the word the electors of Great Britain may be said to be ... the body in which sovereign power is vested ... But this is a political, not a legal fact.[34]

Similarly, defenders of sovereignty insisted that there was no contradiction between monistic sovereignty and a federalist state structure, or a constitutional political order. "Constitutional law does not limit . . . sovereignty," the Australian judge and jurist W. Jethro Brown explained. The constitution "*defines* the mode of its structure and exercise . . . The structure may be complex; but this complexity does not limit the sovereign when once it is established."[35]

The best example is the United States, encompassing "national and state legislative bodies, including the President and state governors because of their veto," provisions for amendments to the constitution itself, for initiatives, referendums, and so forth, all of whose "enactments unless brought into question . . . are recognized as laws,—i.e. vested with proper legal authority." This multiplicity does not constitute divided sovereignty as long as the court system, headed by a Supreme Court, can tie the system together by *preventing a conflict of laws.*[36]

The conflict between legal or political sovereignty and individual moral autonomy is not, to be sure, so easily resolved, since it is at bottom the age-old conflict between law and justice. Pluralists like Duguit, and emphatically those like Laski (who, as the American political scientist John Dickinson recognized, seemed "to be seeking primarily for a way to regularize and legalize disobedience to existing positive law")[37] adopted the classic position of the anarchists; and their opponents, the classic 'law and order' position.

Laski contended, as did many others, that obedience to duly constituted authority was essentially the arbitrary submission of one man's will to another, without moral justification whenever the law itself was unjust.

Dickinson, as did many others, disagreed. "If there were no question but of a conflict between two opposing wills, the will of the citizen as one individual and the will of the sovereign as another," there would be no contest. The "individual could not fairly be expected to surrender his will until convinced intellectually and morally that he was wrong."[38]

But the problem was not so simple. The issue raised by claiming the *right* to disobey the law is whether or not civil society is worth having. The "thing which we strike at whenever we disobey or resist the sovereign," Dickinson claimed, is "the desirability of preserving public authority and civil society itself." The real conflict is not between one individual will and another, but "between the individual and all that the sovereign stands for . . . the advantage, not merely to all individuals but to each individual, of having a legally ordered society to live in, *and of the price he must perforce pay to get it.*" The disputes between men over who is entitled to what are inevitable. They spring from deep differences over justice as much as they do, say, over the interpretation of a contract between two individuals who accept the principle of contracts. The real question is whether these differences will be "settled peaceably by a publicly authorized arbiter, and, so far as possible, by impartial rules, rather than by the rough arbitrament of force and chance."[39] Justice is not inevitable in a sovereign state; but the probability of getting it is greater than under anarchy.

Pluralists such as Duguit argued that only "metaphysical" constructs, like individual rights and private property, stood in the way of individuals immediately and spontaneously grasping what is necessary to promote "solidarity." Critics observed that the pluralists couldn't agree among themselves now on crucial political and legal rules that would govern the post-sovereign society.[40]

Commentary: Representation of Interests?

Several other critics of pluralism wondered whether the champions of intermediate groups had overlooked the question of fairness or democracy *inside* the group. "Small groups or communities," the American philosopher Morris R. Cohen observed,

> may be far more oppressive to individuals than larger ones. . . . Indeed it is precisely because of the intolerable oppression by local and guild sovereignties in medieval society that the modern national state was able to replace it. It is because the kings' courts were able to deal out what was on the whole better justice that they were gradually able to replace the local and vocational courts.

"No one," Cohen added,

> who has had intimate knowledge of the working of our trade unions as well as of our political parties has as yet shown that bosses or oligarchic machines are any more absent in one than in the other . . . The fact that our trade unions or southern states do not have absolute sovereignty in their own realms and that there is a possible appeal from their acts to the law of the land, certainly prevents them from oppressing some of their members more than they do.[41]

Similarly, the desire by pluralists of the right or the left to base political representation on economic or 'functional' lines did not appear to be a reasonable solution to the problem of social disharmony. As the economist and social reformer Paul H. Douglas noted in a strongly argued essay, the classification of occupational groups in modern industrial society, on which the political units of a pluralist society would be based, was far more complicated and tenuous than most people realized. Except for certain highly skilled workers, the assumption "that the personnel of an industry is relatively permanent" was quite wrongheaded; turnover, "the flux of labor from job to job and from industry to industry" was actually the norm.[42]

Occupational representation would accordingly freeze political power in a jurisdictional configuration that would be obsolete almost as soon as it was determined. The redistricting problem would be endless, presenting opportunities for protracted conflicts that would make traditional political gerrymandering seem tame and insignificant by comparison. Recall G. D. H. Cole, who had seriously proposed giving men as many votes as they had interests. This proposal, Harvard political scientist W. Y. Elliott observed, was "calculated to turn the old fashioned" ward heeler "green with envy."[43]

On the face of it, pluralist versions of industrial democracy, of the right or of the left, seem to be extraordinarily prone to *conflict* rather than to peace. Politically potent but economically obsolete groups might stand in the way of change, or they might force the rest of society to run up huge deficits to buy off what would amount to parasitic public sector unions and their robber-baron leaders. W. Y. Elliott thought that Duguit's version of solidarism and corporativism was particularly ominous. After all, once the "concept of public services be extended to the whole economic structure of the nation, as a productive unit which stands or falls together, it becomes Fascism."[44]

If "groups are destined to gain new ground," the English political scientist Ernest Barker hypothesized in the midst of World War I, it is actually more than likely that, contrary to pluralist theory, "the State will also gain, perhaps even more than it loses, because it will be forced to deal with ever graver and ever weightier problems of adjustment."[45] And so it was.

England: From Criminal Conspiracy to Estate of the Realm

England was the country where the status of the collective agreement changed least from the principles animating the free market. There was no statutory 'right to organize' in English law that protected employees from discrimination by private employers (or unions). There was no legislation compelling unions and employers to bargain collectively, or to submit irreconcilable differences to arbitration. English unions were not exclusive bargaining representatives; nor were collective bargaining agreements legally binding contracts.[46]

Unions in England, in short, remained fully voluntary associations representing only their members, and employers were under no obligation to bargain with them. The law tended to "stay out" of labor disputes— with one immensely significant and far-reaching exception, the Trade Disputes Act (TDA) of 1906 (6 Edward VII, c. 47).*

The TDA was a reaction to developments in the law courts after the Conspiracy and Protection of Property Act, 1875, which developments union leaders felt unfairly limited their collective freedom of action in labor disputes (see chapter two *supra* for a discussion of the law of labor disputes after the Conspiracy and Protection of Property Act, 1875). Unions were upset about the limits placed on their violent or intimidatory behavior. They were also exceedingly vexed by what appeared to be the development of a double standard in the law regarding the boundaries of economically 'coercive' activity permitted them. The unions' anger revolved around the implications of the famous Trilogy cases.

In the leading case of *Mogul Steamship Co.* v. *McGregor, Gow, & Co.* (23 Q.B.D. 598, 1889, affirmed [1892] A.C. 25), a combination of shipowners sought to exclude rivals from their trade and monopolize a market. The

---

*Reproduced in full as Appendix 9 below.

combination offered rebates to all shippers who used their lines exclusively, but refused to ship the goods of anyone who used their competitors. This was a form of aggressive competition that common lawyers also looked at as a kind of secondary boycott: A refuses to deal with B unless B refuses to deal with C, D, . . . The combined shipowners were sued by a rival but found innocent of conspiracy in restraint of trade. (The difference between English and American commercial law after the Sherman Act on this point should be apparent.)

Several years later, the trade union case of *Allen* v. *Flood* ([1898] A.C. 1) reached its dénouement. In this dispute, a group of workers, through their union agent, announced their refusal to continue to work (they were employed at will) for an employer unless he discharged all members of a *rival* union. Here, too, the House of Lords (the final court of appeal in England) refused to declare this secondary boycott threat to be an unlawful conspiracy in restraint of trade.*

Three years later, in *Quinn* v. *Leathem* ([1901] A.C. 495), the House of Lords seemed to take it all back. In this case, a union attempted to monopolize the labor supply of an employer's shop—although they didn't have any members in the shop to begin with. They did so by threatening to strike *one of his customers.* (A tertiary boycott, one may say: A refuses to deal with B, unless B refuses to deal with C, in order to get C to deal with A and cease dealing with D.) All of the contracts in this case—between the employer and his present employees, between the employer and his customer—were "at will." The House of Lords declared the union boycott/strike threat to be an unlawful conspiracy in restraint of trade—though it did not overturn the *Mogul* decision. Thus, it seemed to many that, after *Quinn,* there was one law for business competition and a more restrictive law for labor disputes.[47]

Given the rising tide of pro-union collectivist opinion, and the growing political muscle of organized laborers, some reaction was probably inevitable to reverse the trend of the courts after 1875 to reproduce via the doctrines of tort and civil conspiracy the same obstacles to unions' monopolistic designs previously accomplished by the law of criminal conspiracy. But the straw that broke the camel's back did not involve any arcane rules of conspiracy and secondary boycotts, or of the difference between peaceable and intimidatory picketing. It did not even turn on the 'double standard'. But it did involve a question that pluralists were not wont to raise, namely the degree to which the corporate group was responsible to others for the acts of its agents, officers, and members.

---

*This case was particularly celebrated for a dictum that seemingly swept away a pillar of the 'conversion' principle in conspiracy law. Henceforth, as the headnote writer for this case wrote, "[a]n act lawful in itself is not converted by a malicious or bad motive into an unlawful act so as to make the doer of the act liable to a civil action." (p. 1)

The Taff Vale Case (*Taff Vale Railway Co.* v. *The Amalgamated Society of Railway Servants,* [1901] A.C. 426) involved a suit for damages against a union whose members had participated in a disorderly, violent strike. (The employees of the railway were hired 'by the term', meaning that they could not quit, nor could they be fired, without notice: failure rendered the employee or the employer liable to suit for damages.) The only interesting wrinkle in the case was that the company sued the union *in its common name* for the acts committed by agents on the union's behalf, and sought damages from the union's general treasury.

Since the 1870s, most unions had believed—or had professed to believe—that their *organization* could not be sued, only individual union officers or agents (which, given these individuals' financial situation, meant that they were more often than not judgment-proof). But the House of Lords let the suit stand. The damages assessed against the union, arrived at in a later case, came to 23,000 pounds sterling.[48]

Taff Vale came on the heels of others that qualified fairly sharply the lawfulness of union attempts to induce workers to quit or strike, to induce others via secondary boycotts to make union rules stick, and other decisions that sharply limited 'peaceful picketing'. In response, the English Trades Union Congress launched a crusade to rewrite, once and for all, the conspiracy law.[49]

Parliament appointed a commission to investigate the matter. The Royal Commission on Trade Disputes issued a report that contained a mixed bag of recommendations. It endorsed abolishing the 'conversion principle' of *civil* conspiracy in labor conflicts as the Conspiracy and Protection of Property Act had earlier abolished it from the law of criminal conspiracy. It suggested rewriting the law of picketing to legalize its presumably peaceful, non-intimidatory manifestations; and it suggested pruning back the tort of interfering with contractual relations so as to permit strikes and picketing, if not in all cases, at least when the nonstriking employees whom the strikers wanted to leave were not themselves employed by the term (or did not have to give notice). Some members of the Commission thought that unions should be permitted to incorporate fully to enter binding contracts with their own members as well as with employers; and, to protect the interests of union members, the Commission's Report urged separation of union benefit and general treasury (including its strike) funds.

The Commission (including its socialist member, Sidney Webb) nevertheless *supported* the principle of corporate responsibility affirmed in Taff Vale:

> [W]hen Trade Unions come in contact by reason of their actions with outsiders, and *ex hypothesi,* wrong those outsiders, there can be no more reason that they should be beyond the reach of

the law than any other individual, partnership, or institution. Such a claim has indeed in former times been made by the spiritual as against the civil authority, and has been consistently disallowed. What was denied to religion ought not in our judgment to be conceded to Trade Unionism.[50]

Yet the labor legislation that emerged out of Parliament accomplished exactly the opposite. It established a kind of collective irresponsibility in English labor law, with ramifications that, even in the 1980s, have yet to be fully addressed.

The TDA completely swept away the law of civil conspiracy in restraint of trade from trade disputes (and *only* in trade disputes), banishing once and for all the 'conversion' principle. Henceforth, unless some act was actionable when done by an individual, a mere agreement or combination (however motivated) to accomplish that act, would not convert it into an actionable (or enjoinable) conspiracy. (Section 1) There was to be, in short, no juridically recognized difference between individual acts and group acts.

The TDA also abolished (again, in trade disputes only) the tort of inducing or procuring a breach of an employment contract, whether the behavior was engaged in by an individual or by a union: not only for prospective contracts, and not only for employment contracts terminable at will—but in *all* cases. Thus, an individual worker, or an individual businessman, might be liable for damages for breaking a contract of employment (as they might be for breaking contracts generally). And in the case of most contracts, third parties who singly or in combination induced or procured contract breaking could, in a wide variety of circumstances, also be liable to suit (or an injunction). But this legal principle no longer restrained unions. Section 3 abolished any grounds for civil action "on the ground only that it induces some other person to break a contract of employment or that it is an interference with the trade, business, or employment of some other person, or with the right of some other person to dispose of his capital or his labour as he wills."

The TDA went further still. Trade unions (of employers or employees), again only in the context of a trade dispute, were granted immunity from any tort liability:

> An action against a trade union, whether of workmen or mas-
> ters, or against any members or officials thereof on behalf of
> themselves and all other members of the trade union in respect
> of any tortious act alleged to have been committed by or on
> behalf of the trade union, shall not be entertained by any court.
> (Section 4)

The range of privilege created by this last provision was very large. As one contemporary legal scholar noted in astonishment, the union's immunity applies to tortious acts of every kind committed by or on behalf of the Trade Union, i.e. to such acts as libel, fraud, damage to person or property which, if committed by or on behalf of any individual or body, would render that individual or body liable to pay compensation to the sufferer and to be restrained by injunction from continuing or repeating such wrongful acts. It applies not only to intentional, but also to merely negligent acts. If, for instance, a driver in the course of his duties on behalf of a firm or company negligently runs over a person in the street, the firm or company is liable: if the driver had been in the employment of a trade union who sent him out with a cart to distribute packets of placards or handbills the union would incur no liability for any such negligence on his part.[51]

The TDA also expressly legalized mass picketing, not only at a work place, but at homes as well—as long as it was for "peacefully obtaining or communicating information, or of peacefully persuading any person to work or abstain from working." (Section 2)

Commentary: The Reaction in America to the British Trade Disputes Act

Since 1890 Americans had been moving *away* from a laissez-faire approach to competition. The wide latitude granted to businessmen under the English rule announced in *Mogul Steamship* had little parallel in America after the Sherman Act; indeed, it was to ban such activity that the law was passed. The British TDA was incompatible with the public policy enshrined in the Sherman Act (not to mention its possibly unconstitutional invasion of individual property rights).[52]

Nevertheless, American champions of industrial democracy hailed the British TDA as a great breakthrough, and it was held up in this country as a worthy model to emulate. According to John R. Commons and his star pupil, Edwin Witte, the British TDA put "labor and capital upon an exact legal equality" and did not unduly favor trade unions at the expense of employers, nonunion workers or the public. The law gave unions only "a free hand to fight by peaceable and legitimate methods" employers' blacklists, lockouts, yellow-dog contracts, and the like. "Let the state keep 'hands off' in the struggle between capital and labor," Witte wrote in a popular college text, "until either party oversteps the bounds of peace and order. Then neither party will have an unfair advantage."[53]

Progressive intellectuals in the vanguard of labor reform did not *actually* mean that they endorsed laissez faire, of course, still less that they wanted to do away with antitrust. On the contrary, they wanted to establish their own version of the double standard—to favor unions. Thus, progressive reformers and labor union leaders sought to prohibit employer boycotts of union labor (and to continue to subject businessmen to the full brunt of the Sherman Act and then later the Clayton Act) while exempting unions from antitrust or common law conspiracy restraints entirely. The upshot of their efforts was the Norris-La Guardia Anti-Injunction Act, which will be discussed in chapter eight *infra.*

Bargaining Pluralism in France

American reformers came to know about the French laws governing collective labor relations through the writings of Duguit and other French jurists who were highly critical of that country's failure to establish corporative reforms. French law prior to 1936 "recognized" the collective bargain as legally binding, but only on those party to it. Collective contracts did not automatically preclude individual bargaining. French law established no duty to bargain; and unions in France did not have the power of an exclusive bargaining representative.[54]

Most French unions belonged to one of three highly politicized federations, each committed to the ultimate abolition of capitalism and its replacement by some kind of socialism, syndicalism, or corporativism. Nevertheless, cooperative collective bargaining was a fact of life, since there was "sufficient consensus among the various unions on the performance of their essential," that is their economic, "functions" *in the workplace.*[55]

The existence of rival unionism throughout the economy, and the highly politicized nature of French labor unions, meant that "[e]xclusive representation by the majority union, in almost any place of employment, would violate the real scruples of a minority's political and religious beliefs."[56] French law prohibited yellow-dog contracts and other forms of anti-union discrimination by employers; and it also prohibited closed shop strikes or closed shop agreements, particularly where employees in a plant who were already members of one union would have to join another.

The French law of collective bargains had major drawbacks as far as American progressives were concerned. Ralph Fuchs, a respected international labor law expert at the University of Wisconsin, wrote in the *Yale Law Journal* on the eve of the New Deal that "French unionism on the whole has not been strong, but weak, with only partial and unstable organization," particularly because of the "competition between the organized and the unorganized." This was no model for Americans, since, from the standpoint of industrial democracy, "anything less than complete control of a competitive field by a collective agreement is unsatisfactory."[57]

The 'Extended Agreement' in New Zealand

A third model of collective labor law, widely noted and admired by Americans in the years before the New Deal, was based on compulsory arbitration and the so-called 'extended' agreement. The extended agreement, which established the legal essence (if not the legal fact) of exclusive representation, first appeared in New Zealand in the 1890s, from which it spread into Australia; then it reappeared at the birth of the short and unhappy life of the Weimar Republic.[58]

New Zealand's Industrial Conciliation and Arbitration Act (1894)* established a system in which unions could compel employers to submit to an arbitration court. This system eventually allowed unions to name as parties to a dispute as many *employers in a given geographical area or industry* as they wanted to, whether or not these unions represented a majority or even a plurality of any given employer's workers. The arbitration court's nonreviewable wage awards could be extended to cover, that is, declared binding on *all employers,* and thus all employees, in a given trade or territory. The arbitration award, in other words, was *extended* to govern the employment rules of employers and employees who were not in fact parties to the original dispute. The weakness of the labor movement in New Zealand (its inability to overcome the geographic dispersal of the population and the resistance of employers to collective bargaining) was the very reason that the authors of this statute granted to unions in New Zealand this power to virtually compel industry-wide collective bargaining.[59]

New Zealand came to be known as the 'country without strikes' because it prohibited strikes and lockouts both during the arbitration process and after an award was made. Moreover, very early on in the history of the system, the arbitration court attempted to settle the always-explosive closed shop issue by an ingenious device, the preferential union shop. Unions could demand, and employers could be ordered to accept, clauses in a collective agreement that compelled the latter to hire union members *in preference to* (that is, ahead of) nonunion workers wherever or whenever union members were available (although already-employed nonunion workers could not be dismissed solely to provide spaces for

*Appendix 8 below.

them). Needless to say, a compulsory preferential shop is a *very* strong incentive for an individual worker to choose union affiliation (and insofar as arbitration awards fix wage rates above market-clearing levels, there will no doubt be an ample supply of unemployed union workers available for preferential hiring if conditions change and more labor is needed). The arbitration court assumed one more power as well: that of *ordering* employers to reinstate workers discharged for union affiliation, and to pay damages—to the union.[60]

The Australasian Model in America

The New Zealand system and its successors in Australia were heavily publicized and highly praised in America before World War I, particularly by Henry Demarest Lloyd. Lloyd published a stream of books and articles lavishly praising the institution, particularly the extension device, as democracy in action. New Zealand, he explained, had shown how the "law" of compulsory arbitration became "the instrument through which democracy equips a majority to maintain its welfare against the attacks of an anti-social minority."[61]

New Zealand's system was also probably what the American socialist theoretician Laurence Gronlund had in mind in 1898 when he advocated both exclusive representation in the context of compulsory arbitration, and other laws to " 'persuade' every workman to join his trades-union, or other labor-organization" by so arranging "conditions that it will be made as disadvantageous for him as possible to remain outside."[62]

The "preferential shop" device engineered in New Zealand was incorporated into the famous "Protocol of Peace" (1910-1916) in the garment industries of New York and Chicago, an almost-industry-wide system of collective bargaining established after a wave of bitter, destructive organizational strikes. The principle authors of the Protocol—Louis Brandeis, Morris Hillquit, and E. A. Filene—looked on their version of industrial democracy as a model for the American economy as a whole. The attorney for the employers' association, Julius H. Cohen, also championed industry-wide collective bargaining between national unions and national employer associations as the path to industrial peace, "law and order." Cohen proposed that the federal government create a "national industrial board, constituted of leading trades unionists, employers and public men and women" who could "utilize Federal power" to make collective bargains " 'voluntarily come to' binding upon the unscrupulous and illegitimate minority employer."[63]

The influential law school professor Robert Hale thought Cohen's ideas "a step in the right direction." It was true, Hale admitted, that the kind of corporativist scheme Cohen proposed would "give to unofficial boards," that is, to groups of private citizens, "the power to make rules governing the legal relations governing individuals." This delegation of legislative power did not bother him however, since, " 'unofficial minorities' " like capitalists already usurped governmental power to make law.[64]

The New Zealand system demonstrated, according to Henry Demarest Lloyd, that the traditional objections to compulsory arbitration were unsound. Experience in New Zealand showed that awards could indeed be enforced and obeyed:

> There has not been a strike by organised labor, with one insignificant exception, since its passage. [The compulsory arbitration system] has harmonised all the labor troubles brought under its cognisance. . . . Capital has not fled, but, on the contrary, industries have been flourishing as never before. There have been a few attempts to evade or disregard the decisions of the courts; these the judges have proved themselves fully able to control and punish.[65]

The abolition of strikes, incidentally, was the primary reason American labor leaders such as Samuel Gompers *opposed* compulsory arbitration (under the New Zealand or any other system), which he fatuously likened to slavery.[66] Actually, there was little to fear. Compulsory arbitration in New Zealand successfully averted strikes only so far, and only so long as, the unions got favorable awards. Once the economic situation turned sour, as it did after 1900, the arbitration courts began to rule in favor of employer demands. This turned even moderate, craft union opinion against the system, as it did the rising young militants of the industrial unions. The 'no strikes' era in New Zealand thereupon gradually evaporated and was a dead letter by World War I, swept away like a dead leaf in a hurricane. But that development escaped notice in America—as did the further reform in New Zealand's labor laws in the 1920s and 1930s, which *mandated closed shops* in any industry covered by an industrial arbitration award.[67]

Industrial Democracy in Weimar Germany

The extended agreement device reappeared in Germany at the end of World War I, due in no small part to the urging of pluralist political scientists, jurists, and economists, as well as to the pressure of cartel-oriented big businessmen and union leaders. It was thereafter copied by several European nations.[68]

The Ordinance of December 23, 1918 provided that collective labor agreements would automatically supersede individual labor contracts, with two interesting exceptions (interesting in light of arguments in America in the 1930s and 1940s that these things were impossible or impolitic). The collective agreement could, if the signatories so chose, exempt individual workers from its terms; and individual workers could negotiate better terms than those provided for in the collective agreement (unless the collective agreement specifically prohibited them).

The Ordinance of 1918 also permitted the Cabinet-level "National Ministry of Labor" to "declare generally binding such collective agreements as have acquired outstanding importance in the fixing of terms of employment in certain occupations in the areas covered by the agreements."[69] The extended agreement automatically replaced individual labor contracts in a given territory or occupation; and employers who disregarded these statutory agreements to hire labor cheaper could be *sued* by other employers—for unfair competition.

The Weimar Republic originally neglected to compel collective bargaining and arbitration, a loophole that upset many of the social democrats, including Lujo Brentano. In 1923, however, compulsory arbitration became the law of the land. Thereafter employers or unions could compel each other to submit to arbitration, and the Ministry of Labor could extend compulsory arbitration awards, at its discretion.

Through the extended agreement, German unions could bind individual, nonunion workers and their employers to terms of employment not of their own choosing. Even so, German unions did not enjoy the status of a true exclusive representative. Bargaining pluralism was a fact of life in Germany as in France, and probably for the same reason, namely the existence of three politicized trade union federations, each one jealous of its autonomy. The legal system was very reluctant to allow one union to disenfranchise members of any others through such devices as the closed shop.

The 'right not to organize' versus the closed shop was a controversial issue in the Weimar Republic. During World War I, the Reichstag conscripted labor for industrial work and outlawed strikes. But the political price the government had to pay organized labor for their cooperation in this matter was legal protection against dismissal by private employers for union membership or activity. (The German unions' deal was, absent the labor conscription element, rather similar to the deal the AFL cut during World War I; see chapter eight *infra*.) Partly to enforce the anti-discrimination principle, the government established committees of workers in all factories to settle labor disputes directly with employers. Late in 1918, in the midst of the great postwar crisis, the various major employer associations and union federations reached a private treaty cementing the right of employers and employees to self-organization without interference or discrimination by the other.

The Weimar *Constitution* (1919) guaranteed individual workers the freedom to join or organize unions and prohibited anti-union discrimination by private parties. This was accomplished by Article 118, which gave every individual "the right within the limits of the general laws, to express his opinion orally, in writing, in print, pictorially, or in any other way," and which declared that "[n]o circumstance arising out of his work or employment shall hinder him in the exercise of this right, and no one shall discriminate against him if he makes use of such right." Article 159, in turn, guaranteed "freedom of association . . . to everyone and to all professions," banning "[a]ll agreements and provisions which attempt to limit this freedom or seek to hinder its exercise. . . . " Anti-union discrimination by employers during the Weimar Republic was an actionable offense, triable in labor courts, and those found guilty of it could be ordered to pay compensatory damages. The courts could not order reinstatement, however, unless an employer was willing.[70]

Since German unions and their federations were highly politicized, as in France, membership in a labor organization was as much a political as an economic act. The closed shop strike or closed shop agreement, therefore, collided with *both* Articles 118 and 159 of the constitution. Most legal opinion held that so-called 'obligatory' (union security) provisions of a collective agreement were not only illegal but unconstitutional (the wages and hours provisions were called 'normative' provisions). Although the courts shied away from unequivocally banning all forms of union security, they did rule fairly consistently against them; and as a matter of policy the National Minister of Labor usually refused to extend any collective agreement with an obligatory or 'organizational' clause.[71]

The Weimar constitution (and those of other postwar European nations modeled on it, such as Austria's) also anticipated what we would today call 'tripartite industrial policy'. Article 165 of the Weimar constitution, implemented by legislation in 1920, established a system of workers' councils on a plant, regional, and national level "to cooperate in common with employers, and on an equal footing, in the regulation of salaries and working conditions, as well as in the entire field of economic development of the forces of production." Paralleling these workers' councils was a system of employers' associations on a regional and national level. Representatives of these groups were to meet with the workers in economic councils "for the purpose of performing economic functions and for the cooperation in the execution of the laws of socialization." That is to say, these employer/employee cartels would be the organizations that would in some manner manage and administer such industries as the Reichstag *chose to nationalize.* Provision for nationalization (with compensation) appeared in Article 156, which envisioned the possibility of a total corporative reorganization of the economy into cartels managed jointly by employers and employees, but owned and supervised by the state.

The worker council system and the potential for a corporativist reorganization of the economy lay dormant during the Weimar Republic, but their intellectual lineage is revealing. The worker councils themselves were born during the war as shop committees, and were then championed by far left revolutionary organizations who saw in them a means of breaking free from the bureaucratically oriented socialist unions, and as the means for eventually establishing direct worker control of industry on the 'Soviet' model (although in the 1920s the councils were essentially absorbed or 'co-opted' by the main-line unions, and few industries were nationalized or forced into cartels). Intellectual support for the 'joint control' method arose from an important group of businessmen/politicians spearheaded by Walter Rathenau and Wichard von Möllendorff. Rathenau was president of the *Allgemeine Elektrizitäts-Gesellschaft* (AEG), a gigantic electric power generation and distribution combine. One of Germany's most powerful businessmen, Rathenau became during the war the originator and coordinator of the economic mobilization—a kind of super Bernard Baruch. But Rathenau was also a dreamy, romantic writer given to utopian visions of a non-Marxist, corporativist collectivism. His popular wartime book, *Von Kommenden Dingen*, [translated as *In Days to Come*], 1917, sought to convince Germans to permanently institutionalize in peacetime the 'War Economy' mobilization.[72]

Commentary: The Weimar Model in America

The influence, if any, of German-type corporative schemes on those American businessmen who led the 'trade association' movement in the 1920s is hard to trace. Actually, what the trade association movement mainly wanted was exemption from the antitrust laws—which is not the same thing as demanding that the government corral all competitors into a giant coercive cartel. Nevertheless, Gerard Swope, whose 'Swope Plan' (which did entail government muscle to enforce trade association price-fixing rules) was a major inspiration of the National Industrial Recovery Act, was a long-time acquaintance of Walter Rathenau.[73]

American champions of union-oriented industrial democracy, particularly in the academy, were much more in tune with the social and intellectual currents of the Weimar Republic, a country which they considered the most advanced social democracy in the world. The significance of Germany's labor law reforms did not go unnoticed.

Professor Ralph Fuchs of Washington University, for instance, was a well-informed student of international labor law and an ardent champion of progressive labor legislation during the 1920s. In a number of law review articles, he strongly commended the Weimar system to reformers here. "The American student of modern democratic organization," Fuchs confessed late in the decade,

> can hardly avoid allowing a wistful note to creep into his appraisal of the German system of control of employment by collective agreement. There is indicated by the system a creative ability in devising social mechanisms which is decades in advance of anything that has been developed in the United States . . . By the extension of existing voluntary agreements, backward producers may be brought up to prevailing standards; and by the imposition of new agreements through state action strikes and lockouts are in many instances outlawed.

Its "basic ideas are simple and admirably suited to the realities of modern industrial organization," he contended, most importantly its "abandonment of all pretense that the individual labor contract is a democratic means of establishing standards of employment."[74]

As far as Fuchs was concerned, there were only a few clouds on the horizon. German employers, he opined, might begin to emulate their American counterparts, and, by establishing company unions, win workers' loyalty away from traditional, adversarial labor organizations. The German legal system's 'open shop' interpretation of the 'right to organize' principle (that is, no discrimination from any quarter) was, also, to Fuchs' way of thinking, most unfortunate. "If the labor organizations are to be charged with the responsibility of creating and maintaining a just and permanent system of employment relations," he didn't see why they shouldn't be "entitled to the financial support of all the workers whom they benefit."[75]

Despite this endorsement of compulsory unionism, Fuchs went on to praise the existence of three rival union federations "which exist side by side in some of the larger industries," and owned that if the German experiment in industrial democracy were to survive and flourish, there "would have to be a safeguard against the more powerful of these making use of legal machinery to crowd the others from the field."[76] Yet Fuchs did not address the problem of how compulsory financial contributions and the closed shop—which would amount in practice to a kind of one-party industrial democracy with taxes levied for the support of the incumbent political organization—could be squared with a viable system of rival unionism.

Fuchs detected some other quirks in the Weimar labor system. Though established to bring about industrial peace, it did so *only when it was in the interest of the parties to remain at peace.* In somewhat oracular prose, Fuchs explained that even "from a theoretical standpoint it must be admitted that skepticism as to the power of a court actually to enforce its decrees against a determined group of workers or employers" was well-warranted. German law, unlike its counterparts in England or America, *permits* judges to enjoin the specific performance of a personal service contract. That is, it permits a court to order someone *to work.* Yet, for some unexplained reason, there are no reported cases in German courts of last resort in which a union or an employers' association was sued for the purpose of actually compelling it to live up to its obligation under a collective agreement. A union could sue an employer for damages, and vice versa; but what remedy an employer might have in the case of a wildcat strike was uncertain. In the latter case, Fuchs thought that "effective legal measures for checking violations" ought to be adopted; but he did not specify any.[77]

Finally, Fuchs noted a relative decline in the number of workers covered by collective agreements that paralleled the growing unemployment problem in the German economy generally, and particularly in the heavily organized industries. Fuchs chalked up this problem to technological displacement.[78]

Commentary: The Weimar System in Germany

The collective bargaining system Fuchs recommended so highly to Americans was actually imploding, even as he sang its praises. Following the currency collapse of 1923, German unions voiced great support for the labor relations system, particularly with the addition of compulsory arbitration. They rode the crest of the return to prosperity, demanding and getting higher and higher wage rates. But this exacerbated the unemployment problem and undermined the "solidarity" of labor, creating a bitterly resentful, alienated underclass of unemployed workers.[79]

The resort to inflation and deficit spending to increase employment (a solution proposed and to some degree adopted in England and America in the 1930s)—to restore lost profit margins by pumping up aggregate demand, widening markets and lowering real wages (all the while hoping that unions and employers wouldn't catch on and build inflationary expectations into their wage and price demands)—was not available to Weimar politicians. Not after 1923.

The result was that high wage costs helped price German goods out of the international market. Employers pressed for wage reductions, or at least for an end to spiralling increases. Now, however, the unions grew alienated under the system that helped them wax fat; and by the very late 1920s and early 1930s the collective bargaining system as a whole was at an impasse. Indeed, authentic *bargaining* virtually disappeared. The compulsory arbitration system encouraged not a meeting of the minds, but a pattern of irresponsible demands coupled with a political 'fight for the soul of the arbitrator' that "made employer-employee relations worse than before." Power ineluctably slipped from the hands of the private sector and into the government's. Compulsory arbitration became "a means of enforcing state policy in a mild dictatorship." Eventually, the "mild dictatorship" was superseded by brutally harsh one that wasted no time with pluralism.[80]

Fascist Syndicalism: Monopoly Unionism in Italy

The system of "fascist syndicalism" engineered in Italy by Benito Mussolini and his cohorts developed the theory of the 'statutory agreement' to perfection, although they too dispensed with the notion of political pluralism. Fascist Italy was the only significant industralized country before America to establish the principle of exclusive representation in its labor law.[81]

The Fascist Labor Charter* of 1927 summarized the labor relations system that had been emerging since Mussolini came to power in 1922.[82] The Charter did not compel workers to join any labor organization. But "only the legally recognised syndicate, under the control of the State, has the right to *legally represent the whole category of employers or workers for which it is constituted.*" These exclusive bargaining representatives were to "defend their interests *vis-a-vis* the State and other professional associations"; "stipulate collective labour contracts which are obligatory for all who belong to the category"; "impose contributions" [sic]; and "exercise the function of delegate of the public interest." (Article 3, emphasis added)

The Fascist state recognized as representative those national associations (loyal to the Party) whose membership constituted at least one-tenth of the total number of employees (or employers) in a given category in a given area. These organizations became exclusive bargaining agents and were "recognised by law as organs of the State" (Article 6), under the

*Appendix 10 below.

affirmative legal duty, not merely to bargain, but to reach an agreement (backed up, if need be, by compulsory arbitration). Like the extended agreement device in Weimar Germany, the terms of the collective agreement automatically displaced individual contracts to the contrary but permitted individual labor contracts with more favorable terms.[83] The exclusive representatives, in addition, had "the duty and the right" to represent the interests of all employees, whether they were members of the syndicates or not (Article 29).

Alfredo Rocco, the first Fascist Minister of Justice, explained that plural unionism or individual bargaining was both inefficient and disorderly: "One syndicate competes with the other at the expense of the workers collectively." The "liberty of syndicates," that is, voluntary organization and members-only collective bargaining, was unacceptable because it "led to a multiplication of workers' organizations." Unions in Italy, as in many other western European countries, were highly politicized and often allied with political parties. Thus, as Rocco went on to say,

> [p]olitical parties divided the workers into so many groups that they were placed in a very disadvantageous position when they had to face their employers who never had more than one organization. In fact the interests of a single category of workers . . . can not be adequately defended except by a single organization, and the unitary principle of syndicate organization is a logical presupposition of the practical utility of collective labor contracts.[84]

Since the syndicate certified by the state had the right and the duty to represent fairly and secure the interests of all employees, the rationale for compulsory dues followed inevitably. "As the benefits are enjoyed by all, whether inscribed in the syndicates or not, it is only fair that all should contribute to the syndical funds."[85]

Collective bargaining agreements had the force of public law, and they were sanctioned by a mixture of civil and criminal penalties. Employers and employees who violated collective contracts were liable to a fine established by law. They also had to pay for damages to the employee or employer harmed, to his own syndicate, and to the other syndicate. The syndicate itself was liable for damages inflicted on another, and to the employer or employee for violation of its end of the bargain, "and also when the association has failed to do all in its power to compel the offender to observe the contract or when the association has guaranteed the execution of the contract."[86] Strikes and lockouts were illegal, punishable by fine or even imprisonment.

A dual labor court system processed grievances. An individual worker had access to one court in which he *alone* could be heard, without the intermediary of his exclusive bargaining representative. Another court heard disputes about collective matters; and in these *only* the syndicates had standing.[87]

The Italian system of collective bargaining (copied to a greater or lesser degree by Spain, Portugal, and Bulgaria in the 1930s) was the structural core of a larger and more ambitious plan to reorganize society itself. The syndicates of workers and employers were to be components of a complicated territorial and occupational system of "corporations"; and these quasi-economic, quasi-political organs were eventually to be represented in Parliament itself. But imperialistic adventures and a world war cut short this experiment in industrial democracy.[88]

The Italian system of fascist syndicalism evolved in the 1920s just as American progressive intellectuals and trade union leaders sought answers to the question about how best to democratize industry in this country. The kinds of solutions they came up with, together with their reaction to the Italian experiment, are explored in the next chapter.

8. The Promise of American Life

Industrial democracy emerged as the organizing principle and popular goal of labor relations reform in America at least as early as the 1890s, and by the eve of World War I, there was hardly anyone who didn't have a good word for it. The *meaning* of the concept, to be sure, varied enormously. Although industrial democracy was usually applied to union-management relations, it was sometimes applied to efforts at labor market restrictionism generally (to the minimum wage for women or for men and women, or to the abolition of child labor) and it was sometimes applied to virtually anything that could be pigeonholed under the social reform rubric. Even in the labor relations field it had all sorts of meanings.

Socialists had one version; syndicalists another; corporativists still another. Businessmen and those who purported to speak on their behalf picked it up. Some applied it hesitantly to their own attempts to organize the economy into cartels through the trade association. Several thought industrial democracy meant accommodating themselves to the 'conservative', established unions of the AFL in order to avoid the more radical alternatives; some sought to establish it through profit sharing or by company unions; a few envisioned, even in the early years of the century, a re-organization of the economy along corporative lines not dissimilar from the kind attempted by the National Industrial Recovery Act. Academic reformers attached to it a variety of meanings; and union leaders of the AFL had still others.[1]

Despite its growing popularity in the early years of this century, those champions of industrial democratic reform intent on using the power of government to vest in unions the power to establish the terms and conditions of employment faced what appeared to be formidable legal and constitutional obstacles. The common law doctrines of criminal and civil conspiracy in restraint of trade were one such obstacle. The law and public policy represented by the Sherman Act, which regulated combinations even more stringently, was another. And on top of these, there was the United States Constitution, a document which, as interpreted by the Supreme Court, recognized and protected numerous individual economic liberties against legislative invasion or infringement.

Yet, in the face of these bulwarks of the capitalist economy, those who sought compulsory unionism—those who sought to compel employers to cease boycotting union laborers, to compel them to 'recognize' and deal with unions as the exclusive representatives of their employees, and to compel them to honor collective bargains as they would any other contracts—prevailed, and prevailed decisively. This chapter will discuss the kinds of arguments they used to do so, and the larger end-result toward which industrial democrats of the unionist and progressive persuasions were headed by the eve of the New Deal.

The Juristic Critique of Economic Liberty: Police Power, Public Policy, and the General Welfare

Legal reformers overcame the inherited traditions of contractual liberty that stood in the way of compulsory unionism with what was essentially a very simple argument. They insisted that freedom of contract did not 'practically' exist in the modern employment relationship, because of the worker's lack of bargaining power. Individual wage competition no longer served the laborer's, or society's, interest or welfare, and was, indeed, inimical to it.

To understand the significance of this argument, it must be recalled from the discussion in chapter two of this study that neither the English common law (that long predated the formation of the American Republic, and served—and still serves—as the basis for American common law), nor the U.S. Constitution, secured or was intended to secure property or contractual rights 'absolutely'.

From the *juristic* standpoint, property and contract rights in the Anglo-American common law tradition have virtually always been recognized and protected from government interference not on the basis of a political philosophy of natural rights, but only insofar as they were consistent with or did not conflict with a 'larger' 'public interest' or 'public policy' consideration. The significance of this juristic point of view—for the differential treatment of individual and group action, for instance—has already been discussed in the second chapter of this study. The interesting question is the effect of the U.S. Constitution on this tradition.

The political philosophy of natural rights reached its height in America when the Constitution was written; and among its most fundamental goals, the Constitution was written to secure individual economic liberties (individual property rights) from legislative invasion, particularly by the states. This was accomplished, or so the framers of the Constitution believed, by prohibiting the states from passing laws impairing the obligation of contracts, by guaranteeing that the citizens of each state would be entitled to all the privileges and immunities of citizens in the several states, by making domestic free trade the constitutional norm, and by reserving to Congress alone the power to regulate commerce among the several states. Federal government power, moreover, was divided between the executive, legislative, and judicial branches; and among its other virtues, the "separation of powers" was considered important in order to prevent the legislative power—the power to make the general rules to which all individuals must conform—from being delegated to or assumed by the other branches. Also, since the people of the several states were already living under state constitutions which guaranteed individual rights and freedoms, the federal government powers, though wide, were 'enumerated'; what was not enumerated remained either a right of individuals or a power of the states. This was the underlying philosophy of the federal constitution as a whole, but, rather than leaving it implicit, the Bill of Rights reinforced the concept explicitly. (See also chapter two *supra*.)

Nevertheless, the Constitution did not abolish, but only qualified, three broad economic powers that have ever been claimed 'inherent' in the concept of sovereignty. These are: the power to tax, the power to take private property for public purposes (eminent domain), and the police power. The third power is most significant for this study.

Common law courts, and certainly the Supreme Court, *never* denied that the state legislatures had an 'inherent police power' (a power whose roots are deep in English history) to regulate economic or social conditions or otherwise curtail individual freedom of action in order to protect society's 'health, welfare, or morals'. (The authority to outlaw pornography, for instance, or prohibit the ingestion of alcohol or other drugs, derives from the states' police power; nor was the Bill of Rights intended to effect any change in this, as the constitutional guarantees in the first ten amendments applied only to the U.S. Congress.) The boundaries between economic liberty and the police power have been drawn and redrawn throughout American history by legislatures, and by the state and federal judiciaries.

The tension between individual economic rights and the police power existed in the early decades of the 19th century, when the natural rights political philosophy was still influential among American jurists. Just how deeply rooted this tension was can be demonstrated by looking at a celebrated early 19th century federal decision already mentioned in the second chapter of this book, *Corfield* v. *Coryell* (6 F. Cases (No. 3230) 546 (C.C.E.D. Pa., 1823)).

In that case, Justice Bushrod Washington delivered a famous encomium to the individual American citizen's economic liberties. He explained that the "privileges and immunities" in the Constitution referred to the fundamental rights such as "the right to acquire and possess property of every kind, and to pursue and obtain happiness and safety"; the "right of a citizen of one state to pass through, or to reside in any other state, for purposes of trade, agriculture, professional pursuits, or otherwise"; and the right "to take, hold and dispose of property . . ." Proponents of property rights have cited this sturdy defense of economic liberties endlessly in the years that followed. How Washington actually *applied* the principle of privileges and immunities has often escaped notice. The court *denied* that citizens of each state "are permitted to participate in all the rights which belong exclusively to the citizens" of any particular state, and it *denied* that state legislatures were "bound to extend to the citizens of all the other states the same advantages as are secured to their own citizens." (pp. 551-552) And the Court justified its very narrow interpretation of the "privileges and immunities" clause precisely by deferring to the police power of the states.[2]

Later in the century, in the heyday of what has been erroneously called 'laissez-faire constitutionalism', the story was similar. In case after case where Supreme Court justices affirmed the individual's freedom to contract, they always qualified these affirmations with some proviso to the effect that, as one of them put it, "[i]ndividual liberty of action must give way to the greater right of the collective people in the assertion of well-defined policy, designed and intended for the general welfare."[3]

This police-power exception undercut any philosophical, or even legal, consistency to the Supreme Court (or state court) decisions upholding property and contract rights against legislative intervention throughout the last decades of the 19th century and the opening decades of the 20th century. Thus, the Court that struck down, in stentorian terms, a state's attempts to fix the maximum hours during which bakers could work in the famous (or infamous) case of *Lochner* v. *New York* (198 U.S. 45 (1905)), acquiesced—to take but a few of the many examples—in state regulation of the hours of labor in mines or the maximum hours women could work, state prohibition of the manufacture and sale of oleomargarine and liquor, state zoning laws and rent control.

On the national level, the power of the Congress to regulate commerce among the several states gradually became the federal proxy for the state's police power, and the vehicle Congress used to restructure the labor market in order to permit the needs of collective bargaining to take precedence over individual contractual rights.

This study concerns the evolution of ideas rather than the twists and turns of Supreme Court doctrine regarding property rights, and it cannot explore the complex, even tortuous, history of the case law bearing on conflict between property, contract, and the police power that eventually resulted in the virtual abdication of federal judicial review with regard to economic regulation. Nevertheless, as a loose generalization, the following may be concluded. Even in its most individualistic, pro-competitive eras, Supreme Court cases reveal: (1) ringing claims on behalf of constitutionally protected liberty of contract, though often as not in cases where laws trampling such liberty were upheld, on the basis of (2) equally vociferous affirmations of an ill-defined police power. And the Court never attempted (3) to define a boundary between the two.[4]

The police-power exception to contractual liberty provided progressive labor reformers with the wedge they needed. Over time, they simply convinced enough judges that there was an overwhelming consensus against the individual justice or social utility of the individual wage bargain and of the employer's common law rights to hire and fire at will; and therefore, that these judges must defer to the legislatures which were rewriting the economic rules of the game in order to advance what these legislators believed was the general welfare.

There were different styles or tendencies among legal reformers who criticized individual freedom generally, and in the labor market particularly. Individuals of the 'sociological jurisprudence' school didn't deny that equality under the law existed for employers and unions, but argued that changed industrial conditions made equality of right obsolete public policy. They typically sought interventionist legislation that would help introduce or mandate democracy in industry. Several 'legal realists' were closer to the unionists in spirit. The 'realists' wanted the government to 'stop intervening' in the economy on the side of employers—that is, to stop protecting employers' rights.

Sociological Jurisprudence and the Ideal of Status Law

Sociological jurisprudence in America was essentially the creation of the learned and influential legal philosopher and Harvard Law School professor Roscoe Pound.[5] Pound's theories, which he explicitly intended would permit the law to "absorb the new economics and the new social science"[6] were propagated by progressives elsewhere and served as a point of departure or rallying point for a vast number of others in the legal profession who came to a similar position either on their own or as students of his writings. Among the former, two must be singled out for their far-reaching contributions to the cause of organized labor: Louis Brandeis[7] and Felix Frankfurter.[8] As teachers, mentors, or seers, Pound, Brandeis, and Frankfurter are the supreme figures in 20th century American jurisprudence.

Pound's theory of sociological jurisprudence, which he adapted from a 19th century German legal theorist, Rudolf von Jhering, amounted to Benthamism without the latter's economics. "The individualist conception of justice," Pound wrote, was that of "the liberty of each limited by the like liberties of all." This, Pound said, was an obsolete notion; to anyone "acquainted at first hand with actual industrial conditions," the equal right to contract for the sale of one's labor was "'utterly hollow'." The new school of social scientists—Pound was referring to individuals such as Lester Frank Ward—had shown that *"wants,"* not *rights,* are the basis for resolving the conflicting claims of individuals in the social order. Henceforth, the public good, or "justice," must be defined, not as the constitutional protection of private rights, but by legislatures engaged in the process of "social engineering" according to a formula of social justice he defined as "the satisfaction of everyone's wants so far as they are not outweighed by others' wants."[9]

This new general welfare state required a very basic, very far-reaching change in the legal position of the individual adult citizen. As Pound observed, the

> conception that rights should belong or duties attach to a person of full age and natural capacity *because of the position he occupies* in society or of the *occupation in which he is engaged,* is repugnant to the spirit of the common law.

But, as he went on to explain, in the welfare state social justice *demands* the reinstitution of the idea of *status law:*

> When the standard is equality of freedom of action, all classes other than those few and simple ones, based on so-called natural incapacities, such as infancy and lunacy, are repugnant to the idea of justice. *When the standard is equality in the satisfaction of*

wants, such classification and such return in part to the idea of status are inevitable.[10]

The reforms that individuals imbued with the sociological perspective of the law favored were more often than not 'paternalistic', in the sense that they involved state intervention in the economy to 'rescue' those who were considered to have little or no bargaining power from the consequences of their own weakness, as a parent would protect a child. But there was another possibility, namely to 'empower' weak individuals or groups with special privileges and immunities so that they could 'bargain' more 'equally'; in other words, to help them help themselves. This kind of reform was a specialty (though not a monopoly) of the legal realists.

Legal Realism vs. the Rule of Law

Sociological writers argued that contracts between unequals were unfair. Legal realists argued that they were not contracts at all, and that the relationship subsumed under the concept of contract was *always* one of mutual coercion, rather than mutual incentive.[11]

According to Brooks Adams, historian, law professor, and one of the earliest proponents of legal realism, a contract is usually considered to be "a voluntary agreement to do or not to do some specific thing." But if one of the parties has "no choice but to accept the terms offered, the party constrained is under duress, and whatever his act may be called, it is not a contract." The transaction was actually a servitude:

> When the law confers upon any man or class of men an exclusive privilege to fix upon some object which is a matter of necessity or even of desire to others, it concedes a sovereign power to the vendor, and subjects the purchaser to a servitude . . . When such a privilege is enjoyed through the operation of law by a private person or corporation that person participates in the prerogatives of sovereignty; and those who deal with him or it do not contract, since they are subject to more or less complete duress.

Adams was an economic determinist who claimed that "rules of law" were really only "established by the self-interest of the dominant class, so far as it can impose its will upon those who are weaker." This conservative scion of one of America's first families applied his analysis of servitudes only to the suppliers of state-franchised monopolies (like public utilities). But his analysis provided aid and comfort to those economic determinists bent on a more radical analysis. What, these others asked, was the difference between a legal monopoly and ownership of private property?[12]

None, according to Robert Hale, a popular and influential lecturer in law and economics at Columbia University in the 1920s and 1930s, and a champion of progressive labor reform. Hale completely jettisoned the concept of contract as exchange for mutual benefit and gain. The entire world of contract was, according to Hale and to others who followed his analysis, one of duress and servitude. It "is a network of coercive pressures and counter pressures of varying strengths, each pressure consisting in the last analysis either of the power to lock or unlock the bars which the law erects against the non-owners of each piece of property, or else of the power to withhold or not to withhold labor." The "law," Hale added,

> compels people to desist from consuming the products of [another] . . . They can escape, of course, by going without the product. *But that does not prevent the payment from being compulsory,* any more than it prevents the payment of the government tax on tobacco from being compulsory.[13]

The "freedom of the 'market'," as one of Hale's intellectual acolytes later proclaimed enthusiastically, "was essentially a freedom of individuals and groups to coerce one another, with the power to coerce reinforced by the agencies of the state."[14]

The president of the American Federation of Labor agreed with this 'realistic' analysis of the law. "What is any legislation," Samuel Gompers asked rhetorically, "but class legislation or the formulation by one group of people what they deem a policy in their interests"? After all,

> [f]ew laws are passed by unanimous consent. It follows, then, that tariff legislation is 'class legislation' in the interests of manufacturers; that free trade is 'class legislation' in the interests of consumers . . .

And most significantly of all, it follows that "our laws protecting 'property' are class legislation handed down from the middle ages when the property holding classes controlled the government, made the laws, and directed their administration."[15]

The trade union leaders' agenda combined elements of statism and syndicalism, as well as sociological jurisprudence and legal realism. For the unorganized and what they saw as the unorganizable classes of labor (women and children), many trade union leaders favored laws that would either directly fix wage contracts (minimum wages) or remove the contractors from the market entirely (abolition of child labor, immigration restriction). But for organized or easily organizable workers, their agenda was more syndicalist and less statist—an approach which one scholar has aptly summarized in another context as a policy of having the government become "the ally of the labor organizations against the employer, supplying the power" to override individual rights, but "not dictating to what ends it shall be used."[16]

The Right to Organize and the Right to Use Organized Power: Unions in the Age of 'Government by Injunction'

Like their English counterparts, American unions throughout the 19th and 20th century were typically unincorporated associations. Most American unions had no corporate legal existence, and could not enter binding contracts of any sort, nor could they sue or be sued in their common name. And like their counterparts in England, they often resorted to violence, vandalism, or intimidation when they thought they could get away with it. Virtually the only way for courts of law to control their violent or otherwise unlawful behavior was through injunctions. Police and not injunctions were and still are the first line of defense against criminal violence, trespass, etc., in a labor dispute or in any other riotous setting. But police (and other law enforcement officials) were not always willing to maintain the peace; in some cases the purpose of the court order was to make them do their duty. And injunctions are in any event the only practicable remedy to prevent unlawful assemblies and other public nuisances, particularly repeated ones, from taking place, or to stop union officials and others aiding and abetting them.[17]

Not too many years after the first reported English injunction to restrain a labor union occurred, American law courts in the states also began to use their equity power in labor disputes. The number and frequency of labor injunction cases in the federal and state courts involving unions and employers after 1880 and before 1932 has been vastly overstated, to be sure; and the lion's share of injunction cases involved physical coercion of the nasty variety.[18] Nevertheless, not too many years after federal and state courts began to enjoin unlawful union conduct—because it was in restraint of trade (under the common law or the Sherman Act)—unions began a crusade to eliminate entirely the use of injunctions in labor disputes.

One major difference between England and America was the much greater variability, and complexity, of the legal situation facing unions in America. Quite apart from the problem of violence—which, to repeat, was the *fundamental* issue in the era of 'government by injunction' in the half-century following 1880—the rules of law governing nonviolent restraint of trade, including the always-controversial principle of 'conversion' in conspiracy law (according to which, as explored in chapter two *supra,* a combination of individuals to accomplish some end might be unlawful whereas the same end, when sought by individuals in isolation, might not), had to be decided by each state court, in light of its own statutes and precedents and applicable state court rulings elsewhere. The federal courts and the Supreme Court added its own layer of law, based particularly on the Sherman Act. And in many of the leading cases, American courts also leaned on the reasoning of English courts.[19]

Several states, of which New York was the outstanding example, tolerated peaceful strikes to obtain or maintain a closed shop in most (though not in all) contexts, taking as their cue Judge Lemuel Shaw's reasoning in the Massachusetts case of *Commonwealth* v. *Hunt,* and the English decision in *Allen* v. *Flood.* Several other states, of which Massachusetts was the leading exemplar, took *their* lead on the general *illegality* of the closed shop strike from the New York case of *Master Stevedore's Association* v. *Walsh,* 2 Daly 1 (C.P.N.Y.C. 1867) and from *Quinn* v. *Leathem.* And in at least one other state, New Jersey, closed shops were unlawful "only where they covered an entire industry or a substantial geographic area."[20]

Following English precedents, American courts came to recognize the tort of inducing or procuring a breach of contract. The application of this legal principle to labor disputes raised the same problems in both countries—although in England the tort typically limited or qualified the right of already organized workers to strike, while in America it more often impinged on the right of unions to organize workers. Thus sympathy strikes or other forms of secondary boycotting of products or raw materials were outlawed by several (though not all) state courts on the grounds that these activities unlawfully restrained trade, or amounted to a tortious interference with (or constituted an inducement to breach) contracts. The most significant form of secondary boycotting, picketing, raised complex problems of its own.

It was always unlawful for employees to strike when their own employment contract was for a definite term, and it was unlawful as well to induce others to break their employment contracts when these were for a definite term. Similarly, secondary boycotting, of the type that occurred when a union exerted pressure on an employer to sever a binding contractual relationship with a customer or supplier, was also unlawful. But a great deal of trouble brewed when courts applied this principle to employment contracts terminable at will—or to merely prospective contractual relations.

One of the most controversial applications of the tort of interfering with contractual relations involved the yellow-dog contract. An employer who obtained a nonunion pledge from each worker he hired did not protect himself by arranging a reason ahead of time for dismissing a worker who joined a union. At common law, employers could discharge men for joining a union whether or not they had agreed, before they were hired, not to join a union. Indeed, employers could discharge workers hired at will for any reason or for no reason, just as workers could quit for any reason or for no reason. A pre-nuptial nonunion clause added nothing of legal value to an employer vis-a-vis *his employees,* except "that he could sue them for any breach if he could prove damages." But,

> as a matter of fact, it has never occurred in the entire history of yellow-dog contracts that any employer has sued any workman for violating such a contract. Employees who sign non-union agreements may feel morally obligated to observe them, but for practical purposes, such contracts are not legally enforceable against the signers.[21]

The reason employers had workers agree to such clauses was, rather, to secure tranquil labor relations and protect themselves against union organizers. Yellow dog contracts *were* enforceable against third parties— that is, unions—who attempted to get workers to agree to join their organizations even while they remained in the employ of someone to whom they previously promised they would not join.

The Hitchman Case

The leading case here (though not the first) was *Hitchman Coal & Coke Co.* v. *Mitchell,* 245 U.S. 229 (1917).[22] The United Mine Workers (UMW), in league with the mine operators in western Pennsylvania, Ohio, Illinois, and Indiana (the so-called Central Competitive Field or CCF), had been trying since 1898 to unionize unorganized coal mines in West Virginia— where the Hitchman Company was operating—and in Kentucky. The physical cost of mining in these latter regions was so much lower than in the CCF that the mine operators in the CCF faced competitive ruin. Indeed, the costs of production were so much lower that *unorganized miners* in West Virginia were able to earn more (in some cases substantially more) than the union miners, even while the operators were able to undersell their CCF competitors. The bulk of the UMW membership was in the CCF, that is, in the high cost mines; and evidence brought to light during the testimony given at one stage of the Hitchman case made it apparent that if the West Virginia miners and mine operators were ever completely organized—that is, if they were dragged into the UMW-CCF cartel—their interests would be sacrificed.

The Hitchman Company, though it had operated as a (closed) union shop, nevertheless got entangled in a series of quite violent organizational strikes called by the UMW to organize other West Virginia operators. (When a strike occurred anywhere, everyone had to shut down.) During one of them, several miners approached the operator of a Hitchman Company mine and offered to work, at union wages, though renouncing their membership in the union. Why they would have done so is pretty clear from the record; they, as well as the Hitchman Company, were simply pawns in a larger struggle. The agreement arrived at between the company and these employees—which then became a general labor policy of the company applicable to all—provided that the Hitchman company would no longer recognize the United Mine Workers (UMW) or hire any union members.

The UMW nevertheless got some workers at the Hitchman Company to secretly agree to join the union and to go out on strike when the union called a strike (but nevertheless to remain on the job until the time was ripe). The company discovered what was going on and got an injunction to restrain the UMW from interfering with the nonunion employment relationship, on the grounds that the secret agreement between the union and the workers was an unlawful inducement to breach their nonunion employment agreement. The case wended its way through the federal courts, but eventually the Supreme Court upheld (though it modified in some particulars) the original injunction.

Justice Pitney delivered the opinion of the Supreme Court. "Every Hitchman miner who joined" the union's "'secret order' and permitted his name to be entered upon" the union's "list was guilty of a breach of his contract of employment and acted a lie whenever thereafter he entered plaintiff's mine to work." (pp. 254-255) Justice Louis Brandeis disagreed, however. Since the union merely attempted to get the employees "to *agree* to join the Union," but not to actually join it, he argued that it had not induced them to break their contracts, since they did not have to leave their jobs until they had actually joined. (p. 272, emphasis in original) Pitney would have none of this:

> [I]n a court of equity, which looks to the substance and essence of things and disregards matters of form and technical nicety, it is sufficient to say that to induce men to *agree* to join is but a mode of inducing them to join . . . their uniting with the Union in the plan to subvert the system of employment at the Hitchman mine,

to which they had voluntarily agreed and upon which their employer and their fellow employees were relying, was sufficient [to make them members.] (pp. 255-256, emphasis in original)[23]

Helping Unions to Help Themselves

Union leaders recognized in the power of federal (and state) courts to enjoin unlawful union conduct a serious, perhaps insurmountable obstacle to the achievement of their brand of industrial democracy. After Eugene Debs was jailed in 1894 for defying a federal court injunction ordering him to cease aiding and abetting a violent, illegal secondary boycott of the Pullman Company, unions launched a decades-long crusade to eliminate the use of injunctions in labor disputes and exempt labor organizations from *any* liability under the Sherman Act. And they were joined in this crusade by leading progressive academics and jurists—by men such as Louis Brandeis, Felix Frankfurter, Edwin Witte (John R. Common's student), Walter Nelles, Francis B. Sayre, and many, many others.

Injunctions were employed in a variety of contexts during labor disputes (by unions as well as by employers, though this has often been overlooked).[24] But their chief role was to prevent violence and the destruction of property, an unpleasant reality that would somehow have to be explained away before the public would seriously entertain the prospect of limiting or abolishing equity in labor disputes. The easiest way to deal with the violence factor was simply to ignore it, or blame it on anyone but its perpetrators.

Discussion of union violence by proponents of industrial democracy, accordingly, took a number of forms. First, there was a tendency to overlook it. This tendency still exists today, particularly in journalistic accounts of strikes and their aftermaths—when, for instance, it is reported in foggy, euphemistic prose that employers have dismissed strikers or police have arrested 'demonstrators' for 'picket-line activities'. Second, apologists for unions claimed or insinuated that employers were the instigators of violence, through spies, private detectives, or *agents provocateurs*. Finally, 'the system', capitalism, was blamed. Employers, so the argument ran, who denied the right of workers to join unions by refusing to recognize and bargain collectively with unions, by "forcing" employees to agree to yellow-dog contracts, or by hiring nonstrikers, had only themselves to blame for industrial strife. "[V]iolence, dynamite, terror," if not justifiable, were at least understandable, according to Samuel

Gompers, "as the only defense left . . . against the grinding, conscienceless tyranny of those controlling hours, wages, and conditions of work."[25]

Unionists also argued as a point of legal principle that equitable remedies had no part to play in violent labor disputes, since violence was the business of the criminal law. The rejoinder to that complaint was that equity will intervene where the repeated commission of criminal acts also threatens the destruction of property, and where the plaintiff has no adequate remedy at law. Still, "injunction judges," according to one union lawyer, declare that "'Labor is property' and is therefore, a proper subject of injunction," though labor "is an attribute of life, inseparable from man," and "cannot be property unless man himself is property." There was, furthermore, no equality before the law in the area of injunctions, according to the unionists. Employers were always the plaintiffs; workers could never get injunctions, and businessmen could never get injunctions to restrain each other.[26]

Progressive academics like Edwin Witte, whose writings on injunctions were extremely influential after World War I, stressed not so much the legal injustice or the unconstitutionality of labor injunctions, but their inutility. Rightly or wrongly, he wrote, injunctions were passionately opposed by workingmen and their leaders. Believing themselves wronged, they grow ever more contemptuous of law and order generally. Thus injunctions are themselves a cause of further violence, not a cure. "Despite all the injunctions which have been issued in labor disputes, violence is very much more common in strikes in the United States than in any other country." Witte reasoned that the complete abolition of injunctions would in and of itself be a victory for labor peace.[27]

Other progressive jurists, such as Frankfurter, intimated that federal court judges were generally abusing their equity powers: they were too ready to issue sweeping injunctions prohibiting legal acts (peaceful picketing to 'communicate information about a strike') as well as illegal acts, all on the unsupported pleadings of employers, with no opportunity for unions to respond. And once the injunction "broke the strike," union appeals to higher courts to set aside or substantially modify the original order and let the strike go on were essentially futile. Most of these charges of abuse were exaggerated; there are some grounds for wondering if they were sincerely held, since organs of progressive opinion, such as *The New Republic,* urged, as did Witte, that the *use* of injunctions was the real *abuse.*[28]

Again, unionists argued that Congress "never intended" the Sherman Act to apply to labor unions. Insofar as the Sherman Act was not intended to *abolish* labor unions, or declare them *per se* combinations in restraint of trade, they were undoubtedly correct. Insofar as they meant that nothing unions could do in the context of a labor dispute could be held unlawful in restraint of trade, they were mistaken. Even the passage of the Clayton

Antitrust Act of 1914, on which union leaders pinned fond hopes (because it clarified equity powers) failed to accomplish *that* end.[29]

The intellectually more significant argument was not that unions weren't meant to be subject to the Sherman Act, but that they shouldn't be: unions deserved special privileges and immunities because of larger public policy considerations. Progressive intellectuals emphasized this argument after the British Trades Disputes Act (TDA) in 1906, as discussed in chapter seven *supra,* and unionists agreed.

"In the case of the price bargain," Commons wrote (for a minority) in the *Final Report* of President Wilson's prestigious Commission on Industrial Relations, "the public is interested in securing low prices"; therefore combinations of businessmen must be continually distrusted. But "in the case of the wage bargain," the public interest is "high wages"; therefore, public policy ought to favor labor combinations. Of course, Commons added, "the public needs protection against abuses of labor unions as it does against the abuses of trusts"; but he asserted that "employers' associations are a better protection to the public against the abuses of unions than are the courts." How can these sentiments be reconciled? According to Commons, by carving out a separate domain in the law:

> It would, therefore, seem to be proper and constitutional classification in the interest of public policy to treat manufacturers under a law prohibiting or regulating trusts and public utilities and to treat the same persons as employers under different laws, . . . where both employers' associations and trade-unions are given immunities for the use of peaceful coercive weapons which they do not possess under the antitrust laws.[30]

Commons's position was a fairly common one. His student, Witte, wrote that however "useful" the antitrust laws were for business, they

> have no proper place in labor controversies. Labor unions are not trusts and should not be treated as such. Their activities should be judged by their social effects, not on the basis of incidental restraint of trade which they may involve.[31]

The noted 'people's lawyer', Louis Brandeis, agreed. "A proper application of the anti-trust law," Brandeis said in 1913 (and held consistently during his tenure on the Supreme Court), "would permit of a 'reasonable' restraint of trade by the unions in the promotion of their proper interests." The new rule of reason was the essence of simplicity. "Public policy, in turn, will not declare that labor shall be prohibited from taking *whatever action may prove to be essential to the preservation of its rights, the legitimate advancement of its cause.*"[32]

The Commission on Industrial Relations itself lent its weight and its prestige to a proposal based on the TDA. It recommended constitutional recognition of an "unlimited right of individuals to form associations, *not for the sake of profit* but for the advancement of their individual and collective interests," and sought a federal statute that would completely eliminate the 'conversion' principle of conspiracy law—not for businessmen, but for labor organizations: "action on the part of an association of individuals *not organized for profit* shall not be held to be unlawful where such action would not be unlawful in the case of an individual." This demand eventually bore fruit in 1932, with the passage of the Norris-LaGuardia Anti-Injunction Act (which will be discussed *infra*.)[33]

Several union leaders denounced antitrust principles (applied under the common law doctrines of restraint of trade or via the Sherman Act) because they violated freedom of contract, particularly their right to seek and maintain a closed shop. "The ideal of trade unionism," John Mitchell, President of the UMW, wrote, is

> the ideal of two separate, strong, self-respecting and mutually respecting parties, freely contracting with each other, and with no limitations upon this right of perfect and absolute freedom of contract, save that which a community in its wisdom may determine necessary for its own protection.[34]

If "organized workmen have the right to refuse to work with non-union workman," Gompers asserted, then such a "refusal is an exercise of their own right of contract" and doesn't violate anyone else's rights. After all, "employers are free . . . to choose between the organized and the unorganized." Should an employer want the former "for economic reasons, because they are more efficient and productive, the latter have no grievance either against him or against the workmen chosen." *"This,"* Gompers took great pains to emphasize, *"is the meaning of the free market";* this is the meaning of "free bargaining."[35]

The right to contract implied the right not to contract; and so the champions of industrial democracy insisted that the right to boycott should be absolute. "If we assume that a boycott to injure the sale of a product injures a property right," John P. Frey, the vice-president of the International Molders and Foundry Worker's Union of North America, declared,

> then we assume that the manufacturer has a property right in the customer; and no man has a property right in a customer or in the laborer who works for him. . . . No one can have a property right in the goodwill of his customers which the customers are bound to respect. They may quit patronizing him at any time from any motive. *If they do so from fear of personal injury, it is they and not the seller whose rights are assailed.*[36]

Or to put this idea in context: even violent picketing by a union which shuts down access to a plant does not violate the *employer's* rights. The trade unionist in short, Gompers concluded in a highly significant passage, *"holds that no right to continue the relation of employer and employee can lawfully be construed as property."*[37]

Few in the trade union camp really believed this. For what does a strike—what does the very word 'scab'—imply, if not the strikers' property right in their jobs? And when it came to protecting *that* property right, pro-union civil libertarians such as Louis Brandeis made it abundantly clear where progressive opinion stood. In an interview of 1913, Brandeis reminded his fellow industrial democrats that

> [i]t is not good for us that we should ever lose the fighting quality, the stamina, and the courage to battle for what we want when we are convinced that we are entitled to it, and other means fail. . . . We shall have lost something vital and beyond price on the day when the State denies us the right to resort to force in defense of a just cause.

The just cause he had in mind was that of a striking worker's property right to his job. "The Courts," he explained, "have gone too far" in protecting non-striking workers' access to the workplace.

> In the control of picketing the old common law of *trespass* should be born in mind, as expressed in the Latin rule, *'Molliter manus imposuit'*. (He used force with moderation.) Everyone is permitted by law to impound *trespassing cattle* by driving them and shutting them up. Everyone may induce a trespasser to *leave his premises* by the exercise of such force as strictly may be required. The same principle holds when a picket seeks by similar means to induce another workman not to enter the employment of the business against which the strike is in force.[38]

The Right to Organize vs. Liberty of Contract

The demands by industrial democrats for an absolute right by unions to boycott employers was not matched by their equal respect for employers' right to boycott unions.

A few years after the Pullman Boycott, Congress passed the Erdman Act in 1898 (30 Stat. 424). This law established a voluntary arbitration system to help prevent the violent and destructive strikes that had occurred on the railroads, particularly the kind experienced in Chicago in 1894. The authority of Congress to adopt such a system stemmed from its power to regulate commerce among the several states—the same power on which it based the Interstate Commerce Act of 1887. As an incident of this voluntary arbitration scheme, Section 10 of the Erdman Act made yellow-dog contracts a misdemeanor punishable by fine, and made it unlawful for an employer to "threaten any employee with loss of employment, or . . . unjustly discriminate against any employee because of his membership in" a labor union. There were two rationales for including this provision: one, that the discrimination against union labor by employers was itself a cause of industrial strife; and two, that it made no sense to have an arbitration scheme to settle disputes between employers and union laborers if employers could render the process moot by dismissing the latter at will.[39]

Several states in the later 1880s, the 1890s and thereafter also enacted laws declaring the yellow-dog contract a criminal offense, and some twenty-odd states tried to prohibit in some way or another employers from discharging or otherwise discriminating against employees for union membership or activity. The police power rationale offered in defense of these measures was typically that of the theory of the laborer's unequal bargaining power. As the Attorney General for the State of Kansas argued in favor of one of these statutes,

> [i]f all men are to be equal within the law, as provided for in the 14th Amendment; if the laboring man is to be the equal of the corporate officer; if the wage earner is to be the equal of his employer; if the poor man is to be the equal of the rich man; if the 14th Amendment is not to be distorted into a rod of oppression,—then

the state had the right to make unlawful any attempt by an employer

> to coerce, require, demand, or influence any person or persons to enter into any agreement, either written or verbal, not to join or become or remain a member of any labor organization or association, as a condition

of getting or keeping his job.[40]

A majority of the Supreme Court declared unconstitutional both the state and federal laws prohibiting yellow-dog contracts or otherwise circumscribing employers' rights to discriminate against union laborers. The Court maintained that these laws were not a proper exercise of the legislature's inherent police power, but an *arbitrary* invasion of constitutionally protected property rights and personal civil liberties. And because the interference was *arbitrary,* the court claimed that it was a denial of due process of law and of equal protection of the law.[41]

In *Adair* v. *United States*, 208 U.S. 161 (1908), which concerned the Erdman Act, the Court came close to saying that *any* limit on an employer's right to hire and fire whom he wanted would be tantamount to compulsory association. The majority opinion insisted that

> it is not within the functions of government—at least, in the absence of contract between the parties—to compel any person, in the course of his business and against his will, to accept or

retain the personal services of another, or to compel any person, against his will, to perform personal services for another. (p. 174)

Moreover, the *kind* of restriction represented by antidiscrimination laws was always unequal in operation. It limited the right of the employer to terminate his association with an employee, while it did not (and, given the common law rules governing employment, could not) impose any analogous limit on the right of employees to quit. Nevertheless, "the right of the employee to quit the service of the employer, for whatever reason, is the same as the right of the employer, for whatever reason, to dispense with the services of such employee." (pp. 174-175)

In *Coppage* v. *Kansas,* 236 U.S. 1 (1915), which concerned a Kansas statute, the Court gave short shrift to the argument that parties who are not equal in wealth, power, or position cannot or do not bargain equally. Peckham's view of this matter was one of the bluntest defenses of liberty, property, and inequality that ever appeared, in a Supreme Court decision or anywhere else.

> No doubt, wherever the right of private property exists, there must and will be inequalities of fortune; and thus it naturally happens that parties negotiating about a contract are not equally unhampered by circumstances. This applies to all contracts, and not merely to that between employer and employee. Indeed, a little reflection will show that wherever the right of private property and the right of free contract coexist, each party when contracting is inevitably more or less influenced by the question whether he has much property, or little, or none; for the contract is made to the very end that each may gain something that he needs or desires more urgently that that which he proposes to give in exchange. And, since it is self-evident that, unless all things are held in common, some persons must have more property than others, it is from the nature of things impossible to uphold freedom of contract and the right of private property without at the same time recognizing as legitimate those inequalities of fortune that are the necessary result of the exercise of those rights. (p. 17)

The Court found other defects in antidiscrimination laws, particularly the disparity between the standards an employer might use to choose his employees and those a union might use to choose its members. "Can it be doubted," the majority opinion in *Coppage* declared, that the union

> has the inherent and constitutional right to deny membership to any man who will not agree that during such membership he will not accept or retain employment in company with nonunion men? *Or that a union man has the constitutional right to de-*

*cline proffered employment unless the employer will agree not
to employ any nonunion man?* . . . And can there be one rule of
liberty for the labor organization and its members, and a different
and more restrictive rule for employers? We think not . . . (pp.
19-20, emphasis added)

The Court vented a similar view of equal liberty two years later in the
Hitchman case. "Whatever may be the advantages of 'collective bargaining', " the majority opinion held, "it is not bargaining at all, in any just
sense, unless it is voluntary on both sides." It declared that

the employer is as free to make nonmembership in a union a condition of employment, as the working man is free to join the
union, and that this is a part of the constitutional rights of
personal liberty and private property, not to be taken away even
by legislation, *unless through some proper exercise of the
paramount police power.* (pp. 250-251, emphasis added)[42]

Finally, in *Adair,* the Court noted in passing that if the Erdman Act, which
made it a "crime against the United States" for a railroad employer to
discharge a union employee, was constitutional, then what was to prohibit
the United States from requiring that the railroads hire *only* union members or *only* nonunion members? Nothing, in its opinion; and certainly,
this was "a power which could not be recognized as existing under the
Constitution." (p. 179)

Although the Supreme Court had spoken twice, within ten years, about
the unconstitutionality of "right to organize" legislation, and had done so
in no uncertain terms, the precedents of *Adair* and *Coppage* lasted less
than a single generation. They were a dead letter even before the New Deal
began.

The seemingly impregnable, absolutist condemnations of interference
with liberty of contract in *Adair* and *Coppage* were far less than they were
cracked up to be, either by critics or supporters. In the first place, the
Court littered its decisions with repeated affirmations of the legislature's
police power. Harlan explained in *Adair* that, while "personal liberty, as
well as . . . the right of property, [is] guaranteed by the" Constitution, "no
contract, whatever its subject-matter, can be sustained which the law,
upon reasonable grounds, forbids as inconsistent with the public interests,
or as hurtful to the public order, or as detrimental to the common good."
(p. 172) But who was to say what is reasonable, if not the legislature acting
under its police power? The Court had in numerous cases sanctioned
legislative interference with, or regulation of, contract and property
rights, including those in employment. It is clear in retrospect that with
different personnel, a different interpretation of the police power with
regard to discrimination against union labor was eminently possible.

On a subtler level, the claim by the Supreme Court that the law *did* treat employers and employees equally was not beyond dispute. In *Adair,* the Court equated the right of the employee *to quit* "for whatever reason" with the right of the employer to *fire him* "for whatever reason." In *Coppage,* the Court asked rhetorically whether it could be doubted that the union man had a constitutional right to *decline employment,* unless his employer agreed *to employ only union men.* It could certainly be doubted. The Court's undoubtedly correct depiction of the right of employees to leave the employer's service for any reason was not the *whole* story, not at least if they left in a body. What the Court left out (actually, what it noted in a passing comment) was conspiracy law.

The "natural inference" of the Court's statement about legal equality, the lawyer Charles Darling wrote in the *American Law Review,*

> would be that, when we come to a question of the workmen's right to leave the service of the employer, *any question of motive, including malice,* would in like manner be excluded and that the right would be recognized as absolute and un-qualified.
>
> In fact we find the situation, under the authorities, to be quite otherwise, since a certain class of strikes, viz., sympathetic and secondary strikes and sometimes even primary strikes, are held, by the Federal and some other courts, to be unlawful, ... It would seem, therefore, that the propositions of law contained in the Adair case do not mean all that they appear to. . . . The employer can declare a lockout at any time and for whatever reason; no one can question his motives in doing it. But the workmen cannot declare a strike with equal freedom.

"To be sure," Darling added, "it would be said in explanation of this that the apparent inconsistency that the decisions referred to proceed on the ground of combination and conspiracy." But that was just the point.

> This explanation merely emphasizes the fact that the right of the workmen, which is supposed to correspond to the right of the employer, is limited to cases where the workmen act singly, and excludes cases where the workmen act in a body,—in short the right is practically of no avail in matters affecting the general body of workmen but only in those affecting individual work-men. Can this be fairly described as an equality of right?[43]

The decisions of the Supreme Court in *Adair* and *Coppage* (and their interpretation of the Clayton Antitrust Act, by which labor unions could still be liable to injunctions for restraint of trade) only redoubled the efforts of union leaders and their champions among progressive intellec-tuals to prohibit employer boycotts of union labor while providing virtually limitless power to unions to boycott nonunion labor.

Thus the U.S. Commission on Industrial Relations demanded, in the teeth of *Adair* and *Coppage,* "statutes specifically protecting" the "unlimited right of individuals to form associations" and prohibiting "the discharge of any person because of his membership in a labor organization." The Report wanted to empower the Federal Trade Commission to include among its standards for "determining unfair methods of competition" refusal by employers to allow their "employees to become members of labor organizations," or "to meet or confer with the authorized representatives of employees." Similarly, the AFL included among its post World War I reconstruction demands "effective legislation . . . which would make it a criminal offense for any employer to interfere with or hamper the exercise of a" worker's "right to organize into trade unions," "or to interfere with the legitimate activities of trade unions."[44]

The Right to Organize and its Limits:
The Norris-La Guardia Act

The crusade against government by injunction (that is, the crusade to eliminate restraint of trade in labor disputes) and to prohibit employer discrimination against union labor was essentially won before the New Deal began. The Norris-La Guardia (Anti-Injunction) Act (47 Stat. 70, March 23, 1932)* was written into law and signed by President Hoover in 1932. The statutory "right to organize" was achieved on the nation's railroads by 1930, when the Supreme Court essentially overturned its precedents in *Adair* and *Coppage.*

The Norris-La Guardia Act was the American analogue of the British Trade Disputes Act of 1906. It virtually abolished restraint of trade (under the Sherman Act) as it applied to unions involved in labor disputes.[45] The Progressive authors of this statute boldly wrote the theory of labor's unequal bargaining power right into the "public policy of the United States," declaring that

> the individual unorganized worker is commonly helpless to exercise actual liberty of contract and to protect his freedom of labor, and thereby to obtain acceptable terms and conditions of employment[.]

The statute noted, perfunctorily, that the worker "should be free to decline to associate with his fellows," but made it clear that public policy was on the side of unionization;

*See Appendix 11 below.

it is necessary that he have full freedom of association, self-organization, and designation of representatives of his own choosing, to negotiate the terms and conditions of his employment, and that he shall be free from the interference, restraint, or coercion of employers of labor, or their agents, in the designation of such representatives or in self-organization or in other concerted activities for the purpose of collective bargaining or other mutual aid or protection . . .

The Norris-La Guardia Act did not positively prohibit employers from interfering with employees' right to join unions or engage in collective bargaining, strikes, etc. What it did do was to prohibit or severely limit federal courts from protecting employers who sought to exercise *their* rights to resist unions. The law, as the following paragraphs will explain, helped unions to help themselves.

The Norris-La Guardia Act did not make yellow-dog contracts a crime, but it declared them contrary to public policy, and thus, *unenforceable*; they could no longer serve as the basis for an injunction. The rule announced in the *Hitchman* case was eviscerated. (Section 3)

The legal definition of a labor dispute was expanded, in order to immunize sympathy strikes, consumer boycotts, and the like. Traditionally, only individuals in the proximate relation of employer and employee could be regarded as being involved in a labor quarrel. Now anyone with any direct or even indirect *interest* in a labor dispute was to be regarded as a participant. (Sections 4, 5)

The Norris-La Guardia Act cancelled the conspiracy law from labor disputes. Section 4 specified activities an individual person or persons might commit which were now beyond the jurisdiction of federal courts to enjoin. Without going into detail, these were generally striking, threatening to strike, "causing or inducing without fraud or violence" anyone else to strike or otherwise break a yellow-dog contract, picketing (without fraud or violence), or in any way contributing advice or money to these activities. Section 5 abolished the much-hated and always problematic 'conversion' principle. No context or circumstance surrounding a Section 4 activity performed in combination could convert a combination into an unlawful "combination or conspiracy."

Section 6 limited union liability for torts committed by "individual officers, members, or agents" to those cases where it could clearly be proved that the union or its officials actually participated, authorized, or ratified the acts. This was intended to make, and in practice has made, it difficult to affix responsibility to union officials for damages in violent picketing cases. It did not go so far in the direction of corporate irresponsibility as the British did in the Trade Disputes Act of 1906. But it suspended the principle of vicarious responsibility that applies to corporations. Officers of business corporations are held strictly liable for any tort (or in some cases for crimes) committed by an employee while that employee is engaged in some activity within the scope of his employment. They don't have to participate in it, authorize it, or even know about it.

Sections 7 (a) and 9 together eliminated so-called 'blanket injunctions'. Courts could only enjoin specific acts, and only enjoin specific persons or associations. The practical import of this reform can be envisioned by one example. A union might set up a mass picket line. The picketing might become disorderly, violent, and otherwise enmeshed in intimidatory and threatening behavior. When this occurred, a court could formerly order an end to *all picketing* when this occurred; now it could *only* enjoin violence or overt threats. This rule *seems* fair, as a means to protect free speech. But it ignores a real problem, as a pithy comment made by a federal judge in an injunction case years later explains: "Certainly there is a threat of violence when the man who has just knocked me down my front steps continues to stand ground at my door." (*United Mine Workers* v. *Gibbs,* 343 F. 2d at 616 (1965)) Is it too farfetched to regard mass picketing as inherently threatening?[46]

Sections 7 through 12 revised the procedures for issuing injunctions in labor disputes in the only context left where federal judges could issue them—cases of overt violence, vandalism, or damage to property, where no other form of relief was available. Here Congress (or more precisely, Felix Frankfurter and his cohorts, who drafted the statute) redefined the principles of fairness (of equity) in labor disputes in some novel ways. Two of these innovations are particularly noteworthy.

Section 7 prohibited federal courts from issuing injunctions in violent labor disputes, "except after hearing the testimony of witnesses in open court (with opportunity for cross-examination) in support of the allegations of a complaint made under oath, and testimony in opposition thereto, if offered, and except after findings of fact by the court, to the effect" that, (Section 7 (e)) "the public officers charged with the duty to protect complainant's property are unable or unwilling to furnish adequate protection." This rule was defended on the rather peculiar grounds that the "integrity" of local law officials should not "be impugned without giving them opportunity to be heard on the matter."[47]

In practice, as modern authorities have explained, the courts' implementation of this rule has required a standard of proof very difficult to satisfy. A common-sense consideration—if the evidentiary testimony of ongoing unlawful activity in the hearing is sufficient for a temporary injunction, why isn't *that fact alone* sufficient evidence that the police can't (or won't) handle the situation?—has been ignored.[48]

Another innovation was that federal courts could no longer enjoin violent mob activity in a labor dispute except when, "as to each item of relief granted greater injury will be inflicted upon complainant by the denial of relief than will be inflicted upon defendants by the granting of relief." (Section 7 (c)). Furthermore,

> No restraining order or injunctive relief shall be granted to any complainant who has failed to comply with any obligation imposed by law which is involved in the labor dispute in question, *or who has failed to make every reasonable effort to settle such dispute either by negotiation* or with the aid of any available governmental machinery of mediation or voluntary arbitration. (Section 8, emphasis added)

The 'duty to bargain' principle embedded in Section 8 has to be reread to be fully believed. (Bear in mind that the provisions just enunciated refer to injuries that are violations of criminal law). "It has generally been supposed," as one outraged and astounded critic pungently observed of these provisions, "that when a man engaged in an act that was wrong in itself it was time for the law to call a halt." But now, in the brave new world of labor law, the victim of a slugging, so to speak, has to prove first that he has made every effort to negotiate with the sluggers, and then that the harm he suffers from being slugged is greater than the harm the sluggers will suffer from stopping! If "the fraud be great enough and the violence be prodigious enough to be of greater profit to the defendant than it may be of harm to the plaintiff, the law is helpless," this attorney claimed.[49]

Industrial Democracy: World War I

Adair and *Coppage* notwithstanding, union leaders and their progressive allies sought to prohibit employers from boycotting union labor and, what is more, to compel employers to negotiate with unions on the basis of majority rule.

The first victory came during World War I. The political power of organized labor became clear very soon after America entered the war, when the combined railway brotherhoods virtually extorted Congress into passing their long-sought Eight Hours Law (the Adamson Act).[50] The Supreme Court upheld this legislation in *Wilson v. New,* 243 U.S. 332 (1917), reversing its own precedents. The decision was five-to-four. The decisive vote was cast by Woodrow Wilson's new appointee, Louis Brandeis. But on a much wider scale, the AFL, through Samuel Gompers's, and Felix Frankfurter's, role on the various executive agencies that handled labor relations during the war, successfully used its strike threat power to extract from the federal government a promise to protect union labor from discrimination by private employers.

Thus the National War Labor Board (NWLB) affirmed the "right of workers to organize in trade-unions and to bargain collectively" and insisted that "[e]mployers should not discharge workers for membership in trade-unions, nor for legitimate trade-union activities." The NWLB's policy on employers discharging workers for *nonmembership* in trade unions was a compromise. The NWLB declared that "workers, in the exercise of their right to organize, should not use coercive measures of any kind to induce persons to join their organizations nor to induce employers to bargain or deal therewith." But the NWLB refused to apply this declaration retroactively to establishments where the closed shop already existed.[51]

The policy of the federal labor agencies on the "duty to bargain" was also a compromise. Where employers had bargained with unions in the past, they were required to continue to do so; but not if they were presented with this demand for the first time. In unorganized plants, with no history of collective bargaining, the NWLB began to establish what amounted to 'works councils'. Under the Board plan, the employees of each *department,* voting separately on the basis of majority rule, elected representatives to serve on a department committee. The elected representatives of each department committee, taken together, formed a *shop committee* with which the employer was legally bound to bargain.

These shop committees did not establish the principle of exclusive representation by majority vote as we know it today, since all departmental representatives were not necessarily affiliated with one association or organization (union). Moreover, there was even some provision for minority representation on the departmental level.[52]

The uneasy 'co-operation' between employers and unions collapsed after the war. The representatives of organized labor and of employers (or their associations) who participated in President Wilson's postwar Industrial Conference could not arrive at any common policy on the fundamental right to organize. Union spokesmen and their progressive sympathizers insisted that the closed union shop was within their contractual rights, and not a violation of the right of nonunion laborers. Employers just as resolutely demanded the right to run their businesses on a nonunion basis, an 'open shop' basis (no discrimination between union and nonunion men) or a closed shop basis, as they so pleased. The "public representatives" to the Conference endorsed the right of a union laborer to be free from employer discrimination, and the right of a nonunion worker "to refrain from joining any organization or to deal directly with his employer, if he so chooses." And there matters stood.[53]

The Railroad Industry

The railroad industry was a noticeable exception to the postwar 'return to normalcy', insofar as government intervention in employment was concerned. The course of labor relations law in this largest of American businesses during the 1920s served as a dress rehearsal for the big show in the 1930s.

Even before America entered World War I, the Secretary of the Miner's Federation explained, in language strongly reminiscent of the argument of the guild socialists in England and elsewhere, that *"nationalization in the old sense is no longer attractive,"* unless workers, through unions,

> exercise some form of control as producers[.] If not, the whole tendency will be toward the power of the bureaucracy. . . . Under state ownership the workmen should be desirous of having . . . some directive power in the industry in which they are engaged. Now how are we going to have this power under state control?[54]

His colleagues on the railroads agreed. They fought hard to keep the railways under federal ownership after World War I and to share control of them with the federal government and representatives of the management (though not representatives of the *investors*) in a tripartite scheme called the Plumb Plan. This scheme, named after the union attorney who hatched it, was modeled on wartime British coal-industry nationalization proposals. The author of the Plumb Plan recommended it for all industries engaged in interstate commerce.[55]

Congress failed to enact the Plumb Plan, and the railroads were returned to their owners. But the Transportation Act of 1920 established a Railroad Labor Board (RLB) to regulate the carriers' labor relations. This Board attempted, through a broad interpretation of its administrative powers, to establish a version of industrial democracy on the railroads.[56]

Early in its existence, the RLB announced that henceforth there would be no employment discrimination, *Adair* v. *United States* to the contrary notwithstanding.

> No discrimination shall be practiced by management as between members and non members of organizations or as between

members of different organizations, nor shall members of organizations discriminate against non members or use other methods than lawful persuasion to secure their membership.[57]

The RLB meant it. A case arose in which a member of one union was dismissed by his employer pursuant to a 'preferential shop' agreement with another union. The Board vetoed the discharge and ordered the employer to reinstate the fired worker, with back pay. And the RLB also held employers culpable for discharging employees who joined labor unions.[58]

Nevertheless, the RLB's commitment to 'free employee choice' was severely qualified, if not entirely undercut, by its equally firm commitment to the principle of exclusive representation by majority rule. In the same case where the 'no discrimination' principle was announced, the RLB declared that henceforth the

> majority of any craft or class of employees shall have the right to determine what organization shall represent members of such craft or class. Such organization shall have the right to make an agreement which shall apply to all employees in such craft or class. No such agreement shall infringe, however, upon the right of employees not members of the organization representing the majority to present grievances either in person or by representatives of their own choice.[59]

The RLB's commitment to majority rule unionism *and* free employee choice raised some serious problems, quite apart from the questionable authority the RLB claimed to have to establish them, or their substantive constitutionality. One issue concerned the determination of the class or craft for bargaining purposes. Who was to determine the appropriate bargaining unit now that individual employees, by their own designation of bargaining representative, could not?

In one case, a railroad corporation sought to avoid bargaining with a federation of craft unions and demanded the right to bargain with each union individually. In this case, the RLB insisted that the aggregate unit was the proper one. In another case, a carrier whose *company union* won the allegiance of a majority of workers in four out of six crafts then demanded that the company union become the exclusive representative of all *six* crafts, swallowing up the other two, which had voted for an AFL affiliate. Here the Board decided that the two AFL unions should be permitted to bargain separately. And in another case, the Pennsylvania Railroad established a company-wide union to match the structure of a federation of AFL shop crafts. Both organizations proceeded to hold elections on their own, neither of which included the other on the ballot. In this case, the RLB ordered a new election, in which all employees were to be given a choice between the two organizations.[60]

The Pennsylvania Railroad challenged the Board's authority in this case. In 1923 the Supreme Court decided that the Transportation Act gave the RLB only voluntary, advisory powers in their role as arbiter of labor disputes. It could not legally compel anyone to do anything.[61]

While employers resisted the RLB's representation decisions, the AFL unions resisted its wage decisions. Early wage arbitration awards favored union demands for wage increases, in the context of the general inflation of 1920. But employers demanded wage reductions after a sharp recession set in at the end of 1921, and the Board granted these. The result was the famous railroad shopcraft strike of 1922—one of the bloodiest conflicts in American history.[62]

The railroad strike of 1922, coupled with the Supreme Court's decision in the Pennsylvania Railroad Case of 1923, effectively destroyed the RLB, but not before it made one last decision. Soon after the shopcraft strike erupted, the Board declared that the striking unions' defiance of the Board deprived them of their (Board-created) right to represent non-striking employees. The RLB also announced that

> it will be desirable, if not a practical necessity, for the employees of each class on each carrier to form some sort of association or organization to function in the representation of said employees before the Railroad Labor Board.[63]

The railroad corporations accepted this virtual invitation to establish company unions, and in the next few years many of them introduced closed shop company unions maintained by a compulsory dues checkoff. This closed shop company union threat led directly to the Railway Labor Act of 1926, drafted largely by a railway union attorney, Donald Richberg (with the help of Felix Frankfurter's young protégé, David Lilienthal), who was later to play such a controversial role during the NRA.[64]

The Railway Labor Act of 1926 (44 Stat 577) provided for a statutory 'right to organize' and also established an employer's 'duty to bargain'[65] with the "designated and authorized" representatives of their employees. But it did not prohibit company unions, and perhaps, for that reason, it did not establish the principle of exclusive representation by majority rule. As such, it was not clear with whom the railroads were duty-bound to bargain. Section 2 merely stated that

> Representatives, for the purposes of this Act, shall be designated by the respective parties in such manner as may be provided in their corporate organization or unincorporated association, or by other means of collective action, without interference, influence, or coercion exercised by either party over the self-organization or designation of representatives, by the other.

The Railway Labor Act seemed to fly in the face of the Supreme Court's decisions in *Adair* and *Coppage,* and a suit was brought to test the law's constitutionality. But this time around, the Supreme Court *upheld* Congress's power to interfere with employers' rights to hire, retain, or fire employees.

In *Texas and New Orleans Railroad Company* v. *Brotherhood of Railway and Steamship Clerks* (281 U.S. 548 (1930)), the Court, now speaking unanimously (with the exception of McReynolds, who did not participate in the case), emphasized that the purpose of the Railway Labor Act was to provide for the "amicable" settlement of disputes (p. 569) that threatened to shut down transportation by making "collective action" on the part of organized employees "an instrument of peace rather than of strife." But "collective action would be a mockery if representation were made futile by interferences with freedom of choice" by employers. Thus Congress, in exercising its power to regulate commerce and to enact "'all appropriate legislation'" for its "'protection and advancement'," could prohibit such interference

> with the selection of representatives for the purpose of negotiation and conference between employer and employees, [and] instead of being an invasion of the constitutional right of either, [this regulation] was based on the recognition of the rights of both. (p. 570)

The Court *denied* that it was overruling *Adair* and *Coppage*. It asserted that the Railway Labor Act did "not interfere with the normal exercise of the right of the carrier to select its employees or to discharge them" (p. 571). But two sentences later the Court made the real basis of its decision clear; the railroad carriers "have no constitutional right to interfere with the freedom of employees in making their selections" (p. 571).

Railroad unions by the end of the 1920s already had at least half a loaf. They were an exception. Elsewhere, the membership as well as the power of unions generally declined while the country prospered, and employers in many industries established company unions to serve as an alternative to adversarial organizations. And in some industries where there were no company unions, the situation, from the union point of view, was even worse.

In the coal industry, for instance, collective bargaining virtually collapsed after the war. Miners in Southern coal fields could not and would not be organized, yet the efflux of coal from this region disrupted the price and wage structure in the old UMW stronghold, the Central Competitive Fields (Indiana, Illinois, western Pennsylvania, and Ohio). Unable to organize the miners, the UMW leadership set its sights on organizing the employers. Throughout the 1920s, union leaders, sympathetic academics, and legislators advocated schemes whereby every coal operator would have to secure a federal license to operate in interstate commerce. Among the requirements for this license would be recognition of the UMW and a pledge to bargain collectively with it as the sole representative of the employees. The collective agreements were to be legally binding. The resemblance of reforms espoused for the coal industry to the "extended agreement" system in Europe—and to the NRA adopted in America in 1933 (see chapter nine *infra.*)—are clear.[66]

The Collective Agreement under the Common Law

One other subject has to be discussed. This is the ultimate meaning of the collective bargain and its role in the vision of industrial democracy entertained by champions of organized labor both inside and outside the labor movement.

At common law, the collective agreement in America had very little legal value or effect. Unions typically had no distinct legal identity apart from their members. There was no entity an employer could sue in case of an unauthorized strike, and there was nothing in the collective agreement to make the individual worker a "responsible person in the world of con-tracts," to use Henry Carter Adams's formulation. As John R. Commons aptly remarked in 1918,

> The so-called 'contract' which a trade union makes with an em-ployer or employers' association is merely a 'gentlemen's agree-ment', a mutual understanding, not enforceable against anybody. It is an understanding that, when *the real labor contract* is made between the individual employer and the individual employee, it shall be made according to the terms previously agreed upon. But there is no legal penalty if the individual contract is made differently.

Occasionally, a court might hold that "the collective agreement establishes a usage which enters into individual contracts unless rejected" by employer or employee; but no court would "enforce the collective contract" over an express agreement to the contrary and thereby deny "the individual's liberty to make his own contract."[67]

The union's legal 'irresponsibility' was a reason businessmen often gave for refusing to bargain collectively. The bitterness of "open shop" employers, such as those of the National Association of Manufacturers (NAM), on this issue was unbounded.[68] But the 'enlightened' employers associated with organizations like the National Civic Federation made the same complaint. Though this organization was sympathetic to unions and to collective agreements, its businessmen members were extremely reluctant to sign or verbally agree to terms that had no legal teeth. George

W. Perkins, who was J. P. Morgan's right-hand man, testified before Wood-row Wilson's Commission on Industrial Relations that laborers ought to organize and employers ought to bargain collectively. But when it was pointed out to him that *none* of the major industrial empires on whose Boards of Directors he sat either recognized or bargained collectively with their men, he responded no differently than would a representative of the NAM.

> I did not mean to say that I believed in the organization of labor as it is . . . labor should be required to incorporate and be under Federal regulation and to be of known responsibility in its nego-tiations, which is not now the case.[69]

Unions' legal nonaccountability bothered some progressives, too. Louis Brandeis admitted in 1902 that "the practical immunity of the unions from legal liability" was a major obstacle to good relations with employers. It "creates" on the employers' part "a bitter antagonism, not so much on account of lawless acts as from a deep rooted sense of injustice, arising from the feeling that while the employer is subject to law, the union" is not. The solution appeared to be simple: unions should incorporate. It was not.[70]

The position of major American union leaders such as Samuel Gompers was constant from the 1880s to the 1920s. They were adamantly opposed to making collective agreements legally binding on the union or on the individual worker. The collective agreement, in Gompers's view, must have *no connection* to the apparati of the state or its court systems; it must be "voluntary."

Against those who urged unions to incorporate if they wanted employ-ers to live up to collective agreements, Gompers argued, first of all, that it was employers, not unions, who typically ignored collective agreements. Moreover,

> it is not in accord with mutual rights and equal justice for em-ployers to demand in return for . . . the full recognition of the right of the workers to organize and bargain collectively . . . that trade unions must assume financial responsibilities which do not apply to employers and their associations.[71]

Gompers and others, like Clarence Darrow, claimed that incorporation would unfairly subject unions to double indemnity, making them finan-cially responsible "for the wrongdoing of any individual member" and giving "employers an additional opportunity" for harassing them through litigation.[72]

Incorporation also posed a threat to union 'solidarity', insofar as factions within the union could tie up the organization in the courts. Gompers, for instance, imagined that "in an incorporated trade union it would be within the power of a minority to enjoin a union from expending its funds even in accordance with its own laws."[73]

The arguments unionists gave against incorporation revealed a great deal, perhaps unwittingly, about their notion of the obligation of contract. Their objection to imposing financial responsibility on unions for breaching collective agreements because employers were not legally liable was simply a form of circular reasoning. Employers were not legally liable for breaking collective bargains *because* unions were not. No one expected or supposed that employers would go scot-free if unions were made liable. Moreover, union incorporation, like the incorporation of a business, was a means for *limiting* the liability of the organization. After incorporation the union itself would not be responsible for the wrongdoing of any or every individual member, though it would, like corporations, be responsible for the unlawful acts committed by officers, agents, or other employees engaged in union business.

On the other hand, were it true that unions were the victims and not the aggressors in most labor disputes, Louis Brandeis argued that incorporation would do wonders for their tarnished public image.

> Nearly every large strike is attended by acts of flagrant lawlessness. The employers, and a large part of the public, charge these acts to the unions. . . . What an immense gain would come to the unions from a full and fair trial of such charges if the innocence of the unions were established, and perhaps even the guilt of the employer [established]![74]

As it stood, legal proceedings on these matters occurred almost entirely in the unpublicized equity hearings. Yet unions complained that these hearings did not permit them their day in court.

Finally, proponents of incorporation explained that incorporation could introduce more democracy—*into unions*. Incorporation would give unions the power to sue members for dues; and each worker would have "the right to enforce the payment of his benefits, whether for sickness, injury, unemployment, or other purpose . . . instead of trusting to the good faith of the officers of the organization."[75]

Whose Industrial Democracy Is It, Anyway?

But that, unfortunately, was just the problem. One labor lawyer revealed this in 1903, while the controversy surrounding the Taff Vale decision was still swirling on both sides of the Atlantic. The "fundamental advantage of an unincorporated association," John P. Frankenheimer correctly explained to the participants in a symposium of the National Civic Federation, "is the greater power [it] possesses over its members and over the management of its internal affairs, and its greater freedom from interference by the courts in these matters." If "from the trade union standpoint the object desired is untrammeled disciplinary power over its members," incorporation must be avoided.[76]

Years later, Gompers explained even more clearly just how high a price union leaders were prepared to make workers pay for "unity" or "solidarity." Soon after World War I, the problem of labor racketeering in the New York City building trades prompted the State legislature to launch an investigation. The counsel to the committee was the impeccably progressive Samuel Untermyer. Gompers was asked to testify as a representative of the labor movement, and he gladly did. At one point, the colloquy veered away from the particular problem of New York City to more general questions about the proper relationship between the union, its members, and the law:

Q [Untermyer]: Suppose an employer brings a suit to enjoin a labor union in connection with a transaction in which the employer thinks he is in the right and the union is in the wrong, and one of the members of the union makes an affidavit on request as to the facts as he understands them; do you think that is the proper subject of a fine being imposed against that member?

A [Gompers]: If it is done, if the affidavit is made to help the employer in his contention against the union, I think it is wrong.

Q: But suppose the employer is telling the truth?

A: That may be.

Q: You don't think he should assist in the administration of justice by telling the truth?

A: I do not think he should assist the employer in a contention with the Union of his trade or calling.

. . .

Q: . . . Would you permit any kind of review in the courts from the expulsion of a member of a labor union?

A: I would not.

. . .

Q: You think that the Labor Unions should be permitted to exercise this autocratic and despotic power . . . without any say-so by the courts?

A: God save Labor from the courts.

. . .

A: I . . . would not give my assent or approval to any measure that would increase the power of the courts in any matter affecting the organization of the working people of our country or our State.[77]

The legal nature of the collective bargain also came under examination. And here the president of the AFL explained that *there was never any intention* but that the collective agreement was meant to bind only the employer, leaving the union to honor it or scrap it as it suited their immediate interests:

Q: If all the trade unions in New York engaged in the Building Trades agree with all the employers engaged in the building trades that the rate of wages for a plasterer for the year should be nine dollars it would be a gross breach of contract for the employers, because of a depression of business to get them to work for eight dollars, wouldn't it?

A: Yes sir.

Q: Wouldn't it be an equal breach of contract on the part of the union and its members to take advantage of an activity to try to get ten or twelve dollars in the face of its contract to work for nine dollars?

A: No.

. . .

Q: Where is the mutuality, if the employer is bound to pay the same rate, even if he can get men for less, and the employee is not bound . . . to work for the same scale, if he can get more, notwithstanding the contract, where is the mutuality of the contract?

A: The contract is based upon a minimum wage, not a maximum.

. . .

Q: Why shouldn't the employer have the same right to enforce a contract of that kind against the union?

A: Because one is an organization dealing with material things, inanimate: and the other is dealing with human beings.

. . .

Q: Is that any reason why it should not be enforced against him?

. . .

A: Yes sir.

Q: Then what is the good of a contract if it cannot be enforced?

A: Because time develops self-discipline.[78]

What, then, did the whole notion of 'voluntarism' in relationship to industrial democracy ultimately boil down to?

Q: . . . isn't the power to control an industry by a labor union a proper aspiration for the union?

A: To control the industry, no.

Q: Not to control the labor in the industry?

A: To control the labor of the industry, yes.

. . .

Q: . . . Does the fact that the aspiration of the union to control the labor in an industry is a noble one . . . justify . . . abuses or acts of oppression in reaching that aspiration?

A: No, I don't justify that.

. . .

Q: But you do insist that [abuses or acts of oppression] should not be suppressed because they are aspirations?

A: Not suppressed by the Government; Yes, I am opposed to that.[79]

And even as Gompers spoke, the court system of New York was slowly beginning to accommodate itself to this new conception of contract.

Schlesinger v. *Quinto* (192 N.Y.S. 564, 194 N.Y.S. 401, 201 App. Div 487 (1922)) involved an effort by the International Ladies Garment Workers Union (ILGWU) to force the Cloak, Suit, and Shirt Manufacturers Protective Association to abide by a collective agreement dating back to May, 1919 and supposed to run until June, 1922.[80]

But in November, 1919 the union demanded a revision of the wage scale. The Association refused, and the result was a series of unauthorized but uncontrollable wildcat strikes (and lockouts) in defiance of the no-strike clause of the master agreement. The governor of New York intervened in this dispute, convened an arbitration board, and the board recommended a revision of the wage scale favorable to the workers. The Union and the Association accepted the award, but differed sharply in its interpretation. Once again, several strikes erupted, not all of which the ILGWU was capable of settling.

This time around the Association announced its intention of withdrawing from the arbitration features of the original collective agreement of May, 1919, since the arbitration mechanism was obviously not keeping the peace. A few months later the Association also demanded a downward revision of the wage scale, and invited the union to a conference to discuss the matter. While the conference was in session, the Association unilaterally put the reduction into effect (the union had refused even to discuss a 'giveback'), touching off a wave of strikes. But at this point, the union sought an injunction to compel the employers to cease violating any of the terms of the original, May 1919 agreement.[81]

The judge of the New York Supreme Court to whom the ILGWU applied granted the union's request for a temporary restraining order, and his decision was upheld on appeal a few months later in the Appellate Division (194 N.Y.S. 412). The unprecedented nature of this decision is best gathered from the remarks of the lone dissenting judge on appeal.

> It is sought by the injunction to enforce an agreement between the parties [the agreement of May 1919], the very existence of which at the time of bringing the action is denied, an agreement which had been violated or treated as abandoned by both parties thereto, and the responsibility for the breach of which is open to serious doubt, if, indeed, both did not equally break and disregard it. (p. 412)

The union's *original* "demand for an increase in the scale of wages" was itself a breach of the agreement, as the appellate court judges upholding the injunction recognized (p. 407). The 'clean hands' doctrine, one would assume, would prohibit a court order from providing equitable relief to the union, which had acted improperly with relation to the contract beforehand. Similarly, both the judge in the original case and his brethren on appeal ignored the union officials' inability to stop the wildcat shop strikes, despite the no-strike clause in the May 1919 agreement. Moreover, the employers, had they been the plaintiffs, "could not compel the performance by court order of the covenants made by the employees" (p. 411). Then why should the employers be held to the bargain?

Despite these considerations, the Appellate Division found much with which to agree in the reasoning of the Supreme Court judge who had issued the original restraining order upholding this thoroughly modern collective bargain. "Precedent," this injunction judge declared, "is not our only guide in deciding these disputes, for many are worn out by time and made useless by the more enlightened and humane conception of social justice." Obsolete notions of equal rights must give way to a more perfect "understanding of the trials and hardships experienced by the workers in their just struggle for better living conditions." "Our decisions should be in harmony with that modern conception, and not in defiance of it" (192 N.Y.S. 564, 569). The author of these words was Robert F. Wagner.

The Promise of American Life

"Collective bargaining in industry," Gompers wrote in an often cited article soon after World War I, "does not imply that wage earners shall assume control of industry, or responsibility for financial management." It meant "that the employees shall have the right to organize and to deal with the employer through selected representatives as to wages and working conditions." "But there is no belief held in the trades unions," at least those of which he was spokesman, "that its members shall control the plant or usurp the rights of the owners."[82]

This famous 'minimalist' version of industrial democracy formulated by the AFL president fit in with a long-held belief in a philosophy of 'voluntarism'. Voluntarism meant that labor unions should achieve their demands on their own, through strikes, boycotts, and other forms of collective action, such as collective bargaining—but not through government 'interference' in the struggle. As the Executive Council of the AFL put it, "[d]emocracy cannot come into industry through the state" but must be achieved "from below."[83]

Despite their strong anti-statist overtones, these statements cannot be taken at face-value. They conflict with the demand by the AFL for the prohibition, by statute, of employer boycotts of union labor; for the prohibition, by statute, of child labor; for the restriction, by statute, of the hours of women in industry (who would otherwise compete with higher-priced union labor); and with other legislative goals, such as immigration restriction.

Gompers and the AFL were never, to be sure, in favor of *socialism*. But "whether there is government ownership or private ownership" was not, Gompers wrote, so important as socialist intellectuals made it out to be. "The main issue is the question of control and operation." The crucial issue was union power in industry. Government ownership or operation that interfered "with the right to collectively cease work" would be far worse than private ownership that did not. Put plainly, so long as the American public would not tolerate public sector strikes, nationalization of the means of production would be fatal for the aims and methods of organized labor.[84]

The voluntarist philosophy of the conservative AFL was closer in spirit to pluralism, as that term was defined in the previous chapter of this study. This was brought into focus by William English Walling, an influential former socialist intellectual who became a close confidante of Gompers after World War I.[85]

In his semi-official exposition of the AFL ideology, *American Labor and American Democracy* (1926), Walling explained in somewhat oracular prose that

> *[i]ndustrial democracy may be developed both by a tendency away from outside [governmental] political control within the workshop and within the industry and at the same time by an extension of outside political control over the economic and industrial structure at external points.*

The extension of government control at "external points," however, must "develop only in proportion as new governmental organs"—and here Walling had in mind such entities as federal regulatory commissions—"shake off their present purely political forms and take on a semi-economic character." Perhaps this may be rendered more plainly by saying that government control of the economy will be acceptable to organized labor when governmental organs actually become *controlled* by economic interest groups, such as organized labor.[86]

The dual tendencies of "voluntary economic organization," which is to say, internal trade union control via collective agreements and *highly politicized* external regulation, will "tend at the same time to industrialize the state and democratize industry, and will pave the way for semi-official and official recognition of the economic organizations that will rule industry from within."[87]

Ultimately, the process of control from within and recognition from without would be resolved; business unionism would slough its antistatist skin and the blue eagle of a corporative state would emerge. In the distant future, as Gompers himself reflected in his autobiography, "those things which concern all industry" will "be determined by a national economic body, truly representative, competent to make decisions and to secure compliance." Or as Walling explained,

> The government must be controlled, in the main, by economic organizations rather than by political parties or sectarian bodies; Congress must be organized by the great economic groups representing the entire population, or at least every economic function; the government must be divided mainly into economic bodies, representing the chief economic activities of the nation rather than the largely antiquated and often unworkable executive, legislative, and judicial departments; and, finally, these new governmental bodies must be representative of economic groups rather than political parties or geographic sections.[88]

The family resemblance of these musings to the pluralist ideas and systems then being floated abroad, as well as in America (as in the Plumb Plan), is apparent; and Gompers's appraisal of the various post-World War I, European proposals to reorganize the economy and give to organized workers a share in the control and operation of it reflect this affinity.[89] So did his appraisal of industrial democracy in Italy.

Gompers died before the Fascist Labor Charter *formally* announced the principle of exclusive representation and outlawed strikes. Nevertheless, he penned a long, extremely interesting editorial late in 1923 about the Italian experiment, in the form of a book review (the book was *Fascism*, by Odon Por). Gompers condemned Fascism's political autocracy—which is more than one can say about many of Mussolini's American businessmen-admirers—but he praised its evolving industrial syndicalism. The

> structure of trade union organizations and of corporations . . . being erected in Italy [lead to] a prospect of something akin to compulsory trade unionism, the meaning of which will be, it appears, that each person who is occupied in a productive capacity must belong to an organization of fellow workers in that occupation. This is logical because if there is to be created a structure of industrial democracy it can not come into being without thorough and complete organization of all who are engaged in productive effort.

Actually, though the more syndicalistic of the Italian fascists favored it, compulsory unionism in Italy never went *that far*. Workers were not required to actually *belong* to the 'recognized' union, even though everyone had to pay dues. At any rate, the prospect of universal compulsory unionism was one that Gompers found very promising; he could

> not escape the conviction [that] there is in the process of development an industrial franchise which with the promised revival of the political franchise will give the Italian people a voice in the conduct of their daily affairs such as they have never enjoyed before.

Gompers concluded his examination of fascist syndicalism with an arresting remark: the "promise of industrial democracy in Italy, pledged in declarations and phrases which might easily enough have been taken from the mouths of American trade unionists" was "one of tremendous and exciting interest."[90]

9. The Formation of American Industrial Democracy, 1933-1947

The Great Depression of the 1930s engendered a crisis atmosphere during which time the American people tried, through their elected officials, to cope with what they had been taught for years to believe were some 'bottom line' lessons about the competitive system.

(1) The unhampered market economy was not self-regulating or self-correcting, but rather liable to spin out of control, exacting a huge and needless toll in human suffering, particularly through unemployment. To preserve the benefits of a capitalistic form of economy within a democratic framework, government must exercise overall control and direction. This is the basal concept of the 'mixed economy'.

(2) The individual was a pawn in the grip of larger economic or social forces that rendered such old-fashioned virtues as self-reliance, 'negative' freedom, and voluntary self-help (in the form of private charity, for instance) obsolete. If a man were poor or unemployed, it wasn't his fault; indeed it wasn't anybody's fault—but it was everybody's responsibility, best discharged by the federal government. This, we might say, is the basal concept of the 'welfare state'.

(3) Individual workers exercised no actual liberty of contract and therefore could not obtain fair wages or working conditions, unless they were organized into unions. The government must guarantee the right to

organize, strike, and bargain collectively against private discrimination by employers, in order to secure the public interest in promoting industrial peace by removing the cause of industrial strife, and to stabilize wage rates, purchasing power, and employment at high levels. This is the basal concept of industrial democracy.

The intellectual relationships between industrial democracy, the mixed economy, and the welfare state spring from their common anti-capitalistic heritage; the political relationship was, and is, a close one: most mixed economy and welfare state legislation has for half a century worn a union label.

The remarkable variety of socialist, fascist, syndicalist, and corporativist experiments through which the various levels of government in the United States tinkered with social, political, and economic institutions during the New Deal was not unprecedented, not in America, and certainly not in other industrialized nations. Moreover, the *ideas* that were at the basis of these experiments had long been in the culture; the earliest chapters of this book attempt to account for them. At any rate, rightly or wrongly, these ideas about bargaining power, underconsumption and unemployment, and the role of unions were held by a culturally and politically significant cross-section of Americans on the eve of the New Deal. As a result of the trauma of the Depression, these ideas spread more widely still. This chapter describes the steps, and the arguments, by which collective bargaining reforms were enacted during the 1930s, and the fate of these reforms in the American court system.

The NRA and Collective Bargaining: Initial Skirmishes

After a failed first attempt on the railroads after World War I (described in the previous chapter) majority rule unionism reappeared in America during the National Recovery Administration period (1933-1935). The NRA experiment in industrial democracy did not last. But its labor policies were the basis of the Wagner Act and have survived virtually intact.

The NRA experiment in industrial self-government might be characterized as an unsuccessful attempt to achieve an 'Italian' solution to the problem of competition by 'German' means. The crucial legislative mechanism was an 'extended' collective agreement for *both* prices and wages, to be arrived at by business trade associations in each industry or economic sector. When and if the President approved these associations or groups as "truly representative of such industries thereof," their private "codes of fair competition" would have the force of law, superseding the rights of the nonassenting, 'twentieth man' minorities and individuals. If no trade association existed in an industry, or if an agreement could not be reached, the President could promulgate a code and impose it directly on the industry.[1]

The heavy support for the National Industrial Recovery Act (48 Stat. 195)* by leaders of organized labor inside and outside of Congress was based on a declaration of public policy (Title I, Section 1) favoring collective bargaining between employers and employees, and on the provisions of Section 7. Section 7 guaranteed to laborers the 'right to organize' free of employer discrimination, and contemplated, or appeared to contemplate, the organization of laborers on a nationwide basis, paralleling the structure of the business trade association (and industry-wide collective bargaining between the two). But the labor provisions of the NIRA were ambiguously drafted, and this helped cause the NRA to self-destruct.

Sections 7(a) and 7(b) provided for the 'right to organize' and for extended collective agreements much like those in Weimar Germany or fascist Italy. Section 7(a) made a condition of every "code of fair competition, agreement, and license"

> (1) That employees shall have the right to organize and bargain collectively through representatives of their own choosing, and shall be free from interference, restraint, or coercion of employers of labor, or their agents, in the designation of such representatives or in self-organization or in other concerted activities for the purpose of collective bargaining or other mutual aid or protection;
> (2) that no employee and no one seeking employment shall be required as a condition of employment *to join any company union or to refrain from joining, organizing, or assisting a labor organization of his own choosing* (emphasis added) . . .

Section 7(b) directed the President to "afford every opportunity to employers and employees" to mutually agree to "maximum hours of labor, minimum rates of pay, and . . . other conditions of employment," and stipulated that "such agreements, when approved by the President, shall have the same effect as a code of fair competition." Section 7(c) provided that where "mutual agreements" were not forthcoming, the President could establish them by fiat.

Section 7(a) established the 'right to organize', but what about the right

---

*Appendix 12 below.

not to organize? Did Section 7 (a) prohibit closed union shops as well as closed non-union or closed company union shops? Did Section 7 taken as a whole *mandate* collective bargaining? And if so, with whom must employers bargain, and over what?

The administrators of the NRA, General Hugh S. Johnson and Donald Richberg, interpreted Section 7 somewhat as if it were the Railway Labor Act of 1926. According to them, there should be no discrimination *of any kind* against employees on the basis of union affiliation or lack of union affiliation. Thus, the yellow-dog contract was illegal, but so was the closed shop agreement. Company unions of the voluntary kind were permissible, and collective 'dealing' between a company and its own in-house union was a legitimate means of satisfying Section 7. Moreover, neither Johnson nor Richberg believed that there was an employer duty to bargain, because language to this effect nowhere appeared in the law. They insisted that individual laborers and minority groups had the right to bargain for themselves at all times.

Not surprisingly, businessmen favored the Johnson/Richberg interpretation of Section 7, particularly the approval of company unions. Indeed, the passage of the NIRA was followed by (if it did not lead to) a big expansion of company unions, even in industries where previously there were none. Incidentally, most of the new company unions of the early 1930s were 'industrial' and not 'craft' organizations, and employers usually treated these company unions as the exclusive representatives of their men.

Was the Johnson/Richberg interpretation of the 'right to organize' sound? It was surely consistent with one of the early *drafts* of Section 7 (a), particularly the version that granted employees "the right to organize and bargain collectively through representatives of their own choosing" and added that "no employee and no one seeking employment shall be required as a condition of employment *to join any organization* or *to refrain from joining a labor organization* of his own choosing."[2] The wording of the Bill, when it became a law, was different from that of the draft just quoted, since Section 7 (a) (2) explicitly eliminated only the closed company union shop and explicitly outlawed only the yellow-dog contract. Section 7 (a) (1) was rephrased to coincide with the 'public policy' enunciated in Section 2 of the Norris-La Guardia Act (see chapter eight *supra*).

Even so, Section 7 (a) (1) *might* still be read as a ban on the closed shop, for how can an employee have the right to organize and bargain collectively through a representative of *his own choosing,* if, as a condition of employment, he must be a member of a labor union *not of his own choosing*? The amendments to the federal Bankruptcy Act, passed on

March 3, 1933, for instance, looked toward the abolition of both yellow-dog contracts *and* closed union shop agreements.[3]

But that was *not* how Robert F. Wagner (in whose office Section 7 was drafted) and his fellow members of the National Labor Board (established in August, 1933) and the 'first', or 'old', National Labor Relations Board (established in June, 1934) interpreted it.[4] They read Section 7 as a mandate for industrial democracy in the sense with which we are familiar today: compulsory collective bargaining between employers and majority unions exercising complete and unalloyed exclusive bargaining power. What was fundamental, in their view, was that collective agreements *take place*; no interpretation of the 'right to organize' that interfered with this overarching policy goal was permissible. In pursuit of this goal, the NLB and the NLRB handed down a series of administrative law decisions in 1933 and 1934 that became the basis of the Wagner Act in 1935.[5]

The National Labor Board's commitment to majority rule unionism and to compulsory collective bargaining was implicit in its first great decision, the Reading Mills case.[6] The Board conducted secret-ballot elections to determine who were the true representatives of the men. Yet holding an election *by itself* is a commitment to something more than the 'right to organize' and is not required by it. If the latter were primary, a worker who desired representation by some organization would simply join it.

When employers resisted the Board's authority to conduct elections, the NLB sought and obtained explicit power from the President to hold them. On February 1, 1934, Roosevelt issued an Executive Order authorizing the NLB to conduct elections to determine representatives by majority vote, and authorized the NLB to seek "appropriate action" from the NRA if an employer thereafter "declined to recognize or deal with said representatives." But two days later, Johnson and Richberg virtually sabotaged the order by publicly reaffirming "the right of minority groups of employees or of individual employees to deal with their employer."[7]

A stalemate came in March, 1934, when Johnson and Richberg got Roosevelt to agree to a *proportional representation* settlement in the automobile industry. Employers were to "bargain collectively with the freely chosen representatives of groups"; and "[i]f there be more than one group, each bargaining committee shall have total membership pro rata to the number of men each member represents."[8] The NLB was committed to majority rule, but the automobile settlement, since it involved one of the nation's largest industries, undermined the NLB's credibility. Wagner wanted Congressional authority for a refurbished, newly named National Labor Relations Board. In the meantime he pressed for an omnibus statute to surmount the infirmities of Section 7 (a).

Wagner's Labor Bill, 1934

Wagner's 1934 labor disputes Bill (S 2926, introduced on March 1, 1934) sought to establish the right of workers to "organize and join labor organizations, and to engage in concerted activities, either in labor organizations or otherwise, for the purposes of organizing or bargaining collectively." It prohibited a number of employer "unfair labor prac-tice[s]," including the establishment of company unions and yellow-dog contracts, but it specifically permitted closed union shop agreements. The Bill also compelled an employer "to recognize and/or deal with represent-atives of his employees" and "to exert every reasonable effort to make and maintain agreements with such representatives concerning wages, hours, and other conditions of employment."[9]

The Bill authorized representation elections and granted its Labor Board discretionary authority to determine voting eligibility and the appropriate unit for election purposes. It did not mandate exclusive representation by majority rule in so many words, but it disenfranchised scabs. One section provided that "the term 'employee' shall not include an individual who has replaced a striking employee."

Wagner's Bill also revived 'government by injunction', although in a novel form. The Bill reinvested federal courts with the "jurisdiction to restrain any unfair labor practice" employers might commit. But the excruciatingly punctilious procedures governing the issuance of injunc-tions by federal courts under the Norris-La Guardia Act would not apply to unfair labor practice injunctions demanded by the National Labor Board in Wagner's Bill. In National Labor Board hearings, on the basis of which the NLB could demand that the Attorney General seek injunctions, "the examiner or the Board shall not be bound by the rules of evidence prevailing in courts of law or equity." If an employer appealed to the federal courts, however, the "findings of the Board as to the facts, if supported by evidence," *any evidence,* "shall be conclusive." NLB-generated injunctions could order employers to "cease and desist" from unfair labor practices, to "pay damages," and also "to take affirmative action," including the reinstatement of illegally dismissed employees.

Wagner's Bill aroused a storm of controversy, and even though some of its provisions were watered down after the hearings, the bill did not become law. Instead, Congress promulgated a Joint Resolution, creating the first, or old, NLRB to administer Section 7 (a) of the NRA. But Congress did amend the Railway Labor Act of 1926. The Railway Labor Act of 1934 (48 Stat. 1185) abolished company unions and yellow-dog contracts and established exclusive representation by majority rule, ordering employers to "exert every reasonable effort to make and maintain" collective agreements with majority unions. It also outlawed the closed shop (which remained unlawful on the railroads, although the Railway Labor Act of 1951 permitted union security agreements similar to those allowed elsewhere under federal law).[10]

Majority Rule and the Duty to Bargain under the NRA

NRA labor boards hammered out a series of decisions in 1934 that tried to establish, through administrative regulation, the principles that Wagner and his colleagues failed to obtain from Congress until 1935. Some of the important cases are worth review for the light they shed on what progressives and trade union leaders sought in the Wagner Act itself.

The Denver Tramway Case involved an employer who had cooperated with a Board-sponsored election.[11] An AFL union (the Amalgamated Association of Street and Railway Employees) beat a company union (the Employees Representative Committee) by a very narrow margin. The company negotiated with the majority union but continued to meet with the minority organization. The AFL union protested to the NLB "that the company would not recognize it as the exclusive collective bargaining agency of all the employees." Nevertheless, the AFL union submitted a proposal to management "in which it was provided, among other things, that said agreement was to govern 'the relations to exist during the term of this Agreement between the company and the members of the said Association'." (p. 64)

The apparent contradiction between the union's "members-only" proposal and its demand for exclusivity was not explained in the published record of the case and has gone unremarked upon in the literature. One hypothesis is that the union all along wanted both exclusive bargaining rights and a closed shop. If this is correct, one can infer that the company refused to negotiate *that* kind of members-only agreement, and that the company was probably fortified in its decision by the existence of a minority (company) union that held the allegiance of a substantial number of employees. Perhaps this lack of 'solidarity' kept the majority union from calling a strike, and impelled them instead to look to the law for help.

At any rate, the NLB insisted that the organization "selected by a majority of those voting" (p. 64) must bargain for all the corporation's employees and process any grievances between the employees and the management. The Board threw out the "members-only" proposal.[12]

The legality of *individual* bargaining between employer and employee after a majority representative had been chosen arose in the E.F. Caldwell Company Case.[13] The company offered all its employees individual, written labor contracts, as had been its custom, as an alternative to a collective agreement. The union, "feeling that the circulation of the individual agreements revealed the company's unwillingness to bargain collectively" (p. 12), went out on strike.

The NLRB (successor to the NLB) announced that the mere *offer* of individual bargaining as an alternative to collective bargaining was an interference with the employees' "right to bargain collectively through representatives of their own choosing." According to the Board, it would "empty the employees' right of collective bargaining of all significance and purpose." (p. 13) The right to strike was not enough.

Would an employer who bargained to an impasse, and then 'took a strike' rather than come to an agreement, interfere with the "right to bargain collectively"? Would an employer be justified in offering to take back striking workers on an individual basis? Would an employer who hired nonstrikers or scabs interfere with strikers' "right to bargain collectively"? Would the continued operation of a struck plant by *any* means (say by supervisors) "empty the employees' right of collective bargaining of all significance and purpose"? The NLRB didn't say.

The Board further clarified its evolving common law of collective bargaining in the celebrated Houde Engineering Company Case, decided soon after the Caldwell Case.[14] The representation situation in this automobile parts manufacturer's plant was similar to what existed in the Denver Tramway Company, but Houde was unwilling to negotiate a collective agreement of any type either with the minority representative (the Houde Welfare and Athletic Association, a former company union), or with the majority choice (the United Automobile Workers). The company conferred independently with each group on working conditions and grievances, but not with both.

The union did not charge, nor did the Board find, that the employer deliberately attempted to keep the two organizations apart. Nor did the Board find that Houde dominated the minority organization. The company itself suggested a composite bargaining committee based on proportional electoral strength, perhaps modeling its proposal on the recent settlement in the automobile industry (of which it, Houde, was a satellite firm). But the UAW refused to participate in this plan, as it was refusing to participate in the ill-fated proportional representation scheme in the automobile industry.

The Board declared that the company interfered with the employees' 'right to organize' by refusing to bargain exclusively with the majority union. "It seems clear," the Board claimed, "that the company's policy of dealing first with one group and then with the other" enabled "it to favor one organization at the expense of the other." This policy alone could "check at will the growth of either organization" and "confuse the employees," making "them uncertain which organization they should from time to time adhere to." Thus the company could "maintain a permanent and artificial division in the ranks." (p. 39) Why the employees or their representatives could not see this and take the appropriate action, if the division in the ranks were *really* artificial, the Board didn't say.

At any rate, the Board ruled that the existence of multiple bargaining agents violated the workers' statutory right to organize and "resulted, whether intentionally or not, in defeating the objects of the statute." The object of the National Industrial Recovery Act "was to encourage collective bargaining, with all that implies." "Collective bargaining," of course, was "simply a means to an end. The end is an agreement." "[A]ny interpretation of Section 7(a) which in practice would hamper self-organization and the making of collective agreements cannot be sound"; thus the "right of employees to bargain collectively implies a duty on the part of the employer to bargain with their representatives. Without this duty to bargain the right to bargain would be sterile." (pp. 39, 35, 37)[15]

Why did the Board rule "that the only interpretation of Section 7(a) which can give effect to its purposes" was "that the representatives of the majority" must "constitute the exclusive agency for collective bargaining with the employer"? (p. 40) Majority rule, the Board answered, "is in accord with American traditions of political democracy, which empower representatives elected by the majority of voters to speak for all the people." (p. 43) The concept may seem reasonable, since there is generally only one representative for a political district; but no American tradition of political democracy mandates a one-party government.

The Board's 'duty to bargain' doctrine in the Houde Case, like its restriction of individual bargaining in the Caldwell Case, is as interesting for what it omits as for what it includes. If *any* interpretation of Section 7(a) which in practice hampers the making of collective agreements cannot be sound, then why doesn't 7(a) imply compulsory agreements? Why isn't failure on an employer's part to agree to *any* or *all* union demands an interference with the right to organize and bargain collectively? Would not an employer's willingness to 'take a strike', not to mention his decision to operate during a strike, be proof that he never intended to bargain in good faith and always intended to 'bust the union' by demonstrating its ineffectiveness to the workers concerned? Do not the doctrines of *Caldwell* and *Houde* point toward a rule (and reflect the kind of thinking) that would prohibit an employer from ever bargaining individually once a majority representative has been selected?

The National Labor Relations Act, 1935

After the mid-term Congressional elections in 1934 returned an overwhelmingly Democratic Congress, and in a climate of violent 'recognition' strikes, Wagner reintroduced his labor disputes bill in February, 1935 (S 1958). Representative William P. Connery introduced a similar measure concurrently in the House of Representatives. Hearings were held in both the Senate (where the important testimony was taken) and the House in March. The Senate Committee reported the Bill favorably in May, and, following a climactic debate, it passed. The House Committee reported its version favorably later in May, and, following a debate early in June, it too passed. A Conference Committee issued its reconciliation measure late in June. President Roosevelt signed the measure into law in the first week of July.

The National Labor Relations Act (NLRA, also called the Wagner Act)* was the climax of a very long and very complicated political-ideological journey that radically restructured the market to favor monopolistic collective bargaining over competition and individual contracting. Like the similarly motivated measures that immediately preceded it—the Railway Labor Acts of 1926 and 1934, the Norris-La Guardia Act of 1932, and the National Industrial Recovery Act of 1933—the Wagner Act was based squarely and explicitly on the theory that individual laborers could not bargain equally with employers, that inadequate bargaining power led to inadequate purchasing power which in turn led to unemployment, and that, through organization and through collective bargaining, wages, purchasing power, and employment could be 'stabilized'.

The authors of the Wagner Act, as well as its fervent supporters throughout American society, looked ultimately toward industry-wide unions bargaining collectively with employers and employer associations operating on the basis of universal closed shops. But the law did not *mandate* closed shops, nor did it impose any *particular* bargaining unit standard for the American economy. The function of the law was, in effect, to supplement union power. The unions would go about organizing and bargaining, without having to worry overmuch about the power of the federal courts to bring their violent or otherwise unlawful activities to heel, while the NLRB would systematically weaken or destroy employers', and nonunion workers', power to resist. The 'right to organize', the 'duty to bargain', the principle of exclusive representation by majority rule, and the employer's obligation to abide by collective bargains were all instruments to facilitate or achieve the larger end: a 'cartellized' labor market. Each provision of the law supported, and was supported by, the

---

*Appendix 13 below.

others; the law as a whole was meant to help unions to organize workers, and to supplement unions' strike threat power.

Free Employee Choice vs. Union Security

The 'instrumental' nature of the Wagner Act provisions is most apparent in its 'right to organize' principle, and in the debate over the meaning of this principle in Congress. The right to organize is very prominent in the Act. It appears in Section 1 as a declaration of policy; in Section 7 as a general provision; and in Section 8 it is protected against various "unfair labor practice[s]" by employers, including discrimination in hiring, discharge and promotion, formation of company unions, yellow-dog contracts—indeed, generally any act "to encourage or discourage membership in any labor organization"—with one overwhelmingly significant exception: the closed shop agreement with a majority union.

It is revealing as an indicator of the distance the country had traveled that hardly anyone publicly defended the simple right of the employer to hire or fire workers for any reason, including joining a union or going out on strike, on the grounds of freedom of association. Nevertheless, throughout the hearings and debates of 1934 and 1935, the opponents of closed union shops (employers, leaders of rival, minority unions, and conservative intellectuals and opinion leaders) insisted, time and time again, on an amendment to eliminate "coercion" from *any* source that would encourage or discourage membership in a labor organization. It seemed evident to these individuals that passage of the NLRA, as written, would bring in its wake an increase of union coercion of individual employers—and through employers, of individual employees—the likes of which the country had never seen. How could anyone permit himself to believe otherwise, given the well-nigh universal demand by unions for closed shops, and the means they had used from time immemorial to obtain them?[16]

The opponents' efforts went for naught. The proponents of the Wagner Act as written stonewalled any or all objections, insisting (correctly) that the statute does not mandate the closed shop, but blandly denying that there is any such thing as employee or union coercion of other employees. Senator Walsh, for instance, testifed that "[t]here is no such thing as economic pressure between employee and employee." After all,

> [n]o one workman can dismiss another from the shop. The workman would probably have the protection of his employer if he should resist an urgent invitation [sic] to join a labor organization.[17]

Senator Wagner was the master of this argument, however, and he used it over and over again. In one place, for instance, he claimed that

> there is no possibility that the same coercive power can be exercised by one employee against another that can be exercised by the employer against the employee. If the employee does not do what is wanted by the employer, he does not retain his job. To lump employers and employees together is to bewilder the listener and confuse the situation.

Yet there is a problem with this line of reasoning, given the labor reformer's own ends and means. A colloquy between Wagner and Senator Tydings, leader of the amendment forces in the Senate, is apropos:

> Mr. Tydings: . . . My theory is that there may be men who do not want to join the union who will be coerced under the Senator's bill into joining a union where really they are happy and contented as they are and do not want to be forced to join a union.
>
> Mr. Wagner: How is that possible? . . . We are extending the right to the workers to elect any individual or organization they choose, instead of being restricted. How is that compelling anybody to do anything? The charge of compulsion is a gross misrepresentation that has circled the country. . . . Closed-shop agreements are made all over the country, and they are matters of agreement. The question of compulsion is not in them. They are matters of agreement.[18]

If a closed shop is a matter of voluntary agreement, then why isn't a yellow-dog contract, or an agreement to join a company union? What about the rights of individual workers to union representation (or no union representation) *of their own, individual choosing*? Shouldn't there be some consistency, one way or another? Exasperated with Wagner's obfuscation, Tydings threw up his hands:

> As I see this particular section, it looks to me like an effort to force every man in America to join a certain kind of union, whether or not he wishes to join that union; and the coercion and intimidation features are not to be inserted in this section because a certain union desires a free hand to take the workers from the groups in which they now belong into groups into which they may not wish to go.
> That is the naked fact back of the opposition to this amendment. It is an amendment to force all working people into a particular union, and every Senator on this floor knows that to be the truth.[19]

Of course, Wagner did also, because elsewhere he admitted that all this stuff about abstract 'rights' was so much nonsense; it was all a matter of power. The right to organize, he correctly stated,

> has been interpreted repeatedly to mean that any employee at any time may choose his own representative or may elect to deal individually with his employer. Such an interpretation, which illegalizes the closed union shop, strikes a death blow at the practice and theory of collective bargaining . . . It has been claimed that in order to be fair, the bill should prohibit employees and labor organizations, as well as employers, from coercing employees in the choice of representatives. This argument rests upon a misconception of the needs which give rise to this measure. Violence and intimidation by either employers or workers are adequately prevented by the common law . . . This measure deals with the subtler forms of economic pressure. Such pressure cannot be exerted by employees upon one another *to an extent justifying* Congressional action.

If economic 'coercion' *by unions* is to be eliminated from labor relations in the name of employee free choice, Wagner also correctly noted that "it will repeal all the salutary features of the Norris Anti-Injunction Act. . . . *It would be better to have no law at all than to make this legislation a vehicle for the revival of the labor injunction*."[20]

The Duty to Bargain and the Obligation of Contract

The proponents of compulsory collective bargaining insisted, as had the majority on the NLB and the first NLRB, that without it the 'right to organize', as well as the principle of majority rule, would be, in the words of the Senate Report accompanying and explaining the Wagner Act, "a mere delusion . . . of little worth. . . . Experience has proved that neither obedience to law nor respect for law is encouraged by holding forth a right unaccompanied by fulfillment."[21]

Opposition to this 'instrumental' or 'positive' theory of rights arose from a variety of quarters. Some asked why anyone should be forced to associate with an organization that might be pledged to destroy him. "I take it," Walter G. Merritt, of the employer-oriented League for Industrial Rights, testified, that

> so far as the wording of this bill goes, that I have to carry on relations, . . . [if] the majority of my employees want it, with a communist organization pledged to my destruction. Absurd, you may say . . . but extreme illustrations are useful in developing an

idea . . . it is absolutely an unsound legislative policy . . . to say that you will have to do business with these organizations, regardless of their wrongdoings, . . . regardless of the fact that they are devoted to illegal practices. . . .[22]

It was left to James E. Emery, counsel to the NAM, to puncture the balloon of the whole 'positive' theory of rights—upon which the progressive social conscience rested, then as now.

Does the right to lend create in anybody the duty to borrow? Does the right to rent on the part of a landlord excite in any person the duty to accept the tenancy which is offered to him? Does the right to marry include the right . . . to compel her to accept your suit without regard to the competition of others? . . . Never before has anyone in this field suggested that the right to engage in contractual relations placed on somebody else, without a mutual right to reject the contract, the duty of agreement to it.[23]

The proponents of the duty to bargain vehemently denied that it implied any duty to agree. But one employer, probably reflecting the edgy feeling on the part of many, wondered if the NLRB would hold the duty to bargain in reserve, like a "club over the heads of all of the employers" and practically compel them to make concessions, even to agree, whenever the unions didn't feel like risking a strike to get their demands.[24]

The old problem of mutuality that plagued the collective agreement was not much discussed in 1934 and 1935. The unilateral breach of a collective agreement was not mentioned explicitly among the unfair labor practices an employer might commit, though it is obvious that the NLRB would punish this behavior (either as a violation of the employer's duty to bargain or as an interference with the worker's right to organize). But there was no question that unions would *not* be legally bound to their end of the bargain, since Section 13 of the Wagner Act read that "[n]othing in this Act shall be construed so as to interfere with or impede or diminish the right to strike."

Majority Rule

Section 9 (a) established majority rule unionism:

Representatives designated or selected for the purposes of collective bargaining by the majority of the employees in a unit appropriate for such purposes, shall be the exclusive representa-

tives of all the employees in such unit for the purposes of collective bargaining in respect to rates of pay, wages, hours of
employment, or other conditions of employment: *Provided,*
That any individual employee or a group of employees shall have
the right at any time to present grievances to their employer.

Section 9 (b) gave the NLRB the power to

decide . . . whether . . . the unit appropriate for the purposes of
collective bargaining shall be the employer unit, craft unit, plant
unit, or subdivision thereof.

The authors of the majority rule principle were at pains to indicate the
effect this provision would have on individual bargaining. The Senate
Committee Report stated that

[m]ajority rule carries the clear implication that employers *shall
not interfere* with the *practical* application of the right of
employees to bargain collectively through chosen representatives *by bargaining with individuals or minority groups in
their own behalf,* after representatives have been picked by the
majority to represent all.

The House Committee Report had virtually identical language.[25]

The champions of exclusive representation by majority rule stressed
two themes during the course of the legislative hearings. The first, in the
words of the Senate Committee Report, was that it was "wellnigh
universally recognized that it is practically impossible to apply two or
more sets of [collective] *agreements* to one unit of workers at the same
time, or to apply the terms of one agreement to only a portion of the
workers in a single unit."[26] The second theme was that collective
bargaining on the basis of proportional representation, or the individual's
right to bargain for himself, even to arrive at a unitary agreement, was
impracticable. Minority representation allegedly led to industrial strife,
permitted employers to evade their duty to bargain, and generally was at
loggerheads with the purpose of the act as a whole.

Francis Biddle and Lloyd Garrison, both law professors and members of
the old NLRB in 1934, testified to the alleged impossibility of collective
agreements on any other terms than majority rule. Biddle asserted that
members-only collective agreements necessarily conflicted with the
provisions of the law prohibiting employer discrimination. "Failure of the
employer to give equally advantageous terms to nonmembers of the union
negotiating the agreement," Biddle claimed, "would immediately result in
a marked increase of the union's membership." But "the giving of better
terms to nonmembers of the union negotiating the agreement would
immediately result in a marked increase [obviously, Biddle meant de-

crease] in the union's membership" and "would result in a strike." There would arise, in the words of the House Committee Report, "a wholly unworkable arrangement whereby men performing comparable duties were paid according to different scales of wages and hours."[27]

"An employer," Garrison insisted,

> cannot give one set of wages and hours to one group and another set to another where they are all doing the same type of work. It has to be an agreement applying to all. Then the only question is where there are two groups of employees, a majority and a minority group, with which shall the agreement be negotiated? It cannot be negotiated with both, because there is going to be only one agreement, and it is to apply to everybody. Is it at all sensible that the employer should negotiate . . . with the [minority] group [?]

Edwin Witte also strongly deprecated collective bargaining with minority representatives, going so far as to claim that the alternative to exclusivity was anarchy:

> In industrial government, just as in political government, there has to be majority rule, when it comes to actual government. . . . The right of petition, the right to lay grievances before Congress, is a right that any individual and every group must have. Similarly, in industrial government, the right of petition, the right to lay grievances before the employer seems to me a right that every group should be accorded, and every individual . . . but if it comes to determining conditions of employment by making some kind of rules governing wages and hours, there obviously has to be determination on the basis of majority rule, or you have pure anarchy, just as you would have in government.[28]

Proponents of majority rule also argued that employers would utilize members-only bargaining or proportional representation to evade their duty to bargain and avoid coming to an agreement by using company dominated unions to create artificial divisions in the work force and playing one group off against the other. The problem with this contention was that the NLRA was going to eliminate company unions. Most of the other independent unions were communist. If there was a division in the workforce because of divided loyalties in that case, it was hardly artificial or created by the employer.

Testifying about minority representation in the automobile industry in 1934, William Green, president of the AFL, claimed that it "caused turmoil and strife," that it "cannot work," and that it "will not work" elsewhere. Why? Perhaps because of the obstinacy of the AFL unions themselves. "While the device of proportional representation," Monsignor John A. Ryan observed, "has a certain appearance of fairness, it is entirely impracticable at the present time in the United States." The reason? The

> representatives of the regular [AFL] unions will not sit down on
> the same side of the bargaining table with the representatives of a
> company union or with the representatives of a Communist
> union. This may be deplorable, but it is a fact that cannot be
> changed by any amount of preaching or legislation in the near
> future.[29]

Even more pertinent, Dean Harry A. Millis of the University of Chicago observed that proportionality "in a plant or industry tends to keep the organizational situation open and plastic, while majority rule tends to maintain and to increase the strength" of the majority union. If "under such an arrangement" the organizations do not cooperate in the first place, "the workers will certainly not cooperate in making a show of strength by withdrawing their labor power." Majority rule, in other words, was useful for solidifying a majority union's strike-threat power. Finally, a proponent of exclusivity claimed that minority representation and plural bargaining, particularly where company unions were part of the scheme, were defective because they would not serve as a suitable basis for taking wages out of competition in the context of the future development of a corporative state. The logical level for plural bargaining (such as might take place with a company union and an independent union), Lloyd Garrison pointed out, is the plant. But

> the great thing to work for in this country is the making of
> industry-wide agreements such as we have in the coal industry
> and in the garment industry, and several others. . . . With the
> company union set-up it is impossible ever to conceive of reach-
> ing industry-wide agreements, because each plant . . . is treated as
> a thing in itself . . .[30]

Commentary: Majority Rule

One problem with Biddle's impossibility theorem is that it begs the question of an "appropriate bargaining unit." Jurisdiction is often part of the problem. What if all the men in a unit are *not* doing the same kind of work? What if a smaller group is absorbed by a larger, whose interests are different—say a craft by an industrial union? That is exactly what happened later in the 1930s, when NLRB unit elections began to favor CIO unions that swallowed up smaller, craft-oriented AFL unions. The situation reached the stage where some leaders of the AFL demanded that the

NLRB's discretion to establish appropriate bargaining units be significantly limited.[31]

There are other problems with the argument for exclusivity, though these were not voiced during the Wagner Act hearings. The last clause of Section 9 (a) admits that the majority union may not fairly represent the interests (grievances) of the individual worker, and there was nothing in the Wagner Act to guarantee that the exclusive bargaining representative would. In other words, it held "forth a right unaccompanied by fulfillment"; for what is the worth of the individual or minority group right to present grievances to an employer if the majority representative, operating with a closed shop agreement, for instance, could kick the griever out of the union for doing so? The evolution of a "duty of fair representation" in the law after 1944, seems to indicate that this problem was very real.

The objection to members-only agreements pertaining to their discriminatory effect on union membership is harder to fathom. The ability of unions to cut a better deal for their members is presumably the reason why workers join them in the first place, so why object if an employer pays union members higher wages than nonmembers? Suppose the employer pays higher wages to nonmembers to undermine union loyalty. Why is this so horrible? Unions 'pay' workers, as it were, to join and remain members; why can't employers pay them to stay out? If an employer reneges on promises he makes to keep unions out, he won't stay nonunion for long.

Leaving non-exclusive agreements for a moment for the question of non-exclusive bargaining, Garrison's and Witte's arguments were also not compelling. There is nothing remotely impossible about rules that govern all but are arrived at through representatives of different interests and points of view. Congress passes legislation governing all citizens, yet representatives of different parties exist and function during legislative deliberations. It is true that differences in Congress often prevent the passage of legislation at all; but this has rarely been regarded as an overwhelming defect of democracy.

Some opponents of majority rule understood this well enough. As Walter Merritt testified, exclusivity was not really compatible with *American* ideals of democracy:

> I think this majority rule comes pretty nearly to the idea with which Mr. Mussolini originally started, in effect if you got a bare plurality the other party is rooted out. It would be almost like saying our Senate must be made up exclusively of Democrats.[32]

Other opponents insisted that majority rule unionism was radically flawed *in principle,* because it applied a political metaphor to relationships that should properly be governed voluntarily, by private contract. "Our country being the democracy it is," one employer testified, and based on the principles it is, has always recognized the necessity of electing candidates by majorities. . . . But when it comes to the question of negotiating as to your right to work for someone else, I think the situation is vastly different. . . . I think the right to earn a living is vastly different from the right to vote, no matter how sacred the right to vote is.

The right to contract for the sale of one's labor was a far more fundamental civil liberty, James Emery reminded the Senators, than the right to vote. Recalling Abraham Lincoln's famous anti-slavery remark that " '[n]o man is good enough to govern another man without his consent'," Emery questioned whether the relationship between an individual worker and a union "representative" clothed with the public power of exclusivity was compatible with the constitutional basis of American society. Along these lines, James L. Donnelly of the Illinois Manufacturing Association claimed that there "has never been anything in the history of this country to compare with" exclusivity "aside from slavery and war-time conscription."[33]

Well, almost not. After all, most employers and employers' associations had supported majority rule a few years ago—when the issue was *price fixing* under the codes of competition of the NRA! For that matter, most employers who established company unions prior to or in response to the NRA always insisted on exclusivity (and often the closed company union shop as well). The author of the Wagner Act did not let this hypocrisy go unnoticed.[34]

Communist union leaders and their supporters stood to lose by majority rule, and they too lined up solidly against it (though not for individual bargaining rights). In 1934, Mr. Isidore Polier of the International Juridical Association submitted a lengthy memorandum to Congress, with suggestions for amending Wagner's Bill that included a '10 percent' solution. Closed shop agreements with majority unions would be all right, but only if such agreements would "permit any employee to join any other labor organization of his own choice which represents at least 10 percent of [the] employees." Polier's group would also provide for minority representation whenever 10 percent or more of the employees indicated a desire for this. But in all cases the minority would retain the right "to strike or picket."[35]

Industrial Democracy: Initial Constitutional Skirmishes

The National Labor Relations Board operated under a cloud between 1935 and 1937. Employers resisted the Board mightily because they were convinced that the Wagner Act invaded their constitutional rights. The Supreme Court had declared the NIRA unconstitutional in 1935 and the Bituminous Coal Conservation Act (BCCA) unconstitutional in 1936; both these measures contained provisions similar to those of the Wagner Act.[36]

The best-known and most often discussed question regarding the constitutionality of the NIRA, and its companion measure in the coal industry, concerned the limits of Congressional authority to regulate commerce among the several states, in light of the Supreme Court's hoary distinctions between "manufacturing" and "commerce" and between "interstate" and "intrastate" commerce. Less well-known, but even more pertinent for the law of labor relations, were the twin issues of 'separation of powers' and the problem surrounding the Congressional delegation of legislative powers to the Executive, and to private parties.

The NIRA and the BCCA both provided for the 'extension' of collective price and wage agreements by executive authority on the German model. In each instance, the Supreme Court found this corporative state device at odds with the Constitution.

"Congress," the Supreme Court declared in *A.L.A. Schechter Poultry Corporation* v. *United States* (295 U.S. 495 (1935)), "is not permitted to abdicate or to transfer to others the essential legislative functions with which it is thus vested" by the Constitution. "The codes of fair competition which the" NIRA "attempts to authorize are codes of laws. If valid, they place all persons within their reach under the obligation of positive law, binding equally those who assent and those who do not assent." But "[s]uch a delegation of legislative power is unknown to our law and is utterly inconsistent with the constitutional prerogatives and duties of Congress." (pp. 529-530, 537)

The delegation of legislative power to the President was impermissible under the Constitution; its delegation to private citizens—the formation of private governments—was profoundly shocking. Thus the Court denounced the corporativist provision of the BCCA in *Carter* v. *Carter Coal Company* (298 U.S. 238 (1936)):

> The power conferred upon the majority [in the Coal Commission, made up of representatives of the operators and the miners] is, in effect, the power to regulate the affairs of an unruly minority. This is legislative delegation in its most obnoxious form; for it is not even delegation to an official or an official body, presumptively disinterested, *but to private persons whose interests may and often are adverse to the interests of others in the same business* . . . a statute which attempts to confer such power undertakes an intolerable and unconstitutional interference with personal liberty and private property. The delegation is so clearly arbitrary, and so clearly a denial of rights safeguarded by the due process clause of the Fifth Amendment,

that it is unnecessary to do more than refer to decisions of this Court which foreclose the question. (p. 311, emphasis added)

Now, the power conferred on a majority union (*vis-a-vis* nonunion workers) to exercise its exclusive bargaining rights under Section 9 (a) of the National Labor Relations Act, and under Section 2, Fourth, of the Railway Labor Act of 1934, was analogous to the power of the code authorities under the NIRA and the Guffey Coal Act. Thus, when the Wagner Act came up for review, it would have been logical for the Supreme Court either to declare exclusive representation unconstitutional or to overturn its precedents in *Schechter* and *Carter*. But the Court did neither; or rather, it upheld majority rule unionism without overturning its precedents against the delegation of government power to private groups!

How and why the Court managed this feat historians and legal scholars have yet to fully explain,[37] but one facet of this episode is clear. The Court misread and misconstrued the *meaning* of majority rule unionism insofar as it affected the individual employer's right to bargain individually with employees, and the individual employee's right to bargain with employers. Part of the reason for this confusion lay in some dubious, even misleading, statements made by the government attorneys who argued the cases.

Virginian Railway Co. v. *AFL* (300 U.S. 515 (1937)) involved the constitutionality of the Railway Labor Act of 1934. The attorney for the corporation complained during the oral arguments that the employer's duty to bargain with a majority union was unconstitutional. But he did not seem to believe that exclusivity violated *employers'* rights:

> We say . . . that the right to give the majority the control over the minority in important matters of rules and rates of pay is, as this Court said, in *Carter* v. *Carter Coal Co.* (298 U.S. 238), the delegation of an authority of the most obnoxious kind. *But that is a matter for the employees to argue, not for us.* I just merely mention it in passing.[38]

Government lawyers denied that the employer's duty to bargain with the majority union usurped individual employee or employer rights. "We do not construe" the Railway Labor Act, Mr. Stanley Reed (the U.S. Solicitor General) opined, "to mean that the employer is restrained from contracting with individuals," but *only* that he may not enter "into agreements and undertakings which affect the *whole* of any particular craft" with other than a majority union. The "language" of the injunction issued on behalf of the Railroad Labor Board to enforce the law is "inapplicable to individual contracts with individual employees . . . it forbids only those agreements which cover an entire craft." *"Practically"* speaking, of course, Reed added, "it is impossible to have different contracts with different groups of employees—to have representatives of the majority and the minority, *or of individuals.*"[39]

The federal government argued that majority rule unionism did preclude individual contracting, *except* on terms agreeable to the majority representative (should it choose to demand a collective agreement). But this, the government contended in its written brief, was not a matter of *law*.

> When the majority of a craft or class has (either by secret ballot or otherwise) selected a representative, the carrier cannot make with anyone other than the representative *a collective contract* . . . whether the contract covers the class as a whole or a part thereof. *Neither the statute nor the decree prevents the carrier from refusing to make a collective contract and hiring individuals on whatever terms the carrier may by unilateral action determine.* In hirings of that sort the individual does not deal in a representative capacity with the carrier and hiring does not set general rates of pay, rules, or working conditions.[40]

The Court agreed with this reasoning. Majority rule and the duty to bargain, the Court explained,

> must be taken to prohibit the negotiation of labor contracts, generally applicable to employees . . . with any representative other than the respondent, but as not precluding such individual contracts as petitioner may elect to make directly with individual employees . . . The obligation imposed on the employer . . . to treat with the true representative of the employees . . . imposes the affirmative duty to treat only with the true representative, and hence the negative duty to treat with no other [representative]. (pp. 549, 548)

Given this reading of the law, the Court did not profess to see any conflict between majority rule and individual rights such as had arisen under the NIRA and the BCCA.

Their interpretation of exclusivity under the Railway Labor Act also permitted the Supreme Court to rule favorably on the Wagner Act, despite the clear evidence of Congressional intent to the contrary, as expressed in the Senate and House Committee Reports on the Wagner Act (see text *supra*, accompanying note 25.). In oral argument, counsel for Associated Press lambasted majority rule as an arbitrary invasion of the individual rights of both employer and employee: "to deny the right of the minority to deal with the employer is to deny to the employer the right to deal with the minority." But the government attorney sidestepped this problem by reminding the Court that "this provision is not invoked against the petitioner in this case" and hence "a decision on its validity would seem clearly unnecessary." Similarly, Stanley Reed, in the Jones and Laughlin case (*NLRB* v. *Jones and Laughlin Steel Corporation*, 301 U.S. 1 (1937)), reminded the Court that the "section as to exclusive representation—that is not before the Court at this time."[41]

In *Jones and Laughlin*, the Court nevertheless did rule on Section 9 (a), and followed their own reading of exclusive representation in the *Virginian Railway* case. Emphasizing the allegedly benign effect of majority rule on individual bargaining rights, the Court wrote that "the obligation to treat with the true representative" does not preclude

> 'such individual contracts' as the Company might 'elect to make directly with individual employees' . . . The Act does not compel agreements between employers and employees. It does not compel any agreement whatever. It does not prevent the employer 'from refusing to make a collective contract and hiring individuals on whatever terms' the employer 'may by unilateral action determine'. (pp. 44-45)

The Period of Legal Limbo, 1937-1944

The Supreme Court notwithstanding, the National Labor Relations Board faithfully executed the principle of majority rule unionism as its legislative authors intended, and in accord with the body of administrative 'common law' built up in the NRA era. In 1934 individual bargaining between employer and employee *as an alternative* to collective bargaining after a majority union was chosen had been declared a violation of the "right to organize." After 1937, the NLRB declared it a violation of the employer's "duty to bargain."[42]

Similarly, the scope of the employer's duty to bargain had (and still has) yet to be decided. Were there any limits on the subjects employers could be compelled to bargain about? Wages and hours are explicitly named, but what is the reach of "working conditions"? Were there any so-called 'management prerogatives' beyond the reach of the duty to bargain (if not beyond the power of the strike)?

In *theory*, there are not; because there is nothing the managers of a firm may do with its assets that does not directly or indirectly affect employee working conditions. Union leaders have always had an open-ended view of their mandate. As one of them put it, "there are no managerial prerogatives." And as the scholar Neil Chamberlain explained,

> One of the management members of the President's National Labor-Management Conference following World War II reported subsequently: 'Labor wouldn't even agree to an effort to define the functions of management, although we made a real effort to

get that issue settled. We drew up a list of some thirty odd specified acts, such as the determination of prices, accounting procedures, and so forth, which it seemed clear to us must be reserved to management. Labor refused to accept a single one, and we are told officially by one of the labor delegates that the reason they had refused was that at some future time labor may want to bring any one of these functions into the realm of collective bargaining'.[43]

In a publication reflecting his research during the 1940s, Chamberlain concluded that

if the strength and power of labor unions continue to expand in the future as in the past there will continue at the same time a slow but marked penetration of organized labor into the field of management prerogatives,

especially manifest in the "trend toward industry-wide collective bargaining." He found that there had already

been collective bargaining on questions involving the building or the extension or contraction of the plant or the industry, the location of the plant or the industry, the co-ordination and integration of the work, the general organization of the plant, the determination of the type of personnel, the types of machinery and equipment, the purchase of materials and supplies, the nature and quality of the product or service to be produced, the fixing of the price of the product or service, the quantity of production, the sales and distribution policy, and the policy as to extensions and improvements, as well as general labor policies.

Chamberlain found growing evidence of a "pattern of industrial organization resembling a loose system of industrial corporatism" throughout the economy, wherever unions gained a foothold.[44]

The collective agreement itself in these years bound only the employer. Unions retained the right to strike at any time; and the NLRB was indisposed to enjoin strikes or picketing *even if called by minority unions* in defiance of a lawfully negotiated collective agreement by a majority union.[45] Actually, the Board went much further. They prohibited employers from insisting, as a precondition for signing a collective agreement, that unions assume contractual responsibility for their actions by incorporating, posting a bond, or agreeing to a "no strike" clause.[46]

The political scientist and legal scholar John Dickinson, a veteran of the debate about pluralism and sovereignty during the 1920s, put it all into an interesting perspective. The evolving American system of industrial democracy, he wrote in 1943, was rapidly coming to resemble "a regime of status," at least as far as employers were concerned. They were "passively subjected to duties without voluntarily assuming them," while "from the standpoint of employees, many of the advantages of contract persist."

> The substance . . . of what may be said of the status of collective labor agreements or contracts is that as against the employer, they are apparently contracts in the full legal sense, capable of judicial enforcement; but, on the other hand, as against the employees, not merely is there usually a lack of procedure to enforce them, but in addition governmental agencies can, and frequently do, support labor organizations in their efforts to compel more favorable terms in the teeth of the provisions of an existing agreement.[47]

Nevertheless, the entire system of industrial democracy being (sometimes, all too literally) hammered out in the years after 1937 existed in a kind of legal limbo, with respect to one fundamental issue. The Court had yet to fully face the conflict between individual rights and majority rule, since its interpretation of exclusive representation in 1937 was profoundly at variance with legislative intent and administrative policy.

This problem did not go unnoticed within the legal profession. To what degree was the collective contract, to recall Herbert Croly's phrase of a generation past, "absolute within the limits contained in the bond"?[48] A few argued that individual contracts with terms inferior to those negotiated by the majority representative should be legal. Others (and this had been Croly's position) argued that collective terms should be construed as minimums, much as the "extended agreements" in Europe always were; individual terms better than those negotiated by the union ought to be permissible. But a larger group, including an influential number of 'social democrat' refugees from fascist countries themselves, insisted that *no* individual deviations should be permitted. The Supreme Court eventually came to agree with this *Weltanschauung*.[49]

The Triumph of Fascist Syndicalism

In *J. I. Case Co. v. NLRB* (321 U.S. 332 (1944)), the Supreme Court announced that individual bargaining between an employer and an employee as an alternative to collective bargaining after the majority representative was selected was a violation of the employer's duty to bargain.

In the dispute at hand, some of the individual terms the employer offered workers in lieu of collective bargaining were *better* than the union's demands. Nonetheless, the Court found this impermissible, since the "practice and philosophy of collective bargaining looks with suspicion on such individual advantages." The Court recognized that collective agreements might establish only minimums—but that was at the discretion of the union; and

> except as so provided, advantages to individuals may prove as disruptive of industrial peace as disadvantages. They are a fruitful way of interfering with organization and choice of representatives; increased compensation, if individually deserved, is often earned at the cost of breaking down some other standard thought to be for the welfare of the group. . . . (p. 338)[50]

The *J. I. Case Company* decision thus dissipated the legal fog the Supreme Court had itself created in 1937. Majority rule unionism *was* incompatible with individual bargaining rights. But was exclusive representation compatible with the Constitution? Oddly enough, the Court didn't really say. In the *Schechter* and *Carter Coal* cases, the Court found the delegation of legislative power to private groups unconstitutional, but it passed favorably on exclusive representation in the *Jones and Laughlin* case, by misreading the legal meaning of majority rule as it affected individual rights. In 1944, the Court correctly *construed* the meaning of majority rule. But the *constitutionality* of exclusive representation was not contested by either side, so the precedents of *Schecter* and *Carter Coal* remained—and still remain—valid. The result is a profound irony. The political core of American industrial democracy survived intact by virtue of a judicial sleight-of-hand. It still does.[51]

The exact nature of the new property right secured through "collective bargaining and the formal labor contract," to recall Henry Carter Adams's phrase of a generation past, was further clarified by the Supreme Court in the companion case of *Medo Photo Supply Corporation* v. *NLRB* (321 U.S. 678 (1944)). Here a majority of the employees repudiated the bargaining authority of their own exclusive agent and approached the employer directly, as a group, to negotiate terms of employment. The *union* filed an unfair labor practice charge against the employer, which the Supreme Court found meritorious.

> Bargaining carried on by the employer directly with the employees, whether a minority or majority, who have not revoked their designation of a bargaining agent, would be subversive of the mode of collective bargaining which the statute has ordained . . . The statute was enacted in the public interest for the protection of the employees' right to collective bargaining and *it may not be ignored by the employer, even though the employees consent.* (pp. 684, 687, emphasis added)

Justice Rutledge dissented against the syndicalist theory of unionism reflected by the majority of his brethren, and argued in favor of a 'contractual' approach. "The statute purports to be drawn in favor of protecting the interests of employees, *not those of unions as such."* Therefore, "after the employees took matters into their own hands and showed to the employer by that act that they wanted to deal with him themselves, not through the union," they *had revoked* their designation. "In all normal agency relations, . . . the principal can revoke them by exercising the agency himself," and "need not notify the agent." When the principal, in this case, the worker, "acts on his own behalf, he exhausts the subject matter of the agency and it comes to an end." Rutledge added that

> [u]nless a designated union acquires, by its selection, a thraldom over the men who designate it . . . it would seem that any powers the union may acquire by virtue of the designation would end whenever those who confer them and on whose behalf they are to be exercised take them back of their own accord into their own hands and exercise them for themselves. (pp. 695, 696, emphasis added)

"[W]hich is to prevail," Rutledge asked rhetorically—one of those rhetorical questions that manages to compress an entire political philosophy into a single alternative—"the agent's interest and right or the principal's, the unions or the employees?" (p. 696) The answer the Court gave was clear, as Professor Clyde Summers observed a few years later. Under the American version of industrial democracy, he surmised, the real "locus of power" is "not vested in the majority" of workers, "but in the union as an entity wholly apart from the governed employees . . . Whether the union is still approved by the majority is irrelevant. Its power continues." The Wagner Act had created a hybrid social organization, private in origin but exercising public power over individual rights; the majority union became something akin to a private government, a legally created 'state within the state':

> Unions, in bargaining, are not private organizations but are governmental agencies garbed with the cloak of legal authority to represent all employees in the unit and armed with the legal right to participate in all decisions affecting terms and conditions of employment. . . . It is . . . necessary to state . . . explicitly the nature of union power . . . the union is . . . the employees' economic government. The union's power is the power to govern.[52]

More expansively still, Professor Ruth Weyand, the NLRB's attorney in the *Medo* case, observed that Congress's "adoption of the majority rule principle as the central concept of the collective bargaining structure constitutes a complete repudiation" of the free market and the regime of contract.

> In contrast to the concern of the common law with the assumed intent of each employee, the majority rule principle makes the intent of any or all of the individual employees immaterial. Instead, by analogy to the political process, each employee, union and non-union alike, who falls within the unit over which the elected representative has jurisdiction, is subject to all provisions respecting his employment upon which the representatives and his employer agree. Like the legislative branch of the government, effecting changes in the law, the union and the employer, by changing from time to time the rules governing hours, wages, and conditions of employment, bind the employee to each change effected irrespective of the employees' intent in the matter. Nor can the employee by any individual contract alter the rules governing his employment fixed by the collective agreement entered into by the union selected by the majority of the employees in the unit any more than a citizen by private contract alter the rules of the legislature.[53]

But just as the guilds of old eventually discovered that they could not exercise monopoly power granted to them by the government without sooner or later being called to account, the Supreme Court decided in yet another profoundly important case in 1944 (*Steele* v. *Louisville and Nashville Railroad,* 323 U.S. 192), that the majority union had a legally enforceable *duty* to represent "fairly" the interests of all employees for whom it bargained. The Court observed that

> Congress has seen fit to clothe the bargaining representative with powers comparable to those possessed by a legislative body both to create and restrict the rights of those whom it represents.

Therefore, the Court reasoned,

> the Railway Labor Act imposes upon the statutory representative of a craft at least as exacting a duty to protect equally the interests of the members of the craft as the Constitution imposes upon a legislature to give equal protection to the interests of those for whom it legislates. (p. 202)

Individual workers were at least subject to relief from some of the grosser forms of abuse by their representatives (in this case, racial discrimination).

The federal government thereafter gradually assumed the authority, even the duty, to make unions conform their policies to standards, such as due process, that previously only applied to the government itself. Years have passed and a mountain of 'duty of fair representation' litigation has accumulated. Yet no one has been able to consistently explain how a representative can fairly represent the interests of those individuals who never wanted representation in the first place, and who stand to lose by it.[54]

Similarly, great public uneasiness over the unions' exercise of legally-created monopolistic power led to legislation in 1947 (Taft-Hartley Act, 61 Stat. 136) and in 1959 (Landrum-Griffin Act, 73 Stat. 519), which attempted to regulate and restrict these private governments.

The Taft-Hartley Act prohibited closed shops and union shops where more is required of the individual employee than the payment of dues; and permitted states to go even further and prohibit virtually all kinds of union security agreements. Several states had already passed "right to work laws" before 1947; and several more followed thereafter (see Introduction, *supra*.) But union security is a fundamental goal of virtually all unions—both as an end in itself (to secure union power against dissenters and free riders) and as a means to obtain further ends. Feeling threatened by these statutory inroads on their power (power obtained by virtue of legislative restriction of freedom of contract) some unions unsuccessfully challenged the constitutionality of these measures—on the grounds of liberty of contract. This did not mean that these unions suddenly became advocates of laissez faire. On the contrary, in a display of what may only be characterized as spectacular chutzpah, they asserted in *Lincoln Federal Labor Union* v. *Northwestern Iron & Metal Co* (335 U.S. 525 (1948))

> 'that the right to work as a non-unionist is in no way equivalent to or the parallel of the right to work as a union member; that there exists no constitutional right to work as a non-unionist on the one hand while the right to maintain employment free from discrimination because of union membership is constitutionally protected'. (p. 531)

The Supreme Court made short work of the idea that the Constitution allowed legislatures to protect union members from discrimination yet prohibited legislatures from protecting nonunion members from discrimination.[55]

Following the startling revelations in the 1950s of union crime, violence, corruption, and undemocratic practices, Congress passed the Landrum-Griffin Act, which attempted to regulate the internal affairs of unions, in order to prevent these abuses.[56] Landrum-Griffin created a 'Bill of Rights' for employees represented by a majority union, established an elaborate set of financial reporting and other standards, and prohibited communist party members or persons convicted of various felonies from serving as union officers or employees for a period of several years. These various regulatory measures were, and are, fairly remarkable intrusions into private, non-governmental organizations. Congressional representatives, for instance, do not have to pass fitness tests such as those required of union officers or employees. On the other hand, these kinds of standards have been applied to government employees; and to that extent our 'free trade unions' have become incorporated into the state—a disturbing process that may fairly be described as the beginning of a fascistic regulation of our quasi-syndicalist system of industrial democracy.

Appendix 1. The Ordinance of Labourers, 1349
(Complete Text)

Edward *by the grace of God,* &c. *to the reverend father in Christ,* William, *by the same grace archbishop of* Canterbury, *primate of all* England, *greeting. Because a great part of the people, and especially of workmen and servants, late died of the pestilence, many seeing the necessity of masters, and great scarcity of servants, will not serve unless they may receive excessive wages, (2) and some rather willing to beg in idleness, than by labour to get their living; we, considering the grievous incommodities, which of the lack especially of ploughmen and such labourers may hereafter come, have upon deliberation and treaty with the prelates and the nobles, and learned men assisting us, of their mutual counsel, ordained:*

CAP. I.
Every person able in body under the age of sixty years, not having to live on, being required, shall be bound to serve him that doth require him, or else committed to the gaol, until he find surety to serve.

That every man and woman of our realm of *England,* of what condition he be, free or bond, able in body, and within the age of threescore years, not living in merchandize, nor exercising any craft, nor having of his own whereof he may live, nor proper land, about whose tillage he may himself occupy, and not serving any other, if he in convenient service (his Estate considered) be required to serve, he shall be bounden to serve him which so shall him require. And take only the wages, livery, meed, or salary, which were accustomed to be given in the places where he oweth to serve, the xx. year of our reign of *England,* or five or six other common years next before. Provided always, That the lords be preferred before other in their bondmen or their land tenants, so in their service to be retained: so that nevertheless the said lords shall retain no more than be necessary for them. And if any such man or woman, being so required to serve, will not the same do, that proved by two true men before the sheriff or the bailiffs of our sovereign lord the King, or the constables of the town where the same shall happen to be done, he shall anon be taken by them or any of them, and committed to the next gaol, there to remain under strait keeping, till he find surety to serve in the form aforesaid.

CAP. II.
If a workman or servant depart from service before the time agreed upon, he shall be imprisoned.
Item, If any reaper, mower, or other workman or servant, of what estate or condition that he be, retained in any man's service, do depart from the said service without reasonable cause or licence, before the term agreed, he shall have pain of imprisonment. And that none under the same pain presume to receive or to retain any such in his service.

CAP. III.
The old wages, and no more, shall be given to servants.
Item, That no man pay, or promise to pay, any servant any more wages, liveries, meed, or salary than was wont, as afore is said. Nor that any in other manner shall demand or receive the same, upon pain of doubling of that, that so shall be paid, promised, required, or received, to him which thereof shall feel himself grieved, pursuing for the same. And if none such will pursue, then the same to be applied to any of the people that will pursue. And such pursuit shall be in the court of the lord of the place where such case shall happen.

CAP. IV.
If the lord of a town or manor do offend against this statute in any point, he shall forfeit the treble value.
Item, if the lords of the towns or manors presume in any point to come against this present ordinance either by them, or by their servants, then pursuit shall be made against them in the counties, wapentakes, tithings, or such other courts, for the treble pain paid or promised by them or their servants in the form aforesaid. And if any before this present ordinance hath covenanted with any so to serve for more wages, he shall not be bound by reason of the same convenant, to pay more than at another time was wont to be paid to such person. Nor upon the said pain shall presume any more to pay.

CAP. V.
If any artificer or workman take more wages than were wont to be paid, he shall be committed to the gaol.
Item, That sadlers, skinners, white-tawers, cordwainers, taylors, smiths, carpenters, masons, tilers, shipwrights, carters, and all other artificers and workmen, shall not take for their labour and workmanship above the same that was wont to be paid to such persons the said twentieth year, and other common years next before, as afore is said, in the place where they shall happen to work. And if any man take more, he shall be committed to the next gaol, in manner as afore is said.

CAP. VI.
Victuals shall be sold at reasonable prices.
Item, That butchers, fishmongers, regrators, hostelers, brewers, bakers, pulters, and all other sellers of all manner of victual, shall be bound to sell the same victual for a reasonable price, having respect to the price that such victual be sold at in the places adjoining, so that the same sellers have moderate gains, and not excessive, reasonably to be required according to the distance of the place from whence the said victuals be carried. (2) And if any sell such victuals in any other manner, and thereof be convict in the manner and form aforesaid, he shall pay the double of the same that he so received, to the party damnified, or, in default of him, to any

other that will pursue in this behalf. (3) And the mayors and bailiffs of cities, boroughs, merchant-towns, and others, and of the ports of the sea, and other places, shall have power to inquire of all and singular which shall in any thing offend the same, and to levy the said pain to the use of them at whose suit such offenders shall be convict. (4) And in case that the same mayors and bailiffs be negligent in doing execution of the premises, and thereof be convict before our justices, by us to be assigned, then the same mayors and bailiffs shall be compelled by the same justices to pay the treble of the thing so sold to the party damnified, or to any other in default of him that will pursue; and nevertheless towards us they shall be grievously punished.

CAP. VII.

No person shall give any thing to a beggar that is able to labour.
Item, *because that many valiant beggars, as long as they may live of begging, do refuse to labour, giving themselves to idleness and vice, and sometime to theft and other abominations; none upon the said pain of imprisonment shall, under the colour of pity or alms, give any thing to such, which may labour, or presume to favour them towards their desires, so that thereby they may be compelled to labour for their necessary living:* Wherefore our said sovereign lord the King, the xiiii. day of *June,* the xxiii. year of his reign, hath commanded to all sheriffs of *England* by divers writs, that they shall do openly to be proclaimed and holden, all and singular the premises in the counties, boroughs, merchant-towns, sea-ports, and other places in their bailiwicks, where to them shall seem expedient: and that they do thereof due execution, as afore is said.

CAP. VIII.

He that taketh more wages than is accustomably given, shall pay the surplusage to the town where he dwelleth, towards a payment to the King of a tenth and fifteenth granted to him.
Subsequently *our sovereign lord the King, perceiving by the common complaint, that his people, for such excessive stipend, liveries, and prices, which to such servants, labourers, and workmen were constrainedly paid, be oppressed, and that the disme and quinzime to him attaining might not be paid, unless remedy were therefore provided: regarding also the coactions and manifest extortions, and that there was no man, which against such offenders, did pursue for the said commodity so ordained to be obtained: wherefore it was consonant, that that thing which was ordained to be applied to singular uses, seeing that the same persons did not, nor would not, pursue, should be converted to a publick and common profit, by the advice of his counsel,* Hath ordained, That all and singular workmen, servants and artificers, as well men as women, of whatsoever estate or condition they be, taking more for their labours, services, and workmanship, than they were wont to take the said xx. year, and other years aforesaid, should be assessed to the same sum, which they shall receive over and above, with other sums as well for the time past, when the stipend, wages, liveries, and prices were augmented, as for the time then to come. And that the said whole sum received over and above, should be levied of every of them, and gathered to the King's use, in alleviation of every of the towns, whereof the said artificers, servants, and labourers be, towards the payments of the sums of the disme and quinzime yet running, whereunto the same towns or people of the same were assessed. So that always, the same disme and quinzime ended, all the same money, liveries, and prices, or the value of the same liveries, which, (as afore is said) should be over and above received of them, and every of them, should be levied and gathered by them, whom the King will thereto assign, to the King's use, in alleviation, and supportation of the realm of *England.* And that they which for the same to serve, or the said sums so by them over and above received, and before assessed to pay, and their crafts and work to exercise do refuse, they shall be incontinently arrested by the taxers and collectors

of the said disme and quinzime, or any of them, in every of the said towns deputed to execute the premises, or by the bailiffs of the places, or constables of the towns, when they be thereof certified, and committed to the gaol, there to remain till they have found surety to serve, and shall pay that that they shall above receive, according to the same ordinances, or till the King shall some other thing thereof demand. And always it is the intent of the King and of his council, that according to the first ordinance it should be lawful, and shall be lawful to every man, to pursue against all exceeding the same, or not obeying to the same, and the thing recovered to be applied to his own use. *And therefore our said sovereign lord the King hath commanded all archbishops, and bishops, that they do to be published the premises in all places of their dioceses, commanding the curates and other subdiocesans, that they compel their parochians to labour, according to the necessity of the time, and also their stipendiary priests of their said dioceses, which do now excessively take, and will not, as it is said, serve for a competent salary, as hath been accustomed, upon pain of suspension and interdiction. And that in no wise ye omit the same, as ye love us and the commonwealth of our realm. Dated the day and year aforesaid.*

Appendix 2. The Bill of Conspiracies of Victuallers and Craftsmen, 1548

(Complete Text)

Forasmuch *as of late divers sellers of victuals, not contented with moderate and reasonable gain, but minding to have and to take for their victuals so much as list them, have conspired and covenanted together to sell their victuals at unreasonable prices:* (2) *And likewise artificers, handicraftsmen and labourers have made confederacies and promises, and have sworn mutual oaths not only that they should not meddle one with another's work, and perform and finish that another hath begun, but also to constitute and appoint how much work they shall do in a day, and what hours and times they shall work, contrary to the laws and statutes of this realm, and to the great hurt and impoverishment of the King's majesty's subjects:* (3) For reformation thereof it is ordained and enacted by the King our sovereign lord, the lords and commons in this present parliament assembled, and by the authority of the same, That if any butchers, brewers, bakers, poulterers, cooks, costermongers or fruiterers, shall at any time from and after the first day of *March* next coming, conspire, covenant, promise or make any oaths, that they shall not sell their victuals but at certain prices; (4) or if any artificers, workmen or labourers do conspire, covenant, or promise together, or make any oaths, that they shall not make or do their works but at a certain price or rate, or shall not enterprize or take upon them to finish that another hath begun, or shall do but a certain work in a day, or shall not work but at certain hours and times, (5) that then every person so conspiring, covenanting, swearing or offending, being lawfully convict thereof by witness, confession or otherwise, shall forfeit for the first offence ten pounds to the King's highness; and if he have sufficient to pay the same, and do also pay the same within six days next after his conviction; or else shall suffer for the same offence twenty days imprisonment, and shall only have bread and water for his sustenance: (6) And for the second offence shall forfeit twenty pound to the King, if he have sufficient to pay the same, and do pay the same within six days next after his conviction, or else shall suffer for the second offence punishment of the pillory; (7) and for the third offence shall forfeit forty pound to the King, if he have sufficient to pay the same, and also do pay the same within six days next after his conviction, or else shall sit on the pillory and lose one of his ears, and also shall at all times after that be taken as a man infamous, and his saying, depositions or oath not to be credited at any time in any matters of judgment.

II. And if it fortune any such conspiracy, covenant or promise to be had and made by any society, brotherhood or company of any craft, mystery or occupation of the victuallers above mentioned, with the presence or consent of the more part of them, that then immediately upon such act of conspiracy, covenant or promise had or made, over and besides the particular punishment before in this act appointed for the offender, their corporation shall be dissolved to all intents, constructions and purposes.

III. And it is further ordained and enacted by the authority aforesaid, That all and singular justices of assise, justices of peace, mayors, bailiffs and stewards of leets, at all and every their sessions, leets and courts, shall have full power and authority to inquire, hear and determine all and singular offences committed against this statute, and to punish or cause to be punished the offender, according to the tenor of this statute.

IV. And it is ordained and enacted by the authority aforesaid, That no person or persons shall at any time after the first day of *April* next coming interrupt, deny, let or disturb any free-mason, rough-mason, carpenter, bricklayer, plasterer, joiner, hardhewer, sawyer, tiler, paver, glasier, lime-burner, brick-maker, tile-maker, plummer or labourer, born in this realm or made denizen, to work in any of the said crafts in any city, borough or town corporate, with any person or persons that will retain him or them, albeit the said person and persons so retained or any of them do not inhabit or dwell in the city, borough or town corporate where he or they shall work, nor be free of the same city, borough or town; any statute, law, ordinance, or other thing whatsoever had or made to the contrary in any wise notwithstanding; (2) and that upon pain of forfeiture of five pound for every interruption or disturbance done contrary to this statute; the one moiety of every such forfeiture to be to the King, and the other moiety thereof to be to him or them that will sue for the same in any of the King's courts of record, by bill, plaint, action of debt or information, wherein no wager of law, essoin nor protection shall be allowed. *Continued by 22 & 23 Car. 2. c. 19. except as to such things as are thereby altered or repealed.*

Appendix 3. The Statute of Artificers, 1563
(Extracts)

Although *there remain and stand in force presently a great number of acts and statutes concerning the retaining, departing, wages and orders of apprentices, servants and labourers, as well in husbandry as in divers other arts, mysteries and occupations; (2) yet partly for the imperfection and contrariety that is found, and doth appear in sundry of the said laws, and for the variety and number of them, (3) and chiefly for that the wages and allowances limited and rated in many of the said statutes, are in divers places too small and not answerable to this time, respecting the advancement of prices of all things belonging to the said servants and labourers; (4) the said laws cannot conveniently, without the great grief and burden of the poor labourer and hired man, be put in good and due execution: (5) and as the said several acts and statutes were, at the time of the making of them, thought to be very good and beneficial for the commonwealth of this realm (as divers of them are:) so if the substance of as many of the said laws as are meet to be continued, shall be digested and reduced into one sole law and statute, and in the same an uniform order prescribed and limited concerning the wages and other orders for apprentices, servants and labourers, there is good hope that it will come to pass, that the same law (being duly executed) should banish idleness, advance husbandry, and yield unto the hired person, both in the time of scarcity, and in the time of plenty, a convenient proportion of wages.*

III. And be it further enacted by the authority aforesaid, That no manner of person or persons, after the aforesaid last day of *September* now next ensuing, shall retain, hire or take into service, or cause to be retained, hired or taken into service, nor any person shall be retained, hired or taken into service, by any means or colour, to work for any less time or term than for one whole year, in any of the sciences, crafts, mysteries or arts of clothiers, woolen cloth weavers, tuckers, fullers, clothworkers, sheremen, dyers, hosiers, taylors, shoemakers, tanners, pewterers, bakers, brewers, glovers, cutlers, smiths, farriers, curriers, sadlers, spurriers, turners, cappers, hatmakers or feltmakers, bowyers, fletchers, arrow-head-makers, butchers, cooks or millers.

IV. And be it further enacted, That every person being unmarried; (2) and every other person being under the age of thirty years, that after the feast of *Easter* next shall marry, (3) and having been brought up in any of the said arts, crafts or sciences; (4) or that hath used or exercised any of them by the space of three years or more; (5) and not having lands, tenements, rents or hereditaments, copyhold or freehold, of an estate of inheritance, or for term of any life or lives, of the clear yearly value of forty shillings; (6) nor being worth of his own goods the clear value of ten pound; (7) and so allowed by two justices of the peace of the county where he hath most commonly inhabited by the space of one whole year, and under their hands and seals, (8) or by the mayor or other head officer of the city, borough or town corporate where such person hath most commonly dwelt by the space of one whole year, and two aldermen, or two other discreet burgesses of the same city, borough or town corporate, if there be no aldermen, under their hands and seals; (9) nor being retained with any person in husbandry, or in any of the aforesaid arts and sciences, according to this statute; (10) nor lawfully retained in any other art or science; (11) nor being lawfully retained in household, or in any office, with any nobleman, gentleman or others, according to the laws of this realm; (12) nor have a convenient farm, or other holding in tillage, whereupon he may employ his labour: (13) shall, during the time that he or they shall be so unmarried, or under the said age of thirty years, upon request made by any person using the art or mystery wherein the said person so required hath been exercised (as is aforesaid) be retained; (14) and shall not refuse to serve according to the tenor of this statute, upon the pain and penalty hereafter mentioned.

V. And be it further enacted, That no person which shall retain any servant, shall put away his or her said servant, (2) and that no person retained according to this statute, shall depart from his master, mistress or dame, before the end of his or her term; (3) upon the pain hereafter mentioned; (4) unless it be for some reasonable and sufficient cause or matter to be allowed before two justices of peace, or one at the least, within the said county, or before the mayor or other chief officer of the city, borough or town corporate wherein the said master, mistress or dame inhabiteth, to whom any of the parties grieved shall complain; (5) which said justices or justice, mayor or chief officer, shall have and take upon them or him the hearing and ordering of the matter betwixt the said master or mistress, or dame and servant, according to the equity of the cause.

VI. And that no such master, mistress or dame, shall put away any such servant at the end of his term, or that any such servant shall depart from his said master, mistress or dame at the end of his term, without one quarter's warning given before the end of his said term, either by the said master, mistress or dame, or servant, the one to the other, upon the pain hereafter ensuing.

VII. And be it further enacted by the authority aforesaid, That every person between the age of twelve years and the age of sixty years, not being lawfully retained, nor apprentice with any fisherman or mariner haunting the seas; (2) nor being in service with any kidder or carrier of any corn, grain or meal, for provision of the city of *London*; (3) nor with any husband-man in husbandry; (4) nor in any city, town corporate or market-town, in any of the arts or sciences limited or appointed by this estatute to have or take apprentices; (5) nor being retained by the year, or half the year at the least, for the digging, seeking, finding, getting, melting, fining, working, trying, making of any silver, tin, lead, iron, copper, stone, sea-coal, stone-coal, moor-coal or cherk-coal; (6) nor being occupied in or about the making of any glass; (7) nor being a gentleman born, nor being a student or scholar in any of the universities, or in any school; (8) nor having lands, tenements, rents or hereditaments, for term of life, or of one estate of inheritance, of the clear yearly value of forty shillings; (9) nor being worth in goods and chattels to the value of ten pound; (10) nor having a father or mother then living, or other ancestor whose heir apparent he is, then having lands, tenements or hereditaments, of the yearly value of ten pound or above, or goods or chattels of the value of forty pound; (11) nor being a necessary or convenient officer or servant lawfully retained, as is aforesaid; (12) nor having a convenient farm or holding, whereupon he may or shall imploy his labour; (13) nor being otherwise lawfully retained, according to the true meaning of this estatute; (14) shall after the aforesaid last day of *September* now next ensuing, by virtue of this estatute, be compelled to be retained to serve in husbandry by the year, with any person that keepeth husbandry, and will require any such person so to serve, within the same shire where he shall be so required.

VIII. And be it further enacted by the authority of this present parliament, That if any person after he hath retained any servant, shall put away the same servant before the end of his term, unless it be for some reasonable and sufficient cause to be allowed, as is aforesaid; (2) or if any such master, mistress or dame, shall put away any such servant at the end of his term, without one quarter's warning given before the said end, as is above remembered; (3) that then every such master, mistress or dame so offending, unless he or they be able to prove by two such sufficient witnesses such reasonable and sufficient cause of putting away of their servant or servants, during their term, or a quarter's warning given afore the end of the said term, as is aforesaid, before the justices of *oyer* and *terminer,* justices of assise, justices of peace in the quarter-sessions, or before the mayor or other head officer of any city, borough or town corporate, and two aldermen, or two other discreet burgesses of the same city, borough or town corporate, if there be no aldermen, or before the lord president and council established in the marches of *Wales,* or before the lord president and council for the time being established in the north parts, shall forfeit the sum of forty shillings.

IX. And if any servant retained according to the form of this estatute, depart from his master, mistress or dame's service, before the end of his term, unless it be for some reasonable and sufficient cause to be allowed, as is aforesaid; (2) or if any servant at the end of his term depart from his said master, mistress or dame's service without one quarter's warning given before the end of his said term, in form aforesaid, and before two lawful witnesses; (3) or if any person or persons compellable and bounden to be retained, and to serve in husbandry, or in any other the arts, sciences or mysteries above remembred, by the year or otherwise, do (upon request made) refuse to serve for the wages that shall be limited, rated and appointed, according to the form of this statute; (4) or promise or covenant to serve, and do not serve according to the tenor of the same: (5) that then every servant so departing away, and every person so refusing to serve for such wages, upon complaint thereof made by the master, mistress or dame of the said servant, or by the party to or with whom the said refusal is made, or promise not kept, to two justices of peace of the county, or to the mayor or other head officer of the city, borough or town corporate, and two aldermen, or two other discreet burgesses of the same city, borough or town corporate, if there be no aldermen, where the said master, mistress or dame, or the said party to or with whom the said refusal is made, and promise not kept, dwelleth, or to either of the said lords presidents and council, of *Wales,* and the north, the said justices, lords presidents and councils, and also the said mayors or other head officers, and other persons of cities, boroughs or towns corporate, or any of them, as is aforesaid, shall have power by force of this statute, to hear and examine the matter; (6) and finding the said servant, or the said party so refusing faulty in the premisses, upon such proofs and good matter as to their discretions shall be thought sufficient, to commit him or them to ward, there to remain without bail or mainprise, until the said servant or party so offending shall be bound to the party to whom the offence shall be made, to serve and continue with him for the wages that then shall be limited and appointed, according to the tenor and form of this estatute, and to be discharged upon his delivery, without paying any fee to the gaoler where he or they shall be so imprisoned.

X. And be it likewise enacted by the authority aforesaid, That none of the said retained persons in husbandry, or in any the arts or sciences above remembred, after the time of his retainer expired, shall depart forth of one city, town or parish to another; (2) nor out of the lath, rape, wapentake or hundred; (3) nor out of the county or shire where he last served, to serve in any other city, town corporate, lath, rape, wapentake, hundred, shire or county; (4) unless he have a testimonial under the seal of the said city or town corporate, or of the constable or constables, or other head officer or officers, and of two other honest housholders of the city, town or parish, where he last served, declaring his lawful departure, and the name of the shire and place where he dwelled last before his departure, according to the form hereafter expressed in this act: (5) which certificate or testimonial shall be written and delivered unto the said servant, and also registered by the parson, vicar or curate of the parish where such master, mistress or dame doth or shall dwell, taking for the doing thereof two-pence, and not above: and the form thereof shall be as followeth:

Memorandum, That *A. B.* late servant to *C. D.* of *E.* husbandman, or taylor, *&c.* in the county, *&c.* is licensed to depart from his said master, and is at his liberty to serve elsewhere, according to the statute in that case made and provided. In witness whereof, *&c.* Dated the day, month, year and place, *&c.* of the making thereof.

XI. And be it further enacted by the authority aforesaid, That no person or persons that shall depart out of a service, shall be retained or accepted into any other service, without shewing before his retainer, such testimonial as is above-remembred, to the chief officer of the town corporate, and in every other town and place, to the constable, curate, churchwarden, or other head officer of the same, where he shall be retained to serve; (2) upon the pain that every such servant so departing without such certificate or testimonial, shall be imprisoned until he procure a testimonial or certificate; (3) the which if he cannot do within the space of one and twenty days next after the first day of his imprisonment, then the said person to be whipped and used as a vagabond according to the laws in such cases provided; (4) and that every person retaining any such servant, without shewing such testimonial or certificate, as is aforesaid, shall forfeit for every such offence five pounds: (5) and if any such person shall be taken with any counterfeit or forged testimonial, then to be whipped as a vagabond.

XII. And be it further enacted by the authority aforesaid, That all artificers and labourers, being hired for wages by the day or week, shall betwixt the midst of the months of *March* and *September* be and continue at their work at or before five of the clock in the morning, and continue at work and not depart until betwixt seven and eight of the clock at night (except it be in the time of breakfast, dinner or drinking, the which times at the most shall not exceed above two hours and a half in a day, that is to say, at every drinking one half hour, for his dinner one hour, and for his sleep when he is allowed to sleep, the which is from the midst of *May* to the midst of *August,* half an hour at the most, and at every breakfast one half hour: (2) and all the said artificers and labourers, between the midst of *September* and the midst of *March,* shall be and continue at their work from the spring of the day in the morning until the night of the same day, except it be in time afore appointed for breakfast and dinner; (3) upon pain to lose and forfeit one penny for every hour's absence, to be deducted and defaulked out of his wages that shall so offend.

XIII. And be it also enacted by the authority aforesaid, That every artificer and labourer that shall be lawfully retained in and for the building or repairing of any church, house, ship, mill or every other piece of work taken in great, in task or in gross, or that shall hereafter take upon him to make or finish any such thing or work, shall continue and not depart from the same, unless it be for not paying of his wages or hire agreed on, or otherwise lawfully taken or appointed to serve the Queen's majesty, her heirs or successors, or for other lawful cause, or without licence of the master or owner of the work, or of him that hath the charge thereof, before the finishing of the said work; (2) upon pain of imprisonment by one month, without bail or mainprise; (3) and the forfeiture of the sum of five pounds to the party from whom he shall so depart; for the which the said party may have his action of debt against him that shall so depart, in any of the Queen's majesty's courts of record, over and besides such ordinary costs and damages as may or ought to be recovered by the common laws, for or concerning any such offence: in which action no protection, wager of law or essoin shall be admitted.

XIV. And that no other artificer or labourer retained in any service, to work with the Queen's majesty or any other person, depart from her said Majesty or from the said other person, until such time as the work be finished, if the person so retaining the artificer or labourer so long will have him, and pay him his wages or other duties; upon pain of imprisonment of every person so departing, by the space of one month.

XV. And for the declaration and limitation what wages servants, labourers and artificers, either by the year or day or otherwise, shall have and receive, Be it enacted by the authority of this present parliament, That the justices of peace of every shire, riding and liberty within the limits of their several commissions, or the more part of them, being then resiant within the same, and the sheriff of that county if he conveniently may, and every mayor, bailiff or other head officer within any city or town corporate wherein is any justice of peace, within the limits of the said city or town corporate, and of the said corporation, shall before the tenth day of *June* next coming, and afterward shall yearly at every general sessions first to be holden and kept after *Easter* or at some time convenient within six weeks next following every of the said feasts of *Easter,* assemble themselves together; (2) and they (so assembled) calling unto them such discreet and grave persons of the said county or of the said city or town corporate, as they shall think meet, and conferring together, respecting the plenty or scarcity of the time and other circumstances necessarily to be considered, shall have authority by virtue thereof, within the limits and precincts of their several commissions, to limit, rate and appoint the wages, as well of such and so many of the said artificers, handicrafts-men, husbandmen or any other labourer, servant or workman, whose wages in time past hath been by any law or statute rated and appointed, (3) as also the wages of all other labourers, artificers, workmen or apprentices of husbandry, which have not been rated, . . .

XVIII. And be it further enacted by the authority aforesaid, That if any person after the said proclamation shall be so sent down and published, shall by any secret ways or means, directly or indirectly retain or keep any servant, workman or labourer, or shall give any more or greater wages or other commodity, contrary to the true intent and purport of this estatute, or contrary to the rates or wages that shall be assessed or appointed in the said proclamations; that then every person that shall so offend, and be thereof lawfully convicted before any the justices or other head officers above-remembred, or either of the said presidents and councils, shall suffer imprisonment by the space of ten days, without bail or mainprise, and shall lose and forfeit five pounds of lawful money of *England.*

XIX. And that every person that shall be so retained and take wages contrary to this estatute or any branch thereof, or of the said proclamation, and shall be thereof convicted before the justices aforesaid, or any two of them, or before the mayor or other head officers aforesaid, shall suffer imprisonment by the space of one and twenty days, without bail or mainprise.

XX. And that every retainer, promise, gift or payment of wages or other thing whatsoever contrary to the true meaning of this estatute, and every writing and bond to be made for that purpose, shall be utterly void and of none effect.

XXI. And be it enacted by the authority aforesaid, That if any servant, workman or labourer, shall wilfully or maliciously make any assault or affray upon his master, mistress or dame, or upon any other that shall at the time of such assault or affray, have the charge or oversight of any such servant, workman or labourer, or of the work wherein the said servant, workman or labourer is appointed or hired to work, and being thereof convicted before any two of the justices, mayor or other head officer aforesaid, where the said offense is committed, or before either of the said lords presidents and council before remembred, by confession of the said servant, workman or labourer, or by the testimony, witness and oath of two honest men; that then every such offender shall suffer imprisonment by the space of one whole year or less, by the discretion of two justices of peace if it be without a town corporate; (2) and if it be within a town corporate, then by the discretion of the mayor or head officer of the same town corporate, with two others of the discreetest persons of the same corporation at the least: (3) And if the offence shall require further punishment, then to receive such other open punishment, so as it extend not to life nor limb, as the justices of peace in open sessions, or as the more part of them, or the said mayor or head officer, and six or four at the least of the discreetest persons of the same corporation, before whom the offence shall be examined, shall think convenient for the quality of the said offence so done or committed.

XXII. Provided always, and be it enacted by the authority aforesaid, That in the time of hay or corn harvest, the justices of peace and every of them, and also the constable or other head officer of every township upon request, and for the avoiding of the loss of any corn, grain or hay, shall and may cause all such artificers and persons as be meet to labour, by the discretions of the said justices or constables, or other head officers, or by any of them, to serve by the day for the mowing, reaping, shearing, setting or inning of corn, grain and hay, according to the skill and quality of the person; (2) and that none of the said persons shall refuse so to do, upon pain to suffer imprisonment in the stocks by the space of two days and one night: (3) And the constable of the town or other head officer of the same, where the said refusal shall be made, upon complaint to him made, shall have authority by virtue hereof to set the said offender in the stocks for the time aforesaid, and shall punish him accordingly, upon pain to lose and forfeit for not doing thereof the sum of forty shillings.

XXIV. And be it further enacted by the authority aforesaid, That two justices of peace, the mayor or other head officer of any city, borough or town corporate, and two aldermen, or two other discreet burgesses of the same city, borough or town corporate, if there be no aldermen, shall and may, by virtue hereof, appoint any such woman as is of the age of twelve years, and under the age of forty years and unmarried, and forth of service, as they shall think meet to serve, to be retained or serve by the year, or by the week or day, for such wages, and in such reasonable sort and manner as they shall think meet; (2) and if any such woman shall refuse so to serve, then it shall be lawful for the said justices of peace, mayor or head officers, to commit such woman to ward, until she shall be bounden to serve as is aforesaid.

XXV. And for the better advancement of husbandry and tillage, and to the intent that such as are fit to be made apprentices to husbandry, may be bounden thereunto, (2) be it enacted by the authority of this present parliament, That every person being an housholder, and having and using half a ploughland at the least in tillage, may have and receive as an apprentice any person above the age of ten years, and under the age of eighteen years, to serve in husbandry, until his age of one and twenty years at the least, or until the age of twenty-four years, as the parties can agree, and the said retainer and taking of an apprentice, to be made and done by indenture.

XXVI. And be it further enacted, That every person being an housholder, and twenty-four years old at the least, dwelling or inhabiting, or which shall dwell and inhabit in any city or town corporate, and using and exercising any art, mystery or manual occupation there, shall and may, after the feast of Saint *John Baptist* next coming, during the time that he shall so dwell or inhabit in any such city or town corporate, and use and exercise any such mystery, art or manual occupation, have and retain the son of any freeman, not occupying husbandry, nor being a labourer, and inhabiting in the same, or in any other city or town that now is or hereafter shall be and continue incorporate, to serve and be bound as an apprentice after the custom and order of the city of *London,* for seven years at the least, so as the term and years of such apprentice do not expire or determine afore such apprentice shall be of the age of twenty-four years at the least.

XXXI. And be it further enacted by the authority aforesaid, That after the first day of *May* next coming, it shall not be lawful to any person or persons, other than such as now do lawfully use or exercise any art, mystery or manual occupation, (2) to set up, occupy, use or exercise any craft, mystery or occupation, now used or occupied within the realm of *England* or *Wales*; except he shall have been brought up therein seven years at the least as an apprentice, in manner and form abovesaid; (4) nor to set any person on work in such mystery, art or occupation, being not a workman at this day; (5) except he shall have been apprentice as is aforesaid; (6) or else having served as an apprentice as is aforesaid, shall or will become a journeyman, or be hired by the year; (7) upon pain that every person willingly offending or doing the contrary, shall forfeit and lose for every default forty shillings for every month.

XXXIII. And be it further enacted by the authority aforesaid, That all and every person and persons that shall have three apprentices in any of the said crafts, mysteries or occupations of a cloth-maker, fuller, sheerman, weaver, taylor or shoemaker, shall retain and keep one journeyman, and for every other apprentice above the number of the said three apprentices, one other journeyman, upon pain for every default therein ten pounds.

XXXV. And be it further enacted, That if any person shall be required by any housholder, having and using half a ploughland at the least in tillage, to be an apprentice, and to serve in husbandry, or in any other kind of art, mystery or science before expressed, and shall refuse so to do, that then upon the complaint of such housekeeper made to one justice of the peace of the country wherein the said refusal is or shall be made, or of such housholder inhabiting in any city, town corporate or market-town, to the mayor, bailiffs or head officer of the said city, town corporate or market-town, if any such refusal shall there be, they shall have full power and authority by virtue hereof, to send for the same person so refusing: (2) And if the said justice, or the said mayor or head officer shall think the said person meet and convenient to serve as an apprentice in that art, labour science or mystery, wherein he shall be so then required to serve: That then the said justice, or the said mayor or head officer, shall have power and authority by virtue hereof, if the said person refuse to be bound as an apprentice, to commit him unto ward, there to remain until he be contented, and will be bounden to serve as an apprentice should serve, according to the true intent and meaning of this present act. (3) And if any such master shall misuse or evil intreat his apprentice, or that the said apprentice shall have any just cause to complain, or the apprentice do not his duty to his master, then the said master or apprentice being grieved, and having cause to complain, shall repair unto one justice of peace within the said county, or to the mayor or other head officer of the city, town corporate, market-town or other place where the said master dwelleth, who shall by his wisdom and discretion take such order and direction between the said master and his apprentice, as the equity of the cause shall require; . . .

XL. Provided always, That this act, or any thing therein contained or mentioned, shall not be prejudicial or hurtful to the cities of *London* and *Norwich,* or to the lawful liberties, usages, customs or privileges of the same cities, for or concerning the having or taking of any apprentice or apprentices; but that the citizens and freemen of the same cities shall and may take, have and retain apprentices there, in such manner and form as they might lawfully have done before the making of this statute; this act, or any thing therein contained, to the contrary in any wise notwithstanding.

XLI. And be it also further enacted, That all indentures, covenants, promises and bargains of or for the having, taking or keeping of any apprentice, otherwise hereafter to be made or taken, than is by this statute limited, ordained and appointed, shall be clearly void in the law, to all intents and purposes; (2) and that every person that shall from henceforth take or newly retain any apprentice contrary to the tenor and true meaning of this act, shall forfeit and lose for every apprentice so by him taken, the sum of ten pounds.

XLVI. Provided always, That this act, or any thing therein contained, shall not extend to any lawful retainings or covenants had or made before the making of this act, but that all and every the parties to such retainings or covenants shall and may have the same and like advantages of such retainings and covenants, and of the statutes heretofore in that behalf provided, as if this act had never been had or made; any clause of repeal or other matter whatsoever in this act to the contrary in any wise notwithstanding.

XLVII. And be it further enacted by the authority aforesaid, That if any servant or apprentice of husbandry, or of any art, science or occupation aforesaid, unlawfully depart or flee into any other shire; that it shall be lawful to the said justices of peace, and to the said mayors, bailiffs and other head officers of cities and towns corporate, for the time being justices of peace there, to make and grant writs of *Capias,* so many, and such as shall be needful, to be directed to the sheriffs of the counties, or to other head officers of the places whither such servants or apprentices shall so depart or flee, to take their bodies, returnable before them at what time shall please them; so that if they come by such process, that they be put in prison till they shall find sufficient surety well and honestly to serve their masters, mistresses or dames from whom they so departed or fled, according to the order of the law.

Appendix 4: The Masters and Servants Act, 1823

(Complete Text)

Whereas an Act was passed in the Twentieth Year of the Reign of His Majesty King *George* the Second, intituled *An Act for the better adjusting and more easy Recovery of the Wages of certain Servants, and for the better Regulation of such Servants, and of certain Apprentices;* and another Act was passed in the Sixth Year of the Reign of His late Majesty King *George* the Third, intituled *An Act for better regulating Apprentices, and Persons working under Contract;* and also another Act was passed in this present Session of Parliament, intituled *An Act to increase the Power of Magistrates in cases of Apprenticeships;* and it is expedient to extend the Powers of the said Acts;' Be it therefore enacted by the King's most Excellent Majesty, by and with the Advice and Consent of the Lords Spiritual and Temporal, and Commons, in this present Parliament assembled, and by the Authority of the same, That it shall and may be lawful, not only for any Master or Mistress, but also for his or her Steward, Manager or Agent, to make Complaint upon Oath against any Apprentice, within the Meaning of the said before recited Acts, to any Justice of the Peace of the County or Place where such Apprentice shall be employed, of or for any Misdemeanor, Misconduct or ill Behaviour of any such Apprentice; or if such Apprentice shall have absconded, it shall be lawful for any Justice of the Peace of the County or Place where such Apprentice shall be found, or where such Apprentice shall have been employed, and any such Justice is hereby empowered, upon Complaint thereof made upon Oath by such Master, Mistress, Steward, Manager or Agent, which Oath the said Justice is hereby empowered to administer, to issue his Warrant for apprehending every such Apprentice; and further, that it shall be lawful for any such Justice to hear and determine the same Complaint, and to punish the Offender by abating the Whole or any Part of his or her Wages, or otherwise by Commitment to the House of Correction, there to remain and be held to hard Labour for a reasonable Time, not exceeding Three Months.

    II. And be it further enacted, That all Complaints, Differences and Disputes which shall arise between Masters or Mistresses and their Apprentices, within the Meaning of the said before recited Acts, or any of them, touching or concerning any Wages which may be due to such Apprentices, shall and may be heard and determined by One or more Justice or Justices of the Peace of the County or Place where such Apprentice or Apprentices shall be employed, which said Justice or Justices is and are hereby empowered to examine on Oath any such Master or Mistress, Apprentice or Apprentices, or any Witness or Witnesses, touching any such Complaint, Difference or Dispute, and to summon such Master or Mistress to appear before such Justice or Justices at a reasonable Time to be named in such Summons, and to make such Order for Payment of so much Wages to such Apprentice or Apprentices, as according to the Terms of his, her or their Indentures of Apprenticeship shall appear to such Justice or Justices, under all the Circumstances of the Case, to be justly due, (provided that the Sum in question do not exceed the Sum of Ten Pounds,) the Amount of such Wages to be paid within such Period as the said Justice or Justices shall think proper, and shall order the same to be paid; and in case of a Refusal or Nonpayment thereof, such Justice and Justices shall and may issue forth his and their Warrant, to levy the same by distress and Sale of the Goods and Chattels of such Master or Mistress, rendering the Overplus to the Owners, after Payment of the Charges of such Distress and Sale.

III. And be it further enacted, That if any Servant in Husbandry or any Artificer, Calico Printer, Handicraftsman, Miner, Collier, Keelman, Pitman, Glassman, Potter, Labourer or other Person, shall contract with any Person or Persons whomsoever, to serve him, her or them for any Time or Times whatsoever, or in any other Manner, and shall not enter into or commence his or her Service according to his or her Contract (such Contract being in Writing, and signed by the contracting Parties), or having entered into such Service shall absent himself or herself from his or her Service before the Term of his or her Contract, whether such Contract shall be in Writing or not in Writing, shall be completed, or neglect to fulfil the same, or be guilty of any other Misconduct or Misdemeanor in the Execution thereof, or otherwise respecting the same, then and in every such Case it shall and may be lawful for any Justice of the Peace of the County or Place where such Servant in Husbandry, Artificer, Calico Printer, Handicraftsman, Miner, Collier, Keelman, Pitman, Glassman, Potter, Labourer or other Person, shall have so contracted, or be employed or be found, and such Justice is hereby authorized and empowered, upon Complaint thereof made upon Oath to him by the Person or Persons, or any of them, with whom such Servant in Husbandry, Artificer, Calico Printer, Handicraftsman, Miner, Collier, Keelman, Pitman, Glassman, Potter, Labourer or other Person shall have so contracted, or by his, her or their Steward, Manager or Agent, which Oath such Justice is hereby empowered to administer, to issue his Warrant for the apprehending every such Servant in Husbandry, Artificer, Calico Printer, Handicraftsman, Miner, Collier, Keelman, Pitman, Glassman, Potter, Labourer or other Person, and to examine into the Nature of the Complaint; and if it shall appear to such Justice that any such Servant in Husbandry, Artificer, Calico Printer, Handicraftsman, Miner, Collier, Keelman, Pitman, Glassman, Potter, Labourer or other Person, shall not have fulfilled such Contract, or hath been guilty of any other Misconduct or Misdemeanour as aforesaid, it shall and may be lawful for such Justice to commit every such Person to the House of Correction, there to remain and be held to hard Labour for a reasonable Time, not exceeding Three Months, and to abate a proportionable Part of his or her Wages, for and during such Period as he or she shall be so confined in the House of Correction, or in lieu thereof, to punish the Offender by abating the Whole or any Part of his or her Wages, or to discharge such Servant in Husbandry, Artificer, Calico Printer, Handicraftsman, Miner, Collier, Keelman, Pitman, Glassman, Potter, Labourer or other Person from his or her Contract, Service or Employment, which Discharge shall be given under the Hand and Seal of such Justice *gratis*.

IV. And Whereas it frequently happens that such Masters, Mistresses or Employers reside at considerable Distances from the Parishes or Places where their Business is carried on, or are occasionally absent for long Periods of Time, either beyond the Seas, or at considerable Distances from such Parishes or Places, and during such Residence or occasional Absences entrust their Business to the Management and Superintendence of Stewards, Agents, Bailiffs, Foremen or Managers, whereby such Servants, Artificers, Handicraftsmen, Miners, Colliers, Keelmen, Pitmen, Glassmen, Potters, Labourers or other Persons and Apprentices, are or may be subjected to great Difficulties and Hardships, and put to great Expence in recovering their Wages;' Be it therefore enacted, That in either of the said Cases, it shall and may be lawful to and for any Justice or Justices of the County or Place where such Servant in Husbandry, Artificer, Handicraftsman, Miner, Collier, Keelman, Pitman, Glassman, Potter, Labourer or other Person or Apprentice shall be employed, upon the Complaint of any such Servant, Artificer, Handicraftsman, Miner, Collier, Keelman, Pitman, Glassman, Potter, Labourer or other Person in Apprentice touching or concerning the Nonpayment of his or her Wages, to summon such Steward, Agent, Bailiff, Foreman or Manager, to be and appear before him or them at a reasonable Time to be named in such Summons, and to hear and determine the Matter of Complaint in such and the like manner as Complaints of the like Nature against any Master, Mistress or Employer are directed to be heard and determined in and by this and the before recited Acts, and also to make an Order for the Payment by such Steward, Agent, Bailiff, Foreman or Manager, to such Servant, Artificer, Handicraftsman, Miner, Collier, Keelman, Pitman, Glassman, Potter, Labourer or other Person or Apprentice, of so much Wages as to such Justice or Justices shall appear to be justly due; provided that the Sum in question do not exceed the Sum of Ten Pounds; and in case of Refusal or Nonpayment of any Sum so ordered to be paid by such Steward, Agent, Foreman, Bailiff or Manager, for the Space of Twenty one Days from the Date of such Order, such Justice or Justices as aforesaid shall and may issue forth his or their Warrant to levy the same by Distress and Sale of the Goods and Chattels of such Master, Mistress or Employer, rendering the Overplus to the Owner or Owners, or to such Steward, Agent, Bailiff, Foreman or Manager, for the Use of such Master, Mistress or Employer, after Payment of the Charges of such Distress and Sale.

V. And be it further enacted, That every Justice or Justices of the Peace before whom any Complaint shall be made, in pursuance of the said before recited Act made in the Twentieth Year of the Reign of His late Majesty King *George* the Second, or of another Act made in the Thirty first Year of the Reign of His said late Majesty, intituled *An Act to amend an Act made in the Third Year of the Reign of King* William *and Queen* Mary, *intituled 'An Act for the better Explanation and supplying the Defects of the former Laws for the Settlement of the Poor,' so far as the same relates to Apprentices gaining a Settlement by Indenture; and also to empower Justices of the Peace to determine Differences between Masters and Mistresses and their Servants in Husbandry, touching their Wages, though such Servants are hired for less Time than a Year,* shall and may order the Amount of the Wages that shall appear due to any Servants in Husbandry, Artificers, Labourers or other Person named in the said Acts, or either of them, to be paid to the Person entitled thereto, within such Period as the said Justice or Justices shall think proper; and in case of Refusal or Nonpayment thereof, shall and may levy the same by Distress and Sale, in manner directed by the said first mentioned Act; and every Order or Determination of such Justice or Justices made under this Act shall be final and conclusive, any thing in either of the said Acts contained to the contrary in any wise notwithstanding.

VI. Provided always, and be it enacted, That nothing in this Act contained shall extend to impeach or lessen the Jurisdiction of the Chamberlain of the City of *London,* or of any other Court within the said City, touching Apprentices.

Appendix 5. The Combination Act of 1824

(Sections I-VIII)

Whereas it is expedient that the Laws relative to the Combination of Workmen, and to fixing the Wages of Labour should be repealed; that certain Combinations of Masters and Workmen should be exempted from Punishment; and that the Attempt to deter Workmen from Work should be punished in a summary Manner; Be it therefore enacted by the King's most Excellent Majesty, by and with the Advice and Consent of the Lords Spiritual and Temporal, and Commons, in this present Parliament assembled, and by the Authority of the same, That from and after the passing of this Act, so much of a certain Act passed in the Thirty third Year of King *Edward* the First, intituled *Who be Conspirators and who be Champertors,* as relates to Combinations or Conspiracies of Workmen or other Persons to obtain an Advance or to fix the Rate of Wages, or to lessen or alter the Hours or Duration of the Time of working, or to decrease the Quantity of Work, or to regulate or controul the Mode of carrying on any Manufacture, Trade or Business, or the Management thereof, and as relates to Combinations or Conspiracies of Masters, Manufacturers or other Persons, to lower or fix the Rate of Wages, or to increase or alter the Hours or Duration of the Time of working, or to increase the Quantity of Work, or to regulate or controul the Mode of carrying on any Manufacture, Trade or Business, or the Management thereof, or to oblige Workmen to enter into Work; and also a certain other Act passed in the Third Year of King *Henry* the Sixth, intituled *Masons shall not confederate themselves in Chapiters and Assemblies;* also a certain other Act passed in the Parliament of *Ireland,* in the Thirty third Year of King *Henry* the Eighth, intituled *An Act for Servants' Wages;* also a certain other Act passed in the Second and Third Years of King *Edward* the Sixth, intituled *The Bill of Conspiracies of Victuallers and Craftsmen;* also a certain other Act passed in the Parliament of *Scotland,* in the Fifth Parliament of King *James* the First of *Scotland,* intituled *Of the Fees of Craftsmen and the Price of their Worke;* also a certain other Act passed in the Parliament of *Scotland,* in the Fifth Parliament of King *James* the First of *Scotland,* intituled *Of the Fees of Workmen;* also a certain other Act passed in the Parliament of *Scotland,* in the Fifth Parliament of King *James* the First of *Scotland,* intituled

Of Writches and Masones; also a certain other Act passed in the Parliament of *Scotland,* in the Seventh Parliament of King *James* the First of *Scotland,* intituled *The Price of ilk Workmanshippe;* also a certain other Act, passed in the Parliament of *Scotland,* in the Fifth Parliament of Queen *Mary* of *Scotland,* intituled *The Price of Craftesmenne's Wark, of Meate and Drinke in Tavernes;* also a certain other Act passed in the Parliament of *Scotland,* in the Seventh Parliament of King *James* the Sixth of *Scotland,* intituled *Anent the setting of Ordour and Price in all Stuffe;* also so much of a certain other Act passed in the Thirteenth and Fourteenth Years of King *Charles* the Second, intituled *An Act for regulating the Trade of Silk Throwing,* as provides and enacts, that the Corporation of Silk Throwers should not, by virtue of that Act, nor any Thing therein contained, make any Orders, Ordinances or Bye Laws, to set any Rates or Prices whatsoever upon the throwing of Silk, to bind or enforce their Members to work at; also a certain other Act passed in the Seventh Year of King *George* the First, intituled *An Act for regulating the Journeymen Tailors within the Weekly Bills of Mortality,* excepting so much thereof as relates to the Recovery of Wages, or to Journeymen Tailors or Servants departing from their Service, or refusing to enter into Work or Employment, as therein mentioned; also so much of an Act passed in the Twelfth Year of King *George* the First, intituled *An Act to prevent unlawful Combinations of Workmen employed in the Woollen Manufactures, and for better Payment of their Wages,* as provides that Contracts, Covenants or Agreements, Bye Laws, Ordinances, Rules and Orders, made or entered into by or between Persons brought up in, or professing, using or exercising the Art and Mystery of a Woolcomber or Weaver, or Journeyman Woolcomber or Journeyman Weaver, as therein mentioned, shall be illegal, null and void, and as punishes Woolcombers, Weavers, Journeyman Woolcombers and Weavers, and other Persons concerned in the Woollen Manufactures, for keeping up, continuing, acting in, making, entering into, signing, sealing or being knowingly concerned in, presuming or attempting to put in Execution such Agreements, Bye Laws, Ordinances, Rules or Orders, as therein mentioned, and as provides that the Provisions of the said Act of the Twelfth of *George* the First, just recited, shall extend to the Persons therein mentioned; also so much of a certain other Act passed in the Parliament of *Ireland,* in the Third Year of King *George* the Second, intituled *An Act to prevent unlawful Combinations of Workmen, Artificers and Labourers, employed in the several Trades and Manufactures of this Kingdom, and for the better Payment of their Wages; as also to prevent Abuses in making of Bricks, and to ascertain their Dimensions,* as declares illegal, null and void the Contracts, Covenants, Agreements, Bye Laws, Ordinances, Rules and Orders therein mentioned, and makes it an Offence to keep up, continue, act in, make, enter into, sign, seal or to be knowingly concerned therein, and to presume or attempt to put the same into Execution, as therein mentioned; also so much of a certain other Act passed in the Parliament of *Ireland,* in the Seventeenth Year of King *George* the Second, intituled *An Act for continuing several Statutes now near expiring, and for amending other Statutes, and for other Purposes therein mentioned,* as declares the Assemblies therein mentioned to be unlawful Assemblies, the Houses where they meet common Nuisances, and punishes the Master and Mistress thereof, as likewise those who enter into the Contracts, Covenants or Articles therein mentioned, or collect or pay Money for the Support of Persons as therein mentioned; also so much of a certain other Act passed in the Twenty second Year of King *George* the Second, intituled *An Act for the more effectual preventing of Frauds and Abuses committed by Persons employed in the Manufacture of Hats, and in the Woollen, Linen, Fustian, Cotton, Iron, Leather, Fur, Hemp, Flax, Mohair and Silk Manufactures, and for preventing unlawful Combinations of Journeymen Dyers and Journeymen Hotpressers, and of all Persons employed in the said several Manufactures, and for the better Payment of their Wages,* as extends those Provisions of the said Act of the Twelfth of *George* the First herein mentioned to the Persons therein mentioned; also so much of a certain other Act passed in the Twenty ninth Year of King *George* the Second, intituled *An Act to render more effectual an Act passed in the Twelfth Year of the Reign of His late Majesty King* George, *to prevent unlawful Combinations of Workmen employed in the Woollen Manufactures, and for better Payment of their Wages; and also an Act passed in the Thirteenth Year of the Reign of His said late Majesty, for the better Regulation of the Woollen Manufacture, and for preventing Disputes among the Persons concerned therein, and for limiting a Time for Prosecution for the Forfeiture appointed by the aforesaid Act, in case of the Payment of the Workmen's Wages in any other Manner than in Money,* as relates to the making of Rates for the Payment of Wages, continuing and altering and notifying them as therein mentioned; also so much of a certain other Act passed in the Parliament of *Ireland,* in the Third Year of King *George* the Third, intituled *An Act for continuing and amending certain temporary Statutes heretofore made, for the better Regulation of the City of* Cork, *and for enlarging the Salary of the Treasurer, and for the better regulating the Sale of Coals in the said City, and for erecting and continuing Lamps in the same, and for the better preserving the Streets and Highways therein, and for confirming and establishing a Court of Conscience in the said City, and for regulating the Assize of Bread therein, and for securing the Quays of Parapet Walls,* as relates to the Assemblies and Combinations of Artificers, Journeymen, Apprentices, Labourers and Manufacturers therein mentioned; also so much of a certain other Act passed in the Parliament of *Ireland,* in the Third Year of King *George* the Third, intituled *An Act for the better Regulation of the Linen and Hempen Manufactures,* as relates to meeting in order to consult upon or enter into Rules, Agreements or Combinations to ascertain or fix the Price of Labour or Workmanship, and as relates to administering Oaths or Declarations tending to fix the Price of Wages or Workmanship, and as relates to issuing and delivering Tickets, Certificates and Tokens of Parties being licensed to work, and as relates to Rules, Orders and Regulations relating to the Price or Wages of Labour or Workmanship, and as relates to Oaths to enter into Combinations or Agreements to ascertain or fix the Price of Wages or Workmanship, and to Oaths and Combinations not to work for a particular Employer, as therein mentioned; also a certain other Act, passed in the Eighth Year of King *George* the Third, intituled *An Act to amend an Act made in the Seventh Year of King George the First, intituled 'An Act for regulating the Journeymen Tailors within the Weekly Bills of Mortality;'* also so much of a certain other Act, passed in the Parliament of *Ireland* in the Eleventh and Twelfth Years of King *George* the Third, intituled *An Act for the Regulation of the City of* Cork, *and for other Purposes therein mentioned relative to the said City,* as relates to the Meetings and Assemblies therein mentioned, the administering and taking Oaths and Declarations, to the Tickets, Certificates, Advertisements and Writings, and to the Rules, Orders, Agreements and Regulations, and to the Combinations and Agreements to ascertain or fix the Price of Wages, Labour or Workmanship, or not to work, and as relates to the Refusal or Neglect, by Persons not in actual Service, to work on Application made, and as relates to the Detection and Discovery of Assemblies and Combinations for any of the above recited Purposes, and as relates to ascertaining Wages as therein mentioned; also so much of a certain other Act, passed in the Parliament of *Ireland* in the Eleventh and Twelfth Years of King *George* the Third, intituled *An Act for regulating the Journeymen Tailors and Journeymen Shipwrights of the City of* Dublin *and the Liberties thereof, and of the County of* Dublin, as punishes those who permit the Clubs and Societies therein mentioned to be kept or held in their Houses or Apartments, and as makes the Contracts, Covenants and Agreements therein mentioned, and Oaths to enforce them, illegal, and as punishes Persons for keeping up, continuing, acting in, making, entering into, signing, sealing or being knowingly interested or concerned in such Contracts, Covenants or Agreements, and as punishes Persons not retained or employed for refusing to enter into Work or Employment on Request made, as therein mentioned, and as regulates the Hours of Work and the Rate of Wages as therein mentioned; also so much of a certain other Act, passed in the Thirteenth Year of King *George* the Third, intituled *An Act to empower the Magistrates therein mentioned to settle and regulate the Wages of Persons employed in the Silk Manufacture within their respective Jurisdictions,* as relates to settling, regulating, ordering and declaring the Wages and Prices of Work, and the Notification thereof, and makes it an Offence to deviate from such Settlement, Regulation, Order and Declaration, or to ask, receive or take more or less Wages or larger or less Prices than shall be so settled, or to enter into Combinations, or for that Purpose to decoy or solicit, or to assemble, as therein mentioned, and as relates to the Detection of such Offences, and as makes it an Offence to retain or employ Journeymen Weavers, or to give, allow or pay, or cause to be given, allowed or paid, more or less Wages than shall be settled, as therein mentioned; also so much of a certain other Act, passed in the Seventeenth Year of King *George* the Third, intituled *An Act for the better regulating the Hat Manufactory,* as relates to the keeping up, acting in, making, entering into, signing, sealing or being knowingly concerned in the Contracts, Covenants or Agreements, Bye Laws, Ordinances, Rules or Orders of the Clubs, Societies or Combinations therein mentioned, or the presuming or attempting to put the Agreements, Bye Laws, Ordinances, Rules or Orders in Execution, or to the attending Meetings, Clubs, Societies or Combinations, or to the Summoning, giving Notice to or calling upon, collecting, demanding or receiving, persuading, enticing or inveigling, or endeavouring to persuade, entice or inveigle, paying Money, making or entering into Subscriptions or Contributions, as therein mentioned; also so much of a certain other Act, passed in the Parliament of *Ireland* in the Nineteenth and Twentieth Years of King *George* the Third, intituled *An Act to prevent Combinations, and for further Encouragement of Trade,* as declares that Combinations in Trade are public Nuisances, and that the Acts therein enumerated shall be considered as Evidences of unlawful Combinations, and sufficient for the Conviction of any Person who shall be guilty of the same, and as avoids Rules, Bye Laws and Regulations contrary to its Provisions and Oaths for obeying or executing the same, and as provides for the Case of an Act of Combination for which no specific Punishment is pointed out, as therein mentioned; also so much of a certain other Act, passed in the Parliament of *Ireland* in the Nineteenth and Twentieth Years of King *George* the Third, intituled *An Act for the better Regulation of the Silk Manufacture,* as relates to the Wages and Prices for Work, to Combinations to raise Wages, and the decoying or soliciting Journeymen Weavers, as therein mentioned; also so much of a certain other Act, passed in the Parliament of *Ireland* in the Nineteenth and Twentieth Years of King *George* the Third, intituled *An Act for regulating the curing and preparing Provisions, and for preventing Combinations among the several Tradesmen and other Persons employed in making up such Provisions, and for regulating the Butter Trade in the City of* Dublin, *and for other Purposes therein mentioned,* as relates to summoning Persons to appear at Meetings and Assemblies, and as relates to administering Oaths or Declarations, to the issuing and delivering of Messages, Tickets, Certificates and Tokens, Advertisements or Writings, to making or joining in making Rules, Orders, Agreements and Regulations as therein mentioned, and as relates to taking Oaths, or entering into Combinations or Agreements to ascertain or fix the Price of Wages or of Labour or Workmanship, or to make any Rule, Order, Agreement or Regulation, and to taking Oaths and entering into Combinations and Agreements not to work for a particular Person, as therein mentioned, and as relates to the fixing of Wages; also so much of a certain other Act, passed in the Parliament of *Ireland* in the Twenty fifth Year of King *George* the Third intituled *An Act for granting the Sums of Twenty thousand Pounds, Five thousand Pounds, and Four thousand Pounds, to certain Trustees, and for promoting the several Manufactures therein named,* as relates to ascertaining the Rates of Labour and Prices of Workmanship, as therein mentioned, and as requires an Affidavit to be filed previous to the Commencement of a Suit, as therein mentioned; also so much of a certain other Act, passed in the Thirty second Year of King *George* the Third, intituled *An Act for extending the Provisions of an Act made in the Thirteenth Year of the Reign of His present Majesty, intituled 'An Act to empower the Magistrates therein mentioned to settle and regulate the Wages of Persons employed in the Silk Manufacture within their respective Jurisdictions,' to Manufactories of Silk mixed with other Materials, and for the more effectual Punishment of Buyers and Receivers of Silk purloined and embezzled by Persons employed in the Manufacture thereof* as extend the Provisions of the said Act of the Thirteenth of *George* the Third, hereby repealed, to the Persons therein mentioned; also a certain other Act, passed in the Thirty sixth Year of King *George* the Third, intituled *An Act to prevent unlawful Combinations of Workmen employed in the Paper Manufactory;* also so much of a certain other Act passed in the Thirty ninth Year of King *George* the Third, intituled *An Act to explain and amend the Laws relative to Colliers in that Part of* Great Britain *called* Scotland, as relates to the fixing and appointing of Hire and Wages; also an Act passed in the Thirty ninth and Fortieth Years of King *George* the Third, intituled *An Act to repeal an Act passed in the last Session of Parliament, intituled 'An Act to prevent unlawful Combinations of Workmen,' and to substitute other Provisions in lieu thereof,* excepting so much thereof as relates to the Adjustment of Disputes between Masters and Workmen, as therein mentioned; also so much of a certain other Act passed in the Forty third Year of King *George* the Third, intituled *An Act to prevent unlawful Combinations of Workmen, Artificers, Journeymen and Labourers, in* Ireland, *and for other Purposes relating thereto,* as makes illegal and void Contracts, Covenants and Agreements for obtaining an Advance of Wages, or for lessening or altering the Hours or Time of working, or for decreasing the Quantity of Work, or for controlling or affecting the Conduct or Management of any Manufacture, Trade or Business, and as prohibits the making or entering into or being concerned in the same, and as punishes Persons for so doing, and as relates to the Combinations therein mentioned, and as relates to endeavouring by Gift, Persuasion or Solicitation to prevent Persons hiring themselves, and as relates to attending the Meetings therein mentioned, or endeavouring to induce the Attendance of others, and collecting, demanding, asking or receiving Money for the Purposes therein mentioned, and as relates to persuading, enticing, soliciting or endeavouring to induce others to enter into or be concerned in the Combinations therein mentioned, and to paying Money, making or entering into Subscriptions or Contributions, and to Oaths and Declarations, and to Tickets, Certificates and Tokens, and to Contributions supporting and maintaining others, as therein mentioned, and as punishes Persons for permitting Assemblies in their Houses or Apartments, as therein mentioned; also a certain other Act passed in the Forty seventh Year of King *George* the Third, intituled *An Act to declare that the Provisions of an Act, made in the Parliament of* Ireland *in the Thirty third Year of King* Henry *the Eighth, relating to Servants Wages, shall extend to all Counties of Cities and Counties of Towns in* Ireland; also so much of a certain other Act passed in the Fifty seventh Year of King *George* the Third, intituled *An Act to extend the Provisions of an Act of the Twelfth Year of His late Majesty King* George *the First, and an Act of the Twenty second Year of His late Majesty King* George *the Second, against Payment of Labourers in Goods or by Truck, and to secure their Payment in the lawful Money of this Realm, to Labourers employed in the Collieries, or in the working and getting of Coal, in the United Kingdom of* Great Britain *and* Ireland, *and for extending the Provisions of the said Acts to* Scotland *and* Ireland, as extends such of the Provisions of the said Acts as are hereby repealed to *Scotland and Ireland;* together with all other Laws, Statutes and Enactments now in force throughout or in any Part of the United Kingdom of *Great Britain* and *Ireland,* relative to Combinations to obtain an Advance of Wages, or to lessen or alter the Hours or Duration of the Time of working, or to decrease the Quantity of Work, or to regulate or controul the Mode of carrying on any Manufacture, Trade or Business, or the Management thereof; relative also to Combinations to lower the Rate of Wages, or to increase or alter the Hours of Duration of the Time of working, or to increase the Quantity of Work, or to regulate or controul the Mode of carrying on any Manufacture, Trade or Business, or the Management thereof; relative also to fixing the Amount of the Wages of Labour; relative also to obliging Workmen not hired to enter into Work; together with every other Act and Enactment enforcing or extending the Application of any of the Acts or Enactments repealed by this Act, shall be and the same are hereby repealed, save and except in as far as the same may have repealed any prior Act or Enactment. [*See Section 6. post.*]

II. And be it further enacted, That Journeymen, Workmen or other Persons who shall enter into any Combination to obtain an Advance, or to fix the Rate of Wages, or to lessen or alter the Hours or Duration of the Time of working, or to decrease the Quantity of Work, or to induce another to depart from his Service before the End of the Time or Term for which he is hired, or to quit or return his Work before the same shall be finished, or not being hired, to refuse to enter into Work or Employment, or to regulate the Mode of carrying on any Manufacture, Trade or Business, or the Management thereof, shall not therefore be subject or liable to any Indictment or Prosecution for Conspiracy, or to any other Criminal Information or Punishment whatever, under the Common or the Statute Law.

III. And be it further enacted, That Masters, Employers or other Persons, who shall enter into any Combination to lower or to fix the Rate of Wages, or to increase or alter the Hours or Duration of the Time of working, or to increase the Quantity of Work, or to regulate the Mode of carrying on any Manufacture, Trade or Business, or the Management thereof, shall not therefore be subject or liable to any Indictment or Prosecution, or, for Conspiracy, or to any other Criminal Information or Punishment whatever, under the Common or the Statute Law.

IV. And be it further enacted, That all penal Proceedings for any Act or Omission against any Enactment hereby repealed, and not made punishable by the Provisions of this Act or for any Act or Omission hereby exempted from Punishment, shall become null and void; and that no penal Proceedings for any Act or Omission against any Enactment hereby repealed, and not made punishable by the Provisions of this Act, or for any Act or Omission hereby exempted from Punishment, shall be instituted against any one in relation to any such Offence already incurred; provided that no Person shall be subjected to Loss or Liability for any Thing already done, touching any Act or Omission, the penal Proceedings against which are hereby made null and void, or shall lose any Privilege or Protection to which the Enactments hereby repealed entitle him.

V. And be it further enacted, That if any Person by Violence to the Person or Property, by Threats or by Intimidation, shall wilfully or maliciously force another to depart from his Hiring or Work before the End of the Time or Term for which he is hired, or return his Work before the same shall be finished, or damnify, spoil or destroy any Machinery, Tools, Goods, Wares or Work, or prevent any Person not being hired from accepting any Work or Employment; or if any Person shall wilfully or maliciously use or employ Violence to the Person or Property, Threats or Intimidation towards another on account of his not complying with or conforming to any Rules, Orders, Resolutions or Regulations made to obtain an Advance of Wages, or to lessen or alter the Hours of working, or to decrease the Quantity of Work, or to regulate the Mode of carrying on any Manufacture, Trade or Business, or the Management thereof; or if any Person, by Violence to the Person or Property, by Threats or by Intimidation, shall wilfully or maliciously force any Master or Mistress Manufacturer, his or her Foreman or Agent, to make any Alteration in their Mode of regulating, managing, conducting or carrying on their Manufacture, Trade or Business; every Person so offending, or causing, procuring, aiding, abetting or assisting in such Offence, being convicted thereof in Manner hereafter mentioned, shall be imprisoned only, or imprisoned and kept to hard Labour, for any Time not exceeding Two Calendar Months.

VI. And be it further enacted, That if any Persons shall combine, and by Violence to the Person or Property, or by Threats or Intimidation, wilfully and maliciously force another to depart from his Service before the End of the Time or Term for which he or she is hired, or return his or her Work before the same shall be finished, or damnify, spoil or destroy any Machinery, Tools, Goods, Wares or Work, or prevent any Person not being hired from accepting any Work or Employment; or if any Persons so combined shall wilfully or maliciously use or employ Violence to the Person or Property, or Threats or Intimidation towards another, on account of his or her not complying with or conforming to any Rules, Orders, Resolutions or Regulations made to obtain an Advance of Wages, or to lessen or alter the Hours of working, or to decrease the Quantity of Work, or to regulate the Mode of carrying on any Manufacture, Trade or Business, or the Management thereof; or if any Persons shall combine, and by Violence to the Person or Property, or by Threats or Intimidation, wilfully or maliciously force any Master or Mistress Manufacturer, his or her Foreman or Agent, to make any Alteration in their Mode of regulating, managing, conducting or carrying on their Manufacture, Trade or Business; each and every Person so offending, or causing, procuring, aiding, abetting or assisting in such Offence, being convicted thereof in Manner hereinafter mentioned, shall be imprisoned only, or imprisoned and kept to hard Labour, for any Time not exceeding Two Calendar Months: Provided always, that nothing herein contained shall alter or affect any Law now in force for the Prosecution and Punishment of the said several offences; only that a Conviction under this Act for any of such Offence shall exempt the Offender from Prosecution under any other Law or Statute. [*See Section* 1. *ante.*]

VII. And for the more effectual Prosecution of Offenders against this Act, be it further enacted, That on Complaint and Information upon Oath before any One or more Justice or Justices of the Peace, of any Offence having been committed against this Act within his or their respective Jurisdictions, such Justice or Justices are hereby authorized and required to summon the Person or Persons charged with any such Offence against this Act to appear before any Two Justices at a certain Time and Place to be specified, such Place to be as near to the Place where Cause of such Complaint shall have arisen as may be; and if any Person or Persons so summoned shall not appear according to such Summons, then such Justices (Proof on Oath having been first made before them or him of the due Service of such Summons upon such Person or Persons, by delivering the same to him or her personally, or leaving the same at his or her usual Place of Abode, provided the same shall be so left Twenty four Hours at the least before the Time which shall be appointed to attend the said Justices upon such Summons) shall make and issue their or his Warrants or Warrant for apprehending the Person or Persons so summoned and not appearing as aforesaid, and bringing him or her before such Justices; or it shall be lawful for such Justices, if they shall think fit, without issuing any previous Summons, and instead of issuing the same, upon such Complaint and Information upon Oath as aforesaid, to make and issue their Warrant or Warrants for apprehending the Person or Persons by such Information charged to have offended against this Act, and bringing him or her before such Justices; such Justices shall and they are hereby authorized and required forthwith to make Enquiry touching the Matters complained of, and to examine into the same, and to hear and determine the Matter of every such Complaint; and upon Confession by the Party, or Proof by Two or more credible Witnesses upon Oath, (which Oath such Justice or Justices are hereby authorized to administer,) to convict or acquit the Party against whom Complaint shall have been made as aforesaid; such Conviction, and the Commitment thereon, to be in the Form or to the Effect of the Form in the Schedule to this Act annexed.

VIII. Provided always, and be it further enacted, That no Justice of the Peace, being also a Master, or the Father or Son of any Master, in any Trade or Manufacture, shall act as such Justice under this Act.

Appendix 6. The Combination Act of 1825

(Sections III-VI)

III. And be it further enacted, That from and after the passing of this Act, if any Person shall by Violence to the Person or Property, or by Threats or Intimidation, or by molesting or in any way obstructing another, force or endeavour to force any Journeyman, Manufacturer, Workman or other Person hired or employed in any Manufacture, Trade or Business, to depart from his Hiring, Employment or Work, or to return his Work before the same shall be finished, or prevent or endeavour to prevent any Journeyman, Manufacturer, Workman or other Person not being hired or employed from hiring himself to, or from accepting Work or Employment from any Person or Persons; or if any Person shall use or employ Violence to the Person or Property of another, or Threats or Intimidation, or shall molest or in any way obstruct another for the Purpose of forcing or inducing such Person to belong to any Club or Association, or to contribute to any common Fund, or to pay any Fine or Penalty, or on account of his not belonging to any particular Club or Association, or not having contributed or having refused to contribute to any common Fund, or to pay any Fine or Penalty; or on account of his not having complied or of his refusing to comply with any Rules, Orders, Resolutions, or Regulations made to obtain an Advance or to reduce the Rate of Wages, or to lessen or alter the Hours of working, or to decrease or alter the Quantity of Work, or to regulate the Mode of carrying on any Manufacture, Trade or Business, or the Management thereof; or if any Person shall by violence to the Person or Property of another, or by Threats or Intimidation, or by molesting or in any way obstructing another, force or endeavour to force any Manufacturer or Person carrying on any Trade or Business, to make any Alteration in his Mode of regulating, managing, conducting or carrying on such Manufacture, Trade or Business, or to limit the Number of his Apprentices, or the Number or Description of his Journeymen, Workmen or Servants; every Person so offending or aiding, abetting or assisting therein, being convicted thereof in Manner hereinafter mentioned, shall be imprisoned only, or shall and may be imprisoned and kept to Hard Labour, for any Time not exceeding Three Calendar Months.

IV. Provided always, and be it enacted, That this Act shall not extend to subject any Persons to Punishment, who shall meet together for the sole Purpose of consulting upon and determining the Rate of Wages or Prices, which the Persons present at such Meeting or any of them, shall require or demand for his or their Work, or the Hours or Time for which he or they shall work in any Manufacture, Trade or Business, or who shall enter into any Agreement, verbal or written, among themselves, for the Purpose of fixing the Rate of Wages or Prices which the Parties entering into such Agreement, or any of them, shall require or demand for his or their Work, or the Hours of Time for which he or they will work, in any Manufacture, Trade or Business; and that Persons so meeting for the Purposes aforesaid, or entering into any such Agreement as aforesaid, shall not be liable to any Prosecution or Penalty for so doing; any Law or Statute to the contrary notwithstanding.

V. Provided also, and be it further enacted, That this Act shall not extend to subject any Persons to Punishment who shall meet together for the sole Purpose of consulting upon and determining the Rate of Wages or Prices which the Persons present at such Meeting, or any of them, shall pay to his or their Journeymen, Workmen or Servants, for their Work, or the Hours or Time of working in any Manufacture, Trade or Business, or who shall enter into any Agreement, verbal or written, among themselves, for the Purpose of fixing the Rate of Wages or Prices, which the Parties entering into such Agreement, or any of them, shall pay to his or their Journeymen, Workmen or Servants, for their Work or the Hours or Time of working in any Manufacture, Trade or Business; and that Persons so meeting for the Purposes aforesaid, or entering into any such Agreement as aforesaid, shall not be liable to any Prosecution or Penalty for so doing, any Law or Statute to the contrary notwithstanding.

VI. And be it further enacted, That all and every Persons and Person who shall or may offend against this Act, shall and may, equally with all other Persons, be called upon and compelled to give his or her Testimony and Evidence as a Witness or Witnesses on behalf of His Majesty, or of the Prosecutor or Informer, upon any Information to be made or exhibited under this Act, against any other Person or Persons not being such Witness or Witnesses as aforesaid, and that in all such Cases every Person having given his or her Testimony or Evidence as aforesaid, shall be and is hereby indemnified of, from and against any Information to be laid, or Prosecution to be commenced against him or her, for having offended in the Matter wherein or relative to which he, she or they shall have given Testimony or Evidence as aforesaid.

Appendix 7. The Conspiracy and Protection of Property Act, 1875

(Sections 3-7)

3. An agreement or combination by two or more persons to do or procure to be done any act in contemplation or furtherance of a trade dispute between employers and workmen shall not be indictable as a conspiracy if such act committed by one person would not be punishable as a crime.

Nothing in this section shall exempt from punishment any persons guilty of a conspiracy for which a punishment is awarded by any Act of Parliament.

Nothing in this section shall affect the law relating to riot, unlawful assembly, breach of the peace, or sedition, or any offence against the State, or the Sovereign.

A crime for the purposes of this section means an offence punishable on indictment, or an offence which is punishable on summary conviction, and for the commission of which the offender is liable under the statute making the offence punishable to be imprisoned either absolutely or at the discretion of the court as an alternative for some other punishment.

Where a person is convicted of any such agreement or combination as aforesaid to do or procure to be done an act which is punishable only on summary conviction, and is sentenced to imprisonment, the imprisonment shall not exceed three months, or such longer time, if any, as may have been prescribed by the statute for the punishment of the said act when committed by one person.

4. Where a person employed by a municipal authority or by any company or contractor upon whom is imposed by Act of Parliament the duty, or who have otherwise assumed the duty of supplying any city, borough, town, or place, or any part thereof, with gas or water, wilfully and maliciously breaks a contract of service with that authority or company or contractor, knowing or having reasonable cause to believe that the probable consequences of his so doing, either alone or in combination with others, will be to deprive the inhabitants of that city, borough, town, place, or part, wholly or to a great extent of their supply of gas or water, he shall on conviction thereof by a court of summary jurisdiction, or on indictment as

herein-after mentioned, be liable either to pay a penalty not exceeding twenty pounds or to be imprisoned for a term not exceeding three months, with or without hard labour.

Every such municipal authority, company, or contractor as is mentioned in this section shall cause to be posted up, at the gasworks or waterworks, as the case may be, belonging to such authority or company or contractor, a printed copy of this section in some conspicuous place where the same may be conveniently read by the persons employed, and as often as such copy becomes defaced, obliterated, or destroyed, shall cause it to be renewed with all reasonable despatch.

If any municipal authority or company or contractor make default in complying with the provisions of this section in relation to such notice as aforesaid, they or he shall incur on summary conviction a penalty not exceeding five pounds for every day during which such default continues, and every person who unlawfully injures, defaces, or covers up any notice so posted up as aforesaid in pursuance of this Act, shall be liable on summary conviction to a penalty not exceeding forty shillings.

5. Where any person wilfully and maliciously breaks a contract of service or of hiring, knowing or having reasonable cause to believe that the probable consequences of his so doing, either alone or in combination with others, will be to endanger human life, or cause serious bodily injury, or to expose valuable property whether real or personal to destruction or serious injury, he shall on conviction thereof by a court of summary jurisdiction, or on indictment as hereinafter mentioned, be liable either to pay a penalty not exceeding twenty pounds, or to be imprisoned for a term not exceeding three months, with or without hard labour.

Miscellaneous.

6. Where a master, being legally liable to provide for his servant or apprentice necessary food, clothing, medical aid, or lodging, wilfully and without lawful excuse refuses or neglects to provide the same, whereby the health of the servant or apprentice is or is likely to be seriously or permanently injured, he shall on summary conviction be liable either to pay a penalty not exceeding twenty pounds, or to be imprisoned for a term not exceeding six months, with or without hard labour.

7. Every person who, with a view to compel any other person to abstain from doing or to do any act which such other person has a legal right to do or abstain from doing, wrongfully and without legal authority,—

1. Uses violence to or intimidates such other person or his wife or children, or injures his property; or,
2. Persistently follows such other person about from place to place; or,
3. Hides any tools, clothes, or other property owned or used by such other person, or deprives him of or hinders him in the use thereof; or,
4. Watches or besets the house or other place where such other person resides, or works, or carries on business, or happens to be, or the approach to such house or place; or,
5. Follows such other person with two or more other persons in a disorderly manner in or through any street or road,

shall, on conviction thereof by a court of summary jurisdiction, or on indictment as hereinafter mentioned, be liable either to pay a penalty not exceeding twenty pounds, or to be imprisoned for a term not exceeding three months, with or without hard labour.

Attending at or near the house or place where a person resides, or works, or carries on business, or happens to be, or the approach to such house or place, in order merely to obtain or communicate information, shall not be deemed a watching or besetting within the meaning of this section.

Appendix 8. The New Zealand Industrial Conciliation and Arbitration Act, 1894

(Extracts)*

"An Act to encourage the formation of industrial unions and associations and to facilitate the settlement of industrial disputes by conciliation and arbitration"

17. The parties to industrial agreements may be (1) trade unions, (2) industrial unions, (3) industrial associations, (4) employers, and any such agreement may provide for any matter or thing affecting any industrial matter, or in relation thereto, or for the prevention or settlement of an industrial dispute.

21. Every industrial agreement duly made and executed shall be binding on the parties thereto and on every person who at any time during the term of such agreement is a member of any industrial union, trade union, or association party thereto, and on every employer who shall in the prescribed manner signify to the registrar of the supreme court where such agreement is filed concurrence therein, and every such employer shall be entitled to the benefit thereof, and be deemed to be a party thereto.

24. (1) The governor may from time to time divide New Zealand, or any portion thereof, into such districts as he shall think fit, to be called "industrial districts," and notice of the constitution of every such district shall be given in the Gazette as occasion requires. . . .

29. Whenever an industrial dispute shall be referred to a board or court as hereinafter provided, no industrial union or association, trade union, or society, whether of employers or workers, and no employer who may be a party to the proceedings before the board or court shall, on account of such industrial dispute, do any act or thing in the nature of a strike or lockout, or suspend or discontinue employment or work in any industry affected by such proceedings, but each party shall continue to employ or be employed, as the case may be, until the board or court shall have come to a final decision in accordance with this act. But nothing herein shall be deemed to prevent any suspension or discontinuance of any industry, or from working therein, for any other good cause.

*Source: U.S. Industrial Commission, *Report* (Washington, D.C.: GPO, 1901), Volume XVI

42. Any industrial dispute may be referred for settlement to a board either by or pursuant to an industrial agreement, or in the manner hereinafter provided.

(1) Any party to such a dispute may, in the prescribed manner, lodge an application with the clerk requesting that such dispute be referred for settlement to a board.

(2) The parties to such dispute may comprise—

(a) An individual employer, or several employers, and an industrial union, trade union, or association of workers, or several such unions or associations.

(b) An industrial union, trade union, or association of employers, or an individual employer, or several employers, and an industrial union, trade union, or association of workers, or several such unions or associations.

But the mention of the various kinds of parties shall not be deemed to interfere with any arrangement thereof that may be necessary to insure an industrial dispute being brought in a complete shape before the board; and a party or parties may be withdrawn or removed from the proceedings and another or others substituted after the reference to the board and before any report is made, as the board shall allow or think best adapted for the purpose of giving effect to this act, and the board may make any recommendation or give any direction for any such purpose accordingly. . . .

(7) . . . When any industrial dispute has been referred for settlement to a board or the court, any employer, association, trade union, or industrial union may, on application, if the board or the court deem it equitable, be joined as party thereto at any stage of the proceedings, and on such terms as the board or the court deems equitable. [added by amendment, 1896]

43. . . . Where an industrial dispute relates to employment or wages, the jurisdiction of the board or court to deal therewith shall not be voided or affected by the fact that the relationship of employer and employed has ceased to exist, unless it so ceased at least 6 weeks before the industrial dispute was first referred to the board or to the court, if there has been no prior reference to the board. [added by amendment, 1895]

47. There shall be one court of arbitration for the whole colony for the settlement of industrial disputes pursuant to this act. . . .

48. (1) The court shall consist of three members to be appointed by the governor, one to be so appointed on the recommendation of the councils or a majority of the councils of the industrial associations of workers in the colony, and one to be so appointed on the recommendation of the councils or a majority of the councils of the industrial associations of employers of the colony: . . . the third member . . . shall be a judge of the Supreme Court. . . .

67. . . . In order to enable the court the more effectually to dispose of any matter before it according to the substantial merits and equities of the case, it may, at any stage of the proceedings, of its own motion or on the application of any of the parties, and upon such terms as it thinks fit, by order: (1) Direct parties to be joined or struck out; . . . [added by amendment, 1898]

72. Proceedings in the court shall not be impeached or held bad for want of form, nor shall the same be removable to any court by *certiorari* or otherwise; and no award or proceeding of the court shall be liable to be challenged, appealed against, reviewed, quashed, or called in question by any court of judicature on any account whatsoever. . . .

74. Every award of the court shall specify each industrial union, trade union, association, person, or persons on which or on whom it is intended that it shall be binding, and the period, not exceeding 2 years from the making thereof, during which its provisions may be enforced; and during the period within which the provisions of such award may be enforced such award shall be binding upon every industrial union, trade union, association, or person upon which it shall be thereby declared such award shall be binding: *Provided,* That if the members of any industrial union or trade union are mentioned generally in such award, all persons who are members at the date thereof of such award, or may thereafter become so during its subsistence, shall be included in the direction given or made by the award.

Appendix 9. The Trade Disputes Act, 1906

(Complete Text)

Be it enacted by the King's most Excellent Majesty, by and with the advice and consent of the Lords Spiritual and Temporal, and Commons, in this present Parliament assembled, and by the authority of the same, as follows:

1. The following paragraph shall be added as a new paragraph after the first paragraph of section three of the Conspiracy and Protection of Property Act, 1875:—

"An act done in pursuance of an agreement or combination by two or more persons shall, if done in contemplation or furtherance of a trade dispute, not be actionable unless the act, if done without any such agreement or combination, would be actionable."

2.—(1) It shall be lawful for one or more persons, acting on their own behalf or on behalf of a trade union or of an individual employer or firm in contemplation or furtherance of a trade dispute, to attend at or near a house or place where a person resides or works or carries on business or happens to be, if they so attend merely for the purpose of peacefully obtaining or communicating information, or of peacefully persuading any person to work or abstain from working.

(2) Section seven of the Conspiracy and Protection of Property Act, 1875, is hereby repealed from "attending at or near" to the end of the section.

3. An act done by a person in contemplation or furtherance of a trade dispute shall not be actionable on the ground only that it induces some other person to break a contract of employment or that it is an interference with the trade, business, or employment of some other person, or with the right of some other person to dispose of his capital or his labour as he wills.

4.—(1) An action against a trade union, whether of workmen or masters, or against any members or officials thereof on behalf of themselves and all other members of the trade union in respect of any tortious act alleged to have been committed by or on behalf of the trade union, shall not be entertained by any court.

(2) Nothing in this section shall affect the liability of the trustees of a trade union to be

sued in the events provided for by the Trades Union Act, 1871, section nine, except in respect of any tortious act committed by or on behalf of the union in contemplation or in furtherance of a trade dispute.

5.—(1) This Act may be cited as the Trade Disputes Act, 1906, and the Trade Union Acts, 1871 and 1876, and this Act may be cited together as the Trade Union Acts, 1871 to 1906.

(2) In this Act the expression "trade union" has the same meaning as in the Trade Union Acts, 1871 and 1876, and shall include any combination as therein defined, notwithstanding that such combination may be the branch of a trade union.

(3) In this Act and in the Conspiracy and Protection of Property Act, 1875, the expression "trade dispute" means any dispute between employers and workmen, or between workmen and workmen, which is connected with the employment or non-employment, or the terms of the employment, or with the conditions of labour, of any person, and the expression "workmen" means all persons employed in trade or industry, whether or not in the employment of the employer with whom a trade dispute arises; and, in section three of the last-mentioned Act, the words "between employers and workmen" shall be repealed.

Appendix 10. The Fascist Labor Charter, 1927

(Complete Text)*

(1)

The Italian nation is an organism having aims, life and means of action superior in power and duration to those of the individuals, divided or in groups, which compose it. It is a moral, political and economic unity which is realised integrally in the Fascist State.

(2)

Work, in all forms—administrative, executive, technical, intellectual and manual, is a social duty. For this reason, and only for this reason, it is safeguarded by the State. The many factors of production are accounted as one from the national point of view, its objects are one and are united for the well-being of individuals and the development of national power.

(3)

Syndical and professional organisation is free, but only the legally recognised syndicate, under the control of the State, has the right to legally represent the whole category of employers or workers for which it is constituted. To defend their interests *vis-a-vis* the State and the other professional associations. To stipulate collective labour contracts which are obligatory for all who belong to the category and to impose contributions and to exercise the function of delegate of the public interest.

(4)

Solidarity between the various factors of production finds its concrete expression in the collective labour contract by way of conciliation of the opposing interests of employers and employees and their subordination to the superior interests of production.

*Source: Raffaelo Viglione, *The Structure of the Corporate State,* 4th ed., translated and abridged by Anne Waring (London: British Empire Fascist Party, 1933)

(5)

The Labour Court is the organ through which the State intervenes to regulate labour controversies, whether in regard to the observance of pacts and other existing rules, or in regard to determination of new conditions of labour.

(6)

The legally-recognised associations ensure legal equality between employer and employee and maintain the discipline of production and of labour, and promote the general perfection of production. The Corporations are the organs of unification of the forces of production and represent integrally their interests.

By virtue of this integral representation, the interests of production being national interests, the Corporations are recognised by law as organs of the State.

In so much as they represent the united interests of production the Corporations can make obligatory rules for the discipline of labour relations, and also for the co-ordination of production, whenever they are given the necessary authority by the dependent associations.

(7)

The Corporate State considers private initiative in the field of production as the most efficacious and useful instrument in the National interest.

Private organisation of production being a function of national interest, the organiser of the business is responsible for the direction of production to the State. From collaboration the forces of production derive reciprocity of rights and duties. The employee, technical, intellectual or manual, is an active collaborator in the business, the direction of which is in the hands of the employer and whose responsibility it is.

(8)

The associations of employers are obliged to promote in every way the augmentation and improvement of production and the reduction of costs. The representatives of those who are occupied in independent professions or arts and the associations of public dependents, contribute to the progress of art, science, and letters, to the improvement of production and consequently to the moral aims of the corporate State.

(9)

The intervention of the State in economic production takes place only where private initiative is insufficient or lacking, or where the political interests of the State are in question. Such intervention can assume the form of control, encouragement or direct management.

(10)

In collective labour controversies legal action cannot be taken if the Corporation has not first attempted a conciliation.

In industrial controversies concerning the interpretation and application of collective labour contracts the associations have power to arbitrate.

The final arbitration for such controversies devolves on the ordinary Courts of Law, with the addition of assistants appointed by the interested associations.

(11)

The associations are obliged to regulate, by means of collective contracts, labour relations between the categories of employers and employees which they represent.

Collective labour-contracts are stipulated between associations of 1st grade under the guidance and control of the central organisations, or of the association of higher grade in certain cases, provided for by the law and statutes.

Every collective labour contract should, under pain of nullity, contain precise rules on disciplinary relations, on the length of probation, on the amount and payment of salaries, and the hours of work.

(12)

The actions of the syndicate, the conciliating work of the Corporate organs and the sentence of the Labour Courts guarantee that the salary should correspond to the normal necessities of life, the possibilities of production and the amount of work. The determination of salary is withdrawn from any general rule and confirmed by the agreement of the parties in the collective contract.

(13)

The data supplied by the public administrations of the Central Institute of Statistics and the legally-recognised associations, concerning the conditions of labour and production, the state of the money-market and the variations in the standards of living of the workers, when co-ordinated and elaborated by the Ministry of Corporations, give the criterion for proportioning the interests of the different categories and classes between themselves and between them and the superior interests of production.

(14)

Payment should correspond in the way most suitable to the exigencies of the worker and the business. Payment for piece-work should be made weekly or fortnightly if the time required for finishing the work exceeds 15 days.

Night work, not included in the regular shifts, is paid a percentage more than day labour. When the worker is paid by piece-work the amount of payment should be determined in such a way that the worker, of normal capacity, should be able to gain a minimum sum over and above the minimum wage.

(15)

The employee has a right to a weekly rest on Sunday, also on civil and religious feast days, according to local tradition and bearing in mind the existing laws, and exigencies of the business.

The time-table should be scrupulously observed by the worker.

(16)

After a year of uninterrupted service the worker has a right to an annual paid holiday.

(17)

The worker has the right, in case of dismissal for no fault of his own, to an indemnity proportionate to years of service. An indemnity is also payable in the event of the death of the worker.

(18)

A business changing hands does not break the labour contract and the personnel retain their rights under the new ownership.

If the illness of a worker does not exceed a certain time limit, it does not break the labour contract.

A call to arms or military service is not a reason for dismissal.

(19)

Infraction of discipline and acts which disturb the normal progress of the business committed by the worker are punished according to the gravity of the case, with a fine, with suspension from work, and in the most serious cases, with dismissal without indemnity. The cases must be specified in which the employer can punish with a fine, suspension or immediate dismissal without indemnity.

(20)

The newly engaged worker is subject to a period of probation during which the rights of terminating the contract are reciprocal. Payment is only made for work done.

(21)

The collective labour contract also extends its benefits and its discipline to the workers at home. Special rules will be given by the State to assure cleanliness and hygiene in work done at home.

(22)

The State ascertains and controls the employment and unemployment of workers. These are an indication of the condition of production.

(23)

The Labour Exchanges are under the control of the Corporate organs of the State. The employer is obliged to engage labour by way of these exchanges. They may select from those inscribed in the register giving preference to those who belong to the "Partito Nazionale Fascista" (the National Fascist Party) and the Fascist Syndicates according to the date of registration.

(24)

The associations of workers are obliged to exercise a selective function with the object of raising technical capacity and moral worth.

(25)

The Corporate organs supervise the observance of the laws regarding hygiene in conditions of labour and prevention of accidents by individuals in the association.

(26)

Foresight is a necessary principle of collaboration and should be encouraged by employers and employees.

The State, through the Corporate organs and the associations, promotes, as much as possible, co-ordination and unification between the systems and institutions of insurance.

(27)

The Fascist State promotes:—

The improvement of insurance against accidents.

The improvement and extension of insurance for maternity.

Insurance against industrial diseases and tuberculosis, as the beginning of general insurance against all diseases.

The improvement of insurance against involuntary unemployment.

The adoption of special forms of endowment insurance for young workers.

(28)

It is the task of the associations of workers to assist them in everything relative to insurance against illness and social insurance. In the collective labour contracts, whenever technically possible, provision should be made for instituting "mutual savings banks" with contributions from employers and employees, and administered by their representatives and under the control of the Corporate organs.

(29)

It is the duty and the right of the associations to assist their associates whether they are members or not. They should exercise the function of assistance themselves and cannot delegate it to other Bodies or Institutions, except for objectives of a general nature and exceeding the interests of individual categories.

(30)

Educational or professional instruction for their associates, whether members or not, is one of the principal duties of the associations. They should support the activity of the "Opera Nazionale Dopolavoro" (National Leisure Hours Institution), and other educational activities.

Appendix 11. The Norris-La Guardia (Anti-Injunction) Act, 1932

(Complete Text)

Be it enacted by the Senate and House of Representatives of the United States of America in Congress assembled, That no court of the United States, as herein defined, shall have jurisdiction to issue any restraining order or temporary or permanent injunction in a case involving or growing out of a labor dispute, except in a strict conformity with the provisions of this Act; nor shall any such restraining order or temporary or permanent injunction be issued contrary to the public policy declared in this Act.

Sec. 2. In the interpretation of this Act and in determining the jurisdiction and authority of the courts of the United States, as such jurisdiction and authority are herein defined and limited, the public policy of the United States is hereby declared as follows:

Whereas under prevailing economic conditions, developed with the aid of governmental authority for owners of property to organize in the corporate and other forms of ownership association, the individual unorganized worker is commonly helpless to exercise actual liberty of contract and to protect his freedom of labor, and thereby to obtain acceptable terms and conditions of employment, wherefore, though he should be free to decline to associate with his fellows, it is necessary that he have full freedom of association, self-organization, and designation of representatives of his own choosing, to negotiate the terms and conditions of his employment, and that he shall be free from the interference, restraint, or coercion of employers of labor, or their agents, in the designation of such representatives or in self-organization or in other concerted activities for the purpose of collective bargaining or other mutual aid or protection; therefore, the following definitions of, and limitations upon, the jurisdiction and authority of the courts of the United States are hereby enacted.

Sec. 3. Any undertaking or promise, such as is described in this section, or any other undertaking or promise in conflict with the public policy declared in section 2 of this Act, is hereby declared to be contrary to the public policy of the United States, shall not be enforceable in any court of the United States and shall not afford any basis for the granting of legal or equitable relief by any such court, including specifically the following:

Every undertaking or promise hereafter made, whether written or oral, express or implied, constituting or contained in any contract or agreement of hiring or employment between any individual, firm, company, association, or corporation, and any employee or prospective employee of the same, whereby

(a) Either party to such contract or agreement undertakes or promises not to join, become, or remain a member of any labor organization or of any employer organization; or

(b) Either party to such contract or agreement undertakes or promises that he will withdraw from an employment relation in the event that he joins, becomes, or remains a member of any labor organization or of any employer organization.

Sec. 4. No court of the United States shall have jurisdiction to issue any restraining order or temporary or permanent injunction in any case involving or growing out of any labor dispute to prohibit any person or persons participating or interested in such dispute (as these terms are herein defined) from doing, whether singly or in concert, any of the following acts:

(a) Ceasing or refusing to perform any work or to remain in any relation of employment;

(b) Becoming or remaining a member of any labor organization or of any employer organization, regardless of any such undertaking or promise as is described in section 3 of this Act;

(c) Paying or giving to, or withholding from, any person participating or interested in such labor dispute, any strike or unemployment benefits or insurance, or other moneys or things of value;

(d) By all lawful means aiding any person participating or interested in any labor dispute who is being proceeded against in, or is prosecuting, any action or suit in any court of the United States or of any State;

(e) Giving publicity to the existence of, or the facts involved in, any labor dispute, whether by advertising, speaking, patrolling, or by any other method not involving fraud or violence;

(f) Assembling peaceably to act or to organize to act in promotion of their interests in a labor dispute;

(g) Advising or notifying any person of an intention to do any of the acts heretofore specified;

(h) Agreeing with other persons to do or not to do any of the acts heretofore specified; and

(i) Advising, urging, or otherwise causing or inducing without fraud or violence the acts heretofore specified, regardless of any such undertaking or promise as is described in section 3 of this Act.

Sec. 5. No court of the United States shall have jurisdiction to issue a restraining order or temporary or permanent injunction upon the ground that any of the persons participating or interested in a labor dispute constitute or are engaged in an unlawful combination or conspiracy because of the doing in concert of the acts enumerated in section 4 of this Act.

Sec. 6. No officer or member of any association or organization, and no association or organization participating or interested in a labor dispute, shall be held responsible or liable in any court of the United States for the unlawful acts of individual officers, members, or agents, except upon clear proof of actual participation in, or actual authorization of, such acts, or of ratification of such acts after actual knowledge thereof.

Sec. 7. No court of the United States shall have jurisdiction to issue a temporary or permanent injunction in any case involving or growing out of a labor dispute, as herein defined, except after hearing the testimony of witnesses in open court (with opportunity for cross-examination) in support of the allegations of a complaint made under oath, and testimony in opposition thereto, if offered, and except after findings of fact by the court, to the effect—

(a) That unlawful acts have been threatened and will be committed unless restrained or have been committed and will be continued unless restrained, but no injunction or temporary restraining order shall be issued on account of any threat or unlawful act excepting against the person or persons, association, or organization making the threat or committing the unlawful act or actually authorizing or ratifying the same after actual knowledge thereof;

(b) That substantial and irreparable injury to complainant's property will follow;

(c) That as to each item of relief granted greater injury will be inflicted upon complainant by the denial of relief than will be inflicted upon defendants by the granting of relief;

(d) That complainant has no adequate remedy at law; and

(e) That the public officers charged with the duty to protect complainant's property are unable or unwilling to furnish adequate protection.

Such hearing shall be held after due and personal notice thereof has been given, in such manner as the court shall direct, to all known persons against whom relief is sought, and also to the chief of those public officials of the county and city within which the unlawful acts have been threatened or committed charged with the duty to protect complainant's property: *Provided, however,* That if a complainant shall also allege that, unless a temporary restraining order shall be issued without notice, a substantial and irreparable injury to complainant's property will be unavoidable, such a temporary restraining order may be issued upon testimony under oath, sufficient, if sustained, to justify the court in issuing a temporary injunction upon a hearing after notice. Such a temporary restraining order shall be effective for no longer than five days and shall become void at the expiration of said five days. No temporary restraining order or temporary injunction shall be issued except on condition that complainant shall first file an undertaking with adequate security in an amount to be fixed by the court sufficient to recompense those enjoined for any loss, expense, or damage caused by the improvident or erroneous issuance of such order or injunction, including all reasonable costs (together with a reasonable attorney's fee) and expense of defense against the order or against the granting of any injunctive relief sought in the same proceeding and subsequently denied by the court.

The undertaking herein mentioned shall be understood to signify an agreement entered into by the complainant and the surety upon which a decree may be rendered in the same suit or proceeding against said complainant and surety, upon a hearing to assess damages of which hearing complainant and surety shall have reasonable notice, the said complainant and surety submitting themselves to the jurisdiction of the court for that purpose. But nothing herein contained shall deprive any party having a claim or cause of action under or upon such undertaking from electing to pursue his ordinary remedy by suit at law or in equity.

SEC. 8. No restraining order or injunctive relief shall be granted to any complainant who has failed to comply with any obligation imposed by law which is involved in the labor dispute in question, or who has failed to make every reasonable effort to settle such dispute either by negotiation or with the aid of any available governmental machinery of mediation or voluntary arbitration.

SEC. 9. No restraining order or temporary or permanent injunction shall be granted in a case involving or growing out of a labor dispute, except on the basis of findings of fact made and filed by the court in the record of the case prior to the issuance of such restraining order or injunction; and every restraining order or injunction granted in a case involving or growing out of a labor dispute shall include only a prohibition of such specific act or acts as may be expressly complained of in the bill of complaint or petition filed in such case and as shall be expressly included in said findings of fact made and filed by the court as provided herein.

SEC. 10. Whenever any court of the United States shall issue or deny any temporary injunction in a case involving or growing out of a labor dispute, the court shall, upon the request of any party to the proceedings and on his filing the usual bond for costs, forthwith certify as in ordinary cases the record of the case to the circuit court of appeals for its review.

Upon the filing of such record in the circuit court of appeals, the appeal shall be heard and the temporary injunctive order affirmed, modified, or set aside with the greatest possible expedition, giving the proceedings precedence over all other matters except older matters of the same character.

SEC. 11. In all cases arising under this Act in which a person shall be charged with contempt in a court of the United States (as herein defined), the accused shall enjoy the right to a speedy and public trial by an impartial jury of the State and district wherein the contempt shall have been committed: *Provided,* That this right shall not apply to contempts committed in the presence of the court or so near thereto as to interfere directly with the administration of justice or to apply to the misbehavior, misconduct, or disobedience of any officer of the court in respect to the writs, orders, or process of the court.

SEC. 12. The defendant in any proceeding for contempt of court may file with the court a demand for the retirement of the judge sitting in the proceeding, if the contempt arises from an attack upon the character or conduct of such judge and if the attack occurred elsewhere than in the presence of the court or so near thereto as to interfere directly with the administration of justice. Upon the filing of any such demand the judge shall thereupon proceed no further, but another judge shall be designated in the same manner as is provided by law. The demand shall be filed prior to the hearing in the contempt proceeding.

SEC. 13. When used in this Act, and for the purposes of this Act—

(a) A case shall be held to involve or to grow out of a labor dispute when the case involves persons who are engaged in the same industry, trade, craft, or occupation; or have direct or indirect interests therein; or who are employees of the same employer; or who are members of the same or an affiliated organization of employers or employees; whether such dispute is (1) between one or more employers or associations of employers and one or more employees or associations of employees; (2) between one or more employers or associations of employers and one or more employers or associations of employers; or (3) between one or more employees or associations of employees and one or more employees or associations of employees; or when the case involves any conflicting or competing interests in a "labor dispute" (as hereinafter defined) of "persons participating or interested" therein (as hereinafter defined).

(b) A person or association shall be held to be a person participating or interested in a labor dispute if relief is sought against him or it, and if he or it is engaged in the same industry, trade, craft, or occupation in which such dispute occurs, or has a direct or indirect interest therein, or is a member, officer, or agent of any association composed in whole or in part of employers or employees engaged in such industry, trade, craft, or occupation.

(c) The term "labor dispute" includes any controversy concerning terms or conditions of employment, or concerning the association or representation of persons in negotiating, fixing, maintaining, changing, or seeking to arrange terms or conditions of employment, regardless of whether or not the disputants stand in the proximate relation of employer and employee.

(d) The term "court of the United States" means any court of the United States whose jurisdiction has been or may be conferred or defined or limited by Act of Congress, including the courts of the District of Columbia.

SEC. 14. If any provision of this Act or the application thereof to any person or circumstance is held unconstitutional or otherwise invalid, the remaining provisions of the Act and the application of such provisions to other persons or circumstances shall not be affected thereby.

SEC. 15. All Acts and parts of Acts in conflict with the provisions of this Act are hereby repealed.

Appendix 12. The National Industrial Recovery Act, 1933

(Title I, Sections 1-7 and 10)

Declaration of Policy

SECTION 1. A national emergency productive of widespread unemployment and disorganization of industry, which burdens interstate and foreign commerce, affects the public welfare, and undermines the standards of living of the American people, is hereby declared to exist. It is hereby declared to be the policy of Congress to remove obstructions to the free flow of interstate and foreign commerce which tend to diminish the amount thereof; and to provide for the general welfare by promoting the organization of industry for the purpose of cooperative action among trade groups, to induce and maintain united action of labor and management under adequate governmental sanctions and supervision, to eliminate unfair competitive practices, to promote the fullest possible utilization of the present productive capacity of industries, to avoid undue restriction of production (except as may be temporarily required), to increase the consumption of industrial and agricultural products by increasing purchasing power, to reduce and relieve unemployment, to improve standards of labor, and otherwise to rehabilitate industry and to conserve natural resources.

Administrative Agencies

SEC. 2. (a) To effectuate the policy of this title, the President is hereby authorized to establish such agencies, to accept and utilize such voluntary and uncompensated services, to appoint, without regard to the provisions of the civil service laws, such officers and employees, and to utilize such Federal officers and employees, and, with the consent of the State, such State and local officers and employees, as he may find necessary, to prescribe their authorities, duties, responsibilities, and tenure, and, without regard to the Classification Act of 1923, as amended, to fix the compensation of any officers and employees so appointed.

(b) The President may delegate any of his functions and powers under this title to such officers, agents, and employees as he may designate or appoint, and may establish an industrial planning and research agency to aid in carrying out his functions under this title.

(c) This title shall cease to be in effect and any agencies established hereunder shall cease to exist at the expiration of two years after the date of enactment of this Act, or sooner if the President shall by proclamation or the Congress shall by joint resolution declare that the emergency recognized by section 1 has ended.

Codes of Fair Competition

Sec. 3. (a) Upon the application to the President by one or more trade or industrial associations or groups, the President may approve a code or codes of fair competition for the trade or industry or subdivision thereof, represented by the applicant or applicants, if the President finds (1) that such associations or groups impose no inequitable restrictions on admission to membership therein and are truly representative of such trades or industries or subdivisions thereof, and (2) that such code or codes are not designed to promote monopolies or to eliminate or oppress small enterprises and will not operate to discriminate against them, and will tend to effectuate the policy of this title: *Provided*, That such code or codes shall not permit monopolies or monopolistic practices: *Provided further*, That where such code or codes affect the services and welfare of persons engaged in other steps of the economic process, nothing in this section shall deprive such persons of the right to be heard prior to approval by the President of such code or codes. The President may, as a condition of his approval of any such code, impose such conditions (including requirements for the making of reports and the keeping of accounts) for the protection of consumers, competitors, employees, and others, and in furtherance of the public interest, and may provide such exceptions to and exemptions from the provisions of such code, as the President in his discretion deems necessary to effectuate the policy herein declared.

(b) After the President shall have approved any such code, the provisions of such code shall be the standards of fair competition for such trade or industry or subdivision thereof. Any violation of such standards in any transaction in or affecting interstate or foreign commerce shall be deemed an unfair method of competition in commerce within the meaning of the Federal Trade Commission Act, as amended; but nothing in this title shall be construed to impair the powers of the Federal Trade Commission under such Act, as amended.

(c) The several district courts of the United States are hereby invested with jurisdiction to prevent and restrain violations of any code of fair competition approved under this title; and it shall be the duty of the several district attorneys of the United States, in their respective districts, under the direction of the Attorney General, to institute proceedings in equity to prevent and restrain such violations.

(d) Upon his own motion, or if complaint is made to the President that abuses inimical to the public interest and contrary to the policy herein declared are prevalent in any trade or industry or subdivision thereof, and if no code of fair competition therefor has theretofore been approved by the President, the President, after such public notice and hearing as he shall specify, may prescribe and approve a code of fair competition for such trade or industry or subdivision thereof, which shall have the same effect as a code of fair competition approved by the President under subsection (a) of this section.

(e) On his own motion, or if any labor organization, or any trade or industrial organization, association, or group, which has complied with the provisions of this title, shall make complaint to the President that any article or articles are being imported into the United States in substantial quantities or increasing ratio to domestic production of any competitive article or articles and on such terms or under such conditions as to render ineffective or seriously to endanger the maintenance of any code or agreement under this title, the President may cause an immediate investigation to be made by the United States Tariff Commission, which shall give precedence to investigations under this subsection, and if, after such investigation and such public notice and hearing as he shall specify, the President shall find the existence of such facts, he shall, in order to effectuate the policy of this title, direct that the article or articles concerned shall be permitted entry into the United States only upon such terms and conditions and subject to the payment of such fees and to such limitations in the total quantity which may be imported (in the course of any specified period or periods) as he shall find it necessary to prescribe in order that the entry thereof shall not render or tend to render ineffective any code or agreement made under this title. In order to enforce any limitations imposed on the total quantity of imports, in any specified period or periods, of any article or articles under this subsection, the President may forbid the importation of such article or articles unless the importer shall have first obtained from the Secretary of the Treasury a license pursuant to such regulations as the President may prescribe. Upon information of any action by the President under this subsection the Secretary of the Treasury shall, through the proper officers, permit entry of the article or articles specified only upon such terms and conditions and subject to such fees, to such limitations in the quantity which may be imported, and to such requirements of license, as the President shall have directed. The decision of the President as to facts shall be conclusive. Any condition or limitation of entry under this subsection shall continue in effect until the President shall find and inform the Secretary of the Treasury that the conditions which led to the imposition of such condition or limitation upon entry no longer exists.

(f) When a code of fair competition has been approved or prescribed by the President under this title, any violation of any provision thereof in any transaction in or affecting interstate or foreign commerce shall be a misdemeanor and upon conviction thereof an offender shall be fined not more than $500 for each offense, and each day such violation continues shall be deemed a separate offense.

Agreements and Licenses

Sec. 4. (a) The President is authorized to enter into agreements with, and to approve voluntary agreements between and among, persons engaged in a trade or industry, labor organizations, and trade or industrial organizations, associations, or groups, relating to any trade or industry, if in his judgment such agreements will aid in effectuating the policy of this title with respect to transactions in or affecting interstate or foreign commerce, and will be consistent with the requirements of clause (2) of subsection (a) of section 3 for a code of fair competition.

(b) Whenever the President shall find that destructive wage or price cutting or other activities contrary to the policy of this title are being practiced in any trade or industry or any subdivision thereof, and, after such public notice and hearing as he shall specify, shall find it essential to license business enterprises in order to make effective a code of fair competition or an agreement under this title or otherwise to effectuate the policy of this title, and shall publicly so announce, no person shall, after a date fixed in such announcement, engage in or carry on any business, in or affecting interstate or foreign commerce, specified in such announcement, unless he shall have first obtained a license issued pursuant to such regulations as the President shall prescribe. The President may suspend or revoke any such license, after due notice and opportunity for hearing, for violations of the terms or conditions thereof. Any order of the President suspending or revoking any such license shall be final if in accordance with law. Any person who, without such a license or in violation of any condition thereof, carries on any such business for which a license is so required, shall, upon conviction thereof, be fined not more than $500, or imprisoned not more than six months, or both, and each day such violation continues shall be deemed a separate offense. Notwithstanding the provisions of section 2 (c), this subsection shall cease to be in effect at the expiration of one year after the date of enactment of this Act or sooner if the President shall by proclamation or the Congress shall by joint resolution declare that the emergency recognized by section 1 has ended.

SEC. 5. While this title is in effect (or in the case of a license, while section 4(a) is in effect) and for sixty days thereafter, any code, agreement, or license approved, prescribed, or issued and in effect under this title, and any action complying with the provisions thereof taken during such period, shall be exempt from the provisions of the antitrust laws of the United States.

Nothing in this Act, and no regulation thereunder, shall prevent an individual from pursuing the vocation of manual labor and selling or trading the products thereof; nor shall anything in this Act, or regulation thereunder, prevent anyone from marketing or trading the produce of his farm.

Limitations Upon Application of Title

SEC. 6. (a) No trade or industrial association or group shall be eligible to receive the benefit of the provisions of this title until it files with the President a statement containing such information relating to the activities of the association or group as the President shall by regulation prescribe.

(b) The President is authorized to prescribe rules and regulations designed to insure that any organization availing itself of the benefits of this title shall be truly representative of the trade or industry or subdivision thereof represented by such organization. Any organization violating any such rule or regulation shall cease to be entitled to the benefits of this title.

(c) Upon the request of the President, the Federal Trade Commission shall make such investigations as may be necessary to enable the President to carry out the provisions of this title, and for such purposes the Commission shall have all the powers vested in it with respect of investigations under the Federal Trade Commission Act, as amended.

SEC. 7. (a) Every code of fair competition, agreement, and license approved, prescribed, or issued under this title shall contain the following conditions: (1) That employees shall have the right to organize and bargain collectively through representatives of their own choosing, and shall be free from the interference, restraint, or coercion of employers of labor, or their agents, in the designation of such representatives or in self-organization or in other concerted activities for the purpose of collective bargaining or other mutual aid or protection; (2) that no employee and no one seeking employment shall be required as a condition of employment to join any company union or to refrain from joining, organizing, or assisting a labor organization of his own choosing; and (3) that employers shall comply with the maximum hours of labor, minimum rates of pay, and other conditions of employment, approved or prescribed by the President.

(b) The President shall, so far as practicable, afford every opportunity to employers and employees in any trade or industry or subdivision thereof with respect to which the conditions referred to in clauses (1) and (2) of subsection (a) prevail, to establish by mutual agreement, the standards as to the maximum hours of labor, minimum rates of pay, and such other conditions of employment as may be necessary in such trade or industry or subdivision thereof to effectuate the policy of this title; and the standards established in such agreements, when approved by the President, shall have the same effect as a code of fair competition, approved by the President under subsection (a) of section 3.

(c) Where no such mutual agreement has been approved by the President he may investigate the labor practices, policies, wages, hours of labor, and conditions of employment in such trade or industry or subdivision thereof; and upon the basis of such investigations, and after such hearings as the President finds advisable, he is authorized to prescribe a limited code of fair competition fixing such maximum hours of labor, minimum rates of pay, and other conditions of employment in the trade or industry or subdivision thereof investigated as he finds to be necessary to effectuate the policy of this title, which shall have the same effect as a code of fair competition approved by the President under subsection (a) of section 3. The President may differentiate according to experience and skill of the employees affected and according to the locality of employment; but no attempt shall be made to introduce any classification according to the nature of the work involved which might tend to set a maximum as well as a minimum wage.

(d) As used in this title, the term "person" includes any individual, partnership, association, trust, or corporation; and the terms "interstate and foreign commerce" and "interstate or foreign commerce" include, except where otherwise indicated, trade or commerce among the several States and with foreign nations, or between the District of Columbia or any Territory of the United States and any State, Territory, or foreign nation, or between any insular possessions or other places under the jurisdiction of the United States, or between any such possession or place and any State or Territory of the United States or the District of Columbia or any foreign nation, or within the District of Columbia or any Territory or any insular possession or other place under the jurisdiction of the United States.

Rules and Regulations
Sec. 10. (a) The President is authorized to prescribe such rules and regulations as may be necessary to carry out the purposes of this title, and fees for licenses and for filing codes of fair competition and agreements, and any violation of any such rule or regulation shall be punishable by fine of not to exceed $500, or imprisonment for not to exceed six months, or both.

(b) The President may from time to time cancel or modify any order, approval, license, rule, or regulation issued under this title; and each agreement, code of fair competition, or license approved, prescribed, or issued under this title shall contain an express provision to that effect.

Appendix 13. The National Labor Relations Act (Wagner Act), 1935

(Complete Text)

Be it enacted by the Senate and House of Representatives of the United States of America in Congress assembled,

Findings and Policy

SECTION 1. The denial by employers of the right of employees to organize and the refusal by employers to accept the procedure of collective bargaining lead to strikes and other forms of industrial strife or unrest, which have the intent or the necessary effect of burdening or obstructing commerce by (a) impairing the efficiency, safety, or operation of the instrumentalities of commerce; (b) occurring in the current of commerce; (c) materially affecting, restraining, or controlling the flow of raw materials or manufactured or processed goods from or into the channels of commerce, or the prices of such materials or goods in commerce; or (d) causing diminution of employment and wages in such volume as substantially to impair or disrupt the market for goods flowing from or into the channels of commerce.

The inequality of bargaining power between employees who do not possess full freedom of association or actual liberty of contract, and employers who are organized in the corporate or other forms of ownership association substantially burdens and affects the flow of commerce, and tends to aggravate recurrent business depressions, by depressing wage rates and the purchasing power of wage earners in industry and by preventing the stabilization of competitive wage rates and working conditions within and between industries.

Experience has proved that protection by law of the right of employees to organize and bargain collectively safeguards commerce from injury, impairment, or interruption, and promotes the flow of commerce by removing certain recognized sources of industrial strife and unrest, by encouraging practices fundamental to the friendly adjustment of industrial disputes arising out of differences as to wages, hours, or other working conditions, and by restoring equality of bargaining power between employers and employees.

It is hereby declared to be the policy of the United States to eliminate the causes of certain substantial obstructions to the free flow of commerce and to mitigate and eliminate these obstructions when they have occurred by encouraging the practice and procedure of collective bargaining and by protecting the exercise by workers of full freedom of association, self-organization, and designation of representatives of their own choosing, for the purpose of negotiating the terms and conditions of their employment or other mutual aid or protection.

Definitions

Sec. 2. When used in this Act—

(1) The term "person" includes one or more individuals, partnerships, associations, corporations, legal representatives, trustees, trustees in bankruptcy, or receivers.

(2) The term "employer" includes any person acting in the interest of an employer, directly or indirectly, but shall not include the United States, or any State or political subdivision thereof, or any person subject to the Railway Labor Act, as amended from time to time, or any labor organization (other than when acting as an employer), or anyone acting in the capacity of officer or agent of such labor organization.

(3) The term "employee" shall include any employee, and shall not be limited to the employees of a particular employer, unless the Act explicitly states otherwise, and shall include any individual whose work has ceased as a consequence of, or in connection with, any current labor dispute or because of any unfair labor practice, and who has not obtained any other regular and substantially equivalent employment, but shall not include any individual employed as an agricultural laborer, or in the domestic service of any family or person at his home, or any individual employed by his parent or spouse.

(4) The term "representatives" includes any individual or labor organization.

(5) The term "labor organization" means any organization of any kind, or any agency or employee representation committee or plan, in which employees participate and which exists for the purpose, in whole or in part, of dealing with employers concerning grievances, labor disputes, wages, rates of pay, hours of employment, or conditions of work.

(6) The term "commerce" means trade, traffic, commerce, transportation, or communication among the several States, or between the District of Columbia or any Territory of the United States and any State or other Territory, or between any foreign country and any State, Territory, or the District of Columbia, or within the District of Columbia or any Territory, or between points in the same State but through any other State or any Territory or the District of Columbia or any foreign country.

(7) The term "affecting commerce" means in commerce, or burdening or obstructing commerce or the free flow of commerce, or having led or tending to lead to a labor dispute burdening or obstructing commerce or the free flow of commerce.

(8) The term "unfair labor practice" means any unfair labor practice listed in section 8.

(9) The term "labor dispute" includes any controversy concerning terms, tenure or conditions of employment, or concerning the association or representation of persons in negotiating, fixing, maintaining, changing, or seeking to arrange terms or conditions of employment, regardless of whether the disputants stand in the proximate relation of employer and employee.

(10) The term "National Labor Relations Board" means the National Labor Relations Board created by section 3 of this Act.

(11) The term "old Board" means the National Labor Relations Board established by Executive Order Numbered 6763 of the President on June 29, 1934, pursuant to Public Resolution Numbered 44, approved June 19, 1934 (48 Stat. 1183), and reestablished and continued by Executive Order Numbered 7074 of the President of June 15, 1935, pursuant to

Title I of the National Industrial Recovery Act (48 Stat. 195) as amended and continued by Senate Joint Resolution 133[1] approved June 14, 1935.

National Labor Relations Board

SEC. 3. (a) There is hereby created a board, to be known as the "National Labor Relations Board" (hereinafter referred to as the "Board"), which shall be composed of three members, who shall be appointed by the President, by and with the advice and consent of the Senate. One of the original members shall be appointed for a term of one year, one for a term of three years, and one for a term of five years, but their successors shall be appointed for terms of five years each, except that any individual chosen to fill a vacancy shall be appointed only for the unexpired term of the member whom he shall succeed. The President shall designate one member to serve as chairman of the Board. Any member of the Board may be removed by the President, upon notice and hearing, for neglect of duty or malfeasance in office, but for no other cause.

(b) A vacancy in the Board shall not impair the right of the remaining members to exercise all the powers of the Board, and two members of the Board shall, at all times, constitute a quorum. The Board shall have an official seal which shall be judicially noticed.

(c) The Board shall at the close of each fiscal year make a report in writing to Congress and to the President stating in detail the cases it has heard, the decisions it has rendered, the names, salaries, and duties of all employees and officers in the employ or under the supervision of the Board, and an account of all moneys it has disbursed.

SEC. 4. (a) Each member of the Board shall receive a salary of $10,000 a year, shall be eligible for reappointment, and shall not engage in any other business, vocation, or employment. The Board shall appoint, without regard for the provisions of the civil-service laws but subject to the Classification Act of 1923, as amended, an executive secretary, and such attorneys, examiners, and regional directors, and shall appoint such other employees with regard to existing laws applicable to the employment and compensation of officers and employees of the United States, as it may from time to time find necessary for the proper performance of its duties and as may be from time to time appropriated for by Congress. The Board may establish or utilize such regional, local, or other agencies, and utilize such voluntary and uncompensated services, as may from time to time be needed. Attorneys appointed under this section may, at the direction of the Board, appear for and represent the Board in any case in court. Nothing in this Act shall be construed to authorize the Board to appoint individuals for the purpose of conciliation or mediation (or for statistical work), where such service may be obtained from the Department of Labor.

(b) Upon the appointment of the three original members of the Board and the designation of its chairman, the old Board shall cease to exist. All employees of the old Board shall be transferred to and become employees of the Board with salaries under the Classification Act of 1923, as amended, without acquiring by such transfer a permanent or civil service status. All records, papers, and property of the old Board shall become records, papers, and property of the Board, and all unexpended funds and appropriations for the use and maintenance of the old Board shall become funds and appropriations available to be expended by the Board in the exercise of the powers, authority, and duties conferred on it by this Act.

(c) All of the expenses of the Board, including all necessary traveling and subsistence expenses outside the District of Columbia incurred by the members or employees of the Board under its orders, shall be allowed and paid on the presentation of itemized vouchers therefor approved by the Board or by any individual it designates for that purpose.

[1]So in original.

Sec. 5. The principal office of the Board shall be in the District of Columbia, but it may meet and exercise any or all of its powers at any other place. The Board may, by one or more of its members or by such agents or agencies as it may designate, prosecute any inquiry necessary to its functions in any part of the United States. A member who participates in such an inquiry shall not be disqualified from subsequently participating in a decision of the Board in the same case.

Sec. 6. (a) The Board shall have authority from time to time to make, amend, and rescind such rules and regulations as may be necessary to carry out the provisions of this Act. Such rules and regulations shall be effective upon publication in the manner which the Board shall prescribe.

Rights of Employees

Sec. 7. Employees shall have the right to self-organization, to form, join, or assist labor organizations, to bargain collectively through representatives of their own choosing, and to engage in concerted activities, for the purpose of collective bargaining or other mutual aid or protection.

Sec. 8. It shall be an unfair labor practice for an employer—

(1) To interfere with, restrain, or coerce employees in the exercise of the rights guaranteed in section 7.

(2) To dominate or interfere with the formation or administration of any labor organization or contribute financial or other support to it: *Provided*, That subject to rules and regulations made and published by the Board pursuant to section 6 (a), an employer shall not be prohibited from permitting employees to confer with him during working hours without loss of time or pay.

(3) By discrimination in regard to hire or tenure of employment or any term or condition of employment to encourage or discourage membership in any labor organization: *Provided*, That nothing in this Act, or in the National Industrial Recovery Act (U. S. C., Supp. VII, title 15, secs. 701-712), as amended from time to time, or in any code or agreement approved or prescribed thereunder, or in any other statute of the United States, shall preclude an employer from making an agreement with a labor organization (not established, maintained, or assisted by any action defined in this Act as an unfair labor practice) to require as a condition of employment membership therein, if such labor organization is the representative of the employees as provided in section 9 (a), in the appropriate collective bargaining unit covered by such agreement when made.

(4) To discharge or otherwise discriminate against an employee because he has filed charges or given testimony under this Act.

(5) To refuse to bargain collectively with the representatives of his employees, subject to the provisions of Section 9 (a).

Representatives and Elections

Sec. 9. (a) Representatives designated or selected for the purposes of collective bargaining by the majority of the employees in a unit appropriate for such purposes, shall be the exclusive representatives of all the employees in such unit for the purposes of collective bargaining in respect to rates of pay, wages, hours of employment, or other conditions of employment: *Provided*, That any individual employee or a group of employees shall have the right at any time to present grievances to their employer.

(b) The Board shall decide in each case whether, in order to insure to employees the full benefit of their right to self-organization and to collective bargaining, and otherwise to effectuate the policies of this Act, the unit appropriate for the purposes of collective bargaining shall be the employer unit, craft unit, plant unit, or subdivision thereof.

(c) Whenever a question affecting commerce arises concerning the representation of employees, the Board may investigate such controversy and certify to the parties, in writing, the name or names of the representatives that have been designated or selected. In any such investigation, the Board shall provide for an appropriate hearing upon due notice, either in conjunction with a proceeding under section 10 or otherwise, and may take a secret ballot of employees, or utilize any other suitable method to ascertin[1] such representatives.

(d) Whenever an order of the Board made pursuant to section 10 (c) is based in whole or in part upon facts certified following an investigation pursuant to subsection (c) of this section, and there is a petition for the enforcement or review of such order, such certification and the record of such investigation shall be included in the transcript of the entire record required to be filed under subsections 10 (e) or 10 (f), and thereupon the decree of the court enforcing, modifying, or setting aside in whole or in part the order of the Board shall be made and entered upon the pleadings, testimony, and proceedings set forth in such transcript.

Prevention of Unfair Labor Practices

SEC. 10. (a) The Board is empowered, as hereinafter provided, to prevent any person from engaging in any unfair labor practice (listed in section 8) affecting commerce. This power shall be exclusive, and shall not be affected by any other means of adjustment or prevention that has been or may be established by agreement, code, law, or otherwise.

(b) Whenever it is charged that any person has engaged in or is engaging in any such unfair labor practice, the Board, or any agent or agency designated by the Board for such purposes, shall have power to issue and cause to be served upon such person a complaint stating the charges in that respect, and containing a notice of hearing before the Board or a member thereof, or before a designated agent or agency, at a place therein fixed, not less than five days after the serving of said complaint. Any such complaint may be amended by the member, agent, or agency conducting the hearing or the Board in its discretion at any time prior to the issuance of an order based thereon. The person so complained of shall have the right to file an answer to the original or amended complaint and to appear in person or otherwise and give testimony at the place and time fixed in the complaint. In the discretion of the member, agent or agency conducting the hearing or the Board, any other person may be allowed to intervene in the said proceeding and to present testimony. In any such proceeding the rules of evidence prevailing in courts of law or equity shall not be controlling.

(c) The testimony taken by such member, agent or agency or the Board shall be reduced to writing and filed with the Board. Thereafter, in its discretion, the Board upon notice may take further testimony or hear argument. If upon all the testimony taken the Board shall be of the opinion that any person named in the complaint has engaged in or is engaging in any such unfair labor practice, then the Board shall state its findings of fact and shall issue and cause to be served on such person an order requiring such person to cease and desist from such unfair labor practice, and to take such affirmative action, including reinstatement of employees with or without back pay, as will effectuate the policies of this Act. Such order may further require such person to make reports from time to time showing the extent to which it has complied with the order. If upon all the testimony taken the Board shall be of the opinion that no person named in the complaint has engaged in or is engaging in any such unfair labor practice, then the Board shall state its findings of fact and shall issue an order dismissing the said complaint.

(d) Until a transcript of the record in a case shall have been filed in a court, as hereinafter provided, the Board may at any time, upon reasonable notice and in such manner as it shall deem proper, modify or set aside, in whole or in part, any finding or order made or issued by it.

(e) The Board shall have power to petition any circuit court of appeals of the United States (including the Court of Appeals of the District of Columbia), or if all the circuit courts of appeals to which application may be made are in vacation, any district court of the United States (including the Supreme Court of the District of Columbia), within any circuit or district, respectively, wherein the unfair labor practice in question occurred or wherein such person resides or transacts business, for the enforcement of such order and for appropriate temporary relief or restraining order, and shall certify and file in the court a transcript of the entire record in the proceeding, including the pleadings and testimony upon which such order was entered and the findings and order of the Board. Upon such filing, the court shall cause notice thereof to be served upon such person, and thereupon shall have jurisdiction of the proceeding and of the question determined therein, and shall have power to grant such temporary relief or restraining order as it deems just and proper, and to make and enter upon the pleadings, testimony, and proceedings set forth in such transcript a decree enforcing, modifying, and enforcing as so modified, or setting aside in whole or in part the order of the Board. No objection that has not been urged before the Board, its member, agent or agency, shall be considered by the court, unless the failure or neglect to urge such objection shall be excused because of extraordinary circumstances. The findings of the Board as to the facts, if supported by evidence, shall be conclusive. If either party shall apply to the court for leave to adduce additional evidence and shall show to the satisfaction of the court that such additional evidence is material and that there were reasonable grounds for the failure to adduce such evidence in the hearing before the Board, its member, agent, or agency, the court may order such additional evidence to be taken before the Board, its member, agent, or agency, and to be made a part of the transcript. The Board may modify its findings as to the facts, or make new findings, by reason of additional evidence so taken and filed, and it shall file such modified or new findings, which, if supported by evidence, shall be conclusive, and shall file its recommendations, if any, for the modification or setting aside of its original order. The jurisdiction of the court shall be exclusive and its judgment and decrees shall be final, except that the same shall be subject to review by the appropriate circuit court of appeals if application was made to the district court as hereinabove provided, and by the Supreme Court of the United States upon writ of certiorari or certification as provided in sections 239 and 240 of the Judicial Code, as amended (U.S.C., title 28, secs. 346 and 347).

(f) Any person aggrieved by a final order of the Board granting or denying in whole or in part the relief sought may obtain a review of such order in any circuit court of appeals of the United States in the circuit wherein the unfair labor practice in question was alleged to have been engaged in or wherein such person resides or transacts business, or in the Court of Appeals of the District of Columbia, by filing in such court a written petition praying that the order of the Board be modified or set aside. A copy of such petition shall be forthwith served upon the Board, and thereupon the aggrieved party shall file in the court a transcript of the entire record in the proceeding, certified by the Board, including the pleading and testimony upon which the order complained of was entered and the findings and order of the Board. Upon such filing, the court shall proceed in the same manner as in the case of an application by the Board under subsection (e), and shall have the same exclusive jurisdiction to grant to the Board such temporary relief or restraining order as it deems just and proper, and in like manner to make and enter a decree enforcing, modifying, and enforcing as so modified, or setting aside in whole or in part the order of the Board; and the findings of the Board as to the facts, if supported by evidence, shall in like manner be conclusive.

(g) The commencement of proceedings under subsection (e) or (f) of this section shall not, unless specifically ordered by the court, operate as a stay of the Board's order.

(h) When granting appropriate temporary relief or a restraining order, or making and entering a decree enforcing, modifying, and enforcing as so modified or setting aside in whole or in part an order of the Board, as provided in this section, the jurisdiction of courts sitting in equity shall not be limited by the Act entitled "An Act to amend the Judicial Code and to define and limit the jurisdiction of courts sitting in equity, and for other purposes", approved March 23, 1932 (U.S.C., Supp. VII, title 29, secs. 101-115).

(i) Petitions filed under this Act shall be heard expeditiously, and if possible within ten days after they have been docketed.

Investigatory Powers

SEC. 11. For the purpose of all hearings and investigations, which, in the opinion of the Board, are necessary and proper for the exercise of the powers vested in it by section 9 and section 10—

(1) The Board, or its duly authorized agents or agencies, shall at all reasonable times have access to, for the purpose of examination, and the right to copy any evidence of any person being investigated or proceeded against that relates to any matter under investigation or in question. Any member of the Board shall have power to issue subpenas requiring the attendance and testimony of witnesses and the production of any evidence that relates to any matter under investigation or in question, before the Board, its member, agent, or agency conducting the hearing or investigation. Any member of the Board, or any agent or agency designated by the Board for such purposes, may administer oaths and affirmations, examine witnesses, and receive evidence. Such attendance of witnesses and the production of such evidence may be required from any place in the United States or any Territory or possession thereof, at any designated place of hearing.

(2) In case of contumacy or refusal to obey a subpena issued to any person, any District court of the United States or the United States courts of any Territory or possession, or the Supreme Court of the District of Columbia, within the jurisdiction of which the inquiry is carried on or within the jurisdiction of which said person guilty of contumacy or refusal to obey is found or resides or transacts business, upon application by the Board shall have jurisdiction to issue to such person an order requiring such person to appear before the Board, its member, agent, or agency, there to produce evidence if so ordered, or there to give testimony touching the matter under investigation or in question; and any failure to obey such order of the court may be punished by said court as a contempt thereof.

(3) No person shall be excused from attending and testifying or from producing books, records, correspondence, documents, or other evidence in obedience to the subpena of the Board, on the ground that the testimony or evidence required of him may tend to incriminate him or subject him to a penalty or forfeiture; but no individual shall be prosecuted or subjected to any penalty or forfeiture for or on account of any transaction, matter, or thing concerning which he is compelled, after having claimed his privilege against self-incrimination, to testify or produce evidence, except that such individual so testifying shall not be exempt from prosecution and punishment for perjury committed in so testifying.

(4) Complaints, orders, and other process and papers of the Board, its member, agent, or agency, may be served either personally or by registered mail or by telegraph or by leaving a copy thereof at the principal office or place of business of the person required to be served. The verified return by the individual so serving the same setting forth the manner of such service shall be proof of the same, and the return post office receipt or telegraph receipt therefor when registered and mailed or telegraphed as aforesaid shall be proof of service of the same. Witnesses summoned before the Board, its member, agent, or agency, shall be paid the same fees and mileage that are paid witnesses in the courts of the United States, and witnesses whose depositions are taken and the persons taking the same shall severally be entitled to the same fees as are paid for like services in the courts of the United States.

(5) All process of any court to which application may be made under this Act may be served in the judicial district wherein the defendant or other person required to be served resides or may be found.

(6) The several departments and agencies of the Government, when directed by the

President, shall furnish the Board, upon its request, all records, papers, and information in their possession relating to any matter before the Board.

SEC. 12. Any person who shall willfully resist, prevent, impede, or interfere with any member of the Board or any of its agents or agencies in the performance of duties pursuant to this Act shall be punished by a fine of not more than $5,000 or by imprisonment for not more than one year, or both.

Limitations

SEC. 13. Nothing in this Act shall be construed so as to interfere with or impede or diminish in any way the right to strike.

SEC. 14. Wherever the application of the provisions of section 7 (a) of the National Industrial Recovery Act (U.S.C., Supp. VII, title 15, sec. 707 (a)), as amended from time to time, or of section 77 B, paragraphs (l) and (m) of the Act approved June 7, 1934, entitled "An Act to amend an Act entitled 'An Act to establish a uniform system of bankruptcy throughout the United States' approved July 1, 1898, and Acts amendatory thereof and supplementary thereto" (48 Stat. 922, pars (l) and (m)), as amended from time to time, or of Public Resolution Numbered 44, approved June 19, 1934 (48 Stat. 1183), conflicts with the application of the provisions of this Act, this Act shall prevail: *Provided,* That in any situation where the provisions of this Act cannot be validly enforced, the provisions of such other Acts shall remain in full force and effect.

SEC. 15. If any provision of this Act, or the application of such provision to any person or circumstance, shall be held invalid, the remainder of this Act, or the application of such provision to persons or circumstances other than those as to which it is held invalid, shall not be affected thereby.

SEC. 16. This Act may be cited as the "National Labor Relations Act."

Notes

Introduction

[1]See the Appendix for the full text of the Wagner Act and of some related statutes discussed later on in this book.

[2]A brief historiographical note. Milton Derber, *The American Idea of Industrial Democracy, 1865-1965* (Urbana, Illinois: University of Illinois Press, 1970), has traced the various meanings Americans attached to the concept of industrial democracy from after the Civil War down to the present, as, in a similar fashion, Mark Perlman, *Labor Union Theories in America: Background and Development* (Evanston, IL: Row, Peterson, 1958) has explained the various theories of the organized labor movement in America over roughly the same time period—including the most famous theory of them all (his father's), Selig Perlman, *A Theory of the Labor Movement* (New York: Macmillan, 1928); and see also John A. DeBrizzi, *Ideology and the Rise of Labor Theory in America*, Contributions in Labor History, Number 14 (Westport, CT: Greenwood Press, 1983), a sociological interpretation of some of the important "progressive" economists. On a more general plane, Sidney Fine, *Laissez Faire and the General-Welfare State: A Study of Conflict in American Thought, 1865-1901* (Ann Arbor: The University of Michigan Press, 1956) is the single most comprehensive canvass of social reform thought for this most critical period in modern American history. See also Frank Tariello, *The Reconstruction of American Political Ideology, 1865-1897* (Charlottesville: University Press of Virginia, 1982).

Irving Bernstein, *The New Deal Collective Bargaining Policy* (Los Angeles: University of California Press, 1950) is a concise analytical and historical guide to the legislative history of the Wagner Act, best read in conjunction with Grant N. Farr, *The Origins of Recent Labor Policy*, University of Colorado, Series in Economics, No. 3 (Boulder: University of Colorado Press, 1959), an investigation of the origins of the collective bargaining provisions of the National Industrial Recovery Act; and with James A. Gross, *The Making of the National Labor Relations Board* Volume I: 1933-1937 (Albany: State University of New York Press, 1974).

The present work covers material discussed in all of the above-mentioned studies, but there are a number of differences. First, I begin this investigation far earlier than the Civil War, in order to track down the intellectual sources of industrial democratic thought to their wellsprings. Second, the focus of this book is more general than most of the previous ones cited. I place theories of industrial democracy in America in the context of the evolution of political economy during the 19th century, specifically in the framework of free market liberalism—a framework which, for historical reasons, is invaluable for understanding the evolution of anti-competitive doctrines and institutions. (Free market liberalism, or more precisely, laissez-faire capitalism, is also my own intellectual framework—another difference between this book and most of those mentioned above.)

Third (or fourth), I believe that many who write about the evolution of American labor relations laws have unduly neglected or overlooked the significance of English and European industrial democratic thought and reforms for American progressive intellectuals and trade union leaders in the early decades of this century; see for instance, Summers, "American and European Labor Law: The Use and Usefulness of Foreign Experience," 16 *Buffalo Law Review* 210 (1966), and Bok, "Reflections on the Distinctive Character of American Labor Laws," 84 *Harvard Law Review* 1394 (1971).

³Between 1935 and 1946, union membership in this country grew from 3.7 million to 15.4 million. The number of workers employed under collective agreements rose from 9.3 million in 1941 to 14.9 million in 1946; of these, the number employed under closed-shop and union-shop agreements was 3.7 million in 1941 and 7.5 million in 1946. See U.S., Department of Labor, Bureau of Labor Statistics, *Handbook of Labor Statistics* (Bulletin 961), 1947, p. 130; and "Extent of Collective Bargaining and Union Recognition, 1946," *Monthly Labor Review* LXIV (May 1947), p. 767.

⁴Readers not conversant with the labor relations jargon may find the following terminology useful. A closed shop usually refers to an arrangement whereby an employee must be a member of a union before he can be hired, and must remain a member to keep his job. A union shop usually refers to an arrangement whereby a nonunion employee can be hired, but must become a union member within thirty days thereafter, and must remain a union member to keep his job. An agency shop usually refers to an arrangement whereby an employee must, to retain his job, pay to a union the equivalent of membership dues and fees (or at least that portion of dues and fees which represents the cost of collective bargaining and contract administration, but not that portion used for, say, political lobbying), but who is *not* required to become or remain a union *member.* Employees who are not true union members are not subject to internal union rules or disciplinary procedures, such as fines or expulsion for refusing to honor a strike call or for crossing a picket line. Under a true union shop, in other words, an employee expelled from the union loses his job; under the agency shop he can lose his job *only* if he doesn't pay dues or collective bargaining fees.

Haggard, "Right-to-work Laws in the Southern States," 59 *North Carolina Law Review* 29 (1980), explains in concise terms the complicated federal and state law on union security agreements; for his comprehensive study, see *Compulsory Unionism, the NLRB, and the Courts: A Legal Analysis of Union Security Agreements,* Industrial Research Unit, the Wharton School, Labor Relations and Public Policy Series, No. 15 (Philadelphia: University of Pennsylvania, 1977).

⁵The administration and enforcement of national labor policy by a quasi-judicial administrative agency, the National Labor Relations Board (NLRB), is another vital characteristic of our system of industrial democracy, but it is not discussed in this book. For a stinging legal and constitutional critique of NLRB performance over the years, see Petro, "Expertise, the NLRB, and the Constitution: Things Abused and Things Forgotten," 14 *Wayne Law Review* 1126 (1968).

⁶See chapter two, *infra.*

⁷45 Mass. 111, 133, 130 (1842); see also chapter two, *infra.*

⁸For an indication of the difficulties judges had in defining and hence defending the right to

strike, see the perceptive discussion in Vieira, "Of Syndicalism, Slavery and the Thirteenth Amendment: The Unconstitutionality of 'Exclusive Representation' in Public-Sector Employment," 12 *Wake Forest Law Review* 515, 715-716 (1976). The distinction between primary and secondary boycotts used here is taken from Sylvester Petro; see "Unions and the Southern Courts: Part I—Boycotts in the Southern Courts," 59 *North Carolina Law Review* 100, 103-106 (1980).

[9]Under the Taft-Hartley Amendments to the Wagner Act, courts in certain circumstances may enjoin a strike and issue a 'back to work' order. This provision is referred to occasionally as 'slave labor'. But employees remain free to quit, 'back to work order' or not.

[10]As Mr. Justice Pitney said in *Hitchman Coal and Coke Co.* v. *Mitchell,* 245 U.S. 229, 250 (1917): "Whatever may be the advantages of 'collective bargaining', it is not bargaining at all, in any just sense, unless it is voluntary on both sides."

[11]The doctrine of employment at will under the common law was enunciated with great clarity in *Payne* v. *Western & Atlantic R.R. Co.,* 81 Tenn. 507, 518-519 (1884):

> [M]en must be left, without interference to buy and sell where they please, and to discharge or retain employees at will for good cause or for no cause, or even for bad cause without thereby being guilty of an unlawful act *per se*. It is a right which an employe may exercise in the same way, to the same extent, for the same cause or want of cause as the employer.

Cf. *Adair* v. *United States,* 208 U.S. 161, 174-175 (1908):

> The right of a person to sell his labor upon such terms as he deems proper is, in its essence, the same as the right of the purchaser of labor to prescribe the conditions upon which he will accept such labor from the person offering to sell it. So the right of the employee to quit the service of the employer, for whatever reason, is the same as the right of the employer, for whatever reason, to dispense with the services of such employee.

See also Jay Feinman, "The Development of the Employment at Will Rule," *American Journal of Legal History* XX (April 1976): 118-135; Epstein, "In Defense of the Contract at Will," 51 *University of Chicago Law Review* 947 (1984); and Epstein, "A Common Law of Labor Relations? A Critique of the New Deal," 92 *Yale Law Journal* 1357 (1983).

[12]See chapter eight, *infra* for more discussion of the antecedents, and of the logic, behind the 'Hitchman' doctrine.

[13]See chapter eight, *infra,* for more discussion. The 'free rider' is a worker who reaps the benefits of unionism (such as higher wage rates) without having to shoulder some share of the cost (and not only the monetary cost of dues, but also obedience to strike votes, etc.). This is claimed to be unfair to those who do bear the costs; moreover, so the argument goes, if one worker rides free, every one would have an incentive to do so, and the union would fall apart. See the discussion in Haggard, *Compulsory Unionism,* pp. 271-294; and Mancur Olson, Jr., *The Logic of Collective Action* (New York: Schocken Books, 1969 [1965]), pp. 66-97.

Because I don't intend to discuss this issue at great length elsewhere, a few passing comments are appropriate here.

Surprisingly, the reform economist John R. Commons rebutted the "fairness" argument against free riders in 1907:

> The trade unionist feels that a man who is getting the advantages which the unions have secured in high wages is an ungrateful man, greedy and selfish, if he does not pay union dues and help out the organization. This sentimental reason cannot stand alone. Every one of us gets advantages in society that we do not pay for. We receive advantages which others have secured for us. If we do not contribute in a proper way to promote the common advantage of our fellows and ourselves, that is something which must be left to our private judgment, influenced by the opinion of our fellows.

See "The Organization of Public Employees," an address before the Women's Trade Union

League of Illinois at Hull House, Chicago, 1907, in John R. Commons, *Labor and Administration* (New York: Macmillan, 1913), p. 108.

There are problems with the economic analysis of the free rider. First, not all union services are nondivisible, certainly not grievance arbitration, or union-run welfare activities. To the extent these benefits can be offered to members and denied to nonmembers, the free rider case for union security agreements is unavailing. Second, the free rider argument in favor of union security is always asserted, but it is rarely if ever demonstrated. The free rider phenomenon no doubt exists; nevertheless, its logic is not fully compatible with the existence of certain social institutions such as the Red Cross or political parties which flourish without a compulsory dues or membership mechanism.

Third, not all 'collective good' union benefits are shared by those within the cartel. There are workers who could do better with a merit, rather than with a seniority, employment system. There are conflicts between the skilled and the unskilled. There are conflicts between younger and older workers regarding the relative merits of higher wages or more job security; and there are conflicts between workers who are deeply aggrieved by the social and political agendas of their 'benefit providers'. These conflicts are real; to force workers to contribute to institutions which they believe (or which do) harm their interests is to make them *forced riders,* not free riders.

Fourth, and most important, unions do not provide 'collective good' benefits to *all workers,* or to society as a whole. On the contrary, such benefits as higher wages are mostly obtained at the expense of other workers (*qua* workers, or *qua* consumers).

I do not question the existence of the free rider. But the inability of a cartel or monopoly (of businessmen or laborers) to push (or maintain) prices above a competitive level because of the free rider (cheating) is not a social problem requiring special legal privileges or immunities making it easier for such combinations to do so. Neither is the existence of combinations or contracts in restraint of trade (by laborers or employers) grounds for outlawing them, by such measures as the Sherman Act. My opinion on this fundamental issue of political economy (and thus my disagreement with the argument of those with whom I am so often in agreement, that our economic house would be put in order if only labor unions could be subject to antitrust) is the same as that of Adam Smith; see *The Wealth of Nations,* ed. Edwin Cannan (New York: Modern Library, 1937 [1776]), Book I, c. 10, p. 128:

> People of the same trade seldom meet together, even for merriment and diversion, but the conversation ends in a conspiracy against the public, or in some contrivance to raise prices. It is impossible indeed to prevent such meetings, by any law which either could be executed, or would be consistent with liberty and justice. But though the law cannot hinder people of the same trade from sometimes assembling together, it ought to do nothing to facilitate such assemblies; much less to render them necessary.

The rise of giant enterprise in the late 19th century and early 20th century should not shake anyone's confidence in the robust vitality of competition, either; in this regard, see Dominick T. Armentano, *Antitrust and Monopoly: Anatomy of a Policy Failure* (New York: John Wiley and Sons, 1982). Finally, the free rider argument ignores the rights and the interests of workers (actual or potential) who fear the impact that the *costs* of union benefits may have on an employer's decision to hire or retain *them.*

[14]NLRA, Section 8 (3). See also chapter nine *infra*

[15]NLRA, Section 7, Section 8 (a) (3) (5), 8 (b) (2), 14 (b), as amended by Public Law No. 101, 61 Stat. 136 (1947). See also National Right to Work Committee, *State Right to Work Laws with Annotations* (National Right to Work Committee: Fairfax, Virginia, 1977); and Haggard, "Right-to-Work Laws in the Southern States."

[16]See Petro, "Civil Liberty, Syndicalism, and the NLRA," 5 *University of Toledo Law Review* 447, 452-459 (1974), and see chapter eight, *infra* The Taft-Hartley Amendments, Section 301 has made it possible for employers to sue a union for breach of a collective agreement.

[17]In the Matter of Houde Engineering Corporation and United Automobile Workers Federal Labor Union No. 18839, *Decisions of the National Labor Relations Board,* July 9, 1934-December 1934 (Washington, D.C.: GPO, 1935), p. 43. See also U.S. Congress, Senate, Committee on Education and Labor, Senate Report No. 573 on S. 1958, in U.S., National Labor Relations Board, *Legislative History of the National Labor Relations Act, 1935* (Washington, D.C.: GPO, 1949), p. 2313: "the rule is sanctioned by our governmental practices, by business procedure, and by the whole philosophy of democratic institutions." See also chapter nine, *infra.*

[18]Since no one has a right to a job without an employer's consent, exclusivity is, first of all, an interference with an *employer's* right to contract individually with employees. Because of his rights, exclusivity also interferes with the rights of already employed workers at the time when a majority union is certified, and of potential employees who, but for the majority union, would work on terms different than those demanded by the majority union.

[19]Weyand, "Majority Rule in Collective Bargaining," 45 *Columbia Law Review* 556, 561 (1945).

[20]Summers, "Union Powers and Workers' Rights," 49 *Michigan Law Review* 805, 811, 815-816 (1951) (emphasis added).

[21]American Federation of Labor Reconstruction Program, 1918, quoted in David Saposs, ed., *Readings in Trade Unionism* (New York: George H. Doran, 1926), p. 46.

[22]J. P. Kay Shuttleworth, "Report of the Trades' Societies Committee," in National Association for the Promotion of Social Science, *Trades' Societies and Strikes* (London: John W. Parker and Son, 1860), p. x. Compare with John P. Mitchell, *Organized Labor* (Philadelphia: American Book and Bible House, 1903), p. 3:

> [w]hile the employer engages hundreds or thousands of men and can easily do without the services of any particular individual, the workingman, if bargaining on his own account and for himself alone, is at an enormous disadvantage. . . .

and with Chief Justice William H. Taft—whom the leaders of organized labor counted an enemy—in *American Steel Foundries v. Tri-City Central Trades Council* 257 U.S. 184, 209 (1921):

> A single employee was helpless in dealing with an employer. He was dependent ordinarily on his daily wage for the maintenance of himself and family. If the employer refused to pay him the wages that he thought fair, he was nevertheless unable to leave the employ and to resist arbitrary and unfair treatment.

[23]Sidney and Beatrice Webb, *Industrial Democracy* (New York: Augustus Kelley, 1964 [1897]), pp. 217, 561, 654-701 *passim* (emphasis in original).

[24]Richard T. Ely, *An Introduction to Political Economy* (New York: Chautauqua Press, 1889), p. 236.

[25]Henry Demarest Lloyd, "The Safety of the Future Lies in Organized Labor," a paper read before the thirteenth annual convention of the American Federation of Labor, 1893, in Lloyd, *Men, The Workers* (New York: Doubleday, Page, 1909), pp. 90-91 (emphasis added). Lloyd's essay was distributed in pamphlet form by the American Federation of Labor.

[26]T. J. Dunning, *Trades' Unions and Strikes: Their Philosophy and Intention* (London: By the Author, 1860), p. 7.

[27]*American Steel Foundries v. Tri-City Central Trades Council,* 257 U.S. 184, 209 (1921).

[28]For a typical expression of this view, see American Federation of Labor Reconstruction Program, 1918, in Saposs, *Readings in Trade Unionism,* p. 47:

> Unemployment is due to underconsumption. Underconsumption is caused by low or insufficient wages.
>
> Just wages will prevent industrial stagnation and lessen periodical unemployment.
>
> Give the workers just wages and their consuming capacity is correspon-

dingly increased. A man's ability to consume is controlled by the wages received. Just wages will create a market at home which will far surpass any market that may exist elsewhere and will lessen unemployment.

[29]William H. Hutt, *The Theory of Collective Bargaining: A History, Analysis and Criticism of the Principal Theories Which Have Sought to Explain the Effects of Trade Unions and Employers' Associations on the Distribution of the Product of Industry* (Glencoe, NY: The Free Press, 1954 [London, 1930]), summarized the contending positions as they had evolved up to the eve of the Great Depression, and he concluded that the theory of collective bargaining was false. For a lengthier discussion and citations to modern studies, see chapters five and six, *infra*.

[30]For a discussion of this theory as it arose in America, see chapter six, *infra*.

[31]Paul F. Brissenden, "Genesis and Import of the Collective-Bargaining Provisions of the Recovery Act," in *Economic Essays in Honor of Wesley Clair Mitchell* (New York: Columbia University Press, 1935), p. 33, captures the logic of both the National Recovery Administration (NRA) and that of the Wagner Act. National labor policy, he explains,

> deliberately tilts the *law* against the employer sufficiently to balance an *economic* set up which would otherwise operate lopsidedly to frustrate the achievement of any 'recovery', except the conventional return to a prosperity which, because not widely distributed, would be pretty sure to wind up in another tail spin. (emphasis in original)

The "Findings and Policies" of Section One of the Wagner Act reflect this imperative as well. Unions' demands for *special* rights, i.e., for legal favoritism, masquerading in the guise of a demand for *equal* rights was well recognized (and applauded) by Herbert Croly in his enormously influential book, *The Promise of American Life* (New York: E.P. Dutton, 1963 [1909]), pp. 386 *et seq.*

[32]In the Matter of Houde Engineering Corporation, *Decisions*, p. 35; and see chapter eight, *infra*.

[33]This situation changed as the result of the Supreme Court's invention of a "duty of fair representation" in *Steele* v. *Louisville & Nashville Railroad*, 323 U.S. 192 (1944). In 1959, Congress passed the Landrum-Griffith Act (Labor-Management Reporting and Disclosure Act, 73 Stat. 519), which gave to labor union members a "Bill of Rights" (Section 101). See chapter nine, *infra*.

[34]See chapters seven and eight, *infra*.

[35]Frank A. Fetter, *The Principles of Economics*, 1913, as quoted in Ludwig von Mises, *Socialism: An Economic and Sociological Analysis*, trans. J. Kahane (Indianapolis, Indiana: Liberty Classics, 1981 [1951, 1922]) p. 400n.

The metaphor of the market as a democracy implies that individuals have *more* than one vote, and that individuals exercise an *unequal* number of votes. This fact has usually been held up for scorn, as demonstrating the moral or political inferiority of the marketplace to government. I believe it shows just the opposite—it is the political disposition of economic resources under a 'one man, one vote' representative model which is inferior. In the first place, experience demonstrates that the individual, even the poor individual, is materially better off—has more votes, so to speak—under capitalism than under socialism, inequality notwithstanding.

But there is a deeper issue of 'political economy' here. In the market, the consumer casts each of his dollar votes on the basis of (and to achieve) *his own individual preferences and interests*. In a politically controlled economy—let us take an imaginary 'democratic socialism' as a paradigm—the individual citizen casts one vote for a representative. Even assuming his preferred candidate wins, the individual citizen-voter has typically bought a 'package deal', that is, an 'agent' who has other citizen's interests to serve and possibly his own (only partially known) agenda, only some of whose items the individual citizen may agree with. Individual preferences are bound to be frustrated in a way they are not in the nearest market analogue to political representation, that is, the relationship between principal and agent. Interestingly enough, G. D. H. Cole in his guild socialist phase recognized this defect in traditional political models of representation and devised his own solution (each citizen to have as many votes as interests); see chapter seven, *infra.*

I should like to take this opportunity to acknowledge my intellectual debt to the novelist and philosopher Ayn Rand, whose moral defense of capitalism has greatly influenced me; to Ludwig von Mises, whose writings on the logic of the economy have also proved instructive; to William H. Hutt, whose previously cited essay on the theory of collective bargaining helped clarify my own thinking on the issues of unionism and collective bargaining; and to the many works of Sylvester Petro, whose understanding and analysis of American labor relations law is unmatched. Needless to say, the analysis and point of view in this book is my own. The following books and articles also proved useful: Fritz Machlup, *The Political Economy of Monopoly: Business, Labor, and Government Policies* (Baltimore: The Johns Hopkins University Press, 1952), pp. 317-435; Lionel Robbins, *Wages: An Introductory Analysis of the Wage System Under Modern Capitalism* (London: Jarrolds, 1926), especially pp. 58-69; Henry Simons, "Reflections on Syndicalism," *Journal of Political Economy* LII (March 1944): 1-25; Charles Lindblom, *Unions and Capitalism* (New Haven: Yale University Press, 1949); Philip Bradley, ed., *The Public Stake in Union Power* (Charlottesville: University Press of Virginia, 1959); F. A. Hayek, *The Constitution of Liberty* (Chicago: University of Chicago Press, 1960), pp. 267-284; E. H. Chamberlain, ed., *Labor Unions and Public Policy* (Washington, D.C.: American Enterprise Institute, 1958); David McCord Wright, ed., *The Impact of the Union* (New York: Harcourt, Brace, 1951); Charles Baird, *Opportunity or Privilege: Labor Legislation in America* (Bowling Green, OH: Social Philosophy and Policy Center, 1984); Schatzki, "Majority Rule, Exclusive Representation, and the Interests of Individual Workers: Should Exclusivity Be Abolished?" 123 *University of Pennsylvania Law Review* 897 (1975); and the two articles by Richard Epstein cited in note 11 *supra.*

[36]*Coppage v. Kansas,* 236 U.S. 1, 17 (1915).

[37]Dunning, *Trade Unions,* p. 7.

Chapter One

[1]George Sabine, *A History of Political Theory,* 3d edition (New York: Holt, Rinehart, and Winston, 1961), p. 249. See also Walter Ullman, *The Individual and Society in the Middle Ages* (Baltimore: The Johns Hopkins University Press, 1966); Otto Gierke, *Political Theories of the Middle Ages,* trans. F. W. Maitland (Cambridge: Cambridge University Press, 1900), especially pp. 22-30; and Ernest Troeltsch, *The Social Teaching of the Christian Churches,* trans. Olive Wyon (New York: Macmillan, 1931), Volume I, pp. 284-328, and Volume II, pp. 528-576, 617-625.

[2]Leonard Peikoff, "Nazi Politics (II)," *The Objectivist* VIII (March 1969), p. 2. The collision of the organic and individualist world view was captured in a short conversation said to have occurred between Samuel Taylor Coleridge and Harriet Martineau. "You seem to regard society," the poet accused the economist, as nothing more than an "aggregate of individuals." Her economical reply: "Of course I do." (Quoted in G. M. Young, *Victorian England: Portrait of An Age* (New York: Oxford University Press, 1964), p. 68n.)

[3]Edgar S. Furniss, *The Position of the Laborer in a System of Nationalism: A Study in the*

Labor Theories of the Later English Mercantilists (Boston: Houghton Mifflin, 1920), p. 222.
[4]Id.

[5]See Rehbinder, "Status, Contract, and the Welfare State," 23 *Stanford Law Review* 941 (1971); Ronald Graveson, *Status in the Common Law* (London: Athlone Press, 1953), pp. 2-6, 112-113, 129-136; Carleton K. Allen, "Status and Capacity," in *Legal Duties and Other Essays in Jurisprudence* (Oxford: Clarendon Press, 1931), pp. 28-70; and Sir Henry Sumner Maine, *Ancient Law: Its Connection with the Early History of Society and its Relation to Modern Ideas* (New York: Henry Holt and Company, 1906 [1861]), pp. 163-165.

[6]On wage and price controls, see Ephraim Lipson, *The Economic History of England* (London: A. & C. Black, Ltd., 1937-1947), Volume I, pp. 96-100, 348-352, Volume III, pp. 251-278; William J. Cunningham, *The Growth of English Industry and Commerce* (Cambridge: At the University Press, 1896), Volume I, pp. 329-336, 534-541, Volume II, pp. 25-52; Nassau Senior, "English Poor Laws," *Edinburgh Review*, October 1841, reprinted in Nassau Senior, *Historical and Philosophical Essays* (London: Longman, 1865), Volume II, pp. 45-115; and Thorold Rogers, *Six Centuries of Work and Wages* (London: George Allen and Unwin, 1949 [1884]), *passim*.

[7]Quoted in Pauline Gregg, *Black Death to Industrial Revolution: A Social and Economic History of England* (New York: Harper and Row, 1974), p. 85.

[8]See, for instance, the Ordinance of Labourers, 23 Edward III (1349) (Appendix 1 of this book); Statute of Labourers, 25 Edward III (1350-1351); Act of 34 Edward III (1360); Act of 12 Richard II (1388); the infamous 1 Edward VI, c.3 (1547); or the Statute of Artificers, Act of 5 Elizabeth (1563) (Appendix 3 of this book).

[9]See, for instance, 12 Richard II (1388); 11 Henry VII (1495); 22 Henry VIII (1531); 27 Henry VIII (1536); 1 Edward VI (1547), and the discussion in Adam Smith, *The Wealth of Nations,* ed. Edwin Cannan (New York: Modern Library, 1937 [1776]), (hereinafter cited as *WN*), Book I, c. 10, part II, pp. 135-141.

[10]As quoted in Jay M. Feinman, "The Development of the Employment at Will Rule," *American Journal of Legal History* XX (April 1976), p. 120.

[11]See Smith, *WN,* Book III, c. 5, pp. 490-510 for a discussion of the food trade regulations. For the laws against forestalling, regrating, and engrossing generally (which were eventually applied to all manner of commodities), see the excellent discussion in William Letwin, *Law and Economic Policy in America: The Evolution of the Sherman Act* (New York: Random House, 1965), pp. 32-39; Jones, "Historical Development of the Law of Business Competition," 35 *Yale Law Journal* 905, 906-920 (1926); Lipson, *Economic History,* Volume I, pp. 196-238, 266-273; and Donald Dewey, *Monopoly in Economics and Law* (Chicago: University of Chicago Press, 1959), pp. 112-115.

[12]*Farmer's Tour Through the East of England* (1771), IV, quoted in Furniss, *Position of the Laborer,* p. 118. On the theory of low wages, see ibid., pp. 117-156, 178-197; and D. C. Coleman, "Labour in the English Economy in the 17th Century," *Economic History Review* VIII (April 1956): 280-295.

[13]On the guilds and the guild system, see Georges Renard, *Guilds in the Middle Ages,* trans. Dorothy Terry (London: G. Bell and Sons, 1918); Lujo Brentano, *On the History and Development of Guilds, and the Origin of Trade Unions,* 2d edition (London: Trubner and Co., 1870); and Austin Evans, "The Problem of Control in Medieval Industry," *Political Science Quarterly* XXXVI (December 1921): 603-616.

On the English guilds in particular, see Charles Gross, *The Gild Merchant: A Contribution to British Municipal History* (Oxford: Clarendon Press, 1927 [1890]); Stella Kramer, *The England Craft Guilds: Studies in Their Progress and Decline* (New York: Columbia University Press, 1927); J. A. Kellett, "The Breakdown of Guild and Corporation Control Over the Handicraft and Retail Trade of London," *Economic History Review* X (April 1957): 381-394; Lipson, *Economic History,* Volume I, pp. 238-390, Volume III, pp. 330-351; Gregg,

Black Death, pp. 124-137; and Cunningham, *Growth of English Industry,* Volume I, pp. 219-229, 336-352, 506-525.

[14]See, for instance, 22 Henry VIII, c. 4 (1531); 28 Henry VIII, c. 5 (1537); 3 & 4 Edward VI, c. 22 (1550); 2 & 3 Ph and M, c. 11 (1555); and Act of 5 Elizabeth, c. 4 (1563), section 33.

[15]Quoted in Lipson, *Economic History,* Volume I, p. 315 (emphasis in original). These are examples of what modern economists call the 'lump of labor' fallacy (which, if acted upon, becomes a self-fulfilling prophecy).

[16]Lipson, *Economic History,* Volume I, pp. 308, 244, 295-296. Selig Perlman, *A Theory of Labor Movement* (New York: Macmillan, 1928), pp. 254-279 develops the parallels between "job conscious" unionism and the medieval guild ethic in absorbing detail.

[17]See Lipson, *Economic History,* Volume I, pp. 315-316; and Kramer, *English Craft Guilds,* p. 53n. See Renard, *Guilds,* pp. 37-39.

[18]*Select Cases in Chancery* (Selden Society, 1896), quoted in Jones, "Law of Competition," p. 924; Lipson, *Economic History,* Volume I, pp. 302-303.

[19]Quoted in Sidney and Beatrice Webb, *The History of Trade Unionism,* revised edition (New York: Augustus Kelley, 1973 [1920, 1894]), p. 3; see also pp. 36-37.

[20]Renard, *Guilds,* p. 89.

[21]See Cunningham, *Growth of English Industry,* Volume I, pp. 444-445; and Sylvia Thrupp, "Medieval Guilds Reconsidered," *Journal of Economic History* II (November 1942), pp. 167-168.

[22]See Lipson, *Economic History,* Volume I, pp. 369-373; Cunningham, *Growth of English Industry,* Volume I, pp. 445, 511.

[23]There are discussions of these cases in Letwin, *Law and Economic Policy,* pp. 23-32; Donald O. Wagner, "Coke and the Rise of Economic Liberalism," *Economic History Review* VI (October 1935): 30-44; and Donald O. Wagner, "The Common Law and Free Enterprise: An Early Case of Monopoly," *Economic History Review* VII (November 1936): 217-220.

On the role of Sir Edward Coke in the evolution of economic liberalism, see Charles T. Mullett, "Coke and the American Revolution," *Economica* XII (November 1932): 457-471; and Edward S. Corwin, *Liberty Against Government: The Rise, Flowering, and Decline of a Famous Juridical Concept* (Baton Rouge: Louisiana State University Press, 1948), pp. 34-43. See also Lipson, *Economic History,* Volume III, pp. 352-386 for a discussion of the 17th century anti-monopoly movement.

[24]Letwin, *Law and Economic Policy,* p. 24.

[25]Holdsworth, "Industrial Combinations and the Law in the 18th Century," 18 *Minnesota Law Review* 369, 372 (1934) (emphasis added).

[26]Sir William Erle, *The Law Relating to Trade Unions* (London: Macmillan, 1869), p. 44.

[27]Letwin, "The English Common Law Concerning Monopolies," 21 *University of Chicago Law Review* 355, 367 (1954).

[28]See Sabine, *History of Political Thought,* pp. 415-572; Caroline Robbins, *The Eighteenth-Century Commonwealthman* (Cambridge: Harvard University Press, 1959); Kingsley Martin, *French Liberal Thought in the Eighteenth Century: A Study of Political Ideas from Bayle to Condorcet* (Boston: Little Brown & Co., 1929); Corwin, *Liberty Against Government,* pp. 44-57; Crawford MacPherson, *The Political Theory of Possessive Individualism: Hobbes to Locke* (Oxford: Clarendon Press, 1962); and Karen Vaughn, *John Locke: Economist and Social Scientist* (Chicago: University of Chicago Press, 1980).

[29]John Locke, *Two Treatises on Government,* ed. Thomas I. Cook (New York: Hafner Publishing Company, 1966 [1690]), Second Treatise, c. 6, sec. 57, p. 148; c. 2, sec. 4, p. 122; c. 11, sec. 135, p. 189; and see also c. 9, sec. 123-124, p. 184.

[30]Quoted in translation by W. Walker Stephens, ed., *Life and Writings of Turgot* (London: Longmans, Green and Co., 1895), p. 130. This right to work did not imply a right to a job.

[31]*Éphémérides,* 1768, quoted in Charles Gide and Charles Rist, *A History of Economic*

Doctrines from the Time of the Physiocrats to the Present Day 2d English edition, trans. R.
Richard (Boston: D.C. Heath, 1948 [1909]) p. 45n. The "royal privileges" concept Beaudeau
attacked appears as an assumption in the preamble to Turgot's famous Edict on the Jurandes,
1776; see A. R. J. Turgot, *Ouevres De Turgot* (Paris: Librairie Félix Alcan, 1923), Volume V,
p. 242.

³²Smith, *WN,* Book I, c. 10, Part II, pp. 121f.

³³For some typical and famous passages connecting individual freedom and self-interest, and social happiness, see Smith, *WN,* Book I, c. 10, p. 99; Book IV, c. 2, pp. 421, 423; c. 4,
p. 508.

There are comments on the two traditions (the one emphasizing individual self-interest
and natural rights, and the other social utility) in the history of economic liberalism in Albert
Venn Dicey, *Lectures on the Relation Between Law and Public Opinion During the 19th
Century,* 2d edition (London: Macmillan, 1919 [1905]), pp. 146-147; Lionel Robbins, *The
Theory of Economic Policy in English Classical Political Economy,* 2d edition (London:
Macmillan, 1978 [1952]), pp. 46-49; Ellen Frankel Paul, *Moral Revolution and Economic
Science: The Demise of Laissez-Faire in Nineteenth-Century British Political Economy*
(Westport: Greenwood Press, 1979), pp. 4-5; Alasdair MacIntyre, *A Short History of Ethics*
(New York: Macmillan, 1966) pp. 162-177, 232f; and Milton L. Myers, *The Soul of Modern
Economic Man: Ideas of Self-Interest, Thomas Hobbes to Adam Smith* (Chicago: University
of Chicago Press, 1983).

On Adam Smith, see Paul, *Moral Revolution,* pp. 9-44; Samuel Hollander, *The Economics of
Adam Smith* (Toronto, Canada: University of Toronto Press, 1973); J. Ralph Lindgren, *The
Social Philosophy of Adam Smith* (The Hague, Netherlands: Martinus Nijhoff, 1973);
Thomas D. Campbell, *Adam Smith's Science of Morals* (London: George Allen and Unwin,
1971); Andrew S. Skinner, *Adam Smith and the Role of the State* (Glasgow, Scotland:
University of Glasgow Press, 1974); Andrew Skinner and Thomas Wilson, eds., *Essays on
Adam Smith* (Oxford: Clarendon Press, 1975); Gerald P. O'Driscoll, Jr., ed., *Adam Smith and
Modern Political Economy: Bicentennial Essays on the Wealth of Nations* (Ames, Iowa:
Iowa State University Press, 1979); Fred R. Glahe, ed., *Adam Smith and the Wealth of Nations:
1776-1976 Bicentennial Essays* (Boulder: Colorado Associated University Press, 1978); John
M. Clark, *et al., Adam Smith, 1776-1926; Lectures to Commemorate the Sesquicentennial of
the Publication of The Wealth of Nations* (Chicago: University of Chicago Press, 1928); and
A. L. MacFie, ed., *The Individual in Society: Papers on Adam Smith* (London: George Allen
and Unwin, 1967).

³⁴Smith, *WN,* Book I, c. 2, p. 14. Cf. Book I, and c. 10, p. 99; and c. 11, Part III, pp. 248-250.

³⁵For a discussion and a defense of this latter contention, see Mises, *Human Action,* pp.
598-600, 770-779; and Murray N. Rothbard, *Man, Economy, and State: A Treatise on
Economic Principles* (Los Angeles: Nash Publishing Co., 1970 [1962]), pp. 522-528, 679-687.

³⁶See Smith, *WN,* Book I, c. 10, *passim.*. For some modern discussions, see Lionel Robbins,
Wages: An Introductory Analysis of the Wage System Under Modern Capitalism (London:
Jarrolds, 1926), pp. 27-40; Albert Rees, "Compensating Wage Differentials," in Skinner and
Wilson, *Essays on Adam Smith,* pp. 336-349; and Simon Rottenberg, "On Choice in Labor
Markets," *Industrial and Labor Relations Review* IX (January 1956): 183-199 (and the
controversy generated by this article: IX (July 1956): 629-643; and XI (October 1957):
96-103).

³⁷Smith, *WN,* Book I, c. 8, pp. 81, 78-79; see also pp. 82-83. On the waning appeal of the "low
wages" theory, see A. W. Coats, "Changing Attitudes To Labour in the Mid-Eighteenth
Century," *Economic History Review* XI (August 1958): 35-51; on the classical economists'
attitudes toward laborers, see A. W. Coats, "The Classical Economists and the Labourer," in E.
L. Jones and G. E. Mingay, eds., *Land, Labour and Population in the Industrial Revolution:
Essays Presented to J. D. Chambers* (London: Edward Arnold, 1967), pp. 100-130.

³⁸Smith, *WN,* Book I., c. 10, p. 129; and see pp. 118-123.

³⁹Ibid, Book IV, c. 5, pp. 490-510.

[40]The wages fund doctrine will be discussed further in chapters two and five of this study. The most useful sources on the doctrine and the controversy it generated are: Frank W. Taussig, *Wages and Capital: An Examination of the Wages Fund Doctrine* (New York: Augustus M. Kelley, 1968 [1896]); Doris Phillips, "The Wages Fund in Historical Context," *Journal of Economic Issues* I (December 1967): 321-334; Pedro Schwartz, *The New Political Economy of J. S. Mill* (London: George Weidenfield and Nicolson Ltd, 1972), pp. 67-105; Frank W. Taussig, "The Wages-Fund at the Hands of German Economists," *Quarterly Journal of Economics* IX (October 1894): 1-25; James W. Crook, *German Wages Theories: A History of Their Development,* Columbia University Studies in History, Economics and Public Law, Volume IX, Number 2 (New York: Columbia University Press, 1898), pp. 67-103; Francis A. Walker, *The Wages Question: A Treatise on Wages and the Wages Class* (New York: Henry Holt, 1876), pp. 128-151; William Breit, "Some Neglected Early Critics of the Wages Fund Theory," *Southwestern Social Science Quarterly* XLVIII (June 1967): 54-60, and his "The Wages Fund Controversy Revisited," *Canadian Journal of Economics and Political Science* XXX (Nov 1967): 509-528; and Scott Gordon, "The Wage-Fund Controversy: The Second Round," *History of Political Economy* V (Spring 1973): 14-35.

[41]Smith, *WN,* Book I, c. 8, p. 69; and see Taussig, *Wages and Capital,* pp. 142-151. In this passage "revenue" refers to what employers spend on personal servants, liverymen, and so forth.

[42]Smith, *WN,* Book I, c. 8, pp. 83, 68.

[43]Ibid., Book I, c. 8, p. 86; c. 11, pp. 242-243; c. 1, p. 7.

[44]See ibid., Book I, c. 8, p. 65.

[45]Taussig, *Wages and Capital,* pp. 98-99 (emphasis added).

[46]Smith, *WN,* Book I, c. 8, p. 66 (emphasis added). See chapter two of this study for more discussion about the law of combinations in the 18th and 19th centuries.

[47]Smith, *WN,* Book I, c. 8, pp. 66.

[48]Ibid., Book I, c. 8, pp. 67, 68.

[49]Ibid., Book I, c. 8, p. 68; c. 10, p. 114.

[50]Ibid., Book I, c. 8, pp. 71, 73.

[51]Ibid., Book I, c. 8, pp. 66-67 (emphasis added); cf. c. 10, p. 142:

> When masters combine together in order to reduce the wages of their workmen, they commonly enter into a private bond or agreement, not to give more than a certain wage under a certain penalty.

T. S. Ashton, *The Industrial Revolution, 1760-1830* (London: Oxford University Press, 1955 [1948]), p. 135 found evidence of employer combinations in the late 18th century. He did not say if they were defensive (formed in reaction to trade unions), an hypothesis that Hutt, *Theory of Collective Bargaining,* pp. 18-23 provides some evidential support for; and on this point, see also the discussion and the additional sources in J. A. McKenna and Richard G. Roger, "Control by Coercion: Employers' Associations and the Establishment of Industrial Order in the Building Industry of England and Wales, 1860-1914," *Business History Review* LIX (Summer 1985): 203-231. For that matter, there is some real question whether Smith took his own analysis all that seriously; see Hutt, *op. cit.,* p. 18.

[52]Smith, *WN,* Book I, c. 8, p. 67.

[53]Ibid., Book I, c. 10, p. 128 (emphasis added); and see p. 142.

[54]Ibid., Book I, c. 5, p. 30.

[55]Ibid., Book I, c. 6, p. 47; and see c. 5, p. 31.

[56]Ibid., Book I, c. 8, p. 64; see also c. 6, p. 47.

[57]Ibid., Book I, c. 5, p. 30 (emphasis added); and see p. 31.

[58]Le Trosne, *Intérêt Social,* quoted in Gide and Rist, *History of Economic Doctrines,* pp. 45-46n: "Exchange is a contract of equality, equal value being given in exchange for equal value. Consequently it is not a means of increasing wealth, for one gives as much as the other receives, but it is a means of satisfying wants and of varying enjoyment." On this fallacy, see Mises, *Human Action,* pp. 204-206.

[59]James Buchanan, "The Justice of Natural Liberty," in O'Driscoll, *Adam Smith and Modern Political Economy,* p. 122.

[60]Smith, *WN,* Book II, c. 2, p. 308. Adam Smith's moral theory is beyond the scope of this study. Despite his authentic respect for self-interest, and his understanding of how it operated in society, he still retained some of the old, religious traditionalism; see the famous (or infamous) statement in *The Theory of Moral Sentiments* (Indianapolis, IN: Liberty Classics, 1969 [1759]), Part VI, Section II, c. 3, p. 384:

> The wise and virtuous man is at all times willing that his own private interest should be sacrificed to the public interest of his own particular order of society. He is at all times willing, too, that the interest of this order or society should be sacrificed to the greater interest of the state or sovereignty of which it is only a subordinate part: he should, therefore, be equally willing that all those inferior interests should be sacrificed to the greater interest of the universe, to the interest of that great society of all sensible and intelligent beings, of which God himself is the immediate administrator and director.

[61]See the famous denunciation of natural rights in Jeremy Bentham's essay, "Anarchical Fallacies," 1793, in John Hill Burton, ed., *Benthamania* (Philadelphia: Lea and Blanchard, 1844), pp. 60-83.

[62]See John Stuart Mill, *Utilitarianism,* 1861, in *Collected Works of John Stuart Mill,* ed. J. M. Robson (Toronto: University of Toronto Press, 1969), Volume X, p. 258 (emphasis in original):

> All persons are deemed to have a *right* to equality of treatment, except when some recognised social expediency requires the reverse.

The significance of Mill's utilitarianism for monopolistic unionism is discussed in chapter five, *infra.* The scholar alluded to in the text is Ellen Frankel Paul; see *Moral Revolution and Economic Science.*

[63]John Neal, *Principles of Legislation* from the MS. of Jeremy Bentham, by M. Dumont, translated from the second corrected and enlarged edition (Boston: Wells and Lilly, 1830), pp. 119-120; cf. Bentham, "Anarchical Fallacies," *Benthamania,* p. 67 (emphasis in original):

> What is the language of reason and plain sense upon this same subject? That in proportion as it is *right* or *proper,* i.e. advantageous to the society in question, that this or that right . . . should be established and maintained, in that same proportion it is *wrong* that it should be abrogated: but that as there is no *right,* which ought to be maintained so long as it is upon the whole advantageous to the society that it should be maintained, so there is no right which, when the abolition of it is advantageous to society, should not be abolished.

See also the very interesting article by Paul A. Palmer, "Benthamism in England and America," *American Political Science Review* XXXV (October 1941): 855-871, especially pp. 862-864, showing how one of Bentham's American followers used utilitarian principles to defend black slavery.

[64]As quoted in Pound, "Liberty of Contract," 18 *Yale Law Review* 454, 461 (1909).

Chapter Two

[1]Letwin, "The English Common Law Concerning Monopolies," 21 *University of Chicago Law Review* 355, 367 (1954).

[2]Holdsworth, "Industrial Combinations and the Law in the 18th Century," 18 *Minnesota Law Review* 369, 372 (1934) (emphasis added).

[3]The account of the conspiracy doctrine in this chapter is my own interpretation of the following secondary sources: Alpheus T. Mason, *Organized Labor and the Law* (Princeton: Princeton University Press, 1925), pp. 1-116; Holdsworth, "Industrial Combinations"; Holdsworth, *History of English Law,* Volume III, pp. 400-407; Volume VIII, pp. 378-397; Volume XI, pp. 475-500; Volume XV, pp. 61-82; M. Dorothy George, "The Combination Laws Reconsidered," *Economic Journal* History Supplement, Number 1 (May 1927): 214-228; Lipson, *Economic History of England,* Volume III, pp. 386-409; Sir William Erle, *The Law Relating to Trade Unions* (London: Macmillan, 1869); John R. Commons and E. A. Gilmore, eds., *Documentary History of American Industrial Society* (New York: Russell and Russell, 1958 [1910-1911]), Volumes III-IV; Morris Forkosh, "The Doctrine of Criminal Conspiracy and Its Application to Labor," 40 *Texas Law Review* 303, 473 (1962); Witte, "Early American Labor Cases," 35 *Yale Law Journal* 825 (1926); Marjorie S. Turner, *The Early American Labor Conspiracy Cases. Their Place in Labor Law: A Reinterpretation,* Social Science Monograph Series, Volume 1—Number 3 (San Diego: San Diego State College Press 1967); Haggard, *Compulsory Unionism,* pp. 11-33; Dicey, "The Combination Laws as Illustrating the Relation Between Law and Opinion in England During the Nineteenth Century," 17 *Harvard Law Review* 511 (1904); and finally, the extremely important reappraisal of the entire literature on conspiracy in Petro, "Unions and the Southern Courts: Part III—The Conspiracy and Tort Foundations of the Labor Injunction," 60 *North Carolina Law Review* 544 (1982).

[4]All of the anti-combination statutes are collected in the preamble to the Combination Act of 1824 (5 George IV, c. 95) (See Appendix 5 of this book). See also Paul Mantoux, *The Industrial Revolution in the 18th Century,* revised edition, trans. Majorie Vernon (New York: Harper and Row, 1965 [1928]), pp. 440 et seq.; and Lipson, *Economic History,* Volume III, pp. 386-409.

[5]The Combination Act of 1800, unlike the Act of 1799, declared "illegal, null, and void" any contracts or agreements among employers to reduce the wages or increase the hours of work of their employees, and subjected them to a fine (but not, like the workmen, automatically to a jail sentence). Also, the Act of 1800 prohibited employers who were also justices of the peace from serving as judge in a conspiracy case involving their own "particular trade or manufacture"; and finally, it provided a mechanism for the arbitration of wage disputes between employers and employees.

[6]See Letwin, *Law and Economic Policy,* pp. 39-46; Petro, "Conspiracy and Tort in Labor Law," pp. 607-609; Donald Dewey, *Monopoly in Economics and Law* (Chicago: Rand McNally, 1959), pp. 123-138; and Holdsworth, *History of English Law,* Volume VIII, pp. 54-62.

[7]For some typical judicial expressions of the belief that acts performed by groups may be unlawful whereas the same act performed by an individual would be lawful, see Lord Bowen in *The Mogul Steamship Co. Ltd.* v. *McGregor, Gow and Co.,* 23 Q.B.D. 1889, 598, 616:

> Of the general proposition, that certain kinds of conduct not criminal in any one individual may become criminal if done by combination among several, there can be no doubt. The distinction is based on sound reason, for a combination may make oppressive or dangerous that which if it proceeded only from a single person would be otherwise, and the very fact of the combination may shew that the object is simply to harm, and not to exercise one's own just rights.

Or see Lord Brampton in *Quinn* v. *Leathem,* 1901 A.C. 495, 530:

> Much consideration of the matter has led me to be convinced that a number of actions and things not in themselves actionable or unlawful if done separately without conspiracy may, with conspiracy, become dangerous and alarming, just as a grain of gunpowder is harmless but a pound may be highly destructive, or the administration of one grain of a particular

drug may be most beneficial as a medicine but administered frequently in
larger quantities with a view to harm may be fatal as a poison.
See also the discussion in Dicey, "The Combination Laws," 512-515, and *Law and Opinion*,
pp. 150-158.

[8]W. Hawkins, *A Treatise of the Pleas of the Crown*, 1716, as quoted in Francis B. Sayre, ed.,
Cases on Labor Law (Cambridge: Harvard University Press, 1922), p. 42.

[9]See Holdsworth, "Industrial Combinations," p. 373, and *History of English Law*, Volume
VIII, p. 382; and see p. 383:

> ... just as in the law of contract the courts used the doctrine of public policy
> to control certain of the activities of the citizen, so in the criminal law it
> used this wide conception of conspiracy for the same purpose.

[10]Adam Smith complained (in *The Wealth of Nations*) that the law prohibited combinations
of employees to raise wages while it did not prohibit combinations of employers to lower
them. See chapter one, *supra*. Given the drift of the common law decisions just discussed, his
understanding of the law may not have been totally accurate.

[11]Francis Jeffrey [Lord Jeffrey], "Combinations of Workmen: Substance of the Speech of
Francis Jeffrey, ... at the Public Dinner Given at Edinburgh to Joseph Hume," 1825, reprinted
in *Repeal of the Combination Acts: Five Pamphlets and One Broadside, 1825* (New York:
Arno Press, 1972), pp. 6-7.

[12]J. R. McCulloch, *Essay on the Circumstances Which Determine the Rate of Wages and the
Condition of the Labouring Classes*, 1826, as quoted in Robbins, *Theory of Economic Policy*,
p. 107, and "Combination Laws—Restraints on Emigration," *Edinburgh Review*, 1824, as
quoted in Dennis P. O'Brien, *J. R. McCulloch: A Study in Classical Economics* (London:
George Allen and Unwin, 1970), p. 366 (emphasis in original). Compare with J. R. McCulloch,
*A Treatise on the Circumstances Which Determine the Rate of Wages and the Condition of
the Labouring Classes, Including an Inquiry into the Influence of Combinations*, 2d
edition, corrected and improved (London: G. Routledge & Co., 1854 [1826]), p. 78.

[13]Taussig, *Wages and Capital*, pp. 189-214, 212-213, and O'Brien, *J. R. McCulloch*, pp.
355-360, discuss McCulloch's importance as an economist in the first few decades of the 19th
century.

[14]McCulloch, *Treatise on Wages*, p. 49; see also Robbins, *Theory of Economic Policy*, p. 84.
Nevertheless, even McCulloch didn't make the distinction clearly enough; see the *Treatise on
Wages*, pp. 49-50.

[15]McCulloch, *Treatise on Wages*, pp. 4-5.

[16]Ibid., pp. 78-80.

[17]Ibid., p. 80.

[18]Ibid., pp. 80-81 (emphasis in original). For a definitive restatement based on modern
economic science, see Ludwig von Mises, *Human Action*, 3d revised edition (Chicago:
Henry Regnery, 1966 [1949]), pp. 592-598.

[19]McCulloch, *Treatise on Wages*, p. 81, 82.

[20]Ibid., pp. 83, 86. On page 83 of the *Treatise*, McCulloch also says that the machines
"invented and introduced because of the capricious and unreasonable demands and
proceedings" of textile workers "have materially improved and cheapened the products of
the manufactures into which they have been introduced." Union apologists have made much
of this relationship via the so-called 'shock theory' of technological change; see chapter six,
infra.

[21]The views of some other classical economists on labor unions in the competitive process
are discussed in Lionel Robbins, *Robert Torrens and the Evolution of Classical Economics*
(London: Macmillan, 1958), pp. 49-51; Marian Bowley, *Nassau Senior and Classical
Economics* (London: George Allen and Unwin, 1937), pp. 277-281; Henry Fawcett,
Economic Position of the British Labourer (London: Macmillan, 1865), pp. 119-120, and
Henry Fawcett, *Manual of Political Economy* 5th revised edition (London: Macmillan,

1876), pp. 240-254; and Frédéric Bastiat, "Speech on the Suppression of Industrial Combinations," 1849, in *Selected Essays on Political Economy by Frédéric Bastiat*, trans. Seymour Cain (Irvington-on-Hudson, N.Y.: Foundation for Economic Education, 1964), pp. 301-316. See also Taussig, *Wages and Capital*, pp. 152-216.

A cursory examination of the texts of several major American economists in the early and mid-19th century yields views similar to (though usually not as detailed or as well-developed as) the English followers of Smith. See, for instance, Henry Vethake, *The Principles of Political Economy*, 2d edition (New York: Augustus Kelley, 1971 [1844]), pp. 325-331; Alonzo Potter, *Political Economy* (New York: Harper and Brothers, 1876 [1840]), pp. 233-302; Francis Lieber, *Essays on Property and Labour* (New York: Harper and Brothers, 1843), pp. 186-190; Henry Carey, *Essay on the Rate of Wages* (Philadelphia: Carey, Lea and Blanchard, 1835), and Henry Carey, *Principles of Political Economy* (Philadelphia: Carey, Lea and Blanchard, 1838), Part II pp. 31-33; Francis Wayland, *The Elements of Political Economy*, 4th edition (Boston: Gould, Kendall and Lincoln, 1841), pp. 300-305; Francis Bowen, *The Principles of Political Economy* (Boston: Little Brown and Company, 1859), pp. 228-236; Amasa Walker, *The Science of Wealth: A Manual of Political Economy*, 7th revised edition (Boston: Little Brown and Co., 1874 [1866]), pp. 269-273; Arthur Latham Perry, *Elements of Political Economy*, 7th revised edition (New York: Charles Scribner and Company, 1872), pp. 133-150, and Arthur Latham Perry, *Political Economy*, 18th edition (New York: Charles Scribner's Sons, 1883), pp. 232-250. See also Michael J. O'Connor, *Origins of Academic Economics in the United States* (New York: Columbia University Press, 1944), pp. 190-191, 197-198, 211-213.

For the views of William Graham Sumner, a late 19th century libertarian, see "Industrial War," *The Forum*, 1886, in William Graham Sumner, *The Challenge of Facts and Other Essays* (New Haven: Yale University Press, 1914), pp. 93-102; "Strikes and Industrial Organization," 1887, in Maurice R. Davie, ed., *Sumner Today: Selected Essays of William Graham Sumner* (New Haven: Yale University Press, 1940), pp. 61-64; and "Do We Want Industrial Peace?", 1889, in William Graham Sumner, *War and Other Essays* (New Haven: Yale University Press, 1911), pp. 229-243.

[22]He did have kind words for Friendly Societies, Savings Banks, and other self-help organizations; see *Treatise on Wages*, pp. 102-110. There was very little discussion (see p. 83) at all about workingmen standing out in a body to resist arbitrary treatment of one of their number.

[23]See Graham Wallas, *Life of Francis Place, 1771-1854* (New York: Burt Franklin, 1951 [1898]), pp 197-240; Dicey, *Law and Opinion*, pp. 191-201; O'Brien, *McCulloch*, pp. 27, 366-370; Barry Gordon, *Political Economy in Parliament, 1819-1823* (London: Macmillan, 1976), pp. 165-175; and Barry Gordon, *Economic Doctrine and Tory Liberalism, 1824-1830* (London: Macmillan, 1979), pp. 26-38.

[24]Nassau Senior, "Combinations and Strikes," in *Historical and Philosophical Essays*, Volume II, pp. 118; see pp. 116-172 for the details. See also William Trant, *Trade Unions, Their Origin and Objects, Influence and Efficacy* (London: Kegan Paul, Trench & Co., 1884 [1873]), p. 40, quoting William Saunders on the famous "Sheffield Outrages" of 1867:

> In order to compel men to join their unions and comply with the rules, a system had been adopted of taking away the tools and driving bands of independent or defaulting workmen, and this system had become so universal that when tools or bands had been stolen, the sufferers applied systematically to the secretary of the union to know on what terms the old articles would be restored. But the unionists were not long content with this exercise of their power, and proceeded to the execution of a series of outrages and crimes which are perhaps almost without parallel in the history of communities supposed to be civilized. Masters and workmen who refused or failed to comply with their rules, were subjected to

treatment of the most diabolical character. Their cattle were hamstrung, or otherwise mutilated, their ricks set on fire. They were shot at, and in one instance a master was killed by an air gun fired into a crowded room. Gunpowder was usually employed in the case of obnoxious workmen. Canisters were thrown down chimneys, bottles filled with the explosive, to which lighted fuses were attached, were thrown through windows of the workmen's dwelling-houses, thus exposing women and children to its terrible effects. It was a common practice to place gunpowder in grinding troughs, which exploded as soon as work was commenced.

Violence, to be sure, was not universal—particularly when the police or the military were present in force; for an example (the famous Spinners Strike at Preston, 1836-1837), see Henry Asworth, *An Inquiry into the Origins, Progress and Results of the Strike of the Operative Cotton Spinners of Preston,* 1838, reprinted in *Rebirth of the Trade Unions: Five Pamphlets, 1838-1847* (New York: Arno Press, 1972).

[25]See Feinman, "Employment at Will," pp. 121-122.

[26]In *Hornby* v. *Close* (Queen's Bench, 1867 L.R. 2, Q.B. 153) the Court ruled that because a union was a combination in restraint of trade, it could not even sue to recover money purloined by a member. In America the nonenforceability rule for contracts in restraint of trade was jettisoned in favor of (what in my opinion was a reactionary policy of) criminal penalties by the Sherman Anti-trust Act of 1890.

[27]See H. W. McCready, "British Labour and the Royal Commission on Trade Unions, 1867-1869," *University of Toronto Quarterly* XXIV (July 1955): 390-409; Royden Harrison, *Before the Socialists: Studies in Labour and Politics, 1861-1881* (London: Routledge and Kegan Paul, 1965), pp. 277-307; and Henry Pelling, *A History of British Trade Unionism,* 3d edition (London: Macmillan, 1976), pp. 58-70.

[28]The Criminal Law Amendment Act of 1871 (34 and 35 Victoria, c. 32) prohibited individuals who were interested parties (employers or their relatives, etc.) from acting as members of the courts of summary jurisdiction to prosecute criminal conspiracy cases—a disturbing possibility left open by the Combination Act of 1825 and long a sore point among the trade unions.

[29]See *Springhead Spinning Co.* v. *Riley,* Chancery, 1868, L.R. 6 Equity, 551.

[30]*Bowen* v. *Hall,* 1881 (C.A.) Q.B.D., 338. Cf. *Temperton* v. *Russell,* 1893 Q.B.D. (C.A.), 730:

> a person who induces a party to a contract to break it, intending thereby to injure another person or to get a benefit for himself, commits an actionable wrong. . . . I presume that the principle is this, viz., that the contract confers certain rights on the person with whom it is made, and not only binds the parties to it by the obligation entered into, but also imposes on all the world the duty of respecting that contractual obligation.

[31]*Temperton* v. *Russell,* 1893 Q.B.D. (C.A.), 728.

[32]*Allen* v. *Flood,* 1898 A.C. 121.

[33]The tort of "interference with contractual relations" is one of the most complicated and controversial in the legal system. On the advertising example, for instance, the absurdity is in general quite apparent. But what if the advertiser fraudulently disparages his competitor's product in order to get a sale, say by claiming it will damage the consumer's health? Is it enough to say that *only* the consumer's right not to be defrauded has been trespassed, and that the producer has no right that has been violated?

[34]Carl Degler, *Out of Our Past: The Forces that Shaped Modern America,* 2d Revised edition (New York: Harper & Row, 1970), p. 1.

[35]Edgar A. J. Johnson, *American Economic Thought in the 17th Century* (New York: Russell and Russell, Inc., 1961), p. ix.

[36]See William Bradford's postmortem on the experiment with communism in *Of Plymouth Plantation,* ed. Harvey Wish (New York: Capricorn Books, 1962 [1856]), p. 91. The opening

lines of John Winthrop's sermon, "Model of Christian Charity" (1630), [in David and Sheila Rothman, eds., *Souces of the American Social Tradition* (New York: Basic Books, 1975), p. 23] display the status assumptions of the colonists:

> God Almighty in His most holy and wise providence hath so disposed of the condition of mankind, as in all times some must be rich, some poor, some high and eminent in power and dignity, others mean and in subjection.

Johnson, *Economic Thought in the 17th Century, passim,* collects many of the anti-individualist sentiments of the 17th century colonial leaders. The social and economic theories of the two most important Protestant theorists, Luther and Calvin, are discussed by Troeltsch, *Social Teachings of the Christian Churches,* Volume II, pp. 554-569, 617-625.

[37]John Winthrop, *History of New England,* Volume II, as quoted in Johnson, *Economic Thought in the 17th Century,* p. 211.

[38]On wage and price fixing in the colonial era, and the liability of individuals to compulsory labor, see Johnson, *Economic Thought in the 17th Century,* pp. 205-213; Richard B. Morris, *Government and Labor in Early America* (New York: Harper and Row, 1965 [1946]); and Johnathan R. T. Hughes, *Social Control in the Colonial Economy* (Charlottesville: University Press of Virginia, 1976), especially pp. 96-143. On indentured servitude, see David W. Galenson, *White Servitude in Colonial America: An Economic Analysis* (Cambridge: Cambridge University Press, 1981).

[39]On the role of corporate monopolies and guilds in early American history, see the discussion in Jones, "Law of Business Competition," pp. 42-50. On the guilds in America, see also Beverly McNear, "The Place of the Freemen in Old New York," *New York History* XXIII (October 1942): 418-430; Samuel McKee, Jr., *Labor in Colonial New York, 1664-1776,* Columbia University Studies in History, Economics and Public Law, Number 410 (New York: Columbia University Press, 1935), pp. 29-45, 52-54; Morris, *Government and Labor,* pp. 139-156, 365-389; and Jerome Toner, *The Closed Shop in American Trade Unions* (Washington, D.C.: American Council on Public Affairs, 1942), pp. 58-63. On occupational freedom in America in the late 18th and early 19th centuries, see Tench Coxe, *A View of the United States of America* (New York: Augustus M. Kelley, 1965 [1794]), pp. 66-67, 143, 144; and Daniel J. Boorstin, *The Americans: The Colonial Experience* (New York: Random House, 1958), p. 194.

[40]On the liberal political and economic philosophies dominant in America in the late 18th and early 19th centuries, see Bernard Bailyn, *The Ideological Origins of the American Revolution* (Cambridge: Harvard University Press, 1967); Edward S. Corwin, *Liberty Against Government: The Rise, Flowering, and Decline of a Famous Juridical Concept* (Baton Rouge: Louisiana State University Press, 1948), pp. 58 et seq., and his "The Progress of Constitutional Theory Between the Declaration of Independence and the Meeting of the Philadelphia Convention," *American Historial Review* XXX (April 1925): 511-536; Vieira, "Of Syndicalism, Slavery, and the Thirteenth Amendment: The Unconstitutionality of 'Exclusive Representation' in Public-Sector Employment," 12 *Wake Forest Law Review* 515 (1976), especially pp. 626-695; and Bernard Siegan, *Economic Liberties and the Constitution* (Chicago: University of Chicago Press, 1980).

For a classic statement of James Madison in favor of property rights, recalling both Adam Smith and A. R. J. Turgot, see "On Property," *National Gazette,* 1792, in *Writings,* ed. Gaillard Hunt (New York: G. P. Putnam's Sons, 1906), Volume VI, p. 101 (emphasis in original):

> This term [property] in its particular application, means 'that dominion which one man claims and exercises over the external things of the world, in exclusion of every other individual'. In its larger and juster meaning, it embraces everything to which a man may attach a value and have a right; and *which leaves to everyone else the like advantage.* In the former sense, a man's land, or merchandise, or money, is called his property. In the latter sense, a man has a property in his opinions and the free communication of

them. He has a property of peculiar value in his religious opinions, and in the profession and practice dictated by them. He has property very dear to him in the safety and liberty of his person. He has an equal property in the free use of his faculties, and free choice of the objects on which to employ them. In a word, as a man is said to have a right to his property, he may be equally said to have a property in his rights.

For a famous expression of the idea that individuals have a natural liberty to contract, see Chief Justice Marshall in dissent, in *Ogden v. Saunders,* 25 U.S. 212, 346 (1827):

[I]ndividuals do not derive from government their right to contract, but bring that right with them into society; . . . obligation is not conferred on contracts by positive law, but is intrinsic, and is conferred by the acts of the parties. . . . These rights are not given by society, but are brought into it.

[41]Siegan, *Economic Liberties,* especially pp. 60-82, discusses the original intent of the contracts and *ex post facto* clauses, and criticizes their interpretation by the Supreme Court. The Court's evisceration of the "privileges and immunities" clause in the *Slaughter-House* cases (83 U.S. 36 (1873)), discussed in the text *supra.,* has long been a source of consternation among legal commentators of whatever political stripe: see, for instance, Siegan, *Economic Liberties,* pp. 47-53, and Raoul Berger, *Government By Judiciary: The Transformation of the Fourteenth Amendment* (Cambridge: Harvard University Press, 1977), pp. 20-51.

[42]"If all the available evidence is summed up, it may be said that practically every trade union formed prior to the Civil War was in favor of excluding non-members from employment": Frank Stockton, *The Closed Shop in American Trade Unions* (Baltimore: The Johns Hopkins University Press, 1911), p. 34. On the exclusionary admissions policies of the early trade unions, see F. E. Wolfe, *Admission to American Trade Unions* (Baltimore: Johns Hopkins University Press, 1912).

On the violent proclivities of the unions in the early decades of the 19th century, see Witte, "Early American Labor Cases"; Commons and Gilmore, *Documentary History,* Volumes III, IV *passim.;* and Evans Woolen, "Labor Troubles Between 1834 and 1837," *Yale Review* I (May 1892), p. 90:

Catalogues of 'rats' or non-union men were occasionally published by the typographical societies. . . . Indeed, the life of a 'rat' then, as now, was often an hard one. . . . Foolhardy 'scabs', who applied for work at an establishment where a strike was pending, were met and cared for by union 'pickets'. . . . The treatment which non-union applicants might expect from these sentinels can be inferred from manifestoes like the following: 'We would caution all strangers and others who profess the art of horseshoeing, that if they go to work for any employer under the above prices, they must abide by the consequences . . .'

See also the episodes recounted in Richard B. Morris, "Andrew Jackson, Strikebreaker," *American Historical Review* LV (October 1949), pp. 54-68, and Leo Brophy, "Horace Greely, 'Socialist'," *New York History* XXIX (July 1948) p. 313.

[43]Quoted in Commons and Gilmore, *Documentary History,* Volume III, p. 233. On the conspiracy cases, see ibid., Volumes III-IV; Turner, *Early American Conspiracy Cases;* Mason, *Organized Labor,* pp. 53-69; Witte, "Early American Labor Cases"; Richard B. Morris, "Criminal Conspiracy and Early Labor Combinations in New York," *Political Science Quarterly* LII (March 1937): 51-85; and Haggard, *Compulsory Unionism,* pp. 11-17.

[44]See Witte, "Early American Labor Cases," and Mason, *Organized Labor,* pp. 56-65.

[45]See Nelles, "Commonwealth v. Hunt," 32 *Columbia Law Review* 1128 (1932), and Leonard Levy, *The Law of the Commonwealth and Chief Justice Shaw* (Cambridge: Harvard University Press, 1957), pp. 183-206.

[46]The leading state case to the contrary was *Master Stevedores' Association* v. *Walsh,* 2 Daly

1 (C.P.N.Y.C.) 1867; for a discussion of this case and others, see Petro, "Conspiracy and Tort in Labor Law," *passim.*; Haggard, *Compulsory Unionism,* 17-24; Witte, "Early American Labor Cases," pp. 828 *et seq.*; and Mason, *Organized Labor,* pp. 72-99. See also chapter eight *infra.*

Chapter Three

[1]Robert Owen, "Report to the County of New Lanark," in Robert Owen, *A New View of Society and Other Writings,* ed. G. D. H. Cole (New York: E.P. Dutton, 1927), p. 269.

[2]The virulent hatred of selfishness or egoism by 19th century collectivist radicals cannot be overemphasized. For some typical expressions, see Johann Gottlieb Fichte, *The Characteristics of the Present Age,* trans. W. Smith, 4th edition (London: Trübner, 1889 [1804-1805]) pp. 36-37; John Bray, *Labour's Wrongs and Labour's Remedy: Or the Age of Might and the Age of Right,* Reprints of Scarce Tracts in Economic and Political Science (London: London School of Economics, 1931 [1839]), pp. 119, 133-134; Langdon Byllesby, *Observations on the Sources and Effects of Unequal Wealth* (New York: Russell and Russell, 1961 [1826]), p. 27; and see chapter four, *infra.*

[3]As quoted in Alexander Gray, *The Socialist Tradition: Moses to Lenin* (New York: Longmans, Green & Co., 1946), p. 225 (Sir John Marriott's edition). For some similar expressions of this theme, see William Thompson, *An Inquiry into the Principles of the Distribution of Wealth Most Conducive to Human Happiness* (London: Longman, Hurst, Rees, Orme, Brown, and Green, 1824), p. 371; and compare with the (suspiciously similar) comment by Charles Fourier, *Le Nouveau Monde Industriel et Societaire,* 1829, as quoted in Gray, *Socialist Tradition,* p. 177; John Gray, *A Lecture on Human Happiness,* Reprints of Scarce Tracts in Economics and Political Science (London: London School of Economics, 1931 [1825]), p. 46; and Bray, *Labour's Wrong's,* pp. 117-118.

[4]In addition to the specific monographs, biographies, and other sources cited in this chapter and the next on particular socialists, syndicalists, or anarchist thinkers, the following works have valuable general discussions: Anton Menger, *The Right to the Whole Produce of Labour: The Origin and Development of Labour's Claim to the Whole Product of Industry,* trans. M. E. Turner (New York: Augustus M. Kelley, 1962 [1899]); Esther Lowenthal, *The Ricardian Socialists,* Columbia University Studies in History, Economics, and Public Law, Volume 46, Number 1 (New York: Columbia University Press, 1911); G. D. H. Cole, *History of Socialist Thought,* 5 vols. (London: Macmillan, 1953-1960); Max L. Beer, *A History of British Socialism* (London: George Allen & Unwin, 1940); Gray, *The Socialist Tradition;* Charles Gide and Charles Rist, *A History of Economic Doctrines from the Time of the Physiocrats to the Present Day,* 2d English edition., trans. R. Richards (Boston: D.C. Heath and Company, 1948 [1909]); Frank E. Manuel, *The Prophets of Paris* (Cambridge, MA: Harvard University Press, 1962); George Lichtheim, *The Origins of Socialism* (New York: Praeger, 1969); F. A. Hayek, *The Counter-Revolution of Science: Studies on the Abuse of Reason* (New York: The Free Press, 1955); and Ludwig von Mises, *Socialism: An Economic and Sociological Analysis,* trans. J. Kahane (Indianapolis, IN: Liberty Classics, 1981 [1922]).

The following general studies are also useful for establishing the relationships between these foreign ideologies and American pre-Civil War radicalism: David Harris, *Socialist Origins in the United States: American Forerunners of Marx, 1817-1832* (Amsterdam, The Netherlands: Van Gorcum, 1966); Arthur Eugene Bestor, *Backwoods Utopias: The Sectarian Origins and Owenite Phase of Communitarian Socialism in America, 1663-1829* (Philadelphia: University of Pennsylvania Press, 1950); J. F. C. Harrison, *Quest for the New Moral*

World: Robert Owen and the Owenites in Britain and in America (New York: Charles Scribners Sons, 1969); Edward Pessen, *Most Uncommon Jacksonians, The Radical Leaders of the Early Labor Movement* (Albany: State University of New York Press, 1967); Paul Conkin, *Prophets of Prosperity: America's First Political Economists* (Bloomington: Indiana University Press, 1980); Joseph Dorfman, *The Economic Mind in American Civilization,* 5 vols. (New York: The Viking Press, 1946); Maurice Neufeld, "Realms of Thought and Organized Labor in the Age of Jackson," *Labor History* X (Winter 1969): 5-43; John R. Commons, et al., *History of Labor in the United States,* 4 vols. (New York: Macmillan, 1918-1935); and Walter Hugins, *Jacksonian Democracy and the Working Class* (Stanford, California: Stanford University Press, 1960.

⁵See Menger, *Right to the Whole Produce of Labour,* pp. 5-11; and see chapter four, *infra.*

⁶Thomas Spence was a school teacher and radical journalist whose *The Real Rights of Man* (1775) demanded abolition of fee-simple land ownership and restoration of the "commons" under medieval parish authority. On Spence, see Olive Rudkin, *Thomas Spence and His Connections* (New York: International Publishers, 1927).

William Ogilvie was a Professor at King's College in Aberdeen, Scotland, whose views appear in his *An Essay on the Right to Property* (1781); Charles Hall's inflammatory treatise, *The Effects of Civilization on the People in European States,* was published in 1805.

Tom Paine wrote an essay, *Agrarian Justice* (1797), in which he proposed the creation of a national fund to support those who had no access to land and to support people in their old age. It was to be financed by a tax on land. But Paine did not demand the abolition of private property in land, or question its necessity. Moreover, he supported individual wage bargaining; see Frank Tariello, *The Reconstruction of American Political Ideology, 1865-1897* (Charlottesville: University Press of Virginia, 1982), pp. 18-19.

⁷On Owen, see G. D. H. Cole, *Robert Owen* (Boston: Little Brown and Co., 1925); Francis Page, "Robert Owen and the Early Socialists," in F. J. C. Hearnshaw, ed., *The Social and Political Ideas of Some Representative Thinkers of the Age of Reaction and Reconstruction, 1815-1865* (New York: Barnes and Noble, 1967 [1932]), pp. 82-111; and Robert Murray, *Studies in the English Social and Political Thinkers of the Nineteenth Century* (Cambridge, England: W. Heffer and Sons, 1929), Volume I, pp. 128-160. On Owen's influence, see Harrison, *Quest for the New Moral World;* Bestor, *Backwoods Utopias;* and Sidney Pollard and John Salt, eds., *Robert Owen: Prophet of the Poor* (London: Macmillan, 1971).

The most important 'Owenite' or 'Ricardian' socialists were William Thompson, John Gray, Thomas Hodgskin, and John Bray. In addition to the general sources cited in Note 4 *supra,* see Richard K. P. Pankhurst, *William Thompson: Britain's Pioneer Socialist, Feminist, and Co-operator* (London: Watts and Company, 1954); Janet Kimball, *The Economic Doctrines of John Gray, 1799-1833* (Washington, D.C.: Catholic University Press, 1948); Elie Halevy, *Thomas Hodgskin,* ed. and trans. A. J. P. Taylor (London: Ernest Benn, 1956): and C. H. Driver, "Thomas Hodgskin and the Individualists," in Hearnshaw, *Social and Political Ideas,* pp. 191-217.

⁸Among American radicals, several of whom were influential spokesmen for organized labor in this period, are individuals such as Langdon Byllesby, William Heighton, Thomas Skidmore, Robert Dale Owen, Frances Wright, Cornelius Blatchly, George Henry Evans, Albert Brisbane, and Orestes Brownson. In addition to the works cited in Note 4 *supra,* see Louis Arky, "The Mechanics' Union of Trade Associations and the Formation of the Philadelphia Workingmen's Movement," *Pennsylvania Magazine of History and Biography* LXXVI (April 1952): 142-176; Edward Pessen, "Thomas Skidmore, Agrarian Reformer in the Early American Labor Movement," *New York History* XXXV (July 1954): 280-296; and A. J. G. Perkins, *Frances Wright: Free Enquirer* (Philadelphia: Porcupine Press, 1972), especially pp. 245-270.

Proudhon's syndicalist theories were important in the history of the French labor movement, but they were not influential in America until very late in the century, when socialist revolutionaries such as Daniel De Leon grafted them onto a Marxist base. Nevertheless, Proudhon's theory of 'mutualism' influenced American individualist anarchists, some of whom had ties to organized labor; and Proudhonite-like inflationary schemes, together with those of Louis Blanc, were very hospitably received by radical labor leaders in the generation following the American Civil War.

One of these American individualist anarchists, Josiah Warren, was the first individual to have the honor of attempting to implement Robert Owen's labor-as-money ideas. See William Bailie, *Josiah Warren, The First American Anarchist. A Sociological Study* (Boston: Small, Maynard and Company, 1906); and James J. Martin, *Men Against the State: The Expositors of Individualist Anarchism in America, 1827-1908* (De Kalb, IL: Adrian Allen, 1953), pp. 11-108.

The indirect ties of individualist anarchism to AFL-style labor union voluntarism are assessed by George Cotkin, "The Spencerian and Comtian Nexus in Gompers's Labor Philosophy: The Impact of Non-Marxian Evolutionary Thought," *Labor History* XX (Fall 1979): 510-523; and see chapter eight *infra.*

On Proudhon, see Alan Ritter, *The Political Thought of Pierre-Joseph Proudhon* (Princeton, NJ: Princeton University Press, 1969); Shi Yung Lu, *The Political Theories of P. J. Proudhon* (New York: M. R. Gray, 1922); George Woodcock, *Pierre-Joseph Proudhon* (London: Routledge and Kegan Paul, 1956); Edward Hyams, *Pierre-Joseph Proudhon* (New York: Taplinger, 1979); William H. George, "Proudhon and Economic Federalism," *Journal of Political Economy* XXX (August 1922): 531-542; Robert L. Hoffman, *Revolutionary Justice: The Social and Political Theory of P.-J. Proudhon* (Urbana: University of Illinois Press, 1972); and Constance Margaret Hall, *The Sociology of Pierre-Joseph Proudhon, 1809-1865* (New York: Philosophical Library, 1971). See also Louis Levine [Lorwin], *The Labor Movement in France: A Study in Revolutionary Syndicalism,* Columbia University Studies in History, Economics, and Public Law, Volume 46, Number 3 (New York: Columbia University Press, 1912), especially pp. 34-40.

On Fourier, see Nicholas Riasonovsky, *The Teachings of Charles Fourier* (Berkeley: University of California Press, 1969).

[9]See Locke, Second Treatise, c. 5, secs. 27-29, pp. 134-135; and see Karen Vaughn, "John Locke's Theory of Property: Problems of Interpretation," *Literature of Liberty* III (Spring 1980): 5-37.

[10]See Ogilvie, "The Right of Property in Land," especially pp. 40-41, 35, 38, and Spence, "The Real Rights of Man," pp. 5-6, both in Max L. Beer, ed., *The Pioneers of Land Reform* (London: G. Bell and Sons, 1920). Compare with Gray, *Lecture on Human Happiness,* p. 35; Cornelius Blatchly, *An Essay on Common Wealths,* 1822, quoted in Harris, *Socialist Origins,* p. 18; Thomas Skidmore, *The Rights of Man to Property!* (New York: Alexander Ming, Jr., 1829), especially pp. 101, 130; and Pierre-Joseph Proudhon, *What is Property? An Inquiry into the Principle of Right and of Government,* trans. Benjamin Tucker (New York: Humboldt Publishing Co., 1893 [1840]), p. 89.

[11]Proudhon, *Property,* pp. 65f, 82. Compare with Ogilvie, *Property in Land,* pp. 36-38, and Spence, *Real Rights of Man,* pp. 5-6.

[12]Skidmore, *Rights of Man to Property,* p. 60.

[13]Evans, "The Radical," 1834, quoted in Helene Zahler, *Eastern Workingmen and National Land Policy,* 1829-1862 (New York: Columbia University Press, 1941), p. 34n.

[14]There is a fundamental difference between several of these writers, who are often called 'Ricardian Socialists', and Ricardo himself, who taught that rent was only the *difference* between the yield of marginal and supermarginal land, traceable to the "original and indestructible powers of the soil." See David Ricardo, *The Principles of Political Economy and Taxation,* (New York: E.P. Dutton, 1927 [1817]), p. 33.

[15]Thomas Hodgskin, *Labour Defended Against the Claims of Capital, or the Unproductiveness of Capital Proved with Reference to the Present Combinations Amongst Jour-*

neymen (New York: Augustus Kelley, 1963 [1825]), p. 67. (Hodgskin's tract was a defense of trade unions written after the wave of violent strikes in 1824-1825 induced Parliament to rewrite the Combination Act of 1824.) Unappropriated land, not accumulated capital, was usually viewed as the escape valve; Evans's position, for instance, was that

> The abolition of land monopoly was the worker's only hope, since free access to the soil could end his dependence on the employer for the work that gave him bread. If he had a choice between wage-labor and self-employment in the West, the workingman could demand and get the full value of his labor.

(Zahler, *Eastern Workingmen,* pp. 34n, 35)

[16]Thompson, *The Distribution of Wealth,* 1st Edition (1824), p. 171. Cf. Smith, *WN,* Book I, c. 8, pp. 66-67.

[17]Charles Hall, *The Effects of Civilization on the People in European States* (New York: Augustus Kelley, 1965 [1805]), pp. 44, 72-73.

[18]William Heighton, "An Address Delivered Before the Mechanics and Working Classes Generally, of the City and County of Philadelphia," 1827, quoted in Harris, *Socialist Origins,* p. 84. Cf. Orestes Brownson, "The Laboring Classes," *Boston Review,* 1840, in *The Laboring Classes (1840) with Brownson's Defence of the Article on the Laboring Classes* (Delmar, N.Y.: Scholars Facsimiles and Reprints, 1979), p. 48; Hodgskin, *Labour Defended,* p. 80; and Stephen Simpson, *The Workingman's Manual, A New Theory of Political Economy . . .* (Philadelphia: Thomas L. Bonsal, 1831), especially pp. 45, 70-71.

[19]The classic Northern specimen of this type of reasoning was Orestes Brownson; see his "The Laboring Classes," p. 10; and his *Defense,* pp. 49-50. George Fitzhugh was the most noteworthy Southerner to employ this doctrine.

On the fascination of Northern intellectuals with this metaphor of capitalism as wage slavery, see Marcus Cunliffe, *Chattel Slavery and Wage Slavery: The Anglo-American Context, 1830-1860* (Athens: University of Georgia Press, 1979); and Johnathan A. Glickstein, "'Poverty Is Not Slavery': American Abolitionists and the Competitive Labor Market," in Lewis Perry and Michael Fellman, eds., *Antislavery Reconsidered* (Baton Rouge: Louisiana University Press, 1979), pp. 195-218.

[20]Louis Blanc, *Organization of Work,* 1st edition, trans. Marie Paula Dickoré (Cincinnati: University of Cincinnati Press, 1911), pp. 15, 16.

[21]Owen, *A New View of Society,* pp. 143-144.

[22]In *A New View of Society,* p. 9. See also Peter Gorb, "Robert Owen as a Businessman," *Bulletin of the Business Historical Society* XXV (September 1951): 127-148. This notion that higher wages or shorter hours of work 'paid for themselves' became a powerful argument of social reformers and trade unionists in favor of implementing minimum wages and maximum hours, through legislation or by collective bargaining. See chapter six *infra.*

[23]"Report to the County of New Lanark," in *A New View of Society,* p. 258. Yet in 1817 Owen claimed that the industrial overcapacity and unemployment plaguing Britain were the result of the collapse of an artificial, government-inspired boom caused by the Napoleanic Wars; see "Report to the Committee for the Relief of the Manufacturing Poor," in *A New View of Society,* pp. 157-158.

[24]Heighton, "An Address to the Members of Trade Societies," quoted in Harris, *Socialist Origins,* pp. 88, 89 (emphasis in original).

[25]Skidmore, *Rights of Man to Property,* p. 383.

[26]On Say's Law, see William H. Hutt, *A Rehabilitation of Say's Law* (Athens, OH: Ohio University Press, 1974); Thomas Sowell, *Say's Law: An Historical Analysis* (Princeton, NJ: Princeton University Press, 1973); and Tyler Cowen, "Say's Law and Keynesian Economics," in Richard Fink, ed., *Supply-side Economics: A Critical Appraisal* (Frederick, MD: University Publications of America, 1982). Thomas Hazlett, "The Supply-Side's Weak Side: An Austrian Critique," in id. is a corrective to some present-day misunderstandings of Say's Law.

[27]Proudhon, *Property,* pp. 188, 189 (emphasis in original).

[28]Gray, *Lecture on Human Happiness,* pp. 64, 62 (emphasis in original); see also pp. 59-72 generally. See also chapter four *infra.*

[29]Cole, *History of Socialist Thought,* Volume I, p. 117. The Owenite influence on the English trade union movement is discussed by John Saville, "J.E. Smith and the Owenite Movement, 1833-1834," in Pollard, *Robert Owen: Prophet of the Poor,* pp. 115-144.

[30]Thompson, *Labour Rewarded,* pp. 78, 79.

[31]Ibid., pp. 80-81.

[32]Ibid., p. 81-83 (emphasis in original). Thompson's use of the word "justice," in the context of his general discussion, does not seem to be intended as sarcastic or ironic.

[33]Hodgskin, *Travels in the North of Germany,* 1820, quoted in Lowenthal, *Ricardian Socialists,* p. 66. In 1827, however, Hodgskin taught his workingman audiences at the London Mechanics Institute the strange notion that strikes could raise wages because *capital* was immobile:

> . . . except for the acquired and useful abilities of the labourers of a society, and what they can carry with them . . . no part of the capital of a country can be either driven or sent away . . . To talk of sending away roads, bridges, canals, and cultivated fields is a striking absurdity . . .

(*Lectures on Popular Political Economy* (New York: Augustus M. Kelley, 1966 [1827]), p. 253). He even intimated that it might not be a bad thing if unions drove capitalists away, since they would have to leave their capital behind! (Hodgskin, *Labour Defended,* pp. 91-92.) Fixed capital depreciates and must be renewed or replaced; and gradual disinvestment (such as failure to replace worn-out equipment) or failure to invest in new enterprise is what economists actually mean when they talk of strikes driving capital away.

[34]Bray, *Labour's Wrongs,* pp. 100-101.

[35]Pierre-Joseph Proudhon, *General Idea of the Revolution in the 19th Century,* trans. John Beverly Robinson (London: Freedom Press, 1923 [1851]), pp. 79, 83, and see pp. 97-98. Proudhon's quoted statement referred to socialism, not unionism, but his comments about trade unions are quite in this spirit; see Pierre-Joseph Proudhon, *Selected Writings,* trans. Elizabeth Fraser (London: Macmillan, 1969), pp. 181-183. It is unclear whether membership in Louis Blanc's "ateliers sociaux" was to be compulsory; see Leo Loubère, *Louis Blanc: His Life and His Contribution to the Rise of French Jacobin-Socialism* (Evanston, IL: Northwestern University Press, 1961), p. 36.

[36]Thomas Skidmore, for instance, fearlessly maintained that if on Monday all property was distributed equally, it should be redistributed again on Tuesday if a new landless inhabitant appeared; see Skidmore, *Rights of Man to Property,* p. 128, and pp. 125-144 *passim.* See also Ogilvie, *Right of Property in Land,* pp. 92-95; Spence, *Real Rights of Man,* pp. 10-11; and Hall, *Effects of Civilization,* pp. 277-282.

George Henry Evans's land reform ideas did not include free alienation of land held in fee simple; in this sense, he differed profoundly from land law reformers such as Thomas Hart Benton, and from the actual Homestead legislation passed in 1862; see Zahler, *Eastern Workingmen,* pp. 34-35.

[37]See Menger, *Right to the Whole Produce of Labour,* pp. 16-20; and see Frédéric Bastiat's discussion of Victor Considérant's *Theory of the Right to Property and the Right to Work,* in Bastiat, "Property and Plunder," 1848, in *Selected Essays on Political Economy,* trans. Seymour Cain (Irvington-on-Hudson, N.Y.: Foundation for Economic Education, 1964), pp. 191-192, for an assessment of the 'natural-right-to-a-job' principle.

[38]A. L. Morton, *The Life and Ideas of Robert Owen* (London: Lawrence and Wishart, 1962), p. 51.

[39]Robert H. Murray, *Studies in English Social and Political Thinkers of the 19th Century* (Cambridge: W. Heffer & Sons, 1929), Volume I, p. 155.

[40]J. E. Smith, "The Crisis," quoted in Raymond W. Postgate, *The Bolshevik Theory* (London: Grant Richards, 1920) p. 132; and see also chapter seven *infra.*

[41]Menger, *Right to the Whole Produce of Labour,* pp. 120-121. See also Richard Ely, *French*

and German Socialism in Modern Times (New York: Harper and Brothers, 1883), pp. 119-120; and Loubère, *Louis Blanc,* especially pp. 36-39. According to Loubère, Blanc's legislature would still base representation on population and territory, and thus his utopia would not be a true syndicalist, or corporative, state.

[42]Proudhon, *General Idea,* pp. 215-216 (emphasis added).

[43]Smith, *WN,* Book I, c. 6, p. 47, c. 13, p. 64.

[44]Thompson, *Distribution of Wealth,* 1824, p. 7. Cf. Ogilvie, *Right of Property in Land,* p. 69; and Robert Owen, "Report to the County of New Lanark," in *A New View of Society,* p. 250. For the Americans, see Neufeld, "Realms of Thought," pp. 5-43.

[45]Proudhon, *Property,* pp. 112, 113 (emphasis in original); and see the fascinating discussion on pp. 113 *et seq.* Cf. Gray, *Lecture on Human Happiness,* p. 38.

[46]Smith, *WN,* Book I, c. 6, p. 47.

[47]Bray, *Labour's Wrongs,* pp. 44, 48.

[48]Gray, *Lecture on Human Happiness,* p. 39 (emphasis in original).

[49]Owen, "Report to County of New Lanark," in *A New View of Society,* p. 250.

[50]See Bailie, *Josiah Warren,* pp. 9-24, 42-49; and Martin, *Men Against the State,* pp. 16-26.

[51]See Morton, *Life and Ideas of Robert Owen,* p. 48; Gide, *History of Economic Doctrines,* pp. 251-252; and Murray, *English Social and Political Thinkers,* Volume I, pp. 153-154.

[52]John Stuart Mill, *Chapters on Socialism,* 1879, in J. M. Robson, ed., *The Collected Works of John Stuart Mill* (Toronto: University of Toronto Press, 1967), Volume V, p. 729.

[53]Edwin Cannan, *A Review of Economic Theory* (London: P. S. King, 1929), p. 340 (emphasis added).

[54]Owen's apparent claim that higher wages 'pay for themselves' through greater productivity and output is vastly exaggerated; see the discussion in chapter six, *infra.*

[55]There is an excellent historical discussion of the different positions held by economists in Alexander Gourvitch, *Survey of Economic Theory on Technological Change and Employment* (New York: Augustus Kelley, 1966 [1940]), pp. 20-79.

Jean-Baptiste Say's famous arguments are in J. B. Say, *A Treatise on Political Economy,* trans. C. R. Prinsep (New York: Augustus Kelley, 1964 [1821, 1803]), Book I, Chapter VII, pp. 86-90, and J. B. Say, *Letters to Mr. Malthus,* trans. John Richter (New York: Augustus Kelley, 1964 [1821]), Letters IV, V, pp. 62-74.

McCulloch's position, and his critique of Malthus and Ricardo, is explained in his *The Principles of Political Economy,* 4th revised edition (London: Longman, Brown, Green and Longmans, 1849 [1825]), pp. 197-226, 600-602; see also O'Brien, *McCulloch,* pp. 302-306.

The two exceptions to the consensus were Malthus, and more important, Ricardo. Ricardo's famous change of mind was based on some highly restrictive assumptions about diminishing returns in the agricultural sector of the economy forcing an increase in wage rates elsewhere, which in turn forces employers to convert circulating capital to fixed capital, which in turn results in a less-than-proportionate increase in the demand for labor (not a decrease in the demand for labor). The analysis is short-run. See Samuel Hollander, "The Development of Ricardo's Position on Machinery," *History of Political Economy* III (1971): 105-135; Shlomo Maital and Patricia Haswell, "Why Did Ricardo (Not) Change His Mind?" On Machinery and Money," *Economica* XLIV (November 1977): 359-368; Mark Blaug, *Ricardian Economics: A Historical Study* (New Haven: Yale University Press, 1958), pp. 64-79; and Oswald St. Clair, *A Key to Ricardo* (London: Routledge and Kegan Paul, 1957), pp. 172-259, for a discussion of Malthus's and Ricardo's heresies on this issue.

[56]McCulloch, *Principles,* p. 205; cf. Owen, "Report to the Committee of the Manufacturing Poor," 1817, in *A New View of Society,* p. 156.

[57]McCulloch, *Principles,* p. 206; cf. Say, *Letters to Malthus,* pp. 68-69.

[58]See William H. Hutt, *The Strike Threat System: The Economic Consequences of Collective Bargaining* (New Rochelle, N.Y.: Arlington House, 1973), pp. 24-25. Hutt was among several scholars in this century who challenged the notion popularized in the Anglo-American world

by the Webbs and the Hammonds about working class immiseration in England during the early decades of the 19th century. See William H. Hutt, "The Factory System of the Early Nineteenth Century," *Economica*, 1926, in F. A. Hayek, ed., *Capitalism and the Historians* (Chicago: University of Chicago Press, 1954); and William H. Hutt, "The Poor Who Were With Us," *Encounter* XXXIX (November 1972): 84-90. There is an extensive literature on this issue; see the essays in Arthur Seldon, ed., *The Long Debate on Poverty: Eight Essays on Industrialism and the 'Condition of England'* (London: Institute of Economic Affairs, 1972), and the useful collection in Philip A. M. Taylor, ed., *The Industrial Revolution: Triumph or Disaster?* (Boston: D.C. Heath, 1958). One of this century's leading socialist scholars has essentially agreed that living standards increased during the development of the factory system under capitalism; see G. D. H. Cole, *The Meaning of Marxism* (Ann Arbor, Michigan: University of Michigan Press, 1964 [1948]), pp. 84-88.

[59]The wage rates of common labor in America may have risen as well, albeit modestly and unevenly, from 1790-1860; see Stanley Lebergott, *Manpower in Economic Growth: The American Record Since 1800* (New York: McGraw Hill, 1964), especially pp. 149-150.

[60]John Herman Randall, Jr., *The Problem of Group Responsibility to Society: An Interpretation of the History of American Labor* (New York: Arno Press, 1969 [1922]), p. 60 (emphasis added); and see pp. 54-75 generally.

[61]Edward Pessen, *Most Uncommon Jacksonians: The Radical Leaders of the Early Labor Movement* (Albany: State University of New York Press, 1967), p. 167.

One cannot take the anti-monopoly sentiments of all those sympathetic to the antebellum organized labor movement without a large grain of salt. Take the case of Frederic Robinson, a politician. In his "An Oration Delivered Before the Trades' Union of Boston and Vicinity, July 4, 1834," he denounced as themselves monopolists those (recipients of special government privileges, monopoly franchises, and the like) who were denouncing unions as monopolies:

> Who are they who complain of trades unions? Are they not those whose combinations cover the land and who have even contrived to invest some of their combinations with the sanctity of law? Are they not those who are the owners of all kinds of monopolies, who pass their lives in perpetual caucuses, on 'change [the stock exchange], in halls connected with banks, composing insurance companies, manufacturing companies, turnpike, bridge, canal, railroad, and all other legalized combinations?

There was some truth in what Robinson said, because some of the enterprises he mentioned were government monopolies (and general incorporation acts had yet to be passed by the legislatures of the several states). Yet he went on to explain that "when the market is but scantily supplied, the producer receives a more adequate return for his labor, and the nonproducer is obliged to part with a larger portion of his funds," and "[i]n such times things tend to equality. . . . How important then are trades unions, not for the purpose of controlling the price of labor while the market is glutted, for this is impossible," but "for the purpose of seeing that no more is produced than barely enough to supply the demand." (quoted in Joseph Blau, *Social Theories of Jacksonian Democracy* (New York: The Liberal Arts Press, 1954), pp. 330, 338, 339-340)

[62]The importance of utopian, 'associationist' ideals as against the AFL's acceptance of the 'permanent wage earner' is discussed in Gerald Grob, *Workers and Utopia: A Study of the Ideological Conflict in the American Labor Movement, 1865-1900*, Northwestern University Studies in History, Number 11 (Evanston: Northwestern University Press, 1961); see also Neufeld, "Realms of Thought"; Pessen, *Most Uncommon Jacksonians*; and Hugins, *Jacksonian Democracy*, especially pp. 131-202 *passim*.

Prior to the Civil War, champions of organized labor were in favor of hard (specie) money and banks, and against inflation, presumably on the grounds that the cheap credit made available by paper money favored the 'monopolists'. After the Civil War the position was reversed; and influenced by such men as Edward Kellogg (whose monetary ideas were rather similar to those of Proudhon), spokesmen for the organized labor movement touted cheap credit and paper money as the means to restore "the independence of the working class" by permitting anyone to establish his own business, or unions to do so collectively. (Grob, *Workers and Utopia,* p. 8). On Kellogg, see Chester McArthur Destler, *American Radicalism, 1865-1901: Essays and Documents* (New York: Octagon Books, 1965 [1946]), pp. 9, 50-77; and Edward Kellogg, *A New Monetary System* (New York: U.S. Book Company, 1861 [A revised edition of *Labor and Other Capital,* 1849]), especially pp. xi-xxiv.

[63]Decades before the advent of marginalism, some economists contended that utility, not labor, was the source of value. "It is not," as Richard Whately said in 1834, "that pearls fetch a high price because men have dived for them; but on the contrary, men dive for them because they fetch a high price." Or as Nassau Senior argued a few years later, while it is true that, given utility and a scarce labor supply, a commodity will fetch a higher price when more labor is required to produce it, "any other cause limiting supply is just as efficient a cause of value in an article as the necessity of labour to its production." (Both quoted in Edwin Cannan, *A Review of Economic Theory* (London: P. S. King, 1929), pp. 186-187.)

[64]See John Humphrey Noyes, *History of American Socialisms* (New York: Dover, 1961 [1870]), p. 97.

[65]Bray, *Labour's Wrongs,* p. 159. The principle of making work more attractive as a way of getting around the incentive problems of equal rewards was pioneered by Fourier and Owen, but developed in greater detail by state socialists; see chapter four *infra.*

[66]Bray, *Labour's Wrongs,* p. 159.

[67]See Mises, *Socialism,* pp. 154-158 on this and other related issues.

[68]Thompson, *Labour Rewarded,* p. 37.

[69]Thompson, *Distribution of Wealth,* 1st edition, quoted in Gray, *Socialist Tradition,* p. 272.

[70]Hodgskin, *Labour Defended,* pp. 89, 83 (emphasis added).

[71]See Pierre-Joseph Proudhon, *The System of Economical Contradictions, or the Philosophy of Misery,* trans. Benjamin Tucker (Boston: Benjamin R. Tucker, 1888 [1846]), p. 123; but see also Lu, *Political Theory of Proudhon,* pp. 59-60, 99n; and see the selection from *On the Political Capacity of the Working Classes,* 1865, in Fraser, ed., *Selected Writings,* pp. 63-68.

[72]Simpson, *Workingman's Manual,* pp. 27-28 (emphasis in original). On Simpson, see Edward Pessen, "The Ideology of Stephen Simpson, Upperclass Champion of the Early Philadelphia Workingmen's Movement," *Pennsylvania History* XXII (October 1955): 328-340.

[73]See the classic statement in Menger, *Right to the Whole Produce of Labour,* p. 124.

Chapter Four

[1]Mises, *Socialism,* p. 211 (emphasis added).

[2]Christian Socialists' programme typically amounted to one form or another of corporativism, however, and discussion of their views is therefore deferred: see chapter five *infra.*

[3]Gray, *Socialist Tradition,* p. 157. On Saint-Simon, in addition to the general works on socialism cited in chapter three, note 4 *supra,* see Frank E. Manuel, *The New World of Henri Saint-Simon* (Cambridge, MA: Harvard University Press, 1956); and Frank E. Manuel, *The Prophets of Paris* (Cambridge, MA: Harvard University Press, 1962).

[4]"Vivre pour autrui," or "live for others"; see Auguste Comte, *The Catechism of Positive Religion,* trans. Richard Congreve (London: John W. Chapman, 1858 [1853]), p. 313. On

Comte, see Edward Caird, *The Social Philosophy and Religion of Comte* (Glasgow, Scotland: James Maclehose, 1885); Theodora Bosanquet, "Auguste Comte and the Positive Philosophers," in F. J. C. Hearnshaw, ed., *Social and Political Ideas of Some Representative Thinkers of the Age of Reaction and Reconstruction, 1815-1865* (London: Dawson, 1967 [1932]), pp. 134-147; Gertrude Lenzer, Introduction to *Auguste Comte and Positivism: The Essential Writings* (New York: Harper and Row, 1975); and Ronald Fletcher, Introduction to *The Crisis of Industrial Civilization: The Early Days of Auguste Comte* (London: Heinemann Educational Books, 1974).

⁵On the Saint-Simonians, see Georg Iggers, *Cult of Authority: The Political Philosophy of the Saint-Simonians, A Chapter in the Intellectual History of Totalitarianism* (The Hague: Martinus Nijhoff, 1958); Georg Iggers, ed. and trans., *The Doctrine of Saint-Simon: An Exposition, First Year, 1828-1829* (Boston: Beacon Press, 1958); Edward S. Mason, "Saint-Simonism and the Rationalisation of Industry," *Quarterly Journal of Economics* XLV (August 1931): 640-683; and Hayek, *Counter-Revolution of Science*, pp. 143-167.

⁶Though Kant was a political liberal, his metaethical philosophy was a repudiation of everything on which an individualist social order must ultimately rest. Arguing that "empirical principles are not at all suited to serve as the basis of moral laws," Kant maintained that "the principle of one's own happiness is the most objectionable of all" because it "supports morality with incentives which undermine it and destroy all its sublimity." (Immanuel Kant, *Foundations of the Metaphysics of Morals*, trans. L. W. Beck, ed. Robert Paul Wolff (Indianapolis, Indiana: Bobbs-Merrill, 1969), p. 69) Elsewhere he spoke of self-love as "the source of an incalculably great antagonism to morality," "the very source of evil." (*Religion within the Limits of Reason Alone,* as quoted in Leonard Peikoff, "Kant and Self-Sacrifice," *The Objectivist* X (September 1971), p. 11; and see Leonard Peikoff, *The Ominous Parallels: The End of Freedom in America* (New York: Stein and Day, 1982), pp 71-84.

Johann Gottlieb Fichte, Kant's student and his most important early follower, sensed the incompatibility of capitalism and individual rights with the master's ethics of duty and self-sacrifice, and came out in favor of a socialistic welfare state in a seminal volume of 1800, *Der geschlossene Handelsstaat* (The Closed Commercial State). See Helmuth G. Engelbrecht, *Johann Gottlieb Fichte* (New York: Columbia University Press, 1933); Rohan D. Butler, *The Roots of National Socialism, 1783-1933* (New York: E. P. Dutton, 1942), pp. 35-47; and the other general works on socialist thought previously cited in chapter three, note 4 *supra*.

Hegel's well known worship of the state needs no introduction; see Walter Stace, *The Philosophy of Hegel: A Systematic Exposition* (New York: Dover, 1955), pp. 404-438; Karl Popper, *The Open Society and Its Enemies*, 5th revised edition (Princeton: Princeton University Press, 1966), Volume II, pp. 27-80; A. D. Lindsay, "Hegel the German Idealist," in *Political Ideas of the Age of Reaction and Reconstruction*, pp. 52-67; and Sidney Hook, *From Hegel to Marx: Studies in the Intellectual Development of Karl Marx* (New York: The Humanities Press, 1950) pp. 41-47. The connection between Hegel and Comte is discussed in Hayek, *Counter-Revolution of Science*, pp. 191-206. To be sure, Hegel, like Marx, opposed Kant's "abstract ethical idealism"—because it was too individualistic; see Hook, *op. cit.,* pp. 47-53.

Karl Rodbertus was a lawyer, politician, and country squire. A writer of far less philosophical stature than the better known Fichte, Hegel, or Marx, Rodbertus was nevertheless a very influential expositor of (nonrevolutionary, socially conservative) socialist ideas. Directly inspired by French socialists and syndicalists, Rodbertus in turn was Ferdinand Lassalle's economics teacher. He was also the patron saint of the late 19th century *Kathedersozialisten,* a group of interventionist professors who instilled a passion for social and economic reform in several important American graduate students who later became intellectual leaders of American Progressivism (see chapter six *infra*) See E. C. K. Gonner, *Social Philosophy of Rodbertus* (New York: Macmillan, 1899); Herbert Osgood, "Scientific Socialism: Rodbertus,"

Political Science Quarterly I (December 1886): 560-594; and W. H. Dawson, *German Socialism and Ferdinand Lassalle,* 2d edition (London: Swann Sonnenschein, 1899), pp. 61-90.

Ferdinand Lassalle was the founder of Germany's organized workingclass political movement, and was influenced intellectually primarily by Fichte, Rodbertus, Marx, and Louis Blanc. On Lassalle, see David Footman, *The Primrose Path: A Life of Ferdinand Lassalle* (London: Cresset Press, 1946); and George Brandes, *Ferdinand Lassalle* (Westport, CT: Greenwood Press, 1970 [1911]).

The following secondary works proved particularly useful on Marx's ideas for the purposes of this study; G. D. H. Cole, *The Meaning of Marxism* (Ann Arbor, Michigan: University of Michigan Press, 1964 [1948]); Thomas Sowell, "Marx's Increasing Misery Doctrine," *American Economic Review* L (March 1960): 111-119; Thomas Sowell, "Marxian Value Reconsidered," *Economica* XXX (August 1963): 297-308; Thomas Sowell, "Marx's *Capital* after One Hundred Years," *Canadian Journal of Economics and Political Science* XXXIII (February 1967): 50-74; Phillip Wicksteed, "*Das Kapital:* A Criticism," *To-Day,* n.s., II (October 1884): 388-409; T. W. Hutchison, "Friedrich Engels and Marxist Economic Theory," *Journal of Political Economy* LXXXVI (April 1978): 303-319; and W. O. Henderson, *The Life of Friedrich Engels* (London: Frank Cass, 1976).

⁷On Hobson, see Erwin E. Nemmers, *Hobson and Underconsumption* (Amsterdam: North Holland Press, 1956); E. F. M. Durbin, *Purchasing Power and Trade Depression: A Critique of Underconsumption Theories,* revised edition (London: Johnathan Cape, 1934 [1933]); Paul T. Homan, *Contemporary Economic Thought* (New York: Harper Brothers, 1928), pp. 283-374; and T. W. Hutchison, *A Review of Economic Doctrines, 1870-1929* (Oxford: Clarendon Press, 1953), pp. 118-129. Hobson is perhaps better known as the author of *Imperialism* (1902), the essential source used by Lenin for his *Imperialism: The Highest Stage of Capitalism* (1916).

⁸On American socialism generally, the following works proved useful for the purposes of this study; Howard Quint, *The Forging of American Socialism* (Columbia: University of South Carolina Press, 1953); Donald Egbert and Stow Persons, eds., *Socialism and American Life,* 3 vols. (Princeton: Princeton University Press, 1952); David Shannon, *The Socialist Party in America* (New York: Macmillan, 1955); Ira Kipnis, *The American Socialist Movement, 1897-1912* (New York: Columbia University Press, 1952); John H. M. Laslett, *Labor and the Left: A Study of Socialist and Radical Influences on the Labor Movement, 1881-1924* (New York: Basic Books, 1970), and Lewis Feuer, "American Travelers to the Soviet Union: The Formation of a Component of New Deal Ideology, 1917-1932," *American Quarterly* XIV (Summer 1962): 119-149. See chapter six, *infra,* for a discussion of the American Christian Socialists.

⁹Quint, *Forging of American Socialism,* p. 28. On Gronlund, see Solomon Gemorah, "Laurence Gronlund—Utopian or Reformer?" *Science and Society* XXXIII (Fall-Winter 1969): 446-458.

¹⁰John Dewey, "A Great American Prophet," *Common Sense,* 1934, quoted in Elizabeth Sadler, "One Book's Influence: Edward Bellamy's *Looking Backward,*" *New England Quarterly* XVII (December 1944), p. 546. Dewey here was discussing the *future* prospects of Bellamy's books, in light of renewed interest in his work in the early 1930s. I believe Dewey's statement applies even better retrospectively. On Bellamy, see Arthur E. Morgan, *Edward Bellamy* (New York: Columbia University Press, 1944); Everett W. MacNair, *Edward Bellamy and the Nationalist Movement, 1889-1894* (Milwaukee: Fitzgerald Company, 1957); Sylvia Bowman, *The Year 2000: A Critical Biography of Edward Bellamy* (New York: Bookman Associates, 1958); Arthur E. Morgan, *The Philosophy of Edward Bellamy* (New York: King's Crown Press, 1945); John Hope Franklin, "Edward Bellamy and Nationalism," *New England Quarterly* XI (December 1938): 739-772; Arthur E. Morgan, *Plagiarism in Utopia: A Study of the Utopian Tradition with Special Reference to Edward Bellamy's Looking Backward*

(Yellow Springs, OH: A. Morgan, 1944); and Sylvia Bowman, et al., *Edward Bellamy Abroad: An American Prophet's Influence* (New York: Twayne Publishers, 1967).

[11]While the I.W.W. was a syndicalist organization, De Leon was a socialist. In his most famous speech, "The Socialist Reconstruction of Society," 1905, *(The Preamble to the Industrial Workers of the World* (New York: New York Labor News, 1915), p. 38), De Leon provides us with a blueprint for his new state:

> [In] [t]he central administrative organ of the Socialist Republic . . . [the] constituent bodies must be exclusively industrial . . . As the slough shed by the serpent that immediately reappears in its new skin, the political State will have been shed, and society will simultaneously appear in its new administrative garb. The mining, the railroad, the textile, the building industries, . . . regardless of former political boundaries, will be the constituencies of that new central authority . . . Where the General Executive Board of the Industrial Workers of the World will sit, there will be the nation's capital.

That seems to me to imply that the General Executive Board of the I.W.W. will run things, much like a one-party dictatorship runs the Soviet system. The replacement of popular or territorial representation with representation based on economic function also makes the scheme resemble syndicalism, albeit not anarcho-syndicalism.

On De Leon, see L. Glen Seratan, *Daniel De Leon: The Odyssey of an American Marxist* (Cambridge: Harvard University Press, 1979); Don K. McKee, "Daniel de Leon: A Reappraisal," *Labor History* I (Fall 1960): 264-297; and James D. Young, "Daniel de Leon and Anglo-American Socialism," *Labor History* XVII (Summer 1976): 329-350.

[12]Iggers, *Doctrine of Saint Simon*, p. 83, and see also p. 82. Compare with the later, if better-known, statement by Karl Marx, "Wage Labor and Capital," 1849, in *Wage-Labour and Capital and Value, Price and Profit* (New York: International Publishers, 1976), p. 20 (emphasis in original):

> The worker leaves the capitalist, to whom he has sold himself, as often as he sees fit, and the capitalist discharges him as often as he sees fit, as soon as he no longer gets any use, or not the required use, of him. But the worker, whose only source of income is the sale of his labour power, cannot leave the *whole class of buyers, i.e. the capitalist class,* unless he gives up his existence. He does not belong to this or that capitalist, but to the *capitalist class.*

[13]Sidney Webb, "The Difficulties of Individualism," 1891, in Sidney and Beatrice Webb, *Problems of Modern Industry* (London: Longmans, Green, & Co., 1898), pp. 248, 244.

[14]*L'Organisateur,* 1830, as quoted in translation by Iggers, *Cult of Authority,* pp. 140, 141 (emphasis in original). Compare with the (again) later but better-known passage in Karl Marx, *Das Kapital,* Volume I, [1867], quoted in Robert Freedman, ed., *Marx on Economics* (New York: Harcourt, Brace, and World, 1961), pp. 192, 193-194:

> We have seen that the growing accumulation of capital imples its growing concentration. . . . That which is now to be expropriated is no longer the labourer working for himself, but the capitalist exploiting many labourers. This expropriation is accomplished by the action of the immanent laws of capitalistic production itself, by the centralisation of capital. One capitalist always kills many. . . . Along with the constantly diminishing number of the magnates of capital, who usurp and monopolise all advantages of this process of transformation, grows the mass of misery, oppression, slavery, degradation, exploitation; . . . Centralisation of the means of production and socialisation of labour reach a point where they become incompatible with their capitalist integument. This integument is burst asunder. The knell of capitalist private property sounds. The expropriators are expropriated.

and with Engels, *Conditions of the Working Class,* 1844, in *Collected Works of Marx and Engels* (New York: International Publishers, 1975) Volume IV, p. 325; and Marx/Engels, *Manifesto of the Communist Party,* 1848, Volume VI, pp. 491 *et seq.*

[15]Rodbertus's theory of the trade cycle appeared in his Second Social Letter to Von Kirchman, 1850, and has been translated by Julia Franklin in Karl Rodbertus, *Overproduction and Crises* (New York: Charles Scribner's Sons, 1898).

[16]"Zur Beleuchtung der Socialen Frage," ii, 1885, quoted in Gonner, *Rodbertus,* p. 64 (emphasis added).

[17]Ferdinand Lassalle, *Open Letter to the National Labor Association of Germany* (Offenes Antwort Schreiben), 1863, trans. John Ehmann and Fred Bader (Cincinnati: National Executive Committee of the Socialist Labor Party, n.d.), p. 14; and see pp. 17-18.

[18]Marx, "Wage Labor and Capital," pp. 26, 27.

[19]Rodbertus, *Overproduction and Crises,* p. 71.

[20]Ibid., pp. 71-72.

[21]Marx, "Wage Labor and Capital," pp. 36, 37 (emphasis in original). Nevertheless, Marx did not subscribe to the underconsumptionist theory of the trade cycle, sticking to the more basic objection that production under capitalism was not centrally planned, and thus bound to become unbalanced. See Sowell, "Marx's *Capital,*" pp. 56-63, and "Marxian Value Reconsidered," pp. 304-308.

[22]Gonner, *Rodbertus,* p. 87.

[23]Ibid., pp. 87, 89.

[24]Rodbertus, *Overproduction and Crises,* p. 129; Rodbertus, *Das Kapital,* 1884, quoted in Gide and Rist, *History of Economic Doctrines,* p. 421n. Cf. Gray, *Lecture on Human Happiness,* p. 62: "It never enters into the calculations of manufacturers how much cloth would be required to supply the wants of mankind . . . All they ask, all they require to know, is *how much they can dispose of at a profit."* (emphasis in original); and Marx, *Kapital,* Volume III, quoted in Freedman, *Marx on Economics,* pp. 197-198:

> The capitalist mode of production . . . comes to a standstill at a point determined by the production and realisation of profit, not by the satisfaction of social needs.

[25]Hobson's theories about the trade cycle changed over time, and are at any rate scattered throughout his many books and articles. The capsule summary presented here takes up only that interpretation of underconsumption he espoused that was hospitable to union-oriented versions of industrial democracy. See Nemmers, *Hobson and Underconsumption,* pp. 26-32, 60-110.

[26]See, for instance, the testimony of Robert F. Wagner in the Congressional Record, 7 June 1933, page 5256, as quoted in Simon Whitney, *Trade Associations and Industrial Control: A Critique of the NIRA* (New York: Central Book Company, 1934), p. 17 n.1:

> In my opinion the depression arose in large part from the failure to coordinate production and consumption. During the years 1922-1929 corporate earnings rose very much faster than wage rates. This led to an overexpansion in productive equipment, particularly machinery and plant facilities. The great mass of consumers did not receive enough pay to take the goods off the market.

For Franklin Delano Roosevelt's views, see ibid., pp. 16-17; and Daniel Fusfeld, *Economic Thought of FDR and the Origins of the New Deal* (New York: Columbia University Press, 1956), pp. 228, 245, 298 n. 50.

[27]See Edward Bellamy, *Equality* (New York: D. Appleton, 1897), pp. 195-203 *et passim.;* and see Bowman, *Bellamy Abroad,* pp. 71, 138, 166-167, 245, 270-271, 431.

[28]Howard Kershner, "The Hoax That Deceived Millions," in *Dividing the Wealth: Are You Getting Your Share?* (Old Greenwich, CT: Devin Adair, 1971) has some interesting observations about the popularity of De Leon's speech.

[29]De Leon, "Socialist Reconstruction," pp. 11, 4. See also Jack London's apocalyptic novel of 1907, *The Iron Heel* (Westport, CT: Lawrence Hill, 1980), especially chapter nine, "The Mathematics of a Dream."

[30]See, for instance, Auguste Comte, *Cours de Philosophie Positive,* 1830-1842, quoted in Caird, *Social Philosophy of Comte,* p. 61:

> Man is a mere abstraction, and there is nothing real but humanity, regarded intellectually, and yet more morally . . . man as an individual, . . . cannot properly be said to exist save in the too abstract brain of modern metaphysicians . . . individuals should be regarded not as so many distinct beings, but as organs of the One Great Being (Humanity).

Or see Henri de Saint-Simon, *De la physiologie appliqué à L'amélioration des Institutions Sociales,* quoted in Manuel, *New World of Saint-Simon,* p. 321:

> Society is not a simple agglomeration of living beings whose independent actions . . . had no cause but arbitrary individual wills, nor any result but accidents ephemeral or trivial. On the contrary, society is above all a veritable organic machine whose every part contributes in different manner to the movement of the whole.

Or see Laurence Gronlund, *The Co-operative Commonwealth* (Boston: Lee & Shepard, 1884), p. 81 (emphasis in original):

> . . . the State is a living Organism, differing from other organisms in no essential respect. This is not to be understood in a simply metaphorical sense; it is not that the State merely resembles an organism, but that it, including with the people the land and all that the land produces, literally *is an organism,* personal and territorial. . . . It follows that the relation of the State, the body politic, to us, its citizens, is *actually* that of a tree to its cells, and *not* that of a heap of sand to its grains, to which it is entirely indifferent how many other grains of sand are scattered and trodden under foot.

Or see Moses Hess, *About the Socialist Movement in Germany,* quoted in Lichtheim, *Origins of Socialism,* p. 182 (emphasis in original):

> The being of man . . . is social, the cooperation of the various individuals toward a common aim . . . the true doctrine of man, the true humanism, is the theory of human sociability. *That is to say, anthropology is socialism.*

Compare Hess with his student, Karl Marx, *Economic and Social Manuscripts,* 1844, translated by T. B. Bottomore, quoted in Erich Fromm, *Marx's Concept of Man* (New York: Frederic Ungar, 1961), p. 129 (emphasis in original):

> . . . Activity and mind are social in their content as well as in their *origin;* they are *social* activity and *social* mind. The *human* significance of nature only exists for *social* man, because only in this case is nature a *bond* with other men, the basis of his existence for others and of their existence for him.

Hobson's contempt for individualism and commitment to organic collectivism are clearly enunciated in his essay, "Rich Man's Anarchism," *The Humanitarian: A Monthly Review of Sociological Science,* new series, XII (June 1898): 390-397. For a rebuttal, see Auberon Herbert, "Lost in the Region of Phrases," ibid., (May 1899), reprinted in Auberon Herbert, *The Right and Wrong of Compulsion by the State, and Other Essays,* ed. Erick Mack (Indianapolis, IN: Liberty Press, 1978).

[31]Gonner, *Rodbertus,* p. 73.

[32]Bellamy, *Equality,* pp. 88-89; and see his *Looking Backward, 2000-1887* (New York: Modern Library, 1951 [1887]), pp. 107-108. Cf. Comte, *Catechism,* pp. 332-333.

[33]Comte, *Catechism* pp. 331, 332, 313 (emphasis in original). Cf. J. G. Fichte, *Characteristics of the Present Age,* 4th edition, trans. William Smith (London: Trubner, 1889 [1804-1805]), pp. 36-37 (emphasis in original):

... the Life according to Reason consists herein,—that the Individual forget himself in the Race, place his own life in the Life of the Race and dedicate it thereto;—the Life opposed to Reason, on the contrary, consists in this,— that the Individual think of nothing but himself, love nothing but himself and in relation to himself, and set his whole existence in his own personal well-being alone . . . there is but one Virtue,—to forget one's own personality;—and but One Vice,—to make self the object of our thoughts.

These words are to be understood strictly as we have spoken them, in their most rigorous sense. The mitigation of our principle which might be attempted here, namely—that it is only our duty not to think of ourselves *exclusively,* but *also* upon others . . . is inconsequential, and seeks to disguise itself, not having altogether triumphed over shame. He who thinks *at all* of his own person and personal gratification, and desires any kind of life or being, or any joy of life, except *in* the Race and *for* the Race, with whatever vesture of good deeds he may seek to hide his deformity, is nevertheless, at bottom, only a mean, base, and therefore unhappy man.

Or see Louis Blanc, *Histoire de la Revolution de 1848,* quoted in Ely, *French and German Socialism,* p. 121:

Man has received of nature certain faculties . . . But these have by no means been given him in order that he should exercise them solitarily; they are but the supreme indication of that which each one owes to . . . society . . . If you are twice as strong as your neighbor it is a proof that nature has destined you to bear a double burden. . . . Weakness is the creditor of strength; ignorance of learning.

Or see William Godwin, *Political Justice,* 1793, quoted in Gray, *Socialist Tradition,* p. 120:

Not a talent do we possess, not a moment of time, not a shilling of property, for which we are not responsible at the tribunal of the public, which we are not obliged to pay into the general bank of common advantage.

[34]Gronlund, *Cooperative Commonwealth,* pp. 83, 84, 85. Cf. Rodbertus, *Zur Beleuchtung Der Sociale Frage,* quoted in Gonner, *Rodbertus,* pp. 73-74:

... land, capital, and the product of labour, can never belong to the labourer, just as they have never belonged to him since labour first became the subject of division. . . . if society is to attain sound conceptions as regards property, the labourer must never be the owner of land and capital, or even of the product of his own labour. This holds good for all societies organized on the basis of the division of labour, and division of labour . . . is the indispensable foundation of progress and culture.

For the views of Marx see, for instance, his *Critique of the Gotha Program* (New York: International Publishers, 1966) pp. 6-11.

[35]Iggers, *Doctrine of Saint Simon,* pp. 95, 98. Cf. Gronlund, *Cooperative Commonwealth,* pp. 42-44, 106 *et seq.*

[36]See, for instance, Gronlund, *Cooperative Commonwealth,* pp. 27-28, 51.

[37]See ibid., p. 153; and see Menger, *Right to the Whole Produce of Labour,* pp. 5-7, 11-28. For an interesting discussion of the travails the British labor unions faced during World War II, when the English economy was virtually socialized, see Sidney Rolfe, "Trade Unions and Central Planning," in Wayne Leeman, *Capitalism, Market Socialism, and Central Planning: Readings in Comparative Economic Systems* (Boston: Houghton Mifflin, 1963), pp. 224-237.

[38]John Spargo, *Social Democracy Explained* (New York: Harper Brothers, 1916), pp. 276-277; see his *Syndicalism, Industrial Unionism, and Socialism* (New York: B. W. Huebsch, 1913), pp. 190-194. See also Gonner, *Rodbertus,* pp. 17-18; Bowman, *Bellamy*

Abroad, p. 34; and Lawrence Gronlund, *The New Economy* (Chicago: Herbert Stone, 1898), pp. 47-48, 93-96. On the Webbs, see chapter seven *infra.*

[39]See Iggers, *Cult of Authority,* p. 151, and *Doctrine of Saint Simon,* p. xxxviii; Gonner, *Rodbertus,* p. 162; and Cole, *History of Socialist Thought,* Volume II, p. 22.

I have not differentiated in this discussion between the distribution of income and the distribution of wealth. In a socialist society, there should not be, by definition, any ownership of income-producing assets, nor presumably any interest earned on saved income. To the extent an individual spends less than he receives, he may accumulate some degree of wealth.

[40]Morelly, *Le Code de la Nature,* circa 1755. The principle was popularized by Louis Blanc in his *Organisation du Travail.*

[41]Bellamy, *Looking Backward,* pp. 107, 108, 73-74. For Gronlund's different views, see *The Cooperative Commonwealth,* pp. 147-148, and *The New Economy,* pp. 47-48. Cf. Marx, *The German Ideology,* 1845-1846, quoted in Z. A. Jordan, *Karl Marx: Economy, Class, and Social Revolution* (New York: Charles Scribner's Sons, 1971), pp. 303-304 (emphasis in original):

> . . . one of the most vital principles of communism . . . is its . . . view . . . that differences of *brain* and of intellectual capacity do not imply any differences whatsoever in the nature of the *stomach* and of physical *needs;* therefore the false tenet, '*to each according* to his abilities,' must be changed, . . . into the tenet, '*to each according to his need';* in other words, a *different form* of activity, of labour, does not justify *inequality,* confers no *privileges* in respect of possession and enjoyment.

[42]On Fourier, see Gray, *Socialist Tradition,* pp. 185-186; on Rodbertus, see Cole, *History of Socialist Thought,* Volume II, p. 22, and Gray, *Socialist Tradition,* pp. 349-350; on Gronlund, see *Cooperative Commonwealth,* pp. 148-149; and on Bellamy, see *Looking Backward,* pp. 50-51. Reduced hours, to be sure, imply an unequal distribution of leisure time.

[43]Bellamy, *Looking Backward,* pp. 51, 52-53, 101.

[44]Ibid., p. 74.

[45]For Fichte's views (expressed in his *Der geschlossne Handelsstaat*), see Gray, *Socialist Tradition,* p. 111; and Fichte, *The Characteristics of the Present Age,* pp. 164, 167, 168:

> In a Perfect State no just individual purpose can exist which is not included in the purposes of the Community, and for the attainment of which the community does not provide . . . all the individual members of the State, without exception, are subjected to the purpose of the Whole. . . . absolutely no Individual can propose any purpose to himself, and devote himself to its furtherance, which is his own merely, and not at the same time the purpose of the whole Community.

Or see Henri Saint-Simon, *Du System Industriel,* 1821-1822, quoted in Keith Taylor, ed. and trans., *Henri Saint-Simon, 1760-1825: Selected Writings on Science, Industry and Social Organisation* (London: Groom Helm, 1975), p. 229:

> . . . the maintenance of individual liberties can in no case be the object of the social contract . . . if the vague and metaphysical idea of liberty current today continued to be taken as the basis of political doctrines, it would tend severely to impede the actions of the mass on individuals . . . it would be contrary to the development of . . . a well-ordered system . . .

Or the Saint-Simonians, quoted in Iggers, *Doctrine of Saint Simon,* p. 109:

> At the head of the social body are the general administrators whose function it is to assign each man to the place where he is most needed for his sake and for the sake of others.

Or the woman's liberationist Frances Wright, "Communication from the Trustees of Nashoba," *New Harmony Gazette,* 1828, quoted in Bestor, *Backwoods Utopias,* p. 225:

> In a cooperative community, when perfectly organized, the simple relation

between the society and the individual is, that the latter devotes his time and his labor for the public good in any way the public may enjoin, while the society supports each member.

Or compare the comment by Marx in *The German Ideology,* quoted in Note 41 *supra,* with that in *Capital,* Volume I (New York: Modern Library, 1937 [1867]), p. 90:

> ... picture to ourselves ... a community of free individuals carrying on their work with the means of production in common, in which the labour-power of all the different individuals is consciously applied as the combined labour-power of the community ... The total product ... is a social product. [labor is allocated] in accordance with a definite social plan [to maintain] the proper proportion between the definite kinds of work to be done and the various wants of the community.

Finally, consider the philosophical jiu-jitsu of Leon Trotsky, in his speech at the Third Congress of Trade Unions, April 1920, quoted in translation by Isaac Deutscher, "Russia," in Walter Galenson, ed., *Comparative Labor Movements* (New York: Prentice Hall, 1952), pp. 505, 504, who defended "labor armies"—conscript labor—by dismissing the difference between freedom and force altogether:

> We know that every labor is socially compulsory labor. Man must work in order not to die.... the type of labor that is socially regulated on the basis of an economic plan, obligatory for the whole country, compulsory for every worker ... is the basis of socialism ... is the indispensable, basic method for the organization of our labor forces.

[46]Spargo, *Syndicalism,* pp. 190, 191-192 (emphasis added).

[47]Gronlund, *Cooperative Commonwealth,* p. 273 (emphasis added).

[48]United States Commission on Industrial Relations, *Report* (Washington: GPO, 1915) pp. 1451-1452; and see the testimony by Joseph Ettor of the IWW, p. 1555.

Compare with the observations of Luke Grant, in an investigative report prepared for this same commission, *The National Erector's Association and the International Association of Bridge and Structural Ironworkers* (Washington: GPO, 1915), pp. 111, 109-110:

> The views of Mr. St. John are extreme and most labor leaders will openly repudiate them. But there is no denying the fact that Mr. St. John gave public expression to views that are privately entertained by tens of thousands....
> When the door of the factory closes and the employees are paid the wages due them, the employer takes the position that his former workers have no further interest in his factory. The law says he is right in that position. He is not, therefore, violating any written law.... But the workers who were locked out because they refused to accept the conditions imposed, or because they demanded improved conditions, take quite a different view of the situation. They feel they have a property right in the jobs they formerly held. That the law holds they have no such right, and that anyone who is willing to accept the conditions, shall have a right to fill the jobs, without fear of molestation, does not alter the situation in the minds of the workers.... They cannot see the justice of the law. It is quite plainly on the side of the employer, at least in the particular instance in which they are vitally interested. They refuse to accept the dictum of the law and of the employer ... They want the jobs, ... In order that they may get the jobs, it is necessary to prevent others from taking them. ... What is the natural thing for the strikers to do? Prevent new employe[e]s from taking the jobs ... If that can be done by peaceful methods, so much the better. If it cannot, then it must be done by violent methods. The important

thing is that it be done. That is the way the workers view the situation, the law to the contrary notwithstanding. . . .

Compare Grant's comments with those of Jack London, in "The Scab," 1904: "When a striker kills with a brick the man who has taken his place, he has no sense of wrong-doing." (*Novels and Social Writings,* (New York: Viking, 1982), Volume II, p. 1121), or with those of A. J. Muste, "Factional Fights in Trade Unions," in J. B. S. Hardman, ed., *American Labor Dynamics in the Light of Post War Developments* (New York: Harcourt, Brace, 1928), p. 335:

> Be it observed in passing that when we speak of the union as conservative or revolutionary, we are not speaking of what the union says about itself in its preamble or in its official proceedings. We are not speaking of a conscious philosophy, but of the actual functions performed by the union and the attitudes developed in its membership. When the National Association of Manufacturers dubs the A.F. of L. subversive and talks about unionism and Bolshevism in the same breath, it is doubtless, superficially speaking, ignorant and stupid, but in a deeper sense it may be said to fight even pure-and-simple trade unionism not because it misunderstands the situation, but because it understands the situation only too well.

[49]The effects of this propaganda were assessed by two very different observers of the European scene. See Georges Sorel, *Reflections on Violence,* trans. T. E. Hulme and J. Roth (New York: The Free Press, 1950 [1908], pp. 88, 89, 90, 91 (emphasis in original):

> There are plenty of workmen who understand perfectly well that all the trash of Parliamentary literature only serves to disguise the real motives by which the Government is influenced . . . the workers have no money, but they have at their disposal a much more efficacious means of action; they can inspire *fear,* and for several years past they have availed themselves of this resource. . . . the most decisive factor in social politics is the cowardice of the Government. . . . Syndicalist leaders know how to make excellent use of this situation, and they teach the workers that it is not at all a question of demanding favours, but that they must profit by *middle-class cowardice . . .* One of the things which appear to me to have most astonished the workers during the last few years has been the timidity of the forces of law and order in the presence of a riot; magistrates who have the right to demand the services of soldiers dare not use their power to the utmost, and officers allow themselves to be abused and struck with a patience hitherto unknown to them. It is becoming more and more evident every day that working class violence possesses an extraordinary efficacity in strikes; prefects, fearing that they may be obliged to use force against insurrectionary violence, bring pressure to bear on employers in order to compel them to give way; the safety of factories is now looked upon as a favour which the prefect may dispense as he pleases; consequently he arranges the use of his police so as to intimidate the two parties, and skil[l]fully brings them to an agreement. Trades union leaders . . . endeavour to intimidate the prefects by popular demonstrations which might lead to serious conflicts with the police, and they commend violence as the most efficacious means of obtaining concessions. At the end of a certain time the obsessed and frightened administration nearly always intervenes with the masters and forces an agreement upon them, which becomes an encouragement to the propagandists of violence. . . . The theorists of social peace shut their eyes to these embarrassing facts; they are doubtless ashamed to admit their

cowardice, just as the Government is ashamed to admit that its social politics are carried out under the threat of disturbances.

Compare with the remarks by the Italian sociologist Vilfredo Pareto in his *The Mind and Society,* trans. Andrew Bongiorno and Arthur Livingston (New York: Harcourt, Brace, 1935 [1923, 1916]), Volume IV: The General Form of Society, Section 2187, p. 1528:

> If a government . . . sets out to protect employers or strikebreakers from violence by strikers, it is accused of 'interfering' in an economic matter that does not properly concern it. If the police do not allow their heads to be broken without using their weapons, they are said to have 'shown poor judgment', to have acted 'impulsively', 'nervously' [i.e., to have "overreacted"]. Like strike-breakers, they must be denied the right to use arms whenever they are attacked by strikers, for otherwise some striker might be killed, and the crime of assault, assuming but not conceding that there has been such a crime, does not deserve the penalty of death. . . . Court decisions are impugned as 'class decisions'; at any rate, they are always too severe. Amnesties, finally, must wipe out all remembrance of such unpleasantries.

[50]Lloyd, "The New Independence," in Henry Demarest Lloyd, *Men, the Workers* (New York: Macmillan, 1909) pp. 132, 151. On Lloyd and organized labor, see E. Jay Jernigan, *Henry Demarest Lloyd* (Boston: Twayne Publishers, 1976), pp. 78-105, 124-141; and Chester Destler, *Henry Demarest Lloyd and the Empire of Reform* (Philadelphia: University of Pennsylvania Press, 1963), especially pp. 400-423; and see chapter seven *infra.*

[51]Lloyd, "Trade Agreements," in *Men, the Workers,* pp. 242, 243, and p. 234:

> Of course [non-strikers crossing picket lines] are strictly within their legal rights, but to me they seem to violate a moral duty of the highest sanctity, which is that a man must do what he can to help along a necessary struggle for the elevation of his own class and of society at large. . . . The union certainly withdraws no legal protection from them. They are not protected by the union from being visited with that obloquy which properly falls upon a man who will not join in with a common effort for the common good. I should class this man precisely with the Loyalist in the American revolution.

Compare with the comments of the leading Christian Socialist-cum-liberation-theologist of his generation, Walter Rauschenbush, *Christianizing the Social Order* (New York: Macmillan, 1921) pp. 389, 391:

> The group selfishness of the unions is at least a larger and nobler selfishness than that of the strike breaker whom the public sentiment of capitalism praises and rewards . . . Labor unions are fighting organizations, and fighting always abridges personal liberty and stiffens the demand for obedience and subordination. . . . The battle of labor is fought by a few for all . . . Unorganized labor reaps the advantages of the sacrifices made by the unions, yet often thwarts their efforts and defeats the common cause. Bitterness, roughness, and violence are inevitable in such a conflict . . . They doubtless sin, but even the errors of labor are lovable compared with the errors of capitalism.

[52]Lloyd, "The New Independence," in *Men, the Workers,* p. 143. Cf. Norman Thomas, *What Is Industrial Democracy?* (New York: League for Industrial Democracy, 1925), p. 19:

> The right not to belong to a union which is so dear to open shoppers is a shabby and unsocial 'right'. Its exercise makes a man not a hero but a parasite. Every worker owes the general improvement in his condition over

that of the worker of an earlier epoch primarily to the organized labor
movement, and the worker who is deliberately outside a union is no more
to be admired than the man without a country.

[53]Debs's tolerance for strike violence was demonstrated most spectacularly in the famous
American Railway Union strike of 1894 (actually an illegal secondary boycott of the Pullman
Company). The conventional wisdom about this boycott is that the violence was *caused* by
the use of federal troops to keep the trains running (i.e. to "break the strike"), despite the
request of Governor Altgeld of Illinois that President Cleveland *not* send them; or that the
cause of the violence was the decision on the part of the railroads to continue to operate; or
that the *cause* of the violence (on the railroads!) was George Pullman's refusal to restore the
wages of his sleeping-car workers; see Philip Taft and Philip Ross, "American Labor Violence:
Its Causes, Character, and Outcome," in Hugh Davis Graham and Ted Robert Gurr, eds.,
Violence in America: Historical and Comparative Perspectives (New York: Bantam Books,
1970), pp. 298-299. Nevertheless, as far as the first "cause" is concerned, riots broke out
before the troops appeared on the scene; see ibid., p. 298. Generally, on this affair and Debs's
role in it, see Willard King, "The Debs Case," in Colston E. Warne, ed., *The Pullman Boycott of
1894: The Problem of Federal Intervention* (Boston: D.C. Heath, 1955), pp. 85-97.

But what is really at stake in blaming the violence on employers or the government in this,
or in so many other cases, is simply the belief that a union, on the basis of their members'
presumed property right to their jobs, had a right to shut down a plant or industry or even an
entire economy. Suppose the authorities, during the famous GM sitdown strike of 1936 in
Flint, Michigan, had tried to repossess the corporation's property and evict the criminal
trespassers who were occupying it, over the protests of Governor Frank Murphy. Presumably,
a riot would have occurred. Who would have *caused* it?

Harold W. Curie, *Eugene V. Debs* (Boston: Twayne Publishers, 1976), pp. 69-75 absolves
Debs of any charge of sympathy for violence, except "on isolated, extreme occasions." (p. 69)
I find this conclusion bizarre and invite the reader to peruse some of Debs's speeches and
writings and make up his own mind; see Eugene V. Debs, *Writings and Speeches*, ed. Joseph
Bernstein (New York: Hermitage Press, 1948) especially pp. 257-258, 343-350, 350-377,
378-386, 473-480. For that matter, one need look no further than the comments by Debs
Curie himself collects. Of Debs, like a fair number of other socialists, an observation of Samuel
Gompers seems appropriate: "the leaders of socialism are in one breath calling for blood or in
another washing their hands of it . . . " *American Federationist,* 1912, quoted in Samuel
Gompers, *Labor and the Common Welfare* (New York: E.P. Dutton, 1919), p. 189. But of
Gompers, an observation of the socialist Jack London seems appropriate also:

> With all due respect to the labor leaders, who are not to be blamed for
> volubly asseverating otherwise, terrorism is a well-defined and eminently
> successful policy of the labor unions. It has probably won them more
> strikes than all the rest of the weapons in their arsenal. ("The Scab," p. 1124)

[54]See the comments by the Judge in *Altman* v. *Schlesinger,* 198 N.Y.S. 128, 132 (1923):

> The learned and experienced counsel who appeared for the respondents
> [the union], while personally deprecating the individual acts of violence
> and disorder complained of, stated frankly upon the argument, as in
> justification and by way of confession and avoidance: 'It is idle to mince
> matters. These industrial disputes are war'.

The learned counsel appearing for the ILGWU was another self-styled pacifist socialist, Morris
Hillquit.

See *American Steel and Wire Co.* v. *Wire Drawers and Die Makers,* CC N.D. Ohio, E.D., 90 F.
608, 619 *et seq.* (1898) for another example of this type of defense; and see the fascinating
discussion of sabotage in Spargo, *Syndicalism,* pp. 139-178, especially pp. 172 *et seq.* Cf.

Victor S. Yarros, "The Labor Question and the Social Problem," *American Journal of Sociology* IX (May 1904): 768-780.

[55]Bellamy, *Equality,* pp. 363-364, 208, 318.

[56]See De Leon, "Socialist Reconstruction of Society," pp. 23-29; Seratan, *De Leon,* pp. 104-108; and compare with Vincent St. John's testimony before the U.S. Commission on Industrial Relations, *Report,* Volume I, pp. 1450-1451.

Marx published little on collective bargaining that is of any value for this study. He wrote that as between the *"physical minimum of wages"* and the *"maximum rate of profit* an immense scale of variations is possible" that can "only" be "settled by the continuous struggle between capital and labour." Where wages arrive "resolves itself into a question of the respective powers of the combatants." But the "very necessity of *general political action* affords the proof that in its merely economic action capital is the stronger side." (in *Wage-Labour and Capital and Value, Price and Profit,* pp. 58-59 (emphasis in original).)

Marx was indifferent to pure and simple unionism in light of his explicitly revolutionary goals. The "working class . . . ought . . . not to be exclusively absorbed in these unavoidable guerrilla fights incessantly springing up from the never-ceasing encroachments of capital or changes in the market." Paraphrasing the Saint-Simonians, Marx wrote that "[i]nstead of the *conservative* motto, '*A fair day's wage for a fair day's work,*'" the unions "ought to inscribe on their banner the *revolutionary* watchword, '*Abolition of the Wages System*.'" (ibid, p. 61; emphasis in original). Cf. the statement in the Saint-Simonian *L'Organisateur,* 1830, quoted in Iggers, *Cult of Authority,* pp. 148f: "[i]t is no longer a question today of *guaranteeing wages* but of destroying the wage-system and establishing association." (emphasis in original)

[57]Gronlund, *New Economy,* pp. 162, 163, 160-161.

[58]Mill, *Chapters on Socialism,* 1879, in J. M. Robson, ed., *Collected Works of John Stuart Mill* (Toronto: University of Toronto Press, 1967), Volume V, pp. 734, 736.

[59]Mill, *Chapters on Socialism,* pp. 734, 735.

[60]There is a critique of the De Leon speech in Howard Kershner, "The Hoax That Deceived Millions."

[61]Empirical investigations of the 'functional distribution' of the national income began in the very late 19th century. Hutt, *Strike Threat System,* pp. 241-251, provides a short overview of their findings, plus a discussion of the more recent investigations, particularly those which have attempted to assess the impact of collective bargaining. See also Morgan Reynolds, *Power and Privilege: Labor Unions in America* (New York: Universe Books, 1984), pp. 160-161.

[62]A. Pool, *Wage Policy in Relation to Industrial Fluctuations* (London: Macmillan, 1938), p. 84 (·emphasis added); and see pp. 79-85 for a critique of Hobson's theories. See also Nemmers, *Hobson and Underconsumption,* pp. 68-110; E. F. M. Durbin, *Purchasing Power and Trade Depression: A Critique of Underconsumption Theories,* revised edition (London: Johnathan Cape, 1934 [1933]); and Lionel Robbins, "Consumption and the Trade Cycle," *Economica* XII (November 1932): 413-430. Senator Robert Wagner claimed that "corporate earnings rose very much faster than wage rates" in the 1920s (see Note 26 *supra*). So what?

[63]See Mill, *Chapters on Socialism,* pp. 730-731.

[64]A progressing economy is constantly generating new, competitive industries, some of which come to overshadow the older, more concentrated ones. The example of the automobile industry in relation to the railroads comes to mind; the more recent loss of domestic automobile manufacturers to overseas competitors is another example; the astonishing growth of the computer industry is still another.

George Gunton (a trade union theorist about whom more will be said later) thought that most of the anti-monopoly agitation of the 1880s in America, to the degree it derived from the socialistic "inevitability of monopoly" thesis, was based on faulty observation and economic reasoning; see his "The Economic and Social Aspects of the Trusts," *Political Science Quarterly* III (1888): 385-408. There is a literature demonstrating retrospectively the soundness of Gunton's (among many others') confidence in the untrammeled competitive process, and the emptiness of the claim that "where combination is possible, competition is impossible." One of the best sources here is Dominick Armentano, *Antitrust and Monopoly: Anatomy of a Policy Failure* (New York: John Wiley and Sons, 1982). Alfred D. Chandler, Jr., "The Structure of American Industry in the Twentieth Century: A Historical Overview," *Business History Review* XLIII (Autumn 1969): 255-298, assesses the relative stability of overall concentration ratios in American business; and see John M. Vernon, *Market Structure and Industrial Performance: A Review of Statistical Findings* (Boston: Allyn and Bacon, 1972), for a searching critique of the "market structure" numbers racket.

I will only mention in passing some of the more cogent critiques of Marx's "immanent laws of capitalist production"; see Eugen von Böhm-Bawerk, *Karl Marx and the Close of His System* (New York: Augustus Kelley, 1949 [1896]); Böhm-Bawerk, *Capital and Interest* (South Holland, Illinois: Libertarian Press, 1959 [1884-1909]), Volume I, pp. 241-321, and Volume III, pp. 74-77; Wicksteed, *"Das Kapital:* A Criticism"; and see Lewis Feuer, "Indeterminacy and Economic Development," in *Marx and the Intellectuals* (Garden City, New York: Anchor Books, 1969).

[65]Gray, *Lecture on Human Happiness,* pp. 62, 68 (emphasis in original).

[66]Rodbertus, *Das Kapital,* 1865, quoted in Gide and Rist, *History of Economic Doctrines,* p. 421. For some broadly similar expressions of the idea that planning would be a relatively simple matter of statistics-gathering, see Bellamy, *Looking Backward,* pp. 146-151; Gronlund, *Cooperative Commonwealth,* pp. 178-180; Iggers, *Doctrine of Saint Simon,* pp. 95-99, 107-109; and Friedrich Engels, "Principles of Communism," 1847, in *Collected Works,* Volume VI, pp. 347-348.

[67]Gide and Rist, *History of Economic Doctrines,* p. 422.

[68] F. A. Hayek, *Freedom and the Economic System,* University of Chicago Public Policy Pamphlet Number 29 (Chicago: University of Chicago Press, 1939), pp. 20-21; and see also Gide and Rist, *History of Economic Doctrines,* p. 422; and Marshall Goldman, "Marketing: A Lesson for Marx," *Harvard Business Review* XXXVIII (January-February 1960): 79-86.

[69]If one keeps in mind the value of consumer freedom and the fact that no one individual or group can be omniscient, the mistake of those who claim that capitalism is inherently inefficient (because some investments will inevitably fail to pan out) should be obvious.

[70]On the irrationality of economic planning, see Mises, *Socialism,* pp. 111-130, and his *Human Action,* 3d revised edition (Chicago: Henry Regnery Company, 1966 [1949]), pp. 698-715. The publication of Mises' first essay on this matter, "Economic Calculation in the Socialist Commonwealth," 1920, touched off one of the most famous debates in 20th century economic thought. See F. A. Hayek, *Collectivist Economic Planning* (London: George Routledge and Sons, 1935); Trygve J. B. Hoff, *Economic Calculation in the Socialist Society,* trans. M. A. Michael (London: William Hodge, 1949); and see Murray Rothbard, "Ludwig von Mises and Economic Calculation Under Socialism," in Laurence Moss, ed., *The Economics of Ludwig von Mises* (Menlo Park, CA: Institute for Humane Studies, 1976), pp. 67-77. Simon Rottenberg, "Unemployment in Socialist Countries," *Industrial and Labor Relations Review* XV (July 1962): 536-538, well points out that in a socialist society everyone might be assigned a task and kept busy, giving the appearance of "full employment"; but this would only be the reality of disguised unemployment, or underemployment.

[71]There is an innovative discussion of this issue in George Reisman, *The Government Against the Economy* (Ottawa, IL: Caroline House, 1979), pp. 133-187 *passim.*

[72]For Proudhon's rejection of the 'need principle', see Ely, *French and German Socialism,* pp. 133-134, 137. Mill objected to a great deal in Comte's philosophy of positivism, including

the latter's monomaniacal *devotion* to altruism—but *not* to the ideal itself; see John Stuart Mill, *Auguste Comte and Positivism,* 1865, in *Collected Works,* Volume X, especially pp. 335-341. The modern philosopher alluded to in the text is Ayn Rand; the maxim she coined referred to the political programme of the 1972 American presidential candidate George S. McGovern. For her exposition of the implications of the principle of 'From Each According to His Ability, To Each According to His Need', see *Atlas Shrugged* (New York: Random House, 1957), especially pp. 616-627.

Chapter Five

[1]This should not be taken to mean that classical economists were wedded to laissez faire, still less that legislators refrained from interfering with contracts.

[2]John Stuart Mill, "Thornton on Labour and Its Claims," *Fortnightly Review,* May and June 1869, in *Collected Works,* Volume V, p. 646 (emphasis added).

[3]One of the earliest economists to rebut the reformers was Eugen von Böhm-Bawerk; see "Control or Economic Law?" [1914], trans. John Richard Mez, in *Shorter Classics of Eugen von Böhm-Bawerk* (South Holland, IL: Libertarian Press, 1962), Volume I, pp. 139-199.

[4]See Pedro Schwartz, *The New Political Economy of J. S. Mill* (London: George Weidenfield and Nicolson Ltd., 1972), pp. 79, 99-100.

[5]That is, the 1820s, 1830s, and 1840s. Several objections *not* discussed in this study are assessed in William Breit, "Some Neglected Early Critics of the Wages Fund Theory," *Southwestern Social Science Quarterly* XLVIII (June 1967): 54-60.

[6]See Francis A. Walker, "The Wages-Fund Theory," *North American Review* CCXLV (January 1875), pp. 108-111, 112-114, and Francis A. Walker, *The Wages Question: A Treatise on Wages and the Wages Class* (New York: Henry Holt, 1876), pp. 147 *et seq.* For Walker's ideas about competition and the wages system, see chapter six *infra.* Walker's criticism of the wages fund—which in this author's opinion is more perceptive and convincing than those discussed in this study—appeared *after* Mill's recantation. See also the references cited chapter one, Note 40 *supra.*

[7]Frank W. Taussig, "The Wages-Fund Doctrine at the Hands of German Economists," *Quarterly Journal of Economics* IX (October 1894), p. 8. See also Frank W. Taussig, *Wages and Capital: An Examination of the Wages Fund Doctrine* (New York: Augustus M. Kelley, 1968 [1896]), pp. 266-273; and James W. Crook, *German Wages Theories: A History of Their Development* (New York: Columbia University Press, 1898), pp. 23-32. Francis Walker also argued that consumption, and not capital, limited wages; see Walker, *The Wages Question,* pp. 128-137; and Walker, "The Wages Fund Theory."

[8]Taussig, "Wages Fund Doctrine in Germany," pp. 9-10; see also *Wages and Capital,* pp. 270-272.

[9]See Crook, *German Wages Theories,* pp. 28-29.

[10]See T. J. Dunning, *Trades' Unions and Strikes: Their Philosophy and Intention* (London: Published by the Author, 1860). Compare with the fundamentally similar ideas in William Trant, *Trade Unions, Their Origin and Objects, Influence and Efficacy,* 19th edition (Washington: American Federation of Labor, 1921 [1873]). Trant's book was often reprinted by the American Federation of Labor as representing its own views. R. V. Clements, "British Trade Unions and Popular Political Economy, 1850-1873," *Economic History Review* XIV (August 1961): 93-104, discusses trade union leaders' general dismissal of classical economic doctrines, including the wages fund theory; see also Frances E. Gillespie, *Labor and Politics*

in England, 1850-1867 (Durham, N.C.: Duke University Press, 1927), pp. 140-141; and Royden Harrison, *Before the Socialists: Studies in Labour and Politics, 1861-1881* (London: Routledge and Kegan Paul, 1965), pp. 16-18.

[11]Dunning, *Trades' Unions and Strikes,* pp. 6, 7; cf. Trant, *Trade Unions,* pp. 21-30.

[12]See Paul Adelman, "Frederic Harrison and the Positivist Attack on Orthodox Political Economy," *History of Political Economy* III (September 1971): 170-189; H. W. McCready, "British Labour and the Royal Commission on the Trade Unions, 1867-1869," *University of Toronto Quarterly* XXIV (July 1955): 390-407, and his "The British Labour Lobby, 1867-1875," *Canadian Journal of Economics and Political Science* XXII (1956): 141-160; Frederic Harrison, *Autobiographical Memoirs* (London: Macmillan, 1911), Volume I, pp. 245-278, 317-327; and Harrison, *Before the Socialists,* pp. 251-342.

The reform of English trade union law in the early 1870s is discussed in chapter seven *infra.*

[13]"The Iron Masters Trade Union," *Fortnightly Review,* 1865, quoted in Adelman, "Frederic Harrison," p. 180; "The Good and Evil of Trades-Unionism," *Fortnightly Review,* 1865, reprinted in *National and Social Problems* (New York: Macmillan, 1908), pp. 303-304. Cf. the National Association for the Promotion of Social Science, which had commissioned a study and issued a report on unions in 1860, and concluded, on the basis of an "empirical" investigation, that "the constant assertion that strikes are scarcely successful, is [not] at all borne out by facts." (*Trade Societies and Strikes* (London: John W. Parker & Son, 1860, pp. xiii-xiv))

[14]Harrison, "Good and Evil," p. 312.

[15]Ibid., pp. 310-311. For similar complaints in the 1860s about laborers' immobility, see Bishop Ketteler, *Christianity and Labor,* 1864, quoted in Philip Taft, *Movements for Economic Reform* (New York: Rinehart, 1950), pp. 423-424. Cf. Lujo Brentano, *The Relation of Labor to the Law of Today,* trans. Porter Sherman (New York: G. P. Putnams, 1891 [1876]), p. 180. Between 1864, when Ketteler claimed that workers couldn't move, and 1876, when Brentano agreed, at least 1.2 million Germans (the bulk of them wage earners) emigrated to the United States alone (and only a small fraction of them were assisted by public or private charitable organizations).

[16]Harrison, "Good and Evil," p. 313.

[17]Ibid., pp. 310, 311-312.

[18]Dunning, *Trades' Unions,* p. 25 (emphasis added).

[19]See Francis D. Longe, *A Refutation of the Wage-Fund Theory of Modern Political Economy* (Baltimore: The Johns Hopkins University Press, 1904 [1866]); and Taussig, *Wages and Capital,* pp. 241-244.

[20]Longe, *Refutation,* pp. 25, 52 (emphasis in original); see also pp. 27, 44, 47-51.

[21]Ibid., pp. 52-53.

[22]Ibid., p. 53.

[23]Ibid., pp. 37, 30, 68. See also p. 65, where Longe claimed that employers didn't know "the difference between cheap labour and low wages."

[24]Thomas E. Cliffe Leslie, "Political Economy and the Rate of Wages," *Frasers Magazine* LXXVIII (July 1868), p. 94. Leslie was an early advocate of the "historical method," pioneered by a school of German interventionist economists that will be discussed in this chapter. See John Kells Ingram, *A History of Political Economy* (New York: Macmillan, 1888), pp. 228-230.

[25]Longe, *Refutation,* pp. 63-64. Leslie was no champion of combination either; see "Political Economy and the Rate of Wages," p. 94.

[26]Fleeming Jenkin, "Trade Unions: How Far Legitimate," *North British Review* XLVIII (March 1868): 1-34; and "The Graphic Representation of the Laws of Supply and Demand, and Their Application to Labour," in Alexander Grant, ed., *Recess Studies* (Edinburgh: Edmonston

and Douglas, 1870) pp. 151-185. See also A. D. Brownlee and M. F. Lloyd Prichard, "Professor Fleeming Jenkin, 1833-1885: Pioneer in Engineering and Political Economy," *Oxford Economic Papers* XV (November 1963): 204-216. Jenkin's essay of 1870, published after William Thornton's *On Labour* and Mill's recantation, mentions these two works.

[27]Jenkin, "Trade Unions," pp. 4-5.

[28]Ibid., p. 10. See also Jacob Waley, "On Strikes and Combinations with Reference to Wages and Conditions of Labour," *Journal of the Royal Statistical Society* XXX (March 1867), pp. 6-7:

> In these great branches of industry in which, through the fluctuations of good and bad years, there is a continual, though not a steady, increase of the gross returns to be shared between the capitalist and the labourer; in which, from the rapid growth of the trade, its conditions are in a perpetual flux, and never have time to settle into a state of stable equilibrium,—I conceive that there will in general be a large margin of uncertainty as to the division of the returns between profits and wages, and that the precise place at which the line is drawn will to a very considerable extent be determined by circumstances which may fairly be called fortuitous, and may be greatly influenced by a bargain between the employer and the employed. When a question of this sort arises, and is not adjusted by agreement, it seems to me quite possible that a rise in the price of labour may be attained by temporarily withholding the supply, and that the rise so acquired may be permanently held—in other words, that a strike may be successful.

[29]Jenkin, "Graphic Representation," pp. 184, 174.

[30]Ibid., pp. 173, 179.

[31]Jenkin, "Trade Unions," p. 9.

[32]Thornton published parts of his book in article form in the *Fortnightly Review* in 1866 and 1867; see "A New Theory of Supply and Demand," (October 1866), pp. 420-434; "What Determines the Price of Labour," (May 1867), pp. 551-565; and "Stray Chapters From a Forthcoming Work on Labour," (October 1867), pp. 477-500, (November 1867), pp. 592-602, (December 1867), pp. 688-702. Only the second, revised and enlarged edition of *On Labour* (London: Macmillan, 1870) was available to me; it has passages responding to Mill's review of the first edition.

[33]Thornton, *On Labour,* p. 85; see also pp. 84-87.

[34]Ibid., p. 56 (emphasis added).

[35]Ibid., pp. 56-57. While this is plausible, the sole buyer (at 8 shillings) in the Dutch auction example *might* still risk letting the bid drop anyway.

[36]Ibid., pp. 54 ("supply and demand do not . . . govern price"), 44 ("the price, whether of labour or of anything else, in no case whatsoever depends on the proportion between supply and demand . . . "); and see p. 51.

[37]Ibid., pp. 93-94, 95 (emphasis in original).

[38]Ibid., p. 104.

[39]Ibid., p. 107 (emphasis in original).

[40]Ibid., pp. 177, 176.

[41]Ibid., p. 190.

[42]Ibid., pp. 193, 200. Cf. John Stuart Mill, *Principles of Political Economy,* 6th edition, 1865, as quoted in Clements, "Trade Unions," p. 97: "their sole endeavor is to receive as much and return as little, in the shape of service, as possible."

[43]Thornton, *On Labour,* p. 203; but see also p. 202.

[44]Ibid., p. 303f; see also pp. 279-321 *passim.*

[45]Ibid., p. 310 (emphasis added).

[46]Ibid., p. 311.

[47]Ibid., p. 302.

[48]John Stuart Mill, "Thornton on Labour and its Claims," p. 646. On this episode, see Taussig, *Wages and Capital,* pp. 247-256; Hutt, *Theory of Collective Bargaining,* pp. 39-44; and Schwartz, *New Political Economy of John Stuart Mill,* pp. 90-103, the most recent, and best, account.

[49]Mill, "Thornton on Labour," p. 637 (emphasis added).

[50]Ibid., pp. 637, 643.

[51]Ibid., p. 644.

[52]Id.

[53]Ibid., p. 639.

[54]Ibid., p. 645 (emphasis added); see also p. 644. Schwartz, *New Political Economy of John Stuart Mill,* pp. 94-95, is convinced that the artificiality of the period of production analysis, and not the vulnerability of employers to a strike threat, was the real reason Mill rejected the wages fund.

[55]I am indebted to Hutt, *Theory of Collective Bargaining,* pp. 41-42, for catching Mill's carelessness here.

[56]Mill, "Thornton on Labour," pp. 657-658. See also Schwartz, *New Political Economy,* pp. 101-103, who points out that Mill changed little of substance in his discussion of the wages fund in the later edition of his *Principles of Political Economy.*

[57]Mill, "Thornton on Labour," pp. 661-662. Mill did not add that all laborers were consumers and that most consumers were also laborers.

[58]Ibid., pp. 662f.

[59]Consider Thornton's extraordinary defense of intimidatory picketing (*On Labour,* pp. 245-246 (emphasis added)):

> It cannot, indeed, be otherwise than irksome to a shopkeeper to have sour-visaged sentinels mounting guard constantly at his door, and casting black looks on himself or on any friends of his who came nigh his dwelling; but this intrusion on domestic privacy must be admitted to be, at any rate, a smaller evil than such an interference with liberty of rest or locomotion as would prevent anyone with a fancy for the pastime from spending the day in lolling against some particular lamp-post, or promenading up and down some particular street. It cannot be otherwise than irksome either to non-unionists, to be pursued to their homes with taunts and reproaches for merely taking work where they could get it. Yet it might be difficult to say why less license of remonstrance should be allowed to their pursuers than to the active parish priest whom many would praise for his zeal in similarly dogging the steps of wanderers from his fold, and since they would not come to hear him at church, insisting on preaching to them in the streets.... Provided the reproaches of pickets and their emissaries . . . do not go beyond hooting or upbraiding, keeping clear also of obscenity and profanity, they may quite possibly be, in spite of their roughness, *good for the mental health of those against whom they are launched.* . . . Few kinds of knowledge are more useful than the knowledge of what our associates think of us and our conduct, and hooting, hissing, and calling names are, among working people, favourite and effectual ways of interchanging such knowledge. . . . if they are so unfortunate as to be looked upon by their fellows as traitors to the common cause, or opponents of the common interest, it is highly desirable that they should be distinctly apprised accordingly.

[60]Mill, "Thornton on Labour," p. 664. After delivering himself of this opinion, Mill thoughtfully condemned union featherbedding practices as "grave violations of the moral rule, that disputes between classes should not be so conducted as to make the world a worse place for both together, and ultimately for the whole of the community." (p. 665)

[61]James Stirling, "Mr. Mill on Trades-Unions—A Criticism," in Grant, ed., *Recess Studies*, p. 309; for a similar assessment, see Walker, "The Wage Fund Theory," pp. 100-101.

[62]See John Elliott Cairnes, *Some Leading Principles of Political Economy, Newly Expounded* (New York: Harper & Brothers, 1874), pp. 87-96, 156, 191-192; and see also pp. 214-262 *passim.*

[63]Stirling, "Mr. Mill," p. 330.

[64]T. S. Cree, *A Criticism of the Theory of Trades' Unions* (Glasgow, Scotland: Bell and Bain, 1892 [1890]), pp. 29, 28.

[65]Cree, *Criticism of Trades' Unions*, pp. 15-16; cf. Machlup, *Political Economy of Monopoly*, pp. 357-358.

[66]Alfred Marshall, *Elements of the Economics of Industry*, 3d edition (London: Macmillan, 1905 [1892]), pp. 362-363.

[67]Marshall, *Elements*, pp. 353, 392. Cf. Alfred Marshall, *The Economics of Industry*, 3d edition (London: Macmillan, 1885 [1879]), p. 206.

[68]On the German historicists and their influence on Americans, see, in addition to the general works on socialism and syndicalism cited in chapter three *supra*, note 4: Jürgen Herbst, *The German Historical School in American Scholarship* (Middletown, CT: Wesleyan University Press, 1965); Fritz Ringer, *The Decline of the German Mandarins: The German Academic Community, 1890-1933* (Cambridge: Harvard University Press, 1969), pp. 143-162; Joseph Dorfman, "The Role of the German Historical School in American Economic Thought," *American Economic Review*, Supplement, XL (May 1955): 17-28; Ralph Bowen, *German Theories of the Corporative State* (New York: McGraw-Hill, 1947), pp. 119-159; Eugen Philippovich, "The Verein für Sozialpolitik," *Quarterly Journal of Economics* V (January 1891): 220-237; Eugen Philippovich, "The Infusion of Socio-Political Ideas into the Literature of German Economics," *American Journal of Sociology* XVII (September 1912): 145-199; Abraham Ascher, "Professors as Propogandists: The Politics of the *Katheder-sozialisten*," *Journal of Central European Affairs* XXIII (October 1963): 282-303; Crook, *German Wages Theories*, pp. 33-54, 272-274; Ingram, *A History of Political Economy*, pp. 196-239; Ludwig von Mises, *The Historical Setting of the Austrian School of Economics* (New York: Arlington House, 1969); E. Clark, "Adolph Wagner: From National Economist to National Socialist," *Political Science Quarterly* LV (September 1940): 378-411; Thorstein Veblen, "Gustav Schmoller's Economics," *Quarterly Journal of Economics* XVI (November 1901): 69-93; and Frederic C. Lane, "Some Heirs of Gustav Schmoller," in Joseph T. Lambie, ed., *Architects and Craftsmen in History: Festschrift for Abbot Payson Usher* (Tubingen: J.C.B. Mohr, 1956).

See also Herbert S. Foxwell, "The Economic Movement in England," *Quarterly Journal of Economics* II (October 1887): 84-103; A. W. Coats, "The Historist Reaction in English Political Economy, 1870-1890," *Economica* XXI (May 1954): 143-153; T. W. Hutchison, "Economists and Economic Policy in Britain After 1870," *History of Political Economy* I (Fall 1969): 231-255; and Arthur Mann, "British Social Thought and American Reformers of the Progressive Era," *Mississippi Valley Historical Review* XLII (March 1956): 672-692.

[69]Philippovich, "Infusion of Ideas," p. 173; Held, *Jahrbuch für Gesetzgebung*, quoted in Philippovich, "Verein," p. 224.

[70]Thus, according to Adolph Held, the

> new school demands a complete abandonment of the endeavor to set up natural laws of universal application, and with it the abandonment, as far as possible, of that mode of investigation which reasons by deduction from more or less rigid premises. It demands realistic political economy—that economic investigation shall rest, as far as possible, upon historical and statistical material.

(Held, *Jahrbuch für Gesetzgebung*, quoted in Philippovich, "Verein," p. 224.) Of course, in many cases—the 'living wage' is perhaps the paradigmatic case—the economic objection is that minimum wages are not in the interests of members of the class the state wants to help, since the minimum wage will cause unemployment. Working at zero wages is hardly preferable to working at low wages. Denouncing those who oppose minimum wages and favor free wage competition (on that ground) as being 'apologists for greed' is simply irrelevant. It is far beyond our concern here to examine the meaningfulness or validity of the historicist claim about whether men are or are not (or should or should not be) motivated by self-interest, and, whether the answer is yes or no, if this means that economic laws are universally true or only relatively true. All I can do here is ask the reader a question: Suppose A seeks wealth in order to consume it himself, while B seeks wealth in order to give it away to a stranger. If we assume that A is selfish and B is not, why would B not demand more of a good if its price were lower, while A would?

For an examination of the historicist position, see Ludwig von Mises, *The Historical Setting of the Austrian School of Economics* (New York: Arlington House, 1969); and his *A Critique of Interventionism* (New York: Arlington House, 1977), pp. 71-97.

[71]Philippovich, "Infusion of Ideas," p. 173. The first generation, or "older school," of historicists, included Wilhelm Roscher, Bruno Hildebrand, and Karl Knies. The second generation, or "younger school," included Albert Schaeffle, Adolph Wagner, and Gustav Schmoller. The third generation's most famous figure was Werner Sombart, who began as a revolutionary socialist and ended up as a National Socialist.

[72]Brentano received his early academic training by free traders, but he spent his post-graduate years with the interventionist Dr. Ernest Engel, head of the Prussian Statistical Bureau. Engel sent Brentano to England (just about the time the contretemps over the wages fund broke out) to study the cooperative movement, and in England Brentano came under the influence of various Christian Socialists and of Frederic Harrison. Harrison convinced Brentano that unionism was the wave of the future. On Brentano, see James T. Sheehan, *The Career of Lujo Brentano: A Study of Liberalism and Social Reform in Imperial Germany* (Chicago: University of Chicago Press, 1966); Taussig, *Wages and Capital*, pp. 274-280; and Crook, *German Wages Theories*, pp. 33-37.

[73]Lujo Brentano, *The Relation of Labor to the Law of Today*, trans. Porter Sherman (New York: G.P. Putnams, 1891 [1876]), p. 214; see also Crook, *German Wages Theories*, pp. 35-36.

[74]Brentano, *Relation of Labor to Law*, pp. 223, 222.

[75]See John Shields Nicholson, "Capital and Labor: Their Relative Strength," *Economic Journal* II (September 1892), p. 485; Arthur T. Hadley, *Economics* (New York: G.P. Putnam's Sons, 1902 [1896]), pp. 319-320; and W. Stanley Jevons, *The State in Relation to Labor*, 3d edition (London: Macmillan, 1894 [1882]), pp. 107ff.

[76]Sheehan, *Career of Brentano*, p. 143.

[77]Sidney and Beatrice Webb, *Industrial Democracy*, revised edition (New York: Augustus Kelley, 1964 [1920, 1897]), p. 855.

[78]See Robert Dahl, "Workers' Control of Industry and the British Labor Party," *American Political Science Review* XLI (October 1947), especially pp. 875-892; Jack Melitz, "The Trade Unions and Fabian Socialism," *Industrial and Labor Relations Review* XII (July 1959): 554-567; and see the essays, "The Relationship Between Co-operation and Trade Unionism," 1892, by Beatrice Webb, and "The Difficulties of Individualism," 1891, by Sidney Webb, in Sidney and Beatrice Webb, *Problems of Modern Industry* (London: Longmans, Green, 1898).

On the Webbs and Fabianism, see, in addition to the general works on socialism cited in chapter three *supra,* Note 4: Edward R. Pease, *History of the Fabian Society* (New York: E.P. Dutton, 1916); William Irvine, "Shaw, the Fabians, and the Utilitarians," *Journal of the History of Ideas* VIII (April 1947): 218-231; and George Stigler, "Bernard Shaw, Sidney Webb, and the Theory of Fabian Socialism," in *Essays in the History of Economics* (Chicago: University of Chicago Press, 1960), pp. 268-286.

The Webbs' ideas will be explored as they influenced and were influenced by other English, American, and European socialists and social reformers, in the chapters below.

[79]One of the renegade Saint Simonians, Philippe Buchez, along with the priest Félicité Robert de Lamenais, helped launch the Christian Socialist movement in 19th century France. Later in the century, the two most important figures were Albert de Mun and Marquis de La Tour du Pin Chambly. Both de Mun and La Tour du Pin were heavily influenced by the ideas of the great Wilhelm Emanuel, Baron von Ketteler, the epochal figure among 19th Century German Christian Socialists (or as they were called, Social Catholics). Ketteler's social ideas reached the highest level of influence; it is generally held that Pope Leo XIII's famous anti-capitalist encyclical, *Rerum Novarum,* 1891, was based on Ketteler's writings. Ketteler's most important student was Franz Christoph, Canon Moufang; other influential Social Catholics were Franz Hitze, Heinrich Pesch, and Christian Vogelsang.

In England, the 19th century founders of Christian Socialism—Frederic Denison Maurice, Charles Kingsley, and John Malcolm Forbes Ludlow—were inspired by and committed to Owenite socialism. Their successors, particularly the Social Catholics, were hospitable to the Fabians.

In addition to the general works on socialism and syndicalism cited in chapter three *supra,* Note 4, see: Moritz Kaufmann, *Christian Socialism and Social Reform* (London: Kegan Paul, Trench and Co., 1888); Matthew Elbow, *French Corporative Theory, 1789-1945; A Chapter in the History of Ideas* (New York: Columbia University Press, 1953); John N. Moody, *et al.,* eds., *Church and Society: Catholic Social and Political Thought and Movements, 1789-1950* (New York: Arts Press, 1953); Parker T. Moon, *The Labor Problem and the Social Catholic Movement in France* (New York: Macmillan, 1921); Bowen, *German Theories of the Corporative State,* pp. 75-118; Philip Taft, *Movements for Economic Reform* (New York: Rinehart, 1950), pp. 418-440; E. R. A. Seligman, "Owen and the Christian Socialists," *Political Science Quarterly* I (June 1886): 206-249; Moritz Kaufmann, *Charles Kingsley: Christian Socialist and Social Reformer* (London: Metheun and Company, 1892); Neville C. Mastermann, *John Malcolm Ludlow: Builder of Christian Socialism* (Cambridge, England: Cambridge University Press, 1963); William E. Hogan, *The Development of Bishop Wilhelm Emmanuel von Ketteler's Interpretation of the Social Problem* (Washington, D.C.: Catholic University Press, 1946); Richard Mulcahy, *The Economics of Heinrich Pesch* (New York: Henry Holt, 1952); and Abram Harris, "The Scholastic Revival: The Economics of Heinrich Pesch," *Journal of Political Economy* LIV (February 1946): 38-59.

On the American Christian Socialists, see chapter six *infra.*

[80]Bowen, *German Corporative Theories,* pp. 84-85.

[81]Hitze, *Die Soziale Frage, und Die Bestrebung zu Ihrer Losum,* 1877, paraphrased by Moon, *The Labor Problem,* p. 128 (see also p. 145); Hitze, *Kapital und Arbeit und Die Reorganisation Der Gesellschaft,* 1880, quoted in Bowen, *German Corporative Theories,* p. 100 (emphasis in original). Several German Protestant Christian socialists also favored compulsory organization; see Taft, *Movements for Economic Reform,* p. 455, and Bowen, *German Corporative Theories,* pp. 142-143.

Chapter Six

[1]Several general studies take up the rise of organic collectivism, interventionism, etc., in America in the decades following the Civil War, and contain accounts of the individual figures discussed in this chapter and the succeeding ones: Sidney Fine, *Laissez-Faire and the General Welfare State: A Study of Conflict in American Thought, 1865-1901* (Ann Arbor: University of Michigan Press, 1956); Frank Tariello, *The Reconstruction of American*

Political Ideology, 1865-1897 (Charlottesville: University Press of Virginia, 1982); Mark Perlman, *Labor Union Theories in America* (Evanston, Illinois: Row, Peterson, 1958); Milton Derber, *The American Idea of Industrial Democracy, 1865-1965* (Urbana: University of Illinois Press, 1970); and R. Jackson Wilson, *In Quest of Community: Social Philosophy in the United States, 1860-1920* (New York: Wiley, 1960).

[2]Arthur Latham Perry, *Political Economy,* 18th edition (New York: Charles Scribner's Sons, 1883), pp. 236, 247 (emphasis in original).

[3]The orientation of American economic thought in the early and middle decades of the 19th century is discussed in Michael J. O'Connor, *Origins of Academic Economics in the United States* (New York: Columbia University Press, 1944); Joseph Dorfman, *The Economic Mind in American Civilization* (New York: The Viking Press, 1946), Volume II; and Fine, *Laissez-Faire,* pp. 3-166.

[4]Ward, *Dynamic Sociology,* 1883, quoted in Henry Steele Commager, ed., *Lester Ward and the Welfare State* (New York: Bobbs Merrill, 1967), pp. 48, 49.

The ideas and significance of Lester Ward are discussed in Samuel Chugerman, *Lester F. Ward: The American Aristotle* (Durham, NC: Duke University Press, 1939); Charles H. Page, *Class and American Sociology: From Ward to Ross* (New York: Schocken Books, 1969), pp. 29-72; and Harry Elmer Barnes, ed., *An Introduction to the History of Sociology* (Chicago: University of Chicago Press, 1948), pp. 173-190.

Edward A. Ross, Ward's protégé and son-in-law, was a major figure in American sociology in his own right. Ross helped usher in the school of "sociological jurisprudence" (discussed in chapter seven *infra*) through his influence on Roscoe Pound; see Daniel Wigdor, *Roscoe Pound, Philosopher of Law* (Westport: Greenwood Press, 1974), pp. 112-113. On Ross and his influence, see Julius Weinberg, *Edward Alsworth Ross and the Sociology of Progressivism* (Madison: State Historical Society of Wisconsin Press, 1972); Page, *Class and Sociology,* pp. 213-246; and Joyce O. Hertzler, "Edward Alsworth Ross: Sociological Pioneer and Interpreter," *American Sociological Review* XVI (October 1951): 597-613.

Along with Ward and Ross, the third most important sociologist who helped usher in the new collectivism was Albion W. Small. Small studied in Europe. A student of the ideas of Adolph Wagner, Gustav Schmoller, and Richard Ely, Small was also heavily influenced by Albert Schaeffle and Gustav Ratzehofer. Small was Dean of the Arts and Sciences at the University of Chicago Graduate School and editor of the prestigious *American Journal of Sociology.* He was a proponent of a new, class-based 'constitutional' society and an opponent of individual rights. Small's position that "[l]aws that work against the 'morality' or interests of the larger group must be broken for reasons of fairness and morality" (George Christakes, *Albion W. Small* (Boston: Twayne, 1978), p. 81) was one from whose implications he did not shrink. Thus, he approved violence and even murder if committed by aggrieved majority interest groups against minority or individual rights. Small is not known for his defense of labor union violence however; he applied his doctrine to the Ku Klux Klan and the regime of lynch law in the South. On Small, see Christakes, *Small*; Jürgen Herbst, "From Moral Philosophy to Sociology: Albion Woodbury Small," *Harvard Educational Review* XXIX (Summer 1959): 227-244; Vernon Dibble, *The Legacy of Albion Small* (Chicago: University of Chicago Press, 1975); Page, *Class in American Sociology,* pp. 113-142; and Barnes, *Introduction to the History of Sociology,* pp. 766-792.

[5]Richard T. Ely, *The Past and the Present of Political Economy,* Johns Hopkins University Studies in History and Political Science, Volume II (Baltimore: Johns Hopkins University Press, 1884), p. 49; Richard T. Ely, *The Social Law of Service* (New York: Eaton and Mains, 1896), p. 77; and see Richard T. Ely, *et al., Science Economic Discussion* (New York: The Science Company, 1886), p. 54. Cf. John Dewey and James Tufts, *Ethics* (New York: Henry Holt, 1908), p. 445:

> Until there is secured to and imposed upon all members of society the right

  and the duty of work in socially serviceable occupations, with due returns
  in social goods, rights to life and free movement will hardly advance much
  beyond their present largely nominal state.

See also Tariello, *Reconstruction,* pp. 58-59 for some other representative expressions of this idea.

  Ely was a student of Karl Knies at Heidelberg. His basic moral framework was the Christian Socialism of Maurice and Kingsley; his outlook on labor unions was shaped by Lujo Brentano; his theory of depressions similar to John A. Hobson's. Ely was America's first academic "labor historian"; see Richard T. Ely, *The Labor Movement in America* (New York: Thomas Y. Crowell, 1886). On Ely, see Richard T. Ely, *Ground Under Our Feet: An Autobiography* (New York: Macmillan, 1938); Benjamin Rader, "Richard Ely: Lay Spokesman for the Social Gospel," *Journal of American History* LIII (June 1966): 61-74; Benjamin Rader, *The Academic Mind and Reform: The Influence of Richard T. Ely in American Life* (Lexington: University of Kentucky Press, 1966); John R. Everett, *Religion in Economics: A Study of John Bates Clark, Richard T. Ely, Simon N. Patten* (New York: King's Crown Press, 1946), pp. 75-98; James Dombrowski, *The Early Days of Christian Socialism in America* (New York: Columbia University Press, 1936), pp. 50-59; and Sidney Fine, "Richard T. Ely, Forerunner of Progressivism," *Mississippi Valley Historical Review* XXXVII (March 1951): 599-624.

  Ely's many students—among whom were Edward Bemis, John H. Finley, Albert Shaw, Amos G. Warner, Albion Small, John R. Commons, E. A. Ross, and Woodrow Wilson—would help fill a roll-call of leading American progressives. On Commons in particular, see Note 8, *infra.*

[6]Ely, *Ground Under Our Feet,* p. 136. The final, published version of the document eliminated the reference to laissez faire. The similarity between the American Economics Association and the *Verein für Sozialpolitik* is discussed in Fine, *Laissez Faire,* pp. 213-214; see also Jürgen Herbst, *The German Historical School in American Scholarship* (Middletown, CT: Wesleyan University Press, 1965), pp. 44-45, 134, and 144-145. Herbst (p. 144) has a passage from the *Verein's* founding document that is remarkably similar in tone to Ely's AEA prospectus.

  There was even an epistemological *Methodenstreit* in America echoing the better-known controversy in Germany between the 'deductive' and 'historical' economists; see Richard T. Ely, *et al., Science Economic Discussion* (New York: The Science Company, 1886) (a compilation of papers presented at a conference earlier in the year, and first published serially in *Science* magazine).

[7]See generally Herbst, *German Historical School*; Fine, *Laissez Faire*; Joseph Dorfman, "The Role of the German Historical School in American Economic Thought," *American Economic Review, Supplement* XL (May 1955): 17-28; and Arthur Mann, "British Social Thought and American Reformers of the Progressive Era," *Mississippi Valley Historical Review* XLII (March 1956): 672-692.

  On John Bates Clark (whose views on competition changed during his career), see Everett, *Religion in Economics,* pp. 26-74; J. M. Clark, "J. M. Clark on J. B. Clark," in Henry William Spiegel, ed., *The Development of Economic Thought: Great Economists in Perspective* (New York: John Wiley, 1952), pp. 592-612; Paul T. Homan, *Contemporary Economic Thought* (New York: Harper Brothers, 1928), pp. 17-103; *John Bates Clark, A Memorial* (Privately Printed, 1938, copy in University of Michigan Library); and Joel Jalladeau, "The Methodological Conversion of John Bates Clark," *History of Political Economy* VII (Summer 1975): 209-226.

  On Henry Carter Adams, see Joseph Dorfman, "Henry Carter Adams: The Harmonizer of Liberty and Reform," in Joseph Dorfman, ed., *The Relation of the State to Industrial Action and Economics and Jurisprudence: Two Essays by Henry Carter Adams* (New York: Columbia University Press, 1954); Lester Volin, "Henry Carter Adams, Critic of Laissez Faire," *Journal of Social Philosophy* III (April 1938): 235-250; and "Memorial to Henry Carter Adams," *American Economic Review* XII (September 1922): 401-417. Adams's many students included the sociologist Charles Horton Cooley and the historians John Franklin Jameson and James Allen Smith.

[8]Commons's intellectual background is fascinating. He studied under Henry C. Carey, the anti-free trader at Oberlin, before he hooked up with Richard Ely at Johns Hopkins. Dropping out of academia at the turn of the century for five years, Commons became a journalist and took a postgraduate course in radicalism through the efforts and the writings of such individuals as the English socialist William English Walling, Daniel De Leon, and John A. Hobson. At the University of Wisconsin he became head of the American Bureau of Industrial Research—the foremost academic 'think tank' of the pre-New Deal era.

On Commons, see Lafayette G. Harter, *John R. Commons: His Assault on Laissez Faire* (Corvallis: Oregon State University Press, 1962); John R. Commons, *Myself* (Madison: University of Wisconsin Press, 1963 [1934]); and Selig Perlman, "John Rogers Commons, 1862-1945," and Kenneth Parsons, "John R. Commons Point of View," both in John R. Commons, *Economics of Collective Action,* ed. Kenneth Parsons (New York: Macmillan, 1950).

[9]The application of reform ideas to the law is taken up in chapter eight, *infra.* The standard account of the connection between the American pragmatist spirit and philosophy and the politics of collectivism is Morton White, *Social Thought in America: The Revolt Against Formalism* (New York: Viking Press, 1949); see also Tariello, *Reconstruction,* pp. 70-96, 115-137; and see also the illuminating comments by Leonard Peikoff, *The Ominous Parallels: The End of Freedom in America* (New York: Stein and Day, 1982), pp. 126-138, especially the *aperçu* on p. 137: " . . . in every branch of philosophy, the pragmatists stress 'experiment', 'novelty', 'progress', then offer a rehash of traditional theories culminating in the oldest politics of all: statism."

Henry Carter Adams introduced John Dewey to the concept of industrial democracy; see William Brickman, "Dewey's Social and Political Commentary," in Jo Ann Boydston, ed., *Guide to the Works of John Dewey* (Carbondale: Southern Illinois University Press, 1970), p. 218. On Dewey's economic collectivism, see Gary Bullert, *The Politics of John Dewey* (Buffalo: Prometheus Books, 1983), pp. 21-34.

[10]Although the period 1865-1914 was an increasingly secular one, anti-egoistic Christian ethical ideas were still of great importance, even among intellectuals. For some general accounts of Christian Socialism and the American social gospel, see James Dombrowski, *The Early Days of Christian Socialism in America* (New York: Columbia University Press, 1936); Charles Howard Hopkins, *Protestant Churches and Industrial America* (New Haven: Yale University Press, 1940); Donald Meyer, *The Protestant Search for Political Realism, 1919-1939* (Berkeley: University of California Press, 1960); Aaron Abell, *American Catholicism and Social Action: A Search for Social Justice, 1865-1950* (New York: Hanover House, 1960); Quint, *Origin of American Socialism,* pp. 103-141; John N. Moody, *et al.,* eds., *Church and Society: Catholic Social and Political Thought and Movements, 1789-1950* (New York: Arts Press, 1953), pp. 843-904; and Thomas P. Jenkin, "The American Fabian Movement," *Western Political Quarterly* II (June 1948): 113-123. See also Jacob Henry Dorn, *Washington Gladden: Prophet of the Social Gospel* (Columbus: Ohio State University Press, 1967), especially pp. 203-235; and Vernon Bodein, *The Social Gospel of Walter Rauschenbush and Its Relation to Religious Education* (New Haven: Yale University Press, 1944).

On John A. Ryan, see John A. Ryan, *Industrial Democracy From a Catholic Viewpoint* (Washington, D.C.: Rossi-Bryn, 1925); John A. Ryan, *Social Doctrine in Action* (New York: Harper and Brothers, 1944); Patrick W. Gearty, *The Economic Thought of Monsignor John A. Ryan* (Washington, D.C.: Catholic University of America Press, 1953); and Francis Broderick, *Right Reverend New Dealer, John A. Ryan* (New York: Macmillan, 1963).

[11]Thomas Hill Green, "Lecture on Liberal Legislation and Freedom of Contract," 1881, in *Works of Thomas Hill Green* (London: Longmans, Green, 1888), Volume III, pp 370-371. On Green and his importance, see Melvin Richter, *The Politics of Conscience: T. H. Green and His*

Age (Cambridge: Harvard University Press, 1964); K. R. Hoover, "Liberalism and the Philosophy of T. H. Green," *Western Political Quarterly* XXVI (September 1973): 550-565; John Rodman, "What is Living and What is Dead in the Political Philosophy of T. H. Green," *Western Political Quarterly* XXVI (September 1973): 566-586; Michael Freeden, *The New Liberalism: An Ideology of Social Reform* (Oxford: Clarendon Press, 1978); Peter Clarke, *Liberals and Social Democrats* (Cambridge: Cambridge University Press, 1978); and A. J. M. Milne, *The Social Philosophy of English Idealism* (London: George Allen and Unwin, 1962).

[12]Green, "Liberal Legislation," pp. 370, 371.

[13]Ibid., pp. 370, 371, 372 (emphasis added). Cf. Dewey and Tufts, *Ethics,* pp. 482-483:

> The moral criterion by which to try social institutions and political measures . . . is whether a given custom or law sets free individual capacities in such a way as to make them available for the *development of the general happiness or the common good.* (emphasis added)

[14]Richard T. Ely, "Industrial Liberty," *Publications of the American Economic Association,* 3d Series, II (February 1902), pp. 64-65 (emphasis added); Richard T. Ely, "Economic Theory and Labor Legislation," *Publications of the American Economic Association,* 3d Series, IX (April 1908), p. 139.

[15]Ely, "Industrial Liberty," p. 65 (emphasis in original); cf. Henry Carter Adams, "Relation of the State to Industrial Action," *Publications of the American Economic Association,* 1887, in Dorfman, ed., *Two Essays,* p. 93:

> Suppose that of ten manufacturers nine have a keen appreciation of the evils that flow from protracted labor on the part of women and children; and, were it in their power, would gladly produce cottons without destroying family life, and without setting in motion those forces that must ultimately result in race-deterioration. But the tenth man has no such apprehensions. The claims of family life, the rights of childhood, and the maintenance of social well-being are but words to him. He measures success wholly by the rate of profit and controls his business solely with a view to grand sales. If now the state stand as an unconcerned spectator, whose only duty is to put down a riot when a strike occurs (a duty which government in this country is giving to private management), the nine men will be forced to conform to the methods adopted by the one.

And see Hale, "Labor Legislation as an Enlargement of Individual Liberty," 15 *American Labor Legislation Review* 155 (1925).

[16]John Bates Clark, *Philosophy of Wealth,* 1886, quoted in Everett, *Religion in Economics,* p. 41.

[17]Henry Carter Adams, "The Labor Problem," *Scientific American. Supplement* Number 555 (21 August 1886), p. 8861.

[18]Clark, *Philosophy of Wealth,* quoted in Everett, *Religion in Economics,* p. 41.

[19]Adams, "Labor Problem," p. 8862.

[20]Richard T. Ely, *An Introduction to Political Economy* (New York: Chautauqua Press, 1889), p. 236.

[21]Adams, "Relation of the State," pp. 86, 88; Adams, "An Interpretation of the Social Movement of Our Time," *International Journal of Ethics* II (October 1891), p. 42. Cf. Richard T. Ely *Socialism: An Examination of Its Nature, Its Strength and Its Weakness, with Suggestions for Social Reform* (New York: Thomas Y. Crowell, 1894), especially pp. 314-322.

[22]Adams, "Interpretation of the Social Movements," p. 43; "Relation of State," p. 95 (emphasis added).

[23]Commons, Discussion of Arthur T. Hadley, "Economic Theory and Political Morality: Presidential Address," *Publications of the American Economics Association,* 3d Series, I (February 1900), pp. 67-69; see also John R. Commons, "Representation of Interests," *The Independent* LII (June 1900): 1479-1483; and John R. Commons, "Is Class Conflict in America

Growing and Is It Inevitable?" *American Journal of Sociology* XIII (May 1908): 756-783. Cf. Gronlund, *New Economy,* pp. 161-163.

[24]Herbert Croly, *The Promise of American Life* (New York: E.P. Dutton, 1963 [1909]), pp. 130, 129 (and see pp. 385-398); *Progressive Democracy* (New York: Macmillan, 1914), pp. 388, 389, 390. On Herbert Croly and his importance, see Eric Goldman, *Rendezvous With Destiny* (New York: Alfred Knopf, 1952), pp. 188-207; Charles Forcey, *The Crossroads of Liberalism: Croly, Weyl, Lippman and the Progressive Era, 1900-1925* (New York: Oxford University Press, 1961); David Noble, "Herbert Croly and American Progressive Thought," *Western Political Quarterly* VII (December 1954): 537-553; and the articles in the *New Republic,* 16 July 1930. I wonder how many readers of this periodical have ever stopped to consider the significance of its title.

[25]Ricardo, *Principles of Political Economy,* 1817, quoted in Lionel Robbins, *Theory of Economic Policy,* p. 78.

[26]John Ramsay McCulloch, *The Principles of Political Economy,* 4th revised edition (London: Longman, Brown, Green and Longmans, 1849 [1825]), p. 416.

[27]Smith, *WN,* Book I, c. 8, p. 81.

[28]Francis A. Walker, *The Wages Question: A Treatise on Wages and the Wages Class* (New York: Henry Holt, 1876), p. 83.

[29]Ibid., p. 87.

[30]Ibid., p. 86; and see pp. 387, 404.

[31]According to one Leonard Horner, a factory inspector in 1851, quoted in John Rae, "The Eight Hour Movement in England," *Social Economist* IV (May 1893), p. 271, the absence of any decline in output or increase in unemployment, though

> accounted for partly by increased stimulus given to ingenuity to make the machinery more perfect and capable of increased speed . . . arises far more from the workpeople, by improved health, by absence of that weariness and exhaustion which the long hours occasioned, and, by their increased cheerfulness and activity, being enabled to work more steadily and diligently, and to economize time, intervals of rest while at their work being now less necessary.

And of course this was also Robert Owen's claim; see chapter two *supra.*

[32]Lujo Brentano, *Hours and Wages in Relation to Production,* trans. Mrs. William Arnold (London: Swan Sonnenschein, 1894 [1875]), pp. 32, 13-14. Jacob Schoenhof (an American economics writer), in his *The Economy of High Wages* (New York: G.P. Putnam's Sons, 1893), also espoused an 'efficiency' theory.

[33]See, for instance, Sidney Webb, "The Regulation of the Hours of Labour," *Contemporary Review,* 1889, in *Problems of Modern Industry* (London: Longmans, Green, 1898); Sidney Webb and Harold Cox, *The Eight Hours Day* (London: Walter Scott, 1891); and Sidney and Beatrice Webb, *Industrial Democracy,* revised edition (New York: Augustus Kelley, 1964 [1920, 1897]), pp. 749-784. See also Francis A. Walker, "The Eight Hours Agitation," *Atlantic Monthly* LXV (June 1890): 800-810.

[34]On Steward, McNeill, and Gunton, see Dorothy Douglas, "Ira Steward on Consumption and Employment," *Journal of Political Economy* XL (August 1932): 532-543; Jack Blicksilver, "George Gunton: Pioneer Spokesman for a Labor-Big Business Entente," *Business History Review* XXXI (Spring 1957): 1-22; Derber, *American Idea of Industrial Democracy,* pp. 41-46; and David Montgomery, *Beyond Equality: Labor and the Radical Republicans, 1862-1872* (New York: Alfred Knopf, 1967).

The account of the American trade union wage theory presented in this chapter is based on the following additional sources: George P. McNeill, "Hours of Labor," in George P. McNeill, ed., *The Labor Movement, The Problem of Today; The History, Purpose, and Possibilities of Labor Organizations in Europe and America; Guilds, Trades-Unions, and Knights of Labor; Wages and Profits; Hours of Labor; Functions of Capital; Chinese Labor Competition;*

Arbitration; Profit Sharing and Cooperation; Principles of Knights of Labor; Moral and Educational Aspects of the Labor Question (New York: M.W. Hagen, 1892 [1886]), pp. 470-482; George P. McNeill, *The Eight-Hour Primer* (Washington, D.C.: American Federation of Labor, 1911); Ira Steward, "A Reduction of Hours An Increase in Wages," 1865, in Commons and Gilmore, *Documentary History,* Volume IX, pp. 284-301; George Gunton, *Wealth and Progress: A Critical Examination of the Wages Question* (New York: D. Appelton, 1897 [1887]); George P. Gunton, "The Economic and Social Importance of the Eight-Hour Hour Movement," 2d edition, *Eight Hour Series,* Number 2 (Washington, D.C.: American Federation of Labor, 1889); and Lemuel Danryid, *History and Philosophy of the Eight-Hour Movement* (Washington, D.C.: American Federation of Labor, 1899).

See also Raymond Mussey, "Eight-Hour Theory in the American Federation of Labor," in Jacob Hollander, ed., *Economic Essays Contributed in Honor of John Bates Clark* (New York: Macmillan, 1927), pp. 229-243; Jean Tripp McKelvey, *AFL Attitudes Toward Production, 1900-1932* (Ithaca: Cornell University Press, 1952); and David Smelser, *Unemployment and American Trade Unions* (Baltimore: Johns Hopkins University Press, 1919), pp. 34-56.

[35]Gunton, *Wealth and Progress,* pp. 90, 92, 88, 89.

[36]Frank K. Foster, "Sidelights on the Shorter Workday Demand," *American Federationist,* 1900, quoted in Mussey, "Eight-Hour Theory," p. 236; Gunton, *Wealth and Progress,* p. 90.

[37]Gunton, *Wealth and Progress,* pp. 90, and 193-194.

[38]Ibid., p. 58 (emphasis added). Although it is not a point that can be defended here, I suspect that modern 'demand-side' economics was born, not with Keynes in the 20th century, but with American trade union wage theory of the late 19th century, together with the underconsumptionist doctrines of social reformers such as John Hobson.

[39]Hence the ditty, "If you work by the piece, or work by the day/Reducing the hours Increases the pay."

[40]McNeill, *Eight-Hour Primer,* p. 17; see also Steward, "Reduction in Hours," p. 297. Not that this advice was always followed. In one celebrated instance Massachusetts passed a law limiting the number of hours worked per week, but did not establish an hourly or weekly pay floor. The ensuing *decline in workers' wages* precipitated the massive, violent Lawrence Textile Strike of 1912; see Paul F. Brissenden, *The I. W.W.: A Study in American Syndicalism,* 2d edition (New York: Longmans, Green, & Co., 1919), p. 284.

[41]Steward, "Reduction in Hours," p. 285; see also Gunton, *Wealth and Progress,* pp. 260-261.

[42]Gompers, *Proceedings of the AFL,* 1887, quoted in Harry A. Millis, *Labor's Progress and Some Basic Problems* (New York: McGraw-Hill, 1938), p. 494. See Gunton, "Economic and Social Importance," p. 13; *Wealth and Progress,* pp. 253-254. Compare with McNeill, "Hours of Labor," p. 471; and *Eight-Hour Primer,* p. 15; and see Smelser, *Unemployment and American Trade Unions,* pp. 51-53.

Union officials occasionally mentioned the "efficiency" argument popular among progressive intellectuals; see Gompers, "The Philosophy of the Shorter Working Day," *American Federationist,* 1915, quoted in Smelser, *Unemployment and American Trade Unions,* p. 52; see also Mollie Ray Carroll, *Labor and Politics: The Attitude of the American Federation of Labor Toward Legislation and Politics* (Boston: Houghton Mifflin, 1923), p. 63. But this argument was strictly for public consumption. After all, if union leaders believed that higher-wage laborers were more productive because of their higher wages, why did they fear the competition of lower-paid, unorganized or immigrant labor?

[43]Steward, "Reduction in Hours," p. 298, and McNeill, "Hours of Labor," p. 475.

[44]McNeill, "Hours of Labor," p. 475.

[45]George Schilling, "Less Hours, Increased Production—Greater Progress," *American Federationist,* 1900, as quoted in Mussey, "Eight Hour Theory," pp. 239-240. See also the like-minded statements in Saposs, *Readings in Trade Unionism,* pp. 259-261; and Webb, *Industrial Democracy,* pp. 723-724.

[46]McNeill, "Hours of Labor," pp. 475-476 (emphasis added). The first sentence in the quoted passage is, to be sure, uncontroversial.

[47]Sumner Slichter, "The Secret of Higher Wages," *New Republic* LIV (March 8, 1928), p. 185; Roosevelt's Radio Address, June 17, 1933, *New York Times,* as quoted in Simon Whitney, *Trade Associations and Industrial Control* (New York: Central Book Company, 1934), p. 17n.

[48]"Fallacy of Wage Reductions," *Shoe Worker's Journal,* 1924, quoted in Saposs, *Readings in Trade Unionism,* p. 273.

[49]See American Federation of Labor Reconstruction Program, 1919, quoted in Saposs, *Readings in Trade Unionism,* p. 47: "Unemployment is due to underconsumption. Underconsumption is caused by low or insufficient wages. Just wages will prevent industrial stagnation and lessen periodical unemployment."

The unpopularity of downwardly flexible wage rates (as a means for obtaining full employment) among otherwise fairly orthodox economists (who were leery of any claim that unions could *raise* purchasing power through collective bargaining) is discussed in J. Ronnie Davis, *The New Economics and the Old Economists* (Ames: Iowa State University Press, 1971). The ubiquity of the underconsumptionist/purchasing power theories of unemployment in America by the eve of the Great Depression is mentioned or discussed in Simon Whitney, *Trade Associations and Industrial Control: A Critique of the NIRA* (New York: Central Book Company, 1934), pp. 16-19; Leverett S. Lyon, *et al., The National Recovery Administration: An Analysis and Appraisal* (Washington: Brookings Institution, 1935), pp. 343, 415-416, 757-760; and Theodore Rosenhof, *Dogma, Depression and the New Deal: The Debate of Political Leaders Over Economic Recovery* (Port Washington, N.Y.: Kennikat Press, 1975), pp. 39-43. See also Paul Homan, "Economic Planning: The Proposals and the Literature," *Quarterly Journal of Economics* XLVII (November 1932), p. 116:

> One of the most interesting features of the discussion of social-economic planning is the extent to which it is dominated by some variant of Mr. J. A. Hobson's theory of over-saving or under-consumption as the primary cause of economic instability.

[50]Steward, "A Reduction in Hours," pp. 300, 298f.

[51]McNeill, "Hours of Labor," p. 482. See also the similar statement in *Eight-Hour Primer,* pp. 15, 18. McNeill wrote the "Hours of Labor" essay in 1886 when he was still an official of the Knights of Labor, an organization dedicated to the abolition of the wages system and its replacement by "cooperation." He wrote the *Eight-Hour Primer* while an associate of the AFL, an organization resigned to the permanence of the wages system. Yet the analysis was the same in both instances, an interesting fact that has not always been noticed by historians who wax eloquent about the allegedly vast differences between the two organizations, while (usually) gazing wistfully at the former.

[52]Gunton, *Wealth and Progress,* pp. 228, 229, 270-271 (emphasis added).

[53]George Gunton, "Tendencies of Trade Unions," *Social Economist* VII (October 1894), pp. 218-219 (emphasis added); "Economics of Strikes and Boycotts," *Social Economist* IV (May 1893), p. 263.

[54]Another alternative broached in these years that periodically returns for reconsideration is 'profit sharing'. The opposition to profit-sharing plans by union sympathizers arose from a number of related concerns. In the first place, the underlying ideal of profit sharing is that of a *complementarity* of interest between employer and employee in the prosperity of the firm— a notion hard to swallow by those raised on a class conflict-based adversarial view of the relationship between employer and employee. In the lexicon of union propaganda, profit sharing, particularly when it was offered by employers unilaterally, was always 'anti-union'— and in a much deeper sense than when, say, employers tied a profit-sharing arrangement to a yellow-dog contract (which was sometimes, though not always, done).

There was (and still is) another economic objection to profit sharing on the part of union-oriented champions of industrial democracy that is not always appreciated by outsiders. The proponents of profit sharing do not intend investors to lose out by this deal. On the contrary, workers themselves are assumed to create, through 'increased zeal and efficiency', the additional profits that will be paid out along with the dividends. But this concept runs straight into the 'make work' ideals of unionism in the same way that Scientific Management theories do—both are just different kinds of 'speed ups' or 'stretch outs'. For some discussions of profit sharing, see William S. Barnes, ed., *The Labor Problem: Plain Questions and Practical Answers* (New York: Harper and Brothers, 1886), pp. 52-230; and the articles in the *Journal of Social Science* (New York: G. Putnam's Sons, 1887), Number 23 (November 1887), pp. 25-36, 47-67 (in the University of Michigan Library). See also John Shields Nicholson, "Profit Sharing," *Contemporary Review,* 1890, reprinted in his *Strikes and Social Problems* (New York: Macmillan, 1896), pp. 45-69; I. B. Helburn, "Trade Union Response to Profit Sharing Problems: 1886-1966," *Labor History* XII (Winter 1971): 68-80; Derber, *Idea of Industrial Democracy,* pp. 63-65; and Edmund Pree, "Profit Sharing," in Lewis Henry, ed., *Studies in the Labor Problem in the United States* (Ann Arbor: University of Michigan, 1909 typescript in University of Michigan Library).

[55]See Barnes, *The Labor Problem,* pp. 52-199, 231-255; John O'Neill, "Arbitration," in McNeill, *The Labor Movement,* pp. 497-507; Richard T. Ely, "Arbitration," *North American Review* CXLIII (October 1886): 317-328; Joseph D. Weeks, *Labor Differences and Their Settlement: A Plea for Arbitration and Conciliation,* Economic Tracts, XX (New York: Society for Political Education, 1886); Vernon Jenson, "Notes on the Beginnings of Collective Bargaining," *Industrial and Labor Relations Review* IX (January 1956): 225-235; Edwin Witte, *Historical Survey of Labor Arbitration* (Philadelphia: University of Pennsylvania Press, 1952); and Herbert Schreiber, "The Majority Preference Provisions in Early State Labor Arbitration Statutes, 1880-1900," *American Journal of Legal History* XV (April 1971): 186-198.

[56]The attitude of organized labor toward arbitration in the 1870s and 1880s is discussed in Jenson, "Notes," pp. 228-231, and Perlman, *Labor Union Theories,* pp. 250-252. For some direct testimony, see Barnes, *The Labor Problem,* pp. 113-145; and the "Blair Committee" Report: U.S., Senate, Committee on Education and Labor, *Report* (Washington, D.C.: GPO, 1885), Volume I, especially pp. 23 (Robert Layton, Knights of Labor), 85-88 (Frank K. Foster, Knights of Labor), and 377-378 (Samuel Gompers, Cigar Makers Union).

[57]Since arbitration in a commercial setting is always retrospective and concerns the interpretation of a contract already formed, while arbitration as it was being proposed in these years had to do with the negotiation of prospective wage rates in the context of 'at will' employment, employers were technically correct in asserting that there was nothing to arbitrate; see Thornton, *On Labour,* p. 323.

[58]Ely, "Arbitration," p. 325 (emphasis added).

[59]Ibid., pp. 325-326.

[60]George Gunton, "Society and Sympathy Strikes," *Social Economist* VII (November 1894), pp. 264, 267 (emphasis added). See also p. 265 (emphasis added):

> But if we are to maintain the semblance of free government [sic] we must recognize the laborer's full right to fair competition with capital in all labor controversies which can be accomplished *by limiting the contest to the original disputants on both sides.* Let outside capitalists and laborers [keep] hands off until the struggle is ended. Then open the field to all.

Gunton's essay was a defense of the sympathy strike (and by implication, other secondary boycotts) in response to employers who tried to break strikes by importing 'scabs' they had no intention of using as permanent replacements for strikers.

Compare Gunton's discussion with the observation of Henry George, *The Condition of Labor: An Open Letter to Pope Leo XIII* (New York: United States Book Company, 1891), p. 86 (emphasis in original):

> Labor associations can do nothing to raise wages but by force; it may be force applied passively, or force applied actively, or force held in reserve, but it must be force; they *must* coerce or hold the power to coerce employers; they *must* coerce those among their members disposed to straggle; they *must* do their best to get into their hands the whole field of

labor they seek to occupy and to force other workingmen either to join them or to starve. [sic] Those who tell you of trades unions bent on raising wages by moral suasion alone are like those who would tell of you of tigers who live on oranges.

On the virtual equation of 'recognition' with the closed shop, see John R. Commons, Minority Report, Commission on Industrial Relations, *Final Report* (Washington, D.C.: GPO, 1915), p. 208; Lamar T. Beman, comp., *Selected Articles on the Closed Shop* (New York: H.W. Wilson, 1921); and National Association of Manufacturers, *Open Shop Encyclopedia*, 3d revised edition (New York: National Association of Manufacturers, 1922), pp. 64-67.

[61]Gompers, *Report*, Volume I, pp. 377, 378.

[62]Adams, "The Labor Problem," p. 8862; Adams, Contribution to the symposium in Barnes, *The Labor Problem*, pp. 62, 63 (emphasis added). The significance of his ideas are assessed in Dorfman, *Two Essays*, pp. 1-48; Perlman, *Labor Union Theories*, pp. 163-173; and Derber, *Idea of Industrial Democracy*, pp. 72-76.

This account of Adams's theory of industrial democracy is based on the following sources: Henry Carter Adams, "The Labor Problem," *Scientific American, Supplement* Number 555 (21 August 1886): 8861-8863, 8877-8880; Henry Carter Adams, "Economics and Jurisprudence," in Ely, ed., *Science Economic Discussion*, pp. 80-91; Henry Carter Adams, "An Interpretation of the Social Movements of Our Time," *International Journal of Ethics* II (October 1891): 32-50; Henry Carter Adams, *Outline of Lectures on Political Economy*, 2d edition (Ann Arbor: Register Publishing House, 1886), pp. 74-76; Henry Carter Adams, "Relation of the State to Industrial Action," *Publications of the American Economic Association*, 1887, and "Economics and Jurisprudence," *Publications of the American Economic Association*, 1897, in Dorfman, *Two Essays*.

[63]Adams, "Economics and Jurisprudence," 1897, p. 155.

[64]Adams, "The Labor Problem," p. 8862; "Economics and Jurisprudence," 1897, p. 155.

[65]Adams, "The Labor Problem," p. 8862.

[66]Id.

[67]Ibid., pp. 8862-8863.

[68]Id.; "Interpretation of Social Movements," p. 49.

[69]Adams, "Economics and Jurisprudence," 1897, pp. 160, 161; "The Labor Problem," p. 8863.

[70]Adams, "Economics and Jurisprudence," 1897, p. 152.

[71]Ibid., pp. 174, 151, 150.

[72]Adams, "Interpretation of the Social Movements," p. 49.

[73]Franklin Giddings, Discussion of Adams's "Economics and Jurisprudence," 1897, pp. 165-166. See also Charles A. Tuttle, "The Workman's Position in the Light of Economic Progress," *Publications of the American Economic Association* III (February 1902): 199-234; and E. A. Ross, "A Legal Dismissal Wage," *American Economic Review*, Supplement (March 1919): 132-136.

[74]Weeks, *Plea for Arbitration*, p. 57; see also Barnes, *The Labor Problem*, pp. 239, 243; Thornton, *On Labour*, pp. 323-324; and John Bates Clark, "The Modern Appeal to Legal Forces in Economic Life," *Publications of the American Economic Association* IX (December 1894), p. 23.

[75]R. H. Thurston, Discussion following Adams's essay "The Labor Problem," p. 8879.

[76]Henry Farnham and George Gunton, Discussion of Adams's "Economics and Jurisprudence," 1897, pp. 168, 169.

[77]C. S. Walker, Discussion of Adams's "Economics and Jurisprudence," 1897, p. 166.

[78]John Maurice Clark, *Social Control of Business* (Chicago: University of Chicago Press, 1926), pp. 136-137. Cf. the protest by Harry Gideonse, *Organized Scarcity and Public Policy*, Public Policy Pamphlet Number 30 (Chicago: University of Chicago Press, 1939), pp. 30-31, against the New Deal implementation of progressivism's theory of economic democracy:

The pseudo-democratic vocabulary of current monopolist tendencies is one of the chief reasons for their present dominance in public policy. Schemes to increase the price of food by the curtailment of agricultural production are advocated on the ground that they are 'democratic', because a majority of the food producers has voted to accept them. Monopolist trade unions and monopolist employers describe their 'agreements' as 'democratic' because a majority of the monopolists on the producers' side favor their adoption. Thus, a convention of cats might describe its quota scheme for the consumption of robins as 'democratic' if a feline majority approved the 'plan', although the term 'democratic' is obviously inclusive and it is easy to see that consultation of the present victims of the plan might lead to a different outcome. No one would argue that consultation of a majority of the beneficiaries of, say, a steel monopoly without consultation of the consumers of steel was democratic, but the terms goes unchallenged in current politics if the consultation is limited to milk or wheat producers without consultation of the consumer of these products.

For the spread of "industrial democracy" to occupations and professions outside the labor movement, see J. A. C. Grant, "The Gild Returns to America," *Journal of Politics* IV (August 1942): 303-336, 458-477.

[79]Nikolaas G. Pierson, *Principles of Economics,* trans. A. A. Wotzel (London: Macmillan, 1902), p. 325; and see pp. 321-331 generally for an interesting discussion of the arguments and evidence put forth in his day about the 'efficiency' hypothesis. Although the following is purely speculative, it seems more logical to assume that individuals who are paid a time rate work harder or better in order to qualify for a raise, and then regard that higher wage or salary granted as already earned; what spurs them to greater effort thereafter is anticipation of the next increase. It is not, in other words, the higher salary already earned which increases present effort.

[80]Alfred Marshall, *Elements of the Economics of Industry* (London: Macmillan, 1905 [1892]), p. 351; and see pp. 273-296; and see also Alfred Marshall, *The Economics of Industry,* 3d edition (London: Macmillan, 1885 [1879]), pp. 102-103.

[81]John Davidson, *The Bargain Theory of Wages* (New York: G.P. Putnam's, 1898), pp. 87, 88; and see Marshall, *Elements,* pp. 133, 355.

[82]For an example of the shyster tactics Brandeis stooped to to "prove" this, see Albro Martin, *Enterprise Denied: The Origins of the Decline of American Railroads, 1890-1917* (New York: Columbia University Press, 1971), pp. 206-223.

[83]Paul H. Douglas, *The Theory of Wages* (New York: Augustus Kelley, 1964 [1934]), p. 76.

[84]See Machlup, *Political Economy of Monopoly,* pp. 389-392 for a discussion of the problems of the 'shock theory', variously defined; and see also Gordon S. Bloom, "Wage Pressure and Technological Discovery," *American Economic Review* XLI (September 1951): 603-617.

[85]Douglas, *Theory of Wages,* pp. 501, 83; cf. John Hicks, *Theory of Wages* (New York: St. Martin's Press, 1963 [1932]); and A. C. Pigou, *The Theory of Unemployment* (London: Macmillan, 1933).

[86]Alfred Marshall, *Principles of Economics*, 9th (Variorum) edition (London: Macmillan, 1961 [1890]), p. 521. See also Marshall, *Elements,* p. 196; and Marshall, *Economics of Industry,* pp. 199-200. See also Anastasios Petridis, "Alfred Marshall's Attitudes to and Economic Analysis of Trade Unions: A Case of Anomalies in a Competitive System," *History of Political Economy* V (September 1973): 165-198.

[87]See Allan Cartter, *Theory of Wages and Employment* (Homewood, IL: Richard D. Irwin, 1959); George Stigler, *Production and Distribution Theories: The Formative Period* (New York: Macmillan, 1941); Dennis Robertson, "Wage Grumbles," in *Economic Fragments*

(London: P. S. King, 1931); and Eric Roll, *A History of Economic Thought* 4th edition, revised and enlarged (London: Faber and Faber, 1954 [1938]), pp. 374-414, 424-439.

[88]Marshall, *Elements,* p. 240.

[89]John Bates Clark, *The Distribution of Wealth: A Theory of Wages, Interest, and Profit,* (New York: Macmillan, 1914 [1899]), p. viii (emphasis added).

[90]Marshall, *Principles of Economics,* Volume I, p. 518.

[91]Clark, *Distribution of Wealth,* p. viii.

[92]See Jalledeau, "Methodological Conversion." Clark did not become a proponent of laissez faire, however.

[93]Clark, *Distribution of Wealth,* pp. 4, v. The Englishman William Smart (1853-1915) published a treatise in 1899 with a thesis similar to Clark's; see William Smart, *The Distribution of Income,* 2d edition (London: Macmillan, 1912 [1899]), especially pp. 321-333.

[94]Clark, *Distribution of Wealth,* p. 179 (emphasis in original); "Modern Appeal," p. 12.

[95]Clark, "Modern Appeal," p. 16 (emphasis in original).

[96]John Bates Clark, "The Theory of Collective Bargaining," *Publications of the American Economic Association,* 3d series, X (February 1909), pp. 24-25.

[97]Clark, "Modern Appeal," p. 22.

[98]Philip Wicksteed, *The Common Sense of Political Economy,* ed. Lionel Robbins (New York: Augustus Kelley, 1967 [1933, 1910]), Volume II, pp. 694-695; cf. William Graham Sumner, "Industrial War," *The Forum,* 1886, reprinted in William Graham Sumner, *The Challenge of Facts and Other Essays* (New Haven: Yale University Press, 1914), p. 99; and Hutt, *Theory of Collective Bargaining,* p. 101.

[99]Douglas, *Theory of Wages,* pp. 3-96, *passim.,* summarized the claims and counterclaims down to the early 1930s, but it is worthwhile to reread the original debates and discussions themselves, particularly for the light they throw on the fundamentally different world-views of the participants. Though not a comprehensive listing, the following sources are instructive: John Bates Clark, "The Dynamics of the Wages Question," *Publications of the American Economic Association,* 3d series, IV (February 1903): 130-142, followed by the discussion on pp. 143-153; Jacob Hollander, "Present State of the Theory of Distribution," *Publications of the American Economic Association,* VII (February 1906): 23-45, followed by the discussion on pp. 46-60; "The Theory of Collective Bargaining," pp. 24-39, followed by the discussion on pp. 40-59; and John Bates Clark, "On What Principles Should a Court of Arbitration Proceed in Determining the Rate of Wages?" *Publications of the American Economic Association,* 3d series, VII (February 1907): 23-38, followed by the discussion on pp. 29-53. See also the debate: John A. Hobson, "Marginal Units in the Theory of Distribution," *Journal of Political Economy* XII (September 1904): 449-472; Thomas N. Carver, "The Marginal Theory of Distribution," *Journal of Political Economy* XII (March 1905): 257-266; and John A. Hobson, "The Marginal Theory of Distribution: A Reply to Professor Carver," *Journal of Political Economy* XIII (September 1908): 587-590; and Sumner Slichter, *et al.,* "Theory of Wages: A Symposium," *American Economic Review,* Supplement XVI (March 1926): 240-249.

For a relatively more recent replay of this controversy, see Richard Lester, "Shortcomings of Marginal Analysis for Wage Employment Problems," *American Economic Review* XXXVI (March 1946): 63-82, and (March 1947): 135-148; and Fritz Machlup, "Marginal Analysis and Empirical Research," *American Economic Review* XXXVI (September 1946): 519-554, and (March 1947): 148-154.

[100]Hobson, "Marginal Units," p. 451; see also Homan, *Contemporary Economic Theory,* p. 58.

[101]Thomas Nixon Carver, *Principles of Political Economy* (New York: Ginn & Co., 1919), pp. 383-384. See also his "Marginal Theory."

[102]Douglas, *Theory of Wages,* p. 61.

[103]Clark, *Distribution of Wealth,* pp. 321-331. See also Stigler, *Production and Distribution Theories,* pp. 304-305. Later on, Hobson's objection was turned on its head, and some claimed that it was the marginal worker who was fleeced, when an employer faced an upward-sloping supply curve for labor. For a rebuttal, see Machlup, *Political Economy of Monopoly,* pp. 366-367.

[104]John Ryan, Discussion of Clark's "Courts of Arbitration," pp. 44, 45; see also John Ryan, *A Living Wage: Its Ethical and Economic Aspects* (New York: Macmillan, 1906), especially pp. 243-249; and his *Distributive Justice,* (New York: Macmillan, 1916), pp. 347-351.

[105]See S. S. Garrett, "Wages and the Collective Bargain," *American Economic Review* XVIII (December 1928): 670-683.

[106]Henry Demarest Lloyd to Henry Carter Adams, 6 December 1886, letter quoted in Dorfman, *Two Essays,* p. 35.

Chapter Seven

[1]E. D. Ellis, "The Pluralistic State," *American Political Science Review* XIV (August 1920), p. 401; see also Bernard Zylstra, *From Pluralism to Collectivism: The Development of Harold Laski's Thought* (Assen, The Netherlands: Van Gorcum, 1968), p. 16; and Francis W. Coker, "Pluralistic Theories and the Attack upon State Sovereignty," in Charles E. Merriam, ed., *A History of Political Theory—Recent Times* (New York: Macmillan, 1924), p. 90. On Gierke, see Sobei Mogi, *Otto Gierke, His Political Teaching and Jurisprudence* (London: P.S. King, 1932); John D. Lewis, *The Genossenschafts-theorie of Otto von Gierke* (Madison: University of Wisconsin Press, 1935); Francis Coker, *Organismic Theories of the State* (New York: Columbia University Press, 1910); Bowen, *German Corporative Theories,* pp. 65-69; F. W. Maitland, Introduction to Otto Gierke, *Political Theories of the Middle Ages* (Cambridge: Cambridge University Press, 1913); and Ernest Barker, Introduction to Otto Gierke, *Natural Law and the Theory of Society* (Cambridge: Cambridge University Press, 1934).

[2]Hugo Sinzheimer was a labor lawyer whose book, *Ein Arbeitstarifgesetz* [A Law of Wage Contracts, subtitled "The Idea of Social Self Determination in Law"] was one of the bases for the Weimar collective bargaining system. Hugo Preuss was one of the drafters of the Weimar constitution. See Bowen, *German Corporative Theories,* pp. 68-69; Rupert Emerson, *State and Sovereignty in Modern Germany* (New Haven: Yale University Press, 1928), pp. 126-154; and Herman Finer, *Representative Government and a Parliament of Industry* (London: George Allen and Unwin, 1923), pp. 79 *et seq.* On Rathenau and his influence on economic reform, see James Joll, *Intellectuals in Politics* (London: Weidenfeld and Nicolson, 1960), pp. 59-129; Harry Kessler, *Walter Rathenau, His Life and Work,* trans. W. D. Robson-Scott and Lawrence Hyde (New York: Harcourt Brace, 1930); Fritz Redlich, "German Economic Planning for War and Peace," *The Review of Politics* VI (1944): 315-335; and Bowen, *German Corporative Theories,* pp. 164-209. On Brentano and Gierke, see Sheehan, *Career of Lujo Brentano,* p. 42; and Frieda Wunderlich, *Labor Under German Democracy: Arbitration, 1918-1933* (New York: New School for Social Research, 1940), p. 87.

[3]On Figgis, see Henry Magid, *English Political Pluralism* (New York: Columbia University Press, 1941), pp. 10-30; and Maurice Tucker, *J. N. Figgis* (London: SPCK, 1950). The founders of guild socialism—Arthur J. Penty, S. G. Hobson, and A. R. Orage—were aesthetes and medievalists whose patron saints were John Ruskin, William Morris, *et al.,* rather than Karl Marx or Sidney Webb.

On guild socialism, see S. T. Glass, *The Responsible Society* (London: Longmans, Green, 1966); Niles Carpenter, *Guild Socialism* (New York: D. Appleton, 1922); Niles Carpenter,

"The Literature of Guild Socialism," *Quarterly Journal of Economics* XXXIV (August 1920): 763-776; E. D. Ellis, "Guild Socialism and Pluralism," *American Political Science Review* XVII (November 1923): 584-596; W. Y. Elliott, *The Pragmatic Revolt in Politics: Syndicalism, Fascism, and the Constitutional State* (New York: Macmillan, 1928), especially pp. 177-214; Adam Ulam, *Philosophical Foundations of English Socialism* (Cambridge: Harvard University Press, 1951), pp. 80-95; Mary Parker Follett, *The New State* (New York: Longmans, Green, 1918), esp. pp. 258-270; Francis W. Coker, "Pluralistic Theories and the Attack upon State Sovereignty," in Merriam, *A History of Political Theory—Recent Times*; Francis W. Coker, "The Technique of the Pluralist State," *American Political Science Review* XV (May 1921): 186-213; Ernest Barker, "The Discredited State," *Political Quarterly* II (February 1915): 101-121; Ernest Barker, "The Rule of Law," *Political Quarterly* I (May 1914): 117-140; E. D. Ellis, "Political Science at the Crossroads," *American Political Science Review* XXI (November 1927): 773-791; E. D. Ellis, "The Pluralistic State"; George Sabine, "Pluralism: A Point of View," *American Political Science Review* XVII (February 1923): 34-50; Mises, *Socialism,* pp. 229-236; and Asa Sakalow, *The Political Theory of Arthur J. Penty* (New Haven: Yale Literary Magazine, 1940).

On Cole, see Luther B. Carpenter, *G. D. H. Cole: An Intellectual Biography* (Cambridge: Cambridge University Press, 1973); Margaret Cole, *The Life of G. D. H. Cole* (New York: St. Martin's Press, 1972); A.W. Wright, *G. D. H. Cole and Socialist Democracy* (Oxford: Clarendon Press, 1979); and Gerald L. Houseman, *G. D. H. Cole* (Boston: Twayne, 1979). For a striking instance of Cole's guild socialist influence outside his own country, see Otto Bauer, *The Austrian Revolution,* trans. H. J. Slenning (London: Leonard Parsons, 1925), pp. 145-146. On Tawney, whose *The Acquisitive Society* (1921) was much admired by American progressives, see Ross Terrill, *R. H. Tawney and His Times: Socialism as Fellowship* (Cambridge: Harvard University Press, 1973). On the relation between guild socialism and the radical syndicalist faction of the British labor movement, see Brenko Pribicevic, *The Shop Steward's Movement and Worker's Control, 1910-1922* (Oxford: Basil Blackwell, 1959).

[4]See Moon, *The Labor Problem and the Social Catholic Movement in France,* pp. 128, 145; see also Bowen, *German Corporative Theories,* pp. 85, 89, 102-104; and Elbow, *French Corporative Theory.*

[5]Elbow, *French Corporative Theory,* p. 109.

[6]Emile Durkheim, *The Division of Labor in Society,* trans. George Simpson (Glencoe, IL: The Free Press, 1947 [1893]), p. 27; see also Emile Durkheim, *Suicide: A Study in Sociology,* trans. John A. Spaulding and George Simpson (New York: The Free Press, 1951 [1897]), especially pp. 378, 379; and Emile Durkheim, *Socialism and Saint-Simon,* ed. with an Introduction by Alvin Gouldner, trans. Charlotte Suttler (Yellow Springs, OH: Antioch Press, 1958 [1896]). On Durkheim's corporativism and its influence, see Harry Elmer Barnes, "Durkheim's Contribution to the Reconstruction of Political Theory," *Political Science Quarterly* XXXV (June 1920): 236-253; Elbow, *French Corporative Theory,* pp. 108-114; Robert Nisbet, *The Sociology of Emile Durkheim* (London: Heinemann, 1975); Charles E. Gehlke, *Emile Durkheim's Contributions to Sociological Theory* (New York: Columbia University Press, 1935), pp. 150-181; and Stone, "Theories of Law and Justice of Fascist Italy," 1 *Modern Law Review* 177, 182-188 (1937). A French politician active in the 1930s, Joseph Paul-Boncour's 1900 doctoral dissertation, "La Fédéralisme Economique, Etude sur les Rapports de l'Individuel et des Groupements Professionales," (a plea for corporativism) was popular in England and France.

[7]On Duguit, see John M. Matthews, "A Recent Development in Political Theory: Duguit," *Political Science Quarterly* XXIV (June 1909): 284-295; Brown, "The Jurisprudence of M. Duguit," 32 *Law Quarterly Review* 168 (1916); Gavet, "Individualism and Realism," 29 *Yale Law Review* 523, 543 (1920); Roger Saltau, *French Political Thought* (New York: Russell and Russell, 1959 [1931]), pp. 473-485; Westel Willoughby, *The Ethical Basis of Political Authority* (New York: Macmillan, 1930), pp. 385-409; Charles G. Haines, *Revival of Natural*

Law Concepts (New York: Russell and Russell, 1930), pp. 260-273; Harold J. Laski, "M. Duguit's Conception of the State," in W. Ivor Jennings, ed., *Modern Theories of Law* (London: Oxford University Press, 1933); Follett, *The New State,* pp. 271-287; Elbow, *French Corporative Theory,* pp. 115-118; W. Y. Elliott, "The Metaphysics of M. Leon Duguit's Pragmatic Philosophy of Law," *Political Science Quarterly* XXXVII (December 1922): 639-654; Elliott, *Pragmatic Revolt,* pp. 269-312, 503-507; and Harold Laski, Introduction to Leon Duguit, *Les Transformations du Droit Public,* trans. Frida and Harold Laski as *Law in the Modern State* (New York: B.W. Huebsch, 1919 [1913]). Even Laski's translation of the book's title is a piece of advocacy.

⁸See Herbert Deane, *The Political Ideas of Harold J. Laski* (New York: Columbia University Press, 1955); Zylstra, *From Pluralism to Collectivism;* Elliott, *Pragmatic Revolt,* pp. 142-176; George Granville Eastwood, *Harold Laski* (London: Mowbray, 1977); Kingsley Martin, *Harold Laski, 1893-1950* (London: Gollancz, 1953); C. Hawkins, "Harold J. Laski: A Preliminary Analysis," *Political Science Quarterly* LXV (September 1950): 376-392; and Max Kampelman, "Harold Laski: A Current Analysis," *Journal of Politics* X (February 1948): 131-154. Laski taught at Harvard Law School from 1916 to 1920, where he formed deep and lasting intellectual friendships with, among others, Felix Frankfurter. He was a frequent visitor to America (indeed, he was on a first-name basis with Franklin D. Roosevelt).

⁹See Rodney Mott, "The Political Theory of Syndicalism," *Political Science Quarterly* XXXVII (March 1922): 25-40; Val Lorwin, *The French Labor Movement* (Cambridge: Harvard University Press, 1966), pp. 21-46; Saltau, *French Political Thought,* pp. 442-472; Lewis Lorwin, *Syndicalism in France* (New York: Longmans, Green, 1914), pp. 117-154; Bertrand Russell, *Roads to Freedom* (London: G. Allen & Unwin, 1918) pp. 70-98; and Mises, *Socialism,* pp. 239-244. On Sorel, see James Meisel, *The Genesis of Georges Sorel* (Ann Arbor: G. Whar, 1951); Irving Horowitz, *Radicalism and the Revolt Against Reason* (Carbondale: Southern Illinois University Press, 1968); Richard D. Humphrey, *Georges Sorel, Prophet Without Honor* (Cambridge: Harvard University Press, 1951); S. C. Lyttle, "Georges Sorel, Apostle of Fanaticism," in Edward Meade Earle, ed., *Modern France* (Princeton: Princeton University Press, 1951); and Elliott, *Pragmatic Revolt,* 111-141.

¹⁰Coker, "Pluralistic Theories of the State," p. 83; cf. Duguit, *Law in the Modern State,* pp. 20-25; and Harold Laski, *Studies in the Problem of Sovereignty* (New Haven: Yale University Press, 1917) pp. 267-285.

¹¹Duguit, *Law of the Constitution,* quoted in Elliott, *Pragmatic Revolt,* p. 271.

¹²Harold Laski, *The Foundations of Sovereignty and Other Essays* (New Haven: Yale University Press, 1921), p. 238.

¹³Harold Laski, *Authority in the Modern State* (New Haven: Yale University Press, 1917), pp. 46, 43; see also his *A Grammar of Politics* (New Haven: Yale University Press, 1925), p. 63; and Duguit, *Law in the Modern State,* pp. 25-31.

¹⁴Harold Laski, *A Grammar of Politics* (London: George Allen and Unwin, 1925), p. viii; cf. Laski, *Authority in the Modern State,* pp. 87-88.

¹⁵G. D. H. Cole, *The World of Labour,* 4th edition (London: Macmillan, 1928 [1913]), p. 288 (emphasis in original).

¹⁶Ramiro de Maeztu, *Authority, Liberty, and Function in Light of the War* (New York: Macmillan, 1916), pp. 199-200. De Maeztu was a student of Duguit's thought. On de Maeztu, see Ricardo Landeira, *Ramiro de Maeztu* (Boston: Twayne, 1978).

¹⁷G. D. H. Cole, *Guild Socialism Restated* (London: Leonard Parsons, 1920), p. 33.

¹⁸The revolutionary syndicalists sought to abolish the wages system in one stroke, through a general strike. They were a bit vague about the details that would follow.

¹⁹Duguit, "The Concept of Public Service," 32 *Yale Law Journal* 425, 429 (1923); *Law in the Modern State,* pp. 32-67.

²⁰Duguit, "Collective Acts as Distinguished from Contracts," 27 *Yale Law Journal* 753, 763 (1918) (emphasis added), and see p. 765; *Law in the Modern State,* p. 121.

[21]Duguit, *Law in the Modern State,* p. 115, and pp. 118-119 cf. Duguit, "Collective Acts," p. 766.

[22]See Elbow, *French Corporative Theory,* pp. 117-118; de Maeztu, *Authority,* p. 220.

[23]Duguit, *Law in the Modern State,* pp. 118, 119, 120.

[24]Cole, *Guild Socialism Restated,* pp. 196, 199. Cf. Laski, *Authority,* p. 87, and Laski, *Foundations,* p. 76.

[25]See Glass, *Responsible Society, passim.*; and Adolph Sturmthal, "Nationalization and Worker's Control in Britain and France," *Journal of Political Economy* LXI (February 1953), pp. 53-54. There is a good, concise explanation of the different guild socialist schemes in Savel Zimand, *Modern Social Movements: Descriptive Summaries and Bibliographies* (New York: H.W. Wilson, 1921), pp. 187-189.

[26]See Sidney and Beatrice Webb, *A Constitution for the Socialist Commonwealth of Great Britain* (New York: Longmans, 1920), pp. 108-146, 168-202 for details.

[27]See Coker, "Pluralistic Theories of the State," p. 101.

[28]Cole, *Guild Socialism Restated,* p. 121; G. D. H. Cole, *Social Theory* (London: Methuen, 1920), pp. 138, 139, 140.

[29]Webb, *Constitution,* pp. 196-197, 121-131.

[30]Ibid., pp. 297-298, 141-142; Laski, *Grammar,* pp. 254-255, 461-462, 515. Duguit, of course, was willing to countenance state force to insure the uninterrupted service of vital industries.

[31]The sovereignty debate was one of the last great debates in political *theory* in this century before political scientists retreated into the kind of hyperrefined, ultimately vacuous empiricism that still dominates the field today. For some of the leading defenses of sovereignty, see John Dickinson, "A Working Theory of Sovereignty," *Political Science Quarterly* XLII (December 1927): 524-558; XLIII (March 1928): 32-63; Brown, "Jurisprudence of Duguit"; Mott, "Political Theory of Syndicalism"; George Sabine, "Pluralism: A Point of View," *American Political Science Review* XVII (February 1923): 34-50; Charles MacIlwain, "Sovereignty Again," *Economica* VI (November 1926): 253-268; Morris R. Cohen, "Communal Ghosts and Other Perils in Social Philosophy," *The Journal of Philosophy* XVI (December 4, 1919): 673-690; Westel Willoughby, "The Juristic Conception of the State," *American Political Science Review* XII (May 1918): 192-214; Matthews, "Recent Developments in Political Theory"; Coker, "Pluralistic Theories of the State"; Elliott, *Pragmatic Revolt,* pp. 86-110; Ellis, "Political Science at the Crossroads"; Barker, "The Rule of Law"; and Barker, "The Discredited State".

[32]MacIlwain, "Sovereignty Again," p. 256.

[33]Locke, *Second Treatise,* c. 13, section 149.

[34]Albert Venn Dicey, *The Law of the Constitution,* 9th edition (London: Macmillan, 1950 [1885]) p. 73. See also MacIlwain, "Sovereignty Again," p. 257; Dickinson, "Working Theory," pp. 528-530; and Coker, "Pluralist Theories of the State," pp. 81-89.

[35]Brown, "Jurisprudence of Duguit," p. 174 (emphasis added).

[36]Dickinson, "Working Theory," pp. 540, 541.

[37]Ibid., p. 35.

[38]Ibid., p. 50.

[39]Ibid., pp. 50-51 (emphasis added).

[40]One of Duguit's French critics observed further that solidarity, that is, human cooperation, is not the *sine qua non* of social progress.

> We are unfortunately tied to each other for evil as well as for good: the sick infect the healthy with their illnesses, the morally diseased contaminate the morally sound, the fools oppose necessary reform, and history . . . is largely the record of efforts made to break a solidarity of evil which becomes the most effective bar to progress of every kind, particularly moral and intellectual: in fact advance has invariably come from individuals defying the law of solidarity by making new departures on their own. Here again,

then the real life of society depends not so much on the *mass* of individual consciences as on each individual being left free to choose as it were his own function, which is equivalent to an admission of individual rights.

M. Archambault, *En Deça de L'Individualisme: Droit Social et Droit Individuel, D'Après M. Duguit*, paraphrased in translation by Saltau, *French Political Theory*, p. 477f (emphasis in original).

[41]Cohen, "Communal Ghosts," p. 687.

[42]Paul H. Douglas, "Occupational versus Proportional Representation," *American Journal of Sociology* XXIX (September 1923), p. 148.

[43]Elliott, *Pragmatic Revolt*, p. 203; see Douglas, "Occupational Representation," pp. 145 *et seq.*

[44]Elliott, *Pragmatic Revolt*, pp. 306, 307.

[45]Ernest Barker, *Political Thought in England from Herbert Spencer to the Present Day* (New York: Henry Holt, 1915), p. 183.

[46]See F. Tillyard and W. A. Robson, "Enforcement of the Collective Bargain in the United Kingdom," *The Economic Journal* 48 (March 1938): 15-25; Otto Kahn-Freund, ed., *Labor Relations and the Law: A Comparative Study* (Boston: Little Brown, and Co., 1965), pp. 21-39, 40-47, 127-153; Allen Flanders, "Great Britain," in Adolf Sturmthal, ed., *Contemporary Collective Bargaining in Seven Countries* (Ithaca: Cornell University Press, 1957); Frederick Meyers, *Ownership of Jobs: A Comparative Study* (Los Angeles: University of California Institute of Industrial Relations, 1964), pp. 18-43; Geldart, "Status of Trade Unions in England," 25 *Harvard Law Review* 579 (1912); and W. N. Geldart, "The Present Law of Trade Disputes and Trade Unions," *Political Quarterly*, 1914, reprinted by Oxford University Press, 1914.

[47]See Charles O. Gregory, *Labor and the Law*, 2d revised edition (New York: W.W. Norton, 1961 [1946]), pp. 31-51; Epstein, "A Common Law for Labor Relations: A Critique of New Deal Labor Legislation," 92 *Yale Law Journal* 1357, 1367-1369 (1983). But see Petro, "Conspiracy and Tort," for a strong defense of *Quinn.* The double standard, if there was one, did *not* mean that employers had a freer hand *in labor disputes* than did trade unions, only that the rules governing aggressive rivalry between businessmen allowed them greater freedom of action.

[48]See also *South Wales Miner's Federation* v. *Glamorgan Coal Co.,* [1905] A.C. 239; and Henry Pelling, *A History of British Trade Unionism* (London: Macmillan, 1963), p. 124.

[49]See Pelling, *A History of British Trade Unionism*, pp. 125-127; Henry Pelling, *Labour and Politics, 1900-1906* (London: Macmillan, 1958); and Royal Commission on Trade Disputes and Trade Combinations, *Report* (London: Wyman and Sons, 1906 [Cd. 2825]). The trade unions did not co-operate with this Commission.

[50]Royal Commission, *Report*, p. 8.

[51]Geldart, "Present Law," pp. 38-39. For a history of post-1906 legislation and court decisions, see *Trade Union Immunities*, Cmnd. 8128 (London: Her Majesty's Stationery Office, 1981).

[52]There was at least one abortive attempt to pass legislation based on the TDA, in Massachusetts; see *In Re Opinion of the Justices*, Supreme Judicial Court of Massachusetts, May 8, 1912, 98 N.E. 337.

[53]Edwin Witte, "Injunctions in Labor Disputes," manuscript prepared for the United States Commission on Industrial Relations, and Edwin Witte, in John R. Commons and John B. Andrews, *Principles of Labor Legislation* (New York: Macmillan, 1916), p. 116, both quoted in Theron Schlabach, *Edwin Witte, Cautious Reformer* (Madison: State Historical Society of Wisconsin Press, 1969), p. 56; see also ibid., pp. 28-31, 52-73; Henry Rogers Seager, "The Attitude of the State Towards Trade Unions and Trusts," *Political Science Quarterly* XXII (September 1907): 611-629, especially pp. 624 *et seq.*; and Samuel Gompers, *Labor and the Common Welfare* (New York: E.P. Dutton, 1919), pp. 67-68. Witte's 'hands-off' beliefs did not stop him from favoring statutes to outlaw anti-union discrimination however, or from testifying in favor of the lopsided Wagner Act; see chapter nine, *infra*.

[54]On the French laws governing union management relations, see International Labour

Office, *Freedom of Association,* Studies and Reports, Series A: Industrial Relations, Nos. 28-32 (Geneva: International Labour Office, 1927-1930), Volume II: France; Fuchs, "The French Law of Collective Labor Agreements," 41 *Yale Law Journal* 1005 (1932); Frederic Meyers, *Ownership of Jobs: A Comparative Study* (Los Angeles: University of California Institute of Industrial Relations, 1964), pp. 44-71; Adolf Sturmthal, "Collective Bargaining in France," in Sturmthal, *Contemporary Collective Bargaining*; Andre Brun, "Collective Agreements in France" and "The Law of Strikes and Lockouts in France," both in Kahn-Freund, ed., *Labor Relations and the Law*; Gaeton Pirou, "The Theory of Collective Labor Contracts in France," *International Labour Review* V (January 1922): 35-50; and Val Lorwin, "Reflections on the History of the French and American Labor Movements," *Journal of Economic History* XVII (March 1957): 25-44.

[55]Lorwin, "French and American Labor Movements," p. 38.

[56]Id.

[57]Fuchs, "The French Law of Collective Labor Agreements," p. 1034.

[58]See L. Hamburger, "The Extension of Collective Agreements to Cover Entire Trades and Industries," *International Labour Review* XL (August 1939): 153-194; Robert Matthews, ed., *Labor Relations and the Law* (Boston: Little Brown, 1953), especially pp. 281-288; and Adolf Sturmthal, "An Essay on Comparative Collective Bargaining," in Sturmthal, *Contemporary Collective Bargaining*; and Kahn-Freund, ed., *Labor Relations and the Law, passim.*

[59]On the New Zealand system, and the system in Australian colonies, see Hamburger, "Extension," pp. 157-161; J. B. Condliffe, "Experiments in State Control in New Zealand," *International Labour Review* IX (March 1924): 334-360; John B. Findlay, "Industrial Peace in New Zealand," *International Labour Review* IV (October 1921): 32-46; and the citations in Note 61 *infra.* The entire law is printed in the *Report* of the United States Industrial Commission (Washington, D.C.: GPO, 1901), Volume XVI, pp. 204-214.

[60]Henry Demarest Lloyd, *A Country Without Strikes: A Visit to the Compulsory Arbitration Court of New Zealand* (New York: Doubleday, Page, 1900), pp. 47, 75.

[61]Ibid., pp. 114-115. See also Henry Demarest Lloyd, *Labor Copartnership* (New York: Harper and Brothers, 1898); Henry Demarest Lloyd, "Australasian Cures for Coal Wars," *Atlantic Monthly* XC (November 1902): 667-674; Henry Demarest Lloyd, "A Visit to the Compulsory Arbitration Court of New Zealand," *The Outlook* LXIII (December 9, 1899): 877-899; Henry Demarest Lloyd, "New Zealand Newest England," *Atlantic Monthly* LXXXIV (December 1899): 789-794; John A. Ryan, "A Country Without Strikes," *Catholic World* LXXII (November 1900): 145-157; Frank Parsons, "Compulsory Arbitration," *Arena* XVII (March 1897): 663-676; Henry MacCrosty, "State Arbitration and the Minimum Wage in Australasia," *Political Science Quarterly* XVIII (March 1903): 112-140; Higgins, "A New Province for Law and Order: Industrial Peace through Minimum Wage and Arbitration," 29 *Harvard Law Review* 13 (1915); James E. Le Rossignol and William D. Stewart, *State Socialism in New Zealand* (New York: Thomas Y. Crowell, 1910); and H. H. Lusk, *Social Welfare in New Zealand: The Result of Twenty Years of Progressive Social Legislation and its Significance for the United States and Other Countries* (New York: Sturgis and Walton, 1915).

[62]Gronlund, *New Economy,* p. 162. Cf. the words of the New Zealand Chief Justice in an appeal case: "the [arbitration] Court can make the contract or agreement that is to exist between the workman and the employer. It abrogates the right of workman and employers to make their own contracts. It in effect abolishes *contract* and restores *status.* . . . " quoted in Condliffe "Experiments in State Control," p. 335 (emphasis in original).

[63]Julius Cohen, *Law and Order in Industry* (New York: Macmillan, 1916), p. 226; see also Cohen, "Collective Bargaining and the Law as a Basis for Industrial Reorganization," *Annals of the American Academy of Political and Social Science* XC (July 1920): 47-49. On the Protocol, see chapter eight *infra.*

[64]Hale, "Law Making by Unofficial Minorities," 20 *Columbia Law Review* 451, 456 (1920).

[65]Lloyd, *Country Without Strikes,* pp. 13-14.

[66]See Samuel Gompers's testimony in the U.S. Commission on Industrial Relations, 1916

Volume I, pp. 720-721; Samuel Gompers, *Labor and the Employer* (New York: E.P. Dutton, 1920), pp. 263-265; and Victor Olander, "Compulsory Arbitration," *Shoemakers Journal,* 1920, in Saposs, *Readings in Trade Unionism,* p. 254.

[67]Industrial Conciliation and Arbitration Amending Act, 1936, paragraph 185, printed in A. J. Mazenbarb, ed., *The Industrial Laws of New Zealand* (Wellington: Butterworth, 1940), p. 133; see also Kurt Braun, *The Right to Organize and Its Limits* (Washington, D.C.: Brookings Institution, 1950), pp. 129-130; A. E. C. Hare, *Report on Industrial Relations in New Zealand* (London: J.M. Dent and Sons, 1946), pp. 177-178. The fate of industrial peace in New Zealand prior to World War I is discussed in Findlay, "Industrial Peace," and Condliffe, "Experiments in State Control."

[68]See Fritz Sitzler, "The Law of Collective Bargaining in Germany," *International Labour Review* VI (October 1922): 511-526; Emil Frankel, "How Germany Settles Industrial Disputes," 17 *Monthly Labor Review* 578 (1923): 578-587; Fritz Sitzler, "The Compulsory Adjustment of Industrial Disputes in Germany," *International Labour Review* XII (October 1925): 457-466; William T. Ham, "The German System of Arbitration," *Journal of Political Economy* XXXIX (February 1931): 1-24; Fuchs, "Collective Labor Agreements in German Law," 15 *St. Louis Law Review* 1 (1929); Fuchs, "Protection of the German System of Controlling Employment by Collective Agreement," 18 *St. Louis Law Review* 221 (1932); Lehmann, "Collective Labor Under the German Republic," 10 *Wisconsin Law Review* 324 (1935); Nathan Reich, *Labor Relations in Republican Germany* (New York: Oxford University Press, 1938); Wunderlich, *German Labor*; ILO, *Freedom of Association,* Volume III, pp. 1-95; Thilo Ramm, "The German Law of Collective Agreements," in Kahn-Freund, *Labor and the Law*; Bowen, *Corporative Theories,* pp. 164-209; and Sheehan, *Lujo Brentano,* pp. 160-165, 196-197.

[69]Quoted in Fuchs, "Collective Labor Agreements in German Law," p. 8.

[70]The Weimar constitution is translated in Howard Lee McBain and Lindsay Rogers, eds., *The New Constitutions of Europe* (New York: Doubleday, Page, and Co., 1922), pp. 176-212.

[71]See Reich, *Labour Relations in Republican Germany,* pp. 36-38; Braun, *Right to Organize,* pp. 206-207, 215-218.

[72]See William Guillebaud, *The Works Council: A German Experiment in Industrial Democracy* (New York: Macmillan, 1928); Bowen, *Corporative Theories,* pp. 160-204; Herman Finer, *Representative Government and a Parliament of Industry: A Study of the German Federal Economic Council* (London: The Fabian Society, 1923); and Redlich, "German Economic Planning."

[73]See David Loth, *Swope of G.E.* (New York: Simon and Schuster, 1958), p. 101.

[74]Fuchs, "Collective Labor Agreements in German Law," pp. 39, 1. See also his "Protection of the German System of Controlling Employment by Collective Agreement."

[75]Fuchs, "German Law of Collective Labor Agreements," p. 41.

[76]Id.

[77]Ibid., p. 42, 24n; Fuchs, "Protection of the German System," p. 232.

[78]Fuchs, "German Law of Collective Agreements," pp. 42-44.

[79]See the haunting remarks in Wunderlich, *German Labor,* p. 85:

> [b]ut the arbitration policy had led to a split of interests within labor itself. Organized labor had been willing to accept unemployment rather than lower the level of wages as a whole. This attitude was deeply resented by its victims. The unemployed unable to get a job, sinking from insurance benefits to emergency relief and to municipal aid, declassed and strictly controlled, formed a new and miserable social stratum which felt no solidarity with organized labor. The employed rank-and-file were threatened with the same fate. They realized that union wages were good only if jobs could be had. Thus union strength was undermined even from within.

[80]Wunderlich, *German Labor,* pp. 83, xii. It would be absurd to pin the blame for Hitler on

the Weimar collective bargaining system; but the system was partly responsible for bringing on and perpetuating the economic crisis.

[81]Unless one includes Russia among the industrialized nations. Like its Italian counterpart, the Soviet Union abolished free, independent trade unions entirely. Some seven years before the Fascist Labor Charter declared the corporations (the combined syndicates of unions and employers) organs of the state, the Ninth Congress of the Communist Party proclaimed that the "trade unions" in communist society "must transform themselves into auxiliary organs of the proletarian State" (Quoted in International Labour Conference, *Methods of Collaboration Between the Public Authorities, Workers' Organizations, and Employers' Organizations* (Geneva: International Labour Office, 1940), p. 85). Trade unions recognized by the Soviet government exercised exclusive jurisdiction over all the workers in the group, and the collective agreements negotiated between them and private employers automatically replaced individual labor contracts—except those with better terms. See International Labour Office, *The Trade Union Movement in Soviet Russia* (London: P. S. King, 1927); and Isaac Deutscher, *Soviet Trade Unions: Their Place in Soviet Labour Policy* (New York: Royal Institute of International Affairs, 1950).

[82]The 1927 Charter of Labor was a declaration of the Grand Council of Fascism, i.e., a declaration of the *party* leadership. But the Charter had quasi-constitutional status, ratifying existing legal regulations of the previous few years and serving as a point of departure for later legislation. Prior to the Labor Charter there were two important "pacts" in 1923 and 1925 (of Chigi Palace and of Vidoni Palace, respectively) between Fascist-led unions and employer associations, recognizing the former as sole legal representatives of the employees. There was also a Fundamental Law of April 3, 1926, elaborated by a Royal Decree of July 1, 1926, that put the evolving policies into statutory form.

Article 23 of the Fascist Labor Charter compelled employers to obtain workers from government-run hiring halls ("Labor Exchanges") and nudged them into adopting an affirmative action hiring program in favor of employees who were members of the Fascist Party or of an official syndicate.

On the theory and practice of fascist syndicalism generally, and in the field of labor relations, see Herbert Schneider, *Making the Fascist State* (New York: H. Fertig, 1968[1928]), pp. 66-214, 321-340; Elliott, *Pragmatic Revolt,* pp. 217-352; Raffaello Viglione, *et al., The Structure of the Corporate State* translated and abridged by Anna Waring (London: The British Empire Fascist Party, 1933); Fausto Pitigliani, *The Italian Corporative State* (London: P.S. King, 1933); G. Lowell Field, *The Syndical and Corporative Institutions of Italian Fascism* (New York: Columbia University Press, 1938); Gino Arias, "Trade Union Reform in Italy," *International Labour Review* XIV (September 1926): 345-356; H. E. Geiuseppe Bottai, "Trade Union Organization in Italy," *International Labour Review* XV (June 1927): 815-827; ILO, *Freedom of Association,* Volume IV, pp. 1-178; and ILC, *Methods of Collaboration,* pp. 58-73, 120-121.

Edmondo Rossoni, one of Mussolini's chief labor lieutenants and a strong champion of fascist syndicalism, was an IWW organizer in the New York City area before World War I; see Edwin Fenton, "Immigrants and Unions, A Case Study: Italians and American Labor, 1870-1920," unpublished dissertation, Department of History, Harvard University, 1957, p. 182; and Arthur Livingston, "Italo-American Fascism," *Survey* LVII (March 1, 1927): 738-740.

[83]"Every conflicting clause of an individual contract of employment, whether previous or subsequent to the collective contract, shall be legally replaced by the clauses of the collective agreement, except where it is more favorable to the workers." Section 54 of the Trade Union Regulations, 1926, quoted in translation in ILO, *Freedom of Association,* Volume IV: Italy, p. 67. This might be fruitfully compared with the decision of the Supreme Court of the United States in the *J.I. Case Company* case in 1944; see chapter nine *infra.*

[84]Quoted in Schneider, *Making the Fascist State,* p. 181.

[85]Viglione, *Corporate State,* p. 18.

[86]Ibid., p. 23; see also ILO, *Freedom of Association,* Volume IV, pp. 68-69.

[87]See Pitigliani, *Italian Corporative State,* pp. 60-90; ILO, *Freedom of Association,* Volume IV, pp. 70-83; and Field, *Syndical Institutions,* pp. 118-133.
[88]See Pitigliani, *Italian Corporative State,* pp. 124-137; Field, *Syndical Institutions,* pp. 137-203.

Chapter Eight

[1]See Milton Derber, "The Idea of Industrial Democracy in America, 1898-1915," *Labor History* VII (Fall 1966): 259-286; Milton Derber, "The Idea of Industrial Democracy in America, 1915-1935," *Labor History* VIII (Spring 1967): 3-29; Derber, *Idea of Industrial Democracy*; William Jett Lauck, *The Industrial Code* (New York: Funk and Wagnalls, 1922); W. Jett Lauck, *Political and Industrial Democracy, 1776-1926* (New York: Funk and Wagnalls, 1926); W. Jett Lauck, *The New Industrial Revolution and Wages* (New York: Funk and Wagnalls, 1929); John Ryan, *Industrial Democracy from a Catholic Viewpoint* (Washington, D.C.: Rossi-Bryn, 1925); and Norman Thomas, *What is Industrial Democracy?* (New York: League for Industrial Democracy, 1925).

For discussions of the degree to which the ideal of a 'planned' society penetrated America, see Paul Homan, "Economic Planning: The Proposals and the Literature," *Quarterly Journal of Economics* XLVII (November 1932): 102-122; Sidney Kaplan, "Social Engineers as Saviours: Effects of World War I on Some American Liberals," *Journal of the History of Ideas* XVII (June 1956): 347-369; and Lewis Feuer, "American Travelers to the Soviet Union: The Formation of a Component of New Deal Ideology, 1917-1932," *American Quarterly* XIV (Summer 1962): 119-149.

On the phenomenon of company unionism, employee representation, and other alternatives to adversarial unionism, see Paul Douglas, "Shop Committees Substitute for, or Supplement to Trades-Unions?" *Journal of Political Economy* XXIX (February 1921): 89-107; Paul Gemmill, "The Literature of Employee Representation," *Quarterly Journal of Economics* XLII (May 1928): 479-494; and Henry Eilbert, "The Development of Personnel Management in the United States," *Business History Review* XXXIII (Autumn 1959): 345-364.

Most of the 'enlightened' businessmen who sought an entente with organized labor were associated with the National Civic Federation; see Marguerite Green, *The National Civic Federation and the American Labor Movement, 1900-1925* (Washington, D.C.: Catholic University of America Press, 1956); and James Weinstein, *The Corporate Ideal in the Liberal State: 1900-1918* (Boston: Beacon Press, 1968), especially pp. 3-39.

The general run of businessmen was much more antagonistic to unionism. The National Association of Manufacturers, for instance, is well-known for its outspoken defiance of union 'recognition' (the closed shop). On the other hand, the NAM was the leading proponent of protection against international competition, of 'fair trade' instead of 'free trade'. This mentality was brilliantly captured in Sinclair Lewis's novel of 1922, *Babbitt* (New York: New American Library, 1964), p. 39:

> As to industrial conditions, however, Babbitt had thought a great deal, and his opinions may be co-ordinated as follows:
> 'A good labor union is of value because it keeps out radical unions, which would destroy property. No one ought to be forced to belong to a union, however. All labor agitators who try to force men to join a union should be hanged. In fact, just between ourselves, there oughtn't to be any unions allowed at all; and as it's the best way of fighting the unions, every business man ought to belong to an employers' association and to the Chamber of

Commerce. In union there is strength. So any selfish hog who doesn't join the Chamber of Commerce ought to be forced to'.

[2]New Jersey had adopted a kind of conservation measure to regulate oyster dredging in its waters in a way that discriminated against out-of-state citizens:

The oyster beds belonging to a state may be abundantly sufficient for the use of the citizens of that state, but might be totally exhausted and destroyed if the legislature could not so regulate the use of them as to exclude the citizens of the other states from taking them, except under such limitations and restrictions as the laws may prescribe. (p. 552)

[3]*Allgeyer v. Louisiana,* 165 U.S. 578, 585 (1897).

[4]The declension of constitutionally-protected economic liberty in American history is assessed in Bernard Siegan, *Economic Liberties and the Constitution* (Chicago: University of Chicago Press, 1980); Edward S. Corwin, *Liberty Against Government: The Rise, Flowering, and Decline of a Famous Juridical Concept* (Baton Rouge: Louisiana State University Press, 1948); William Letwin, "Economic Due Process in the American Constitution," in Robert L. Cunningham, ed., *Liberty and the Rule of Law* (College Station: Texas A & M University Press, 1979); and Thomas R. Haggard, "Government Regulation of the Employment Relationship," in Tibor Machan and M. Bruce Johnson, eds., *Rights and Regulation: Ethical, Political, and Economic Issues* (Cambridge, MA: Ballinger, 1982). See also Clyde Jacobs, *Law Writers and the Courts* (Berkeley: University of California Press, 1954) for discussion of the extent to which economic liberty permeated state and federal court decision-making in the late 19th century.

[5]See Daniel Wigdor, *Roscoe Pound, Philosopher of Law* (Westport: Greenwood Press, 1974); Edwin Patterson, *Jurisprudence: Men and Ideas of the Law* (Brooklyn: The Foundation Press, 1953), pp. 509-527; and Maurice Sheldon Amos, "Roscoe Pound," in W. Ivor Jennings, ed., *Modern Theories of Law* (London: Oxford University Press, 1933). After helping breathe life into the 20th century American Leviathan, Pound ended his career as something of a conservative; see his celebrated "Legal Immunities of Labor Unions," 1957, in E. H. Chamberlain, ed., *Labor Unions and Public Policy* (Washington, D.C.: American Enterprise Institute, 1958).

[6]Wigdor, *Roscoe Pound,* p. 209.

[7]On Brandeis, see Mason, *Organized Labor and the Law,* pp. 203-210; Alpheus T. Mason, *Brandeis* (New York: Viking, 1946); Melvin Urofsky, *A Mind of One Piece: Brandeis and American Reform* (New York: Charles Scribner's Sons, 1971); Samuel Knofesky, *The Legacy of Holmes and Brandeis: A Study in the Influence of Ideas* (New York: Macmillan, 1957); Alexander Bickel, ed., *The Unpublished Opinions of Mr. Justice Brandeis* (Cambridge: Harvard University Press, 1957); and Phillipa Strum, *Louis D. Brandeis: Justice for the People* (Cambridge: Harvard University Press, 1984).

[8]On Frankfurter, see Helen S. Thomas, *Felix Frankfurter, Scholar on the Bench* (Baltimore: Johns Hopkins University Press, 1960); Wallace Mendelson, ed., *Felix Frankfurter: A Tribute* (New York: Reynal, 1964); Liva Baker, *Felix Frankfurter* (New York: Coward McCann, 1969); Philip Kurland, ed., *Felix Frankfurter on the Supreme Court: Extrajudicial Essays on the Court and the Constitution* (Cambridge: Harvard University Press, 1970); and Harlan B. Phillips, *Felix Frankfurter Reminisces* (New York: Reynal, 1960). Frankfurter's reputation in the field of labor relations is based, above all, on the enormously important book he co-authored with Nathan Greene, *The Labor Injunction* (New York: Macmillan, 1930). The scholarly credibility of this book (and the intellectual integrity of its authors) has been brought into serious doubt; see Petro, "Injunctions and Labor Disputes: 1880-1932 Part I: What the Courts Actually Did—and Why," 14 *Wake Forest Law Review* 341 (1978).

[9]Pound, "Need of a Sociological Jurisprudence," 19 *Green Bag* 612 (1907); Pound, "Liberty of Contract," 18 *Yale Law Journal* 454 (1909); and see Roscoe Pound, *The Spirit of the Common Law* (Boston: Marshall Jones, 1921), pp. 195 *et seq.* Compare with the Blackstone definition, as quoted by Pound in "Liberty of Contract," p. 461: "[T]he public good is in

nothing more essentially interested than in the protection of every individual's private rights."

[10]Pound, "Need of Sociological Jurisprudence," pp. 614, 615 (emphasis added); see also Pound, "Social Justice and Legal Justice," 75 *Century Law Journal* 455 (1912).

[11]On legal realism, see Morris R. Cohen, *American Thought: A Critical Sketch* (New York: The Free Press, 1954), pp. 169-176; Wilfred Rumble, *American Legal Realism* (Ithaca: Cornell University Press, 1968); Edward Purcell, "American Jurisprudence Between the Wars: Legal Realism and the Crisis of Democratic Theory," *American Historical Review* LXXV (December 1969): 424-446; and Herman Belz, "The Realist Critique of Constitutionalism in the Era of Reform," *American Journal of Legal History* XV (October 1971): 288-306.

On Brooks Adams, see Thornton Anderson, *Brooks Adams, Constructive Conservative* (Ithaca: Cornell University Press, 1951).

[12]Brooks Adams, "Law Under Inequality: Monopoly," in Melville Bigelow, ed., *Centralization and the Law: Scientific Legal Education* (Boston: Little, Brown, 1906), pp. 64, 90; "Nature of Law," ibid., p. 45. Cohen, *American Thought,* p. 170 points out that Adams's straightforward endorsement of economic determinism in his 1906 lectures was one of the first, true pronouncements of 20th century legal realism, and not the more ambiguous thoughts of the pragmatist Oliver Wendell Holmes, Jr. For an account of some of the non-Marxist European legal theorists who argued the case for economic determinism in the law, see Harry Elmer Barnes, "Some Contributions of Sociology to Modern Political Thought," in Merriam, *History of Political Theory—Recent Times.*

[13]Robert Hale, "Economics and Law," in William Fielding Ogburn and Alexander Goldenweiser, eds., *The Social Sciences and Their Interrelations* (Boston: Houghton-Mifflin, 1927), p. 138; Robert Hale, "Coercion and Distribution in a Supposedly Non-Coercive State," *Political Science Quarterly* XXXVIII (September 1923), p. 473 (emphasis added). Hale was a graduate of Harvard Law School and had a doctorate in economics from Columbia. For some other specimens of his thought, see his "Law Making by Unofficial Minorities," 20 *Columbia Law Review* 451 (1920); "Labor Legislation as an Enlargement of Individual Liberty," 15 *American Labor Legislation Review* 155 (1925); *Legal Factors in Economic Society,* 2d edition, 1937 (no publisher: a copy of this book is in the Michigan Law School Library); "Bargaining, Duress, and Economic Liberty," 43 *Columbia Law Review* 603 (1943); and *Freedom Through Law: Public Control of Private Governing Power* (New York: Columbia University Press, 1952).

Among other fallacies, Hale was cashing in on a crude sophistry of Jeremy Bentham, who claimed that when the state enforced contracts it made the rules of these private agreements part of its law. But "the state in permitting private organizations to act for their own purposes does not make those purposes their own. It only holds men to *their own promises."* See Edwin Patterson, *Jurisprudence: Men and Ideas of the Law* (Brooklyn: The Foundation Press, 1953), p. 171.

The logic of the 'realist' analysis of contract-as-coercion, incidentally, would not be any different even if the bargainers were equal in wealth and position.

[14]Dawson, "Economic Duress: An Essay in Perspective," 45 *Michigan Law Review* 253, 266 (1947). Or as a union lawyer explained: "The law is a game in which everyone slugs. I slug for labor." Hale was the intellectual midwife of an entire cottage industry of law professors dedicated to undermining the obligation of *all* contracts by expanding, via the unequal bargaining power doctrine, the concept of duress (or unconscionability) without limit; see, for example, Dalzell, "Duress by Economic Pressure," 20 *North Carolina Law Review* 237 (1942); and Dawson, *op. cit.* For a much-needed corrective, see Epstein, "Unconscionability: A Critical Reappraisal," *Journal of Law and Economics* XIX (1975): 293-315.

[15]Samuel Gompers, *American Federationist,* 1912, quoted in Gompers, *Labor and the Common Welfare,* pp. 52-53.

[16]Dickinson, "New Conceptions of Contract in Labor Relations," 43 *Columbia Law Review* 688, 703 (1943).

[17]On the issue of violence as the fundamental determinant of injunctions in labor disputes in this era, see Petro, "Injunctions and Labor Disputes," p. 341; or see Jack London, "The Scab," 1905, p. 1125:

> When the scab crumples up and is ready to go down before the fists, bricks, and bullets of the labor group, the capitalist group puts the police and soldiers into the field, and begins a general bombardment of injunctions.

See also Louis Adamic, *Dynamite! The Story of Class Violence in America* (New York: Viking Press, 1931); Philip Taft and Philip Ross, "American Labor Violence: Its Causes, Character, and Outcome," in Hugh D. Graham and Ted Robert Gurr, eds., *Violence in America: Historical and Comparative Perspectives* (New York: Bantam, 1969), pp. 281-395; Howard Gitelman, "Perspectives on American Industrial Violence," *Business History Review* XLVII (Spring 1973): 1-23; and T. S. Adams, "Violence in Labor Disputes," *Publications of the American Economic Association,* 3d Series, VII (February 1906): 176-218.

[18]One of the very earliest federal labor injunction cases, *United States* v. *Kane,* 235 F. 748 (Circuit Court, District Colorado, 1885), is worth reading by all students of labor law, since it lays out the problems of violent labor disputes that were to plague this country for the next half-century; see Note 46 *infra.* Petro, "Injunctions," has counted 524 reported labor-injunction actions during 1880-1932, when there were thousands of strikes; moreover, a few of the major strikes in this era counted for many of these injunctions. This does not account for unreported cases; but an unreported case *meant* that the union did not even bother to contest the restraining order. Since unions did contest hundreds of injunctions, the most probable inference, in cases where they did not, is that they understood that they didn't have a leg to stand on. Privately, Petro has communicated to me that a further investigation on his part has revealed a substantial number of other injunction petitions in this era not dealt with in his published study. Most involved suits by union members against their organizations (to contest expulsions and other grievances).

[19]The effect of 19th (and even early 20th) century English decisions on restraint of trade on judges in America is noted, in passing at least, by several histories of labor law, and can easily be gleaned by reading the cases themselves. No one, to my knowledge, has explored this phenomenon in detail. The complexity and variability of the law governing labor combinations in the early decades of the 19th century preclude any detailed examination; but see generally Charles O. Gregory, *Labor and the Law* (New York: W. W. Norton, 1946); Edwin Witte, *The Government in Labor Disputes* (New York: McGraw Hill, 1932); Mason, *Organized Labor and the Law*; Petro, "Injunctions and Labor Disputes," Petro, "Unions and the Southern Courts: Part III—The Conspiracy and Tort Foundations of the Labor Injunction," 60 *North Carolina Law Review* 544 (1982); and Thomas Haggard, *Compulsory Unionism, the NLRB, and the Courts: A Legal Analysis of Union Security Agreements* (Philadelphia: Industrial Research Unit, The Wharton School, University of Pennsylvania, 1977), pp. 11-33. Petro, "Injunctions and Labor Disputes," has a comprehensive list of additional secondary sources on the issues, and on the crusade against 'government by injunction'. See also Theron Schlabach, *Edwin Witte, Cautious Reformer* (Madison: State Historical Society of Wisconsin, 1969), pp. 52-73.

[20]Haggard, *Compulsory Unionism,* p. 21.

[21]Witte, *Government in Labor Disputes,* pp. 223, and see pp. 220-230.

[22]The rarely-discussed historical background of the Hitchman case can be followed by reading the lower court decisions: *Hitchman Coal & Coke Co.* v. *Mitchell,* 172 F. 963 (Circuit Court, N.D. West Virginia, 1909); *Lewis* v. *Hitchman Coal & Coke Co.,* 176 F. 549 (Circuit Court of Appeals, Fourth Circuit, 1910); *Hitchman Coal & Coke Co.* v. *Mitchell,* 202 F. 512 (District Court, N.D. West Virginia, 1912); and *Mitchell* v. *Hitchman Coal & Coke Co.,* 214 F. 685 (Circuit Court of Appeals, Fourth Circuit, 1914).

[23]See the analysis in Epstein, "A Common Law for Labor Relations: A Critique of the New Deal Labor Legislation," 92 *Yale Law Journal* 1357, 1370-1375 (1983).

[24]See, for instance, Petro, "Injunctions and Labor Disputes," pp. 383-389.

[25]Gompers, *American Federationist,* 1913, quoted in Gompers, *Labor and the Employer,* p. 228; and see pp. 231-232:

> If ever the time shall come . . . when government by dynamite shall be attempted, it will have as its main cause the theory and policy upon which is based government by injunction.

For some typical apologias for violence along the lines mentioned in this paragraph, see *Labor and the Employer,* pp. 218-231 *passim.* Compare with Gompers's comment about the socialists and their advocacy of violence, quoted in chapter four, Note 53 *supra.*

[26]Victor Olander, "Equality Before the Law—A Message from Labor," *Shoe Worker's Journal,* 1921, quoted in Saposs, *Readings on Trade Unionism,* pp. 430, 431. See also John P. Frey, *The Labor Injunction* (Cincinnati: Equity Publishing Co., 1922); and Gompers, *Labor and the Common Welfare,* pp. 61-88 for a representative selection of criticism of injunctions by unionists.

Not a single one of these charges can be sustained, particularly the unfounded claim that injunctions were reserved only for use against striking workers. See "Injunctions Against Industry and Commerce," *Law and Labor* XI (January 1929), pp. 5-7 for a description of the over 1,000 injunctions brought by the Federal government against businessmen alone.

See also Mason, *Organized Labor and the Law,* pp. 101-116; Walter G. Merritt, "An Assault on the Labor Injunction: review of John P. Frey, *The Labor Injunction,*" *Law and Labor* IV (November 1922): 315-317; Zechariah Chaffee, Jr., "Review of John P. Frey, *The Labor Injunction,*" 36 *Harvard Law Review* 503 (1923); Donald L. McMurry, "The Legal Ancestry of the Pullman Strike Injunctions," *Industrial and Labor Relations Review* XIV (January 1961): 237-256; and Petro, "Injunctions and Labor Disputes."

[27]Edwin Witte, "Results of Injunctions in Labor Disputes," *American Labor Legislation Review,* 1922, quoted in Schlabach, *Edwin Witte,* pp. 59; Witte, *Government in Labor Disputes,* pp. 111-117, 298.

[28]See "Labor Injunctions Must Go," *The New Republic* XXXII (September 27, 1922), especially the closing comment on p. 110. The editorial was unsigned. Although George Soule was *TNR*'s economics editor, the legal sophistication of the editorial leads me to suspect that Frankfurter (a frequent contributor on labor matters in the 1920s) wrote it.

As far as the theory of 'informational picketing' goes, perhaps the remarks of Luke Grant, a progressive *sympathizer* of organized labor are *à propos* (in *The National Erector's Association and the International Association of Bridge and Structural Ironworkers* (Washington: GPO, 1915), p. 110):

> The factory is picketed. The courts have held that 'peaceful picketing' is not unlawful. It may be lawful, but it is entirely useless and ineffective. It is not necessary for the courts to restrain 'peaceful picketing' although they have sometimes done it. The only purpose in picketing a factory is to prevent certain workers taking the places vacated by certain other workers. The theory of 'peaceful picketing' is, that the workers seeking employment in that particular factory, will voluntarily turn away when they are told that a strike or lockout is in progress. In actual practice they do nothing of the kind, or only in rare instances. The pickets know that; so do the employers. It is not necessary that the pickets actually assault the employees who desire to enter the factory. If the pickets assemble in sufficient numbers, it is possible to intimidate those seeking employment, without actually assaulting them. But it is the fear of possible assault that brings results; not moral suasion. The 'moral suasion' argument is good in the courtroom or on the public platform, but around the factory it counts for practically nothing. Every one with practical experience of conditions knows that. It is better to meet the facts squarely than to dodge them by subterfuge and hypocrisy.

[29]Section 6 of the Clayton Act (38 Stat. 731, 1914) declared that the "labor of a human being is not a commodity or article of commerce," and prohibited any interpretation of the antitrust laws that would prohibit the existence or operation of labor unions as "illegal combinations or conspiracies in restraint of trade," or prohibit or restrain "individual members of such organizations from *lawfully* carrying out the *legitimate objects* thereof." (emphasis added) Section 20 prohibited injunctions in labor disputes, "unless necessary to prevent irreparable injury to property, or to a property right," prohibited judges from enjoining *peaceful* persuasion, *peaceful* assembly "in a lawful manner, and for lawful purposes; or from doing any act or thing which might *lawfully* be done in the absence of such dispute by any party thereto" (emphasis added). The emphasized words are the operative ones. They do not—and as Mason, *Organized Labor and the Law,* pp. 119-131 persuasively argues, were not intended to—abolish restraint of trade in labor disputes. In this regard, see *Duplex Printing Press Co. v. Deering,* 254 U.S. 443 (1921).

Edward Berman, *Labor and the Sherman Act* (New York: Harper and Brothers, 1930), insisted that Congress did not intend the Sherman Act to apply to unions, but Mason's arguments in *Organized Labor and the Law* are much sounder; see also Walter G. Merritt, "The Rule of Reason and Labor Boycotts," *Law and Labor* XIII (January 1931): 12-14.

[30]John R. Commons, in the U.S. Commission on Industrial Relations, *Final Report of the Commission on Industrial Relations* (Washington: GPO, 1915), pp. 219-220.

[31]Witte, *Government in Labor Disputes,* p. 293; see also Schlabach, *Edwin Witte,* pp. 27-28.

[32]Louis Brandeis, "How Far Have We Come on the Road to Industrial Democracy?" Interview in *La Follette's Weekly Magazine,* May 24, 1913, in Osmond K. Fraenkel, ed., *The Curse of Bigness: Miscellaneous Papers of Louis D. Brandeis* (Port Washington, NY: Kennikat Press, 1965), p. 46 (emphasis added). This interview originally appeared in the *Newark Evening News* in 1913. Brandeis's performance with regard to organized labor and the antitrust laws in the 1920s is critically assessed in Mason, *Organized Labor and the Law,* pp. 208-210, and Mason, *Brandeis,* pp. 539-547; see also Merritt, "Rule of Reason and Labor Boycotts."

[33]Commission on Industrial Relations, *Final Report,* p. 67 (emphasis added), and see also p. 91; and Schlabach, *Edwin Witte,* p. 28.

[34]John P. Mitchell, *Organized Labor* (Philadelphia: American Book and Bible House, 1903), p. 414.

[35]Samuel Gompers, "Labor and Equal Rights," *American Federationist* II (June 1900), p. 165 (emphasis in original). Gompers's rhetoric here probably reflected the influence of Spencerian and even anarchistic thought, via union colleagues such as Frank K. Foster. See George Cotkin, "The Spencerian and Comtian Nexus in Gompers's Labor Philosophy: The Impact of Non-Marxian Evolutionary Thought," *Labor History* XX (Fall 1979): 510-523, especially pp. 513-516.

[36]John P. Frey, "The Principle of the Labor Boycott," *International Molder's Journal,* 1906, quoted in Saposs, *Readings in Trade Unionism,* p. 207 (emphasis added).

[37]Gompers, *Annual Report of the AFL,* 1911, quoted in *Labor and the Common Welfare,* p. 75 (emphasis added). For other sentiments, see Gompers, *Labor and the Employer,* pp. 203-217; and Saposs, *Readings in Trade Unionism,* pp. 205-209.

[38]Louis Brandeis, "How Far Have We Come on the Road to Industrial Democracy?" p. 46.

[39]See Clyde Fisher, "Use of Federal Power in Settlement of Railway Labor Disputes," United States Department of Labor, Bureau of Labor Statistics, *Bulletin 303* (Washington, D.C.: GPO, 1922), pp. 15-37. Samuel Gompers opposed the Erdman Act because he opposed government arbitration of any sort. It made no sense to have an arbitration system if unions could render the process moot by calling a strike to defy an arbitration award, either; and Gompers was dead set against any legal restrictions on strikes. But he did endorse 'right to organize' legislation after World War I; see Gompers, *Labor and the Employer,* p. 305.

[40]John S. Dawson, in *Coppage v. Kansas,* 59 L. Ed. 441, 442 (236 U.S. 1 (1915)); Session Laws

of Kansas, chapter 222 (1903), quoted in *Coppage* v. *Kansas,* p. 443. Cf. *The State* v. *Coppage,* 87 Kan 752 (1912), Smith, J., at pp. 755-756, 759:

> It is a matter of common knowledge, of which legislatures and courts should take cognizance, that many individual laborers are unable to cope on an equal footing with wealthy individual or corporate employers as to the terms of employment . . . To many the demands for housing, food and clothing for their families and the education of their children brook no interruption of wages to the breadwinner. Necessity may compel the acceptance of unreasonable and unjust demands. The state is interested in healthful conditions for its wage-earners and in the moral and intellectual development of their children; also that none should become dependent upon the state for support.

See also Frederic Woodward, "Statutory Limitations of Freedom of Contract Between Employer and Employee," 29 *American Law Review* 236 (1895); Witte, *Government in Labor Disputes,* pp. 211 *et seq.*

[41]The state laws had also been struck down by state courts on liberty of contract grounds; see, for instance, *State* v. *Julow,* 129 Mo. 163 (1895); *Gillespie* v. *People,* 188 Ill 176 (1900); *State* v. *Kreutzberg,* 114 Wis 530 (1903); and *People* v. *Marcus,* 185 N.Y. 257 (1906).

[42]Compulsory arbitration was thus declared unconstitutional in 1923; see *Charles Wolff Packing Co.* v. *Court of Industrial Relations of the State of Kansas,* 262 U.S. 521 (1923).

[43]Darling, "The Adair Case," 42 *American Law Review* 884, 889-890 (1908) (emphasis added). Darling's argument makes sense only if one assumes that the collective right to leave an employer's service is what a strike is all about.

[44]*Final Report,* p. 67; AFL Reconstruction Program, December 1918, quoted in Saposs, *Readings in Trade Unions,* p. 46.

[45]Many states passed similar anti-injunction measures in the 1930s to cover areas not regulated under federal law; see Walter Galenson, *Rival Unionism in the United States* (New York: American Council on Public Affairs, 1940), pp. 116-118; and Monkemeyer, "Five Years of the Norris-La Guardia Act," 2 *Missouri Law Review* 1 (1937). For an account of the steps leading to the passage of the Norris-La Guardia Act, see Schlabach, *Edwin Witte,* pp. 60-71.

[46]Cf. Brewer, J., in *United States* v. *Kane,* 23 F. 748 (Circuit Court, District Colorado, 1885), at pp. 749-750, 754 (emphasis added):

> But supposing . . . one is discharged and the other wants to stay, is satisfied with the employment; and the one that leaves goes around to a number of friends and gathers them, and they come around, a large party of them,—as I suggested yesterday, a party with revolvers and muskets,—and the one that leaves come to the one that wants to stay and says to him: "Now, my friends are here; you had better leave; I request you to leave"; the man looks at the party that is standing there; *there is nothing but a simple request,*— that is, so far as the language which is used; there is no threat; but it is a request backed by a demonstration of force, a demonstration intended to intimidate, calculated to intimidate, and the man says: "Well, I would like to stay, I am willing to work here, yet there are too many men here, there is too much of a demonstration; I am afraid to stay." Now, the common sense of every man tells him that there is not a mere request,—tells him that while the language used may be very polite and be merely in the form of a request, yet it is accompanied with that backing of force intended as a demonstration and calculated to make an impression; and that the man leaves, really because he is intimidated. . . . I have no doubt that some men, who are excessively bold, might have laughed . . . believing that no personal violence would be used; but men are not all equally bold and courageous; the average man has a feeling that it is his duty to regard his personal safety;

we all know that, and we act upon that presumption; and when these men met there in that fever of excitement, when the crowd surged backwards and forwards, . . . they knew, and every man knows, that that kind of a demonstration was calculated to intimidate; and they knew, and every man knows, that ordinarily prudent men are not going to risk their personal safety when there is nothing to be gained by it. They are going to say, "Well, here is a crowd; they are in excitment here . . . they say we cannot do any violence, we cannot order you to leave, but you had better leave; we request you to leave; you are not going back on us, and we had better quit." Every one understands that these men felt overawed, intimidated, and quit work, not because they wanted to,—some of them at least,—but because they felt that their personal safety, personal prudence, required them to do it. It would be, as it seems to me, blinding my eyes to obvious facts to say . . . that that was a mere peaceable gathering of a few men to make a request; . . .

[47]Senator Thomas J. Walsh, Congressional Record, Volume 75, p. 4998 (1932), as quoted in Kerian, "Injunctions in Labor Disputes: The History of the Norris-La Guardia Act," 37 *North Dakota Law Review* 49, 62f (1961).

[48]See Stewart and Townsend, "Strike Violence: The Need for Federal Injunctions," 114 *University of Pennsylvania Law Review* 459 (1966), especially pp. 462-464, and pp. 460-470 generally on cases bearing on Section 7 (e). There are some interesting cases in the 1930s revolving around Section 7 (e), particularly one involving the great Minneapolis truck strike: *Powers Mercantile Co.* v. *Olson, Governor of Minnesota, et al.;* 7 F. Supp 865 (District Court, D. Minnesota, Fourth Division, 1934).

[49]Murray T. Quigg, "The Shipstead Substitute Anti-Injunction Bill," *Law and Labor* XI (January 1929), p. 4; "Issues Raised by the Federal Anti-Injunction Statute," *Law and Labor* XIV (May 1932): 35-37; and see the attack on this provision in Congress by Representative James Beck: "The aggressor may act without notice, but the aggrieved may not defend himself by securing injunctive relief without tolerating the violence until he has gone through various steps of peaceful negotiation." (Congressional Record, Volume 75, p. 5472 (1932), as quoted in Kerian, "Injunctions," p. 64. See the cases discussed in Monkemeyer, "Five Years of the Norris-La Guardia Act," 2 *Missouri Law Review* 1 (1937), pp. 16-21. For a discussion of union violence and modern case law, see Thomas Haggard and Armand Thieblot, *Union Violence: The Record and the Response by Courts, Legislatures, and the NLRB* (Philadelphia: Industrial Research Unit, University of Pennsylvania, 1983), especially pp. 197-244.

The provision in Section 8 of the Norris-La Guardia Act discussed in the text was described in Congress then, and continues to be defended now, as a version of the 'clean hands' doctrine, according to which equitable relief will not be granted to a plaintiff if he has by prior conduct violated some equitable principle such as conscience or good faith negotiations. My own opinion is that the authors of the aforementioned provision had something more sinister in mind.

At the time of its passage, and with the exception of the railroad industry, there was no legal or equitable principle that required an employer (retaining his men individually under at-will employment contracts) to recognize unions, negotiate with men in a body, or retain the services of striking workers. Recall, also, that the *relief* that would be denied employers under this provision is from irreparable injury arising from *criminal* acts (in a context where the police were either unable or unwilling to enforce the law). In light of these factors, one begins to understand why lawyers such as Quigg took such exception to the provision.

Suppose Congress passed a law that created a group of labor mediators; but did not make mediation mandatory in any way. Did this mean that if a body of workers demanded a closed shop, were refused, and then suddenly engaged in a sit-down strike (a case of criminal trespass), employers were entitled under federal law to no injunctive relief if they refused to mediate the dispute while their plant was occupied? What if Congress passed a law (as it did in 1935) establishing a 'right to organize', and the same sit-down situation arose, with the strikers claiming that the employer was violating federal law by refusing to recognize the strikers' rights? What then?

Lest my interpretation of Section 8 seem crude, I ask the reader to read the following cases, in which judges did interpret it as a kind of duty to bargain: *Cinderella Theatre Co.* v. *Sign Writers' Local 591,* 6 F. Supp 164, 170-171 (District Court, E.D. Michigan, S.D., 1934); *United Electric Coal Companies* v. *Rice,* 9 F. Supp. 635 (District Court, E.D. Illinois, 1934) (reversed: *United Electric Companies* v. *Rice,* 80 F. 2d. 1 (Circuit Court of Appeals, Seventh Circuit, 1935)); *Richard H. Oswald Co.* v. *Leader,* 20 F. Supp. 876 (District Court, E.D. Pennsylvania, 1937).

Finally, measure the distance between these speculations and the 'clean hands' objection to employer demands for federal injunctions that the CIO unions actually made in sit-down cases after 1935 (defenses, incidentally, which the NLRB was not loath to entertain); see, for instance, the discussion in Irving Bernstein, *The Turbulent Years: A History of the American Worker, 1933-1941* (Boston: Houghton Mifflin, 1970), pp. 539-540, 678-679. The Supreme Court did not buy these arguments, however; see *NLRB* v. *Fansteel Metallurgical Corporation,* 306 U.S. 240 (1939).

[50]The story is told vividly in Albro Martin, *Enterprise Denied: The Origins of the Decline of American Railroads, 1890-1917* (New York: Columbia University Press, 1971), pp. 319-351; see also Fisher, "Use of Federal Power," pp. 57-68; and *Wilson* v. *New,* 243 U.S. 332 (1917).

[51]"Principles and Policies to Govern Relations Between Employers and Employees in War Industries for the Duration of the War," in Lauck, *Industrial Code,* p. 271. On American war labor policies generally, see Gerald Nash, "FDR and Labor: World War I Origins of Early New Deal Policy," *Labor History* I (Winter 1960): 39-52; Gordon S. Watkins, *Labor Problems and Labor Administration in the United States During the World War,* University of Illinois Studies in the Social Sciences, Volume VIII, Nos. 3, 4 (Urbana: University of Illinois Press, 1919), pp. 123-223; Philip Ross, *The Government as a Source of Union Power* (Providence: Brown University Press, 1965), pp. 10-18; and Galenson, *Rival Unionism,* pp. 203-206.

[52]See Galenson, *Rival Unionism,* pp. 205-206; and "Organization and By-Laws for Collective Bargaining Committees Instituted by the National War Labor Board," in Lauck, *Industrial Code,* pp. 313-325.

[53]*Proceedings of the First Industrial Conference...,* 1919, quoted in Ross, *Government as a Source,* p. 15; see also Samuel Gompers, "President's Industrial Conference," *American Federationist* XXVI (December 1919): 1121-1125.

[54]Frank Hodges, Annual Convention of the Miners Federation, 1918, as quoted in William English Walling, *American Labor and American Democracy* (New York: Harper and Brothers, 1926), Volume II, p. 134 (emphasis added).

[55]See Glen Plumb and William Roylance, *Industrial Democracy: A Plan for Its Achievement* (New York: B.W. Huebsch, 1923), especially pp. 63-65; and see James Gilbert, *Designing the Industrial State: The Intellectual Pursuit of Collectivism in America, 1880-1940* (Chicago: Quadrangle, 1972), pp. 112-115.

[56]See Fisher, "Use of Federal Power," pp. 76-97; Galenson, *Rival Unionism,* pp. 206-215; Ross, *Government as a Source,* pp. 32-42; and Leonard Lecht, *Experience Under Railway Labor Legislation* (New York: Columbia University Press, 1955), pp. 31-46.

[57]*International Association of Machinists* v. *Atchison, Topeka, and Sante Fe Railroad,* 2 R.L.B. 87 (1921), quoted in Galenson, *Rival Unionism,* pp. 213-214.

[58]4 R.L.B. 656, quoted in Galenson, *Rival Unionism,* p. 214:

> A railway employee's membership or non-membership in an organization
> should not be a matter of compulsion. He should not be coerced either by
> the labor organization or by the carrier in connection with the exercise of
> his rights to join an organization or to make choice between rival unions.

See also Ross, *Government as a Source,* pp. 35-36.

[59]2 R.L.B. 87, quoted in Galenson, *Rival Unionism,* p. 208; see also the case mentioned on p. 213.

[60]See Fisher, "Use of Federal Power," pp. 92-93; Galenson, *Rival Unionism,* pp. 208-209; and Ross, *Government as a Source,* p. 36.

[61]See *Pennsylvania Railroad Co.* v. *RLB,* 261 U.S. 72 (1923); and *Pennsylvania R. System* v. *Pennsylvania Railroad Co.,* 267 U.S. 203 (1923).

[62]*See U.S.* v. *Railway Employees Department,* 290 F. 978, especially p. 980 (1923); *U.S.* v. *Railway Employees Dept.,* 283 F. 479 (1922); *U.S.* v. *Railway Employees Dept.,* 286 F. 228 (1923); Petro, "Injunctions," pp. 373, 385 n. 60; and Ross, *Government as a Source,* pp. 37-39.

[63]3 R.L.B. 1139 (1922), quoted in Galenson, *Rival Unionism,* p. 214.

[64]On Richberg and the Railway Labor Act of 1926, see Thomas Vadney, *The Wayward Liberal: A Political Biography of Donald Richberg* (Lexington: University Press of Kentucky, 1970), pp. 53-65; Donald Richberg, *My Hero: The Indiscreet Memoirs of an Eventful but Unheroic Life* (New York: G.P. Putnam's Sons, 1954), pp. 126-133; Ross, *Government as a Source,* pp. 42-47; and Lecht, *Experience,* pp. 47-59.

[65]The first subdivision of Section 2 of the Railway Labor Act of 1926 states that

> [i]t shall be the duty of all carriers, their officers, agents, and employees to exert every reasonable effort to make and maintain agreements concerning rates of pay, rules, and working conditions, and to settle all disputes, whether arising out of the application of such agreements or otherwise, in order to avoid any interruption to commerce or to the operation of any carrier growing out of any dispute between the carrier and the employees thereof.

[66]See James P. Johnson, *The Politics of Soft Coal: The Bituminous Industry from World War I Through the New Deal* (Urbana: University of Illinois Press, 1979), pp. 95-164; and Grant N. Farr, *Origins of Labor Recent Labor Policy,* University of Colorado Studies, Series in Economics, No. 3 (Boulder: University of Colorado Press, 1959), pp. 26-32.

[67]John R. Commons, *Principles of Labor Legislation* (New York: Harper and Brothers, 1920), p. 118 (emphasis in original). For assessments of the legal significance of collective agreements under the common law, see the cases discussed by Fuchs, "Collective Labor Agreements in American Law," 10 *St. Louis Law Review* 1 (1925); Rice, "Collective Labor Agreements in American Law," 44 *Harvard Law Review* 572 (1931); Anderson, "Collective Bargaining Agreements," 15 *Oregon Law Review* 229 (1936); and Petro, "Civil Liberty, Syndicalism and the NLRA," 5 *University of Toledo Law Review* 447 (1974).

[68]See National Association of Manufacturers, *Open Shop Encyclopedia,* 3d revised edition (New York: National Association of Manufacturers, 1922) pp. 70-80, 224-227.

[69]Testimony of George Perkins, *Report of the Commission on Industrial Relations* (Washington: GPO, 1916), Volume VIII, p. 7620; see also p. 7622, and pp. 7598-7599:

> I do not believe that competition is any longer the life of trade. I have long believed that cooperation is the life of trade. I believe this because it is clear that competition, driven to its logical end, gave us the sweatshop, child labor, long hours of labor, insanitary labor conditions, and bred strife and discord between employer and employee. I have long believed that cooperation through large industrial units, properly supervised and regulated by the Federal Government, is the only method of eliminating the abuses from which labor has suffered under the competitive method. I believe in cooperation and organization in industry. I believe in this for both labor and capital. . . .

[70]Louis Brandeis, "The Incorporation of Unions," *Green Bag,* 1903, in Louis Brandeis, *Business: A Profession* (Boston: Small Maynard & Co., 1914), p. 88.

The debate about the incorporation of unions was a long-standing one. For a discussion of the problem in the 1880s, see William S. Barnes, ed., *The Labor Problem* (New York: Harper and Brothers, 1886), pp. 238-255. The Taff Vale decision in England precipitated a controversy in this country as well; see the symposium, "Should Unions Incorporate?"

National Civic Federation Monthly Review I (April 1903): 1-7, 18-20; Samuel Gompers, "Trade Unions Do Not Desire Incorporation," *American Federationist* X (February 1903): 103-104; Samuel Gompers, "New Device to Attempt Organized Labor's Disruption," *American Federationist* X (June 1903); 466-468; Clarence Darrow, "Should Trade Unions Incorporate?" *American Federationist* X (February 1903): 79-80; and Mitchell, *Organized Labor,* pp. 222-232.

In 1922, after the famous Coronado Case (*Coronado Coal Co.* v. *United Mine Workers,* 259 U.W. 344), a sort of American Taff Vale, there was yet another reappraisal; see Forrest R. Black, *Should Trade Unions and Employers' Associations Be Made Legally Responsible?,* National Industrial Conference Board Special Report #10 (Boston: National Industrial Conference Board, 1920); Lauck, *Industrial Code,* pp. 193-197; and see Witte, *Government in Labor Disputes,* pp. 149-151 for citations to other discussions. See also Gompers, *Labor and the Employer,* pp. 272-277.

For an opposing viewpoint, see Walter G. Merritt, "Responsibility of Labor Unions for Acts of Their Officers and Agents," *Law and Labor* II (July 1919): 2-5; Walter G. Merritt, "Responsibility of Labor Unions for Acts of Their Officers and Agents," *Law and Labor* II (July 1919): 2-5; and Walter G. Merritt, "Legal Significance of Collective Agreements," *Law and Labor* III (January 1921): 4-6.

[71]Gompers, "Subtle and Tricky," *American Federationist* XXVI (May 1919), 401. One union lawyer apparently not opposed to incorporation was Isaac Hourwich; see his testimony in U.S., *Industrial Commission* (Washington: GPO, 1902), Volume II, pp. 150-161.

[72]Gompers, "Subtle and Tricky," p. 401; and *Labor and the Employer,* pp. 276, 277. See also Darrow, "Should Unions Incorporate?".

[73]Gompers, *Labor and the Employer,* p. 275 (Testimony of 1899).

[74]Brandeis, "Incorporation," pp. 90, 91. See *Loewe* v. *Lawlor,* 208 U.S. 274 (1908); *Lawler* v. *Loewe,* 235 U.S. 522 (1915). It was *lack* of corporate status that led to the famous *Danbury Hatters* judgment, in which each union member was held liable under the Sherman Act for the unlawful acts in restraint of trade committed by all the others.

[75]Black, *Trade Unions and Employer Associations,* p. 24.

[76]Frankenheimer, "Should Unions Incorporate," p. 20. Cf. Michael Rogin, "Voluntarism: The Political Functions of an Antipolitical Doctrine," *Industrial and Labor Relations Review* XV (July 1962), p. 535:

> Internally, voluntarism meant that the leaders [of unions] were free to coerce the union membership. . . . At times, organizational needs served constituency needs. Voluntarism, however, was above all an organizational ideology, serving organizational needs.

and Witte, *Government in Labor Disputes,* p. 149: "They [union leaders] fear not only suits by employers, but still more, suits by members in matters of discipline and expulsion and concerning pension and other benefits."

[77]Testimony of Samuel Gompers during the Committee of the New York Legislature Investigating Housing Conditions (the Lockwood Committee), reprinted in *Law and Labor* IV (May 1922), pp. 119, 114, 113. See also *Law and Labor* IV (June 1922): 146-162. On the practices under investigation, see F. Lauriston Bullard, "Labor Unions at the Danger Line," *Atlantic Monthly* CXXXIII (December 1923): 721-731.

[78]Gompers, Testimony, *Law and Labor* IV (April 1922), pp. 116-117.

[79]Gompers, Testimony, *Law and Labor* IV (June 1922), p. 157.

[80]For an interesting account of this affair by the attorney for the employers' association, see Julius Cohen, *They Builded Better Than They Knew* (New York: Ronald Press, 1946), pp. 212-214, who makes it clear that the employers were not innocent victims of ILGWU aggression. The attorneys for the union were Morris Hillquit and Samuel Untermyer.

[81]See *Schlesinger* v. *Quinto,* 192 N.Y.S. 564, 566 ff.

[82]Samuel Gompers, *Collective Bargaining: Labor's Proposal to Insure Greater Industrial Peace,* AFL pamphlet, 1920, in *Labor and the Employer,* p. 286. The socialist union leaders, of course, had something else in mind.

[83]Report of the Executive Council of the AFL, 1924, quoted in Thomas, *What is Industrial Democracy,* p. 16. On voluntarism, see David Saposs, "Voluntarism in the American Labor Movement," *Monthly Labor Report* LXXVII (September 1954): 967-971; Louis Reed, *The Labor Philosophy of Samuel Gompers* (Port Washington, NY: Kennikat Press, 1966 [1930]); "Labor and the State," a collection in Saposs, *Readings in Trade Unionism,* pp. 395-418, especially the classic statement by Gompers and Frey in the AFL Convention Proceedings of 1914; Grant McConnell, "The Spirit of Private Government," *American Political Science Review* LII (September 1958): 754-770; Michael Rogin, "Voluntarism: The Political Functions of an Antipolitical Doctrine," *Industrial and Labor Relations Review* XV (July 1962): 521-535; George Higgins, *Voluntarism and Organized Labor in the United States, 1930-1940* (Washington, D.C.: Catholic University of America Press, 1944); Ruth Horowitz, *Political Ideologies of Organized Labor* (New Brunswick, NJ: Transaction Press, 1978); and see the penetrating volume by William Dick, *Labor and Socialism in America: The Gompers Era* (Port Washington, N.Y.: Kennikat Press, 1972), especially pp. 34-35, 38-39, 65-66, 113-131, 140, 147-151, 160-161, 167, and 184, for material from previously unpublished archival source material demonstrating the essentially guild socialist and syndicalist leanings of the union voluntarists.

[84]Gompers, *American Federationist,* 1924, in William English Walling, *American Labor and American Democracy* (New York: Harper and Brothers, 1926), Volume II, p. 149.

[85]On Walling and his role in the AFL, see John R. Commons's introductory remarks to *American Labor and American Democracy;* see also Kelley, *Designing the Industrial State,* pp. 200-239; and Dick, *Labor and Socialism,* pp. 65-66, 117-118, 147-151.

[86]Walling, *American Labor and American Democracy,* Volume II, pp. 107, 108 (emphasis in original). See also the somewhat vaguer "Portland Manifesto," an official report of the AFL Executive Council in 1923 on "Industrial Self Determination," of which Walling's book is, to some degree, a lengthy exegesis. The manifesto is in Saposs, *Readings in Trade Unionism,* pp. 59-66.

[87]Walling, *American Labor and American Democracy,* Volume II, p. 108.

[88]Samuel Gompers, *Seventy Years of Life and Labor,* quoted in Walling, *American Labor and American Democracy,* Volume II, pp. 107-108, 163-164.

[89]See Samuel Gompers, "Labor Representation Essential," *American Federationist* XXV (September 1918): 808-810; and Samuel Gompers, "Significant Movements in Europe," *American Federationist* XXXI (July 1924): 565-569.

[90]Samuel Gompers, "An Analysis of Fascism," *American Federationist* XXX (November 1923), pp. 932, 928-929, 933. See also Ronald Radosh, "The Corporate Ideology of American Labor Leaders from Gompers to Hillman," *Studies on the Left* VI (November-December, 1966): 66-88; and John P. Diggins, *Mussolini and Fascism: The View from America* (Princeton: Princeton University Press, 1972), pp. 144-181 *passim.*

Chapter Nine

[1]National Industrial Recovery Act, 48 Stat. 195, Title I, Section 3 (a) (b), 4 (a) (b). On the origins and the administration of the NRA, see Ellis Hawley, *The New Deal and the Problem of Monopoly* (Princeton: Princeton University Press, 1966); Robert F. Himmelberg, *The Origins of the National Recovery Administration: Business, Government, and the Trade Association Issue, 1921-1933* (New York: Fordham University Press, 1976); Simon Whitney, *Trade Associations and Industrial Control: A Critique of the NIRA* (New York: Central Book Company, 1934); John T. Flynn, "Whose Child is the NRA?" *Harper's* CLXIX (September 1934): 385-394; Charles Roos, *NRA Economic Planning* (Bloomington, Indiana: Principia

Press, 1937); James A. Gross, *The Making of the National Labor Relations Board,* Volume I: 1933-1937 (Albany: State University of New York Press, 1974); Irving Bernstein, "Labor and the Recovery Program, 1933," *Quarterly Journal of Economics* LX (February 1946): 270-288, and his *The New Deal Collective Bargaining Policy* (Berkeley: University of California Press, 1950); Farr, *Origins of Recent Labor Policy;* Lewis Lorwin and Arthur Wubnig, *Labor Relations Boards: The Regulation of Collective Bargaining Under the National Industrial Recovery Act* (Washington: Brookings Institution, 1935); William H. Spencer, *Collective Bargaining Under Section 7 (a) of the National Industrial Recovery Act* (Chicago: University of Chicago Press, 1935); Sargent, "Majority Rule in Collective Bargaining Under Section 7 (a)," 29 *Illinois Law Review* 495 (1935); Paul F. Brissenden, "Genesis and Impact of the Collective Bargaining Provisions of the Recovery Act," in *Economic Essays in Honor of Wesley Clair Mitchell* (New York: Columbia University Press, 1935); Ross, *Government as a Source;* Galenson, *Rival Unionism,* pp. 222-242; Radosh, "Corporate Ideology"; Theodore Rosenhof, *Dogma, Depression and the New Deal: The Debate of Political Leaders Over Economic Recovery* (Port Washington, N.Y.: Kennikat Press, 1975); Arthur Schlesinger, Jr., *The Age of Roosevelt: The Crisis of the Old Order, 1919-1933* (Boston: Houghton Mifflin, 1957), pp. 87-178; and his *The Coming of the New Deal* (Boston: Houghton Mifflin, 1960); Peter Irons, *The New Deal Lawyers* (Princeton: Princeton University Press, 1982); and Irving Bernstein, *The Turbulent Years* (Boston: Houghton Mifflin, 1970).

[2]Quoted in Bernstein, *New Deal Collective Bargaining Policy,* p. 33 (emphasis added).

[3]See Bernstein, *New Deal Collective Bargaining Policy,* p. 22.

[4]According to Bernstein, *New Deal Collective Bargaining Policy,* pp. 31-39, the final draftsmen of the NIRA were Robert F. Wagner, Lewis Douglas, Donald Richberg, and Hugh S. Johnson. The principal draftsmen of Section 7 (a) were Wagner, his law-partner Solomon Rifkind, the United Mine Worker economist W. Jett Lauck, and Representative Clyde Kelley, co-sponsor of the structurally similar labor provisions of the National Bituminous Coal Conservation Act, passed in 1935 after the Supreme Court declared the NRA unconstitutional. See also Farr, *Origins of Recent Labor Policy,* pp. 69-94.

[5]The Chairman of the National Labor Board was Senator Robert F. Wagner; the members of the board most sympathetic to compulsory unionism were William Green (president of the AFL), Francis J. Haas (a Catholic minister and a student of John A. Ryan), John L. Lewis (president of the UMW), and the general counsel, Milton Handler.

Lloyd K. Garrison, Dean of the University of Wisconsin Law School, was the chairman of the 'first', or 'old', National Labor Relations Board. He resigned in November, 1934, and Francis Biddle, a lawyer and former Assistant U.S. Attorney, took his place. The other two members were Harry A. Millis, a labor economist at the University of Chicago who eventually became the first Chairman of the National Labor Relations Board under the Wagner Act, and Edwin Smith, who became an important (and extremely controversial) member of the Wagner Act National Labor Relations Board. The general counsel of the first NLRB was Calvert Magruder, one of the leaders in the crusade against government by injunction.

[6]For discussions of the policies of the NRA labor boards, see generally Ross, *Government as a Source;* Spencer, *Collective Bargaining Under 7 (a);* Lorwin, *Labor Relations Boards;* Gross, *Making of the National Labor Relations Board;* Bernstein, *New Deal Collective Bargaining Policy;* Bernstein, *Turbulent Years;* and Irons, *New Deal Lawyers.*

[7]The Executive Order is in U.S., National Labor Relations Board, *Legislative History of the National Labor Relations Act, 1935* (Washington: GPO, 1949), p. 79; the announcement of Johnson and Richberg is quoted in Galenson, *Rival Unionism,* p. 120. (The *Legislative History* will be hereinafter cited as *LH.*)

[8]The automobile settlement is printed in *LH,* p. 1067.

[9]S296 is in *LH,* pp. 1 *et seq.* The principal authors of the Wagner Bills of 1934 and 1935 were Wagner, Leon Keyserling, William Leiserson, William G. Rice, Milton Handler, and Benedict Wolf. In addition to the *LH,* the following sources proved helpful in understanding the origins

and progress of the Wagner Act: Bernstein, *New Deal Collective Bargaining Policy;* Gross, *The Making of the National Labor Relations Board,* Volume I; Bernstein, *The Turbulent Years,* especially pp. 318-351; Schlesinger, *Coming of the New Deal;* Madden, "Origin and Early History of the NLRB," 20 *George Washington Law Review* 234 (1960-1961); Keyserling, "The Wagner Act: Its Origin and Current Significance," 29 *George Washington Law Review* 199 (1960-1961); Leon Silverberg, ed., *The Wagner Act: After Ten Years* (Washington: Bureau of National Affairs, 1945); Kurt Braun, *The Right to Organize and Its Limits* (Washington, D.C.: Brookings Institution, 1950); Galenson, *Rival Unionism;* and J. Joseph Huthmacher, *Senator Robert F. Wagner and the Rise of Urban Liberalism* (New York: Atheneum, 1968).

[10]See Ross, *Government as Source,* pp. 47-48; Bernstein, *New Deal Collective Bargaining Policy,* pp. 40-56; and Leonard Lecht, *Experience Under Railway Labor Legislation* (New York: Columbia University Press, 1955), pp. 73-87.

[11]In the Matter of the Denver Tramway Corporation and Amalgamated Association of Street and Railway Employees of America, Division 1001, *Decisions of the National Labor Board, August 1933-March 1934* (Washington, D.C.: GPO, 1934), pp. 64-65.

[12]Pierre S. Du Pont, the 'business' representative on the NLB, dissented from the majority opinion and came out squarely in favor of members-only collective bargaining and individual bargaining rights for those who did not choose union affiliation.

[13]In the Matter of Edward F. Caldwell & Company, Inc. and Lighting Equipment Workers Local Union #19427, U.S. National Labor Relations Board, *Decisions of the National Labor Relations Board, July 9, 1934-December 1934* (Washington: GPO, 1935), pp. 12-15. The Caldwell Company's individual contracts used to be of the yellow-dog variety, but the one at issue in 1934 was not, and the NLRB did not concern itself with this matter. The union contended that the employer coerced the individual employees into signing the individual contracts; again, the Board did not agree, and announced its rule of law "on the assumption that it did not occur" (p. 13).

[14]In the Matter of Houde Engineering Corporation and United Automobile Workers Federal Labor Union No. 18839, *Decisions,* 1935, pp. 35-44.

[15]See also, In the Matter of National Lock Company and Federal Labor Union 18830, *Decisions,* 1935, p. 19, a case in which the decision was announced before *Houde,* and which also had a 'duty to bargain' rule.

[16]See, for instance, the testimony of James Emery, counsel for the National Association of Manufacturers, *LH,* pp. 1646, 1648, or the testimony of Walter G. Merritt (editor of *Law and Labor,* the organ of the League for Industrial Rights), pp. 1698, 1697.

[17]Walsh, Debate on Senate Joint Resolution 143, in *LH,* p. 1190.

[18]Wagner, in *LH,* pp. 1236-1238; Debate on Wagner Act in Senate, *LH,* pp. 2392-2393.

[19]Tydings, Senate Debate over the Wagner Act, in *LH,* pp. 2388-2389.

[20]Wagner, *LH,* pp. 16, 1423, 2387 (emphasis added).

[21]Senate Report 573 to accompany S 1958, in *LH,* p. 2312.

[22]Merritt, *LH,* p. 1704; cf. Emery, p. 2243.

[23]Emery, *LH,* p. 2242.

[24]Philip R. Van Duyne, *LH,* p. 540. For vehement denials, see Wagner, pp. 1420-1421; Biddle, pp. 1455-1456; and Lloyd Garrison, p. 1517.

[25]Senate Committee Report 573, in *LH,* p. 2313 (emphasis added); House Committee Report 1147, in *LH,* p. 3070.

[26]Senate Committee Report 573, in *LH,* p. 2313 (emphasis added).

[27]Biddle, *LH,* p. 1457; House Report, in *LH,* p. 2928.

[28]Garrison, *LH,* p. 1507; Witte, p. 273. For additional testimony in favor of majority rule, see *LH,* pp. 16, 2491 (Robert F. Wagner); 1457-1458, 2649 (Francis Biddle); 1508-1509 (Lloyd Garrison); 1445-1446, 2677 (William Green); 1531 (Charlton Ogburn); 1560-1562 (Harry Millis); 2412 (John A. Ryan); and 2437 (Francis J. Haas).

[29]Green, *LH,* 2677; Ryan, p. 2412. A survey conducted by the National Industrial

Conference Board in 1933 revealed that roughly 7 percent of the 3,314 responding manufacturing and mining concerns (representing 18 percent of the total employment of these firms) resorted to individual and collective bargaining simultaneously, or to bargaining with trade unions and company unions; see Sidney Fine, "Proportional Representation of Workers in the Auto Industry, 1934-1935," *Industrial and Labor Relations Review* XII (January 1959), p. 183. Fine studied the proportional representation scheme in the automobile industry in 1934 and 1935. The scheme didn't work well. Neither the automobile companies nor the AFL unions, each for their own reasons, tried very hard to make it work.

[30]Millis, *LH,* p. 1561; Garrison, pp. 1510-1511.

[31]See Harry A. Millis and Emily Clark Brown, *From the Wagner Act to Taft-Hartley* (Chicago: University of Chicago Press, 1950), pp. 138-147, 347-349, and see generally James A. Gross, *The Making of the National Labor Relations Board,* Volume I: 1933-1937 (Albany: State University of New York Press, 1974), and Volume II: 1937-1947 (Albany: State University of New York Press, 1981).

[32]Merritt, *LH,* p. 1705; and see pp. 1335-1336. See also Henry I. Harriman (U.S. Chamber of Commerce) p. 1851.

[33]*LH,* pp. 1920-1921 (Donald Sherwin); 2241 (James Emery); 1897 (James L. Donnelly); see also pp. 1851 (Henry Harriman); 1865-1866 (Howard Dunbar); and 1647 (James Emery).

[34]See, for example, Wagner's remarks in *LH,* pp. 1649, 1651, 1898; and see also pp. 1495, 1508; and p. 1561 (Harry Millis).

[35]Polier, *LH,* pp. 1054-1055, 1053.

[36]The Bituminous Coal Conservation Act (49 Stat. 991, 1935) was hastily passed in August, 1935, *after* the NIRA was declared unconstitutional. Congress, and the President, despite their profound doubts about the BCCA's constitutionality, were nevertheless pressured into passing this law under threat of a nationwide coal strike.

[37]There is a first-rate account of the cases in Gross, *Making of the National Labor Relations Board,* Volume I, pp. 149-230. Gross conveys well the government lawyers' profound uneasiness about the constitutionality of the duty to bargain and the majority rule principle. See also Richard Cortner, *The Wagner Act Cases* (Knoxville: University of Tennessee Press, 1964); and Irons, *New Deal Lawyers,* pp. 254-289.

[38]*Arguments in the Cases Arising Under the Railway Labor Act and the National Labor Relations Act Before the Supreme Court of the United States* (Washington: GPO, 1937), p. 13 (emphasis added).

[39]Reed, in *Arguments,* pp. 33, 34, 38 (emphasis added), and see also p. 37. Reed also tried to wriggle out of the *Carter Coal* case; see p. 40; and see the *Brief for the United States as Amicus Curiae,* on writ of certiorari to the United States Circuit Court of Appeals for the Fourth Circuit, *Virginia Railway* v. *System Federation No. 40, Railway Employees Department of the American Federation of Labor,* Supreme Court, October Term, 1936, No. 324, pp. 97-98.

[40]As quoted by the Court in *Virginia Railway Co,* p. 548, note 6 (emphasis added). See the *Amicus Brief,* pp. 44-53, 89-102. The railroad attorney disagreed with the government's interpretation, but understandably did not press the issue; see *Arguments,* p. 50.

[41]*Arguments,* pp. 68, 88, 118.

[42]See Ward, "The Mechanics of Collective Bargaining," 53 *Harvard Law Review* 754, 763-765, 787-791 (1940); Harold Metz, *Labor Policy of the Federal Government* (Washington, D.C.: Brookings, 1945) p. 74; see also Ross, *Government as a Source,* pp. 104-105, 120-121.

Even so, the law remained (and still remains) cloudy on this fundamental point. Individual bargaining as an alternative to collective bargaining is lawful, but only if an employer, after bargaining in good faith, fails to reach an agreement with a majority union, i.e. in labor relations jargon, reaches an *impasse.* Of course, a union can complain at this point that the employer never intended to bargain in good faith, and the NLRB, if it agrees, can impose costly penalties. In practice (and depending upon the political complexion of the Board), the duty to bargain has indeed become a "club over the head of all" employers to practically compel them to make at least some concessions. For a heroic attempt to introduce some rationality into this area of the law, see Petro, "The Employer's Duty to Bargain," 3 *Labor Law Journal* 515 (1952).

[43]Neil Chamberlain, *The Union Challenge to Management Control* (New York: Harper, 1948), p. 144.

[44]Neil Chamberlain, "The Organized Business in America," *Journal of Political Economy* LII (June 1944), pp. 106, 107, 104-106, 109. See also Chamberlain, *Union Challenge;* Charles Lindblom, *Unions and Capitalism* (New Haven: Yale University Press, 1949), especially the chapter titled "Management's Shrinking Domain"; and Clinton S. Golden and Harold J. Ruttenberg, *The Dynamics of Industrial Democracy* (New York: Harper & Brothers, 1942).

[45]See Harry A. Millis and Emily Clark Brown, *From the Wagner Act to Taft-Hartley* (Chicago: University of Chicago Press, 1950), pp. 216 *et seq.*

[46]See Metz, *Labor Policy,* pp. 58, 77; and Theodore Iserman, *Industrial Peace and the Wagner Act* (New York: McGraw Hill, 1947), pp. 33-34. Ross, *Government as a Source,* pp. 143-144, vociferously disagrees with Metz's conclusions, arguing that in the case at hand the NLRB's decision was based on a finding of *other* employer "unfair labor practices." Nevertheless, Ross's criticism of Metz misses the point entirely. The NLRB's decision itself, which Ross quotes on page 144, announced an unqualified, *prospective* rule.

[47]Dickinson, "New Conceptions of Contract in Labor Relations," 43 *Columbia Law Review* 688, 701, 700 (1943). The Taft-Hartley Act, as explained in the introduction to this book, did make it possible for employers to sue unions for breach of a collective contract.

[48]Croly, *Promise of American Life,* p. 391.

[49]The leading article here was Hoeniger, "The Individual Employment Contract Under the Wagner Act," 10 *Fordham Law Review* 14, 389 (1941). Hoeniger was formerly Professor and Dean of the Law Faculty at Freiburg University. See also Lenhoff, "Present Status of Collective Contracts in the American Legal System," 39 *Michigan Law Review* 1109 (1941); Fuchs, "Collective Labor Agreements Under Administrative Regulation of Employment," 35 *Columbia Law Review* 493 (1935); Latham, "Legislative Purpose and Administrative Policy Under the National Relations Act," 4 *George Washington Law Review* 433 (1936); Mann, "Collective Bargaining Through Majority Representatives as it Effects Freedom of Contract," 22 *Cornell Law Quarterly* 151 (1936); Paul H. Douglas, "American Labor Relations Acts," *American Economic Review* XXVII (December 1937): 735-761; Rice, "The Legal Significance of Labor Contracts Under the NLRA," 37 *Michigan Law Review* 693 (1939); Magruder, "A Half Century of Legal Influence Upon the Development of Collective Bargaining," 50 *Harvard Law Review* 1071 (1937); Hamilton, "Individual Rights Arising From Collective Labor Contracts," 3 *Missouri Law Review* 252 (1938); O. W. Phelps and J. E. Jeuck, "Criticisms of the NLRA," *University of Chicago Journal of Business* XII (January 1939): 30-50; Ward, "The Mechanics of Collective Bargaining," 53 *Harvard Law Review* 754 (1940); and Kurt Braun, "The Dual Nature of Collective Agreements," *Journal of Political Economy* LI (October 1943): 451-462.

[50]See also this same case, pp. 338-339:

> But it is urged that some employees may lose by the collective agreement ... The very purpose of ... collective agreement is to supersede the terms of separate agreements of employees with terms which reflect the strength and bargaining power and *serve the welfare of the group.* ... The workman is free, if he values his own bargaining position more than that of the group, to vote against representation; but the majority rules, and if it collectivizes the employment bargain, individual advantages or favors will generally in practice go in as a *contribution to the collective result.* (emphasis added)

[51]See Petro, "Civil Liberty, Syndicalism, and the NLRA," 5 *University of Toledo Law Review*

447, 451 (1974); and Vieira, "Of Syndicalism, Slavery, and the Thirteenth Amendment: The Unconstitutionality of 'Exclusive Representation' in Public-Sector Employment," 12 *Wake Forest Law Review* 515, 607-609, 616-620 (1976).

[52]Summers, "Union Powers and Workers' Rights," 49 *Michigan Law Review* 805, 812-813, 811, 815 (1951).

[53]Weyand, "Majority Rule in Collective Bargaining," 45 *Columbia Law Review* 556, 559, 561 (1945).

[54]See Timothy J. Boyce, *Fair Representation, the NLRB, and the Courts,* Labor Relations and Public Policy Series Number 18, Industrial Research Unit, The Wharton School (Philadelphia: University of Pennsylvania Press, 1978), *passim.* For a compelling case that the "duty of fair representation" is incoherent, see Petro, "Civil Liberty, Syndicalism, and the NLRA." See also Schatzki, "Majority Rule, Exclusive Representation, and the Interests of Individual Workers: Should Exclusivity Be Abolished?" 123 *University of Pennsylvania Law Review* 897 (1975); and Philip Bradley, "Involuntary Participation in Unionism," in Bradley, ed., *Labor Unions and Public Policy* (Washington, D.C.: American Enterprise Institute, 1958).

[55]See *Lincoln Federal Labor Union* v. *Northwestern Iron & Metal Co.,* 335 U.S. 525 (1949); *Lincoln Federal Labor Union* v. *Northwestern Iron and Metal Co.,* 149 Neb. 507 (1948); *State* v. *Whitaker,* 228 N.C. 352 (1947); and *American Federation of Labor* v. *American Sash & Door,* 335 U.S. 538 (1949).

[56]See, for example, Sylvester Petro, *Power Unlimited: The Corruption of Union Leadership* (New York: Ronald Press, 1959); Robert F. Kennedy, *The Enemy Within* (New York: Harper and Row, 1960); and John L. McClellan, *Crime Without Punishment* (New York: Duell, Sloan and Pearce, 1962)

Index